SALCICCIOLI

AMERICAN GOVERNMENT

AMERICAN GOVERNMENT

ROBERT D. CANTOR
TEMPLE UNIVERSITY

HARPER & ROW, PUBLISHERS
New York, Hagerstown, San Francisco, London

Sponsoring Editor: Dale Tharp
Special Projects Editor: Marlene Ellin
Project Editor: David Nickol
Production Supervisor: Marion A. Palen
Photo Researcher: Myra Schachne
Compositor: TriStar Graphics
Printer and Binder: The Murray Printing Company

Photo Credits: Sources for all photos UPI except as follows:
Culver, pp. 16, 17, 18, 26; Hays, Monkmeyer,
p. 39; Hilton, Monkmeyer, p. 219; World Wide,
pp. 88, 103, 109, 149, 172, 178, 210, 219, 228.

AMERICAN GOVERNMENT

Copyright ©1978 by Robert D. Cantor

All rights reserved. Printed in the United States of America. No part of this book may be used or reproduced in any manner without written permission except in the case of brief quotations embodied in critical articles and reviews. For information address Harper & Row, Publishers, Inc., 10 East 53rd Street, New York, N.Y. 10022.

Library of Congress Cataloging in Publication Data

Cantor, Robert D.
   American Government.

   Bibliography: p.
   Includes index.
   1. United States—Politics and government—Handbooks, manuals, etc. I. Title.
JK274.C2715   320.9'73'092   77-26202
ISBN 0-06-041169-4

CONTENTS

Preface — xiii

Chapter 1. THE AMERICAN POLITICAL FRAMEWORK — 1
- Questions to Consider — 1
- Introduction — 2
- The Political Environment — 2
  - Conflict — 2
  - Power — 3
- American Democracy — 3
  - Representative Government — 3
  - Legitimacy — 4
  - Political Institutions — 5
  - The Group Basis of American Politics — 6
  - Majority Rule Versus Minority Rights — 7
  - Pragmatism in American Politics — 7
- The Challenge of Change — 8
  - The Growth of Government — 9
  - The Economic Dimension — 9
  - Priorities and Resources — 10
  - The Time Element — 11
- Summary — 12
- Notes — 13

Chapter 2. THE CONSTITUTIONAL FRAMEWORK — 14
- Questions to Consider — 14
- Introduction — 15
- The Seeds of Revolution — 15
- British Policy Before the Revolution — 15
- The Breaking Point — 16
- The Declaration of Independence — 16
- The Articles of Confederation — 17
- The Constitutional Convention — 18
  - The Virginia Plan — 18
  - The Emerging Issues — 18
  - The New Jersey Plan — 19
  - The Connecticut Compromise — 19
  - The Slavery Question — 19
  - The Chief Executive — 20
  - The Finished Product — 20
- The Fight for Ratification — 20
- The Meaning of the Constitution — 21
  - Limited Government — 21
  - Separation of Powers and Checks and Balances — 22
  - Judicial Review — 22
  - Enumerated Powers — 23
- Individual Rights — 23
- The Amendment Process — 25
  - Early Constitutional Amendments — 26
  - The Civil War Amendments — 26
  - The Twentieth-Century Amendments — 26
- The Federal System — 27

Other Institutions in the Political System	28
Conclusion	28
Notes	30

Chapter 3. AMERICAN FEDERALISM — 31

Questions to Consider	31
Introduction	32
The Growth of Federal Power	32
McCulloch v. *Maryland* (1819)	32
The Road to Federal Supremacy	33
Matching Needs and Resources	33
The Imbalance of Federal Spending	33
The Federal-State-Local Revenue Balance	34
Values and Resources	34
The Property Tax Dilemma	35
Cities and Suburbs	37
The Role of the Federal Government	39
Grants-in-Aid	40
Revenue Sharing	40
Summary	41
Notes	41

Chapter 4. THE AMERICAN DREAM — 43

Questions to Consider	43
Introduction	44
The Basic Problem	44
The Constitution and Individual Rights	45
Freedom of Speech	45
Freedom of Speech and Subversive Activity	45
Freedom of the Press and Prior Restraint	46
Obscenity	46
The Problem of Libel	47
Freedom of Assembly	47
Freedom of Religion	47
Equality Under the Law	48
The Fight for Racial Equality	49
The Problem of Equal Justice	50
Equal Opportunity	51
Differences in Wealth and Income	52
Inequality of Employment Opportunity	52
Equal Opportunity in Education	56
Summary	58
Notes	59

Chapter 5. PUBLIC OPINION AND POLITICAL PARTICIPATION — 60

Questions to Consider	60
Introduction	61
What Is "the Public"?	61
Opinion Trends	61
Values, Attitudes, and Opinions	62
Characteristics of Opinions	62
Theories of Opinion Formation	63
Psychological Theory	63
Sociological Theory	63
Political Theory	64
The American Political Culture	64
Characteristics of the American Public	65
Income and Education	65
Population Shifts	66
The Ethnic Influence	67
The Liberal-Conservative Dimension	67

Issue Types and Public Opinion … 68
   Domestic Issues … 69
   Foreign Policy Issues … 69
The Measurement of Opinion … 70
The Flow of Information … 71
From Opinion to Action … 72
   Who Are the Activists? … 73
   Opinion, Action, and Influence … 74
Governmental Efforts to Influence Public Opinion … 75
Summary … 75
Notes … 77

Chapter 6. VOTING BEHAVIOR AND THE ELECTORAL PROCESS … 78
Questions to Consider … 79
Introduction … 79
Issues, Candidates, and Parties … 79
   Issues … 80
   Candidates … 80
   Parties … 81
Voting and Public Opinion … 82
   Political Trends … 82
   Psychological Predispositions … 82
   Sociological Factors … 82
The Nominating Process … 83
   Delegate Selection … 84
   The Primary Campaign … 84
   Campaign Strategy … 84
   Favorite Sons … 85
   Voter Perceptions … 85
   State Primary Conventions … 86
The National Conventions … 86
Campaign Financing … 87

The Federal Election Campaign Act … 88
   Reporting Requirements … 89
   Federal Financing and the Political Parties … 89
   Financing the 1976 Election … 89
The Presidential Election Campaign … 89
   Campaign Strategy … 90
   The Campaign Organization … 90
   The Campaign as a "Media Event" … 91
   Presidential Debates … 92
   The Impact of the Campaign … 92
Voting Patterns … 93
   Ticket Splitting … 93
   Voter Participation … 93
The Electoral College … 95
The Ebb and Flow of Presidential Power … 96
Summary … 96
Notes … 96

Chapter 7. INTEREST GROUPS … 99
Questions to Consider … 99
Introduction … 100
The Nature of Interest Groups … 100
The Structure of Interest Groups … 101
The Goals of Interest Groups … 101
Interest Groups and the Political System … 102
Interest Groups and Political Parties … 103
   The Electoral Role of Interest Groups … 104
   The Financial Role of Interest Groups … 105
Interest Groups and Congress … 106

Interest Groups and the President	106
Interest Groups and the Federal Bureaucracy	107
Interest Groups and the Judiciary	108
Interest Groups and the Media	108
Interest Groups Within the Government	108
Representing Foreign Interests	109
The Public Interest	110
The Washington Lobbyist	111
Summary	111
Notes	111

Chapter 8. POLITICAL PARTIES — 113

Questions to Consider	113
Introduction	114
Party Government and Responsible Parties	114
The Development of American Political Parties	115
The Role of the Parties	115
Characteristics of American Political Parties	116
Party Ideology	116
Ideology at the National Level	117
Ideology at the State and Local Levels	118
Party Government and Political Ideology	118
The Two-Party System	118
Third Parties	119
Party Organization	120
Presidential Parties	120
Legislative Parties	120
State and Local Parties	121
Party Leadership	121
The Road to the Top	122
The Rank and File	123
Party Performance	123
Contesting Elections	123
Organizing the Legislature	124
The Party and the People	125
The Balance of Political Power	125
The Future of American Political Parties	125
Summary	126
Notes	126

Chapter 9. THE MEDIA — 128

Questions to Consider	128
Introduction	129
The Modern Media	129
Characteristics of the Media	129
To Publish or Not to Publish	130
The Bay of Pigs	130
Counter-Spy and the CIA	130
Interpretation of the News	131
Reporting Versus Creating News	131
The Impact of Intensive Coverage	132
Creating a Chain Reaction	132
Freedom of the Press and the Judicial Process	133
The Media and the Government	134
The Personal Touch	135
To the People—with Media Support	135
The News Leak	136
The Backgrounder	137
Trial Balloons	137
The Media and the Public	137

Freedom and Fairness	139
Summary	139
Notes	139

Chapter 10. CONGRESS 141

Questions to Consider	142
Introduction	142
Congressional Functions	142
Representation	142
Legislation	142
Oversight	143
The Members of Congress	144
Rewards of Congressional Service	145
Congressional Ethics	146
Congressional Constituencies	147
The Individual Citizen	147
Interest Groups and Elites	147
Political Parties	147
The Media	147
The Electoral Process	148
Congressional Operations	149
Congressional Politics	149
The Leadership	150
The House of Representatives	150
The Senate	151
Party Organization	152
Pressures for Party Unity	153
The Legislative Process	153
Congressional Committees	154
Seniority	155
House Committees	155
House Subcommittees	155
Senate Committees	156
Conference Committees	156
The Budget Committees	157
The General Accounting Office	158
Congressional Procedures	158
Filibuster and Cloture	158
Secrecy	158
Classified Information	158
The Subpoena Power	159
Contempt Citations	159
Summary	159
Notes	159

Chapter 11. THE PRESIDENCY 161

Questions to Consider	161
Introduction	162
Presidential Leadership	162
Leadership Style	163
Presidential Character	164
The President as Political Leader	165
The President as Legislator	166
The Veto Power	168
Impoundment of Funds	169
Executive Privilege	169
The President and the Judiciary	169
The President and Foreign Policy	170
Executive Agreements	170
The President as Commander-in-Chief	170
The President, the Media, and the Public	172
The President as Administrative Leader	173
The White House Staff	173
The Executive Office	174
The National Security Council	174

Contents

The Office of Management and Budget	175
The Council of Economic Advisers	175
The Cabinet	175
Limitations on Presidential Power	176
Commitments and Precedents	176
Availability of Resources	176
Availability and Quality of Information	176
The Political Climate	177
The Appeal of the Presidency	178
The Vice Presidency	178
Presidential Succession	179
Summary	179
Notes	179

Chapter 12. THE FEDERAL BUREAUCRACY — 181

Questions to Consider	181
Introduction	182
Characteristics of the Bureaucracy	182
Administration and Policy	182
Political Orientation	183
Influences on the Bureaucracy	183
Problems of the Bureaucracy	183
The Super Bureaucrats	183
Staffing the Bureaucracy	184
The Hatch Act	185
The Good Old Boy Network	185
Unionization and the Right to Strike	185
The Structure of the Bureaucracy	186
The Cabinet Departments	186
Subcabinet Departments	187
The Executive Agencies	188
Semi-Independent Corporations	188
The Federal Reserve Board	189
Governmental Regulation of Business and Industry	190
The Independent Agencies and Commissions	190
Reform of Governmental Regulation	192
Bureaucratic Accountability	193
Summary	194
Notes	195

Chapter 13. THE JUDICIARY — 196

Questions to Consider	197
Introduction	197
Judicial Review—*Marbury* v. *Madison*	198
Courts and the Political Culture	198
The Basis of American Law	199
Common Law and Civil Law	199
Precedents	199
The American Court System	199
State Courts	199
Federal Courts	200
The Judiciary	202
Federal Judges	202
State Judges	203
The Role of the Judiciary	203
Courts of Original Jurisdiction	203
Appellate Courts	204
The United States Supreme Court	204
Activism Versus Restraint	205

Accepting Cases for Review 205
Court Procedure 206
The Impact of Court Opinions 206
The Court's Political Philosophy 207
Selection of Justices 207
Administration of Federal Courts 209
The Historical Role of the Supreme Court 209
   The Federal-State Relationship 209
   Government-Business Relations 210
   Protection of Individual Rights 211
Landmark Judicial Rulings 211
   The Fourteenth Amendment 211
   Racial Discrimination 211
   Freedom of Expression 212
The Future of the Judicial Process 212
Summary 212
Notes 213

Chapter 14. THE POLITICAL ECONOMY 215

Questions to Consider 215
Introduction 216
Setting Priorities 216
Inflation 218
Unemployment 219
Designing Economic Policy 220
   Arguments for Long-Range Planning 222
   Arguments Against Long-Range Planning 222
The Economic Role of Congress 223

The President's Economic Role 223
The Budgetary Process 223
   The President Initiates 223
   Congress Acts 224
   Review and Audit 224
   Budget Execution and Control 224
The Budget 224
Sources of Revenue 224
The National Debt 225
Taxation 225
Tax Reform 228
The U.S. Economy 228
Fiscal and Monetary Policy 229
   Fiscal Policy 229
   Monetary Policy 230
The Economic Power Structure 230
   Financial Institutions 231
   Employee Pension Funds 232
   Labor Unions 232
   Large Corporations 232
The Role of the Government 233
   Direct Impact of the Economy 234
   The Role of Foreign Trade 235
Summary 235
Notes 237

Chapter 15. MILITARY AND FOREIGN POLICY 238

Questions to Consider 238
Introduction 239
The Interdependence of Nations 239
The Role of Diplomacy 240
The Foreign Policy Establishment 240

Presidential Advisers	241
The Foreign Policy Elite	241
The Foreign Policy Bureaucracy	241
The Professional Diplomats	243
The Intelligence Agencies	243
The Military	245
Congress and Foreign Policy	246
The Defense Industry	247
The Military-Industrial Complex	247
Arms Exports	248
Public Opinion and Foreign Policy	249
The Conduct of Foreign Policy	250
Making Foreign Policy Decisions	250
A Foreign Policy Overview	251
Europe	251
The Middle East	252
Asia	252
Latin America	253
Africa	253
Summary	254
Notes	255

Chapter 16. LOOKING AHEAD	**256**
Introduction	256
Who Will Rule?	256
Mobilizing the People	257
The Politics of Lowered Expectations	257
Conclusion	257

Appendix: The Constitution of The United States	258
Bibliography	270
Answers to Crossword Puzzles	275
Index	281

PREFACE

My objective in preparing this book was to provide the college student with a description of the important elements in the American political framework. It was assumed that the student would have no prior political knowledge. We often hear the phrase, "I'm not interested in politics." The major thrust of this book is to emphasize that politics *is* important to the individual and to demonstrate that the political world cannot be ignored.

There are some innovations in the choice of topics covered in this book. For example, the media are treated as a political institution; a chapter is devoted to a discussion of the role of the media in American political society. I have also emphasized the objects of most governmental action, namely, the economy and foreign policy. While political scientists agree that politics involves allocation of resources by a government with the authority to make allocations, the political process itself receives little attention in most political science textbooks. The material on the political economy is intended to correct this defect. Similarly, the chapter on military and foreign policy links U.S. foreign policy with domestic politics more thoroughly than comparable textbooks. This book, in short, is an attempt to expand the study of American government to include areas that have become increasingly important in political terms.

Many people have generously contributed their advice during the preparation of this book. Many of my colleagues reviewed portions of the manuscript. They include: Murray S. Stedman, Jr.; Earl M. Baker.; Harry A. Bailey, Jr.; Benjamin Schoenfeld of Temple University; James S. Milne of West Chester State College; Randolph Westerfeld of the Wharton School of the University of Pennsylvania; Janice Westerfeld of the Federal Reserve Bank of Philadelphia; Arnold S. Lerner of Radio Station WLLH, Lowell, Mass.; Mitchell Miller of the Delaware Law School; and Harry Jenkins III of Jenkins, Miller and Jenkins. I would also like to thank all of the individuals who reviewed my manuscript for Harper & Row: Lawrence Baum of Ohio State University; William S. Livingston of the University of Texas; Lyman A. Kellstedt of the University of Illinois; Kay Schlozman of Boston University; Barry Wishart of Fullerton Junior College; Beate Kukainis of Texas A&M University; Milton D. Morris of the Brookings Institution; Larry L. Berg of the University of California; James Clotfelter of Texas Tech University; Ronald J. Stupak of the U.S. Civil Service Commission Federal Executive Institute; William W. Lammers of the University of Southern California; Sam W. Hawkins of San Jacinto College; Robert L. Lineberry of Northwestern University; and Steven Mazurana of the University of Northern Colorado. Their suggestions were of immeasurable assistance. Finally, I would like to acknowledge the contributions of Marlene Ellin and Ron Taylor of Harper & Row, Publishers, in preparing the manuscript for publication.

ROBERT D. CANTOR

CHAPTER 1
THE AMERICAN POLITICAL FRAMEWORK

CHAPTER OUTLINE

Questions to Consider
Introduction
The Political Environment
   Conflict
   Power
American Democracy
   Representative Government
   Legitimacy
   Political Institutions
   The Group Basis of American Politics
   Majority Rule Versus Minority Rights
   Pragmatism in American Politics
The Challenge of Change
   The Growth of the Government
   The Economic Dimemsion
   Priorities and Resources
   The Time Element
Summary

QUESTIONS TO CONSIDER

This chapter introduces basic concepts and considerations that are necessary for the study of American government: the nature of the American political environment, the meaning of democracy, and the challenges that the American political system has encountered in the past and faces in the future. The first section will discuss the route by which seemingly nonpolitical issues eventually find their way into the political environment. Why and how do such issues become political questions? How are political issues resolved? In the second section we will describe the American political system. We are aware that the federal government is the cornerstone of the American political framework. What other institutions can be considered integral parts of that framework? Establishing the nature of the American political system enables us to consider the characteristics of American democracy. What does representative government mean? And why did it evolve in the United States? What are the issues involved in the balance between majority rule and the protection of minority rights? What is the prevailing ideological temper of American politics? Finally, the third section will deal with the changes that have taken place in the political system. The United States of today bears little resemblence to the nation founded 200 years ago. What are the important issues of today? How are national priorities established, and what is their relationship to national resources? How has the United States adapted to changing conditions and yet continued to be governed under the original Constitution? These questions will be encountered in different forms throughout the text and will serve as a background for consideration of more specific aspects of the American political system.

Introduction

A major political issue in the United States today is the need to strike a balance between the individual's responsibility for his or her own destiny and the government's responsibility for the welfare of every citizen. This issue is increasingly important because of the steadily growing dependence of many individuals on governmental action in many areas.

The interests of individual citizens are usually referred to in terms of the *groups* with which they are identified. The young want subsidized education and jobs; the middle-aged, tax relief and aid in financing the purchase of homes; the elderly, help in maintaining a reasonable standard of living. Workers look to the federal government to ensure full employment, while industry pressures the government for economic policies that will maintain a healthy business climate and encourage expansion. Environmentalists implore Congress to clean up the nation's rivers and streams, while representatives of the business community lament the cost and point to the potentially harmful effects of limiting the exploitation of national resources.

These demands on the government reflect a change in the citizen's view of the proper role of Washington in their lives. Formerly, the federal government was expected to limit its attention to foreign affairs and national defense and to maintain domestic order. Today, individuals and groups petition their elected representatives in response to virtually any problem, despite their growing discontent with the increased influence of the government on the lives of individuals. The resolution of conflicting demands on the government usually has an economic impact, with the gains of one group being financed with revenue from all segments of society. The economic dimension of political action is an integral part of the process by which the government responds to demands from the people.

The Political Environment

Capital punishment, natural gas, air pollution, and pornography are diverse subjects. However, they have something in common: They have become subjects of controversy and will be resolved within the political environment. The *political environment* includes governmental institutions as well as groups seeking to influence public policy, or having an impact on the political process. Thus, Congress, labor unions, and other groups that attempt to influence legislation, as well as the news media, are all included in the political environment.

Issues become political questions as a result of *conflict* between groups or interests in society and are resolved by the government because it has the *power* to do so. For example, public concern about energy has brought the problem of natural gas supplies to the political environment. Conflict exists between those who favor regulating the price and supply of this energy source and those who would trust economic forces to determine the role of natural gas in the nation's energy supply. Ultimately, this question will be resolved by the government, which possesses the constitutional *power* to impose its will on both groups. Thus conflict and power are key elements of political activity.

Conflict

Conflict is inherent in political systems because resources are limited. Governmental institutions have been created to sort out the demands of various groups in society and allocate resources among them, that is, decide who gets how much of what. No governmental action is beneficial to all citizens—some will benefit more than others as a result of any particular legislation. An increase in unemployment compensation payments must be financed by higher taxes on the employed and on their employers. Increased federal aid to education requires that revenue be diverted from other programs or additional taxes raised. But conflict is not limited to issues with economic overtones. The controversy over abortion has a religious and moral basis, but has become a political issue because of the conflict between right-to-life groups and those that favor abortion on demand. Other issues, such as civil rights and equal rights for women, have a social basis. Each of these issues has entered the political environment as a result of conflict between competing groups.

Picket line violence represents a breakdown in peaceful negotiations between labor and management.

Power

The resolution of conflict depends ultimately on the power of the government. Within the guidelines of the Constitution, the government can impose its will in individuals or organizations. Thus, we are required to pay taxes; airlines must seek approval of their fares and routes; and television and radio programs must meet federal standards of "fairness." Similarly, the government can prohibit certain actions, such as polluting streams or robbing banks. The government's coercive power includes the power to impose penalties, such as jail sentences or fines, for breaking the law.

Power is often exercised through persuasion rather than coercion. The essence of political leadership is the ability to persuade people to cooperate for the common good. Whether coercive power or persuasion will be used in a given situation is determined by the issue at hand. For example, in April 1977 President Carter asked for the voluntary cooperation of labor and industry in taking measures to avoid inflation, although the government had the power to impose wage and price controls.

Persuasion is often used when it is difficult to use coercion effectively. In 1973 energy shortages led to the imposition of a 55-miles-per-hour speed limit on the nation's highways, with penalties for exceeding the limit. In 1977, by contrast, people were asked to voluntarily lower their thermostats in order to conserve energy. The government would have had trouble imposing a penalty for violating this request.

American Democracy

The ways in which the government exercises its constitutional powers have been shaped by the character of American democracy. The simplest meaning of *democracy* is self-government—a democracy is a political system that offers citizens the right to choose their leaders and periodic opportunities to change those leaders. There are as many varieties of democratic governments as there are democracies. This reflects the flexiblility of democracy; self-government can take many forms. The basic difference among democratic systems revolve around the question of the relative authority of various governmental institutions. The form that develops in a particular nation depends largely on that nation's past history. The American experience as a colony of Great Britain and the complaints of the colonists in prerevolutionary times provided the background for the structure and values of American democracy.

Representative Government

The American political system is based on *representative democracy*, in which the individual expresses his or her will through the election of representatives. The fact that those representatives must seek reelection to remain in office gives the voters frequent opportunities to pass judgment on the performance of elected officials. The public has proved quite capable of expressing its displeasure with political leaders. Since 1952, the Democratic and Republican parties have alternated control of the White House every eight years.

The concept of representative democracy is based partly on the size of the nation and the number of political units within it. It would be impossible to hold a public debate on every issue and a referendum on every item of legislation. The other reason for representative democracy as opposed to direct participation by every citizen in the policy-making is the assumption that elected representatives possess the knowledge required to make wise choices in determining the means by which national goals are to be achieved.

The impact of the people on their representatives is not confined to voting. Public opinion is a powerful influence on those who hold positions of power. The development of television contributed to the importance of public opinion. More people are presented with political news in an understandable and, at times, dramatic manner. The U.S. effort in Vietnam was graphically portrayed by the TV networks. The visual impact of the destruction of life and property brought about by the war was much greater

The members of the House of Representatives take their oaths at the start of the 94th Congress. Each member of the House represents over 500,000 Americans.

than the impact of even the most powerful newspaper accounts, and played a major role in changing public attitudes toward the war. The media also reflect, if not encourage, the growing tendency of Americans to question the actions of government officials, including the President. This was made very clear by the coverage of the Watergate affair.

Legitimacy

Elected representatives do not have unlimited authority to rule. Their decisions must be viewed as legitimate if they are to be accepted by the public. *Legitimacy* is the recognition by citizens that the government is acting within accepted standards. This acceptance is dependent on citizens' perceptions that the actions of their government are fair and just. Richard Nixon resigned from the Presidency when it had become clear that his administration was no longer regarded as legitimate. Both public opinion and sentiment within the government, as well as powerful interest groups were in favor of resignation or impeachment, and this is a tide no President can withstand.

The Prohibition era is an example of the futility of governmental action that is not regarded as legitimate by the people. In 1919, Congress passed the Eighteenth Amendment to the Constitution, which outlawed the manufacture, sale, and transportation of alcoholic beverages in the United States. People wanted their "spirits", however, so several new words were added to the American vocabulary: *speakeasy, rumrunner, bootleg, bathtub gin, Elliot Ness.* Prohibition failed despite the efforts of law enforcement agencies, and in 1933, the Twenty-first Amendment repealed the earlier amendment.

The need for legitimacy does not mean that every action of the government must be popular. It simply means that all such actions must be recognized as lawful and within the proper realm of governmental activity. Nobody is in favor of higher taxes, but citizens recognize the need when they are presented with the facts. Above all, they accept the idea that the government is acting within its constitutional powers in raising taxes. The individual realizes that many matters with which elected representatives feel are beyond abilities of the average citizen, and the actions of governmental officials are likely to win acceptance unless the results are obviously harmful. The tide of public opinion turned against U.S. involvement in the Vietnam War when it became ap-

Chief Justice Warren Burger administers the oath of office to President Jimmy Carter. Inaugural ceremonies demonstrate the interdependence of various branches of government.

Antiwar protest in Chicago, 1968. The right of citizens to protest government actions is explicit in the Constitution.

parent, contrary to administration statements, that the effort was an exercise in futility. The attempts of the Johnson Administration to "sell" the war backfired and cost President Johnson legitimacy he needed to govern effectively. His decision not to seek reelection in 1968 was motivated by this loss of support.

In recent years, the nation has experienced a series of events that have weakened the prestige and, therefore, the legitimacy of the government. Vietnam, Watergate, and revelations of illegal activities by the Central Intelligence Agency and the Federal Bureau of Investigation have served to confirm the suspicions of the cynic and shake the confidence of the faithful. The government's legitimacy has also been threatened by a crisis of legitimacy in American society. The data in Table 1-1 clearly show decreased respect for many institutions that were formerly among the most highly regarded in the nation. This effects the popular view of government, since all of these institutions represent authority of some sort, collectively, they provide a foundation for the government's legitimacy. There is little doubt that restoring public acceptance of the government is among the major tasks facing any modern administration.

Political Institutions

One of the hallmarks of a democratic society is the existence of nongovernmental institutions in the political environment. This reflects the freedom of political activity that is possible in a democratic political system. The Presidency, Congress, and the Supreme Court are the governmental institutions provided for in the Constitution. However, they coexist with other groups that have arisen to fill the needs of an expanding society. Political parties are the most visible of these nongovernmental institutions. The parties attempt to win control of the Presidency and Congress in order to implement their programs. The Democratic and Republican parties have dominated American politics for over 100 years and play a central role in organizing Congress and carrying out the election process.

Another nongovernmental institution is the news media. Not only do the media bring political news to the people; they also have the capacity to expose wrongdoing within the government. No one who followed the events leading up to the resignation of President Nixon can have any doubt about the impact of TV and radio networks, newspapers, and news magazines on the nation's political consciousness.

There are other, less visible organizations that operate in the political environment. Usually referred to as *interest groups*, they represent the shared interests of individual citizens or of allied groups. Most of these groups are also active in a nonpolitical environment. For example, the American Bar Association (ABA) is concerned primarily with the maintenance of professional standards among the nation's attorneys. However, it also uses its influence by passing

TABLE 1-1
Index of Public Trust

In March 1976, a nationwide cross-section of 1512 households was asked, "As far as people running these institutions are concerned, would you say you have a great deal of confidence, only some confidence, or hardly any confidence at all in them?" Following are the 1976 responses compared to those from 1972 and 1966.

Great Deal of Confidence in:	1976	1972	1966
Medicine	42%	48%	73%
Military	23	35	62
Education*	31	33	61
Religion	24	30	41
U.S. Supreme Court	22	28	50
Federal executive branch	11	27	41
Major U.S. companies	16	27	55
Congress	9	21	42
The press	20	18	29
Television news	28	17	25
Organized labor	10	15	22

SOURCE: Harris Survey, March 1976, #2521; October 1972, #2236; February 1966, #1574. Copyright 1966, 1972, 1976 by the *Chicago Tribune*. World Rights Reserved.

*Beginning in 1973, this title was changed from "Colleges" to "Higher education."

judgment on the qualifications of potential jurists and these judgments may be taken into account by public officials who appoint judges or voters who elect them. In this sense, the ABA is acting within the political environment.

The Group Basis of American Politics

People form groups in order to communicate their desires to the government more effectively than they could if they acted as individuals. American politics has been influenced by groups since the founding of the nation. Agricultural, banking, and industrial interests are among the powerful groups that have been active throughout the nation's existence. Such groups give a degree of structure to the public will. Group activity also benefits the government, since it offers a means of gaining the support of large numbers of people with common interests. Individuals seeking political power have always measured their support in terms of the backing they could get from interest groups.

The entry of Southern blacks into the ranks of voters, large-scale migration to urban areas, increased levels of education, and exposure to current news via TV have combined to make more people politically aware than ever before. In turn, this trend has brought new groups into the political mainstream as increased numbers of individuals have sought greater representation of their interests. Before World War II, the National Association for the Advancement of Colored People was the dominant organization representing the interests of American blacks. The postwar era brought numerous new civil rights organizations, with a broad range of philosophies and modes of operations, into the political environment. Similarly, increased emphasis on women's rights has stimulated the formation of many new groups with varied goals.

The increased number and variety of interest groups has made it more difficult to agree on national goals. And there is less motivation for groups to cooperate as they compete for the support of the individuals they seek to represent. This places more responsibility on the government. It is harder for political leaders to make choices because any decision is likely to cost them political support. As a result, the government has attempted to offer something to almost every group that presents it with specific demands. This has led to a breakdown in the political process.

The government has also failed to restrict the actions of groups that seek narrow goals through means contrary to the common good. This failure may be viewed as a form of political compromise or as a reflection of the tendency of all levels of authority to yield to activists of every kind. Public employees defy court injunctions against illegal strikes and sanctions imposed, if any, are inadequate to prevent others from doing the same thing. Corporations that violate campaign laws and make corporate contributions to political candidates are given token fines and the officials involved receive little more than a reprimand. Such failures to enforce the law have led to the idea that it can be circumvented or ignored with little penalty. But the vitality of democracy depends on the government's willingness to use its authority effectively. The alternative is increased competition among groups, and the consequences are unpredictable. As Woodrow Wilson said,

> Government is not a warfare of interests. We shall not gain our ends by heat and bitterness, which make it impossible to think either calmly or fairly. Government is a matter of common counsel, and everyone must come into the consultation with the purpose to yield to the general view, which seems most nearly to correspond with the common interest. If any decline frank conference, keep out, hold off, they must take the consequences and blame only themselves if they are in the end badly served.[1]

Traditionally, political activity in the United States has been based on the assumption that the most powerful groups would not press their advantage to extremes. Rather, powerful interests have been expected to make room for less influential groups. This does not mean that the most powerful groups have been eager to share the wealth. Rather, they have recognized the fact that unrestrained use of power runs the risk of provoking a coun-

1971 convention of the National Association for the Advancement of Colored People (NAACP), an influential interest group.

terreaction from other groups within the political environment. The main principle underlying the interaction of interest groups is that the stability of the political system depends on moderation and reasonableness.

Majority Rule Versus Minority Rights

The concept of majority rule flows from the idea that self-rule is most appropriate for a political society and that popular wisdom will preserve democratic institutions. However, there must be limits to the rule of the majority or the minority will have no rights at all. The Constitution sets forth the legal boundaries within which the majority may rule and provides protection for all individuals, whether they are members of the majority or of the minority. Legal restraints on the potential tyranny of the majority are necessary but not entirely sufficient, however. The various groups in the private sector must also support this principle if it is to be meaningful. This requires an understanding that no individual or group has any more freedom than any other individual or group. A majority that imposes its will on the minority without regard for its legitimate interests will ultimately face the most serious political problem of all: loss of legitimacy.

Just as safeguards are necessary to prevent a tyranny of the majority, so a democratic society must guard against a tyranny of the minority. Well organized groups, though they may be minorities, can have an influence far greater than their membership. This is legitimate political activity as long as it does not impede the democratic process. However, when minority demands threaten the rights of others they must be checked. Democracy was never intended to provide a vehicle for minority domination of the majority any more than it can tolerate tyranny by the majority.

Democratic politics is really a politics of consensus. That is, broad agreement on the "rules of the game" that set the standards for political conflict. When either a majority or a minority takes an inflexible stance, the consensus is destroyed and one group or the other will inevitably suffer. There are no simple formulas for ensuring the stability of democracies. One has only to consider the recent demise of democratic practices in nations such as Brazil and the Philippines to appreciate the basic weakness of self-government. Democracy must be carefully fostered by groups within the society if it is to endure; it will not happen automatically. The Constitution can offer guidelines for balancing the interests of the majority and the minority; individuals and groups in the private sector are responsible for making the system work. And if they are to succeed, they must be fliexible.

Pragmatism in American Politics

American politics is *pragmatic* in that policy is not determined by ideology. The key to the pragmatism of democracy is adaptability, the ability as well as the willingness to chart a new course of action if necessary. There is nothing in the idea of self-government that automatically excludes the government from any particular role or function. Democratic practice means

'And we're in here for stealing property ...'

only that the government must act in accordance with the best interests of the citizens.

Pragmatism may be found throughout the American political system. It has encouraged the development of political parties that seek support from all segments of American society. This is a source of concern to those who lament the similarity between the Democratic and Republican parties. But the successful candidates in U.S. politics have always been near the center of the political spectrum and thus have been able to attract the votes of people with a wide variety of political views. Occasionally there is a movement within one of the parties to offer a definitive political doctrine so that the voters will have a meaningful choice. Desirable though this may be, recent elections indicate that this path leads to political suicide. The heaviest losers in the Presidential contests held since World War II—Barry Goldwater in 1964 and George McGovern in 1972—offered highly ideological appeals. Both strayed too far from the political mainstream to attract large numbers of voters.

There is some danger that the concept of pragmatism will be used as an excuse for illegal actions. The excesses of Watergate were undoubtedly viewed by those involved as pragmatic politics. However, there is a vast difference between flexibility, which may lead to long-term benefits, and political expediency, which sacrifices long-term values for immediate gains.

The Challenge of Change

The value of pragmatism in American democracy has been reflected in the ability of political institutions and processes to change with the times. The nation's social, political, and economic environment is in a continual state of flux. The changes may be dramatic, as in the case of the civil rights protests of the 1960s, or may reflect the emergence of important new priorities, as in the case of the energy crisis of the 1970s. In addition to changes in the society within which the government operates, there are changes in the relative power of the executive, legislative, and judicial branches of the government. For example, the Watergate affair led to increased consciousness among congresspeople that the power of the legislative branch had been eroded over several decades by an increasingly powerful presidency. Thus, the government must cope with changes within its own structure as well as with social and economic trends.

In adjusting its priorities and methods of operation in accordance with contemporary demands, the government faces the difficult challenge of keeping its institutions and practices flexible. This is a formidable task because any change in priorities or new legislation necessarily works to the advantage of one segment of society at the expense of others. Policies designed to bring minority groups into the mainstream of American life are a good example. When past injustices are remedied by means of preferential hiring requirements, or affirmative action, the government must deal with accusations of "reverse discrimination." In a similar vein, efforts to ensure energy self-sufficiency for the nation receive widespread support, but when the time comes to implement policies that will achieve this goal, competing interests arise to voice their support or opposition.

Social and political change presents a continuing challenge to government. It is not possible for the government to change its policies with every shift in public opinion, nor would this be desirable. The government must chart a course that is broad enough to take many shades of opinion into consideration but specific enough to offer useful guidelines for the achievement of national goals. Within these guidelines, it is necessary to react with flexiblity to changing social values. This is more difficult than formulating policies designed to solve a specific problem. Social trends are impossible to predict accurately and often contain crosscurrents that complicate matters even further.

A striking example of the evolution of social values is found in the American attitude toward the rule of law. The law had long been regarded as the cornerstone of political stability, and few individuals questioned this value before the civil rights and antiwar protests of the 1960s. These protests relied on civil disobedience rather than the court challenges of former years. The increased use of civil disobedience left the government in a quandary. How much and what kind of civil disobedience can a government tolerate without losing its authority?

Challenges to the concept of the rule of law have not been confined to organized movements. Individuals have begun using this tactic with increasing frequency, feeling that there is a higher moral code than the law. This rationale has been used by such disparate individuals as Daniel Ellsberg, who leaked the Pentagon Papers to the press, and the Nixon zealots, who regarded the reelection of their President as a higher value than the laws they violated.

The government must deal with such changes in the public attitude in a positive way or risk losing its legitimacy. It has responded to challenges to the rule of law in a variety of ways: reduced secrecy in response to the Pentagon Papers case and prosecution of those who had broken the law in the case of Watergate. In the former case the existing laws and procedures were found to be overly restrictive, but in the later case there was little justification for the violations. These examples offer evidence that a democratic society can afford the luxury of questioning existing values as long as new interpretations are consistent with the underlying principle of accountability to the people.

The Growth of the Government

The past fifty years have been marked by increased governmental activity in almost every area of American life. This has resulted in a comparable increase in the individual's dependence on governmental decisions. Every citizen is affected by the actions of the government at all levels—local, state, and national—regardless of his or her political interests and knowledge. In turn, government officials at all levels are dependent on the support of the people. Thus, Americans and their government are firmly linked together; neither is likely to fulfill its potential without help from the other.

The growth of the government reflects the increasing complexity of a highly technological society as well as a growing tendency to look to the government for solutions to social and economic problems. In addition, the role of the United States in foreign affairs requires that significant quantities of national resources be used to protect American interests abroad.

Table 1-2 shows government spending at all levels as a percentage of the *Gross National Product* (GNP)—the total of goods and services produced in the nation in one year. The steady increase in this percentage over the past fifty years—from 10 per cent in 1929 to 33 per cent in 1974—reflects the enlarged role to the government in American society. Since there is little evidence that this trend will be reversed, it appears that we will become increasingly dependent on the actions of political leaders in the future. Individual ability and desire to succeed will always be important, but the destiny of the individual is more closely tied to that of the nation than ever before.

The trend toward increased dependence on the government may also be seen in terms of employment. The data in Table 1-3 indicate that a person has almost one chance in five of eventually working for the government (federal, state, or local), and these odds will increase unless there is an unexpected reversal in the tendency for the government to expand its functions.

The data in Tables 1-2 and 1-3 are only the tip of the iceberg. Government spending creates a ripple effect that spreads throughout the economy. Many workers employed in private industry depend on government contracts for their jobs. Government mortgage guarantees and industrial development loans are other examples of activities that are not included in the GNP but reflect the tremendous impact of political action on the economy.

The Economic Dimension

"The business of America is business," said Calvin Coolidge in 1925. Despite the enlarged role of the government in foreign affairs and the constitutional protection of the rights of the individual, Coolidge's remark is still appropriate. The economic dimension of political life in the United States can hardly be exaggerated; political stability is largely dependent on economic viability. The free-enterprise system is based on the ability of the economy to provide enough jobs so that citizens can maintain a satisfactory standard of living. But "satisfactory" is a rela-

TABLE 1-2
Government Spending (Local, State, Federal) as a Percent of Gross National Product

Year	GNP	Government Spending	Percent of GNP
1929	$ 103 billion	$ 10 billion	10
1940	99	18	18
1950	284	60	21
1960	503	136	27
1970	977	312	32
1974	1397	461	33

SOURCE: *The Wall Street Journal,* April 21, 1975, P. 1.

Internal Revenue Service employees prepare to mail income tax forms. The complicated Federal tax forms are typical examples of the demands made by government on our daily lives.

TABLE 1-3
Government Employees (Local, State, Federal) as a Percent of All Employment

Year	All Employees	Government Employees	Percent of All Employment
1929	31,339,000	3,065,000	9.7
1940	32,376,000	4,202,000	12.9
1950	45,222,000	6,026,000	13.3
1960	54,232,000	8,353,000	15.4
1970	70,920,000	12,561,000	17.7
1974	78,334,000	14,284,000	18.2

SOURCE: Adapted from *The Wall Street Journal*, April 21, 1975, p. 1.

tive term. Individuals continually seek to improve their lot in life, and they can do so only in a healthy economy.

Today governmental policies affect the economic well-being of most Americans. It is widely accepted that no administration can afford to be passive while the unemployment rate rises. At the minimum, unemployment benefits must be increased and the period of coverage lengthened during periods of large-scale economic distress. A more desirable solution is to reduce unemployment by stimulating the economy. This is difficult because increases in federal spending can touch off inflation, which may be more harmful than unemployment.

The government's economic policy is intended to ease the suffering of citizens who are unable to care for themselves and to offer industry incentives to expand and invest. However, these basic purposes have become so distorted as a result of the tendency to yield to demands regardless of their merit that government programs have become more costly and less able to accomplish their goals. The economy is plagued by problems of inflation and unemployment; it is not expanding at a satisfactory rate; and the nation's needy have become ever more dependent on the government for their very existence.

The government's economic role has been complicated by its foreign interests. Economic events abroad have a significant impact on the domestic economy but are largely outside the control of the U.S. government. For example, the Arab oil boycott in 1973 and the resulting fourfold increase in oil prices contributed to the recession and inflation of the mid-1970s.

Priorities and Resources

The government must set priorities in a multitude of areas. Limited resources restrict the range of governmental action and lead to conflict in the setting of priorities. When the Carter administration assumed office in 1977, an assortment of high-priority programs were pending. These ranged from building a fleet of B-1 bombers to designing a national health insurance program. Both proposals involve high costs, and both are backed by influential political leaders and interest groups. These and other proposals must compete with one another for government funding.

Table 1-4 illustrates how priorities have been established over the years.

A major factor in the process of setting priorities is the fact that it is difficult to make significant changes in the way money is raised or spent. Any such change will be harmful to the interests of some segment of society, and will be opposed by that segment. The priorities listed in Table 1-4 also reflect the success of some groups in having their demands met by the government. Note the large percentage of the budget directed to individuals. This includes social security payments as well as veterans' benefits and government pensions. Realistically, this 40 percent of the budget cannot be reduced. Nor can the interest on the national debt or grants to states and localities be eliminated. It is obvious that the flexibility of any administration is severely limited by these factors.

During the twentieth century, the role of the government has changed from one of simply ensuring national security and maintaining domestic order to one that includes a wide range of economic and social objectives. This has further complicated the task of setting priorities and increased the pressure from interest groups. The requirements of practical politics—primarily the need to seek reelection—encourage the government to offer

The 1974 gasoline allotment system was an effort to cope with long lines caused by shortages.

TABLE 1-4 The Budget Dollar (Fiscal Year 1977 Estimate)

WHERE IT COMES FROM....
- Excise Taxes 4¢
- Other 4¢
- Borrowing 11¢
- Corporation Income Taxes 13¢
- Social Insurance Receipts 29¢
- Individual Income Taxes 39¢

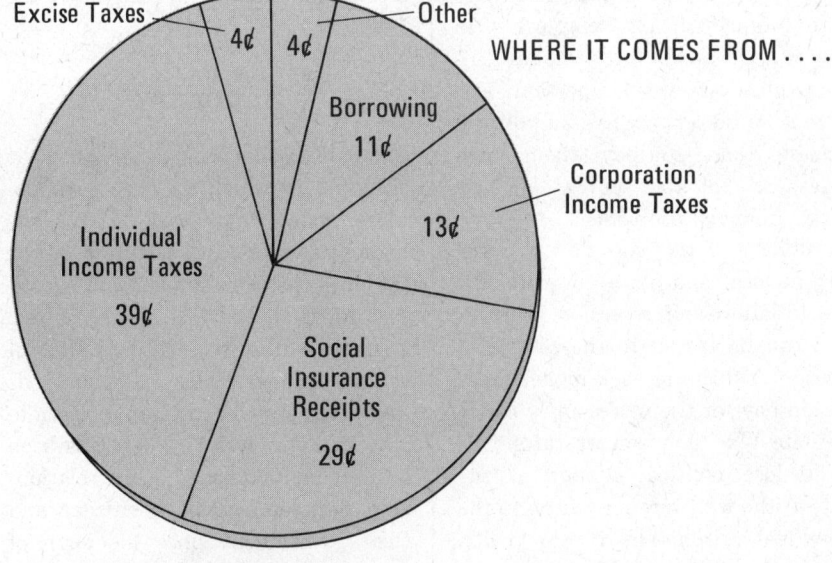

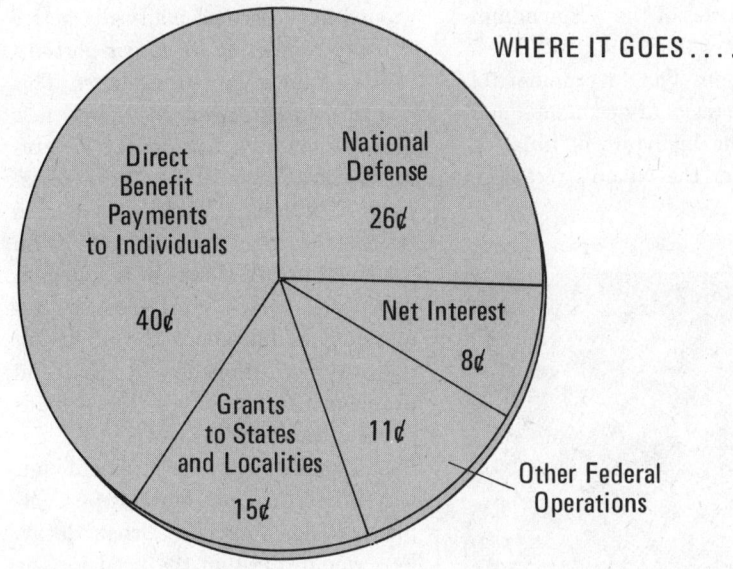

WHERE IT GOES....
- National Defense 26¢
- Net Interest 8¢
- Other Federal Operations 11¢
- Grants to States and Localities 15¢
- Direct Benefit Payments to Individuals 40¢

SOURCE: *The United States Budget in Brief, Fiscal Year 1977.*

something to any influential group that asks the government for help. The failure of so many federal programs to achieve their purpose is evidence that Washington cannot provide the answers to all the nation's problems.

Nor is more money the answer. Billions of dollars have been poured into urban redevelopment projects, but the problems of the inner city have grown more and more serious. Billions have also been spent on "law and order" programs designed to better equip local and state police to cope with mounting crime—but the crime rate continues to rise. The inability to design effective programs to deal with these and other problems has led to even more spending, with no better results. The simple truth is that government was never intended to solve all society's problems and is unable to do so.

Even when basic priorities have been established, it is not easy to decide how those goals should be achieved. The current debate over energy policy is a case in point. There is widespread agreement that reducing energy comsumption is a top priority. But there is no agreement on how to reach this goal. Should domestic oil prices be allowed to fluctuate, or should they be controlled by the government? Will higher prices result in less demand? Will reduced energy consumption cause a recession? What are the relative merits of oil, coal, nuclear, and solar power? The complexity of this issue is obvious, and the failure of the government to chart a policy that can gain widespread approval illustrates the difficulty of choosing among alternative courses of action after a goal has been agreed on. In part, this is a problem of sorting out the arguments of competing groups with conflicting interests. However, it is also due to the inability to be certain that any particular action will achieve the desired end. Nor is it possible to foresee all the possible results of new programs. The problem of choosing alternatives is complicated by conflicting information, and sometimes the same information can be used to support two different proposals. Government programs can also conflict with one another. For example, the government requires cigarette manufacturers to print a warning on cigarette packages alerting purchasers to the hazards of smoking. The Department of Health, Education and Welfare (HEW) has conducted an education campaign to inform smokers and potential smokers about the link between smoking and lung cancer. This program has been well publicized and would appear to represent government action at its best. However, according to a report published by the Health Research Group, a Nader-led organization, the government spends approximately $60 million a year on tobacco price supports and technical aid to tobacco farmers.[2] Thus, HEW is trying to reduce or eliminate smoking while the Department of Agriculture is seeking ways to improve tobacco yields and providing financial aid for tobacco growers.

The Time Element

A basic obstacle to the effectiveness of government programs is the need to balance long-term solutions against the short-term political factors. This is a fundamental weakness of democratic governments. Those who hold elective positions tend to think in time frames corresponding to their terms of office (e.g., two years for a representative, four for the President, six for a senator). Few policies can be successfully carried out in such short periods. The financial crisis faced by New York City in 1975 is an example of what can happen when elected officals fail to plan for the long term. The crisis developed because those in power appropriated money for wages and services far in excess of the available revenues. This policy was stretched out over for many years as long-term debt was used to pay for operating expenses—a financial sin—but eventually the bubble burst when banks and other institutions were no longer willing to buy New York City securities. Thus, the financial capital of the world was a victim of poor financial planning and the political expediency that encourages such practices. The large number of city employees in New York's work force makes this group of voters very important, and there is no better way to gain political support than to pay them high wages—one of the sources of New York's financial problems.

Problems of this sort do not occur only in local and state governments. The inflation and recession of 1973-1975 can be traced to the refusal of Lyndon Jonhson to seek higher taxes to help pay for the increasingly costly Vietnam War. Johnson was afraid he would lose political support if the costs of the war were passed on to the individual citizen. This type of political expediency may also be seen in the economic policies of the Nixon administration just before the 1972 Presidential election. The government followed an expansionary economic policy despite the high rate of inflation, and soon after the Nixon's reelection the nation found itself facing its most serious economic difficulties since the 1930s.

Summary

Samuel Lubell has aptly described the situation in which the American political system finds itself today. "Perhaps," he writes, "we need to drop the pretence that government is a substitute for God, and face up to the real crisis of authority, which is that of self-government. There are not gods among us; only men who must learn to govern themselves."[3] There has been a fundamental change in the relationship between American citizens and their government since the birth of the nation. An increasing number of groups have become politically active and are competing for larger portions of the nation's limited resources. This has pushed the government into new areas of activity. And as the government takes responsibility for more aspects of individual welfare, the citizen becomes increasingly dependent on the government. However, this dependence has been accompanied by increasing doubts about the ability of political institutions to solve all social problems. Not only are there inadequate resources to satisfy all the demands made on the government, but it is difficult to find solutions for complex problems such as urban decay. Few would question the need for the government to be more active today than it was 100 years ago, nor is there reasonable doubt about the growing dependence of most individuals on the government. Today's political controversies revolve around the proper balance between these two factors.

Politics is a dynamic concept, and political institutions must either respond to change or fade away. The Constitution provides a broad outline for the relationship between the individual and the government. Within this outline the American political system has successfully adapted to new realities. It is necessary to understand the principles underlying the Consti-

100,000 people gather in Boston in 1969 to protest the war in Vietnam. The repetition and magnitude of antiwar protests had an effect on government policy during the late 1960s.

tution to judge whether today's political framework will continue to meet the challenge of change. The balance between the responsibilities of the government and those of the citizen will probably change. However, the democratic concept of self-rule requires that the separation between the two be maintained.

CHAPTER 1 CROSSWORD PUZZLE

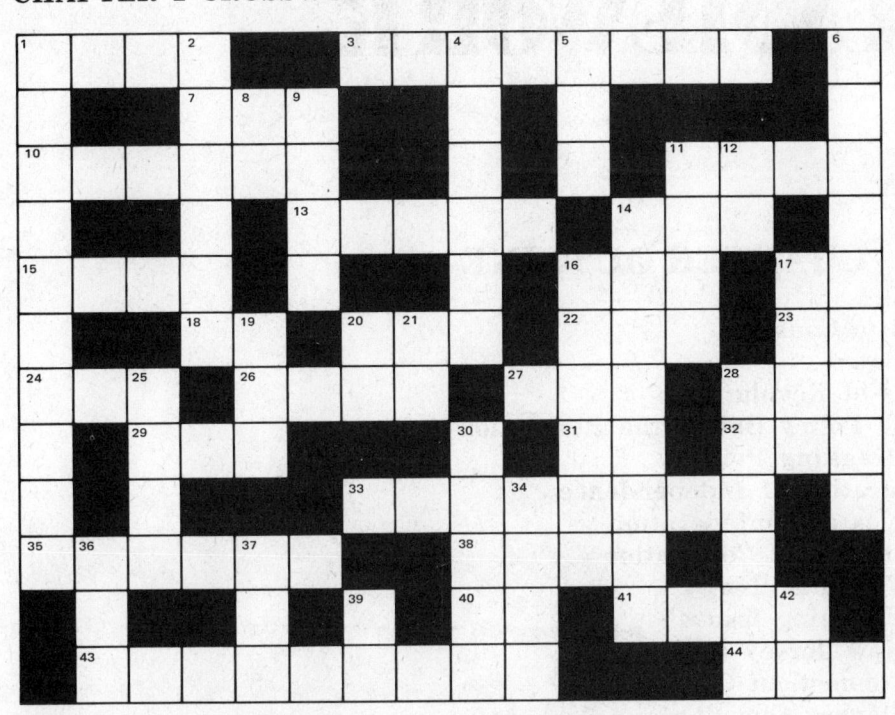

43. It is limited ___ that causes the government to set priorities.
44. Family member

Down
1. ___ is the recognition by citizens that the government is acting within accepted standards.
2. Individuals band together in ___ to more effectively communicate their needs and desires to the government.
4. "The Midnight Ride of Paul ___"
5. Vase
6. The individual has become increasingly ___ on governmental decisions.
8. Opposite of p.m.
9. Job interview question: "How fast do you ___?"
11. Female student
12. First person sing. of verb "to be"
14. The rights of the majority must be balanced against those of the ___.
16. Democracy means that the govt. is accountable to the ___.
17. Villain in Shakespeare's "Othello"
19. Business abbreviation
20. District Attorney (abbr.)
21. Clara Bow: The ___ Girl
25. Horse's flyswatter
28. Performers
30. Occur afterward
34. Commotion; ado
36. Organ of hearing
37. Yoko ___
39. Coffee, tea ___ milk
42. "I ___" (wedding vow)

Across
1. The government balances ___-term national interests against short-term necessities.
3. The ability of the government to ___ people to cooperate for the common good is the essence of leadership.
7. Rodent
10. Dark; dismal
11. Fresh-water fish; complain
13. The constitution gives the government the ___ to impose its will within constitutional guidelines.
14. Dad's companion
15. Journey
16. Apple or cherry ___
17. Opposite of "out"
18. Spanish for "yes"
20. Cease to exist
22. Conclusion
23. Advertisement
24. Floor cover
26. Tidy
27. Place where wild animals are exhibited
28. The ___ of Reason
29. Atomic Energy Commission (abbr.)
31. Puerto Rico (abbr.)
32. Defraud; swindle
33. ___ between interest groups in society turns issues into political questions.
35. Color; cowardly
38. Fat used in cooking
40. We
41. 3 feet = 1 ___

NOTES

[1] Woodrow Wilson, Speech upon accepting the Democratic party nomination for governor of New Jersey (Trenton, September 15, 1910).

[2] Reported by Nancy Hicks in *The New York Times,* August 10, 1975, p. 31.

[3] Samuel Lubell, *The Hidden Crisis in American Politics* (New York: Norton, 1970), p. 297.

CHAPTER 2
THE CONSTITUTIONAL FRAMEWORK

CHAPTER OUTLINE

Questions to Consider
Introduction
The Seeds of Revolution
    British Policy Before the Revolution
    The Breaking Point
The Declaration of Independence
The Articles of Confederation
The Constitutional Convention
    The Virginia Plan
    The Emerging Issues
    The New Jersey Plan
    The Connecticut Compromise
    The Slavery Question
    The Chief Executive
    The Finished Product
The Fight for Ratification
The Meaning of the Constitution
    Limited Government
    Separation of Powers and Checks and Balances
    Judicial Review
    Enumerated Powers
Individual Rights
The Amendment Process
    Early Constitutional Amendments
    The Civil War Amendments
    The Twentieth-Century Amendments
The Federal System
Other Institutions in the Political System
Summary

QUESTIONS TO CONSIDER

The Constitution of the United States has proved flexible enough to allow the political framework to accommodate change, but precise enough to offer guidelines for the government. How did the Constitution evolve? What were the priorities of its framers? The colonial experience resulted in strong feelings about what form the government should take and how it should be limited. How are these reflected in the Constitution? What compromises were made as the thirteen original states tried to reach a workable agreement? Why is the President elected by the people and not by Congress? What is meant by the phrase "checks and balances," which is often used to describe the American political system? And how did the Supreme Court win its powerful position in the political framework?

The American Revolution was a protest against certain actions of the British King and Parliament. What provisions were included in the Constitution to protect individual rights against similar actions by the new government? How can the Constitution be amended to adapt to changing needs? What is the nature of the amendments that have been passed so far? The events leading to the Constitutional Convention and the debates over its form tell us much about the assumptions of the founders. And the amendments tell us much about the Constitution, the evolution of the American nation over the past 200 years.

Introduction

The Constitution of the United States reflects the colonial experience as well as the political philosophy and interests of the nation's founders. Since the delegates represented thirteen states with different problems, potentials, and view points, it was essential that they be willing to compromise in resolving these basic issues. The durability of the Constitution is evidence of their success.

The issues facing the delegates to the Constitutional Convention revolved around (1) the nature of the relationship between the new federal government and the states, (2) protection of the rights of the individual while guaranteeing the ability of the federal government to rule effectively, and, (3) the structure of the federal government.

The Constitution is often called a "living" document. This is a result of the foresight of the framers, who made no effort to dictate the future with an inflexible plan for government, and they provided for an amendment process so that any defects could be remedied. The flexibility of the Constitution is apparent when we consider the changes that have occurred in the relationship between the federal government and the states. The relatively limited national government of the pre-Civil War years has developed into the powerful and highly centralized government of today. The relationship among the three branches of government has also changed in recent years. The power of the Presidency reached a peak during the Johnson and Nixon administrations. However, both the Supreme Court and Congress played key roles in checking the abuses of power by the executive branch that came to light during the Watergate investigations. It is likely that a more balanced relationship among the three branches will result from this experience.

Another area in which changes have occurred is that of individual rights. As the government and society in general have become more complex, protection of individual rights has become more important, and all three branches of the government have moved in this direction since the 1930's.

These changes have taken place within the structure of the Constitution. But the Constitution can best be understood in the light of the time in which it was written: It mirrors the hopes, fears, and political realities of the Revolutionary period.

The Seeds of Revolution

The American Revolution evolved over a period of years as the colonists demanded a greater voice in the management of their own affairs while the British tried to expand their political rule and economic regulation of the American colonies. There was no common economic bond that unified the colonies; they had varying economic bases and, hence, different and often conflicting interests. The clash between the agricultural and commercial segments made it impossible to base a union on anything other than mutual desire to administer the states without outside interference. This attitude enabled the colonists to unite against Great Britain but made it difficult to mold the colonies into a nation.

British Policy Before The Revolution

The British Empire was a rather loose grouping of nations until the Peace of Paris in 1763, which ended the Seven Years War in Europe and the French and Indian War in America. As a result of this treaty, French influence in North America and India was eliminated and Britain set about welding its Empire into a powerful economic unit. This goal included solidifying British control of the American colonies.

One of the first steps in this process was the decision to station a standing army in America to prevent an Indian uprising or renewed activity by French Canadians. The Quartering Act required the colonial governments to quarter the British troops and gave troop commanders the authority to

16 The Constitutional Framework

use unoccupied buildings if adequate quarters were not provided. Adding insult to injury, the British tried to make the colonists pay part of the cost of these garrisons. The colonial legislatures refused to do so.

In 1765 Parliament attempted to raise money by means of the Stamp Act. This act, which provided that all newspapers and legal documents must be printed on stamped paper with the proceeds going to the British government, met with widespread opposition. The fact that the taxes were to be collected by newspapers and lawyers guaranteed the act's failure, since both groups objected and both were influential. Inflamed public opinion led to a boycott of British goods and to repeal of the Stamp Act.

Boycotts and scattered cases of mob violence formed the cutting edge of colonial protest against a series of attempts by the British to raise money by taxing the colonies—attempts that the colonists labeled "taxation without representation." Early opposition to taxation without representation was led by radicals who rejected the very concept of colonial status, while the more prosperous merchants took a conservative view and simply tried to maintain their economic position. But the North Tea Act of 1773, designed to force the colonists to accept tea from the East India Company (in which most members of Parliament and the British royal family were stockholders), threatened the colonial merchants' trade in Dutch tea and raised the fear that they might be further restricted in other areas. Like the Stamp Act, this British action was seized upon by the radicals as a cause for rebellion. At the same time, the conservative merchants abandoned their attitude of protest within the law and supported more militant actions. However, the British tolerated colonial protests during this period, and the purpose of these protests was to force changes in British policy rather than to free the colonies from British rule.

The Breaking Point

In 1774 Parliament decreed that the colonial legislatures must be dissolved. This led to a chain of events that increased the friction between Britain and the colonies and ended in revolution. The military governor of Massachusetts dissolved the Massachusetts legislature in 1774. Its members thereupon formed the Provincial Congress of Massachusetts and prepared for war. Similar events took place in other colonies, and the Virginia legislature called for a Continental Congress. By now the rebellion had gone beyond narrow interests and united the colonies in a common cause.

Delegates from all the colonies except Georgia gathered for the First Continental Congress, held in Philadelphia in September 1774. They stated that they remained loyal to the King but set forth their grievances and called for a complete boycott of British goods. They agreed to meet in May 1775 if the British failed to respond adequately to their protests.

In April 1775 the British commander in Massachusetts, General Gage, moved to seize stores of munitions in Concord and arrest Samuel Adams and John Hancock, the leaders of the rebellion in Massachusetts. The Battles of Concord and Lexington resulted, and revolution became inevitable. The Second Continental Congress met after the Massachusetts battles in order to take control of the Revolution. The delegates recognized the importance of getting all the colonies to participate. They selected a Virginian, George Washington, to command the colonial troops, and John Hancock of Massachusetts was chosen to be President of the Continental Congress.

At this point the colonists' concerns shifted from trying to change British policy to winning political independence. Much of the population still had little desire for rebellion, but the economic status of the elite had been threatened. All that remained to make the break with Britain permanent was military success.

The Declaration of Independence

Thomas Jefferson

The Declaration of Independence, signed in Philadelphia on July 4, 1776, set forth the complaints of the colonies and declared the new nation to be

The Boston Tea Party, December 16, 1773. This was one of the most dramatic protests against British rule.

Signing the Declaration of Independence. This formalized the break between the American colonies and Great Britain.

independent from British rule. It was a remarkable document in that it set forth a political philosophy based on the "natural" political rights of the individual. The Declaration addressed itself to the rest of the world as well as to the colonies: "A decent respect to the opinions of mankind requires that they should declare the causes which impel them to separation." This effort to explain the Revolution to other nations reflected the desire of the colonies to gain worldwide recognition as an independent nation.

The portion of the Declaration that has had the greatest influence on the American political system is the section that sets forth the "natural" rights of the individual and states that governmental power flows from the people. This doctrine is carried to the point of justifying revolution to overthrow an unjust rule:

We hold these truths to be self evident, that all men are created equal, that they are endowed by their Creator with certain unalienable rights, that among these are Life, Liberty and the pursuit of Happiness. That to secure these rights, Governments are instituted among Men, deriving their just Powers from the consent of the governed. That, whenever any Form of Government becomes destructive to these ends, it is the Right of the People to alter or to abolish it, and to institute new Government, laying its foundation on such Principles and organizing its Powers in such form, as to them shall seem most likely to effect their Safety and Happiness.

The Declaration of Independence goes further in the matter of individual rights than might have been expected, given the largely economic causes of the Revolution. It also illustrates the colonists' fear of a government too powerful to be controlled by the people. The idea of a strong central government was unlikely to be popular with the colonists when they had just won freedom from oppressive rule. As a result, the Articles of Confederation, adopted in 1777, proved inadequate to the task of forging thirteen separate colonies into a unified nation.

The Articles of Confederation

The Articles of Confederation were doomed to failure from the beginning. They represented the feelings of people who were determined to live under a government with a minimum of influence over their lives rather than one that had the powers needed to govern effectively. The principles underlying the Articles were largely based on the concepts set forth in the Declaration of Independence: the "natural" rights of the individual and the proposition that governmental power flows from the people. The new government did not have the power to curb either the excesses of a majority or the independent actions of the states. The colonists' bitter experience with royal governors led to the establishment of a government whose actions could, for the most part, be ignored by state legislatures.

The main shortcoming of the Articles was the central government's lack of authority to regulate commerce, levy taxes, and enforce its orders. It was apparent that a political union with so little power could not last long. However, there were fears of a new effort by Britain to regain the former colonies, and it was clear that the individual states could not stand alone against any attack by a European power. Thus there was an obvious need for a new constitution that would ensure the survival of the union. Even the strongest supporters of states' rights were not prepared to allow the union to fail entirely. The weakness of Congress under the Articles of Confederation was apparent from the start. The states charted their own courses in the early days of the Republic, with Congress unable to either help or hinder them. The common economic interests that had brought a degree of unity to the struggle for independence evaporated as economic factions in the commercial states of Massachusetts, Pennsylvania, and New York competed with one another. The southern states— except for Virginia—were unenthusiastic about the idea of union, and even in Virginia political leaders considered the welfare of their state more important than loyalty to the Confederation.

The failure of the Articles to provide adequate funding for the new nation led to widespread issuance of paper money backed only by the credit of governmental units with virtually no assets. The inability of the states to enforce the payment of private debts or the collection of taxes led delegates from five states to meet in Annapolis in 1786 to discuss these problems and ask Congress to call a convention to consider necessary changes in the Articles. This call for change met with little response, but an incident in New England, known as Shays' Rebellion, touched off a series of events that resulted in major changes. The process began when unorganized bands in Massachusetts besieged county courthouses to forestall efforts to collect taxes or force the payment of debts. This open defiance of a state government was on a large enough scale to motivate Congress to issue a call for a constitutional convention to be held in Philadelphia in 1787. It was apparent to all the states that the inability of Massachusetts to deal effectively with its economic problems was an example of the dilemma they all faced.

The Constitutional Convention

The Constitutional Convention met in Philadelphia on May 28, 1787, with 55 delegates eventually taking part (though each state had only one vote). George Washington was elected presiding officer. The revolutionary spirit that had prevailed during the debates over the Articles of Confederation was missing. This time the delegates faced the task of strengthening the national government. They were not enthusiastic about the obvious need to give more power to the federal government at the expense of the states, but they realized that the Articles were inadequate. America's early experience as a nation had shown that a loose federation of states was doomed to failure but had done little to point the way toward the kind of governmental framework that would provide the long-term democratic stability that was lacking under the Articles.

The delegates arrived in Philadelphia convinced that there was an urgent need to build a new political system. Yet the states were still fearful of an all-powerful central government with its potential for tyrannical rules. The task of the Convention was to devise a form of government that could perform the necessary functions but would be structured in such a way as to prevent a small group from gaining ultimate power.

The Virginia Plan

The various proposals for a new government were far-reaching. Rather than simply amending the Articles of Confederation, they offered an entirely new structure. The first proposal placed before the Convention was the Virginia Plan, designed by James Madison and presented to the Convention by Governor Edmund Randolph of Virginia. Randolph expressed the fear of popular rule that was typical of the delegates: "None of the constitutions have proved sufficient checks against popular democracy."[1]

The Virginia Plan proposed to change the structure of the Federal government as well as giving it more power than it had had under the Articles of Confederation. Under the Plan there would be three branches of government instead of only one. The legislature would consist of two houses whose membership and votes would be based on population. One house was to be elected by the people, its members would elect those of the other house. A "national executive" would be elected by the "national legislature," but the Plan did not mention whether the executive would consist of a single person or several people. The judiciary would consist of "one or more supreme tribunals, and of inferior tribunals chosen by the National Legislature." Obviously, under this arrangement most of the power would be in the hands of the national legislature. The legislature was also given the authority to "legislate in all cases to which the separate States are incompetent, or in which the harmony of the United States may be interrupted by the exercise of individual legislation, to negative all laws passed by the several States, contravening in the opinion of the National Legislature the articles of Union." This provision led the way to the idea that the national government should have supremacy over the states but fell short of an acceptable division of powers between it and the states.

The Emerging Issues

One of the major issues faced by the Convention was how to assign seats in the legislature. Should representation be determined by population, as in the Virginia Plan, or be the same for each state? This issue pitted the large states against the smaller ones, although at the time there was little

The Constitutional Convention. Delegates at the convention represented a variety of economic and social interests.

actual difference in population among the 13 states. Virginia had the largest population and Delaware the smallest, but the average of the so-called large states was about 307,000, while that of the small states was 278,000. However, there were differences in land area, and these differences were of greater potential significance than the differences in population size. New Hampshire, Connecticut, New York, New Jersey, Delaware, and Maryland had relatively little untitled land and made up the small-state bloc. The large-state bloc consisted of states with large amounts of "open" land: Massachusetts, Pennsylvania, Virginia, North Carolina, South Carolina, and Georgia. All had land surpluses that would allow for expanding populations.

The New Jersey Plan   *Paterson*

The small states were opposed to the system of proportional representation included in the Virginia Plan. They proposed the New Jersey Plan, which was an effort to amend the Articles of Confederation instead of writing a new Constitution. The smaller states were clearly afraid that the large states would dominate any new governmental structure. Thus, the New Jersey Plan called for a unicameral (one house) legislature, with each state having one vote. Like the Virginia Plan, the New Jersey Plan provided for an executive (consisting of more than one person) to be elected by the legislature. It also provided for a federal judiciary to be appointed by the executive. The basic differences between the two frameworks lay in their conception of the national legislature—one house as opposed to two—and the basis of representation—one per state as opposed to proportional representation.

The small states considered the weakness of the nation under the Articles of Confederation less of a threat than the prospect of being dominated by the large states if representation in the national legislature was based on population as in the Virginia Plan. However, the New Jersey Plan did provide for the supremacy of national law over state law. This was viewed as necessary to the survival of the union. If each state had an equal vote, the large states would be unable to outvote the small states.

The Connecticut Compromise

By a vote of 6-4, the delegates decided to use the Virginia Plan as a basis for further discussion. This reflected the differences in outlook between the large and small states and indicated that major compromises would have to made by both sides. However, the debates over the Virginia and New Jersey Plans revealed important areas of agreement. This encouraged the delegates to proceed with the debate, knowing that the common interest of the delegates in overcoming the weaknesses of the Articles of Confederation was probably stronger than the differences revealed in the two plans. Both the Virginia and New Jersey Plans provided for judicial and executive branches in addition to the legislative branch that had existed under the Articles. They also called for strengthening the authority of the national government over actions of the individual states.   *Sherman*

The delegates were guided as much by the desire to provide for the future prosperity of their states as by the conditions prevailing at the time of the Convention. The western lands offered the large states the prospect of increasing populations, so the proposal for proportional representation contained in the Virginia Plan was attractive to them. They also faced a variety of economic and social problems that made a more authoritative national government desirable.

In contrast, the small states enjoyed greater stability and, having no large tracts of uninhabited land, were inclined to prefer the status quo. Thus, while they recognized the need to enlarge the federal government and give it adequate power, the small states feared domination by the large states and viewed legislative representation based on anything other than equality among the states as potentially damaging to their interests.

The compromise that resolved these differences, known as the Connecticut Compromise owing to the efforts of Oliver Ellsworth and Roger Sherman of Connecticut, recognized the concerns of both blocs. The lower house of Congress was to be chosen on the basis of population, while the upper house would consist of an equal number of representatives from each state.

The Slavery Question

The problem of the divergent interests of the large and small states were largely solved by the Connecticut Compromise. However, this was by no means the only issue that divided the states. The economies of the southern states were based largely on agriculture, while the North depended on trade. The economic differences between North and South also mirrored what would become the key social issue of the new nation: the question of slavery. The southern states considered slaves essential to their agricultural prosperity, whereas slavery was less important in the North. One wonders what would have happened if the northern states had insisted on abolition. Opinions on this subject range from the belief that a firm northern stand would have been successful to the opinion that the South would never have agreed to abolition and that the union might have been dissolved during this period.

The desire to reach a compromise led the delegates to agree that a slave could be counted as three-fifths of a free person in determining the population of a state for the purpose of deciding how many representatives it would send to the House of Representatives. There was also a provision in the Constitution that prevented Congress from interfering with the slave trade for the next twenty years. In return, the southern states had to agree that a slave would also count as three-fifths of a free person for the purpose of assessing taxes.

The Chief Executive

The question of the structure of the executive branch was a perplexing one. The delegates reached agreement that there should be a single chief executive or President, but more difficult was the question of how the President should be elected and what his powers should be. It was originally proposed that Congress elect the President. This posed the problem of giving too much power to the legislative branch, since it would both elect the President and have final authority over the President's appointment of the judiciary. A committee headed by Benjamin Franklin came up with a compromise: the electoral college. The people or the state legislatures—the latter had the authority to choose—would elect a number of electors equal to the total of that state's representatives and senators. The electors would meet in their state on a given day and vote for two individuals, one of whom had to be from another state. The person receiving the most votes would be President and the runner-up vice president.

The President's term of office was set at four years, longer than the two-year term for representatives and shorter than the six-year term for senators. This was an awkward plan, adopted as much out of frustration as out of enthusiasm. It resulted in a fragmented electoral system, but one that served to balance the powers of the executive and legislative branches. For one thing, it increased the possibility that a President from one political party might be faced with a Congress dominated by the opposition party. This was the case during the Eisenhower, Nixon, and Ford administrations—a Republican President had to deal with a Democratic Congress and as a result was often unable to carry out his programs.

The Finished Product

When these issues had been settled, a committee was formed to polish the wording of the Constitution and present it in its final form. The members of the committee were James Madison, Alexander Hamilton, Rufus King of Massachusetts, William S. Johnson of Connecticut, and Gouverneur Morris of Pennsylvania. The latter did most of the writing and is primarily responsible for the Constitution's present form. His influence proved to be more meaningful than the delegates had expected. In presenting the Constitution in the simplest terms possible, many issues were left unresolved. As a result, the Constitution became a living, changing document that has endured over the years rather than an overly restrictive framework in need of continual revision.

The Constitution was signed by 39 of the 42 delegates present on September 17, 1787. In an effort to make it a compact among the American people rather than simply an agreement among the states, the Constitutional Convention called for the elections of delegates to attend a ratifying convention. Approval by nine states would make the Constitution the law of the land, replacing the Articles of Confederation. This method of ratification amounted to a declaration that the national government should be responsible to the people rather than to the states.

The Fight For Ratification

The Constituition was not greeted with universal enthusiasm by the citizens who were eligible to vote for delegates to the state ratification conventions. It has been estimated that only about 4 percent of the eligible voters cast their ballots.[2] The small turnout was due not only to the low level of popular interest in the Constitution but also to a general lack of understanding of the document and its potential impact on the individual citizen. Fear of the unknown also played a role. Many people were satisfied with the Articles of Confederation and would have preferred amending them to meet the nation's needs rather than scrapping them in favor of a new Constitution. The lack of a statement of individual rights also troubled many people. Supporters of ratification argued that the Constitution gave the national government specific rights and that a statement of individual rights would be merely a list of the powers that had not been assigned to the national government. Of course, this was an oversimplification. The failure to include a bill of rights appears to have been more a matter of avoiding potential controversy than a decision to ignore the question because it was unimportant.

The opponents to the new Constitution became known as Antifederalists. They may well have represented the feelings of a majority of the citizens at the time, but their largely rural base gave them little political power. The national government simply was not important to people who lived in rural or frontier areas and had contact only with local government. The Antifederalists also had the disadvantage of having no positive program of their own. Most people regarded the Articles as inadequate, and all the Antifederalists could offer was opposition to the Constitution.

The Federalists, as the supporters of ratification were known, were more unified and in a better position to win support because they had a positive program to offer. At the time of the ratification struggle, they offered the only alternative to the widely recognized weaknesses of the Articles of Confederation. At first the Federalists were successful. Delaware ratified the Constitution in December 1787 and was followed by Pennsylvania and New Jersey in the same month. Georgia and Connecticut ratified in January 1788, and Massachussetts in February 1788. The task of getting the required nine ratifications now became more difficult. It was June 1788 before the ninth state, New Hampshire, ratified the Constitution and it replaced the

Articles. Actually, even ratification by nine states left the Union on shaky ground. The two most powerful states, Virginia and New York, were not among those nine. Virginia finally accepted the compact in June 1788 and New York did so in July of the same year. This late ratification by the two most powerful states is an indication of the controversy surrounding the new Constitution, a controversy that was reflected in the arguments set forth in *The Federalist Papers.*

The Federalist, a group of articles urging ratification of the Constitution, was published in New York newspapers between October 27, 1787 and August 15, 1788. The by-line *Publius* was used throughout, but the authors were James Madison, Alexander Hamilton, and John Jay. *The Federalist* consists of 85 essays, with Jay believed to have written 5, Hamilton 51, and Madison 26.[3] Although there are varying opinions as to how much of an impact *The Federalist* actually had on the ratification process, there is no doubt about its contribution to American political thought. It is still cited in judicial decisions on constitutional questions, since it offers an insight into the intentions of three of the more influential political leaders of the time.

The Federalist presented several arguments for the ratification of the new Constition. It urged the establishment of a strong central government with enough power to avoid political stalemates between the federal and state governments. It also argued that the vast territory controlled by the new nation and the wide range of interests represented by the popultation made it ideally suited to a republican form of government. In *The Federalist* No. 10, Madison dealt with the problem of maintaining a democratic form of government in a nation too large for direct citizen participation in the legislative process:

The two great points of difference between a democracy and a republic are: first, the delegation of the government, in the latter, to a small number of citizens elected by the rest; secondly, the greater number of citizens, and greater sphere of country, over which the latter may be extended.

The effect of the first difference is, on the one hand, to refine and enlarge the public views, by passing them through the medium of a chosen body of citizens, whose wisdom may best discern the true interest of their country, and whose patriotism and love of justice will be least likely to sacrifice it to temporary or partial consideration.

The authors of *The Federalist* also expressed fear that the rights of the individual might be ignored by state governments and greedy majorities. Their concern over the rights of the individual was directed primarily toward those involving property and commercial contracts. This reflects the economic concerns that had led the colonial elite to join the revolutionary movement. In addition, the authors of *The Federalist* discussed the need to limit the power of the central government so that it would be responsive to the people. Finally, while they recognized the wisdom of the principle of majority rule, they stressed the need for legal checks so that the rights of the minority would not be trampled upon.

The Meaning of The Constitution

The Constitution was intended to serve as a compact between the people and the national government. This cured one of the worst defects of the Articles of Confederation: the ability of the states to oppose the national will. The framers of the Constitiution were also concerned with the danger of oppression by a strong central government. The system of checks and balances woven into the constitution was intended to balance each branch of the government against the other two branches, as well as to check the actions of the government in relation to the individual. Thus, the founders had to balance the goals of setting up a national government that would have the resources to endure as a political structure and preventing that government from unduly limiting the freedom of its citizens. The methods used to accomplish these two goals resulted in a constitutional democracy with safeguards against tyranny by the national government.

Limited Government

The Constitution was written by men who wanted to limit the government's power over individual freedom. Thus, the government was given the necessary power to perform its functions, but ultimate political power rested with the people. The ratification of the Bill of Rights shortly after the Constitution shows how important individual rights were to the founders. The concept of limited government also reflects the interests of the delegates to the Constitutional Convention. They had an economic stake in the future of the new nation. Hence, they were concerned with limiting governmental action in the area of property rights as well as that of individual freedom.

There is some disagreement over the extent to which the attitudes of the delegates to the Constitutional Convention were determined by self-interest. In *An Economic Interpretation of the Constitution* Charles A. Beard argues that the wealthy delegates were concerned primarily with protecting their economic interests from both the government and "popular majorities."[4] This view has been challenged by Robert E. Brown in *Charles A. Beard and the Constitution;* Brown found little relation between the delegates' property holdings and their actions at the Convention.[5] However, these contrasting views of the motives of the founders represent the extremes. While it is true that the delegates were well off, it is also true that in many states all adult white males had the right to vote. This was a liberal attitude for the time. It is reasonable to conclude that in pursuing their economic interests the delegates realized that a stable political system was necessary and could not be accomplished by a government with unlimited powers.

Separation of Powers and Checks and Balances

The methods used by the founders to limit governmental power are termed *separation of powers and checks and balances.* James Madison explains the reasoning behind the system of checks and balances in *The Federalist* No. 51:

But the great security against a gradual concentration of the several powers in the same department, consists in giving to those who administer each department, the necessary constitutional means, and personal motives, to resist encroachments of the others. The provision for defense must in this, as in all other cases, be made commensurate to the danger of attack. Ambition must be made to counteract ambition. The interest of the man must be connected with the constitutional rights of the place. It may be a reflection on human nature, that such devices should be necessary to control the abuses of government. But what is government itself, but the greatest of all reflections of human nature? If men were angels, no government would be necessary..... In framing a government, which is to be administered by men over men, the great difficulty lies in this: You must first enable the government to control the governed; and in the next place, oblige it to control itself. A dependence on the people is, no doubt, the primary control on the government, but experience has taught mankind the necessity of auxiliary precautions.

We have only to read this portion of *The Federalist* and relate it to the abuses of governmental power that occurred during the Nixon administration to appreciate Madison's understanding of human nature. Madison recognized that the weaknesses of individuals are magnified when they are given official power, and that a system of representative democracy in which the people choose their leaders would be a necessary but not sufficient check on individual ambition. In recent years political leaders have shown an increasing tendency to ignore constitutional processes in the belief that they are acting in the name of the people. The people's power of election would have been inadequate to check the Watergate abuses, though public opinion and the media played key roles. The constitutional powers of Congress and the Supreme Court were needed to force the Nixon administration to lift its veil of secrecy.

The desire of the Convention delegates to create a strong national government and at the same time guard against the possibility of oppressive rule may be seen in the provision for three branches of government. It was also reflected in the protection of the states as political units. Madison explained the doctrine of separation of powers in *The Federalist* (Nos. 47 and 48):

The accumulation of all powers, legislative, executive, and judiciary, in the same hands, whether of one, a few, or many, and whether hereditary, self-appointed, or elective, may justly be pronounced the very definition of tyranny.....

.... Unless these departments be so far connected and blended, as to give each a constitutional control over the others, the degree of separation ... essential to a free government, can never in practice be duly maintained....

It is agreed on all sides, that the powers properly belonging to one of the departments ought not to be directly and completely administered by either of the other departments.... It will not be denied, that power is of an encroaching nature, and that it ought to be effectually restrained from passing the limits assigned to it.

The separation of powers and the system of checks and balances were carefully planned and have achieved their primary purpose: the denial of final authority to any one branch. Yet the balance of power among the executive, legislative and judicial branches has shifted since the nation's founding. Such changes reflect the personalities of the individuals involved as well as the nature of the problems facing the country at any given time. During the twentieth century, for example, the United States' enlarged international role has combined with the President's responsibility for diplomatic and military affairs to expand the power of the presidency.

The effectiveness of the system of checks and balances may be seen in the war-making powers of Congress and the President. While Congress has the constitutional responsibility for declaring war, in recent years U.S. military forces have been sent into action by presidential order. The massive U.S. involvement in Vietnam resulted when three Presidents — Kennedy, Johnson, and Nixon — committed troops to military action without seeking a formal declaration of war from Congress. Widespread dissatisfaction with this policy and recognition that it disregarded congressional authority led to passage of the War Powers Act of 1973, which limited the President's authority to commit forces without congressional approval.

Judicial Review

Judicial Review is the authority of the Supreme Court to determine whether legislative and executive acts are constitutional. Judicial review is a check on the power of the executive and legislative branches of government. The intention of the founders to provide for judicial review is seen in this passage by Hamilton from *The Federalist* (No. 78):

The judiciary is beyond comparison, the weakest of the three departments of power, ...it can never attack with success either of the other two; and ....all possible care is requisite to enable it to defend itself against their attacks. It equally proves, that, though individual oppression may now and then proceed from the courts of justice, the general liberty of the people can never be endangered from that quarter....

There is no position which depends on clearer principles than that every act of a delegated authority, contrary to the tenor of the commission under which it is exercised, is void. No legislative act, therefore, contrary to the constitution, can be valid....

The interpretation of the laws is the proper and peculiar province of the courts. A constitution is, in fact, and must be, regarded by the judges as a fundamental law. It must therefore belong to them to ascertain its meaning, as well as the meaning of any particular act proceeding from the legislative body....

If then the courts of justice are to be considered as the bulwarks of a limited constitution, against legislative encroachments, this consideration will afford a strong argument for the permanent tenure of judicial officers, since nothing will contribute so much as this to that independence spirit in the judges, which must be essential to the faithful performance of so arduous a duty.

Despite this strong argument in its favor, the Constitution contains no clear provision for judicial review. Article III, Section 1 provides for a Supreme Court, and Congress is given the authority to establish inferior, or lower, courts:

The judicial power of the United States shall be vested in one Supreme Court, and in such inferior courts as the Congress may from time to time ordain and establish. The judges, both of the Supreme and inferior courts, shall hold their offices during good behavior, and shall, at stated times, receive for their services a compensation which shall not be diminished during their continuance in office.

The Court's power of judicial review developed quickly as the nation was learning to live under its new Constitution. The system of checks and balances gave each branch of the government an opportunity to stake out its claim in particular areas. The Court was in an unusual position because of its lack of an independent political power base. Both the President and the members of Congress were elected, while the Supreme Court justices were appointed by the President with the approval of Congress. Thus, the judiciary had to act firmly to gain the power of judicial review since it was not stated clearly in the Constitution.

Enumerated Powers

Recognizing that the ultimate power of the government rested with the people, the nation's founders enumerated the powers of the national government with the balance being reserved to the states and the people. Most of the powers directly granted to the national government are found in Article I, Section 8 of the Constitution:

The Congress shall have power to lay and collect taxes, duties, imposts and excises, to pay the debts and provide for the common defense and general welfare of the United States, but all duties, imposts and excises shall be uniform throughout the United States.

This provision ensures that tax laws will not discriminate against any state or region. It gives the national government the right to tax almost anything or anybody. Some restrictions on this power have been written into the Constitution and some have been established by Supreme Court decisions. There is a provision forbidding the taxation of exports, and the Supreme Court has ruled that interest on state debts may not be taxed by the federal government. The power to tax is fundamental to an effective national government and has been interpreted liberally by the courts. National priorities are reflected in the degree to which various segments of society are taxed and in the exemptions granted for specific purposes.

Article I also contains the other enumerated powers of the national government: the power to borrow money, the power to regulate commerce, the power to set citizenship standards, the power to establish uniform bankruptcy laws, the power to coin money, the power to establish a postal service, the power to regulate patents and copyrights, the power to establish inferior courts, the power to punish piracy and other crimes against nations, the power to maintain armed forces and declare war, the power to use the militia (now called the National Guard) to enforce laws or fight off invasion, the power to govern the national capital, and the power "to make all Laws which shall be necessary and proper for carrying into Execution the foregoing Powers, and all other Powers vested by this Constitution in the Government of the United States, or in any Department or Officer thereof."

These powers are very broad, as they must be if the government is to function. However, they are not all-inclusive, and they do not permit the government to limit the freedom of individuals. The rights of individuals are enumerated in the first ten amendments to the Constitution, the Bill of Rights.

Individual Rights

The Constitution contained fewer provisions regarding individual rights than the Antifederalists would have liked, but those that were included were important. Article I states that "the Privilege of the Writ of Habeas Corpus shall not be suspended, unless when in Cases of Rebellion or Invasion the public Safety may require it." Habeas corpus is fundamental to individual freedom, since it forbids the government to jail a person without specific charges. Article I also prohibits either the federal government or a state government from passing "any Bill of Attainder" (a legislative act that declares a person or persons guilty of a crime and specifies punishment without trial). Finally, Article I prevents both federal and state governments from passing ex post facto laws or laws that seek to enforce or increase penalties for acts committed before the law in question was passed.

Article III deals with the judicial system and guarantees the right to a jury trial to people accused of federal crimes. This article also defines trea-

24   The Constitutional Framework

son so that citizens who oppose the administration that is in power cannot be tried for this offense. Finally, Article VI states that "no religious Test shall ever be required as a Qualification to any Office or public Trust under the United States."

Despite these guarantees of individual rights, the Antifederalists demanded a bill of rights, and this became an issue in the fight for ratification of the Constitution. This issue was especially important in the pivotal states of Virginia and New York. Hamilton held firmly to the view that the limited government provided by the Constitution would fully protect the rights of individuals. But Jefferson persuaded Madison to agree that if Virginia ratified the Constitution in its original form, he would allow a series of amendments setting forth individual rights. In New York, the Federalists were able to achieve ratification only after agreeing to send a letter to the other states calling for a new convention to be held after ratification for the purpose of passing the Bill of Rights.

True to their word, the Federalists proposed 12 amendments to Congress in 1789; by 1791 10 had been ratified. The Antifederalists had succeeded in forcing the Federalist majority to face the entire issue of individual rights within the context of the limited government provided by the Constitution.

The First Amendment guarantees the freedom of speech, press, and assembly and the right to petition the government (i.e. communicate with public officials). It also contains both the guarantee of freedom of religion and a statement forbidding governmental interference in matters of religion: "Congress shall make no law respecting an establishment of religion." This phrase is the cornerstone of the traditional separation of church and state in the United States.

The First Amendment rights have been limited to some extent by the Supreme Court. For example, the guarantee of freedom of religion has been interpreted as implying that religious practices may not violate other legislation. Thus, bigamy is a crime in the United States regardless of religious beliefs. By the same token, freedom of speech does not mean that an individual is free to incite a riot. The First Amendment protects individual rights to the extent that any attempt by the government to limit these rights must be reasonable to be upheld by the Supreme Court. Obviously, the rights of any individual can be no more absolute than the government's responsibility to protect the rights of others.

The Second Amendement gives citizens the right to bear arms in order to protect themselves against domestic as well as foreign threats. Opponents of gun control interpret this amendment as a prohibition against such legislation. In fact, however, the Supreme Court has ruled that the government can control the sale and use of concealed weapons.

The Third Amendment, which prohibits the government from requiring that soldiers be quartered in private homes, is of little significance today.

The Fourth Amendment provides protection against unreasonable search and seizure. Court orders, or warrants, must be obtained before an arrest may be made or the home or property of a suspect searched. There are some exceptions, however. Police officers witnessing a crime are not bound by this prohibition, and their legal power to search such personal property as vehicles has been enlarged to allow for search without a warrant if there is reason to believe that only an immediate search will be possible. Basically, the Supreme Court has interpreted the Fourth Amendment in line with common sense. Arrests or searches without warrants are usually considered legal unless there was not enough evidence or there was time to obtain a court order. The Court has consistently held that only evidence that was obtained legally may be used in federal or state trials. The controversy over the governmental wiretapping, mail interception, and burglaries revealed in recent congressional investigations concerns Fourth Amendment rights. The increasing sophistication of electronic snooping devices has enormously complicated the interpretation of this amendment.

Amendment V deals with the rights of people accused of crimes, ranging from the need to show that a crime has been committed (before a grand jury) to the guarantee that an individual cannot be tried more than once for the same crime (this is termed *double jeopardy*). The Fifth Amendment also states that an accused person may not be forced to testify against himself or herself.

Further, the Fifth Amendment holds that an individual cannot "be deprived of life, liberty, or property without due process of law." *Due process* means that the government must act within the law. It protects the individual from arbitrary and unfair procedures against his or her person or property. The due process guarantees included in the Fifth Amendment apply to the federal government; similar guarantees in the Fourteenth Amendment apply to actions of the states. The due process clause is extremely important. It has served as a basis for numerous court appeals by people who believe the government has acted unlawfully against them. Amendment V also requires the government to pay full value for any private property it acquires and that any such acquisition must be for public use. Property damage is also covered under this amendment on the basis of Supreme Court rulings. For example, if airport noise lowers the value of nearby land, damages can be awarded to the owners of the land.

The Sixth Amendment lists the rights of the accused in criminal trials. The defendant has the right to "a speedy and public trial, by an impartial jury of the State and district wherein the crime shall have been committed . . . and to be informed of the nature and cause of the accusation; to be confronted with the witnesses against him; to have compulsory process for obtaining witnesses in his favor, and to have the assistance of Counsel for his defense." The right to be represented by counsel has been interpreted to mean that the Court must provide legal aid for defendants who are too poor to hire a lawyer.

The Sixth Amendment expands the right to a jury trial set forth in Article III. This is an example of the flexibility of the Constitution. No specific number of jurors is mentioned in the Constitution, nor is there any requirement that a verdict be unanimous. The practice handed down from English common law was for juries to consist of twelve people; it was also necessary for verdicts to be unanimous. This has been changed by Supreme Court rulings, and state courts may provide for as few as six jurors and need not require a unanimous verdict. As a result, juries vary widely among the states.

Every defendant does not have the right to a jury trial; the offense must be one that is punishable by at least six months' imprisonment. Moreover, the Sixth Amendment applies only to criminal cases; the Seventh deals with civil cases and provides that in federal civil trials (not state trials) involving more than $20, the plaintiff and/or the defendant is entitled to a twelve-person jury and a unanimous verdict.

The Eighth Amendment prohibits excessive bail, excessive fines, and cruel and unusual punishment. Suits currently before the Supreme Court claiming that the death penalty is "cruel and unusual" punishment base their arguments on this amendment. This is the type of constitutional provision that is interpreted in the light of the moral attitudes prevailing at any given time.

Amendment Nine is a catchall amendment stating that the government does not have unlimited power over people in areas not specifically covered by the Constitution: "The enumeration in the Constitution, of certain rights, shall not be construed to deny or disparage others retained by the people." This amendment reflects the fear of unrestrained governmental power shared by most of the founders. The Supreme Court has interpreted it to include the right to privacy, a fundamental right not mentioned in the Constitution.

The Tenth Amendment has little to do with individual rights. It was included to satisfy the Antifederalists' demand for the recognition of states' rights as well as (or perhaps more than) individual rights. The Tenth Amendment sets forth the doctrine of federalism: Any rights not given to the federal government or forbidden to the states are "Reserved to the States Respectively, Or to the People."

The Bill of Rights includes the basic constitutional guarantees of individual freedom. They form the core of the idea of limited government as it applies to the individual citizen. Other amendments have been added to these ten as the nation has adjusted to changing conditions.

The Amendment Process

The amendment process has enabled the Constitution to adjust to changing conditions yet has prevented hurried or careless changes. Article V provides that the Constitution may be amended if the proposed amendment is passed by a two-thirds vote of both houses of Congress and ratified by three-fourths of the state legislatures

Suffragettes picketing the White House. These protests were instrumental in securing the right of women to participate in the political process.

or by conventions in three-fourths of the states. Constitutional amendments may also begin with a request to Congress by two-thirds of the states for a constitutional convention to consider the proposed amendment. This method has never beed used.

Most amendments to the Constitution have been ratified by state legislatures. Only the Twenty-first Amendment, which repealed the Eighteenth (Prohibition), was ratified by state conventions. The difficulty of getting three-fourths of the state legislatures to ratify an amendment has limited the number of proposed amendments. (The struggle for ratification of the Equal Rights Amendment is an example.) This, in turn, has emphasized the role of the Supreme Court in interpreting the Constitution. Such controversial questions as abortion and school prayers have led to demands for constitutional amendments, but the difficulty of the amendment process has discouraged serious efforts in this direction. Rather, those who seek change are usually forced to work for new legislation or Supreme Court rulings in favor of their position. Only a relatively small number of amendments have been ratified since the Bill of Rights.

Early Constitutional Amendments

The first amendments passed after the Bill of Rights dealt with political questions that arose soon after the new Constitution went into effect. The Eleventh Amendment (1799) was designed to prevent a flood of civil suits against the states in federal courts. It provides that states cannot be sued without their consent; however, this does not prevent appeals to federal courts from state court decisions.

Amendment XII (1804) was proposed as a result of the Presidential election of 1800, when the Republican-Democratic candidates, Thomas Jefferson and Aaron Burr, received the same number of votes in the electoral college. It provides that Presidential electors should state their choices for President and vice president rather than placing their names on ballots without specifying a choice for President. This amendment also provides that the President will be elected by the House of Representatives if no candidate wins a majority of the electoral votes.

The Civil War Amendments

Not until the Civil War were further constitutional changes believed necessary.

Amendment XIII (1865) banned slavery or involuntary servitude except as punishment for a crime. This amendment forbids individuals to enslave others as well as prohibiting the states from passing any legislation making slavery legal.

The Fourteenth Amendment (1868) states that "all persons born or naturalized in the United States and subject to the jurisdiction thereof, are citizens of the United States and of the State where they reside." There are three classes of American citizens: those born in the United States, those who become citizens through naturalization, and the members of certain Eskimo and Indian tribes. The most important parts of the Fourteenth Amendment are the clauses that prohibit the states from limiting the right of due process (cf. Amendment V). This has had the effect, through Supreme Court decisions, of applying most of the Bill of Rights to state law. The Fourteenth Amendment was designed to protect the rights of all citizens, but was directed primarily toward the newly freed slaves.

Amendment XV (1870) states that the right to vote "shall not be denied or abridged . . . on account of race, color, or previous condition of servitude." This was the last of the nineteenth-century amendments and ended the first century of American government under the Constitution.

The Twentieth-Century Amendments

The first fifteen amendments to the Constitution dealt with two basic issues: the supremacy of the federal government and the protection of individual rights and freedoms. The amendments ratified during the twentieth century cover a broader range of issues. The Sixteenth Amendment (1913) gave Congress the right to im-

A Lincoln-Douglas debate. Lincoln's unwavering stand on human rights as a candidate led to his opposition to slavery when he was President.

pose an income tax. This amendment cleared up earlier confusion regarding the federal government's taxing power and extended it to income "from whatever source derived." The Seventeenth Amendment (1913) provided for direct election of U.S. senators. This was in tune with growing popular participation in the political system, which led to the feeling that senators, like representatives, should be directly accountable to the people. The Seventeenth Amendment replaced the original constitutional provision for election of senators by state legislatures. Actually, some states had already passed laws requiring the state legislators to elect senators according to the will of the people as expressed in state primary elections.

The Eighteenth Amendment (1919), the Prohibition amendment, was repealed by the Twenty-first Amendment in 1933. The federal government spent huge amounts of time and money trying to enforce Prohibition, with very little success. The repeal of Prohibition showed that no constitutional amendment or congressional action will survive without the support of the people.

The Nineteenth Amendment (1920) extended the right to vote to women or, more accurately, stated that women could not be prevented from voting because of their sex. The Twentieth Amendment (1933) changed the inauguration date from March 4 to January 20 so as to shorten the time between the election and the inauguration. It also specified the order of succession to the presidency. The Twenty-second Amendment (1951) limited the length of time the President could hold office to two terms.

The Twenty-third Amendment (1961) gave permanent residents of the District of Columbia the right to vote in federal elections. The Twenty-fourth Amendment (1964) banned poll taxes or any other type of tax as a requirement for voting in federal elections.

The Twenty-fifth Amendment (1967) redefined the order of succession to the presidency and further defined the circumstances in which the vice president may take over the duties of the President. The President may make a written statement that he is unable to fulfill his responsibilities, or the "Vice President and a majority of either the principal officers of the executive departments or of such other body as Congress may by law provide" may make such a statement. In 1974 this amendment provided the means by which President Nixon informed Congress that he was unable to remain in office. The Twenty-fifth Amendment also requires the President to appoint a vice president if that office becomes vacant; a majority of both houses of Congress must confirm the nomination. This is how Gerald Ford became vice president when Spiro Agnew resigned in 1973.

The Twenty-sixth Amendment (1971) granted the right to vote in all elections—local, state, and federal—to citizens 18 years of age and older. The Twenty-seventh Amendment (proposed by Congress in 1972) is now going through the ratification process. Popularly known as the Equal Rights Amendment, it bans discrimination

Women in line to vote in 1920, the first Presidential election in which they were eligible.

based on sex and will become law two years after it has been ratified by three-quarters of the states.

The Federal System

The Articles of Confederation provided for a system of government in which power rested primarily with the states. The Constitution was intended to shift authority to a federal government while at the same time preserving the political autonomy of the states. The question of how to accomplish this was the subject of much debate at the Constitutional Convention. The basic problem that had to be resolved was whether the new Constitution would be a compact between the federal government and the people or an agreement between the federal government and the states, like the Articles of Confederation. Hamilton argued in *The Federalist* (No. 16) that the Constitution must be a compact between the people and the federal government if it was to last:

If it be possible at any rate to construct a federal government capable of regulating the common concerns, and preserving the general tranquility... It must carry its agency to the persons of the citizens. It must stand in need of no intermediate legislations; but must itself be empowered to employ the arm of the ordinary magistrate to execute its own resolutions. The majesty of the national authority must be manifested through the medium of the courts of justice... It must, in short, possess all the means, and have a right to resort to all methods, of executing the powers with which it is entrusted, that are possessed and exercised by the governments of the particular states.

While calling for a national government with the power to fulfill its responsibilities, Hamilton recognized that the state governments had a very important role to play in the new government. The United States was large geographically, and the interests of its population varied greatly. The states were in a unique position to interpret the desires of their citizens. In *The Federalist* (no. 17), Hamilton wrote that "there is one transcendent advantage belonging to the province of the state governments, which alone suffices to place the matter in a clear and satisfactory light—I mean the ordinary administration of criminal and civil justice."

The Constitution limits the powers of the national government to those set forth in Article I. Some of these powers are specific, whicle others are implied. Since the 1930's the Supreme Court has usually interpreted the powers of the national government liberally, thereby allowing it to steadily expand its activities. On the other hand, the states retain whatever powers have not been given to the national government or reserved to the people. Both national and state governments are also forbidden certain actions; other powers are shared. The more important powers and limitations of the national government are listed in Table 2-1.

Other Institutions in The Political System

The framework of American government is contained in the Constitution, modified through the amendment process, and kept vital by a variety of institutions that are continually changing in response to changing conditions in the political environment. But some institutions that are vital to the American political system are not provided for in the Constitution. The vast size of the executive branch in the late twentieth century was not foreseen and is due more to the President's implied powers than to those actually listed in the Constitution. Even the cabinet is a result of custom; it was not mentioned in the Constitution but developed during Washington's presidency. Similarly, though only three branches of government are provided for in the Constitution, there is really a fourth branch: the regulatory agencies and commissions, which have tremendous power in their areas of operation.

Perhaps the most important institution not mentioned in the Constitution is the political party, which serves as a link between the citizen and the government and provides the means by which candidates are nominated, elections held, and political programs explained to the nation. Another significant institution is the interest group, which represents citizens who have interests in common. Finally, judicial review by the Supreme Court, though not explicitly stated in the Constitution, ensures that the intentions of the Constitution will be carried out.

Conclusion

The development of political institutions that were not provided for in the Constitution is a good example of the flexibility of that document. It is this flexibility that has enabled the nation to experience the Industrial Revolution, the Civil War, and sweeping technological and sociological changes while continuing to be governed under the Constitution. The colonial distrust of centralized power is reflected throughout the Constitution—in the system of checks and balances and the

---

TABLE 2-1
Constitutional Distribution of Power

1. Powers exercised *exclusively* by the national government:
    A. Regulating domestic and foreign commerce
    B. Conducting international relations
    C. Settling disputes between states
    D. Admitting new states to the union
2. Powers exercised *exclusively* by state governments:
    A. Creating local units of state government such as counties and cities
    B. Providing laws to deal with relationships between individuals
    C. Ratifying constitutional amendments
3. Powers exercised *concurrently* by national and state governments:
    A. Taxation and borrowing to meet financial needs
    B. Maintaining armed forces appropriate to their respective responsibilities
    C. Maintenance of appropriate judicial systems.
4. Powers *prohibited* to the national government:
    A. Depriving individuals of the protection of the Bill of Rights
5. Powers *prohibited* to state governments:
    A. Depriving individuals of constitutional rights
    B. Restriction of interstate commerce
    C. Coining money or impairing the obligations of contracts.
6. Powers *prohibited* to both national and state governments:
    A. Depriving persons of life, liberty, and property without due process of law
    B. Taking private property without just compensation
    C. Depriving citizens of the right to vote because of race, religion, or sex
    D. Passing *ex post facto* laws
    E. Passing bills of attainder

SOURCE: Adapted from Edward F. Cooke, A Detailed Analysis of the Constitution (Totowa, N.J.: Little field, Adams, 1966), pp. 136-137.

separation of powers within the national government and between Washington and the states. The high priority placed on individual freedom is shown by the early ratification of the Bill of Rights. However, the increasing dependence of the individual on the government that has accompanied the growing complexity of American society could not have been foreseen. Here, too, the flexibility of the Constitution has enabled American society to adapt to changing conditions.

The dominant role of the states in the colonial period and the early nineteenth century made it unlikely that the national government would become very powerful early in its history. However, the increased involvement of the nation in relations with European powers led to increased international trade and a strong emphasis on diplomacy in the years before the Civil War. And the spanning of the continent by railroad and telegraph created a favorable environment for rapid growth and increased dependence on Washington. This new relationship between the national government and the states—popularly called *federalism*—is a significant aspect of the American governmental process today.

CHAPTER 2 CROSSWORD PUZZLE

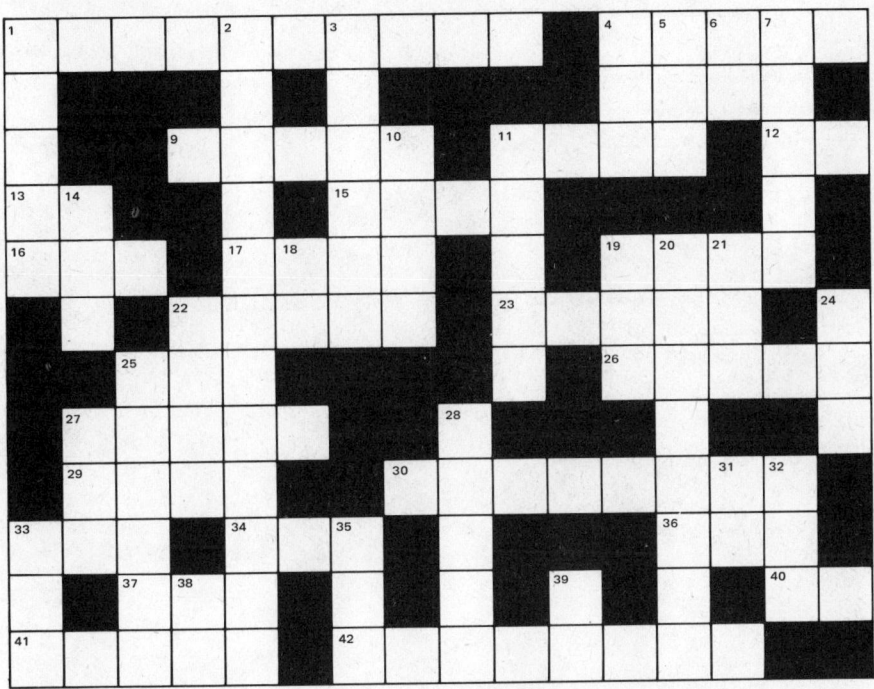

Across
1. The intentions of the framers of the Constitution are reflected in the ___ Papers.
4. An important political institution not mentioned in the Constitution is the political ___.
8. "Hey, what's the big ___?"
9. Kitchen appliance
11. Small beds
12. Possessive word
13. "___ what?"
15. Twelfth of a foot (There are 12 in one foot)
16. Attempt
17. ___ off intruders
19. Ended
22. What Frank Sinatra does in the shower
23. Companion to a table
25. Securities and Exchange Commission (abbr.)
26. Path
27. Fragrant oil
29. Tallest part of a ship
30. ___ review is the authority of the Supreme Court to rule on the constitutionality of legislative and executive acts.
33. "Brevity is the soul of ___."
34. Fluid for writing
36. Direction (abbr.)
37. Freudian term
40. Military Police (abbr.)
41. Buffalo
42. The powers of the ___ government are enumerated in the Constitution with the balance being reserved to the states and the people

Down
1. Freedom of speech, religion, the press, and assembly are guaranteed in the ___ Amendment.
2. While there are three possible ways to amend the Constitution, ___ by state legislatures has been the only procedure by which amendments have been enacted.
3. The inherent flexibility of the Constitution has led to it being described as a ___ document.
4. The center of a peach
5. Want ___
6. Do, ___, mi
7. More docile
10. Terminates
11. The relationship between the three branches of government was designed to erect a ___ on the ability of any one branch becoming dominant.
14. Iron ___
18. Fourteenth letter of the alphabet
19. Grain
20. The proposal in the Constitutional Convention to establish three branches of government was advanced in the ___ Plan.
21. Time period
22. Mathematical groupings
24. Palestine Liberation Organization (abbr.)
25. The most important problems that surfaced under the Constitution involved the relationship between the national government and the ___.
27. French friend
28. Explode
31. Article
32. Moon vehicle
33. Spider's creation
35. Kith and ___
38. Don't stay
39. ___ and fro

NOTES

[1] Quoted in Forrest McDonald, Leslie E. Decker, and Thomas P. Govan, *The Last Best Hope* (Reading, Mass.: Addison-Wesley, 1972), p. 216.

[2] Robert E. Grown, *Charles Beard and the Constitution* (Princeton, N.J.: Princeton University Press, 1956), p. 170.

[3] Gottfried Dietze, *The Federalist* (Baltimore: Johns Hopkins Press, 1960), p. 19ff.

[4] Charles A. Beard, *An Economic Interpretation of the Constitution of the United States* (New York: Macmillan, 1913).

[5] Ibid.

CHAPTER 3
AMERICAN FEDERALISM

CHAPTER OUTLINE

Questions to Consider
Introduction
The Growth of Federal Power
    McCulloch v. *Maryland*
    The Road to Federal Supremacy
Matching Needs and Resources
    The Imbalance of Federal Spending
    The Federal-State-Local Revenue Balance
    Values and Resources
    The Property Tax Dilemma
    Cities and Suburbs
The Role of the Federal Government
    Grants-in-Aid
    Revenue Sharing
Summary

QUESTIONS TO CONSIDER

The federal system of government reflects the differences among the states in terms of both the needs of the citizens and the resources to meet those needs. How relevant are these differences today? Consideration of the role of the states in the federal system is essential to understanding the "hows" and "whys" of American government.

The 50 states exist as political units within the political framework of federalism. But what does the term *federalism* really mean? How has the relationship between the states and national government changed in the past 200 years? What issues have brought the role of the states into focus? These questions will be discussed in the first section of the chapter.

Today we have a powerful national government that appears to dominate the states, and yet, we are aware of serious problems facing the individual states. What is the nature of these problems? How does the urban crisis affect the states? How do these political questions affect the individual citizen? These matters will be the subject of the second section.

The states have become increasingly dependent on actions of the national government. What forms do federal aid take? And what restrictions are placed on the use of that aid? These questions will be discussed in the final section.

Introduction

Federalism is the constitutional arrangement that divides authority between the national and state governments. The power of the national government has grown relative to that of state and local governments because of the national government's greater resources and as a result of Supreme Court decisions that have given the national government more flexibility in the years since the Constitution was written.

The dominance of the national government has become increasingly controversial as the political system has attempted to meet the demands of a changing society. The average citizen's increasing dependence on the government and dissatisfaction with governmental programs and services have combined to raise the question of which level of government can best perform certain tasks. And just as the individual is increasingly likely to look to the government for the solutions to social problems, so state and local governments are seeking greater amounts of federal assistance in solving such problems. Their dependence stems largely from the national government's larger tax base and greater administrative skills.

Many people believe the federal government has grown too large to be responsive to the needs of the people. Local and state governments may more closely mirror the needs and desires of their citizens than a national government, which must consider the needs of a larger and more varied population. During the 1976 Presidential campaign both Gerald Ford and Jimmy Carter spoke on this theme. The basic obstacle to returning power to state and local governments lies in the tangled web of relationships that already exists. Also, some people doubt the ability of state and local governments to be fully responsive to the needs of their citizens.

Within the constitutional framework of separation and sharing of powers, the dynamics of the political system have resulted in a major change in the federal-state relationship, and the balance of power continues to change. The call for greater state influence reflects the gap between the expectations of the American people and the ability of the national government to provide the "good life". Disappointment with the performance of the federal government, whether stemming from the government's failure to solve social problems, the Watergate affair, or the misbehavior of congresspeople, has led some people to argue that returning power to the states may be the best way to deal with such problems.

The constitutional framework does not allow for an equal division of power, but it demands a high level of cooperation if the government is to serve the people rather than simply providing jobs for officeholders. Yet the federal relationship is hard to define. A 1974 study by the Advisory Commission on Intergovernmental Relations (ACIR) noted this problem and described the federal system as follows: "It is a highly complex and infinitely subtle blend of contrasting needs, values, and institutions rooted in a society that is pluralistic, an economy that is diversified, and political parties that are neither centralized nor ideological."[1] This description emphasizes the often conflicting pressures that come into play as the federal and state governments interact.

The Growth of Federal Power

As we have seen, the pluralist nature of the American people and the vast territory covered by the United States lend themselves to a federal form of government. The national government was originally intended to guarantee the nation's security from invasion and to unify the actions of the states in the common interest. The states had different historical backgrounds, were settled by varied groups of immigrants, and had differing political cultures. In the early days of the nation, the decisions that had the greatest impact on the average citizen were made in the state capitals.

The boundaries to which the power of the federal government could be extended were not defined in the Constitution. There was controversy over the question of whether the powers listed in Article I should serve as a limit or a starting point for federal authority. In 1819, however, the Supreme Court issued a landmark ruling on this issue.

McCulloch v. Maryland (1819)

The influence of the Supreme Court on the development of the federal system as we know it today cannot be exaggerated. It began when Chief Justice John Marshall set forth the doctrine of implied powers and the supremacy of national over state law in *McCulloch* v. *Maryland*. The case dealt with an attempt by the state of Maryland to tax a Baltimore branch of the National Bank of the United States, which had been established by Congress. Two issues were involved: first, whether Congress had the authority to establish a national bank, and second, whether the state had the right to tax an institution of the federal government. Marshall held that the powers of the national government are not limited to those listed in the Constitution:

[The Constitution's] "nature," therefore, requires that only its great outlines should be marked, its important objects designated, and the minor ingredients which compose those objects be deduced from the nature of the objects themselves ... Although, among the enumerated powers of government, we do not find the word "bank," or "incorporation," we find the great powers to lay and collect taxes; to borrow money; to regulate commerce; to declare and conduct a war; and to raise and support armies and navies ... It can never be pretended that these vast powers draw after them others of inferior importance ...

Marshall rejected the argument that the State of Maryland had a constitutional right to tax a national bank, stating that "a power to create implied a power to preserve" and that "the power to tax involved the power to destroy."

The Road to Federal Supremacy

The political question of federal supremacy was settled by the Civil War. However, true national power developed during the postwar period. East and west were linked by the steady growth of rail transportation, and the telegraph played a similar role. The nation's vast expanse was made more manageable by rapid communication and modern transportation.

The turn of the century found the nation expanding its territory as a result of the Spanish-American War. This made the United States a world power and increased the role of the national government. The great waves of immigration in the late nineteenth and early twentieth centuries resulted in rapid population growth and created a need for new federal programs to deal with an increasingly complex economy. As a result, the period before World War I was marked by an increase in the rate at which power shifted from the states to the federal government.

The growth of the federal government that we know today, with its multitude of programs, can be traced to the Great Depression of the 1930s. During these years, the role of the federal government expanded with the introduction of social-welfare programs such as social security and unemployment compensation. At the same time, the states became increasingly dependent on federal funds. In the years since the Depression, there has been much debate over the effectiveness of governmental programs and the use of federal revenues.

Matching Needs and Resources

Since the 1930s, the government has played a dominant role in matching national resources with the needs of state and local governments. By *resources* we usually mean tax revenues. These funds are used according to the priorities set by the government and the needs of various regions of the country. But the balance between needs and resources is hard to find. The 1974 ACIR report mentions four areas of imbalance in the federal system: [2]

1. The revenue imbalance that favors the federal government and leaves inadequate resources for state and local governments.
2. The differences in values that lead some states to spend far more on welfare, educational, and social services than others.
3. The problems involved in using property taxes as the major source of school funding.
4. The imbalances in resources and needs between cities and suburbs.

The basic problem illustrated by this list is that the limited nature of national resources requires that many choices be made regarding how much to spend on which programs at any given time. The federal system allows the national government to set broad guidelines for such choices, but these should reflect the demands of the people, which are funneled through state and local governments. Classroom size in Mesa, Arizona; the adequacy of water filtration in Boston; and crime rates in Detroit may appear to be purely local problems. However, the ability to solve these problems depends largely on the resources made available by officials at several levels of government. Federalism may result in a system that is responsive to the people, but this requires effective matching of needs and resources.

The Imbalance of Federal Spending

Table 3-1 shows the amount of federal money spent in the states for each $1 of tax revenue. The figures represent all federal expenditures, including social programs and defense spending. The imbalance of federal spending does not in itself prove that revenues are distributed unfairly. Walter Heller, an economic adviser during the Kennedy and Johnson administrations, put it this way: "This is part of what Democratic liberalism is all about — transferring money from richer states to poorer states." [3] Many people would disagree with this view,

TABLE 3-1
Where the Tax Money Goes: Federal Funds Returned to States for Each Dollar of Taxes, 1973

Alaska	$2.71
Mississippi	2.34
New Mexico	1.96
North Dakota	1.94
Wyoming	1.93
South Dakota	1.77
West Virginia	1.71
Hawaii	1.58
Utah	1.57
Arkansas	1.56
Montana	1.56
New Jersey	1.51
South Carolina	1.39
Alabama	1.34
Maine	1.30
Arizona	1.29
Washington	1.28
Vermont	1.27
Virginia	1.26
New Hampshire	1.20
Kansas	1.11
Louisiana	1.11
California	1.07
Oklahoma	1.04
Florida	.97
Tennessee	.96
Idaho	.87
Georgia	.86
Rhode Island	.86
Texas	.84
Iowa	.84
Maryland	.83
Massachusetts	.83
Oregon	.78
Kentucky	.77
Nevada	.75
Nebraska	.72
North Carolina	.70
Missouri	.69
Wisconsin	.62
Pennsylvania	.61
Indiana	.58
Minnesota	.57
Colorado	.56
Connecticut	.51
Ohio	.51
New York	.47
Illinois	.39
Michigan	.36
Delaware	.40

SOURCE: *The Philadelphia Inquirer*, February 15, 1976, P. I-1. Reprinted by permission.

however. Money is power, and conservative political leaders like Ronald Reagan believe power should be returned to the states on the theory that state officials can be more responsive to the citizens of that state than federal officials, who must use blanket solutions that may or may not work. This was the reasoning behind the revenue-sharing plan proposed by President Nixon in 1972.

Interesting arguments flow from the data in Table 3-1. When New York City faced a financial crisis in 1975, there was much controversy over what role, if any, the federal government should play in helping the city avoid going bankrupt. Opponents of federal aid claimed that the city had used its revenues unwisely, mentioning its tuition-free city university system and higher-than-average level of welfare payments as among the causes of its financial problems. New Yorkers pointed to the small amounts of federal money returned to the state as the real problem.

While New York's financial problems have received much public attention, Table 3-1 indicates many other imbalances that cannot be explained as a transfer of funds from rich states to poor states. Part of the problem is defining "rich" and "poor." New York is rich in terms of economic assets but poor in terms of the adequacy of its resources.

The Federal-State-Local Revenue Balance

A large portion of federal revenue comes from individual income taxes (39 percent) and corporate income taxes (13 percent)[4]. Most of the remainder comes from programs such as social security, which earmark funds for specific purposes. Current levels of federal taxes on personal and corporate incomes have served to limit sources of revenue for states and cities. Where states or cities do impose personal income taxes, they are usually well under 10 percent, often in the 2-3 percent range. The same is true of corporate income taxes—the federal government gets the lion's share, while states are forced to settle for rates of 10 percent or less. This forces states and cities to rely on sales taxes and similar ways of raising money (e.g., taxes on tickets to movies and sports events). Local governments are also handicapped by independent school boards that fund their operations from property taxes, leaving little or nothing to serve as a base for local taxes. This system has favored the wealthier suburbs over the cities, and left most cities dependent on federal aid to attack such problems as housing, crime, and mass transit.

State and local governments have increased their revenues in recent years; many states have imposed income taxes for the first time, and the federal government has provided increased funding for a variety of social programs. Table 3-2 shows major types and amounts of federal and state spending on social-welfare programs. While most social insurance, veterans, and housing programs are funded by the federal government, education expenditures are largely the responsibility of state and local governments. The relatively small federal contribution to education and the large sum—almost $75 billion — spent by the states for this purpose indicate that this is a major area of imbalance. In the areas of public aid, and health and medical care, federal, state, and local government participation is more nearly equal.

In 1973, state and local governments received 20.6 percent of their total revenues from the federal government.[5] The combination of increased federal assistance and new taxes enabled state and local government to record a $14.8 billion surplus in 1972, a year in which the federal government had a budget deficit of $23 billion.[6] These figures indicate that the problem is not so much lack of money as inability to use it where it is needed most because of the difficulty of matching federal programs with state and local needs. On the other hand, the idea of putting the responsibility for many programs in the hands of state and local authorities is disturbing to those who believe the federal government is more skilled in this area. Yet, it could be argued that state and local governments would become equally skilled with increased resources and control over expenditures. Regardless of any future shifts in the balance of responsibilities among federal, state, and local governments, however, it is clear that any such change must be accompanied by the resources to do the job.

Values and Resources

A major obstacle to the correction of imbalances between needs and resources lies in the differences among the states themselves. There are obvious differences in resources. It is easier for California and Texas to raise revenues than for West Virginia or Mississippi. This is partly because of differences in size, but mostly because of differences in natural resources and industrial concentration. However, resources alone do not determine policy. A state's priorities reflect its values and determine what it will do with whatever resources it has. Thus, when the federal government wants to correct revenue imbalances, it is not enough to consider the resources of the area in question; its values are an important factor too.

Table 3-3 shows state expenditures per capita (i.e., per person) for basic programs. Note that California spends about the same amount of money per person on highways as on health and hospitals. In contrast, New York spends twice as much on health and hospitals as on highways. While California's larger geographic area accounts for some of the difference, the different values of the residents of the two states explain most of it. It is possible for governments to provide a wide variety of services, and state and local governments usually can determine how their resources will be spent. New York City long prided itself on its generous welfare payments and its free city college system, which at one point served over 250,000 students. But the financial crunch of 1975 forced New York to change its policies; among other things, the city college began charging tuition.

There are many differences in the ways state and local governments share health, education, and welfare costs. Some of the underlying problems are beyond the control of state governments. The welfare costs of states with large urban areas reflect the tendency of the rural poor to move to the cities. The states have no control over such migration but must bear the costs. While it can be argued that part of the welfare burden is self-imposed (i.e., the payments are too high), the problem is really a national one and should be dealt with at the national level. Congress took the first step in this direction in 1972 with programs to aid the blind, aged, and disabled. As the financial problems of urban areas and states become more serious, there will be added pressure on Washington to take over the entire welfare burden.

The Property Tax Dilemma

The problem of how to pay for public education has not been solved satisfactorily. The desire for local control of the public schools is strong, and so is the effort to keep politics out of the school system by electing "independent" school boards, many of which have the power to impose taxes. Revenues for education have traditionally come from property taxes, but this system is under attack on two fronts. First, most urban areas have already raised property taxes so high that people are moving to the suburbs to escape them. School boards also find in many cases that they must compete with local governments for revenue from property taxes. Second, the idea of paying for education by means of property taxes has been challenged in court on the ground that the amount

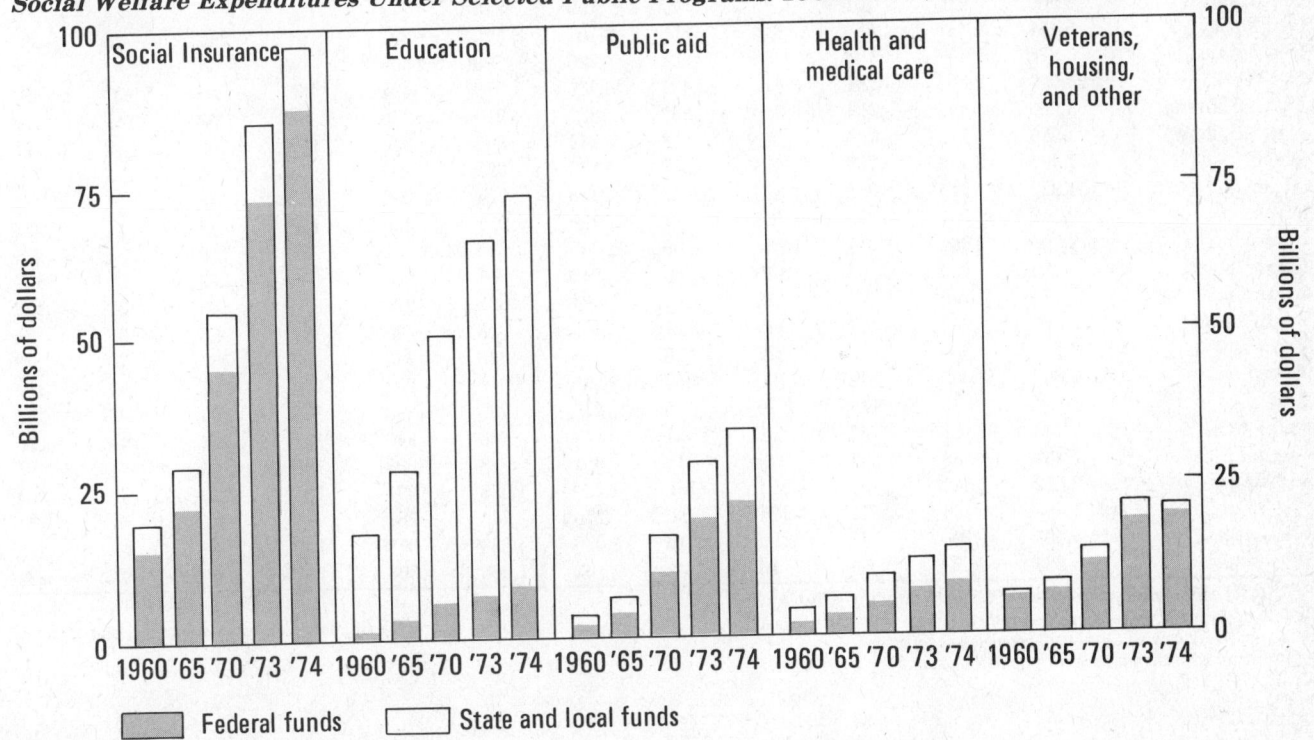

TABLE 3-2
Social Welfare Expenditures Under Selected Public Programs: 1960-1974 (Fiscal Year Data)

SOURCE: *Statistical Abstract of the United States*, 1975, p. 276.

TABLE 3-3
Direct General Expenditure of State and Local Governments—States: 1973

State	Total	Education	Highways	Public Welfare	Health and Hospitals	All Other*	Total	Education	Highways	Public Welfare	Health and Hospitals	All Other*
	\multicolumn{6}{c}{Expenditure (millions of dollars)}	\multicolumn{6}{c}{Expenditures per Capita** (dollars)}
U.S.	181,086	69,573	18,615	23,582	13,844	55,472	863	332	89	112	66	264
Alabama	2,254	851	285	289	243	586	637	240	81	82	69	166
Alaska	784	286	127	40	21	310	2,376	867	284	122	63	940
Arizona	1,685	794	184	90	105	512	819	386	90	44	51	249
Arkansas	1,118	428	161	161	93	275	549	210	79	79	46	135
California	21,082	7,284	1,496	3,866	1,432	7,005	1,023	354	73	188	70	340
Colorado	2,065	933	219	236	147	530	847	383	90	97	60	217
Connecticut	2,770	1,048	267	307	152	997	900	341	87	100	49	324
Deleware	643	290	83	49	31	191	1,117	504	143	85	53	331
District of Columbia	1,176	252	52	199	139	533	1,576	338	70	267	186	715
Florida	5,292	1,910	622	415	509	1,836	689	249	81	54	66	239
Georgia	3,574	1,273	400	499	467	936	747	266	84	104	98	196
Hawaii	1,091	348	100	107	67	470	1,311	418	120	129	80	564
Idaho	569	212	96	53	42	168	740	275	124	68	54	219
Illinois	9,813	4,015	941	1,484	590	2,783	873	357	84	132	53	248
Indiana	3,600	1,765	391	303	287	854	677	332	73	57	54	161
Iowa	2,136	1,004	370	168	144	449	735	346	127	58	50	155
Kansas	1,702	716	258	177	126	426	747	314	113	78	55	187
Kentucky	2,240	874	412	267	136	551	670	261	123	80	41	165
Louisiana	2,882	1,028	386	335	281	852	766	273	103	89	75	226
Maine	782	284	125	118	37	217	761	276	122	115	36	211
Maryland	3,829	1,525	364	404	273	1,263	941	375	89	99	67	310
Massachusetts	5,742	1,991	378	1,055	441	1,877	987	342	65	181	76	323
Michigan	8,582	3,546	705	1,298	649	2,385	949	392	78	143	72	264
Minnesota	3,763	1,653	460	428	244	978	966	424	118	110	62	251
Mississippi	1,519	552	243	210	164	350	666	242	107	92	72	153
Missouri	3,238	1,349	363	347	264	915	681	284	76	73	55	192
Montana	640	251	128	48	32	182	887	348	178	66	44	251
Nebraska	1,127	464	185	101	79	298	731	301	120	65	51	194
Nevada	602	206	82	34	53	227	1,098	376	150	63	97	413
New Hampshire	566	216	101	63	27	159	716	273	127	80	34	201
New Jersey	6,451	2,437	694	814	356	2,151	876	331	94	111	48	292
New Mexico	878	407	104	86	56	226	793	368	94	77	51	204
New York	24,099	7,702	1,261	3,674	2,497	8,966	1,319	422	69	201	137	491
North Carolina	3,260	1,441	424	306	252	837	618	273	80	58	48	159
North Dakota	515	213	100	40	18	144	805	333	157	62	29	225
Ohio	7,497	3,158	787	813	569	2,170	699	294	73	76	53	202
Oklahoma	1,929	715	258	318	149	490	724	268	97	119	56	184
Oregon	2,116	797	278	161	91	789	951	358	125	72	41	354
Pennsylvania	9,700	3,960	1,017	1,364	609	2,749	815	333	85	115	51	231
Rhode Island	780	280	56	145	56	242	801	288	58	149	57	249
South Carolina	1,725	745	194	123	182	481	633	273	71	45	67	177
South Dakota	560	258	117	45	21	118	818	377	171	66	31	173
Tennessee	2,633	989	343	276	290	736	638	240	83	67	70	178
Texas	7,895	3,385	872	790	557	2,292	669	287	74	67	47	194
Utah	914	455	119	79	45	216	790	393	103	69	39	187
Vermont	448	161	87	61	21	119	965	346	187	132	44	255
Virginia	3,432	1,433	515	323	210	951	713	298	107	67	44	198
Washington	3,612	1,342	465	394	162	1,250	1,053	391	136	115	47	364
West Virginia	1,334	468	378	121	92	276	744	261	211	67	51	154
Wisconsin	4,061	1,706	489	480	310	1,078	889	373	107	105	68	236
Wyoming	383	177	76	16	32	82	1,085	501	215	45	91	233

SOURCE: *Statistical Abstract of the United States, 1975,* Table 429.

*Includes police protection, fire protection, natural resources, sanitation, local parks and recreation, financial administration, general control, and interest on general debt as well as miscellaneous lesser functions.

**Based on estimated resident population as of July 1, 1973.

spent per pupil varies widely from one city to another and between cities and suburbs, thereby denying some children the right to an equal education.

In 1974, the wealthy suburban community of Englewood Cliffs, New Jersey spent $2000 a year per student, with a property tax of $0.99 per $100 valuation. In contrast, the city of Camden, New Jersey spent only $1000 per student despite a tax rate of $1.94 per $100 valuation. This difference was explained by the fact that Englewood Cliffs had $246,000 in taxable property per student, while Camden had only $18,000 per student on which to base property taxes. Thus, the problem of school funding based on property taxes extends beyond the willingness of parents to pay for better education for their children. People who live in decaying urban areas or poor rural areas simply do not have enough taxable property.[7] The New Jersey Supreme Court has recently declared that the system of property taxation is a violation of the state constitution. Similar rulings have been laid down by several state supreme courts and lower federal courts.

In 1973, the United States Supreme Court ruled (*Rodriquez* v. *San Antonio School District*) that while the use of property taxes for school revenues is unfair, it is not unconstitutional. The Court suggested that the states act to correct the situation. Even before the *Rodriquez* opinion, many states had begun to take such action. For example, Minnesota increased state aid to local school districts (1971); Maryland took over responsibility for school construction (1971); California reduced property taxes and increased state aid (1972); and Florida appropriated state funds in amounts designed to equalize the resources of school districts accross the state (1973).[8] Today all the states are grappling with this problem, some more successfully than others. This is a highly emotional issue because most people believe they have a right to give their children a superior education by living in a school district that offers above-average programs.

Mexican farm workers in California harvest lettuce. States with migrant farm workers face the problems of coping with a large poverty-stricken population.

The national government has played a minor role in the property tax issue, since most people want to keep public education under local control. However, the increased role of the states in this important area may well lead to demands for more federal aid. Until now such aid has been limited to remedial programs like Head Start, school lunch programs, and the funding of new construction for colleges and universities. Education, thus, provides an example of an area in which the desire of individuals to control their own lives conflicts with increasing dependence on financial aid from the Federal government.

Cities and Suburbs

The changing composition of American cities is clearly shown in Table 3-4. The move to the suburbs by upper- and middle-income families has reduced the cities' tax base and intensified their social problems as lower-income families have become the dominant group. These trends have also reduced job opportunities as industries have built modern facilities in more pleasant surroundings. Table 3-5 shows how this movement has further weakened the financial resources of the cities. Yet despite the move to the suburbs and the decay of the cities, the suburbs depend on the city for their existence.

The cities face the dual burden of a shrinking tax base and the need to provide services for nonresidents. The financial burden is outlined in Table 3-6; both debt and taxes increase along with the size of the city. Most suburban areas owe their existence to the economy of the city, which provides not only jobs but social and cultural advantages as well. A U.S. government study found that in 1970, 36.2 percent of the managerial jobs and 25 percent of the professional and technical jobs in New York City were held by suburban residents.[9] Even the industries that have migrated away from the cities usually depend on urban transportation systems. Since the suburbs do not have an independent source of survival, the decay of the cities will eventually be felt in the suburbs. The problem that must be faced is the regional nature of cities and their suburbs.

It is easier to describe the problems of the cities and point out the interdependence of city and suburb than to find solutions. But sociologist Edwin C. Banfield believes that most American cities can avoid large debt increases without depending on additional state and federal aid. Banfield notes that school enrollments will shrink, resulting in savings, and that governmental activities could be made more efficient.[10] Moreover, not all cities are experiencing these trends. The older cities of the northeast and north central regions have been especially hard hit by urban decay. Large cities in the Southwest such as Houston, Dallas, and Phoenix face the social problems of rapid expansion but are still on the upswing. Both groups, however, have to look toward regional

TABLE 3-4

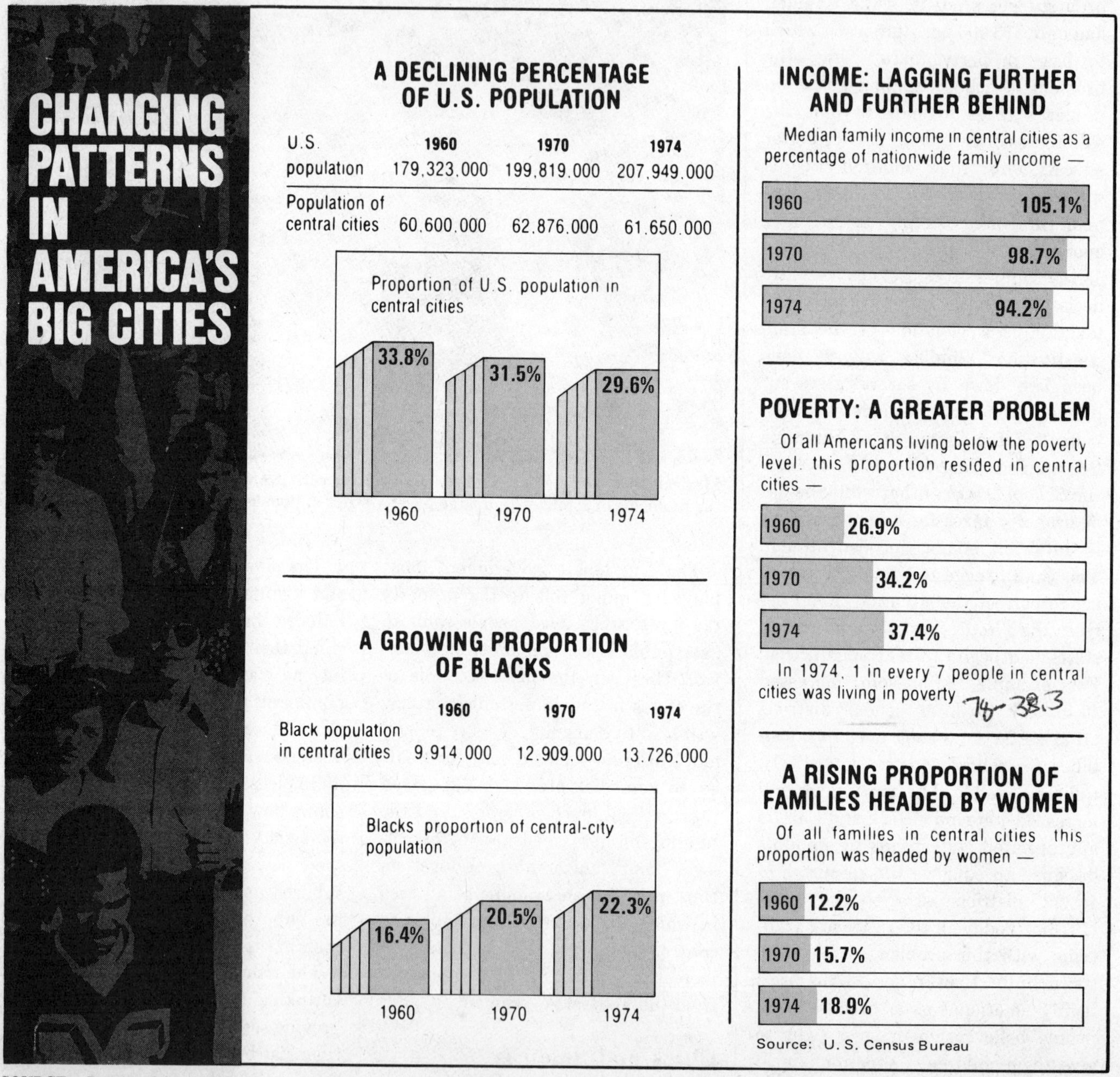

CHANGING PATTERNS IN AMERICA'S BIG CITIES

A DECLINING PERCENTAGE OF U.S. POPULATION

	1960	1970	1974
U.S. population	179,323,000	199,819,000	207,949,000
Population of central cities	60,600,000	62,876,000	61,650,000

Proportion of U.S. population in central cities
- 1960: 33.8%
- 1970: 31.5%
- 1974: 29.6%

A GROWING PROPORTION OF BLACKS

	1960	1970	1974
Black population in central cities	9,914,000	12,909,000	13,726,000

Blacks proportion of central-city population
- 1960: 16.4%
- 1970: 20.5%
- 1974: 22.3%

INCOME: LAGGING FURTHER AND FURTHER BEHIND

Median family income in central cities as a percentage of nationwide family income —
- 1960: 105.1%
- 1970: 98.7%
- 1974: 94.2%

POVERTY: A GREATER PROBLEM

Of all Americans living below the poverty level, this proportion resided in central cities —
- 1960: 26.9%
- 1970: 34.2%
- 1974: 37.4%

In 1974, 1 in every 7 people in central cities was living in poverty

A RISING PROPORTION OF FAMILIES HEADED BY WOMEN

Of all families in central cities this proportion was headed by women —
- 1960: 12.2%
- 1970: 15.7%
- 1974: 18.9%

Source: U.S. Census Bureau

SOURCE: Reprinted from *U.S. News & World Report,* November 3, 1975. Copyright 1975 U.S. News & World Report, Inc.

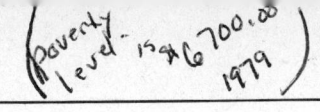

solutions to find long-range answers to their needs.

Urban areas and their suburbs are governed under a multitude of political arrangements. Some cities are combinations of city and county governments with a wide range of responsibilities—New York, Philadelphia, and Baltimore are examples. Their financial burdens are magnified by the lack of a county government that includes the city and its suburbs. Other cities have successfully met this challenge through the merging of city and suburban services. The best example of this is Dade County, Florida, which includes 26 incorporated cities, among them Miami and Miami Beach. The metropolitan government, known as Metro, has the power to provide and operate mass transit systems, recreational facilities, and major highways and to regulate zoning, building codes, and utilities. This is a form of regional federalism in which the cities have agreed to place certain functions under Metro control while retaining control in other areas. Still another form of regionalism is the _annexation_ of areas adjacent to large cities. This is a common practice in the Southwest and explains how Los Angeles expanded to its present size. Annexation has the effect of combining city and suburb by eliminating one of the two governments involved.

Despite the attractive possibilities of regionalism, it is not a cure-all. Jacksonville, Florida and surrounding Duval County consolidated their governments in 1967, creating a city of over 500,000. Though this move has been very successful, Jacksonville Mayor Hans Tanzler says "consolidation is not a panacea. No form of government is any better than the people you put in it. But given that, in a democratic society, you don't always have optimum people, cooperation and understanding, consolidation not only reduces the number of government entities you have to deal with but also the abrasive friction between layers of government." [11]

Expressway and rapid transit system in Chicago pass the Sears Tower, world's tallest building. Problems of mass transit are especially acute in urban areas.

The Role of the Federal Government

The problems of state and local governments cannot be separated from those of the federal government, which is responsible for providing for

TABLE 3-5
The Job Market is Shrinking in Many Cities

From 1970 to 1974, even before the wave of recession layoffs, employment was declining in major cities—at a time when jobs in U.S. as a whole increased by 9.3 percent. Among big cities losing jobs—

	People at Work		
	1970	1974	Change
Detroit	577,000	470,000	Down 18.5%
St. Louis	224,000	183,000	Down 18.3%
Baltimore	353,000	308,000	Down 12.7%
Philadelphia	776,000	682,000	Down 12.1%
Washington	342,000	307,000	Down 10.2%
Chicago	1,364,000	1,249,000	Down 8.4%
New York	3,131,000	2,932,000	Down 6.4%
San Francisco	454,000	443,000	Down 2.4%
Los Angeles	1,282,000	1,273,000	Down 0.7%

SOURCE: *U.S. News & World Report*, April 5, 1976, p. 51. Reprinted from *U.S. News & World Report.* Copyright © 1976 U.S. News & World Report, Inc.

TABLE 3-6
The Bigger the City, the Heavier the Financial Burden

Taxes

Average revenues per capita from local sources, in cities with populations of—

1 million and over	$426.90
500,000 to 1 million	285.47
300,000 to 500,000	231.37
All U.S. cities	208.58

Debt

Average local debt per resident in cities with populations of —

1 million and over	$1,052
500,000 to 1 million	569
300,000 to 500,000	526
All U.S. cities	464

SOURCE: *U.S. News & World Report*, April 5, 1976, p. 51. Reprinted from *U.S. News & World Report.* Copyright © 1976 by U.S. News & World Report, Inc.

The most carefully laid government plans are still subject to the laws of nature.

the general welfare of all Americans. There are a variety of programs through which Washington attempts to aid other levels of government as well as the individual citizen. In fiscal 1977, 40 percent of the federal budget consisted of direct payments to individuals — social security, veterans' benefits, retirement benefits to ex-government employees, unemployment payments, food stamp programs, and so forth. In addition, 15 percent of the federal budget went to state and local governments.[12] There are also two major tax laws designed to help state and local governments finance their activities. Interest income from municipal and state bonds is tax free. This allows state and local governments to raise money at a lower interest rate than if the income was taxable. In addition, individuals may deduct state and local taxes when computing their taxable personal income. The combined cost to the government of these two provisions is estimated at $11.2 billion for fiscal 1977.[13]

The benefits from such provisions are not one-sided, however: Federal property cannot be taxed. This provision is estimated to have cost New York City almost $14 million in fiscal 1976.[14] It is obvious that the federal government taxes with one hand and returns revenue to state and local governments with the other. The question is, how effective is this revenue exchange in meeting the needs of the people? Let us consider the main types of federal grants with this question in mind.

Grants-in-Aid

The grant-in-aid system was established to offer federal funds to state and local governments for specific purposes. In most cases, states were required to provide matching funds and agree to carry out the program in question according to federal guidelines. The original grant programs set quotas for each state, but this system has been replaced by one in which the money is made available on a first-come, first-served basis to state and local governments whose applications meet the requirements for the grant. Some programs offer grants to individuals, and in some cases there is no requirement for matching funds.

The grant-in-aid program gives the federal government an opportunity to channel funds into areas of high priority while getting local authorities to operate the necessary programs. While Washington cannot make the states build highways or offer welfare on a merit system, it can offer grants-in-aid as a reward for doing these things.

There is controversy over the merits of grants-in-aid. The advantages of grants are that they encourage the states to take actions that the federal government considers desirable and give poorer states a chance to provide services that they would not be able to provide otherwise. The disadvantages are that they penalize the richer states by offering more aid to the poorer ones and interfere with the states right to determine what their citizens need. True, states and localities do not have to participate in grant projects, but the financial advantages are usually too great to ignore. There is also criticism of the way grant programs are run. Applying for a grant means wading through oceans of red tape and government forms. Few small governmental units can afford to hire the staff they need to make such applications. Indeed, the problem is so severe that many grants are lost because of lack of knowledge at the local level. Another and more serious criticism is that it is impossible for a federal official to set standards that can apply to grant programs under all conditions and in all areas of the nation. This difficulty has led to new methods of giving federal aid to state and local governments.

Revenue Sharing

During the Nixon administration, Congress passed the Fiscal Assistance Act, or revenue sharing, which provided over $5 billion in 1972 and increased to about $6.6 billion in 1977, the last year provided for in the original Act. (Congress has extended the Act through 1982.) Under revenue sharing, one-third of the money goes to states and the rest to local governmental units. It is divided under a formula based on factors such as population size and tax revenues. The aim of revenue sharing is to offer state and local governments "no strings" funds to be spent according to local priorities rather than federal guidelines. The only limits on the use of revenue-sharing funds are that they may not be used to provide matching funds under existing grant programs and that they must be spent in a nondiscriminatory manner. The total amount offered under revenue sharing accounts for only about 12 percent of the money that flows from Washington to local and state governments. The importance of the Act is that it is an experiment in giving local authorities more leeway in setting priorities and carrying out programs.

The results of the first five years of revenue sharing are unclear. The money has been used for a variety of capital goods and services ranging from paying police salaries to redecorating municipal buildings. In 1976, a group of public-interest organizations, including the League of Women Voters Education Fund, the National Urban Coalition, the Center for Community Changes, and the Center for National Policy Review, published a study that was highly critical of revenue sharing. Among its criticisms are the following: [15]

1. The formula under which funds are divided discriminates against the poor in urban areas because of the higher costs of providing services in cities.
2. The nondiscriminatory provision did not succeed in reducing job discrimination against minorities and women.
3. The "no strings" feature was intended to free state and local governments from accountability to the federal government but had the effect of freeing them from accountability to their own citizens.
4. Not enough money was spent on programs directed toward the poor.

These criticisms imply that the purpose of revenue sharing was to declare a new war on poverty and discrimination. They also imply that the federal government is more effective in designing and carrying out social programs than local and state governments and that state and local officials are less concerned about social problems than federal officials. This is a challenge to those who favor revenue sharing on the ground that smaller units of government are closer to the people and therefore more responsive to their needs. In short, the arguments about revenue sharing are the arguments that have characterized American federalism for the past 200 years.

Summary

The failure of the national government to successfully meet the needs of citizens has raised questions about the future of the federal system. Local and state governments have the advantage of being closer to their citizens, but they lack the resources to effectively carry out necessary programs. They are handicapped by a limited tax base as well as by political boundaries that do not reflect regional needs. Until state and local governments move toward some form of regionalism in seeking solutions to their problems, it is unlikely that real progress can be made.

The financial problems of the states result in part from an imbalance in federal spending, which returns more money to some states than they have paid into the federal treasury while giving others far less. Some redistribution of national wealth is necessary in a strong federal system, but present formulas appear to penalize states that want to offer their citizens above-average educational, health, or welfare benefits. (This has led to the demand that welfare in all its forms be nationalized so that a more equal distribution of wealth can be achieved.) Whatever system is used, the key to the future of American federalism is cooperation among federal, state, and local governments. The way this relationship develops in the future will have an important impact on the life of every American.

NOTES

[1] *American Federalism: Into the Third Century* (Washington, D.C.: Advisory Commission on Intergovernmental Relations, 1974), p. 2.

[2] Ibid., p. 28.

[3] Quoted by Marc Schogol, "We Pay Our Taxes Here: They Spend Them There," reprinted by permission, *The Philadelphia Inquirer,* February 15, 1976, p. 5-I.

[4] *The United States Budget in Brief Fiscal Year 1977* (Washington, D.C.: Office of Management and Budget, 1977), inside cover.

[5] *Statistical Abstract of the United States 1975* (Washington, D.C., Office of Management and Budget, 1975), Table 425.

[6] *American Federalism*, p. 28.

[7] Murray S. Stedman Jr. *State and Local Governments,* (Englewood Cliffs, N.J.: Prentice-Hall 1976), p. 315.

[8] *American Federalism*, p. 32.

[9] Michael Sterne, "Economically Suburbs and Cities Can't Escape Each Other," in *The New York Times,* June 13, 1976, p. E7, citing a study by Herbert L. Bienstock, head of the Bureau of Labor Statistics for the region that includes New York City.

[10] Edwin C. Banfield, "Merger of Cities and Suburbs Seen as Solution," in *The Evening Bulletin,* June 13, 1975, p. A9.

[11] Quoted in *Government Executive,* 8, No. 11 (November 1976) :24.

[12] *The United States Budget in Brief,* inside cover.

[13] Ibid., p. 46.

[14] Gerald Benjamin, "New York's Costly Tax Exemptions," in *The New York Times,* March 28, 1976, p. 14F.

[15] Ernest Holsendolph, "Public Groups Assail Revenue Sharing," in *The New York Times,* March 7, 1976, p. 55. Copyright © 1976 by The New York Times Company. Reprinted by permission.

42 American Federalism

CHAPTER 3 CROSSWORD PUZZLE

Across

1. There are differences in priorities and ___ among the states.
6. Russian ruler
9. Immediately; at once
10. Us
11. Circular
14. Kind of bowl
16. High, rocky hill
17. ___ Coeur (Parisian landmark)
18. The revenue ___ program passed during the Nixon administration provides an unconditional grant of federal funds to state and local government.
21. Money
24. Exclamation
25. Long period of time
26. Vase
27. The constitutional arrangement that divides governmental powers between the national and state governments is called ___.
32. Stunned
33. Stylish; luxurious
34. Carpet
36. Alcoholics Anonymous (abbr.)
39. Sick
42. Type of pigeon
44. The nation's history has been marked by an increase in the power and authority of the ___ government.
45. Crimson

Down

2. Deserves
3. The Supreme Court dealt with inequities in the use of property taxes for school revenues in the ___ case.
4. Printing measure
5. "___ and Lovers" (D. H. Lawrence novel)
6. The national government imposes ___ to fund its operations.
7. Bristlelike appendage of certain grasses
8. ___ government is one approach to the solution of problems that political units cannot effectively handle.
12. Western state
13. Conjunction (neither/___)
14. The Supreme Court decision that set forth the supremacy of national law was issued in ___ vs. Maryland.
15. Gershwin
19. Part of the body
20. Avaricious
22. Part of a ship
23. The migration to the ___ has made the economic and social problems of the nation's cities worse.
27. Mistake; blame; San Andreas ___
28. D___ (initials of 34th President)
29. Associated Press (abbr.)
30. Part of verb "to be"
31. Disgrace
35. ___ and tonic (popular drink)
37. Conditional federal grants to state and local govts. are called grants-in-___.
38. The ___ of Reason
40. Los Angeles (abbr.)
41. ___-go dancer
43. either/___

CHAPTER 4
THE AMERICAN DREAM

CHAPTER OUTLINE

Questions to Consider
Introduction
The Basic Problem
The Constitution and Individual Rights
Freedom of Speech
    Freedom of Speech and Subversive Activity
    Freedom of the Press and Prior Restraint
    Obscenity
    The Problem of Libel
    Freedom of Assembly
    Freedom of Religion
Equality Under the Law
    The Fight for Racial Equality
    The Problem of Equal Justice
Equal Opportunity
    Differences in Wealth and Income
    Inequality of Employment Opportunity
Equal Opportunity in Education
Summary

QUESTIONS TO CONSIDER

What do we mean when we refer to "the American Dream?" To what extent has the American Dream been achieved in the eyes of the individual citizen? A basic element of the American Dream is the protection of individual freedoms from governmental interference. Can such rights be absolute? How is the freedom of the individual balanced against the rights of society? Has a reasonable balance been achieved?

The American Dream also promises equality. What does equality mean in its political sense? How equal are Americans? We are aware of great differences in income and education among Americans. Are these a result of inequality? An issue that has been very controversial in the past decade is the busing of children to achieve school desegregation. What is the relationship of busing to educational opportunity? Should the government concern itself with this matter?

The question of equality in the judicial system is often raised. Are all citizens treated equally by the judicial system? Is this an attainable goal?

Consideration of these various aspects of the American Dream will enable us to judge the extent to which today's citizen has achieved his or her potential within the political system.

Introduction

The waves of immigrants that came to the United States in the nineteenth and early twentieth centuries were attracted by the image of a society in which individuals were allowed a high degree of personal freedom and had the opportunity to rise as far as their ability and ambition would allow. This promise of opportunity and freedom is often called the American Dream. However, the American Dream was not open to everyone. Black Americans, Chicanos, and Asiatics are among the groups who were excluded from the mainstream of national life until after World War II. Since that time, governmental action has focused on making sure the opportunities available to most citizens would be available to all. Yet the American Dream, while widely accepted as an ideal, remains to be achieved in reality.

The term equality is used in referring to many political and social questions. Some have been dealt with through governmental action, while others reflect the prejudices of society and respond to changes in attitudes rather than legislation or court rulings. The effort to achieve equal opportunity is not merely a concern of minority groups who have been deprived of a full role in society for generations; it is a major goal for all citizens who want to improve their standard of living, whether they want material things such as cars and summer homes or the social status that comes with achievement in a highly competitive society. Equality also involves applying the rule of law to all citizens equally. Members of lower-income groups often find themselves less equal in many ways, whether measured by their treatment by the legal system or by the lack of employment and educational opportunities.

The Basic Problem

As everyone knows, the Declaration of Independence states that "we hold these truths to be self-evident, that all men are created equal"—and everyone also knows that the circumstances of birth create major inequalities that are difficult to overcome. Aided by higher family income or greater ability, some people have a better chance of reaching their goals than others. Recent attempts to use governmental power to help overcome such inequalities have given rise to a new issue: "reverse discrimination." In fields ranging from the construction trades to college teaching, quota systems have been designed to correct discriminatory employment practices. But such efforts can achieve their goal only by creating new forms of inequality. If colleges favor women when hiring faculty members in order to correct past discrimination, men who seek faculty positions are discriminated against. Similarly, programs designed to improve the opportunities of blacks, Chicanos, and other minority groups can do so only by establishing new patterns of discrimination.

Governmental efforts to achieve equality of opportunity do not guarantee equality of outcome. The government can provide improved opportunities for groups who formerly did not have a reasonable chance to succeed, but the final outcome depends largely on the individual's ability and willingness to make the necessary effort.

The American people have long been noted for their desire for a higher standard of living. Their efforts to achieve this goal have been based on a realistic understanding of the nation's economic future. In turn, the economic growth of the nation has provided the government with the means to carry out new social programs designed to improve the lot of those who were not receiving their share of the nation's wealth. However, certain events of the 1970s have cast doubt on the economic future of the United States and limited the resources available to the government to satisfy growing demands for federal assistance. The increased cost of energy, for example, has created a situation that will result in higher prices for almost all goods and services in the future, reducing the amount of money most families can spend on luxuries they have become used to as part of "the good life." The government's ability to solve social problems will likewise be hampered by the inadequate financial resources resulting from a slower rate of economic growth.

The government's efforts have been very successful in such areas as ending legal segregation and barriers to voting in southern states. The racial situation in northern states has been harder to overcome. This is an example of the limitations of governmental power. Legal barriers to equal opportunity can be removed, but social walls are more difficult to break down.

The civil rights movement of the 1960s resulted in increased awareness that many Americans were not getting their share of the nation's wealth. Today, problems of poverty, aging, education, urban decay, the judicial system, and individual rights are demanding solutions.

The actions of the government in dealing with issues like those just mentioned reflect both the potentials and the limitations of political structures. Social changes involve either a redistribution of national resources, as in welfare programs, or a breaking down of social and economic barriers, as in questions involving suburban zoning codes that prevent people with low incomes from living in more attractive areas. The major role of the government in our daily lives encourages us to look to Washington for the solutions to such problems, but often the solution can come only from a change in attitudes.

Closely related to the concept of equal opportunity is the constitutional guarantee of individual freedom and protection against abuses of governmental power. In a sense, this is another form of equality—the rights of the individual are given equal status under law with the powers of the government. The concept of individual freedom is an important part of the American Dream.

The rapid rate of change that has marked the past fifteen years has raised new questions about the relationship of the government to the people, the responsibilities of the individual, and the proper balance between conflicting groups in society. These interactions are at the heart of the political system, and the methods the government uses in trying to deal with them reflect the values of Americans at any given time.

The Constitution and Individual Rights

The rights of the individual are balanced against the rights of society and the government. Thus, no rights are absolute. The protection of individual rights is provided for in the Bill of Rights. The task of making sure these rights are not violated is in the hands of the courts, particularly the Supreme Court, whose decisions are binding on lower courts.

The First Amendment to the Constitution contains clear guarantees of freedom of speech, assembly, religion, and the right to petition the government: "Congress shall make no law respecting an establishment of religion, or prohibiting the free exercise thereof; or abridging the freedom of speech, or of the press; or the right of the people peaceably to assemble, and to petition the Government for a redress of grievances." However, these constitutional guarantees are not enough. The need to balance the rights of each individual against those of other individuals as well as the larger public interest has involved the Supreme Court in a never-ending series of cases dealing with these basic freedoms. As a result, the meaning of the First Amendment has been further clarified by Court rulings, especially with regard to freedom of speech, which is the cornerstone of a democratic political system.

Freedom of Speech

Freedom of speech has been expanded by court decisions to include freedom of the press in all its forms. In recent years, the important role of the mass media in American life has resulted in a large number of cases involving freedom of the press. Most Americans agree that freedom of speech is desirable, yet at times they have demanded legislation against obscenity, "dangerous" statements by communists, and other types of speech that oppose the views of the majority.

Finding out exactly how "free" speech may be and still remain within the protection of the First Amendment revolves around the question of how much harm a particular expression of opinion can do to a community or the nation. This must be balanced against the weakening of the democratic process that would result from any limitation on freedom of speech. As Justice Holmes said, in 1919, "Yelling 'fire' in a crowded theatre, is an infringement of the ideal of free speech if there is no fire because of the possible danger to patrons seeking to flee." But short of such clear-cut abuses of freedom of speech, Holmes argued, expressions of opinion should not be limited unless "they so imminently threaten immediate interference with the lawful and pressing purposes of the law that an immediate check is required to save the country." [1] This statement of Justice Holmes, delivered in a dissent to a majority Court opinion, is a clear expression of the view that freedom of speech should not be limited except in cases of extreme public danger. This was a minority opinion, however; the majority of the Court favored such limitations. One of the turning points in the swing towards the view advanced by Justice Holmes occurred in the aftermath of the Communist witch hunts of the Joseph McCarthy era in the 1950s.

Freedom of Speech and Subversive Activity

Concern over subversive activity arises when people feel that their way of life is threatened, and particularly in time of war. The most recent example of such concern occurred in 1951, when the government prosecuted Eugene Dennis and ten other leaders of the American Communist party. (*Dennis v. United States*). The defendants were charged under the Smith Act of 1940, which made it unlawful to advocate the unconstitutional overthrow of the government of the United States or to participate in any activities with this goal. The Supreme Court upheld the convictions of Dennis and his codefendants. Chief Justice Vinson delivered the majority (6-2) opinion, in which he stated that "it is the conspiracy that creates the danger to the nation." [2] The dissenting opinions, delivered by Justices Black and Douglas, denied that the "danger" was great enough to justify placing limits on First Amendment freedoms.

Justice Black also mentioned the anticommunist feelings prevailing at the time and expressed the hope "that in calmer times, when pressures, passions and fears subside, this or some later Court will restore the First Amendment liberties to the high preferred place where they belong in a free society." [3] This has indeed happened. This case, as most that fall within freedom of speech guarantees, rested implicitly on the "clear and present danger" doctrine.

Dennis proved to be a turning point in Supreme Court rulings on subversive activity. Later decisions pointed out the difference between "the statement of philosophical belief and the advocacy of an illegal action,"[4] and the Court's decision in *Yates v. United States* (1957) was based on this distinction.[5] Thus, the *Dennis* ruling, while not overturned, has been reinterpreted in such a way as to bring almost any expression of political dissent under the First Amendment umbrella.

Freedom of the Press and Prior Restraint

During the 1970s, one of the most controversial issues involving freedom of speech has been the matter of *prior restraint*, or legal prevention of certain material from being published. This issue was raised in the famous *Pentagon Papers* case and is the basis of the "gag orders" imposed on the press by judges who want to limit pretrial publicity in criminal cases. In both situations, the goal is to prevent publication of information. The alternative is to seek legal penalties after publication (and possible damage to the public interest).

The Pentagon papers case revolved around the release of "classified" (i.e., secret) material to the newspapers by Daniel Ellsberg. The papers consisted of documents regarding governmental decisions in Vietnam and revealed numerous differences between the government's intentions and its public statements. After the first of a series of articles based on these documents had appeared in several newspapers, the government obtained a temporary restraining order halting further publication of the series by *The New York Times*.[6] However, the Supreme Court ruled that the government could not prevent the *Times* and other newspapers from publishing the articles. The Court's decision challenged the government's practice of classifying documents as secret merely to keep them from public knowledge, though it did not strike down such classification when it could be shown to be in the national interest. The Pentagon papers concerned past events; much of the information had previously been made public, and the "clear and present danger" guideline could not be applied. The Court's ruling did not settle the question of prior restraint, but implied that it would be preferable for the government to seek damages after publication.

A 1976 Supreme Court ruling settled the issue of prior restraint in the courtroom. The case involved a Nebraska judge's order that the local press refrain from printing facts about a case before the jury was picked. The defendant in the case, Erwin Simants, was accused of murdering six members of a Sutherland, Nebraska family, and the judge feared that pretrial publicity would prejudice potential jurors. While the Court did not ban such gag orders, it established requirements that make such orders unlikely to be used in the future. Chief Justice Warren Burger summed up the Court's attitude as follows: "Prior restraints on speech and publication are the most serious and least tolerable infringement on First Amendment rights."[7]

Obscenity

The question of obscenity illustrates the problems that arise when the judicial branch tries to deal with issues of public taste and morals. The underlying problem is the variety of impressions that any form of sexual illustration or public display may create. What appears obscene to one person may seem praiseworthy to another. The difficulty of defining obscenity in precise terms has led the Supreme Court to follow a zig-zag course in this area. In the *Roth* and *Alberts* cases (1957), the Court tried to define obscenity by establishing a test for the material in question. Justice Brennan wrote that only material that was "totally without redeeming social importance" could be judged obscene.[8] It

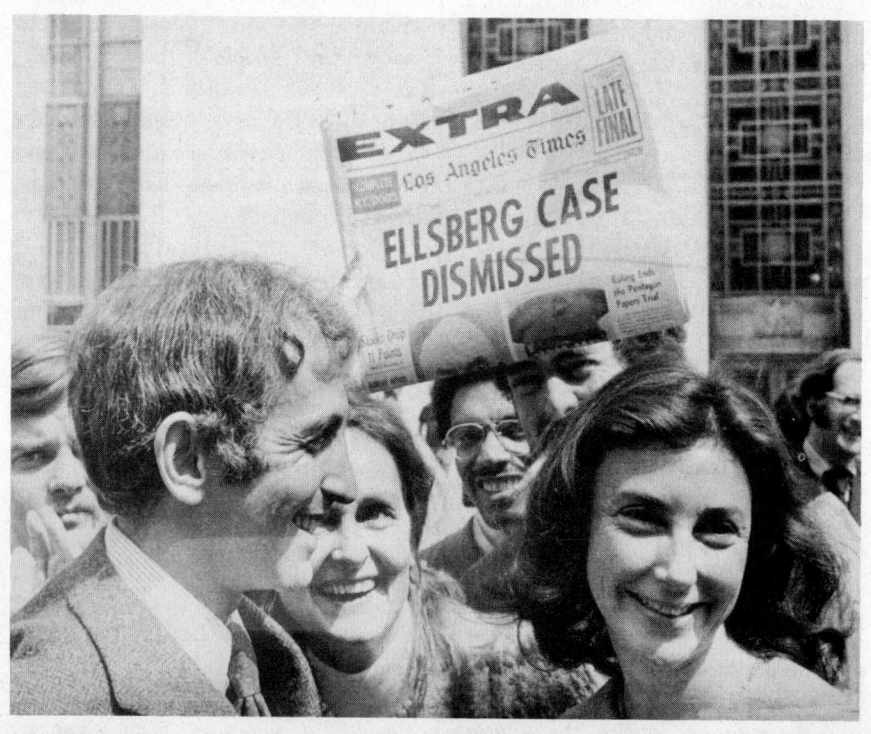

Daniel Ellsberg and friends after a U.S. District Judge dismissed government charges in the Pentagon Papers case because of violation of the defendant's rights.

turned out that "redeeming social importance" was as hard to define as obscenity itself. There followed a series of cases in which the Court tended to interpret the *Roth-Alberts* guidelines liberally. More recently, the Court dealt with obscenity in *Miller v. California* (1973), which concerned advertisement through the mail of a book about sex orgies. The key element in the Court's decision was the ruling that each community may set its own standards regarding obscenity.

The Problem of Libel

The term *libel* refers to any false or malicious written or spoken statement that is damaging to a person's reputation. It is not uncommon to read of entertainers, athletes, politicians, and other public figures threatening to bring libel suits against those who criticize them. Such cases raise the question of whether protection against libel violates the First Amendment. Formerly, the courts often granted damages in such cases. However, a 1964 Supreme Court ruling limited the situations in which such damages can be obtained. Public figures can collect libel damages only if the statement in question is a deliberate falsehood. This is more restrictive than previous interpretations, which held individuals responsible for any false statement. Private citizens who believe they have been libeled can collect damages only if they can prove that the false statement was negligent. This interpretation severely limits the possibility of winning a libel case. This is another example of the extension of First Amendment protection. While this aspect of freedom of speech may be abused, it serves the important function of protecting the citizen's right to criticize government officials without fear of legal penalties.

Freedom of Assembly

Like freedom of speech, freedom of assembly is close to the heart of the democratic process. It is generally accepted that government at any level has the right to require notice of parades or large assemblies that might interfere with normal traffic patterns or the activities of other citizens. At the same time, it is well established that such gatherings cannot be banned simply because government officials disapprove of their purpose. However, there is often a thin line between demonstrations that are intended to express an opinion and those that are intended to incite violence in order to dramatize a cause. Similarly, it is often difficult to sort out the motives of officials who deny certain groups the right to assemble.

The Amish are a religious sect who cling to traditional ways, such as the use of the horse and buggy. Time-honored practices in isolated populations may conflict with modern laws.

A more difficult situation arises when groups attempt to demonstrate in illegal ways, such as the antiwar demonstration in Washington D.C., in 1971, which disrupted traffic and was a clear violation of the rights of others, who were unable to move freely. The question of whether an individual or group has the right to violate the law as a means of protest looms large in times of widespread discontent. The anti-war and civil rights demonstrations of the 1960s have led to a more tolerant attitude by officials who realize that too rigid a stance may lead to more violence.

Freedom of Religion

The First Amendment guarantee of religious freedom is closely linked to freedom of speech, assembly, and petition. Like those freedoms, it includes limitations on actions that might trespass on the rights of others. Justice Roberts made this point in 1940 in a case involving the solicitation of funds by Jehovah's Witnesses: "Without a doubt a State may protect its citizens from fraudulent solicitations by requiring a stranger in the community, before permitting him to solicit funds for any purpose, to establish his identity and his authority for the cause which he purports to represent ... But to condition the solicitation of aid for the perpetuation of religious views or systems upon a license, the grant of which rests in the exercise of a determination by state authority as to what is a religious cause, is to lay a forbidden burden upon the exercise of liberty protected by the Constitution." [9]

One of the problems facing the Supreme Court in cases based on First Amendment protection of religious freedom is that of determining what constitutes a religion. In recent years, "religion" has been defined broadly. During the Vietnam War, for example, conscientious objectors were excused from military duty if their objections were based on "religious" rather than purely moral grounds; that is, the

Court required affiliation with an organized religion that prohibits military service rather than "personal" religious beliefs as a basis for exemption from service.

Separation of church and state (i.e., government at any level) is an important part of the American political heritage, and the Court has usually struck down laws that interfered with religious practices unless those practices violated community standards. Court-ordered medical treatment for children of Christian Scientists is an example of an interference with religious beliefs that has been ruled constitutional. A current issue in the area of separation of church and state is the question of public aid to parochial schools. The Court has upheld state aid to religious schools if that aid is limited to nonreligious uses such as school buses, books, and equipment. This issue is of great practical importance in urban areas in which a large percentage of children attend parochial schools. Many cities would be hard pressed to fit these students into public schools, and the sentiment to aid parochial schools has been encouraged for pragmatic reasons.

The First Amendment freedoms are at the core of the relationship between the individual and the government. They have been expanded by Supreme Court interpretations that have limited the government's right to interfere with those freedoms. However, the Court has upheld certain restrictions on personal freedom. In 1975-1976, it made the following rulings in the area of individual rights:

Upheld the authority of the military to ban political campaign activities on bases and to refuse to allow legal counsel for persons tried by summary courts-martial.

Refused to extend First Amendment protection to labor pickets forbidden to carry their protests into a privately owned shopping mall, holding that their challenge to that ban must be resolved under federal labor law instead.

Held that a defendant could be convicted of selling illegal drugs even though undercover government agents supplied him with the drugs and other agents bought them from him. The Court said that such a defendant was guilty because he was "predisposed" to commit the crime.

Granted absolute immunity to prosecutors from federal damage suits brought by persons who charged that their constitutional rights had been infringed upon by prosecutorial decisions to initiate proceedings or to use certain evidence.[10] What all these decisions have in common is that they place certain limitations on individual freedom and remove certain restraints from the actions of public officials.

The First Amendment freedoms are important safeguards of democracy only to the extent that they are protected by legislative and court action. The former is important because few people have the financial resources to appeal to the courts; unless public-interest organizations sponsor their cause, legal action is often impractical. The latter is important because individual rights mean little unless they are applied to all citizens equally. Supreme Court rulings may consistently protect First Amendment freedoms, but the day-to-day decisions are made in the lower courts, to which the public must appeal for justice.

Equality Under the Law

The legitimacy of a democratic society rests on the concept of equality under the law. Ideally, all citizens should have equal access to the courts, and all should be treated equally by the judicial system. In practice, however, such equality has been difficult to achieve.

There are two dimensions to the problem of equality. One concerns the legal exclusion of certain groups in society from political, educational, and economic opportunity. The other concerns the way individuals are treated by the judicial system. This includes situations in which people must defend themselves against criminal or civil charges as well as those in which they seek the court's help against other individuals or governmental institutions. These individual situations are more difficult to correct because of the multitude of cases involved. Discriminatory practices that involve large groups can be dealt with more readily because they are more visible. Thus, it was easier for the Supreme Court to strike down state laws providing for segregated schools than it is to provide equal justice for the countless individuals who come before the judiciary.

The matter of equality has long been a major concern for blacks who were denied their constitutional rights for almost two centuries, first as slaves and then as second-class citizens. But blacks are not the only group in American society to have been handicapped by unconstitutional legislation that was allowed to stand by Court rulings. Other minority groups, such as Mexican-Americans and Spanish-speaking Americans, as well as people of Asian ancestry, have at various times and in many ways been denied the rights of citizens. In addition, in recent years the women's movement has called attention to many kinds of discrimination against women. All of these cases of inequality stem from social attitudes that have been given the force of law by legislation designed to maintain the status quo and by judicial decisions that have done little to change them.

The problems of equality are not limited to minority groups or women. Individuals who lack political or economic power have been deprived of the equal treatment in the courts. Equality under the law requires a single standard of justice, but people who cannot afford to hire a good lawyer have often found themselves at a disadvantage in the courts. The appeals process, too, is costly. In some cases, groups such as the American Civil Liberties Union may finance an appeal, but such cases offer promise only to a very small number of people.

In the following pages, we will examine the more important struggles for equality that have taken place in recent years. They illustrate the process by which the nation has attempted to move closer to fulfillment of the American Dream.

The Fight for Racial Equality

The intergration of black Americans into the political process was achieved through a series of actions by the three branches of government, spurred by the demands of the black population and the support of influential multiracial organizations. The abuses of the past were so obvious that they were easy to identify; the solutions required only the will to uphold the Constitution.

Unequal status for blacks was written into the Constitution: the second section of Article I states that "Representatives and direct Taxes shall be apportioned among the several States ... according to their respective Numbers, which shall be determined by adding to the whole Number of free Persons ... three-fifths of all other persons." The phrase "all other persons" referred to slaves, and in this way the Constitution recognized slavery as legal.

The Thirteenth Amendment (1865) outlawed slavery, and since that time the matter of equal rights for black Americans has been a political issue rather than simply "the slavery question." The events of the century following the Civil War show how hard it is to overcome deep-seated prejudice through legislative and judicial action. The Fourteenth Amendment (1868) guaranteed equality to all citizens, and the Fifteenth Amendment (1870) dealt specifically with the right to vote. Yet little progress was made in the march toward equality for blacks until the 1930s, and significant Supreme Court decisions and congressional action in this area did not occur until the 1950s. This painfully slow progress occurred in spite of constitutional guarantees of equality and shows the need for legislative and judicial action in support of constitutional principles.

In 1900, almost 90 percent of the nation's blacks lived in the South, and it was there that legal segregation developed. Blacks were excluded from the political process by poll taxes and literacy tests. Public transportation, restaurants, and hotels were segregated. And so were the schools, with the result that blacks were unable to attain the level of education necessary to succeed in the nation's social and economic structure. In short, blacks were subjected to unequal treatment in all areas of life.

State governments played a key role in placing barriers between the races. In addition, the Supreme Court decision in *Plessy* v. *Ferguson* (1896) legitimized the "separate but equal" doctrine and thereby neutralized the Fourteenth and Fifteenth Amendments. These actions reflected the values of the southern population—but the idea that blacks were "inferior" was accepted by most people in the North as well as in the South. The injustice of the judiciary toward blacks accused of crimes during this period is legendary, and the illegal actions of vigilantes—lynch mobs—were brutal.

Meaningful progress toward racial equality began with the migration of blacks from the rural South to northern cities, which started during World War I and was accelerated during World War II by wartime job opportunities. In turn, the big-city political organizations tried to get the new arrivals to join their party "machines," offering rewards such as municipal jobs in return for votes. The plight of the nation's blacks gained increased recognition during the period between the two World Wars, and it became fashionable for politicians to at least pay lip service to the ideal of bringing the blacks into the mainstream of American life. The Roosevelt administration notably Eleanor Roosevelt—was more outspoken on this subject, but the nation entered World War II with segregated armed forces and southern barriers to racial equality still in force.

Although public support for an end to discrimination increased after World War II, the pressure for change was not strong enough to push Congress into action. The Senate voted down legislation to outlaw the poll tax in 1945, 1947, and 1949, a pattern that illustrates the political power of southern states in Congress. The turning point came in 1948, when President Truman issued an executive order to desegregate the armed forces after Congress had failed to include such a provision in its Selective Service legislation.

Truman's action did more than integrate the armed forces, however. It committed the executive branch to efforts to end unequal treatment of blacks. It also made civil rights a political issue. At the 1948 Democratic Convention, southern states left the party and formed the "Dixiecrat" party, with Senator Strom Thurmond of South Carolina as its Presidential candidate. Truman's narrow victory over Thomas E. Dewey in 1948, despite the loss of much of the South to Thurmond encouraged those who favored integration and weakened the power of the southern bloc.

In 1954, the Supreme Court entered the fray with its landmark decision in *Brown* v. *Board of Education.* This ruling had implications far beyond the case in question, which concerned segregation in public schools. It not only reversed the "separate but equal" doctrine that had been in force since *Plessy* v. *Ferguson* but also established the principle that separate is by definition unequal.[11] The impact of the *Brown* decision spread quickly to almost all areas of racial discrimination. It led to further desegregation action by the executive branch and, finally, Congress. In 1955, President Eisenhower issued an executive order creating a Committee on Government Employment Policy whose task was to end discriminatory hiring, firing, and promotion practices in the federal government. And in 1957 Congress passed the Civil Rights Act of 1957, the first major civil rights act since the period just after the Civil War and the beginning of major congressional participation in the battle for equality. The key features of this act were the granting of jurisdiction to United States district courts in cases involving the right to vote, the establishment of a Civil Rights Division in the Justice Department, and authorization of the federal government to seek injunctions against any actions interferring with voting rights.

Despite the Supreme Court decision in *Brown* v. *Board of Education*, and increased federal activity in the civil rights field, progress was slow as white America continued to pay lip service to the ideal of equality while dragging its feet along the road to change. In 1960, the Eisenhower administration got Congress to pass the Civil Rights Act of 1960, another small but significant step toward political equality for blacks. This Act enabled federal district courts to protect the right of voters to register in state as well as federal elections in areas that failed to remove barriers to voting by blacks. But those who wanted integration to succeed believed progress would continue to be slow until blacks won political power. Widespread resistance in the South to Court decisions and federal legislation in the area of civil rights led to increased activism among blacks who were no longer content to wait patiently for court rulings to protect their constitutional rights.

In 1963, blacks took to the streets in Birmingham, Alabama, using civil disobedience to protest their unequal status. This action, the most widely publicized of many such demonstrations throughout the nation, changed the tempo of the civil rights movement. In August 1963, the street protests climaxed in a march by 200,000 people—a multiracial group—in Washington, D.C. It was here that Rev. Martin Luther King made the famous speech in which he said, "I have a dream that one day this nation will rise up and live out the true meaning of its creed."

The civil rights demonstrations brought home in dramatic terms the fact that 22 million blacks were unwilling to remain second-class citizens. Even the most die-hard segregationist began to see that change was inevitable.

The Civil Rights Act of 1964 was the most sweeping civil rights legislation since the post-Civil War period. It outlawed discrimination in public accommodations and gave the attorney general the power to prosecute violators, authorized the executive branch to withhold federal funds from any program that discriminated against blacks, and forbade discrimination by any business or labor union with 100 or more employees, with the number dropping to 25 by 1968. This Act allowed the federal government to force schools to integrate by threatening to withhold federal funds (which are needed by almost all public and private schools) if they failed to cooperate, and made discrimination by industry and unions potentially expensive because it opened the way for damage suits. The public accommodations provision outlawed one of the most widespread forms of segregation and gave federal prosecutors a means of enforcing equal treatment in buses and trains, hotels, and restaurants. Other legislation dealing with specific problems in the civil rights field followed, but the 1964 Act remains the major legislative effort in this area.

The Johnson administration was active in civil rights and was usually backed by federal judges. However, old habits and attitudes are slow to change. The expectations of blacks had risen because of the progress that had been made, and this made the discrimination that remained more difficult to accept. Continued obstacles to black voting were a major problem in some areas of the South, leading to passage of the *Voting Rights Act of 1965*. This Act banned literacy tests in states in which less than 50 percent of the voting-age population had voted in the 1964 Presidential election, thereby removing a key barrier to black political participation in Alabama, Georgia, Mississippi, Louisiana, South Carolina, and Virginia. The Act also provided criminal penalties for interfering with people who were attempting to register to vote and for actions or threats against civil rights workers, and challenged the poll taxes in Alabama, Mississippi, Texas, and Virginia. The effort to bring about full black participation in the electoral process succeeded to such an extent that black voter registration in (southern states increased from 29.1 percent in 1960 to 58.6 percent in 1971. (In 1971, the figure for white registration in the same states was 65 percent. [12])

The executive, legislative, and judicial actions just described combined to increase the opportunity for blacks, as a group, to gain political influence and power. In a democracy, this is the most effective guarantee that constitutional freedoms will be protected by the government. The number of black elected officials tripled between 1969 and June 1976. While blacks still account for less than 1 percent of the 522,000 elected officials in the nation, this increase reflects greater black participation in all levels of government. [13]

The Problem of Equal Justice

More complex in many ways than the problem of discrimination is that of obtaining equal justice for the individual who is charged with a crime and comes before the court with few resources, no influential friends, and only the wisdom of the judge as a guarantee of justice. The individual is protected by the Constitution, but the way constitutional rights are applied is largely the responsibility of the judicial system. The rights of the accused are important to all citizens because the denial of a fair trial to any person weakens the fiber of democracy. But these rights must be balanced against the right of society to be protected from lawlessness.

It is obvious that American justice is applied unequally and that individuals have unequal access to the courts.

Equal Opportunity **51**

'... except for them pre-verts.'

This inequality is due in part to the differences in criminal law among the states. Not only are there different penalties for various offenses, but the probability that convicted people will actually go to prison varies widely from one state to another. Two major solutions to this problem have been suggested. One is the establishment of a federal criminal code with standardized sentences for common crimes. Of course, this would limit the power of state courts and legislatures. The other major suggestion is decriminalization of offenses that seldom result in jail sentences but are costly both for defendants and for the courts. Possession of small amounts of marijuana, larceny (in the case of first offenses) and other nonviolent crimes netting under $5000 are in this category.[13] This approach would remove some of the inequities experienced by poor defendants. It is difficult to exaggerate the differences in outcome that result from differences in resources.

A wealthy defendant who can afford a skilled lawyer is buying more than legal counsel. He or she is also paying for investigative abilities to be used in building a case that will stand up to the prosecution's attack. F. Lee Bailey's defense of Patricia Hearst in 1976 is a case in point. Expert witnesses were summoned by the defense to testify concerning Miss Hearst's frame of mind, the pressures on her when she allegedly committed the crimes of which she was accused, and the degree to which she was accountable for her actions. Firearms experts were brought to the courtroom to state that the gun Miss Hearst was carrying in a photograph taken during the bank robbery in question was not in firing position. While the Hearst case received more news coverage than most, the actions of Miss Hearst's counsel were not unusual for a case in which the defendant can pay for the best possible defense. The poor defendant has much less chance of getting such a defense.

The Sixth Amendment states that "in all criminal prosecutions the accused shall enjoy the right ... to have the Assistance of Counsel for his defense." This protection for the accused was supported by a 1972 Supreme Court ruling that a poor defendant facing a possible jail term must be provided with counsel. However, a 1975 study by the Law Enforcement Assistance Administration found that poor defendants were still being deprived of their constitutional rights.

Compare the following examples of unequal access to a fair trial with the situation faced by a wealthy defendant:

... judges often "openly" encourage defendants to waive their constitutional right to counsel.

... limited concern with basic procedural fairness continues to be prevalent in lower criminal courts.

... lawyers who are appointed to defend indigents are "often inexperienced or of limited competence" and "not adequately prepared," to represent the client's "best interests."

... most of the legal profession has abdicated its responsibility for the lower criminal courts by condoning the often mediocre judges who serve there and by leaving the burden of representation to public defenders or to lower echelons of the bar.[15]

Judicial inequality is by no means limited to criminal cases. Whether the plaintiff or defendant, the person who can afford a skilled lawyer, endure long and often costly trial delays, and appeal the verdict, if necessary, has a better chance of getting a fair trial. The principle of equal justice for all is one of the most fundamental ideals expressed in the Declaration of Independence and the Constitution, but remains one of the most difficult to achieve.

Equal Opportunity

Equal opportunity is closely related to judicial equality because in many ways equal opportunity depends on combined executive, legislative, and judicial actions. In order to grasp the difficulty of achieving equal opportunity, it is necessary to understand the inequalities that exist in many areas of American life. There are various kinds of opportunity—social, economic, educational, and more. This raises the question of which came first, the chicken or the egg? Are some Americans deprived of equal economic opportunity because of their social status, or is low status a result of low income? Similarly, the link between education and income is well established, but which comes first? It is simplistic to say that increased educa-

52 The American Dream

tion will be followed by higher income, because a reasonable income level is necessary for parents to raise children in an atmosphere that will lead to educational achievement. The problem of equal opportunity is complex, but the idea that any person who has the desire to work can get his or her share of society's benefits is a basic aspect of the American Dream at all levels of society. We all like to feel that we have the opportunity to rise to the limit of our abilities. One of the government's key goals is to make this possibility a reality rather than just a campaign slogan.

Differences in Wealth and Income

Equal opportunity involves more than redistribution of wealth—it means maintaining an economic system in which there is enough room for growth to allow those with low incomes to improve their standard of living. This is very different from simply taking from the rich to give to the poor or attempting to control salaries for various occupations. Financial reward often has little to do with the training required for a particular job or the social benefits flowing from that job. The 216 basketball players in the National Basketball Association (NBA) received average salaries of $107,000 in the 1975-1976 season.[16] This is more than congresspeople, Supreme Court justices, or public officials other than the President receive, and it is also a higher average wage than may be found in any professional field. The level reached by NBA players simply reflects the impact of television revenues on professional sports. People who seek economic gains must try to advance in occupations or professions that appear to offer them the greatest potential earnings. Not everyone can be a professional athlete or a big-name entertainer, but all can try to equip themselves to compete successfully in the job market.

Just as some individuals are more equal than others in terms of justice, so there are great inequalities in economic terms. The top 1 percent of the population controls 25.9 percent of individual wealth in the United States and the top 6 percent controls 52.4 percent.[17] These differences in wealth affect various groups in society in different ways. Thus, there is a wide variation in the potential of individuals to advance economically. Those who are born into wealthy families have a head start over others. Race, age, sex, and other characteristics also make a difference. It is the government's task to make sure the economic system is flexible enough to allow for improvement in standards of living. The extent to which federal action can be effective in bringing about equal opportunity depends on the ability of the economy to expand enough to provide more opportunities as well as the willingness of the individual to help himself or herself.

Inequality of Employment Opportunity

Three groups of Americans have experienced higher levels of unemployment than the general population: teenagers, women, and blacks. They face unusual obstacles to economic equality. Some of these barriers are a result of inadequate training and education, some a result of racial or sex prejudice, and others a result of traditional attitudes among employers toward various segments of the work force. The problems of these groups become worse in periods of economic recession. They are usually the first to be fired and the last to be rehired as the economy improves. Statistics on this problem can be misleading, however. The teenagers and women who suffer the most are blacks and members of other minority groups. And not all teenagers and women reported as unemployed may be seriously seeking permanent jobs. Many women represent a second family income and want part-time employment, while many teenagers are living at home and perhaps going to school as well as looking for work. But regardless of how the statistics are interpreted, there is plenty of evidence that employment opportunities are very unequal.

The black-white income gap remains sizable despite recent progress. Blacks are achieving middle-income status (incomes of over $10,000 per year) at a faster rate than whites, and the percentage of blacks sliding into poverty is lower than the percentage

Unemployment lines in Detroit during the recession in 1975. The economic dependence of individuals on government increases as industry grows more complex.

for whites. Although these figures appear to indicate a closing of the economic gap between blacks and whites, the differences that remain reveal that inequality is still dominant. The average family income of black families is 58 percent of that of white families, and this percentage has actually declined from a peak of 61 percent in 1969. The most significant data indicate that even when "adjusted to account for lower black educational attainment, increased labor force participation by white married women, and the larger percentage of female-headed black families, an income gap of approximately 20 percent remains for which there is no reasonable explanation other than discrimination.[18] Finally, while the percentage of unemployed blacks is impossible to determine accurately, the National Urban League estimated it at 25.7 percent in 1976, and Treasury Secretary William Simon has put the black teenage unemployment rate at 40 percent.

The point of these figures is that black and white Americans are still economically unequal in terms of both attainment and opportunity, and this gap will remain unless discrimination is countered by governmental action. There are federal and state laws against discriminatory hiring and promotion practices, but it is hard to control these practices except in the largest corporations and in the government itself.

Efforts to increase the percentage of blacks in certain fields inevitably raise the issue of quotas or, as noted earlier, "reverse discrimination." This is a political hot potato because whites tend to react negatively to the idea that the government should take steps to increase the percentage of blacks in particular jobs. Such artificial attempts to guarantee equal employment change the concept of equality of opportunity to one of redistribution of resources. Thus, American society faces a dilemma. Obviously, 200 years of discrimination have left the black citizen with a huge economic handicap that cannot be overcome by individual efforts except in exceptional cases. While most whites recognize the injustice of such inequality, few are willing to agree to black progress at the expense of whites. The only solution that stands a chance of being accepted by most people is one that provides increased opportunities for black employment through national economic growth. This would be an ideal solution because it would provide greater equality without taking anything from groups who are already well off. The problem lies in maintaining a level of economic growth that would make such progress possible. The recession and inflation of the early 1970s, coupled with the increased amount of national resources that must be used to meet energy needs, make any plans based on a high rate of future economic growth impractical.

Teenage unemployment has ranged from 14.3 percent in 1973 to 19.2 percent in 1976.[19] These figures illustrate the lasting nature of the problem, which is much worse among teenaged blacks. Even in good economic times (including 1973), the percentage of teenage unemployment has remained high. There are no easy answers to this problem, which creates a variety of social ills in addition to economic hardship. In an increasingly sophisticated technological society, people who are untrained or undereducated will find themselves either unemployed or confined to the low end of the wage scale. Governmental programs that encourage teenagers to complete their high school education, provide technical training, and offer subsidies to industries that give on-the-job training have all failed to solve the problem of teenage unemployment. This is an example of a dilemma everyone agrees must be dealt with but to which there are no satisfactory solutions. Political stability is threatened by large numbers of alienated citizens, and it is feared that today's teenage unemployed, who are not being successfully integrated into the nation's economic structure, may remain outside the mainstream of social and political life and become alienated from the ideals of American democracy.

The expanding role of women as an economic force is illustrated in Table 4-1. Also clearly shown is the difference in average income between men and women. As more women choose to enter the professions, this gap will undoubtedly narrow, but it is only recently that such choices have become available to women. Since World War II, the economic role of women has changed from one of, at best, supplementing the family income, often on a

TABLE 4-1

NUMBER: More Women Than Men

The nation's 109.4 million females comprise 51.2 per cent of total population. In 10 years, they will number 120 million and make up an even larger proportion of population. Today there are 76.8 million women age 18 and over.

RACE: 6 of 7 Are White

Of all females —
- 94.9 million, or 87 per cent, are whites.
- 12.8 million, or 12 per cent, are blacks.
- 1.7 million are of other races.

AGE: Older Than Men on Average

Median age of American females is 30 years, compared with 27.6 years for males. And the female population, on average, is getting older — median age by 1985 will be an estimated 32.3 years, by the year 2000, 36.2 years.

LIFE SPAN: Women Live Much Longer Than Men

The average female lives to an age of almost 76 years, nearly eight years longer than the average male. The gap in life expectancy, moreover, is steadily widening — it was little more than six years two decades ago.

ECONOMIC POWER: Women Control Increasing Share of Nation's Wealth

At latest official count, women owned 47 per cent of the nation's wealth — more than half of all bonds, nearly half of cash and corporate stock. The proportions are rising year in, year out.

POLITICAL POWER: An Edge in Numbers of Voting Age

Nearly 77 million women are of voting age, or 52 per cent of the total of persons age 18 and over — a slightly higher proportion than women's share of population at large. With women living longer, the proportion is growing.

JOBS: Nearly Half of All Women Work

A record 37.4 million women are in the country's work force — 47 per cent of all women age 16 and over. Women hold 2 of every 5 jobs in the U.S. and are increasingly landing better and better positions.

EDUCATION: Women Are Spending More Years in School

Four out of 5 women in the 25-to-34 age bracket have at least a high-school diploma. One in 6 has a four-year college education, up from 1 in 10 a decade ago. All told, there are now 7.1 million women college graduates in the U.S.

MARRIAGE: A Rising Proportion Delaying the Day

In the 20-to-24 age bracket, 2 of every 5 women are not yet married, and by 1990 the proportion is expected to rise to almost half. Although marriage is being delayed longer, few women stay single through their adult years. At last count, there were 47.3 million married women, 9.8 million widows, 3.6 million divorcees, 2.2 million who are separated from husbands.

CHILDREN: Women Want Smaller Families

More than 1 wife in 6 in the 18-to-24 year group expects to remain childless or to bear only one offspring. Seventy-five per cent expect two or three children. Only 8 per cent want four or more. All told, these plans, if fulfilled, would mean little if any growth in U.S. population, except for immigrants.

FAMILIES: Those Headed by Women in Sharp Rise

7.2 million families — 1 in every 8 — are now headed by women. The number has grown 44 per cent in a decade, largely the result of the climbing divorce rate.

SOURCE: Reprinted from *U.S. News & World Report,* December 8, 1975. Copyright 1975 U.S. News & World Report, Inc.

WOMEN MAKE UP A GROWING SHARE OF WORK FORCE...

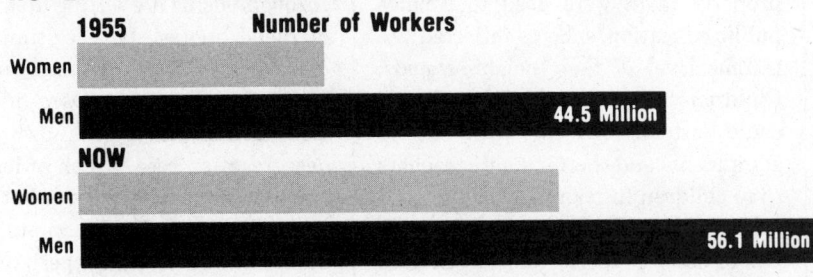

Number of Workers

1955
- Women
- Men — 44.5 Million

NOW
- Women
- Men — 56.1 Million

In the past two decades, nearly 17 million women have joined the labor force, compared with less than 12 million men. If trends continue, there will be as many women as men in the nation's work force before the end of the century.

Source: U.S. Dept. of Labor

...BUT LAG FURTHER BEHIND MEN IN PAY
Median earnings of full-time, year-round workers —

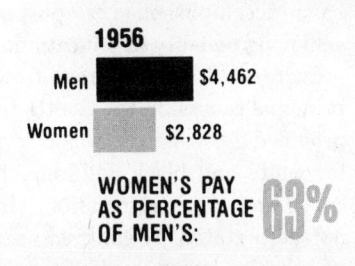

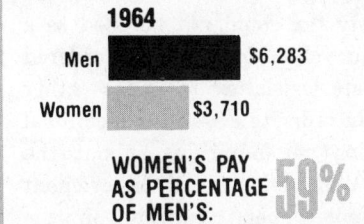

1956
- Men: $4,462
- Women: $2,828
- WOMEN'S PAY AS PERCENTAGE OF MEN'S: 63%

1964
- Men: $6,283
- Women: $3,710
- WOMEN'S PAY AS PERCENTAGE OF MEN'S: 59%

1974
- Men: $12,152
- Women: $6,957
- WOMEN'S PAY AS PERCENTAGE OF MEN'S: 57%

Source: U.S. Dept. of Commerce

...AND EARN LESS, WHATEVER THE JOB

Occupation	Average Earnings Per Week, Full-Time Women Workers	Percentage of Average Earnings of Men
Professional, technical	$208	73%
Managers, administrators	$173	58%
Clerical workers	$138	65%
Craft workers	$138	61%
Laborers	$116	73%
Factory workers	$115	61%
Service workers	$103	64%
Sales workers	$102	44%
Farm workers	$95	84%

Source: U.S. Dept. of Labor

WOMEN SCORE GAINS IN PROFESSIONAL FIELDS...

Women hold nearly 41 per cent of all professional jobs in the U.S., up from 36 per cent in 1964. Changes in the past decade—

Proportion of All Workers Who Were Women	1964	1974
Registered nurses	99%	98%
Elementary-school teachers	88%	84%
Librarians	87%	82%
Social workers	55%	61%
Editors, reporters	36%	44%
Painters, sculptors	38%	42%
Psychologists	23%	41%
Personnel, labor relations	32%	35%
College teachers	23%	31%

Proportion of All Workers Who Were Women	1964	1974
Public relations	15%	29%
Designers	19%	24%
Accountants	18%	24%
Pharmacists	10%	17%
Chemists	7%	14%
Physicians	8%	10%
Drafting technicians	5%	8%
Lawyers, judges	2%	7%

Source: U.S. Dept. of Labor

...AND WITH MORE EDUCATION, ARE IN LINE TO DO BETTER

Proportion of All Students at Professional Schools Who Were Women	1960	1974
Dentistry	1%	7%
Law	4%	19%
Medicine	6%	18%
Optometry	1%	10%
Pharmacy	12%	32%
Veterinary medicine	4%	21%

Source: John B. Parrish, University of Illinois

part-time or temporary basis, to one of full-time employment with opportunities for advancement similar to those traditionally reserved for men.

Table 4-1 shows that the number of men in the work force increased by less than 30 percent between 1955 and 1976, while the number of women almost doubled in the same period. Among other things, this increase has resulted in higher teenage unemployment, since it has added to the number of qualified workers competing with the usually less-qualified teenager.

Thus, the fact that more women are working full-time increases the need for national economic growth.

The key to equality of employment opportunity is an economic climate that offers the opportunity for advancement to all who are able and willing to work. The individual's perception of this opportunity is more important in a political and social sense than its actual existence. Some people set high economic goals and are willing to prepare themselves for whatever competition exists. Others have more modest aims and are satisfied with a job that provides the necessities of life with few luxuries. The political system is threatened when either type of individual is frustrated in his or her efforts to find a satisfactory job and blames governmental inaction or lack of responsiveness. The idea that anyone can "make it" is an important part of the American Dream, and frustration in this area can have serious social and political consequences.

Equal Opportunity in Education

Reasonable ability to use the basic educational skills—reading, writing, arithmetic—is necessary for anyone looking for a job that offers some hope for advancement. Indeed, there are few jobs of any kind available to a person who lacks these skills. But equality of educational opportunity has been denied to many, if not most, Americans. Traditionally, children went to neighborhood schools run by local school districts. In most areas, property taxes were used to finance public education; schools reflected the income level of their neighborhoods. Children in richer neighborhoods could attend schools with better equipment and better-paid teachers than children in poorer districts.

As discussed in Chapter 3, the practice of using property taxes to finance public schools has come under attack in some states. In 1976, the New Jersey Supreme Court ruled that the property tax could not be used as a basis for school financing and ordered the state legislature to impose other taxes in order to equalize educational spending per pupil throughout the state. While educational achievement does not depend entirely on the amount of money spent per pupil, there is little doubt that school financing is an important factor in the quality of education offered. Other states are expected to follow New Jersey's lead in erasing this particular cause of educational inequality.

Higher education also presents an uneven picture. Every state has some form of state college system, and many counties and cities also maintain colleges and universities at minimal cost to the student. College education has traditionally been a luxury that few people could afford, but today a number of federal, state, and other aid programs offer loans to qualified students. It is estimated that the total of outstanding student loans reached $8 billion in 1976. Access to higher education today depends more on getting the required educational background than on financial resources. In this sense, American education has made impressive progress toward opening the doors to higher education to anyone who can qualify.

The busing controversy is at the heart of the question of equality in education because it illustrates the problems that must be faced in attempting to achieve equality. The term busing, refers to the policy of assigning children to schools outside their neighborhoods. In effect, court orders to achieve desegregation through busing are setting up a system of racial quotas. This legitimizes the quota system that was ruled unconstitutional in *Brown* v. *Board of Education* (1954), the best known of the desegregation cases. Such orders have led to new debates over whether reverse discrimination is acceptable as a desegregation tool and, perhaps more important, whether the desegregation efforts that have been made so far have accomplished the purpose of achieving equality in education.

Segregated schools arose from two principal causes. In the South, the law provided for separate school systems for white and black children—this is called *de jure* segregation. In the northern states, by contrast segregated school systems resulted from housing patterns that separated whites and blacks into different neighborhoods and, hence, different schools— this is called *de facto* segregation. The government's early efforts to carry out the 1954 Court decision focused on legal—or *de jure*—segregation, mainly in the South. Today, the majority of southern black children attend desegregated schools. However, progress has been slower in many northern cities, where segregation is a result of housing patterns rather than law and community opposition has been as strong as the early opposition in some southern states. The question of busing is not limited to any particular region. Nor is the de jure or de facto origin of segregated schools important in terms of equality. The real issue is whether or not the goal of educational equality can be achieved through busing programs.

In this, as in any complex area, there are large amounts of conflicting evidence. The differences in opinion cross political party lines and do not show the usual liberal-conservative split often found in social issues. This is illustrated by the statements by two liberal senators, one a Democrat and

Equal Opportunity in Education **57**

Antibusing demonstrators in Louisville. The effort to enforce equality in education has inflamed passions in opposing groups.

the other a Republican:

...Busing is a counterproductive-remedy.... Busing, in effect, codifies the concept that a black is inferior to a white by saying, "The only way you can cut it educationally is if you're with whites." I think this is a horrible concept.—Joseph Biden, Jr. (D., Del.)

I just can't believe we can have a country divided black and white. And if people are to live in an integrated society, part of their preparation must take place in the public-school systems—Senator Edward W. Brooke (R., Mass.)[21]

Just as there are different approaches toward the ideal of equal education, so there are a variety of problems that must be faced. Table 4-2 shows that only 7 of the 20 largest cities had less than 50 percent minority enrollment in their schools in 1973. How is desegregation to be achieved in such situations? One answer is to merge suburban school districts with urban ones in order to achieve a better racial mix. This idea is very hard for suburban residents to accept and is likely to be fought through the courts. Nor is there any evidence that the majority of black parents see busing as the answer to educational inequality. A 1975 Gallup poll showed that among blacks, 40 percent were in favor of busing and 47 percent opposed.[22] Indeed the busing controversy has diverted attention from the real problem, the struggle for equality in education. The problems go far beyond feelings about busing in some areas where racial prejudice runs deep.

The problem of educational equality involves many of the same dilemmas as equality of economic opportunity. The goal is to offer equal opportunity to those who have been deprived in the past without placing the entire burden on those who are better off. It is hard to overcome another person's educational or economic head start. However, the difficulty should not stand in the way of continued governmental efforts to achieve

TABLE 4-2
Major City School Systems with Minority Enrollment Over 50 Percent

Listed are 20 largest U.S. cities, July, 1973 census: only 7 had less than 50 percent minority school enrollment.

City	%	City	%
New York	66%	San Diego	
Chicago	71	San Antonio	
Los Angeles	56	Indianapolis	
Philadelphia	66	Wash. D.C.	97
Detroit	72	Milwaukee	
Houston	60	San Francisco	70
Baltimore	70	Cleveland	60
Dallas	53	Memphis	68
		Phoenix	
		Boston	
		New Orleans	
		St. Louis	70

SOURCE: *The New York Times,* December 21, 1975, p. 3E. Copyright© 1975 by The New York Times Company. Reprinted by permission.

equality within the limits of individual ability and ambition.

Summary

The American Dream includes the ideals of individual freedom, equal justice, and equal educational and economic opportunity. The matter of individual freedom includes protection from abuses of governmental power. The courts provide the most effective guarantee of these First Amendment rights. Equality of justice and equality of opportunity are more difficult to achieve because some people have more money or ability than others. The American Dream remains a goal of both political parties and most political leaders, but the question of how to achieve it is a controversial one. The problem is to overcome the inequality that results from differences in the circumstances of birth without depriving more fortunate individuals of their rights.

Equality in the American sense does not mean redistribution of wealth or a common denominator for education. Rather, it means equal opportunity for all citizens to improve their standard of living. The extent to which a person is able to take advantage of this opportunity depends largely on his or her own ability and desires. The elements of the American Dream are at the heart of American society, and while such complex problems are not easy to solve, the effort to find new ways to bring more citizens into the political, social, and economic mainstream of national life must continue.

CHAPTER 4 CROSSWORD PUZZLE

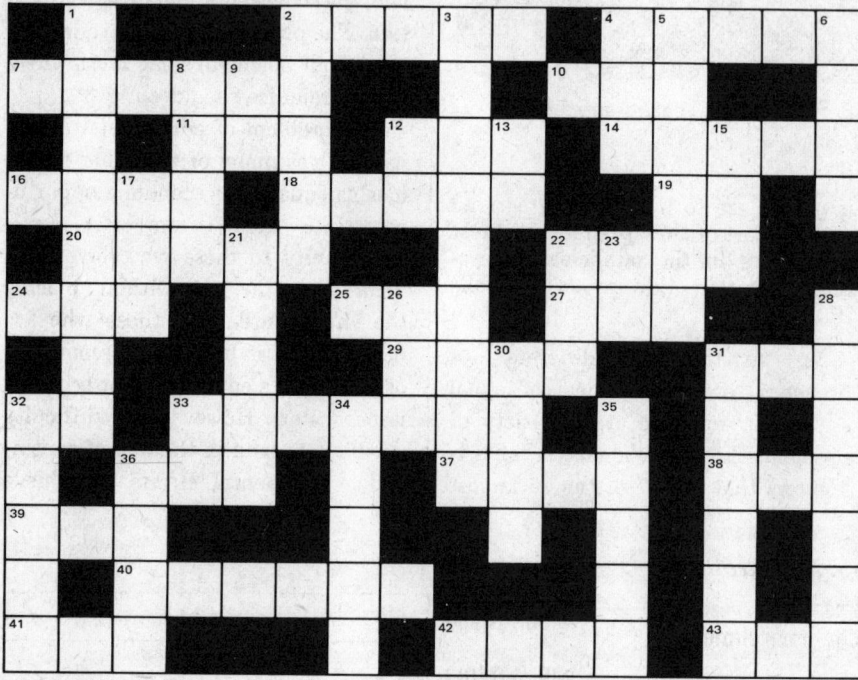

Across
2. Noon meal
4. Brown vs. Board of Education (1954) upset the "separate but ____" doctrine implicit in Plessy vs. Ferguson (1898).
7. Opposite of round
10. Asian ____
11. Type of drink
12. Southern Methodist University (abbr.)
14. Freedom of speech is guaranteed in the ____ Amendment.
16. Intense dislike
18. Wanders
19. ____ cetera
20. Type of material
22. Location
24. "Gunga ____" (Kipling poem)
25. Admirer; aficionado
27. Office of Strategic Services (abbr.)
29. Tears
31. ____-Magnon
32. Possessive pronoun
33. Segregation in schools that has developed because of housing patterns is called ____ segregation.
36. Grassy surface soil
37. 12 months
38. Vase
39. Equality under the ____ has proven a difficult norm to establish.
40. There is a close link between the level of education and level of ____.
41. Uncle ____
42. State; verify
43. Computer in *2001: A Space Odyssey*

Down
1. The American Dream includes assuring all citizens ____ of opportunity.
2. Acquire knowledge
3. The Supreme Court has ruled in Miller vs. California (1973) that each ____ is entitled to set its own standards of obscenity.
4. Sprite; mischeivous creature
5. Silences
6. Behind schedule
8. Egyptian sun god
9. Prefix for "pair" and "veal"
12. South America (abbr.)
13. We
15. Route (abbr.)
17. ____ Pan Alley
21. Over; finished
22. Distress signal
23. Part of verb "to be"
26. Part of a circle
28. The Sixth Amendment guarantees that persons accused of crimes shall have the assistance of ____ in their defense.
30. Writer of verses
31. Separation of ____ and state is part of the American political heritage.
32. Dissolves
33. "I ____" (wedding vow)
34. Odor; scent
35. The Pentagon Papers case involved the issue of ____ restraint.
36. Sink or ____

NOTES

[1] Quoted by Anthony Lewis in "Free Speech: Never Total, Once Again Expanding," in *The New York Times*, February 8, 1976, p. 3E.

[2] *Dennis* v. *United States*, 341 U.S. 494 (1951) at 511.

[3] Ibid., at 581.

[4] Henry J. Abraham, *Freedom and the Court* (London: Oxford University Press, 1967), p. 142.

[5] *Yates* v. *United States*, 354 U.S. 298 (1957).

[6] *New York Times Company* v. *United States*, 403 U.S. 713 (1971).

[7] Quoted in "Judges are Told: You Can't Gag the Press," in *U.S. News & World Report*, July 12, 1976, p. 69.

[8] Quoted in Abraham p. 152; *Roth* v. *United States* and *Alberts* v. *California*, 354 U.S. 476 (1957).

[9] Ibid., p. 187; *Cantwell* v. *Connecticut*, 310 U.S. 296 (1940) at 306.

[10] Elder Witt, "The Individual Is Losing Now in the Court," reprinted by permission, *The Philadelphia Inquirer*, May 2, 1976, p. 1-K.

[11] *Brown* v. *Board of Education of Topeka*, 347 U.S. 296 (1940) at 306.

[12] *Statistical Abstract of the United States 1975* No. 726, "White and Negro Voter Registration in 11 Southern States: 1960 to 1971," p. 449.

[13] "Blacks Increase Share of Elective Offices," *The Philadelphia Inquirer*, August 8, 1976, p. 8-C.

[14] Martha Kwitney, "Shackled Justice—Some Solutions," in *The Wall Street Journal*, October 8, 1975, p. 18.

[15] Lesley Oelsner, "Study Finds Poor Unaided in Court," in *The New York Times*, excerpted from a study commissioned by the Law Enforcement Assistance Administration, November 15, 1975, pp. 1M, 28C. Copyright © 1975 by The New York Times Company. Reprinted by permission.

[16] Leonard Koppett, "Have Athletes' Salaries Hit Ceiling," in *The New York Times*, May 4, 1976, p. 49L.

[17] "Distribution of Personal Wealth in the United States," in *The New York Times*, July 30, 1976, p. D11.

[18] Theodore Cross, "Black and White Incomes: The Gap," in *The New York Times*, July 26, 1975, p. L23.

[19] "Why Its Hard to Cut Teen Age Unemployment, in *U.S. News & World Report*, May 17, 1976, p. 74.

[20] John Allan, "Loans to Students Now Total $8 Billion" in *The New York Times*, November 16, 1975, p. ED15.

[21] Quotes taken from interview "Should School Busing Be Stopped," in *U.S. News and World Report*, October 20, 1975, p. 33-34. Copyright © 1975 *U.S. News & World Report*.

[22] Diane Ravitch, "Busing: The Solution That Has Failed to Solve," in *The New York Times*, December 21, 1975, p. 3E. Copyright © 1975 by The New York Times Company. Reprinted by permission.

CHAPTER 5
PUBLIC OPINION AND POLITICAL PARTICIPATION

CHAPTER OUTLINE

Questions to Consider
Introduction
What Is "the Public"?
Values, Attitudes, and Opinions
Characteristics of Opinions
Theories of Opinion Formation
    Psychological Theory
    Sociological Theory
    Political Theory
The American Political Culture
Characteristics of the American Public
    Income and Education
    Population Shifts
    The Ethnic Influence
    The Liberal-Conservative Dimension
Issue Types and Public Opinion
    Domestic Issues
    Foreign Policy Issues
The Measurement of Opinion
The Flow of Infornation
From Opinion to Action
    Who Are the Activists?
    Opinion, Action, and Influence
Governmental Efforts to Influence Public Opinion
Summary

QUESTIONS TO CONSIDER

A democratic government must be concerned with the opinions of its citizens. This chapter will explore how opinions are formed and how the government is likely to respond to expressions of public opinion. In this chapter we will once again become aware of the interdependence of the government and the people as each tries to influence the other.

The importance of public opinion is continually stressed by the media and by political leaders. But what do we mean by "the public"? How does the public relate to the individual? The formation of individual opinions is a complex process with many potential influences. How important is early childhood in the formation of political opinions? What impact do education and income have on a person's opinions? Is it possible to accurately predict what opinions individuals are likely to form on new issues? The nation's population includes people from a variety of ethnic backgrounds. Is public opinion influenced by these differences? Public figures are often described as conservative or liberal. What is meant by these terms? What do they tell us about a person's political attitudes? Finally, not everyone is interested in the same types of political issues. What issues are likely to receive the most attention?

Public opinion polls are regularly taken in an effort to find out how the public feels about a variety of subjects. How are these polls conducted? Are they accurate barometers of public opinion? To what extent do they affect the decisions of government officials? Does the government attempt to shape public opinion?

Strongly held opinions lead many individuals to try to influence governmental policy. What kind of citizens are most likely to translate their opinions into action? What impact do they have?

Introduction

The opinions of American citizens are a major ingredient of governmental decision making. Every effort is made to see that new policy directions will win public support, and government officials try to respond to public demands for change. Whereas elections offer a periodic opportunity for citizens to express approval or disapproval of their elected representatives, the measurement of public opinion is an ongoing process. Public opinion is expressed in a variety of ways, ranging from responding to polls to trying to influence governmental policy through political activity. These are informal channels of communication between the public and the government, but they are no less important than formal institutions such as voting.

The process by which political opinions are formed and communicated to the government is one of the strongest links between the individual and the political system. It is also through the expression of opinion that groups in society make demands on the government. Many of these demands conflict with those of other groups, and the government must set priorities as to which of these demands will be satisfied. The response of the government varies according to the issues, the group represented, and the conflicting demands from other groups. In the words of V. O. Key, Jr., "The question of who has what kind of opinion is of basic significance in a consideration of interactions between public and government."[1]

What is "The Public"?

Opinion polls report the feelings of the public on a wide variety of issues—"54 percent believe we should not sell computers to the Soviet Union"; "48 percent would sacrifice some environmental quality for less expensive energy." Such statements are supposed to show what "the public" thinks. However, there is no such thing as a single, unified "public." There are many "publics" in society, and public opinion must be interpreted in this light.

Policy makers are very conscious of which publics are important in any given area. For example, economic policy must be acceptable to industry and labor leaders if it is to have any chance of succeeding. A policy such as wage and price controls may evoke opinions from the general public, but these opinions mean little compared with those of the "economic public," whose cooperation is essential if controls are to succeed. In all policy areas, the government must make sure it has the support not only of the publics to whom the subject is important but also of "opinion leaders"—individuals who have access to the media and are respected by the groups they represent.

People are not interested in every public issue; in fact, the level of knowledge on any given issue may be quite low. Therefore, in judging public opinion it is important to define the public that is likely to be both interested in and reasonably well informed on the issue in question. The opinions of this public are important in setting guidelines for acceptable governmental action. The public-at-large that is represented in most newspaper polls is too broad to represent the degree of involvement required for the formation of meaningful opinions. Within the general public, there are many degrees of approval or disapproval of specific actions and widely varying degrees of interest and knowledge.

Opinion Trends

Issues that have been in the spotlight for a long time may attract enough public interest to encourage reasoned opinions. Polls monitoring the public's opinion of the President's performance take advantage of this fact. True, a trip abroad or some similarly dramatic action will increase public approval of the President's performance. However, periodic polls do indicate long-term trends in the President's popularity.

Opinion trends indicate shifts in the public's views of governmental action. Dissatisfaction with the Vietnam War or changes in public attitudes toward amnesty for draft evaders are revealed when responses to similar questions change over time. The impact of opinion trends on governmental policies may be dramatic. Polls taken in the years before President Nixon's trip to the People's Republic of China in February 1972 showed a trend toward public acceptance of the idea of admitting the People's Republic to the United Nations. In 1964, this move was opposed by a majority of 73 percent to 10 percent,[2] but by 1966 the figures were 51 percent to 30 percent,[3] and a Harris survey taken in May 1971 reported that at that time a majority favored the idea.[4] Thus, Nixon went to Peking knowing that the American public would probably approve of his diplomatic efforts.

Values, Attitudes, and Opinions

Opinions are formed within the broad outlines of an individual's *value system,* or general notions of right and wrong or acceptability and unacceptability that remain constant over time. A person's value system is not always consistent, and the opinions that flow fron it may contradict other opinions. Many people believe in the principle of equality but nevertheless display racial or religious prejudice. One of the major reasons for such inconsistencies is the failure to see an issue in the same light as the values underlying it.

Value systems are based on psychological predispositions and therefore play a major role in shaping a person's attitudes. *Attitudes* are more general than opinions. An individual with conservative political values would view strikes by public employees in a conservative light. As a result, his or her attitude would probably be one of disapproval.

The difference between attitudes and opinions is that attitudes are general and opinions are specific. *Opinions* are formed when an issue is relevant to the individual.[5] They develop within general attitudes toward the object or event in question and within the individual's value system. Strongly held opinions are really the tip of the psychological iceberg in that they express deep-seated feelings. The most concrete type of opinion is one that requires some action such as voting.[6]

The Characteristics of Opinions

The conflict that brings an issue to the attention of the public will give rise to opinions that are negative, positive, or somewhere in between. This characteristic, the *direction* of opinion, is the one that is measured by the polls. It is necessary that a person be aware of an issue and perceive it as important if his or her general attitudes in this area are to be converted into specific opinions. The question of whether shale oil deposits in the Rockies should be developed is unlikely to inspire a resident of Maine to form an opinion. Unless a question is relevant to him or her, it is unlikely that the average citizen will pay attention to the information on which opinions are based.

While polls can measure the direction of opinion quite successfully, it is more difficult to measure *intensity*, that is, the strength and stability of opinions. Most poll questions may be answered with a yes or no, ignoring the matter of intensity. Even those that attempt to determine whether a respondent is "strongly in favor," "mildly supportive," or "strongly against" a particular policy are unable to filter out the answers that reflect differences in personality as opposed to degrees of intensity. Some people will choose a middle road if one is offered, while others are likely to go to extremes in expressing an opinion even though they do not feel strongly about the issue itself. The type of intense opinion that reflects personality traits is unlikely to be a stable opinion, but opinions based on knowledge and interest are more likely to be stable. *Stability* is the facet of opinion that is of greatest interest to those whose actions may be affected by the popular will. Stable opinion is possible only when the public has a reasonable knowledge of the issues and alternatives. Opinions that are based on impulse are very changeable and cannot serve as a foundation for political activity.

Opinions that can be translated into action are the most stable and, therefore, the most valuable in terms of judging the public mood. The best example of this type of opinion is voting intentions. The accuracy of polls taken within a week of a Presidential election is well documented, while predictions based on polls taken several weeks earlier are much less dependable. Action is important because the knowledge that one can act in a given situation encourages the careful thought on which a stable opinion must be based.[8]

Few questions have generated more political prose than the rationality—or irrationality—of American political opinions. Simply put, *rationality* means choosing the most appropriate means to a desired end. In order to choose among alternatives, a certain level of knowledge and information is necessary. Rational thinking requires a certain amount of intellectual effort. In terms of opinion formation, only issues that are viewed as relevant are likely to inspire such effort. People are exposed to a constant stream of contradictory statements about public issues. Thus, their rationality is limited by the information available and the extent to which they can sort out the alternatives.

The characteristics of opinion—*direction, intensity, stability,* and *rationality*—are related to the nature of the public being polled. The more specialized the public, the more reasonable it is to expect the levels of knowledge and interest that produce meaningful opinions. When one seeks to judge the national mood, the problems of correctly analyzing broad-based public opinion are complex. The accuracy of such analyses also varies from one issue to another. Questions about issues that are more visible or involve the potential for action are likely to yield more meaningful results than questions dealing with specialized issues that rarely concern the average citizen. Polls can also reveal the degree to which public interest or knowledge is lacking. In fact, Leo Bogart suggests that "the most important and accurate thing that surveys and polls tell us is the extent of public ignorance on matters of fact." [9]

Theories of Opinion Formation

As mentioned earlier, opinions are formed within the context of an individual's value system and attitudes. However, inconsistencies between an individual's values and his or her perceptions of political events can lead to contradictions. For example, it is possible for a strong conviction that "Thou shalt not kill" to conflict with the opinion that murderers deserve capital punishment. The key to the interpretation of public opinion is understanding the individual's perception of a particular issue. Most controversial political issues are not clear-cut. Thus, while value systems form the boundaries within which opinions are formed on most issues, several shades of opinion are possible.

There are three classes of theories that attempt to explain opinion formation: psychological, sociological, and political. All three seem valid, but none can offer a complete explanation. Every opinion is the product of several variables, any of which may be more important in some areas than in others.

Psychological Theory

The key element in psychological theories of opinion formation is the belief that individuals develop their basic values in their early years and that these provide lasting guidelines for the formation of opinions. There is little doubt that likes and dislikes, notions of right and wrong or acceptability and unacceptability are formed in the preschool and school years. The impact of these predispositions on the opinions formed later in life depends on a person's perceptions of an issue and how it relates to him or her.

The family is usually viewed as the primary agent in the development of values. The young child receives his or her first images of the world from this source. During the preschool years, the child's psychological predispositions become part of his or her *personality,* or the way he or she deals with the environment. Exposure to political ideas is limited during the preschool years, but the political world exists within the context of the social environment and early social experiences are likely to be translated to the political area as a child's awareness of his or her surroundings grows.

During the school years political awareness is encouraged. Schoolchildren are taught respect for the nation's flag, history, high government officials, and other political symbols. This training, coupled with increased participation in political discussions at home, shapes early attitudes toward society in general and any political objects, events, or individuals that the child can understand. The school-age child does not have the knowledge on which to base rational opinions or the desire to obtain the necessary information, but political interest usually increases with age.

Family and school are not the only influences on the child. Children are exposed to political issues through the media and conversations with their peers. Few schoolchildren engage in political discussions with their friends, nor are newscasts their favorite form of entertainment. However, these influences tend to reinforce their still-developing values and are important in this sense.

In the later stages of childhood, a person's broad-based values are translated into attitudes toward the political world and finally into opinions on specific issues.[10] The psychological approach stresses the role of early development in this process.

Sociological Theory

Sociological influences on opinion formation include economic status, educational level, ethnic background, and group membership. Sociological theory is based on the belief that an individual's political perceptions are shaped mainly by sociological characteristics.[11] It is clear that such factors play an important role in the interpretation of political issues. For example, education and income are closely linked in the United States. They provide the time to explore political issues as well as the intellectual tools to do so.

Whereas psychological theory emphasizes early childhood and the school years, sociological theory allows for change as a person grows older. An individual may reach a higher socioeconomic level than his or her parents, and his or her ideas of political acceptability may change accordingly. For one thing, he or she may become less sympathetic to social-welfare programs.

Self-interest is a major influence in sociological theory; it is assumed that individuals will react politically according to their social status. In a society such as the United States, with its stress on continual improvement in social status, one would expect to see changes in opinion in people who have risen above their parents' socioeconomic level. Many political issues concern proposals to redistribute resources in some way, with some citizens likely to gain socially or economically and others certain to lose. It is this dimension of the political system that makes sociological theory believable.

However, it is simplistic to assume that a person with an income of $10,000 will view every issue in the same light. Obviously, some issues have a more personal impact than others. In general, domestic issues have the most direct effect on a citizen's pocketbook, and opinions in this area are most likely to be affected by sociological factors. In contrast, foreign policy issues usually have little direct impact on individuals. In this area, sociological factors should have little effect other than to make the issue more understandable to people with higher incomes and more education. Intense, stable opinions on international issues are unlikely to be formed by poorer, less well-educated individuals unless the person is directly affected, as was the case during the later years of the Vietnam War.

The importance of ethnic ties or group membership in the formation of political opinions is often oversimplified.[12] If group membership is to have an effect, the individual must take political cues from the group or identify his or her interests with those of the group. There is also the problem of cross-pressures—a person may identify with several groups and get conflicting political cues from those various groups. For example, an individual may be black (an ethnic identity), Catholic (a religious identity), and a college graduate with an income of $18,000 a year (a socioeconomic identity). Which of these various identities determines his or her opinions and to what extent? Obviously, the answers to such questions lie at the heart of the group basis of opinion formation, and it is unlikely that even the individual just described could accurately sort out the relative importance of his or her various group associations.[13]

Nor should it be assumed that all groups have a unified political outlook. Savers and spenders can be found within almost any group, as can "doves" and "hawks." It is likely that the major effect of group identification is to reinforce previously held opinions.

Although sociological theory rests on different basis than psychological theory, they are not mutually exclusive. One may reinforce the other in some cases or cause confusion in others. People are complex, and both psychological and sociological factors may influence them to varying degrees. Moreover, individuals are likely to form opinions on a wide range of public issues, and the factors that influence this process will vary according to the issue in question.

Political Theory

One of the most important aspects of opinion formation is the impact a person believes a political issue will have on him or her. This fact increases the significance of political and social *trends,* such as a trend toward a more conservative attitude. Such trends may have their roots in geographically based ethnic and racial divisions. For example, the fastest-growing areas of the nation are in the so-called Southern Rim or sun belt, which stretches from Florida across the Southwest to California. People who live in these areas have traditionally taken conservative positions on most political and social issues.[14] The population increase in this region will result in an increase in the percentage of the total population that is conservative in outlook. Any theory that emphasizes political philosophy assumes that people hold fairly consistent views toward political issues. Thus, the conservatism of the sun belt may be contrasted with the liberalism of the large cities of the Northeast. (In the context of everyday American politics, *convervatism* is the view that the role of the government should not be significantly enlarged, while *liberalism* is the idea that the government should take an active role in seeking to provide a better life for all citizens.)

Obviously, individuals representing all socioeconomic levels live in every part of the nation, as do individuals with contrasting value systems. The fact that some sections of the United States can be labeled in terms of political philosophy, despite psychological and socioeconomic differences, shows that political trends play an important role in opinion formation. There are many shades of liberalism and conservatism, and this is where psychological predispositions and socioeconomic status may cause some people to take positions that are different from those of their neighbors. The theory that political trends are important agents in opinion formation is based on the notion that such trends change slowly and thus are a consistent source of reinforcement.

The interplay of psychological, sociological, and political factors in opinion formation is such that the three elements must all be considered key factors in the formation of opinions. One or another may be more important in relation to a particular issue, but it is unlikely that any can be ignored. The assumptions on which these theories are based all appear valid. However, the degree to which people hold consistent opinions is largely related to the relevance of the issue to the individual. When the impact of a political solution is likely to be direct, self-interest becomes the dominant influence. As a result, there is a vast difference between the process of forming opinions on U.S. foreign policy toward Cuba and that of arriving at an opinion on proposals for tax increases.

The American Political Culture

The dominant political and social ideas and customs of a nation are its *political culture,* a system of beliefs that are widely shared. These beliefs consist of the attitudes and values that form the basis for opinions on specific questions. The political culture of the United States is marked by underlying agreement regarding the processes of government and the rights and responsibilities of the individual. This agreement relates to broad questions, however. On specific issues, differing views arise and conflicting opinions are formed.

Perhaps the most elementary aspect of the American political culture is seen in the way government officials are chosen. The election procedure is accepted by all and forms the basis of orderly political change. At the same time, there is widespread cynicism toward politics in general and politicians in particular.[15] This distrust was expressed by the late Walter Lippmann as follows:

With exceptions so rare that they are regarded as miracles and freaks of nature, successful democratic politicians are insecure and intimidated men. They advance politically only as they placate, appease, bribe, seduce, bamboozle, or otherwise manage to manipulate the demanding and threatening elements in their constituencies.[16]

The basic freedoms—speech, religion, assembly—represent beliefs that are shared by most citizens in a general sense.[17] But there is less unanimity on these matters than appears on the surface. Such issues as the release of the Pentagon Papers, Biblereading in public schools, and the right of antiwar demonstrators to protest the nation's policy in Vienam lead to strong demands from some people that the basic freedoms be limited by governmental action. This is an indication that broad agreement on basic democratic values is not necessarily reflected in attitudes and opinions.

There are several possible explanations for this discrepancy. One is the inconsistency that often exists within an individual's value system. A second is the failure of some people to see the relationship between specific events and more general values. Opinions also may clash with basic values if a person feels threatened. Thus, an individual with strong liberal values may react conservatively if the racial makeup of his or her neighborhood is likely to change.

The notion that the individual can and should determine his or her own socioeconomic level is also widely shared—"You get what you work for." This view is an outgrowth of the colonial distrust of centralized government and the belief that the American Dream is open to all. However, as with the rights of citizens, there is a difference between broad agreement on the virtues of independence and specific opinions regarding government programs designed to offer financial aid to some segment of society. Social security, unemployment compensation, and tax relief for industry are examples of the kind of aid that is welcomed even by people who believe firmly in the "work ethic."

Similarly, most people believe citizens should be politically aware and interested, but the level of knowledge on specific issues is low and the level of political participation even lower. To most Americans, political participation means voting, and even voting is not universal. Seldom do more than 60 percent of those who are eligible to vote actually do so. Fewer than 54 percent of the eligible voters cast their ballots in the 1976 Presidential election. Such figures illustrate the extent of political disinterest in the United States. The nation's political stability has allowed the average citizen to sit back, attend to personal concerns, and not worry about which party or candidate is going to win the next election. This disinterest is one reason for the increased importance of political elites and the need to determine the opinions of elite groups as well as those of the general public.

The tendency to be cynical about the government, added to the low level of political interest, has resulted in a politics of the center. Republicans and Democrats argue about how to achieve widely accepted national goals rather than the goals themselves.

Characteristics of the American Public

It is necessary to understand the characteristics of the American people if one is to judge public response to governmental policy. Any profile of the American people includes both demographic characteristics—age, religion, education, income, race, ethnic origin—and political philosophy—liberal or conservative. The relative importance of each of these factors in a particular issue, together with psychological predispositions, shapes public opinion.

Income and Education

The relationship between income and education is shown in Table 5-1, and the distribution of family income is illustrated in Table 5-2. The increasing wealth and educational level of the nation as a whole have an important impact on public opinion for several reasons. First, more Americans are gaining the intellectual tools with which to form political opinions, and this increased awareness will probably result in less dependence on group or elite guidance and more independent judgment. This trend can already be seen in the reduced importance of political parties as sources of political

TABLE 5-1
The Relationship Between Income and Education (Percentage of individuals with varying levels of education, who reach various maximum incomes)

Maximum Annual Income	8th Grade or Less	High School	Some College
Under $5,000	59%	17%	11%
$5,000- 9,999	29	41	26
$10,000- 14,999	9	30	24
$15,000 and over	3	12	39

SOURCE: Robert D. Cantor, *Voting Behavior and Presidential Elections* (Itasca, Ill.: F. E. Peacock, 1975), p. 44.

information. The increase in split-ticket voting (i.e., voting for candidates from more than one party) and crossing of party lines is evidence that the Democratic and Republican parties, once the most important political influence on most citizens, have lost much of their significance.

There is reason to believe that as education and income levels rise, many people will be less dependent on political information from traditional sources such as labor unions, ethnic groups, business organizations, and individuals who have access to the news media owing to their social status. However, this trend is not strong enough to bring about greater political interest and participation. While the influence of traditional information sources has undoubtedly weakened, the American public still is not very well informed about the political system or interested in political issues. The increased trend toward independence in voting may be the first step along the road to increased participation.

Population Shifts

The United States has always been noted for its unusually mobile population. The population shifts illustrated in Table 5-3 will have an impact on the nation's political balance. The House of Representatives is reapportioned every 10 years, and in 1980 the states in the Southern Rim will gain representatives at the expense of those in the Northeast. This shift is important in terms of the political culture it appears to favor, that is, the growing population of the sun belt. Despite the existence of a national political culture with widely agreed-upon goals, these goals are interpreted differently in various geographic regions. The Southern Rim has been described as follows:

If the Southern Rim were an independent nation, its Gross National Product would exceed that of any other country except the Soviet Union.

... the Southern sun shines on a culture especially hospitable to unbridled avarice. The dominant cult of individual achievement measured in dollars and cents and pursued at any

TABLE 5-2
*Income Changes in U.S. from 1956 Projected to 1980 (Percentage of families with various levels of annual income)**

Annual Income	1956	1968	1980 (est.)
Under $10,000	82%	60%	39%
$10,000-14,999	13	25	27
$15,000 and over	5	15	34

SOURCE: Robert D. Cantor, *Voting Behavior and Presidential Elections* (Itasca, Ill.: F. E. Peacock, 1975), p. 45.

*Based on 1968 constant dollars, assuming average inflationary growth of 3.5% per year.

TABLE 5-3
The Rising Power of the Sun Belt: Projected House Apportionment After the 1980 Census

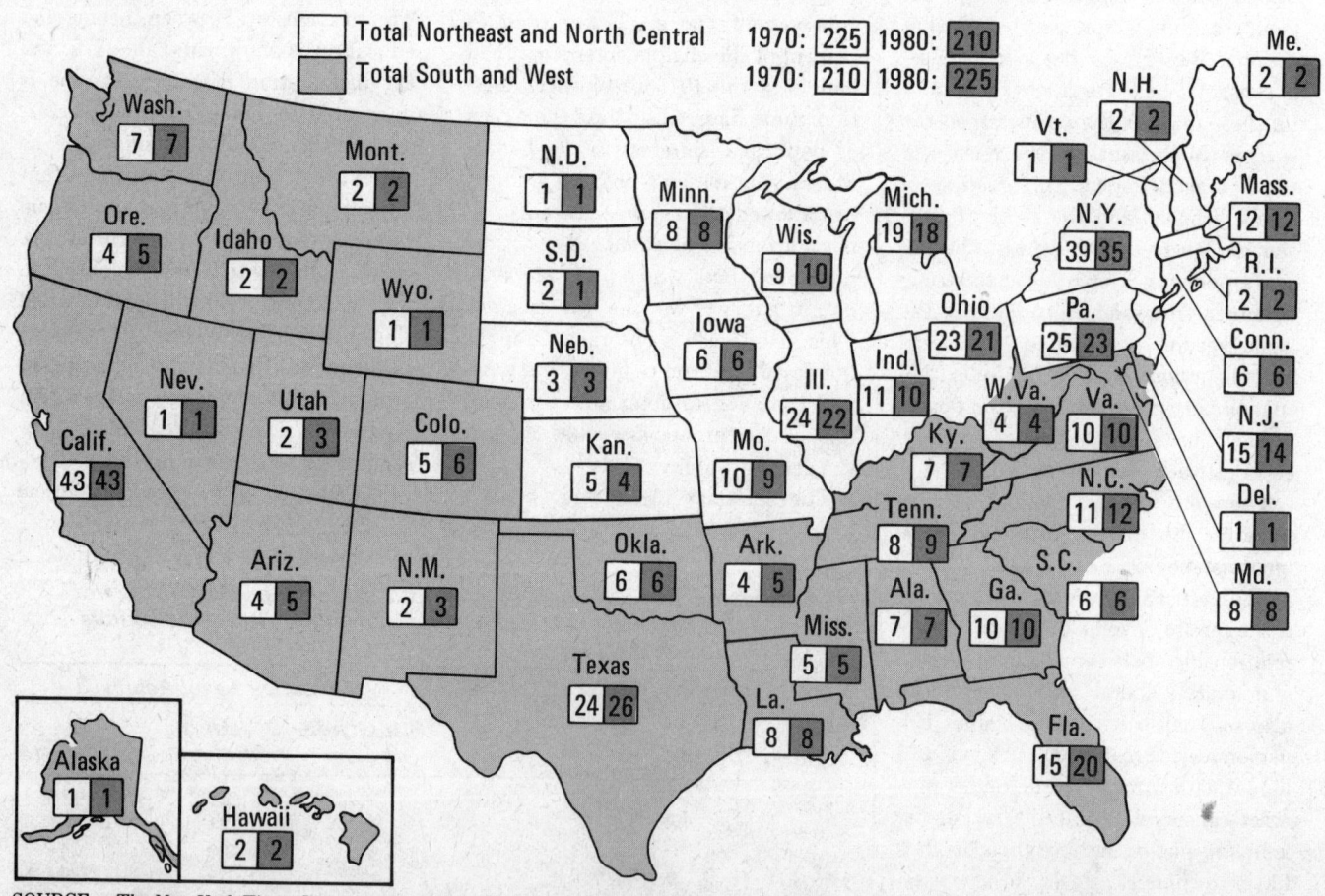

SOURCE: *The New York Times*, January 23, 1976, p. 1. Copyright© 1976 by the New York Times Company. Reprinted by permission.

cost and by any method, legal or otherwise, is abetted by right wing Protestant fundamentalism, virulent anti-Communism, rampant anti-unionism and militant patriotism. The Rim's far right politics are buttressed by the enduring racism of a society historically allied to slavery.[18]

The conservatism of the Southern Rim is marked by increasing dissatisfaction with federal social-welfare programs and criticisms of "big" government by the area's political leaders. It is hard to tell whether the political culture of the Rim is reflecting or influencing the rest of the nation. But the implications are clear: Shifts in public opinion may be triggered by population changes.

The Ethnic Influence

There are an estimated 65 million so-called "hyphenated Americans," that is, citizens of other than English ancestry.[19] Blacks form the largest such group, with about 25 million members, and the next-largest group is the Irish-Americans, with about 13 million members.[20] These groups are believed by some observers to hold fairly unified political views. The fact that many ethnic groups also have their religion in common increases the potential for unity.

The degree to which ethnic factors influence opinion formation depends largely on whether or not the individual is living in a heavily ethnic area. People are likely to live in neighborhoods where incomes are roughly the same. Since the educational level of people with similar incomes is also likely to be similar, their experience and outlook will likewise be similar. If ethnic or religious ties are added to these factors, the ethnic factor may indeed be important. However, if a person has moved away from such a neighborhood, the ethnic influence will be reduced. Unless an individual feels that his or her interests are the same as those of the group he or she identifies with, the group's impact on his or her political views will be minimal. It is possible to have strong ethnic ties without always interpreting political events in ethnic terms.

The Liberal-Conservative Dimension

The degree of unity seen in the widespread agreement of Americans on traditional values such as the basic freedoms and minority rights is not present at the day-to-day level. The average Anerican's political philosophy is pragmatic. Philosophically consistent policies that are unproductive in practical terms would cost any administration much public support. The Nixon administration's use of wage and price controls to combat inflation is an example of political pragmatism: In this case, a conservative Republican President used an economic tool that has traditionally been considered "un-Republican." Similarly, in 1976 the Democratic Presidential candidates proposed no far-reaching social programs of the type normally sponsored by the Democratic party, sensing that they would lose support if they did so.

The conservative-liberal split is not a clear-cut division of public opinion reflecting strongly held political philosophies. Rather, it affects the opinions of those who believe the government should play a more activist role—the liberals—and those who believe federal action should be maintained at present levels or reduced—the conservatives. Almost every citizen is likely to be more or less liberal or conservative, depending on the issue at hand.

The nation has become more liberal over time, but within the trend toward bigger government and less dependence on individual ability and ambition there are pendulum-like swings that shift public opinion back to a more conservative position for a limited period. Table 5-4 indicates that liberalism is associated with increased income and higher educational levels, but that conservatives outnumber liberals. It also shows the increasing conservativism in the South, with much the same pattern true of the entire Southen Rim, the fastest-growing area of the nation.

In considering the liberal-conservative dimension of public opinion, the issues at stake are important. While higher income and education do appear to be accompanied by increased liberalism, this is not true in all areas. Upper socioeconomic groups are more liberal with respect to the rights of others and the need to help the less advantaged members of society—the so-called social issues. They also tend to have a more international outlook

Marchers in New York's Puerto Rican Day Parade demonstrate ethnic pride.

Robert Welch, founder and chairman of the John Birch Society, addressing a meeting in Dallas. This group represents the most conservative sector of political thought.

TABLE 5-4
Relative Changes in Political Philosophy, 1967 to 1972

	Respondent Self-Identification				
	Conservative	Middle Road	Liberal	Radical	Not Sure
Groups Becoming More Liberal					
Total public					
1972	35%	34%	19%	3%	9%
1967	38	37	14	1	10
College educated					
1972	30	34	29	2	5
1967	40	41	13	1	5
Change	−10	−7	+16	+1	—
Under 30					
1972	24	29	31	5	11
1967	38	40	11	2	9
Change	−14	−11	+20	+3	+2
Independent voters					
1972	30	34	23	4	9
1967	34	42	12	1	11
Change	−4	−8	+11	+3	−2
$10,000 and over income					
1972	35	35	24	3	3
1967	39	43	12	1	5
Change	−4	−8	+12	+2	−2
Groups Becoming Middle of the Road and Conservative					
South					
1972	40%	33%	12%	2%	13%
1967	43	26	17	1	13
Change	−3	+7	−5	+1	—
50 and over					
1972	42	36	11	2	9
1967	38	34	14	1	13
Change	+4	+2	−3	+1	−4
Republican					
1972	53	31	8	1	7
1967	50	30	11	—	9
Change	+3	+1	−3	+1	−2

SOURCE: The Harris Survey, November 27, 1972. Copyright 1972 by the *Chicago Tribune*. World Rights Reserved.

than lower socioeconomic groups, who have little interest in foreign affairs. But in the economic area their opinions do not reflect the tendency toward liberalism that they show in social or international matters.

Issue Types and Public Opinion

Public opinion is of most interest to government officials when it is relatively intense. Such opinions tend to be stable and to inspire individuals to express their views. Election years provide the ideal time for the expression of public opinion on various issues because voting is a definite act. At other times strong opinions may be revealed through increased communication with congresspeople, the media, or interest groups.

Intense opinions can form only if an issue is seen as relevant. Mere awareness that a political question has been raised will not give rise to enough intensity for the government to respond. The issue must be important or relevant to the individual. For this reason, domestic issues usually get more attention than foreign policy issues. Federal action to raise social security taxes in order to provide increased benefits is more important to more people than the problems of NATO.

National concerns do not remain constant. There are shifts in focus as once-controversial issues fade into the background and new problems move into the spotlight. Table 5-5 shows the shifts in the relative importance of key issues that occurred over a four-year period. The comparison between 1968 and 1972 is interesting because of the highly visible events that marked this period. Vietnam, riots, and inflation dominated the news. Note the decrease in concern about crime between 1968 and 1972. This reflects the end of the highly publicized riots over racial issues and the Vietnam War. Crime remained a problem, and still does, but the decline in media coverage of spectacular riots and looting reduced public concern. In contrast, the cost of living was a minor concern in 1968, but with inflation on the rise, the 1972 poll showed that the economy ranked with Vietnam as a major concern.

Domestic Issues

The public is better informed on domestic issues than on foreign affairs. Problems such as the economy or social issues such as legalized abortion are understandable to most individuals and therefore generate opinions of moderate to high intensity.

The degree of public knowledge—or lack of it—of political questions has long been a source of interest and controversy. When people are asked about specific aspects of pending legislation, their answers are likely to be vague and indicate a low level of information. However, this may reflect the feeling that the legislation is unimportant rather than lack of knowledge. No issue touches everyone, and most public debates revolve around matters that are difficult to apply to the individual. In the 1970s, for example, unemployment became a national concern. While most people agree that "something should be done" about high levels of unemployment, there is little discussion of this issue on which

TABLE 5-5
The Most Important Problems Facing the Nation, 1968 and 1972 (Percentage of respondents citing problems as most important)

Mid-October, 1968	
Vietnam War	44%
Crime (includes looting, riots)	25
Race relations	17
High cost of living	6
Other problems, no opinion	23
	115%*

Late September, 1972	
Vietnam War	27%
Inflation, high cost of living	27
Crime, lawlessness	8
International problems (general)	10
Drug use, abuse	9
Other problems, don't know	28
	109%*

SOURCE: Robert D. Cantor, Voting *Behavior and Presidential Elections* (Itasca, Ill.: F. E. Peacock, 1975), p. 65.

*Columns add to more than 100 percent because of multiple responses.

solid opinions can be based. Pollsters who ask general questions such as "Do you favor expanded public works programs to deal with unemployment?" will receive answers that are practically meaningless.

It has long been assumed that "pocketbook" issues give rise to the most intense opinions because they have the greatest personal impact. While the logic of this notion is sound, it is not true that economic issues arouse the strongest opinions. Opinion formation requires the existence of conflicting views that are understandable to the public. There is evidence that the public sees little difference between conflicting approaches to economic problems. Some may interpret this fact as being due to lack of understanding, but it is more appropriate to consider it in the light of political debate. Political parties are active in debating economic issues. They discuss the problems and propose solutions. But there is little indication that the public views economic issues in terms of party differences. Thus, there is no real basis for a strong opinion. In 1972, 1288 voting-age individuals were asked, "Looking ahead, do you think your family would get along better financially in the next four years if the Democrats or the Republicans win the election, or wouldn't it make much difference?" Fifty-seven percent said it wouldn't make much difference, while 23 percent favored the Democrats and 20 percent favored the Republicans.[21] This occurred in an election year, a time when candidates are trying to generate party loyalty by debating basic questions such as economic policy. The figures indicate that while the public is aware of the major issues, they simply do not see enough difference between the programs proposed by the parties to encourage intense opinion. Moreover there are very few economic issues on which the parties take clearly opposing positions. This sharply limits the likelihood that public opinion on such issues will be intense.

The domestic issues that are most likely to give rise to conflicting views are in the social area. Issues such as busing or legalized abortion, on which the differences between opposing positions are clear, provides the individual with the opportunity to form an opinion. In addition, in the social area individuals are more likely to see an issue as directly affecting them. This leads to opinions that are both intense and stable. It is for this reason that most politicians prefer to avoid social issues unless the voters in the area they represent share a common viewpoint. Presidential candidates in particular can be expected to play down their positions on social issues wherever possible. In the 1976 Presidential election campaign, Jimmy Carter spoke against a constitutional amendment to ban busing, but he also spoke in favor of "neighborhood schools," using the phrase "ethnic purity." His aides had trouble explaining this phrase, but Carter's message was clear. He offered hope to people who favored busing as well as to those who opposed it by indicating that if he was elected he would not attempt to impose a solution on an unwilling public.

Foreign Policy Issues

American foreign policy is supported by a broad public agreement on the need for military preparedness, the necessity of helping other democratic nations, and the desirability of slowing or halting the nuclear arms race without weakening the military strength of the United States. Differences between liberals and conservatives in this area concern the means of achieving these goals rather than the goals themselves. The opinions generated by foreign policy are not as strong as those generated by some areas of domestic policy. The Vietnam War illustrates the difficulty of trying to interpret foreign policy issues in terms of political philosophy. The Johnson administration probably was responsible for more liberal social legislation than any in history, and yet this liberal President was largely responsible for the war in Southeast Asia. Here he was supported by conservatives, who can usually be counted on to favor a strong stand on any issue that can be viewed as a clash between democracy and communism.

The fact that foreign affairs do not lend themselves to interpretation along party lines discourages the formation of strong opinions. There are differences in opinion regarding how the United States should act in the foreign policy area, but little real differences in value judgments between Democrats and Republicans. For example; after his election victory in 1976 Jimmy Carter did everything possible to assure the world that U.S. foreign policy would not change, despite the fact that President Ford was a Republican. The failure of Americans to see a difference between the Democrats and the Republicans in foreign policy matters parallels the situation with regard to domestic issues. In 1972, 1245 people were asked, "Looking ahead, do you think the problem of keeping out of a bigger war would be better handled in the next four years by the Democrats, by the Republicans, or about the same by both?" Fifteen percent favored the Democrats; 31 percent favored the Republicans; and 54 percent viewed the performance of the two parties as likely to be about the same.[22] The Republicans' edge in foreign affairs probably reflects dissatisfaction with the Democratic administration's unsuccessful Vietnam policy rather than any feeling that the two parties have markedly different approaches to foreign affairs.

The failure of the American public to view either the economy or foreign affairs along party lines does not mean public opinion is unimportant in these areas. The questions asked in both the polls mentioned were of a very general nature, and the responses simply indicated that in the eyes of the public neither party has a monopoly on political wisdom. More specific questions about current problems yield answers that are more useful as indicators of public opinion and serve as a barometer of the public's willingness to accept certain policies. There was considerable debate in February 1976 about the advisability of American aid to an Angolan government facing an uprising backed by the Soviet Union and Cuba. Memories of Vietnam were too vivid to permit the policy favored by President Ford and Secretary of State Kissinger, who wanted to use the CIA to funnel arms and supplies to Angola. Congressional opposition backed by strong public opinion prevented this policy from being carried out. This shows that the public can focus on a particular issue in an area that generally is not viewed as important. Any proposed policy that is seen as leading to increased U.S. activity, possibly of a military nature, will probably arouse intense opinions because the prospect of war is relevant to all citizens.

The Measurement of Opinion

There are several ways of measuring opinion, including telephone surveys, mail questionnaires, and personal interviews. The method used depends largely on the time and money available. Telephone surveys are the quickest and least expensive method, but personal interviews, though costly, are the most reliable. At the heart of opinion measurement is the statistical concept that a small number of answers can be used as a basis from which to generalize about the population being sampled. The results obtained are expressed in terms of probabilities. For example, a nationwide sample of 1500 interviews may be said to represent national opinion to within three percentage points in 95 out of 100 cases.[23] The margin of error can be narrowed and the probability of accuracy increased if the sample size is increased. However, limited time and money as well as the limited gains achieved by using larger samples usually result in the use of a sample of 1500. Smaller samples are used when a lower degree of accuracy is needed or funds are limited.

The sample itself is of primary importance and cannot be chosen by statistical methods alone. Most national polls are based on a few selected areas throughout the nation that, taken together, are representative of the total population. Some of these areas are chosen at random from census materials—these are called *clusters*. Within these clusters, specific blocks are chosen and interviewers are told to call on a set number of households according to a formula such as every fifth house. This introduces the concept of *randomness*, which means that every individual in the cluster has an equal chance of being interviewed. For sampling purposes, children under a certain age are not interviewed.

The way the interview questions are worded may have a significant influence on the answers. Ideally, the questions should be structured so that they do not dictate the answer. This is a simple matter in polls taken before elections because the question is clearcut—"Whom do you intend to vote for for President?" Issue questions are more difficult to structure in this way because of the possibility that the respondent lacks the information necessary to understand the question.

Closely related to this problem is the matter of reporting and interpreting polls. Any survey produces a percentage of responses in the "Don't Know" or "No Opinion" category. The way these are reported (or not reported) has an important effect. It is customary to report the "Don't Know" percentages in polls of people's voting intentions, but this category is seldom mentioned in most other public opinion polls. However, it is impossible to interpret a survey correctly without this information. For example, suppose 1000 people were asked their opinion on whether or not the United Stated should recognize the Castro government in Cuba. Of these, 400 said yes, 300 said no, and 300 said they didn't know. What percentage of the people favor recognizing Castro? If the "don't knows" are included, 40 percent are for recognition and 30 percent against. If the "don't knows" are not included, 57 percent are for recognition and 43 percent against. Obviously, leaving out the "don't knows" exaggerates the positive as well as the negative results.

The difficulty of accurately measuring intensity of opinion was discussed earlier in the chapter. And yet the percentage of people for or against a proposed governmental action is relatively meaningless unless it is possible to determine the intensity of their opinions. Intensity, as we have seen, is closely related to stability, and only stable opinions are of practical value. Some polls make an effort to measure intensity after determining the direction of opinion by asking such questions as "Do you favor the Carter administration's energy program strongly? moderately? or is it barely acceptable?" Such efforts are better than nothing, but they are not enough.

The number of public opinion polls appearing in the nation's newspapers and reported on TV newscasts illustrates the popular appeal of the opinion sampling process. However, the effect of such polls on governmental responsiveness must be measured against their limitations. Consider this example. The Philadelphia Bicentennial Commission hired the Sindlinger Organization in January 1976 to conduct a national survey to determine how many people were likely to visit Philadelphia during the Bicentennial year. This was an important element in the planning process, since the nunber of people expected would determine the scope of the city's preparations for the visitors. In a national survey conducted between March 20 and May 20, 1975, the organization collected data indicating that a maximum of 70 million and a minimum of 19 million people could be expected to visit Philadelphia in 1976. Those responsible for providing housing, transportation, entertainment, police protection, and sanitation facilities for the expected visitors decided to prepare for the lower estimate, 19 million. But even this estimate was far too high: Only about 7 million visitors actually came to Philadelphia during the Bicentennial year.[24] This example illustrates the difficulty of trying to measure what people will do by what they say, particularly when the possible action either is far in the future or involves a minimum of inconvenience.

The Flow of Information

The average American is bombarded with political information every day. The most obvious source of the news is the mass media—radio, television, and newspapers—but these are by no means the only sources of information about political events and issues. Peer groups may also play an important role in communicating news of the political world. The events of the day are discussed in the local bar as well as in the college dorm. The key to opinion formation lies in the *interpretation* of the news rather than with the sources of the facts in question.

The educated, politically aware citizen considers alternative viewpoints before forming an opinion. News magazines and newspaper columnists are more likely to present the alternatives in a meaningful way than front-page headlines or TV newscasts because of their emphasis on analysis. The interested citizen will seek out the basis of a controversy and explore issues that are unlikely to affect him or her directly but appear important in terms of the national interest.

The less educated citizen is likely to be less politically interested and to get information in its most condensed form: TV news. Exposure to such news is no guarantee that a person will understand the issues of the day. Less educated people are unlikely to consider alternative viewpoints because there is little in the news that seems important to them. Only issues that have a direct impact on this segment of the public are likely to lead to more than a superficial opinion, and even then the opinion is probably a product of interpretations provided by peers rather than careful thought about the problem at hand.

While the media are the most obvious source of information and peer groups the most obvious personal influence, there are a variety of social influences that provide news and interpretations of political events. Interest groups such as labor unions and trade and professional associations play a role in making their members aware of political issues that may not have received wide publicity and interpreting these issues in the context of the group's shared interests. This type of influence on opinion formation is very significant because of the high probability that the group's members will trust the interpretations presented by the leaders of the groups. The specialization of interest groups makes such interpretations believable to their members. For example, proposed legislation to limit picketing will arouse the interest of both labor unions and industry groups. Both will interpret the issue and its probable effects on their members, and it is likely that the common interests that bind each group together will lead its members to accept the group's position.

The media are the primary news source and interest groups are important interpreters of political events, but there is another important source of news and analysis: opinion leaders. There are individuals in all fields who, because of their reputations or the positions they hold, can make their views known through the media or interest groups. It is in the area of news interpretation that such people are especially effective. This role is a specialized one, however, and an individual's effectiveness as an opinion leader is largely limited to a particular area. Dr. Jonas Salk is a nationally known opinion leader whose views in the medical field are sought by the media. He is thus in a position to communicate his views to the public, and his reputation as the developer of the Salk polio vaccine makes him believable to the public as far as medical matters are concerned. There are many people with local rather than national reputations who can serve as opinion leaders in a given geographic area. Every city has its so-called "leading citizens," whose views on local matters are respected. As we will see shortly, the two-step theory holds that such individuals are an important link between the media and the public in the interpretation of political events. [25]

From Opinion to Action

Opinion formation does not yield any results in terms of governmental policy unless opinions are transformed into some sort of political activity. Just as there are many publics that must be considered by policy makers, so there are many publics in terms of political participation. The degree of effect individuals have on governmental decisions reflects their political activity. The publics that are most influential are those that actively use the various available channels of communication with the government. Opinion polls are useful in giving government officials an idea of the direction of public opinion, but the difficulty of determining intensity of opinion limits their usefulness. Since opinions that are backed by actions of some sort are likely to be more intense, this form of expression is most meaningful to policy makers.

The most common form of participation in the political process is voting, but there are many other forms of political participation. Table 5-6 illustrates the low rate of participation in activities other than voting. The inactivity of the majority increases the potential influence of the minority who do engage in some type of political activity. However, political participation may extend beyond the activities listed in Table 5-6. People who identify with an interest group such as labor, industry, or professional organizations give the group influence through their support. When the group attempts to influence governmental decisions, the individual is participating in an indirect political action. This is an important idea because it is through some form of group membership that most people communicate with the government.

Political participation can also take the form of efforts to influence the media in the hope that this channel of communication will present a particular point of view to large numbers of people. Individuals write letters to the editor that are published on the editorial pages of newspapers and attract the attention of many people who are interested in political events. This is not a large audience, but their above-average interest makes those who read the editorial page an important political group. Organizations also try to get their views before the public through the media in a more direct way. Leaders of organizations with large memberships have little trouble getting media coverage. Table 5-7 lists such organizations in terms of total membership and shows the percentage of the members that are active. Groups with larger memberships attract media attention through size alone, while smaller organizations are newsworthy if their membership is politically active. Note that Table 5-7 lists only groups who report their membership. To these should be added the large numbers of people who are not dues-paying members of a group but identify with its goals. For example, many nonunion workers see their interests as similar to those of union members. In determining economic policy, political leaders must consider the likelihood that organized labor also speaks for many other workers who are not union members.

Most of the groups listed in Table 5-7 are not involved in political questions on a continuing basis. However, all are likely to take an active role in issues that affect their goals. Garden clubs might support measures for environmental protection; leaders of youth groups may be active in seeking new recreational facilities; and groups associated with the fine arts will do what they can to attract federal support. In short, there are few, if any, activities engaged in by large numbers of people that do not have some political meaning at one time or another.

A more direct form of political participation is communication with government officials to express support of opposition to proposed legislation or policies. Individuals who wish to take such action are usually limited to writing letters to local officials, congresspeople, or the President. These communications are watched carefully as indicators of public opinion because taking the time to write a letter is a sign of a certain amount of intensity of opinion. Letters that follow a format prescribed by such groups as the National Rifle Association are another means of communication with government officials. They are taken seriously because of the sheer weight of numbers. The civil rights protests and anti-war demonstrations of the 1960s illustrate a more dramatic form of direct political participation that, though often going beyond the norms of the political system, can be effective in particular cases.

Who are the Activists?

A recent study of political participation gives us some idea of the type of person who is likely to be more or less active in politics.[26] The lower socioeconomic groups tend to be inactive, though they have the most to gain from political activity. Political participation requires skill and time. A certain level of education and income is more likely to give an individual both the time and the intellectual tools for political activity. There is also less political activity among older and younger people. The former are often disillusioned about their ability to affect the political process, and the younger groups have more immediate personal problems and goals. Thus, while the democratic ideal that all citizens have equal rights is protected by law and the courts, there is no way the government can make sure people

TABLE 5-6
Percentage Engaging in Twelve Different Acts of Political Participation

Type of Political Participation	Percentage
1. Report regularly voting in Presidential elections*	72
2. Report always voting in local elections	47
3. Active in at least one organization involved in community problems**	32
4. Have worked with others in trying to solve some community problems	30
5. Have attempted to persuade others to vote as they were	28
6. Have ever actively worked for a party or candidates during an election	26
7. Have ever contacted a local government official about some issue or problem	20
8. Have attended at least one political meeting or rally in last three years	19
9. Have ever contacted a state or national government official about some issue or problem	18
10. Have ever formed a group or organization to attempt to solve some local community problem.	14
11. Have ever given money to a party or candidate during an election campaign	13
12. Presently a member of a political club or organization	8

Number of Cases: weighted 3095
unweighted 2549

SOURCE: Sidney Verba and Norman H. Nie, *Participation in America* (New York: Harper & Row, 1972), p. 31.

*Composite variable created from reports of voting in 1960 and 1964 Presidential elections. Percentage is equal to those who report they have voted in both elections.

**This variable is a composite index where the proportion presented above is equal to the proportion of those in the sample who are active in at least one voluntary association that, they report, takes an active role in attempting to solve community problems. The procedure utilized was as follows: Each respondent was asked whether he was a member of fifteen types of voluntary associations. For each affirmative answer he was then asked whether he regularly attended meetings or otherwise took a leadership role in the organization. If yes, he was considered an active member. If he was an active member and if he reported that the organization regularly attempted to solve community problems, he was considered to have performed this type of political act. Membership in expressly *political* clubs or organizations was excluded from this index.

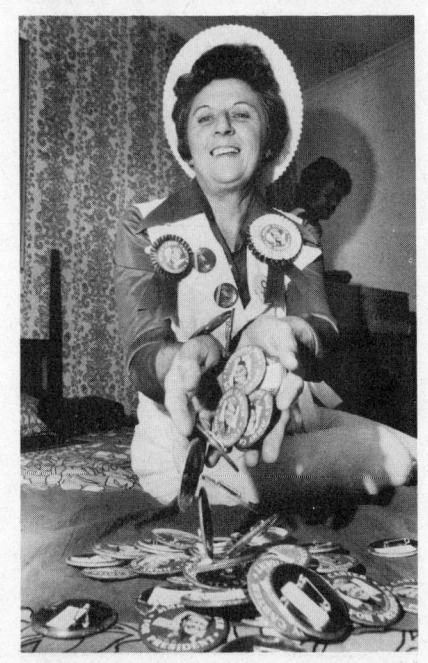

Carter campaign worker showing buttons she designed in Presidential elections to activate the party faithful.

have equal political influence. The groups that are most active have a greater voice in governmental policy than those who participate less.

Participation in America, by Sidney Verba and Norman Nie is the most thorough study of citizen participation to date. These authors summarize the impact of citizen participation in politics as follows:

> The fact that participation comes from a small and unrepresentative sample makes a difference in how leaders respond. Participation is a powerful mechanism for citizen control, but how the mechanism works depends on who participates.[27]

Thus, there is nothing automatic about the government's response to citizen demands. Unless these demands are supported by polical action, they are unlikely to have much impact.

Opinion, Action, and Influence

The impact of public opinion and political activity varies with the situation. In some cases, national opinion polls may have considerable influence, while in others only the opinions of the more active publics will be considered. The way the government responds to expressions of opinion from various groups is an indication of the political influence of those groups.

There are some political issues that affect almost everyone. The Vietnam War, economic recession, and the Arab oil embargo are examples of such situations; the only conflict is over the proper solutions. Since these are broad-based issues, the government takes opinion polls in these areas seriously. While such polls do not dictate a particular course of action, they help offcials judge the acceptability of proposed actions. Wage and price controls were put into effect by the Nixon administration when favorable ratings of Nixon's performance on "keeping down the cost of living" fell from 82 percent to only 14 percent.[28] This was a clear indication that the public would approve of any program that offered the hope of economic stability. It would be simplistic to conclude that the polls were the major reason for Nixon's action, but they did offer some assurance that the public would accept the new policy. This had a special impact because of the "un-Republican" nature of wage and price controls and the desire of any President to stay on good terms with his party.

Conflict is a characteristic of most public issues with various groups in society either supporting a policy, opposing it, or sitting on the sidelines. Almost all governmental policies result in a benefit of some sort for certain groups while others lose in relative terms. It is in such situations that the idea of several publics, each with varying influence in certain areas, becomes important. The clash of interests between labor unions and industry organizations over the right to picket or the minimum wage is an example of conflict between two politically powerful segments of society. In order to maintain their political strength, it is necessary for both groups to constantly pressure government officials at all levels in behalf of their goals. They also attempt to sway the opinions of many publics in order to gain broad-based support.

TABLE 5-7
Membership and Activity Rates in Sixteen Types of Organizations

Type of Organization	Percentage Reporting Membership	Rank	Percentage of Members Active	Rank
Labor unions	17	1	37	16
School service groups, such as PTA or school alumni groups	17	2	60	7
Fraternal groups, such as Elks, Eagles, Masons, and their women's auxiliaries	15	3	65	5
Sports clubs	12	4	53	10
Political groups, such as Democratic or Republican clubs, and political action groups, such as voter's leagues	8	5	66	4
Veteran's groups such as the American Legion	7	6	48	14
Youth groups, such as Boy Scouts and Girl Scouts	7	7	88	1
Miscellaneous groups not covered	7	8	50	12
Professional or academic societies, such as American Dental Association, Phi Beta Kappa	7	9	57	8
Church-related groups, such as women's auxiliary, Bible groups*	6	10	80	2
Service clubs, such as Lions, Rotary, Zenta, Junior Chamber of Commerce	6	11	78	3
Hobby or garden clubs, such as stamp or coin clubs, flower clubs, pet clubs	5	12	42	15
Farm organizations, such as Farmer's Union, Farm Bureau, Grange	4	13	49	13
Literary, art, discussion or study clubs, such as book-review clubs, theater groups	4	14	56	9
School fraternities and sororities, such as Sigma Chi, Delta Gamma	3	15	63	6
Nationality groups, such as Sons of Norway, Hibernian Society	2	16	52	11

SOURCE: Sidney Verba and Norman H. Nie, *Participation in America* (New York: Harper & Row, 1972), p. 42

*This does not include church membership but rather associations emerging around the church or religion.

President Jimmy Carter in town hall meeting in Clinton, Massachusetts, as he attempts to build popular support in the early months of his administration.

Governmental Efforts to Influence Public Opinion

There is a two-way relationship between the government and the public in terms of using public opinion to promote particular goals. Just as a multitude of private groups try to influence government policy by gaining public support on particular issues, so the government makes every effort to win support for its programs and policies. The government is not a single unit any more than there is a single public. Most issues find various government departments, agencies, or branches competing with each other for public support. For example, government agencies and departments compete for congressional funds, and they encourage the groups who support them to put pressure on Congress. The President and Congress also compete for public support. Few issues stir the public to political activity, but neither the President nor Congress wants to arouse public opposition.

Elite groups can place pressure on Congress and the President and thus are more important than the general public in the competition for support. The groups whose support is sought vary with the issue. The endless debate over a national energy program involves gas, oil, and utility companies as well as consumer groups and labor unions. This is the type of issue that has at least a potential impact on everyone, so that efforts to sway public opinion are directed to several specific groups as well as to the public at large. Some issues are narrower in scope, however, and efforts to gain support are correspondingly limited. When the Pentagon announces its intention to close a particular military base, there is a reaction from private groups in the area concerned as well as the congresspeople who represent that area. This issue pits the goal of efficient, economic governmental operations against the cost in terms of the unemployment caused by the closing of military bases on which local economies depend.

Similar conflicts occur between other governmental units. Executive departments such as the Department of Agriculture are interested in maintaining a healthy farm economy. This interest leads Agriculture Department officials to favor grain sales to the Soviet Union, while other departments have conflicting interests. For example, the Labor Department insists that a large percentage of grain sales to the Soviet Union be transported in American ships. The higher wages of American maritime workers compared with Soviet counterparts raises the cost of American wheat and may reduce or prevent wheat sales. Both departments try to win public support for their positions.

Agencies may also attempt to achieve their goals by controlling the media. For example, in 1976 the Senate Intelligence Committee reported that the FBI had tried to influence media coverage of Martin Luther King and the civil rights movement.[29] However, only a thin line separates efforts to influence public opinion from propaganda. *Propaganda* attempts to influence public opinion through selective presentation of the facts as well as complete rejection of opposing views. In democratic nations, most attempts to gain public support for specific programs find it necessary to admit that alternative courses of action might have some merit. This is a result of conflicting views within the government as well as a free press that prevents obvious distortions of the news.

The U.S. government is most likely to use propaganda in relation to foreign affairs, where the President has major responsibility. The President, in turn, becomes the chief interpreter of international events to the people. Efforts by the Johnson administration to present U.S. involvement in Vietnam as necessary and to squelch conflicting views provide an example of the use of propaganda or near-propaganda. Although they were successful in the early stages of the war, these efforts ultimately failed because of the inability of any administration to completely control the news and prevent dissenting opinions from being expressed.

Summary

All political systems are concerned with the opinions of certain key

Public Opinion and Political Participation

groups whose support is necessary to the government if certain policies are to be carried out. However, the number of groups that must be considered and the influence of the general public are greater in democratic nations than in others. The impact of public opinion on those in power and the ways in which competing groups try to influence public opinion are important signs of a healthy democracy. They reflect the interdependence of the government and the people; moreover, the freedom to express opinions is a good indication of the individual freedom. Thus, despite the vague and often contradictory nature of public opinion and the limitations of the opinion measurement process, public opinion remains an important force in the American political system.

Those who engage most actively in political activity are not representative of the population as a whole. They are among the wealthier, better-educated citizens. The significance of this fact from a policy viewpoint is that those who already have an advantage in economic and educational terms are also those who are most likely to be active politically in order to protect their advantage.

In judging the probable impact of public opinion or political activity, it is necessary to consider the issue in question and the nature of the public that is most concerned. Newspaper polls that attempt to reflect public opinion on a national scale can do this only on a very general level. Specialized publics become interested in particular issues, and the intensity of their opinions and the political activity they generate are an important element in governmental policy decisions.

CHAPTER 5 CROSSWORD PUZZLE

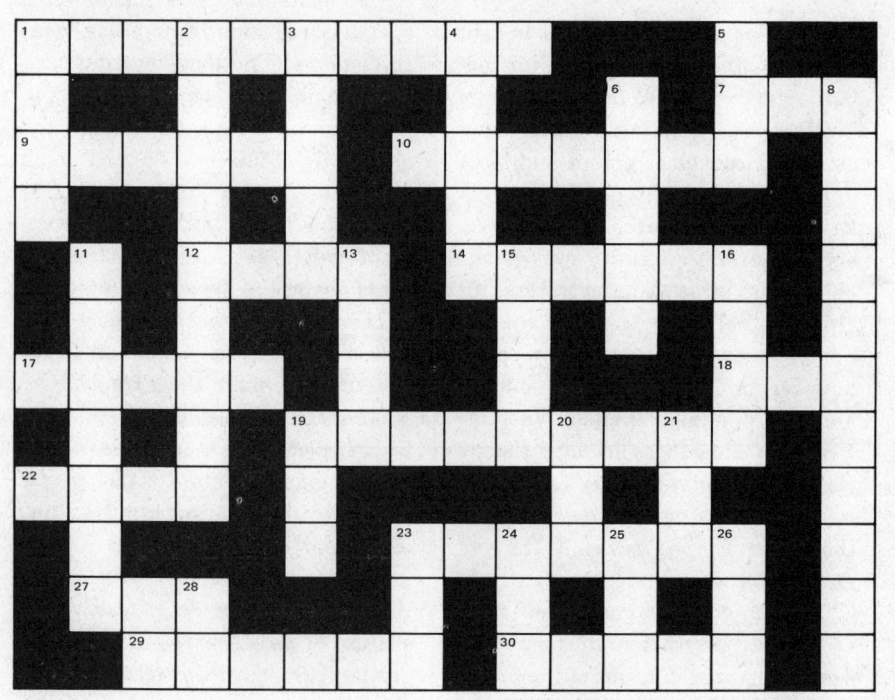

Across
1. Selective presentation of facts and rejection of opposing views is called govt.____.
7. Swiss river
9. Interrogates
10. There are many ____ whose opinions are important in various situations.
12. Job; chore
14. ____ issues are most likely to stir sharp differences of opinion.
17. Solid piece of wood; obstacle
18. Moving ____
19. The strength with which an individual holds an opinion is referred to as ____.
22. The devil's domain
23. The public is better informed about and more interested in domestic issues than ____-policy issues.
27. ____ Pan Alley
29. The most common form of political participation in the United States is ____.
30. Opinion leaders have the opportunity to make their opinions known through the ____ or interest groups.

Down
1. Part of a book; servant
2. Citizens with higher levels of education and income are more likely to participate in various forms of ____ activity.
3. Sudden, violent rushes of wind
4. Percussion instruments
5. ____ de deux
6. Furious; enraged
8. ____ is choosing the most appropriate means to a desired end.
11. Gather
13. Sharp; acute
15. Stove
16. Impose and collect a tax
19. Annoy
20. H. Rider Haggard novel
21. Kind of sale or children's game
23. Hazy atmospheric condition
24. Male sheep
25. Political affiliation (abbr.)
26. National Education Association (abbr.)
28. Opposite of "yes"

NOTES

[1] V. O. Key, Jr., *Public Opinion and American Democracy* (New York: Knopf, 1967), p. 10.

[2] *Harris survey,* November 1964.

[3] Louis Harris, *The Anguish of Change* (New York: Norton, 1974), p. 251.

[4] Ibid., p. 17, citing Harris survey, May 1971.

[5] Leo Bogart, *Silent Politics: Polls and the Awareness of Public Opinion* (New York: Wiley, 1972), p. 99.

[6] Irving Crespi, "What Kind of Attitude Measures are Predictive of Behavior?" *Public Opinion Quarterly,* Fall 1971, p. 334.

[7] Robert E. Lane and David O. Sears, *Public Opinion* (Englewood Cliffs, N.J.: Prentice-Hall, 1964), pp. 7-9.

[8] Daniel Katz, "The Functional Approach to the Study of Attitudes," in William J. Crotty, ed., *Public Opinion and Politics* (New York: Holt, Rinehart & Winston, 1970), p. 295.

[9] Leo Bogart, "No Opinion, Don't Know, and Maybe No Answer," in Robert O. Carlson, ed., *Communications and Public Opinion* (New York: Praeger, 1975), p. 302.

[10] Angus Campbell, Philip E. Converse, Warren E. Miller, and Donald E. Stokes, *The American Voter* (New York: Wiley, 1960), p. 35. Also see pp. 24-37 for a discussion of the concept of the "funnel of causality," which is at the core of psychological theory.

[11] Bernard R. Berelson, Paul F. Lazarsfeld, and William McPhee, *Voting* (Chicago: University of Chicago Press, 1954), p. 147.

[12] Angus Campbell, Gerald Gurin, and Warren F. Miller, *The Voter Decides* (New York: Harper & Row, 1954), p. 85.

[13] Herbert McClosky, "Survey Research in Political Science," in Charles Y. Glock, ed., *Survey Research in the Social Sciences* (New York: Russell Sage Foundation, 1967), pp. 96-97.

[14] Kevin Phillips, *The Emerging Republican Majority* (New York: Arlington House, 1969), p. 470.

[15] Harris, p. 12. Harris poll data show a drop of almost half in confidence level between 1966 and 1972 when applied to the Supreme Court, Congress, and the executive branch of the government.

[16] Walter Lippmann, *The Public Philosopher,* Book 1, Chapter 2, as quoted in Bruce Bohle, ed., *The Apollo Book of American Quotations* (New York: Dodd, Mead, 1967), p. 304:1.

[17] James W. Prothro and Charles M. Grigg, "Fundamental Principles of Democracy: Bases of Agreement and Disagreement," *Journal of Politics,* 22 (Spring 1960): 281.

[18] Robert Lekachman in *The New York Times Book Review,* November 30, 1975, p. 1. Copyright © 1975 by The New York Times Company. Reprinted by permission.

[19] Robert D. Cantor, *Voting Behavior and Presidential Elections* (Itasca, Ill.: F. E. Peacock, 1975), p. 54.

[20] Ibid., p. 55.

[21] Ibid., p. 63, poll taken by the Survey Research Center, University of Michigan.

[22] Ibid.

[23] Harris, Foreward, xi.

[24] Interview with William Rafsky, executive director of Philadelphia '76, Inc., December 2, 1976.

[25] Paul Lazarsfeld, Bernard Berelson, and Hazel Gaudet, *The People's Choice,* 3d ed. (New York: Columbia University Press, 1968), p. 151.

[26] Sidney Verba and Norman Nie, *Participation in America* (New York: Harper & Row, 1972), pp. 118-119.

[27] Ibid., p. 318.

[28] Harris, p. 18.

[29] Reported in *Broadcasting,* May 17, 1976, p. 61.

CHAPTER 6
VOTING BEHAVIOR AND THE ELECTORAL PROCESS

CHAPTER OUTLINE

Questions to Consider
Introduction
Issues, Candidates, and Parties
    Issues
    Candidates
    Parties
Voting and Public Opinion
    Political Trends
    Psychological Predispositions
    Sociological Factors
The Nominating Process
    Delegate Selection
    The Primary Campaign
    Campaign Strategy
    Favorite Sons
    Voter Perceptions
    State Primary Conventions
The National Conventions
Campaign Financing
    The Federal Election Campaign Act
    Reporting Requirements
    Federal Financing and the Political Parties
    Financing the 1976 Election
The Presidential Election Campaign
    Campaign Strategy
    The Campaign Organization
    The Campaign as a "Media Event"
    Presidential Debates
    The Impact of the Campaign
Voting Patterns
    Ticket Splitting
    Voter Participation
The Electoral College
The Ebb and Flow of Presidential Power
Summary

QUESTIONS TO CONSIDER

Elections and electoral behavior are key elements in the American political system. Elections provide the people with a periodic opportunity to change their political leaders. What factors influence the individual's voting decision? How important is loyalty to a political party? These questions are considered in the first two sections of the chapter.

The Democratic and Republican parties dominate the process of nominating candidates for office. In Presidential elections, candidates compete for a party's nomination in a long, hard primary campaign. Are the primaries an effective way of choosing candidates? Do voters have a chance to find out about the abilities and positions of the candidates during the primaries? What determines a candidate's primary campaign strategy? The third section is devoted to the nominating process.

After the primaries are completed, the parties meet to choose their candidates. The person who has dominated the primaries is usually nominated. The national conventions are described in the fourth section.

The Presidential election campaign is the nation's most publicized political event. How are such campaigns financed? How are they organized? How important were the debates between Gerald Ford and Jimmy Carter in 1976? These and related questions are the subject of the fifth section. Finally, recent elections have been marked by an increase in ticket splitting.

Why do people vote for the Presidential candidate of one party and the Congressional candidates of another? Why do so many Americans fail to vote? What is the implication of low levels of voting participation in Presidential elections? Analyses of voting behavior tell us much about the political perceptions of citizens. They also help explain the actions of political leaders.

Introduction

The primary means by which the Constitution guarantees that the government will be responsive to the people is the electoral process, which gives citizens a chance to pass judgment on the performance of elected officials. Many elections are held in the United States at every level from township commissioner to President. The common thread that runs through all such contests is that the people have the final say in choosing their leaders. Voting is really an expression of opinion by means of a definite action.

During election campaigns at any level of government, issues are raised that might not be raised at other times. The impact of these issues on voting behavior is debatable, but the fact that they are raised at all often affects governmental policy. In 1968, for example, Senator Eugene McCarthy's unsuccessful campaign for the Presidential nomination brought the problem of Vietnam onto the stage of political debate. McCarthy's antiwar platform drew a favorable response and encouraged other public officials to speak out on the issue.

Presidential election campaigns offer the most significant look at the American political process because they recieve the most media coverage, raise national issues, and involve citizens in political activity more than at any other time. Therefore, nominating campaigns and the electoral process may be as important to a democratic political system as the election results themselves. Presidential elections and the political activity surrounding them serve to inject life and spirit into the political system of a very complex society. Revelations of recent abuses of power by top-level government officials have reinforced the idea that Presidential elections are not intended to give absolute power to the chief executive. Rather, they are designed to guarantee the accountability of all the nation's elected officials to the people. This is what democratic government is about.

Issues, Candidates, and Parties

Presidential election campaigns send political organizations and officials at all levels into action. The object of this massive effort is the individual voter. The voter views the nominating and election campaigns in terms of three major elements: the political parties, the candidates, and the issues raised in the campaign.[1] The way these three elements are perceived and their relative importance to the voter determine voting behavior.

Voter perceptions result from both long- and short-term factors. There are also many cross-currents affecting the voter. One candidate's personality may be appealing to a particular voter, but his party identification or stands on important issues may leave something to be desired. Voting is a product of the individual's entire collection of political and social experiences and opinions. By looking at these elements individually, we can gain greater understanding of the campaign process as well as the voting decision itself.

Issues

Every candidate for the Presidency announces his intention to "run on the issues," and this theme is repeated throughout the campaign. An issue must meet three major requirements if it is to have any impact on the campaign. First, the voters must be aware that an issue has been raised. Second, they must see the issue as important, and third, they must perceive differences between competing candidates' positions on the issue.

All issues are not equally relevant to all Americans. Candidates attempt to vary their emphasis according to local concerns. Primary contests in New Hampshire bring forth statements on rural and small-town issues; this is not the place to speak of massive expenditures on the nation's inner cities. Similarly, the Nebraska primary is marked by speeches about farm issues, and in the New York campaign the candidate keeps an eye on the concerns of the large bloc of voters who live in New York City. In addition to local issues of this sort, candidates are expected to take positions on the social, economic, and foreign policy issues that affect all Americans.

But it is not enough for candidates to discuss important issues. Voters must perceive differences between the positions of various candidates if those stands are to have any effect on the voting decision. All candidates may speak in favor of a strong national defense. Likewise, all candidates will promise to raise the American standard of living and keep unemployment at a minimum. These statements have little impact on voter decisions because there is not enough difference between the candidates' positions on these issues. When candidates discuss the details of how they intend to achieve these widely agreed-upon goals, the reaction from the electorate is usually one of indifference. This stems from a combination of voter disbelief in the ability of one man, even a President, to make dramatic changes in the political, social, and economic system and insufficient knowledge of issues to generate interest.

A dominant issue in any Presidential election campaign is the record of the current, or *incumbent* administration. This is especially true if the incumbent President is running for reelection. The public has formed an opinion on the effectiveness of the government during the past four years. The candidate of the party in power always gets the credit or takes the blame for whatever has taken place during that period—people vote for or against what has gone before.[2] There is no way to judge what a change of administration will bring, but despite its lack of knowledge when it comes to specific issues, the public is quite capable of voicing its disapproval of the government's past performance.

The pattern just described may be seen in the 1976 campaign. President Ford had to defend the record of his administration while disassociating it from the inglorious end of the Nixon administration. He had to defend the strategy of detente with the Soviet Union, assure the nation that the Soviet arms buildup did not endanger the United States, and still promise to deter Soviet aggression. On the domestic scene, Ford had to blame the continuing high rate of unemployment on previous administrations and Congress while taking credit for the economic recovery that began in 1975. This kind of effort to balance good and bad is the major campaign goal of any incumbent President running for reelection.

The challenger, by contrast, can offer only the promise of a better performance. In the 1976 campaign, for example, the Democrats hoped to direct attention to economic issues, pointing out the high unemployment and inflation that had prevailed during the Ford administration. After the election, however, Patrick H. Caddell, pollster for the Carter campaign, spoke of Carter's inability to take advantage of these issues. His polls revealed that President Ford was seen as more capable than Carter in economic matters.[3] This illustrates the problems faced by any candidate who wants to direct public attention to a particular issue.

Candidates

"I vote for the man, not the party" is a statement often heard at election time. The extent to which a candidate's personality or image affects voting behavior and the particular aspects of personality that are most appealing to voters are interesting questions. The word *charisma* became popular with the election of John F. Kennedy in 1960. It was widely believed that his success signaled a change in Presidential campaigns and that future candidates would have to project the vigor and physical appeal of a Kennedy to be successful. That notion was put to rest only four years later when Lyndon B. Johnson won reelection by a landslide, and again in 1968 when Democrat Hubert H. Humphrey and Republican Richard M. Nixon ran for the Presidency. Neither Johnson nor Humphrey nor Nixon was "charismatic" yet these were the candidates offered to the people.

The overall image of a Presidential candidate appears to be more important than a charismatic personality.

Ability and honesty are probably the traits that are most important to voters when they choose their leaders. Patrick Caddell's polls revealed that the public perceived Carter as more likely to "take charge" than President Ford.[4] It is very possible that Carter's victory was due to this perception rather than to his positions on particular issues. As Caddell put it, "People consistently saw Ford as safe and sound, a man who would not hurt the country. They were not sure what Carter might accomplish. It was our job to convince the public that the risk of Carter was worth taking."[5]

The candidate's personality is probably more important in the primary campaign than in the general election. The latter is basically a media event, with candidates appearing at times and places and under conditions carefully chosen for their suitability. In contrast, the primary campaign is less well organized, with greater opportunity for face-to-face contact with reporters and the public. In the primaries, it is an asset if a candidate can establish that hard-to-define relationship known as rapport.

Carter's 1976 campaign for the Democratic nomination is a good example of the positive influence of a likeable personality in a multicandidate race. Carter faced the formidable task of getting his name known to the public. A CBS/*New York Times* poll taken before the first primary in New Hampshire showed that voters recognized Carter's name almost as often as that of Senator Henry M. Jackson, who had served in Congress for 35 years. This was evidence of Carter's campaign skills and his ability to relate to and identify with potential voters in all parts of the country. Carter achieved this public recognition despite a general lack of knowledge of his views on the issues. As the *Times* said in reporting the poll results:

The bulk of his liberal supporters think him liberal, the bulk of his conservative supporters think him conservative, the bulk of his moderate supporters think him moderate. On a number of issues—race, detente, abortion—his views are not clearly identified by voters.[6]

Candidate Jimmy Carter wears a yarmulke during a campaign visit to a Hebrew school in Miami Beach, Florida. Traditionally, Presidential candidates attempt to show indentification with various groups in the population.

Parties

Table 6-1 shows the extent to which Americans identify with the two major parties and the stability of their party loyalty. However, it is hard to translate this party loyalty into voting behavior in Presidential elections. National, state, and local party organizations may operate under the Democratic or Republican banner with little or no similarity to one another. A person who expresses a party identification may vote along party lines in local elections but show greater independence in other contests. The party has a greater influence in elections that include little-known candidates or issues. This is often the case in congressional races, for example.

The alternation of party control of the Presidency is evidence that voters do not interpret national elections in strictly partisan terms. Table 6-1 shows that the Democrats have an edge of almost two to one over the Republicans, but the latter have won four of the past eight Presidential elections. The makeup of Congress, shown in Table 6-2, more nearly reflects the pattern of party loyalties. Thus, to a certain extent, Presidential elections are viewed as outside the realm of normal party competition. This explains the Republicans' failure

TABLE 6-1
Party Self-Identification

	1952	1956	1960	1964	1968	1972	1976
Democrat	47%	44%	45%	51%	45%	41%	46%
Independent	22	24	24	23	30	34	32
Republican	27	29	27	24	24	23	22
Apolitical, don't know	4	3	4	2	1	2	0
Totals	100%	100%	100%	100%	100%	100%	100%
Number of cases	1,614	1,772	1,954	1,571	1,553	2,703	13,339

SOURCE: Survey Resarch Center.

TABLE 6-2
Party Division in Congress, 1932-1976

Year	House Democratic	House Republican	Senate Democratic	Senate Republican
1932	313	117	59	36
1934	322	103	69	25
1936	333	89	75	17
1938	262	169	69	23
1940	267	162	66	28
1942	222	209	57	38
1944	243	190	57	38
1946	188	246	45	51
1948	263	171	54	42
1950	234	199	48	47
1952	213	221	47	48
1954	232	203	48	47
1956	234	201	49	47
1958	283	154	66	34
1960	263	174	64	36
1962	258	176	68	32
1964	295	140	67	33
1966	248	187	64	36
1968	243	192	58	42
1970	255	180	54	44
1972	242	193	56	42
1974	291	144	62	38
1976	293	142	62	38

Note: Totals reflect party organization in Congress. Sen. Harry Byrd of Virginia was reelected as an Independent in 1976, but joined Democrats for organizational purposes. Similarly, Sen. James Buckley of New York was elected in 1970 as a Conservative, but joined Republicans for organizational purposes.

to match their success in Presidential elections with victory in congressional races.

While people with a strong party identification tend to be more consistent in their loyalty, even this group of voters is by no means a unified bloc that can be counted on in Presidential elections.[7] The parties compete for control of the White House knowing that the contest will be decided by other factors besides party loyalty, which is only one element in the individual's voting decision.

The party organizations are most effective in local and state politics, especially primary elections. The lower turnout in these contests places greater on the skill of party leaders. In many cases, the party endorses candidates in primary elections and is able to maintain party discipline through the organization's ability to control the choice of candidates. Thus, local and state politics are far more likely to be marked by long periods of one-party dominance than Presidential politics.

Voting and Public Opinion

The individual voting decision is an outgrowth of a number of political perceptions regarding issues, candidates, and parties. The way people perceive these elements is determined by the relative strength of the major influences on opinion formation discussed in Chapter 5: political trends, psychological predispositions, and socioeconomic status.

Political Trends

The importance of issues in election campaigns springs from the notion that the liberal-conservative dimension of opinion formation is the primary measure of any national political debate. If the political trend in a particular geographic area, or even in the nation as a whole, is conservative, candidates will try to take conservative positions on the issues. Presidential elections are neither crusades nor educational exercises. They are a democratic political process with the goal of allowing the people to choose their national leader for the next four years. And the people will vote for a candidate whose views are similar to their own. Any candidate who forgets this basic fact of American politics is doomed to failure. Barry Goldwater took issue positions too far to the right—or too conservative—in 1964 and was badly defeated. George McGovern had a similar experience in 1972 when he took positions that were too liberal, or too far to the left, of the prevailing political trend. This is not to say that either Goldwater or McGovern would have been elected if they had taken middle-of-the-road positions. Rather, it is to say that the stands they took were responsible for the large margins by which they were defeated.

Psychological Predispositions

The ability of political parties to win popular support is a product of the psychological predispositions of voters. Some people have never crossed party lines in any election; some have remained loyal only in local or state elections, and many have not only voted for Presidential candidates of both parties but do not hesitate to split their ticket and vote for congresspeople of one party and the Presidential candidate of another. Psychological factors are also important in shaping opinions because most people are more comfortable with their political views if those views do not conflict with their basic values. However, it is interesting to note that in 1976 Jimmy Carter received 51 percent and Gerald Ford 48 percent of the popular vote. If these data are compared to the two-to-one Democratic edge in party self-identification (Table 6-1), it is clear that psychological predispositions are just one of several factors affecting the voting decision.

Sociological Factors

Socioeconomic status affects voting behavior because of the fact that almost all national issues have economic or social aspects, and many include both. Because of the need to attract voters from all sectors of society, candidates usually soft-pedal issue positions that might lead to loss of support at any socioeconomic level. But the way issues are perceived is more important than the way they are presented, and socioeconomic background is an important factor in the perception of issues. It is impossible for Presidential candidates to determine exactly what stand on a particular issue will have the greatest political impact. However, understanding the complexities of opinion formation and voting behavior can help them avoid extreme positions.

Table 6-3 shows the breakdown of voting by socioeconomic group in the 1964, 1968, and 1972 Presidential elections. It is noteworthy that the only group that has consistently supported the Presidential candidate of one party for all three elections is the "Nonwhite" category, which has voted for the Democratic each time. (Another group showing the same pattern but not included in the table is Jewish voters.) The perception of many voters at different levels of society that their best interests are not always served by one particular party has contributed fluidity to American politics and prevented the rise of class-based parties.

There are regular voting patterns within socioeconomic groups that are based on membership in various organizations. The *Americans for Democratic Action* (ADA), for example, is a liberal group of Democratic sympathizers; by contrast, the National Chamber of Commerce is made up of business people and industrialists who consistently support the Republican party. However, Table 6-3 shows that large segments of most groups in American society do not interpret political events solely in terms of group membership. This means that Presidential candidates cannot take the support of any group for granted and must try to take positions that will be acceptable to a cross-section of the public. There is no possible profit in appealing to the rich at the expense of the poor, the young at the expense of the old, or professionals at the expense of blue-collar workers.

Citizens also identify with more than one socioeconomic group, so that one influence may be stronger than others in relation to a particular issue. These cross-pressures are an important element in group voting behavior. The willingness of many people to vote for candidates of either party and the absence of socioeconomic group voting in Presidential elections are responsible for the high level of competition that has existed in national politics since the Roosevelt years.

The Nominating Process

Presidential candidates compete for their party's nomination through state primary elections or state party conventions. Both of these methods are used to select delegates to the party nominating conventions. Since the nominating process is under the control of state law, the dates of elections and conventions vary, as do the rules for delegate selection. Presidential elections dominate the news every four years, but they are held at the same time as elections for the 435-member House of Representatives and one-third of the Senate (33); in 1976, 14 governors were also elected. These other contests may have an impact on the primary struggle in terms of the efforts made by party activists in behalf of various candidates; a highly competitive local or state primary may divert attention from the Presidential primary.

The goal of the primary campaign is to gather the pledges of enough delegates to the national convention to win the party's nomination. The American system of nominating Presidential candidates is complex, physically taxing, and financially burdensome but always fascinating. To a large extent, it removes the process of choosing a candidate from the control of party organizations and opens it to anyone who wants to run in the primaries and conventions.

The choices available to the parties as to the method of delegate selection

TABLE 6-3
Vote by Groups in Presidential Elections, 1964-1972 (in percents)

	1964		1968			1972	
	LBJ	Goldwater	HHH	Nixon	Wallace	McGovern	Nixon
National	61.3	38.7	43.0	43.4	13.6	38	62
Men	60	40	41	43	16	37	63
Women	62	38	45	43	12	38	62
White	59	41	38	47	15	32	68
Nonwhite	94	6	85	12	3	87	13
College	52	48	37	54	9	37	63
High School	62	38	42	43	15	34	66
Grade School	66	34	52	33	15	49	51
Professions & Business	54	46	34	56	10	31	69
White Collar	57	43	41	47	12	36	64
Manual	71	29	50	35	15	43	57
Under 30 years	64	36	47	38	15	48	52
32-49 years	63	37	44	41	15	33	67
50 years & older	59	41	41	47	12	36	64
Protestants	55	45	35	49	16	30	70
Catholics	76	24	59	33	8	48	52
Republicans	20	80	9	86	5	5	95
Democrats	87	13	74	12	14	67	33
Independents	56	44	31	44	25	31	69
Members of labor union families	73	27	56	29	15	46	54

SOURCE: *The Gallup Opinion Index,* December 1972, Report No. 90.

are determined by state law. There are several variations in the system of primaries, and these affect the political impact of the contest. About three-fourths of the delegates to the 1976 Democratic and Republican conventions were chosen in state primary elections. Thirty states held election contests in which both parties participated, while in several others only one party chose the primary method.

Delegate Selection

Voters in state primaries cast their ballots for delegates who are pledged to Presidential candidates or are allocated to candidates according to the votes received by each candidate. Some states have rules binding delegates to vote for the candidate to whom they are pledged, while others allow delegates to make their own choice. In practice, however, delegates rarely stray from the choice expressed in the primaries, especially on the first ballot of the nominating convention.

Most states allow voters to cast their ballots for candidates of the party in which they are registered. Voters registered as "independent" or "no party" cannot participate in such contests. Michigan, Wisconsin, and Vermont allow individuals to vote for delegates of either party regardless of their party registration. Some states have no party registration—Georgia and Indiana are examples—but require voters to state that they have supported candidates of the party in whose primary they wish to take part and will do so in the future.

There are three ways for candidates to have their names placed on the nominating ballot. Some states require petitions signed by a certain number of eligible voters; in others a state official places the names of recognized candidates on the primary ballot, while others list delegates but not candidates. None of these procedures puts a real obstacle in the way of a candidate with any popular support.

The Primary Campaign

State primaries held to select delegates to the national party conventions begin in February and continue throughout the spring. The importance of the staggered system of primaries that has evolved is that it provides a long road along which the candidate must travel. There is no reason for a candidate to enter all of the primaries—limitations of time, money, and staff make this practically impossible. Yet a national candidacy must be tested along the primary trail. In 1976, faced with an unusually strong challenge to an incumbent President, Gerald R. Ford was forced to enter the primaries in order to win the Republican party nomination. Since three-fourths of the 1976 convention delegates were chosen in primary elections, a candidate could not win the nomination by depending on state party conventions alone. If a nominating convention deadlocks, it is possible for a candidate who has not entered the primaries to be selected. But in such a case the candidate would have to have shown considerable political strength throughout the country and within his party.

The primary campaign traditionally starts with the New Hampshire contest, in which less than 1 percent of the convention delegates of either party are at stake. It has become an important, though not crucial, test because of its tremendous media coverage. It gives the candidates an opportunity to work out organizational problems and test their issue stands. Early success also aids the party in its fund-raising efforts. Finally, the small size of the state allows for more face-to-face campaigning than is possible in larger states or during the Presidential election campaign. Therefore, candidates who succeed in New Hampshire demonstrate their ability to win approval on a personal as well as a media basis.

Campaign Strategy

One of the important strategy decisions that must be made by Presidential candidates concerns which primaries to enter and which of these should be their major targets in terms of time, money, and effort. After New Hampshire, there are primaries almost every week, often several on the same day. This means candidates must judge their strengths and weaknesses accurately or risk losing primaries in which they might have done well or spending large amounts of time and money in states where they have little chance of success.

During the 1976 primaries, some interesting strategy choices were made. The Republicans had to choose between an unelected President who had never run for an office above the congressional level and Ronald Reagan, a former governor of California and a seasoned campaigner. It was important for Reagan to get his campaign off to a flying start. Defeating an incumbent President in a primary struggle is an uphill fight at best, and the challenger must establish momentum early in the primary campaign. Reagan chose to have his early contests with Ford in New Hampshire and Florida, the first and fourth primaries. The choice of these states was not a random one. Both have a conservative tradition, and Reagan staked out his issue positions as farther to the right—or more conservative—than President Ford's.

The advantages of being the incumbent President were evident in these early primaries, though Ford's victory margins were unimpressive. But in the May 1, 1976 Texas primary Reagan won a major victory. Reagan's threat to Ford was an indication that the President lacked the support of the conservative wing of the Republican party. Perhaps more important, it was an indication of the anti-Washington feeling that was bound to hurt Ford's bid for reelection.

The Reagan-Ford contests also illustrate the importance of campaign psychology. It is important for any candidate to establish momentum in the early primaries. Ford's narrow margins of victory did not have this effect, and the Republican contest went to the national convention with the result in doubt. The Republican primaries also illustrated that the importance of specific issues is often exaggerated. An incumbent President should have benefited from the improvement of the economy in early 1976. This, combined with the President's ability to dominate the news, would present a major obstacle to a challenger if issues were the dominant element in the campaign. While the power of the Presidency helped Ford gain renomination, issues such as the economy took a back seat to a more basic question — the public's overall judgment of the President. Reagan's strong showing in the primaries was a clear sign that Ford's campaign for reelection was in trouble.

The 1976 Democratic primaries presented a classic picture of a party mounting a challenge to an incumbent administration, with the opportunity for success providing encouragement to many candidates. After eight years of Republican control marred by the Watergate affair, the Democrats had every reason to be hopeful. The primary races attracted a veteran campaigner (Henry Jackson), candidates who had been on the fringes of national politics (Morris Udall, Birch Bayh, Fred Harris, and Sargent Shriver), a former governor with a regional following (Jimmy Carter), perennial candidate George Wallace, and minor political figures such as Governor Milton Shapp of Pennsylvania. All faced the problem of making themselves known as serious candidates who could win in November. Accordingly, the early primaries were of the greatest importance. Only Jackson, who had the advantage of strong political support throughout the nation built up over many years in the government, chose to ignore the New Hampshire primary. Carter's victories in New Hampshire and Florida quickly established him as a major contender, while Jackson won in Massachusetts and adopted a strategy of picking his spots in terms of which primaries he would enter. Bayh, Shapp, and Shriver dropped out during the early primaries and left Morris Udall carrying the banner of the party's liberal wing. Hovering above the primary contests was the image of Hubert Humphrey, an "undeclared" candidate, who was waiting for a deadlock to develop at the Convention. Edmund Muskie, also a national political figure, had the same idea in mind.

The Carter campaign gained momentum with victories in seven of the first nine primaries, and after the Pennsylvania primary in April 1976 Humphrey again declined to enter the race; Jackson ceased campaigning; and the former Georgia governor was on his way to a surprising victory in the Democratic campaign for nomination. His strategy was highlighted by a lack of strong issue positions. The major thrust of the Carter campaign was dissatisfaction with politics-as-usual. His success, coupled with Reagan's strong showing based on a similar appeal, made it apparent that the national mood called for a change in Washington.

Candidates in the struggle for delegates to the national convention all face the task of persuading voters and convention delegates to climb aboard their bandwagons as they roll down the campaign trail. One wonders why candidates who get little support at the outset remain in the race. In fact, candidates have much to gain even if they fall short of victory so long as they make a good showing and make themselves known as national political figures. Many hope for the vice presidential nomination, and there is always the possibility of a cabinet appointment or some other high government office. These possibilities are especially important to candidates who are not members of Congress. They provide a potential springboard to political involvement at the national level.

Favorite Sons

In addition to the national or regional candidates for the nomination, there are always a number of "favorite sons" who enter the national convention with their state's delegates pledged to them rather than to any of the active candidates. This is done by entering a slate of delegates pledged to a well-known state official, such as the governor, on the primary ballot, and attempting to gain political advantage at the convention by trading these delegate votes for future rewards. This tactic is effective if the state's primary is not hotly contested by the major party candidates, in states that choose convention delegates in state party conventions, or where a state official is very popular and can be expected to defeat nationally known candidates in the primary. In the latter case, an influential political leader has a good chance of winning support and entering the national convention in a strong bargaining position.

Voter Perceptions

The primary trail is a step-by-step process in which the results of previous primaries affect voter decisions as well as turnout. In the earlier contests, the voters may have only a vague idea of the candidate's positions or abilities. Primaries are like beauty contests in this respect: A winning personality is very helpful. However, as the campaign continues, the voters' perceptions become sharper. Many early candidates withdraw; the issues become more clearly defined; and a sharper image of the candidates begins to form. Thus, while the early primaries are important in terms of gathering momentum, the later contests give the voters a chance to make more rational choices.

Primaries also give voters an opportunity to express opinions even if it means either voting for a candidate who cannot win or voting for someone whom the voter would not support in the general election. There are usually a few "single-issue candidates" who base their campaigns on positions such as opposition to abortion or busing. These efforts are often limited to a few primaries, and while they have little impact on the final result, they do offer the voters a means of expressing agreement with views that may be outside the political mainstream. The success of George Wallace in the 1968 primaries and even in the Presidential election was a result of this type of protest vote.

Not only do primaries provide a platform for candidates to raise issues that have been submerged by other issues or ignored; they also give the voters a chance to express disapproval of governmental actions that are supported by both parties. Yet despite heavy media coverage, only about one-third of those eligible voted in the 1976 primaries.[8] Regardless of the specific reasons for the low turnout, it is evidence that most Americans did not feel that their interests were threatened by the candidates of either party.

State Primary Conventions

States without direct primary elections choose national convention delegates in congressional district conventions and state party conventions. A few states provide for the election of delegates to such conventions in party primaries. It is in these party conventions that political organizations have the greatest opportunity to influence the primary process because of their role in the selection of delegates to the state and district conventions and the choice of national convention delegates. Every effort is made by the candidates to influence the selection of friendly delegates, and political leaders often line up at this point in favor of one candidate. This early support can prove crucial, and people who can control sizeable blocs of delegates and "deliver" them to the successful candidate will not be forgotten. An alternative strategy is to wait until a clear pattern has emerged from other primaries before taking a stand, or even to wait until the national convention itself begins.

Every politician with any influence dreams of delivering the crucial delegates to the candidate who goes on to be elected President. Events are seldom, if ever, this clear-cut, but the power brokers in both parties try to put all their influence into play in return for future rewards. Even committed delegates are courted by other candidates. Their support is needed in the event that their favorite candidate withdraws along the way or obviously cannot win at the national convention.

The procedure for choosing state convention delegates begins at the precinct level, with the selection of representatives to county or congressional district conventions. The latter choose the delegates to the state party conventions. In an effort to guarantee fair representation, most state Democratic organizations insist that delegates be chosen on a proportional basis, meaning that the number of delegates pledged to a candidate must represent the support that candidate has won in precinct and district conventions. Most Republican organizations, on the other hand, allow winner-take-all elections, a policy that tends to exaggerate the delegate strength of the winner at the expense of other candidates. At-large delegates are also chosen by the state party organizations in order to give a voice to under-represented groups or party officials in public office.

The state convention system of choosing delegates favors candidates who have been politically active in the past. The faithful party member who has taken part in state fund-raising efforts or spoken at political dinners on behalf of candidates in local and state elections accumulates political I.O.U.'s that can often be translated into delegate support. While all candidates attempt to win support at state conventions, the best hope for a previously inactive or little-known candidate is to convince delegates that if their preferred candidate falters, he offers a possible alternative.

The National Conventions

The national conventions are responsible for nominating the party's Presidential and vice presidential candidates. They also give final approval to the party platform, which is hammered out in committee and represents a compromise that the right and left "wings" of the party—its more liberal and more conservative members—can accept.

The Democratic and Republican parties assign delegates to the states on the basis of formulas that reward states that have supported the party's candidates in past elections. The Democrats base their formula on the past three Presidential elections, while the Republicans include gubernatorial and congressional elections; obviously, state delegations are not equal. Table 6-4 shows the number of delegates per state for both parties. In recent years the trend has been toward choosing the delegates themselves by direct primary elections rather than by state party conventions. The parties make their own procedural rules, and this provides a means of challenging delegates on the ground that they have been chosen in a manner that violates party rules.

The nominating process is straightforward. Candidates for the party's nomination are nominated and seconded regardless of their delegate strength. The balloting then begins, continuing until one candidate wins a majority of the delegate votes and is declared the party's candidate. It is unusual for more than one ballot to be needed. The last such case was in

Colorfully attired Uncle Sam greets Jimmy Carter as he arrives in New York to receive the Democratic nomination. Demonstrators such as these are part of the political hoopla that accompanies conventions.

TABLE 6-4
Allocation of Votes—1976

Democratic Convention

Alabama	35	Maine	20	Pennsylvania	178
Alaska	10	Maryland	53	Rhode Island	22
Arizona	25	Massachusetts	104	South Carolina	31
Arkansas	26	Michigan	133	South Dakota	17
California	280	Minnesota	65	Tennessee	46
Colorado	35	Mississippi	24	Texas	130
Connecticut	51	Missouri	71	Utah	18
Delaware	12	Montana	17	Vermont	12
District of Columbia	17	Nebraska	23	Virginia	54
Florida	81	Nevada	11	Washington	53
Georgia	50	New Hampshire	17	West Virginia	33
Hawaii	17	New Jersey	108	Wisconsin	68
Idaho	16	New Mexico	18	Wyoming	10
Illinois	169	New York	274	Canal Zone	3
Indiana	75	North Carolina	61	Guam	3
Iowa	47	North Dakota	13	Puerto Rico	22
Kansas	34	Ohio	152	Virgin Islands	3
Kentucky	46	Oklahoma	37	Democrats abroad	3
Louisiana	41	Oregon	34		

Republican Convention

Alabama	37	Louisiana	41	Oklahoma	36
Alaska	19	Maine	20	Oregon	30
Arizona	29	Maryland	43	Pennsylvania	103
Arkansas	27	Massachusetts	43	Rhode Island	19
California	167	Michigan	84	South Carolina	36
Colorado	31	Minnesota	42	South Dakota	20
Connecticut	35	Mississippi	30	Tennessee	43
Delaware	17	Missouri	49	Texas	100
District of Columbia	14	Montana	20	Utah	20
Florida	66	Nebraska	25	Vermont	18
Georgia	48	Nevada	18	Virginia	51
Hawaii	19	New Hampshire	21	Washington	38
Idaho	21	New Jersey	67	West Virginia	28
Illinois	101	New Mexico	21	Wisconsin	45
Indiana	54	New York	154	Wyoming	17
Iowa	36	North Carolina	54	Guam	4
Kansas	34	North Dakota	18	Puerto Rico	8
Kentucky	37	Ohio	97	Virgin Islands	4

1952, when the Democrats nominated Adlai Stevenson on the third ballot. Usually one candidate enters the convention with enough delegate strength so that, even if it is numerically short of a majority, unpledged delegates or those pledged to favorite sons can be swept into the winner's camp. A candidate who appears to have a chance of being elected has everything going for him, and there is usually a scramble to join his camp while credit may still be gained for doing so.

Choosing a Vice Presidential Candidate

The nomination of a Presidential candidate is followed by the nomination of a vice presidential candidate. In contrast to the long primary battles most Presidential candidates have to fight, the vice presidential candidate is chosen by the Presidential candidate. This choice is based on the potential political gain that may follow from the nomination of a particular individual. Thus, the vice presidential candidate usually balances the Presidential candidate in some way. Lyndon B. Johnson was chosen by John F. Kennedy to attract votes in the southern states and among conservatives. This type of geographic and philosophical balance is often the main consideration in the choice of a vice presidential candidate, but religious balance may also be a consideration. It is unlikely that a Catholic Presidential candidate would be paired with a Catholic running mate. The choice of Thomas Eagleton, a Catholic, by George McGovern, a Protestant, is an example of an effort to provide religious balance. (Eagleton was later dropped for other reasons.)

It is often argued that the vice presidential candidate should be chosen by the nominating convention rather than simply having the delegates approve the Presidential candidate's choice. However, since the vice president has little formal power, the tradition has arisen of allowing the Presidential candidate to choose the person with whom, theoretically, he will work if elected. In practice, political considerations often bring together dissimilar individuals who never develop the close relationship that is desirable in case the vice president should have to become President. In fact, in modern times no vice president has succeeded in breaking into the inner circle of the President's closest advisers.

Campaign Financing

Money and political campaigns have become inseparable in American politics. Spending on Presidential campaigns rose from an estimated $28 million in 1960 to over $100 million in 1972. Even these estimates are low, however; they do not include the costs of primaries or the expenditures of state committees. The cost of political activity at all levels has been estimated by the Citizens Research Council at $200 million in 1964 and $300 million in 1968. [9]

The extent of campaign spending and the dramatic rise in costs led to the widespread opinion that not only was much money being wasted but, more important, the connection between money and electoral success threatened to subvert the idea of democratic elections. As a result, calls for reform became increasingly frequent during the late 1960s.

Candidates Jimmy Carter and Walter Mondale are joined by their wives as they salute the delegates to the Democratic Convention in Madison Square Garden. Carter's nomination was decided in the primaries; the choice of a running-mate is a prerogative of a presidential candidate.

The Federal Election Campaign Act

The Federal Election Campaign Act of 1971 was the first step in the effort to control campaign spending; Effective April 1, 1972, it required candidates to reveal the uses and sources of campaign funds. However, the spending of the Committee to Re-Elect the President reached over $60 million in the 1972 campaign and was clear evidence that such disclosure would not stop the rise in campaign expenditures.[10] The Act was amended in 1974 and further refined by a Supreme Court decision on January 30, 1976. The 1974 Act set spending limits for House and Senate races as well as Presidential contests, but the Court's ruling eliminated restrictions on spending for congressional campaigns. The 1974 act also provided for federal financing of Presidential primary campaigns and Presidential election campaigns.

The campaign spending law set a limit of $1000 on contributions by an individual to any candidate in a primary campaign; a similar limit was set for contributions to candidates in the general election campaign. However, the Court's decision removed limits on campaign spending if an individual wants to make an independent effort on behalf of a particular candidate rather than contributing to a campaign organization. This has the effect of removing restraints from the largest contributors, who can place media advertisements or finance direct mail campaigns without restriction. There are no limits on what congressional candidates and their families may spend in their own behalf, but the $50,000 limit for Presidential candidates holds unless the candidate refuses federal funds.

The 1976 primary campaign was the first to be financed under the 1974 Federal Election Campaign Act, which provides for federal funding of primary and general election campaigns. Presidential candidates may spend up to $10 million in the primary races and $20 million in the general election. There is no limit if a candidate refuses federal funds. In addition, the national party committees can spend up to two cents per eligible voter in behalf of their candidates, including the vice presidential nominee. Fund-raising costs of up to 20 percent are excluded from the spending limits. If candidates in the primaries choose not to use federal funds, they are free to spend unlimited sums before the convention.

Public financing of presidential candidates in primary and general election campaigns is designed to curb the abuses associated with past fund-raising efforts, such as the sale of ambassadorships in return for large contributions. Coupled with limitations on individual contributions, such financing reduces the importance of "fat cats" in the political campaign process. The Supreme Court's ruling allowing individuals to make unlimited expenditures through their own efforts rather than through campaign committees, while it eases the restraints on large contributors, limits the potential for abuse by raising the ante beyond the reach of most people.

In order to qualify for federal matching funds to be used in primary campaigns, a candidate must first raise $5000 in each of 20 states, with no individual contribution over $250 counted in the total. Once he has qualified, the candidate continues to receive matching funds for the first $250 of every contribution. This continues until the total campaign fund—private and federal—reaches the legal limit of $10 million. This arrangement is intended to reserve federal funds for candidates with a reasonably wide base of support. The Act also provides for a $2 million payment to each major party for convention expenses, along with a formula to increase overall spending to compensate for inflation.

The $20 million to be spent in the general election is provided entirely by the federal government; no other funds may be raised except for contributions of no more than $5000 to campaign committees by organizations such as labor unions and professional associations. Thus, it is possible for a large number of political committees to be formed by powerful organizations such as labor unions, which can then contribute $5000 each to campaign committees in 50 states plus the District of Columbia. One of the most significant portions of the Act deals with reporting procedures that make it likely that many past abuses will be avoided.

Reporting Requirements

Early violations of election financing laws were made possible by loose reporting requirements. The current law requires that the names and addresses of all contributors of amounts over $10 be reported and, in addition, that business occupation be reported for all contributors of amounts over $100. Cash contributions of more than $100 are forbidden. This information must be filed with the Federal Election Commission 10 days before and 30 days after each election and within 10 days after the close of each quarter (i.e., March 31, June 30, September 30, and December 31). Each candidate is also required to set up a central organization to record all contributions and expenses over $10. The committee's bank depositories must also be named. These requirements eliminate the worst abuses of campaign financing and, coupled with federal financing of Presidential elections, should be effective in reversing the trend toward ever-larger campaign spending and morally as well as legally questionable fund-raising efforts.

The Federal Election Commission was established in 1974 to oversee the new election financing procedures. The Commission is responsible for enforcing the law and distributing federal funds to candidates who qualify. Its rulings are subject only to court challenges or veto by either the House or the Senate within 30 days. The six-member commission is appointed by the President under a January 30, 1976 Supreme Court decision that overruled the original provision that Congress elect four members.

Federal Financing and Political Parties

The provisions of the Federal Election Campaign Act strengthen the Democratic and Republican parties against third-party challenges. The Act provides for matching funds for all candidates in the primaries, but the outright $20 million grant to the major parties for campaign expenses and $2 million for convention expenses guarantees their ability to campaign effectively and protects them from meaningful third-party competition. While third parties may receive some convention funds based on their past or current voting strength, the advantage of the major parties cannot be overcome by private fund-raising efforts owing to the limitations set by the Act. Whether or not increased party control over campaign funds will bring about more unified national party organizations remains to be seen. The full impact of the new law will not be felt until after several Presidential nomination and election campaigns.

Financing the 1976 Election

During the 1976 primary campaign, total expenditures were reported to be about $70 million, with the 12 Democratic candidates for the nomination spending about $40.4 million and the two Republican contenders spending approximately $29.3 million. This contrasts with the total reported preconvention spending of $52.7 million in 1972.[11] The limits on spending and the provision for federal funding obviously did not reduce the overall cost of primary campaigns, even when inflation is taken into consideration. It is likely that the provision for matching federal funds made it possible for more candidates to enter primary elections than would have been possible if they had been entirely dependent on their own fund-raising efforts.

The Democratic and Republican parties each received $21.8 million for Presidential campaign expenses in 1976. This reflects the provision for inflation that was written into the law. In addition, interpretations of the Federal Election Campaign Act by the Federal Election Commission had the effect of providing each party with another $4.5 million by allowing some campaign expenses to be charged to the candidates themselves rather than to the party organizations.[12] The total of about $50 million that was ultimately spent by the two major party candidates in the general election was significantly below the 1972 total.

The impact of the campaign spending law on the election outcome is hard to determine. Both parties reported that they did not have enough money to provide the bumper stickers, campaign buttons, and other paraphernalia traditionally associated with Presidential campaigns. Whether or not this reduced voter enthusiasm and, hence, turnout is difficult to judge. Herbert Alexander, a leading student of campaign financing, commented as follows:

> My interpretation is that $25 million just isn't enough to mount a national campaign. It means you can't produce and distribute the kinds of banners, buttons and brochures that are helpful in getting people involved. And the consequences are not good for democracy.[13]

As mentioned earlier, the Federal Election Campaign Act limited candidates for the House and Senate to contributions of $1000 from any individual and $5000 from any political committee. The 1976 Supreme Court decision that struck down limits on overall spending in congressional races, as well as limits on individual spending by candidates in their own behalf, allowed spending as usual when candidates could afford to fund their own campaigns. Thus, in 1976 Representative H. J. Heinz (R., Pa.) spent $2.2 million in his successful campaign for a Senate seat.[14] Clearly, limits on political contributions have not put an end to extravagant spending by congressional candidates who can afford it.

The Presidential Election Campaign

Political campaigning has changed markedly in the past twenty years. The decline in the effectiveness of party organizations at all levels has reduced party control over campaign organizations. Calls for party loyalty and references to past party heroes are no longer dominant campaign themes. If anything, more recent Presidential races have actively avoided dependence on the parties; campaign strategy has been designed to stress the personal appeal of the candidate and deal with issues in a way that will not turn off potential supporters.

Campaign Strategy

Candidates rely on their own political skills and those of a few close advisers in planning campaign strategy. People who reach this level of public life have usually taken positions on many public issues and often find their choices limited by their past statements on those issues. In 1976, however, Carter had the advantage of not having to justify previous statements on national issues because he had had little national exposure before the primary campaign and had avoided specific issues during the primaries. A poll taken before the Presidential campaign was in full swing revealed that, by a 55 to 32 percent margin, potential voters agreed with the statement, "At least I know what kind of a President Gerald Ford will be. I'm not so sure about Jimmy Carter."[15]

Polls of this sort are valuable in planning strategy. Presidential candidates always try to judge the public mood so that they can discuss the issues that concern voters most and avoid potentially damaging positions. The defeats experienced by Goldwater and McGovern resulted in part from lack of sensitivity to public opinion. Goldwater depended on the "silent majority," and McGovern counted on 18-21-year-old voters and members of minority groups for his support. In taking positions that would attract these groups, both Presidential candidates alienated many other voters.

Probably the most important element of campaign strategy, and one over which the candidate has little control, is the necessity for the incumbent President to defend the record of his administration and for the challenger to attack that record. In 1976, President Ford took credit for the economic recovery that was then under way while Carter noted the unacceptably high level of unemployment that prevailed despite the recovery. It has also become customary for the incumbent to note the "improvement" in U.S.-Soviet relations while the challenger stresses the "deterioration" of U.S. military power.

There are a large number of side issues in any campaign, many of them regional in nature. Both candidates will promise to support programs that appear to reflect popular demands and avoid those that have little support. Issues may also arise in the course of the campaign, though, short of a confrontation with a foreign power in the midst of the campaign, it is unlikely that such events will change campaign strategy very much.

The challenger has a special problem. He must portray himself as skilled in both domestic and foreign affairs. It is not enough for him to criticize the President; he must also win support by making the voters aware of his own ability. This is not an impossible task. The primaries provide national exposure and allow a candidate to reinforce the weak points either in his program or in the way he presents himself to the public.

How and where the candidate will campaign is determined on the basis of the support a candidate appears to have at the beginning of the campaign. It is well known that campaigns are most effective when they rally the support of the party faithful and win over the undecided voters.[16] Attempting to change the minds of voters who favor the opposition candidate is usually a waste of time. Polls are widely used in an effort to determine areas of strength and weakness throughout the campaign. With the increased emphasis on the media for communication with the public in recent years, the traditional hand-shaking, baby-kissing approach is of limited usefulness. The nation is too large and too populous to base campaigns on a face-to-face effort.

The Campaign Organization

During Presidential elections the party faithful at all organizational levels—local, state, and national—go into action. In the past, the national committee took responsibility for fund raising as well as shaping the loose party structure into a unified campaign force. This effort involved all the party regulars from precinct captains to state party chairmen and other party officials. The recent emphasis on media campaigning and the use of

President Ford at a campaign rally one week before the 1976 Presidential election. A nonelected president, Ford was subject to an unprecedented fight for the nomination as an incumbent.

polling as a source of information have reduced the candidates' dependence on the party organization. There is increasing evidence that the ability of party bosses to deliver the vote in Presidential elections has diminished. There is also much less chance of reward for party workers in Presidential elections than in state and local contests. The ward committeeman may get a city job as a reward for successful party activity in local elections but has little to gain from activity in national elections.

These factors have led to candidate-dominated campaign organizations that make use of the national committees but shape their own strategies. Evidence of the low level of party activity is presented in Table 6-5, which shows that only 12 percent of the Republicans and 9 percent of the Democrats interviewed had been contacted in person or by telephone three weeks before the hotly contested 1968 election. If the debate over the war, the riots in urban areas, and the Wallace candidacy were unable to stimulate party activity, it is unlikely that a candidate who relies on the party organization will be successful.

Still, the party organization, while not crucial, can be of great help to a Presidential candidate. The parties have computerized lists of potential campaign workers and can contact party activists relatively quickly. This "machinery" is an important asset, but it is often hard to set in motion.

Perhaps the party's major contribution to its Presidential candidate is through the interest groups associated with it. Some of these groups are regional in nature; others have ethnic roots; some represent major labor or industry groups; and all can use their organizational structure in support of a candidate. Party leaders serve as a link to these groups. However, even in this type of activity candidates are likely to lean heavily on their own friendships with the leaders of various groups and on the connections of their key supporters. Most Presidential hopefuls have a network of such contacts—otherwise they probably would not have won the nomination in the first place.

The Campaign as a "Media Event"

Hail to B.B.D. & O. It told the nation how to go: It managed by advertisement To sell us a new President.

Eisenhower hits the spot One full general, that's a lot.

Feeling sluggish, feeling sick? Take a dose of Ike and Dick.

Philip Morris, Lucky Strike, Alka Seltzer, I like Ike. [17]

This ditty, written in 1952, expresses the popular notion that Presidential campaigns are largely contests between advertising agencies. It also reflects the important role of public relations in campaign strategy. However, it can be assumed that both candidates will benefit from the skills of public relations advisers so that this aspect of the competition is likely to be a standoff. This is even more probable since the passage of the Federal Election Campaign Act which limits campaign spending and leaves the candidates with equal amounts to spend on advertising and public relations.

The primary reason for using the media to the fullest is to present the candidate favorably and to get him maximum exposure as he follows the campaign trail. Campaign planners commonly schedule a candidate's public appearances at times that allow television reporters to prepare for the evening news. Paid political ads on TV often feature the candidate discussing issues with friendly interviewers. Nixon appeared before selected panels in the 1968 campaign, and in the 1976 campaign President Ford appeared with television personality Joe Garagiola to answer questions that stressed his experience as President.

The length of Presidential campaigns and the intense media coverage they stimulate often result in candidates' having to spend a lot of time explaining their inevitable verbal missteps. The 1976 race was enlivened by Carter's *Playboy* interview, which made "lust" a campaign issue, and Ford's statement during a televised debate that "there is no Soviet domination of Eastern Europe and there never will be under a Ford Administration." [18] Although this sort of coverage led one news correspondent to portray the campaign as "barren and petty," the media encouraged lack of concentration on issues by highlighting candidates' verbal blunders. [19]

Even under the best of conditions, it is very difficult to discuss campaign issues in such a way that the public will be encouraged to make reasoned judgments. The most important issue appears to be the question of which party is in control of the Presidency, but this can be a negative as well as a positive factor. The alternation of Democratic and Republican control of the White House since 1952 suggests that even when the candidate has served less than a full term—as in the case of Ford—or has never been President—as with Nixon in 1960 and Humphrey in 1968—the public is ready for a change of leadership every eight years.

The advertising consultants for the Ford and Carter campaigns shared the feeling that the only real issue was the public's image of the candidate. John Deardourff, Ford's adviser, empha-

TABLE 6-5
Percentage of Voters Contacted by Party Workers, Mid-October, 1968

	Yes—Personal Call	Yes—Telephoned	Neither	Don't Remember
Democrat	6%	2%	91%	1%
Republican	8	4	88	1

SOURCE: Robert D. Cantor, *Voting Behavior and Presidential Elections* (Itasca, Ill.: F. E. Peacock, 1975), p. 98.

"A VERY SOLID PLATFORM... BROAD AND BLURRED."

AUTH in N.Y.C.
© 1976 THE PHILADELPHIA INQUIRER
THE WASHINGTON POST WRITERS GROUP

sized this point in a speech before the American Association of Advertising Agencies in October 1976. Carter's advertising aide, Gerald Rafshoon, agreed: "Issues per se are not what move people to make their choice. The issue is the candidate's character, leadership, and integrity." [20] If both candidates are able to project a favorable image, the matter of which party is in control of the White House becomes a powerful element in the voting decision.

Presidential Debates

An added ingredient in the 1976 campaign—absent since 1960—was the series of debates between Ford and Carter. *Debate* is not really the right word for what is actually a side-by-side press conference with a little exchange between the candidates. Pollsters had a field day after the three Carter-Ford debates, but the significance of their findings is doubtful. Warren Miller, director of the Center for Political Studies at the University of Michigan, spoke of the polls' impact on public opinion, as well as their accuracy, as follows: "I would totally discount their impact, and I would be almost equally willing to discount their credibility." [21] This statement is an indication of the difficulty, if not impossibility, of accurately measuring the value of the debates to the candidates, despite the image they projected or the publicity they received. While the Kennedy-Nixon debates were considered important in determining the election outcome, there is little agreement today about their actual impact. Presidential debates may serve to reinforce the decisions of voters who are already committed. But whether or not they can either change voter decisions or increase turnout is a subject of controversy.

The Impact of the Campaign

Table 6-6 shows the impact of the campaign itself in changing voters' minds about the candidates. In the

Second debate between candidate Jimmy Carter and President Gerald Ford in San Francisco. There has been no clear agreement on the impact of debates on presidential campaigns.

TABLE 6-6
Voter Choice at Early Stages of Campaign, 1964-1976

1964—Postconvention	
Goldwater	31%
Johnson	61
Undecided	8

1968—August 24	
Nixon	40%
Humphrey	34
Wallace	17
Undecided	9

1972—August	
Nixon	57%
McGovern	34
Undecided	8

1976—August	
Carter	45%
Ford	41
Undecided or others	14

SOURCE: *Time Magazine* poll taken by Daniel Yankelovich as reported November 15, 1976, p. 19.

elections covered, there is a consistent relationship between the voters' intentions at the beginning of the campaign and the actual results. Johnson received about 61 percent of the vote in 1964, just about the percentage he started out with. The undecideds appear to have been Republicans who were unenthusiastic about Goldwater in the early stages of the campaign but eventually voted Republican. The 1964 election also illustrates the advantage of the incumbent President over the challenger. The voters know or think they know, what to expect, and their decision comes early in the campaign. A similar pattern emerged in 1972, when Nixon started the campaign with a predicted vote close to the percentage he eventually won. In that election, both candidates had virtually the same degree of support before the campaign as they received in the election; the undecided voters split their votes.

The results of the 1964, 1972, and 1976 elections, in which the incumbent President was seeking reelection, cast doubt on the importance of media coverage of elections. Obviously, in 1964, 1972, and 1976 the hundreds of millions of dollars that were spent had little or no impact on the voters. But neither candidate could risk not campaigning actively. Voters appear to make their choices shortly after the nominating conventions; accordingly, the campaign may be expected to have an impact on voting decisions only in close contests. Even then, while many voters may change their minds, such changes are likely to balance one another. The 1968 election, for example, did not involve an incumbent President and was complicated by the candidacy of George Wallace. About half of the early Wallace strength eventually moved to Humphrey, and the undecideds split their votes between the major party candidates as shown in Table 6-6.

Public opinion polls taken early in the 1976 campaign showed Carter with a commanding lead, but these polls were taken after the Democratic Convention and before the Republican Convention. Such polls are almost meaningless in predicting the outcome of the election because they mirror the media coverage of the nominated candidate at the expense of the one who has not yet been nominated. Table 6-6 shows that a poll taken after the Republican convention in August found Carter with a 4-percentage-point lead over President Ford. This was very close to the final outcome, with the undecideds splitting their votes. Other polls found a larger Carter lead at that point, but by mid-September the poll results were very similar to the final outcome.[22] Thus, there is nothing in the data to indicate that the campaign does more than simply reinforce the voters' original preferences.

Voting Patterns

Two interesting voting patterns that may be seen in recent Presidential elections are the increase in ticket splitting and the continuation of relatively low levels of voter participation. The former reflects greater voter independence, while the latter indicates a continued lack of interest in political participation. It appears that while the percentage of uninterested citizens has remained constant, the voters who do participate in the democratic process have become more aware of political issues and feel able to make independent judgments in Presidential elections. Occasionally, local or state elections are marked by enough controversy to increase their importance to the voter and weaken party ties at these levels as well.

Ticket Splitting
The divided party government that results when the Presidency is controlled by one party while Congress is controlled by the other is a source of concern to many political analysts. There is little question that this situation makes it more difficult for the President to get significant legislation passed, but voters apparently do not consider this a good enough reason not to split their tickets and vote for candidates of both parties. Table 6-7 indicates the extent of ticket splitting in 1960, 1964, and 1968.

The trend toward increased ticket splitting is likely to continue. A Gallup poll taken after the 1972 election revealed that the percentage of ticket splitters reached 60 percent in that election,[23] and in 1976 Carter was elected by about a 3-percentage-point margin, while the Democratic party maintained a better than two-to-one plurality in the House of Representatives. The increase in ticket splitting and the failure of the major parties to attract more support in Presidential elections is evidence that the American public is increasingly independent, unwilling to allow either party to control the White House for long periods, but continuing to vote along party lines in congressional elections.

Voter Participation
The percentage of the voting-age population who cast ballots in Presidential and congressional elections is shown in Table 6-8, and the breakdown by population characteristics is

TABLE 6-7
Straight-and Split-ticket
Voting, 1960-1968
(Including state and local
elections in Presidential years)

1960	
Voted straight Democratic	40.9%
Voted straight Republican	32.0
Split ticket	27.1
No. of cases—1390	100.0%
1964	
Voted straight Democratic	42.3%
Voted straight Republican	17.3
Split ticket	40.4
No. of cases—981	100.0%
1968	
Voted straight Democratic	28.7%
Voted straight Republican	22.7
Split ticket	48.6
No. of cases—990	100.0%

SOURCE: Robert D. Cantor, *Voting Behavior and Presidential Elections* (Itasca, Ill.: F. E. Peacock, 1975), p. 91.

TABLE 6-8
Voter Participation in Election of President and U.S. Representatives, 1932-1976

Year	President	U.S. House of Representatives
1932	52.4%	49.7%
1934	—	41.4
1936	56.9	53.5
1938	—	44.0
1940	58.9	55.4
1942	—	32.5
1944	56.0	52.7
1946	—	37.1
1948	51.1	48.1
1950	—	41.1
1952	61.6	57.6
1954	—	41.7
1956	59.3	55.9
1958	—	43.0
1960	62.8	58.5
1962	—	46.1
1964	61.8	58.1
1966	—	45.4
1968	60.9	55.2
1970	—	43.5
1972	55.7	51.0
1974	—	36.2
1976	53.3	

SOURCE: *Statistical Abstract of the United States,* 1973, No. 611, p. 379.

Note: Percentages based on voting-age population.

Increased levels of education have resulted in slightly higher turnouts in Presidential elections since 1952 (Table 6-8). [The decrease in 1972 and 1976 is due to the entry of 18-year-olds into the voting public and the relatively low level of participation by younger voters (Table 6-9).] Participation in Presidential elections has not increased to the extent that might be expected, however. Obviously, many Americans do not believe the political system can solve the problems they consider relevant. The percentages who vote for representatives are even lower. Less than half of the voting-age population has voted in so-called off-year elections (i.e., those in which a President is not being elected).

The Census Bureau reported before the 1976 election that the voting-age population totaled 150 million. The total vote for President was about 80 million, which means that President Carter was elected by slightly over 25 percent of the voting-age population.[24] This lack of political participation has been explained in the past by such barriers as the exclusion of blacks in many southern states and residency requirements that prevented many people from voting shortly after moving to another state. However, the barriers to black participation in the electoral process have been almost eliminated and the Federal Voting Rights Act of 1970 reduced the residency requirement to 30 days for participation in Presidential and vice presidential contests. In short, non-registered voters are by far the largest block of nonparticipants.

About 12 million registered voters did not participate in the 1972 Presidential election; almost half of them were prevented from doing so by unavoidable circumstances (Table 6-10). It is clear that the great majority of registered voters do participate in Presidential elections. The relatively presented in Table 6-9. Note that the percentage reporting that they voted is greater than the percentage that actually did vote. This indicates that many citizens feel guilty about not voting.

The relationship between education and voting that may be seen in Table 6-9 is striking. Over 78 percent of those with some college education reported voting in both 1968 and 1972. The lower level of participation by the unemployed corresponds to the lower percentages at lower educational levels. It is a paradox that those who have the most to gain from governmental action—which could raise education and income levels—are the least likely to participate in choosing their leaders. This might be attributable to the feeling of people in the lower socioeconomic classes that their vote does not matter because the system is controlled by the upper classes.

TABLE 6-9
Participation in National Elections, by Population Characteristics, 1968-1972

Characteristics	Percent Reporting They Voted 1968	1972
Male	69.8%	64.1%
Female	66.0	62.0
White	69.1	64.5
Negro	57.6	52.1
Age*		
18–20 years	33.3	48.3
21–24 years	51.1	50.7
25–34 years	62.5	59.7
35–44 years	70.8	66.3
45–64 years	74.9	70.8
65 and over	65.8	63.5
Residence		
Metropolitan	68.0	64.3
Nonmetropolitan	67.3	59.4
North and west	71.0	66.4
South	60.1	55.4
Education		
8 years or less	54.5	47.4
9–11 years	61.3	52.0
12 years	72.5	65.4
More than 12 years	81.2	78.8
Employment		
Employed	71.1	66.0
Unemployed	52.1	49.0
Not in labor force	63.2	59.3

SOURCE: Statistical Abstract of the United States, 1973, No. 612. P. 379.

*Covers civilian noninstitutional population 18 years old and over in Georgia and Kentucky, 19 and over in Alaska, 20 and over in Hawaii, and 21 years and older elsewhere in 1968.

TABLE 6-10
Reasons for Nonvoting Given by Registered Voters, 1972 Presidential Election

Health reasons, no transportation, out of town, other unavoidable reasons	48%
Apathetic; dislike of politics, candidates, etc.	27
Other reasons or unknown reasons	25
	100%

SOURCE: U.S. Department of Commerce, Bureau of the Census, *Current Population Reports*, Series P-20, No. 253, October 1973, p. 6

low overall percentage is due to the failure of many voting-age citizens to register.

The Electoral College

The Constitution provides for the election of the President to take place in the *electoral college*. The ballots cast for President on election day are actually for slates of *electors* who have previously been elected by popular vote in each state. The electors meet after the general election to cast their ballots for the candidate to whom they are pledged. The vote is on a winner-take-all basis in each state (except Maine). One potential problem with this procedure is that the electors are not legally bound to vote for the candidate to whom they are pledged. However, only rarely has an elector voted for some other candidate, and this has never changed the result of the election. More serious is the possibility that the candidate who has won a plurality of the popular vote will lose in the electoral college because of the winner-take-all rule.

The winning candidate must receive 270 votes in the electoral college. In 1976, Carter won 297 electoral votes and Ford won 240.[25] If there had been a shift from Carter to Ford, of 2677 votes in Ohio and 3687 votes in Hawaii, these two states and their electoral votes would have been in Ford's column. Thus, despite Carter's plurality of 1.7 million votes, a shift of fewer than 7000 votes in these two states would have given Ford 270 electoral votes and Carter 268.[26] Such situations have arisen before. In three previous elections, the candidate with the highest popular vote in the Presidential election (John Quincy Adams in 1824, Rutherford B. Hayes in 1876, and Benjamin Harrison in 1888) has lost the contest in the electoral college. The 1824 election involved four candidates, and the election went to the House of Representatives because no candidate could win a majority in the electoral college.

A third-party candidate could divert enough electoral votes to prevent the candidate with the highest popular vote from winning the required majority in the electoral college. The election would then go to the House, where a coalition of representatives from states with third-party strength and states that were carried by the other major candidate could elect a President other than the one winning the popular plurality.

The 1976 election, for example was complicated by the candidacy of independent candidate Eugene McCarthy, who, though he won only about 500,000 votes, tipped the scales in some states from Carter to Ford. The McCarthy vote in Ohio, Oregon, Iowa, Maine, and Oklahoma exceeded Ford's margin over Carter. While this meant little in terms of the popular vote, the impact on the electoral vote was substantial if it is assumed that the McCarthy votes were taken away from Carter, a fellow Democrat. It is apparent, thus, that third-party candidacies have an exaggerated impact because of the electoral vote. Even a candidate receiving less than 1 percent, such as McCarthy, have the potential to change the final outcome if their support comes primarily from the party of one of the major candidates.

The possibility that a candidate who was defeated in the general election could gain the Presidency through the mechanism of the electoral college is real enough to cause concern. It is possible to win by the slimmest of margins in the 11 most populous states while losing in the other 39 and still win in the electoral college. Moreover, the original reasons for the electoral college appear to have vanished. The Constitution provided for the electors to be chosen by the states any way they wished, but popular election of electors has developed along with the granting of the right to vote to increasing segments of the population. At the same time, the fear of the industrial states that they could be dominated by less populous rural

96 *Voting Behavior and the Electoral Process*

TABLE 6-11
Popular Vote in Presidential Elections, 1932-1976

	Candidates		Percentage of Popular Vote	
Year	Democratic	Republican	Democratic	Republican
1932	Franklin D. Roosevelt	Herbert C. Hoover	57.4%	39.6%
1936	Franklin D. Roosevelt	Alfred M. Landon	60.8	36.5
1940	Franklin D. Roosevelt	Wendell L. Willkie	54.7	44.8
1944	Franklin D. Roosevelt	Thomas E. Dewey	53.4	45.9
1948	Harry S. Truman	Thomas E. Dewey	49.6	45.1
1952	Adlai E. Stevenson	Dwight D. Eisenhower	44.4	55.1
1956	Adlai E. Stevenson	Dwight D. Eisenhower	42.0	57.4
1960	John F. Kennedy	Richard M. Nixon	49.5	49.3
1964	Lyndon B. Johnson	Barry Goldwater	61.1	38.5
1968	Hubert H. Humphrey	Richard M. Nixon	42.7	43.4
1972	George C. McGovern	Richard M. Nixon	37.5	60.7
1976	Jimmy Carter	Gerald R. Ford	51.0	48.0

SOURCE: *Statistical Abstract of the United States,* 1973, No. 590, p. 364. 1976 data from *The New York Times,* November 7, 1976, p. 3E.

states is no longer a reason to retain the electoral college. As a result of these criticisms, many suggestions for the abolition or restructuring of the electoral college have been made, but they have never gained the momentum necessary for constitutional change.

The Ebb and Flow of Presidential Power

Table 6-11 offers a picture of the pattern of alternating party control of the White House every eight years for the past 24 years. It is also worth noting that even in the landslide elections of 1936, 1964, and 1972 the loser won at least 36.5 percent of the popular vote. This is apparently the minimum any candidate can expect under a variety of conditions. Since 1932, only the 1960 and 1968 elections have been close contests.

No President holding office during the period covered by Table 6-11 has been defeated in a reelection bid except Ford, who had not been elected to the Presidency. In the three cases of an election in which the incumbent President was not running—1952, 1960, and 1968—there was a change of party control. Thus, party power of the White House appears to ebb and flow as the public unhesitatingly votes for a change in party control every eight years while declining to replace a President after only one term. This pattern results from the voters' perceptions of the political system in general and the objects of political life—parties, issues, and candidates—in particular, perceptions that shape the voting decision and thereby determine who will occupy the White House.

Summary

The American electoral process has fulfilled its basic function of giving the citizens a periodic opportunity to review the performance of their leaders. However, there is little indication that even Presidential elections are important enough to many Americans to lift the participation of the voting-age population much above 50 percent. This lack of interest can be explained in several ways. It may mirror a widespread belief that the candidates offer little threat to individual well-being; it may indicate that the public sees little difference between the candidates; or it may reflect dissatisfaction with the governmental process itself. The fact that members of higher socioeconomic classes participate more widely in the electoral process might be interpreted as an indication that widespread satisfaction with the basic outlines of American life has made participation more relevant to those with more education and higher incomes.

Presidential elections do not usually involve flaming issues that inspire high voter turnout or divide the nation into rival political camps. The Democratic and Republican parties still play an important role, but voters are increasingly likely to make independent judgments about the candidates. The parties are still a major force in local, state, and congressional races, however, and while many political observers worry about low voting levels, the public has shown its ability to change the party in control of the White House every eight years. Thus, from the standpoint of encouraging governmental responsiveness to the people, the American electoral process appears to be effective.

NOTES

[1] Angus Campbell, Gerald Gurin, and Warren E. Miller, *The Voter Decides* (New York: Harper & Row, 1954). The use of issues, voters, and candidates as the key variables in voting behavior research was first advanced in this book.

[2] V. O. Key, Jr., with the assistance of Milton Cummings, Jr., *The Responsible Electorate* (New York: Vintage Books, 1968) p. 150.

[3] Warren Weaver, Jr., "Timing Of 3 Debates Held Key To Victory," in *The New York Times,* November 6, 1976, p. 8C. Copyright © 1976 by The New York Times Company. Reprinted by permission.

[4] Ibid.

[5] Ibid.

[6] R. W. Apple, Jr., "Carter And The Poll," in *The New York Times,* February 13, 1976, p. 36M. Copyright © 1976 by The New York Times Company. Reprinted by permission.

[7] Robert D. Cantor, *Voting Behavior and Presidential Elections* (Itasca, Ill: F. E. Peacock, 1975), p. 80.

[8] James Reston, "Over Two Thirds Eligible To Vote in the Primary States Didn't," *The Evening Bulletin,* June 9, 1976, p. 19A.

[9] Cantor, p. 108n.

[10] Warren Weaver, Jr., "By Law This Will Be A Cheaper Campaign," in *The New*

CHAPTER 6 CROSSWORD PUZZLE

Across

1. ___ to national party conventions are selected in state primaries.
9. Vincent ___ Gogh (Dutch painter)
10. Patchwork ___
11. James Bond or Mata Hari
12. Furnish food for a party
14. Street, in Paris
17. ___ offer the people a periodic opportunity to pass judgment on the performance of their government.
19. It is customary for Vice-Presidential candidates to be chosen by the nominee for ___.
21. Type of color
22. Asian holiday
23. ___ estate
25. Unconscious part of the psyche
26. Reverential fear
28. Giggle
30. Since 1952 Democratic and Republican Presidential candidates have been nominated on the ___ ballot in their party conventions.
33. Money left for a waiter; hint
35. Political parties, candidates, and ___ are the major frames of reference that affect the voter's decision.
36. Presidential election campaigns are designed to portray a candidate in a favorable ___.

Down

1. Doctor (abbr.)
2. First woman
3. Fish
4. Indefinite article
5. Identical
6. Girls' name; institute a type of legal action
7. The actual election of the President takes place in the ___ College.
8. Ancient musical instrument
11. The Federal Election Campaign Act limits ___ in Presidential nomination contests and the general election.
13. Recent elections have been marked by an increase in ___ splitting.
15. Carried away with emotion; intent
16. ___ party candidates have the potential to affect the outcome in the Electoral College.
17. ___ nous
20. Stay behind
24. Los Angeles [abbr.]
27. Diminish in size; opposite of "wax"
29. Put to death on a gallows
31. Spanish for "yes"
32. ___ Eliot (American author)
34. Greek letter; math term

[22] Harris, Gallup, and Yankelovich polls as reported in *Time,* November 15, 1976, p. 19.

[23] Cantor, p. 92.

[24] Richard D. Lyons, "Turnout of Voters Largest in History," in *The New York Times,* November 4, 1976, p. 28L.

[25] One elector voted for Ronald Reagan.

[26] Neil R. Peirce, "Electoral College Almost Misfired Again," in *The Philadelphia Inquirer,* November 16, 1976, p. 11-A.

CHAPTER 7
INTEREST GROUPS

CHAPTER OUTLINE

Questions to Consider
Introduction
The Nature of Interest Groups
The Structure of Interest Groups
The Goals of Interest Groups
Interest Groups and the Political System
Interest Groups and Political Parties
    The Electoral Role of Interest Groups
    The Financial Role of Interest Groups
Interest Groups and Congress
Interest Groups and the President
Interest Groups and the Federal Bureaucracy
Interest Groups and the Judiciary
Interest Groups and the Media
Interest Groups Within the Government
Representing Foreign Interests
The Public Interest
The Washington Lobbyist
Summary

QUESTIONS TO CONSIDER

Groups representing a wide variety of interests in every part of the nation have become increasingly important in the political system. These nongovernmental organizations are active at all levels of government. What is the nature of interest groups? What is their relation to competing interest groups? How do such groups go about trying to influence the government? The answers to these questions give a broad picture of interest group strategy.

One of the most controversial aspects of the role of interest groups is the work of lobbyists. What are lobbies and how do they operate? Is their activity beneficial in any way, or are lobbyists a corrupt influence on government officials? The subject of interest groups and their activities tells us much about the way our political system sorts out conflicting demands and the way the government uses its power to allocate resources.

Introduction

The desire of individuals and groups to protect or improve their relative share of society's resources has led to the formation of *interest* or *pressure groups*. What these groups have in common is that they represent individuals or organizations with shared interests within a limited area of activity. They may be labor unions, professional associations representing groups such as architects or engineers, or organizations formed to protect the public interest in environmental affairs.

Interest groups vary in membership from the over 20 million members of labor unions to a few members representing the major auto manufacturers. Large groups such as organized labor are made up of many smaller organizations. While they may form an organization to deal with issues that affect all of them, such as right-to-work laws, there are many issues that affect only particular unions directly. Proposals for changes in mine safety legislation are unlikely to stimulate activity by unions representing hospital workers. The National Farmers Union is concerned primarily with the prosperity of its members, while the Congress of Racial Equality (CORE) devotes its energies to achieving social and economic equality for the blacks it represents.

There have always been interest groups in American society that existed side by side with the political parties as a way for citizens to communicate their needs to the government.[1] The increasing complexity of the government and its expansion into every area of national life has given interest groups new meaning. The Democratic and Republican parties are coalitions of various interest groups and at one time served as the means by which those groups dealt with the government. However, the increased strength of interest groups has enabled them to deal directly with the government, though they may remain important participants in party politics. Thus, while political parties are concerned mainly with the electoral process, the interest group has a much narrower focus and can deal more effectively with the government in its own behalf.

The American labor union movement obviously has enough strength to influence the political system independently of the parties. Like many powerful interest groups, the unions try to affect the political decision-making process by all available means. These include independent interest group activity as well as active participation in the political process through participation in party activities and support of individual candidates. Their activities include participation in nominating and election contests, lobbying among legislators and regulatory commission members, efforts to influence the executive branch, and attempts to win public support through the media.

With the emergence of the United States as an international economic and military power, interest groups have also been formed to represent foreign governments. All of these groups and their activities are an important part of the American political process.

The Nature of Interest Groups

There are almost as many interest groups in the United States as there are shared interests. Obviously, not all groups or associations are classed as interest groups. The local garden club or charitable organization has interests that are unlikely to be political in nature—though it is possible for such groups to become politically active in certain circumstances. The same is true of social organizations or groups formed for a specific purpose, such as a committee to sponsor a neighborhood cleanup campaign. However, when such groups do seek some benefit from the government, they usually do so through the political party organizations. The parties represent the interests of groups that rarely make political demands, just as they stand ready to help individual citizens in their dealings with the government. If a private interest does not have a political basis, it is unlikely to have the skills needed to deal effectively with the government.

An interest group has the organizational structure necessary to deal with the government on a continuing basis. Its strength derives either from the number of people it represents, the wealth or status of the group's members, or the group's potential for political activity. Groups such as the American Medical Association are relatively small in terms of membership but have considerable political influence because of the status and wealth of their members. Organizations such as the National Association for the Advancement of Colored People or the B'nai B'rith, on the other hand, represent large racial and religious blocs that have political influence through the sheer force of number though only a small percentage may actually belong to these groups.

Some political scientists distinguish between groups with a social basis and those with largely economic interests.[2] However, it is difficult to separate the two because their activities in one area often involve them in the other. For example, having largely achieved their original goal of desegregation, groups associated with the civil rights movement are pressing for economic gains for their members.

Many groups exist solely to put pressure on the government. Environmental groups are formed for this purpose and may have few other activities. In contrast, labor unions represent their members in negotiations with management; their interest group role is secondary to their negotiating role. The common denominator of all interest groups is the relatively small number of public issues with which they try to deal. Their strength derives in part from the highly specialized nature of their interests and their willingness to recognize the claims of other groups in certain areas.

Of course, most interest groups face competition from other groups with opposing views. Oil companies pressure the government to allow unlimited offshore oil development, while environmental groups oppose the oil interests at every turn. Unions seek favorable interpretations of laws relating to labor, while management or industry groups take the opposite tack. Even when group activity is designed to gain social or economic benefits for a specific sector of society such as the lower income groups, migrant workers, or recent immigrants from South Vietnam, there is likely to be an opposing group that fears that any redistribution of resources will be harmful to their interests. The allocation of national resources among competing and conflicting interests is a primary function of government, and the way interest groups put pressure on the government to meet their members' needs has an important effect on the distribution of those resources.

The Structure of Interest Groups

Interest groups vary in structure from the formalized, multilevel organization of labor unions to the small but efficient industry association with only one level of organization. There are also groups that organize around specific issues such as the construction of nuclear power plants and may exist only until the issue is resolved. Most effective interest groups have a permanent, professional staff to represent their interests to the government while maintaining contact with their members.

There are also a wide range of reasons for an individual to associate with an interest group; otherwise, members would not be willing to pay the group's dues. Groups that depend on individual memberships must continually remind their members of any threat to their shared interests and the need to maintain a strong organization to protect those interests. The National Rifle Association (NRA) depends largely on the "threat" of gun control legislation to maintain the support of its members. This type of group has a large membership and relatively low dues. The members can see the results of group activity; in the case of the NRA, this fuels the organization's ongoing efforts to preserve the right to own firearms.

Other groups maintain their membership through a mixture of potential benefits such as the chance to meet other people with similar interests. The American Bar Association (ABA) is a powerful group that gives lawyers an opportunity to expand their professional contacts (and income) by participating in any of its many activities. The ABA also uses its influence in such areas as the accreditation of law schools, the enforcement of professional standards, and the recommendation of certain individuals for judicial appointments at all levels of government.

The influence of interest groups cannot be measured solely by their dues-paying membership or the wealth and status of their members. Outside the formal structure of these organizations are large numbers of individuals who sympathize with the group's goals. The government must take this into account in deciding whether to satisfy the group's demands. The American Bankers Association, for example, includes almost all the important banking institutions in the nation. The same is true of the associations representing the steel industry and the commercial airlines. However, groups representing social blocs, such as the Sons of Italy, have a relatively small number of dues-paying members and large numbers of sympathizers. These unofficial "members" must be taken into consideration in judging the group's power or the reasonableness of its goals.

The Goals of Interest Groups

An interest group's goal may be to preserve the status quo in a particular issue area or to seek change through governmental action. The AMA is

Member of National Rifle Association (NRA) recruiting female members for the group's battle against gun control. The NRA is one of the nation's more influential interest groups.

faced with a changing health care environment that includes such far-reaching national programs as medicare and the possibility of national health insurance. Its primary interest is in maintaining the high economic and professional status of its members. In this case, preserving the status quo takes the form of trying to influence any legislation that may affect the medical profession. As often happens, this goal is similar to that of another interest group, the drug industry. Thus, the efforts of each of these powerful groups are reinforced by those of the other.

Group efforts to affect governmental action range from the highly visible activities of the NAACP to the behind-the-scenes efforts of certain economic groups seeking favorable changes in tax laws or beneficial actions by regulatory commissions. Many of the more powerful interest groups get little publicity because it is to their advantage not to arouse counterpressure from other groups. In contrast, groups whose goal is social change usually seek the widest possible coverage of their efforts in order to

TABLE 7-1
Major National Education Interest Groups, 1975

General

Council of Chief State School Officers—Established 1928; 56 state and territorial commissioners of education.

National Association of Secondary School Principals—Established 1916; represents 30,000 principals, assistant principals and other school administrators.

National Catholic Educational Association—Established 1904; represents 12,500 members, including 8,500 Catholic schools.

National Congress of Parents and Teachers (PTA)—Founded 1897; represents more than 8.5 million parents, teachers and school administrators.

National School Boards Association—Established 1940; represents state and local school boards.

Teachers and Students

American Association of University Professors—Established 1915; represents more than 76,000 professors.

American Federation of Teachers (AFT)—Established 1916; union of classroom teachers affiliated with the AFL-CIO, represents 425,000 members.

National Education Association (NEA)—Established as National Teachers Association in 1857, became NEA in 1870; largest professional organization in the world, representing 1.7 million teachers and administrators; a family of organizations including such affiliates as the Association for Educational Communications and Technology and the Home Economics Education Association, and associated organizations such as the Association for Educational Data Systems and the Council for Exceptional Children.

National Student Lobby—Founded 1971; represents 354 members, including 200 institutions of higher education.

U.S. National Student Association—Founded 1947; a confederation of student government associations from 500 institutes of higher education.

Higher Education

American Council on Education—Established 1918; coordinating organization for higher education groups; represents 176 national and regional associations, 1,377 institutions of higher education and affiliated groups.

American Association for Higher Education—Established 1870 as NEA department, independent in 1971; represents more than 8,400 persons working in higher education.

American Association of Community and Junior Colleges—Founded 1920; represents 918 junior and community colleges.

American Association of State Colleges and Universities—Formed 1916 from older organizations, represents 343 state colleges and universities.

Association of American Colleges—Founded 1915; represents about 800 liberal arts colleges; affiliated with National Council of Independent Colleges and Universities, founded in 1967 to speak for private higher education.

Association of American Universities—Established 1900; 48 major universities in the United States.

National Association for Equal Opportunity in Higher Education—Established in 1969 to give visibility to the needs of predominantly black colleges.

National Association of State Universities and Land Grant Colleges—Descendant of oldest higher education associations founded in 1885 and 1895; represents 128 major state universities and land grant institutions.

Graduate Education

Association of American Law Schools—Established 1900; represents 125 law schools.

Association of American Medical Colleges—Founded 1876; represents 115 medical schools, 2,233 individuals interested in medical education.

Council of Graduate Schools in the United States—Established 1961; represents 309 graduate schools.

Adult, Vocational Education

Adult Education Association of the U.S.A.—Founded 1951 to further the concept of continuing education; represents 7,200 members.

American Vocational Association—Established 1926; represents 55,000 vocational education teachers.

National University Extension Association—Founded 1915; represents 199 universities with extension or continuing education divisions.

Libraries and Broadcasters

American Library Association—Founded 1876; represents more than 30,000 librarians, libraries, publishing houses, business firms and individuals.

National Association of Educational Broadcasters—Founded 1925; professional association of individuals and institutions interested in educational television and radio.

SOURCE: *Congressional Quarterly*, September 6, 1975, p. 1919.

---

attract support from their own members as well as other groups that are likely to be sympathetic. There are a large number of organizations representing religious, ethnic, and racial interests that often band together to press for specific governmental actions. For example, the women's rights movement has won the support of many of the interest groups that have fought for civil rights.

The strategy of interest groups is usually to zero in on a few principal targets at any given time rather than trying to affect all governmental activities that might have an impact on members of the group. They recognize that any benefit received by one group inevitably will mean a loss to some other group. As was pointed out earlier, the resources of the government are limited, and this leads interest groups to emphasize the most crucial issues while at the same time trying not to antagonize other groups.

Interest groups in a certain area such as education share basic interests but they may also compete with each other for federal funds. Table 7-1 lists the major educational interest groups. Since the government will allocate only a certain percentage of available revenues to education, these groups must compete for funds. Such competition occurs between groups in any major field whose activities are carried on at all governmental levels and whose memberships include people with conflicting priorities. The interest groups listed in Table 7-1 include school administrators, teachers, students, and parents, as well as related groups such as the American Library Association. These groups are unlikely to agree on anything more specific than the need for increased federal aid to education. The conflict among them would arise from the question of how such funds should be used.

Interest Groups and the Political System

There are many points in the political system where interest groups can ap-

Mohawk Indians in New York State signing a treaty giving them rights to state land. Recent court decisions have restored property rights to many American Indian tribes.

ply pressure in an effort to influence governmental policy. The federal system of national, state, and local governments, plus independent regulatory commissions at all levels, gives the interest group several opportunities to make its presence felt. The level at which a group takes action reflects its capacities as well as the nature of its goals.

Social issues such as integration and equal job opportunities for women lend themselves to group activity at every level of government. In order to present their demands effectively, organizations such as labor unions and civil rights and women's rights groups develop an organizational structure similar to that of the government. In this way they not only use the influence of the group itself but also take advantage of the personal influence of group officials, who are often well known in community or government circles. Any effort to influence the government is more effective if those who make the effort have personal influence as well as an important position in the group.

The action (or lack of it) that a group seeks from the government determines the level at which it applies pressure. Matters that require legislation will stimulate interest group representatives to contact congressional committee members who can recommend action to the full legislature. Other group interests may be better served by contacting state or federal regulatory agencies. The complexity of this task is easy to overlook. In matters such as the regulation of insurance companies, for example, each state has its own regulatory agency. Major companies do business in all the states and thus are forced to deal with 50 independent agencies. The insurance industry sponsors interest group efforts in behalf of proposals such as tax relief or permission to sell stocks to citizens on a state-by-state basis. Appeals for higher rates are usually handled by the individual companies through their own lobbies, but industry groups help set the stage for such appeals.

Communications companies such as American Telephone & Telegraph (AT&T) also face the problem of dealing with regulatory commissions in all states as well as several federal commissions. While large corporations like AT&T can afford to hire their own lobbyists, smaller companies must band together to be heard in state capitals and in Washington.

The activity of pressure groups is a necessary aspect of the relationship between the government and the private sector, especially when the interests represented are those of individuals or businesses that cannot make their needs known otherwise. The type of influence used and the methods used differ according to the level or branch of government being approached. Effective interest group action requires intelligent use of the group's potential political power as well as cooperation with other groups with similar interests. For example, legal challenges to violations of the principle of separation of church and state will usually find several religious groups lined up in opposition to Catholic groups (e.g., educators seeking aid to parochial schools). On other issues, however, the pattern changes: Many Catholic groups joined other religious organizations to oppose American involvement in the Vietnam War. Interest groups usually avoid forming permanent alliances with other groups, however. This flexibility allows them to seek support from a wide variety of other groups when the need arises.

The nature and effectiveness of interest group efforts must be examined in relation to each element of the political system, governmental as well as nongovernmental. The relationships between private interests and political parties, the media, the legislature, the federal bureaucracy, the judiciary, and the executive branch differ in many ways, though in each case interest groups try to achieve the greatest benefit for their members and to prevent any potentially harmful action by the government.

Interest Groups and Political Parties

American political parties may be seen as coalitions of interest groups, with both parties attracting the support of particular groups for long periods. Since the 1930s, the Democratic coalition has consisted of most labor unions, civil rights organizations, and the ethnic groups of the nation's large cities. In contrast, the Republican coalition has included industry and financial groups as well as farmers. These coalitions are not permanent, nor can the various interest groups always deliver the votes of their members. However, interest groups are important to the parties in other ways. Interest group support of party organizations has two major dimensions: electoral and financial. In return for their support, the groups expect favorable treatment from the party organization and especially from the officeholders whom they have helped to win.

The Electoral Role of Interest Groups

The electoral role of interest groups may be seen in primary as well as general elections at the local, state, and national levels. The low turnout for most primary contests increases the importance of any group that can get its members to vote. Labor unions are noted for this ability. They have large memberships, organizational capacity, and continuous contact with both the party regulars and their own members. The actual effectiveness of unions in the electoral process varies with the contest, however, and there is evidence that the unions' ability to influence their members has diminished in national elections and to some extent in local elections.

The popular view of an American labor movement unified behind a Presidential candidate was never accurate, and whatever electoral influence union leaders once had has declined. George Meany, president of the AFL-CIO, the nation's largest labor organization, can endorse a Presidential candidate and contribute the organization's resources to political campaigns, but the roughly 100 unions that make up the AFL-CIO can ignore Meany and either support a different candidate or remain neutral. The political interests of unions vary, and the total union membership of almost 20 million cannot be expected always to fall into line with their leaders. Thus, the political position taken by any interest group is not automatically the same as that of its members. People join local unions to fight for better working conditions or because union membership is a condition of employment. The extent to which union members can be expected to follow their leaders in elections depends on the reward they expect for their loyalty.

Local primary contests and elections are a good example of the connection between interest group activity, electoral influence, and the well-being of the group member. Public-employee unions, especially in metropolitan areas, have been effective in organizing their members in support of a party's candidates for mayor or city council. In turn, the city employees have received hefty wage increases, which in many cases raised their wages above those of comparable employees in private industry. This kind of interest group activity was effective as long as the unions could deliver the expected wage increases. But the financial troubles of New York City and fears of similar situations in many other cities have blunted the power of the unions to use large wage increases as rewards for member support of a particular candidate. Without such rewards, it is doubtful if public employees will be as unified a bloc of voters in the future as in the past.

In the 1976 Presidential primaries, unions were markedly unsuccessful in getting their members to support their leaders' choice. This was illustrated dramatically in the Democratic primary in Pennsylvania. Carter had to change the widespread belief that he could not win in a northeastern industrial state. The unions supported Jackson, but Carter breezed to victory. Within a week, Jackson had withdrawn from the race and Humphrey had decided against entering any primaries. A Philadelphia newspaper editor described union activity in this primary as follows:

A phalanx of about 50 labor leaders ... held a press conference to announce their support for Sen. Jackson. They claimed to represent 1.5 million Pennsylvania union members. They promised to set up phone banks, hand out literature, provide hundreds of thousands of dollars worth of campaign services and turn out 10,000 workers on election day....

All of this was part of a familiar process that Michael Johnson, the former vice-president of the Pennsylvania AFL-CIO, recently described as a "lovely, lovely thing to see."

And it was supposed to produce sure-fire results. "Seven out of 10 times," boasted James Mahoney, Mr. Johnson's successor, "rank-and-file will vote according to what we tell them the facts are."

Well a funny thing happened here in Pennsylvania on April 27, 1976. Sen. Jackson took a drubbing, and so did the labor bosses.[3]

The inability of union leaders to control the votes of their members does not mean unions have no electoral influence. It simply puts this influence in perspective. Any candidate seeks broad-based support as well as endorsement by the leaders of well-known, visible groups. The unions can "deliver" some votes, and this is enough to make a difference in close elections. The Presidential nomination process includes state conventions to select delegates, an area where union efforts can be effective because the delegates are active in local politics and promises of future union support or opposition can be very persuasive. In the past, most national convention delegates were chosen in conventions, so that the unions had more influence than in 1976, when most delegates were chosen in primary elections.

Other interest groups are active in supporting candidates and attempting to deliver the votes of their members. However, they are smaller than the labor groups in terms of membership, and even those that represent specific blocs of voters often disagree on strategy and usually have few followers among the public. Black interest groups are an example of how power can be spread among many organizations. Each such group has relatively few members in relation to the total black population. But even large memberships mean little in terms of effectiveness if organization is lacking. For example, a meeting of the Third National Institute of Black Elected Public Officials in 1976 agreed that there must be more emphasis on getting blacks to vote, but could not decide how to achieve this goal.

The Financial Role of Interest Groups

The failure of interest groups to deliver votes for particular candidates does not mean the end of coalition-based political parties. The money needed for political activity at all levels is largely provided by interest groups seeking to maintain or expand their influence. The fund-raising activities of interest groups are the most visible aspect of their financial role. Party affairs such as the Democrats' Jefferson-Jackson dinners or the Republican party's Lincoln affairs are held at all party levels, with the tickets largely purchased by interest groups such as unions or business organizations. The latter do not have the votes to swing elections but do have the money to contibute to party affairs.

The role of interest groups in campaign finance was changed by the Federal Election Campaign Act, but by no means eliminated. Unions have always been free to contibute to political campaigns and have traditionally done so in behalf of candidates for every office from city councilperson to President. In many cases, candidates of both parties have received contributions from the same organization. The AFL-CIO maintains a full-time political action group—AFL-CIO Committee on Political Education (COPE)—to plan labor's political role at the national level. State labor councils have similar, though less formal, political action groups, and union locals support their favored candidates.

The vast union membership coupled with the organizational resources of the labor movement have given the unions a strong political voice. Traditionally identified with the Democratic party, there is an increased tendency for individual unions to support candidates of both parties according to their perceptions of what would be most beneficial to labor. The many sources of union contributions to political parties and candidates make it impossible to estimate the total of such contributions, but the impact is large enough to give labor an important role in the Republican party and a dominant one in the Democratic party.

It is illegal for corporations to contribute funds to political candidates and parties, but in 1975 it was revealed that this law had been ignored by many of the nation's largest corporations. Some corporations "encouraged" their executives to contribute to a particular party or candidate; others set up secret "slush" funds to be distributed to candidates. A representative of Gulf Oil testified that he had distributed $3.9 million worth of cash contributions between 1961 and 1973. The total of Gulf Oil's contributions was believed to be much higher. [4]

The Federal Election Campaign Act allows companies to set up political committees, and these committees are allowed to contribute $5000 to a candidate for national office before the nomination and another $5000 during the general election campaign. There is no limit on the number of such committees that may be formed. The funds to be contributed may not be taken from the corporate treasury but must be raised by the committees (whose expenses may be paid by the corporation). [5]

While some corporations had raised large sums of money in time for the 1976 campaign, the amounts raised by industry interest groups were really impressive. It was reported in January 1976 that the Associated Milk Producers had raised $1.8 million; the AMA and state medical associations, $1.6 million; and the maritime unions, $1.3 million. [6] These high-powered interest groups have much to gain from favorable governmental action, and this explains their enthusiastic fund-raising activity. For example, the Department of Agriculture provides a floor price for milk, thus taking it out of the competitive market and allowing the government to set the prices and, hence, the profits of the milk producers. In addition, the direct federal cost of milk purchased for various food programs has risen from $52 million to $101 million in the past 15 years. [7] This does not include the indirect benefits to milk producers from such programs as food stamps. Obviously, the political funds raised by the Associated Milk Producers are modest compared with the present and potential gains from favorable governmental action.

As mentioned earlier, the AMA dominates the nation's health industry along with the major drug companies. Increased federal activity in the health field brought spending on medicare and other health programs to $32.1 billion in 1976, with a $2.3 billion increase expected in 1977. [8] Proposals for national health insurance are currently before Congress, and the AMA has a vital interest in these and future programs in the health field. Friendly relations with key congresspeople and leaders of both parties are a necessary element in the AMA's efforts to maintain the health industry's prosperity, and political contributions are closely tied to such friendships.

The political interest of the maritime unions is less widely publicized than that of the milk producers and physicians, but the well-being of their members is even more dependent on governmental policy. The government subsidizes the maritime industry to the tune of over $1 billion a year through regulations, tax breaks, and direct payments. [9] Thus, the welfare of maritime workers is directly tied to governmental action, and the political funds set aside by the maritime unions are a key influence on governmental policy. Common Cause, a public interest group, reported that 30 senators who voted for a tax break for the maritime industry in July 1976 had received a total of $270,000 from maritime unions since 1972. By contrast, seven senators who had received such contributions voted against the bill.[10] We may conclude that the odds are excellent that contributions to congresspeople are often translated into political debts to be repaid later.

The efforts of interest groups to influence the government go beyond financial support for candidates and contributions to political parties. Interest group activity is an ongoing process involving efforts to put pressure on any institution, public or private, that can help achieve the group's goals.

Interest Groups and Congress

Interest groups often try to influence legislative decisions through congressional committees, where the fate of most bills is decided. The potential impact of an interest group representative—or *lobbyist*—is directly related to the group's influence in the congressperson's district or its past financial contributions.

Efforts by interest groups to influence legislation are not based only on what the group can do for congresspeople as individuals. In many cases, information from knowledgeable sources is needed before a committee can make an intelligent decision. The committee holds hearings and invites testimony from the groups that are likely to be affected by the proposed legislation. Much of a lobbyist's work takes the form of providing information in support of the group's position.

While the role of lobbyists is often viewed as a beneficial aspect of interest group activity, it can be a mixed blessing. During the Arab oil embargo of 1973-1974, it was revealed that the American Petroleum Institute's (API) weekly statistical reports were the primary source of information for agencies such as the Federal Energy Administration. In other words, the regulatory agency was relying on information from the group that was to be regulated rather than data provided by an independent source. In November 1976, it was revealed that the API's estimates of fuel imports for the second half of 1976 were too low.[11] While the API, which is the oil and gas industry's trade association, has an excellent reputation for accuracy, one must keep in mind that it has a big stake in governmental regulation.

The choice of a lobbyist is important. Former congresspeople are often hired by interest groups in the hope of making use of their friendships with key legislators. Most groups maintain Washington offices, and their representatives try to develop social relations with key senators and representatives. The work of an interest group in relation to congress is much the same as that of any salesperson in relation to a customer. The major limitation on the effectiveness of interest groups in Congress is competition from other groups with similar personal relationships, financial resources and pressure tactics.

The ability of interest groups to affect legislation also depends on the visibility of the issue involved. It is easier to influence legislation that is not in the public eye than to lobby successfully in areas that get a lot of attention. Congresspeople never lose sight of the next election campaign, and while they would like to reward their friends for their support, they will not risk their own political careers to do so.

The effectiveness of behind-the-scenes lobbying is illustrated by the following example. The Business Roundtable is an interest group with a great deal of power. Its 168 members include "the three largest automobile manufacturers, the three largest banks, seven of the largest oil companies, the largest steel companies, major retailing organizations and many of the largest utilities including the American Telephone and Telegraph Company."[12] This organization charges its members dues ranging from $2,500 to $35,000 and has an annual budget of $1.5 million. In addition, all of these major corporations employ their own lobbyists and thus pay much of the cost of the organization's efforts. Thus, the Business Roundtable is one of the nation's most influential though least visible interest groups.

In late 1975, legislation was being prepared in Congress that would have amended the antitrust laws. The new law would have given the states the authority to bring suit under antitrust law against corporations found guilty of violations. The proposed bill would also have allowed the states to collect damages on behalf of citizens who were overcharged as a result of illegal practices such as price fixing. Obviously, opening up the field of antitrust action to the individual states would pose a tremendous threat to large corporations which might be forced to defend themselves against ambitious legal attacks from 50 directions. The lobbyists representing the Business Roundtable and its members succeeded in blocking this proposed legislation in the House Rules Committee.[13] In this case, the Business Roundtable's stand had some merit, since the new legislation did not change the existing antitrust restrictions but opened the way for lawsuits from every state, thereby threatening to place an enormous burden on individual corporations. If the Roundtable had not conducted an all-out campaign to block the proposed legislation, it probably would have become law (it had already been approved by the House Judiciary Committee). The success of the Roundtable may be attributed to the lack of support for the bill from a public that was unaware of the issue, as well as lack of interest on the part of other organized groups.

Interest Groups and the President

The pressure of interest group activity on the President is more subtle but just as real as the pressure on Congress. This is especially evident during the transition period before a new administration takes office, when the newly elected President is appointing the cabinet and other high government officials. Every President must build his own coalition among the nation's more powerful interest groups so that his administration will have their trust and cooperation. Banking interests, the military-industrial complex, and organized labor are among the powerful groups that play a direct role in the selection of cabinet officials. One of Carter's campaign promises was that he would bring "new faces" to Washington. But when his key cabinet choices were announced it was clear that he had been under pressure to choose people who had served in previous administrations and were acceptable to the major interest groups. His first appointment, Cyrus R. Vance as secretary of state, brought to that post a man who had served in the Kennedy and Johnson administrations and was associated with the Council on Foreign Relations (CFR), the nation's foremost foreign policy interest group. Almost anyone who has any influence in American foreign policy is a member of this group, which includes former Secretaries of State Dean Acheson, John Foster Dulles, Dean Rusk, and Henry Kissinger. The CFR also includes major U.S. corporations with foreign interests such as Chase Manhattan Bank, General Motors, Gulf Oil, and General Electric.[14] Carter's appointments in the area of foreign policy were also members of the Trilateral Commission, a foreign affairs organization of which he had once been a member. Most of the active members of this commission are also associated with the CFR.

Cabinet appointments in every administration have reflected the President's need to win the support of powerful interest groups. Commenting on the people who had been named as possible candidates for Secretary of the Treasury in the Carter administration, Ralph Nader said, "There is not one who is not an old-line, money, Establishment type."[15] Nader's comment is typical of the way many people react to this relationship between the government and powerful interest groups, regardless of the party in control. However, it can be argued that those most directly affected by governmental policy in a particular field should have the greatest influence on that policy. The governmental process is based largely on trust and interest group leaders are more comfortable with government officials whom they know and respect. In any case, it is clear that even a President who spoke against the Establishment in his campaign cannot ignore the nation's more important interest groups in staffing his administration.

Since interest groups form part of a President's political base, they have ready access to the President. Carter received support from many labor unions, big-city political organizations, and black groups, especially in the South. All of these groups will try to translate their support of the President into governmental actions favorable to their members.

Like every other recent President, Jimmy Carter will open that door marked reorganization expecting to find bureaucrats with green eyeshades who have pulled the wires on those buttons on his desk. Instead, he'll find every special interest constituency which made him President. And he'll close that door... Government has become so pervasive that special interests have multiplied 10-fold and become infinitely more sophisticated. They've had to either get theirs or protect themselves against injury.[16]

New York construction workers demonstrating in support of President Nixon's policy in Indochina. Interest groups may take stands on broad political issues as well as on issues which relate to their own narrow interests.

Interest Groups and the Federal Bureaucracy

The vast power of the regulatory commissions has made them a major target of interest group activity. More important than the actual legislation passed by Congress to regulate business or administer social programs is the way the federal bureaucracy carries out these laws. The increase in governmental regulation of business and industry has made many industries completely dependent on federal action.

The maritime, airline, securities, and banking industries are among those that are almost entirely under governmental supervision. Favorable action by the appropriate regulatory commissions can guarantee profits, while unfavorable rulings can spell disaster. Governmental regulation has been attacked as reducing competition and leading to higher consumer prices. On the other hand, changes that would allow for more competition threaten the stability of companies that have prospered under governmental regulation. Hence, there is intense interest group activity on matters concerning any heavily regulated industry.

Typical of the high stakes of regulated industries in the decisions of regulatory commissions is the ongoing struggle before the Federal Communications Commission (FCC), which regulates the radio and television industry. On one side is the cable TV industry, which is seeking more freedom to operate than is allowed under present FCC regulations. Opposing such change are the major networks, which want to protect their virtual monopoly and guaranteed profits. In 1975, the FCC limited the number of films and sports events cable TV can broadcast and thus limited the appeal of cable TV. The *New York Times* reported that FCC officials had 350 private contacts with representatives of the industries concerned between July 19, 1972, when the new rules were proposed, and March 21, 1975, when the rules went into effect. In contrast, FCC members and staff had only 20 private contacts with representatives of other government agencies or public interest groups with no stake in the outcome. More than 40 different organizations sent representatives to testify at the FCC hearings.[17] The contrast between the private contacts of the affected industries and those of the public interest groups indicates the importance of regulatory commission decisions in economic terms. Private contacts are hard to control because they are often conducted by attorneys for the groups involved. It is difficult to separate behind-the-scenes lobbying from legitimate contacts between groups with shared concerns. In any case, efforts to influence decisions on such matters as cable TV will be far more extensive when the group has a direct interest in the outcome than when the group represents the public interest.

The federal bureaucracy is also the target of lobbying efforts by groups concerned with social issues. Whether the issue is increased funds for day care centers, more federal aid to the elderly, or environmental protection, government agencies have a powerful voice in determining how and when funds will be spent. Interest group activity is associated with any center of federal authority just as political parties are associated with any elective office.

Interest Groups and the Judiciary

Interest groups attempt to influence judicial decisions in two ways: (1) investigating the qualifications of Presidential appointees to the federal judiciary and (2) bringing test cases to the courts to test the constitutionality of a law or the way it is carried out. An example of the first method is the American Bar Association's Special Committee on the Federal Judiciary, formed in 1949 to examine the qualifications of appointees to the federal judiciary, including Supreme Court justices. The influence of the ABA in this area varies, depending on the attitude of the President. The ABA is not the only group trying to influence judicial appointments, however. The NAACP, the American Civil Liberties Union (ACLU), and the Americans for Democratic Action (ADA) may also play a role in Senate confirmation of judicial appointments. In addition, well-known legal scholars sometimes form temporary groups to support or oppose particular nominations.

Interest groups are active in bringing test cases to challenge legislation or practices that they believe violate constitutional guarantees of individual rights. The NAACP, ADA, and ACLU, leaders in the civil rights movement, have used court challenges as their main weapon. Court decisions in this area as well as in relation to the rights of the accused have often been made in response to interest group challenges. While the civil rights interest groups have been most active in using the judiciary, other groups may also choose this course. Labor unions may test federal laws relating to picketing or strikes by creating a confrontation that will lead to a court test of a particular law. The judicial system thus provides an important means by which interest groups can achieve their goals. While this form of activity is very different from the work of lobbyists who seek to influence legislation or interest group efforts to affect media coverage of their activities, it is no less important than these other types of group activity.

Interest Groups and the Media

While groups such as the Business Roundtable often operate behind the scenes, others make full use of media exposure in seeking public support for their views. Public support is probably the greatest asset any interest group can have in dealing with the government. It makes congresspeople feel that it would be unwise to buck the tide of public opinion and places pressure on the bureaucracy that is hard to resist. Such groups as the Sierra Club, an environmental protection organization, or any of Ralph Nader's public interest lobbies communicate their views to the public by all possible means. Media coverage is attractive because it is free, and well-known groups have ready access to such coverage.

Media coverage is used on a day-to-day basis by broad-based organizations such as labor unions and civil rights and women's rights groups. The large number of people who can identify with their programs makes any meeting or policy statement by such groups newsworthy. The success of campaigns by women's organizations to achieve equal employment opportunity and end discriminatory lending practices is probably due to the success of these groups in shaping public opinion through the media rather than to their lobbying efforts. Congress and state legislatures have been presented with overwhelming evidence of the public's desire to remove the remaining barriers to equality for women, and this is the most persuasive argument of all.

Interest Groups Within the Government

Interest groups are usually discussed in terms of private influences on gov-

Bible-toting woman handing out literature in a shopping center for the Save Our Children group headed by Anita Bryant debates with volunteer campaigning for homosexual rights. In a Dade County referendum vote in 1977, an ordinance giving gays equal rights in public employment was reversed by the electorate.

ernmental action. But the increase in governmental activity in the twentieth century has created interest groups within the government itself that compete for resources with as much enthusiasm and use many of the same methods as private interest groups. In some cases, the interests of such a group are shared by a private group creating a powerful combined public-private interest group. Government regulatory agencies such as the Federal Maritime Commission are closely tied to the industries they regulate. In fact, the interests of the Maritime Commission are almost inseparable from those of the industry. Maritime Commission members and staff thus become unofficial lobbyists for the industry that is responsible for the Commission's very existence. The tendency of the government to expand encourages this sharing of interests by the bureaucracy and the private sector.

The most striking example of such a combination of interests is the so-called military-industrial complex. The 1977 federal budget provides over $100 billion for national defense, and the military departments have an important stake in that budget. This is true of military officers as well as the civilian employees of the Department of Defense. Their personal interests are served by an ever-growing military establishment with plans for new weapon systems. Therefore, their interests are shared by the defense contractors that will profit from higher defense spending.

Table 7-2 lists the top military contractors; the amounts involved give some idea of the importance of defense contracts to these corporations. This type of shared interest creates a powerful lobby, a situation that is not harmful to the nation unless the desire for ever-higher budgets derives more from personal motivations than from real defense needs. However, it is hard to set precise limits on defense spending because of the impossibility of determining military needs in advance.

The military-industrial complex also has an important impact on U.S. foreign policy. One reason for the United States' consistent support of Israel, in addition to the desire to help a small democratic state surrounded by hostile nations, is that the military-industrial complex benefits from massive U.S. arms aid to foreign nations. Thus, it is sometimes hard to distinguish between policies that are a response to the public will and those that are intended to benefit a powerful interest group.

Representing Foreign Interests

Interest group activity in Washington is not limited to domestic questions. The international role of the United States has brought lobbyists to Capitol Hill to represent most of the non-communist nations as well as many Soviet-dominated countries. These nations have a stake in America's economic policy abroad as well as its diplomatic activities. Some seek increased military and economic aid; some seek expanded trade opportunities; some seek stronger military ties; and all want to be informed of any changes in attitude that may affect the governments they represent.

The international activities of major U.S. corporations often bring their interests into line with those of the nations in which they do business. Economic investment requires political stability for maximum profit, and domestic interest groups therefore have a stake in maintaining the U.S. role abroad. Some foreign nations use Washington law firms as their lobby-

TABLE 7-2
U.S. Military Sales Orders (from abroad)

Fiscal Year	Amount (in thousands)
1950-65	$8,513,602
1966	1,627,136
1967	978,742
1968	793,558
1969	1,551,231
1970	952,593
1971	1,656,818
1972	3,261,192
1973	4,368,437
1974	10,808,926
1975	9,510,727
*1976	12,000,000

SOURCE: *The Philadelphia Inquirer*, May 12, 1976, p. 4-A. Reprinted by permission.
*Estimate from Sen. Hubert Humphrey.

Army Major General John Singlaub prepares to testify before the House Armed Services Committee after he was removed from his Korean post by President Carter. Singlaub's public protest against the proposed withdrawal from Korea is an example of a member of a government department attempting to influence government policy.

ists, while others have permanent staffs to maintain contact with appropriate government agencies. The foreign interest groups that are most effective are those with strong domestic support. An example is the American Israel Public Affairs Committee, a domestic group representing Israel in the United States. Morris Amitay, the director of this group, expresses the importance of such ties as follows:

If we have to make a case solely on the basis of the interest of Israel, we've had it. Basically I think we are effective because we have a good cause—what is good for Israel is good for the United States. We stick by it. We're effective as a lobby because we've got a lot of people we can call on immediately.[18]

The activities of lobbyists like Mr. Amitay and others who represent domestic and foreign interests inevitably arouse resentment in some congresspeople. However, lobbyists for foreign nations often have no base of public support in the United States to use as a lever in their efforts to influence Congress. Instead, they may use inducements such as trips abroad, financial donations, or female companionship. In reporting such a case, the *New York Times* said, "That was not the first time, nor, most certainly, was it the last, that a foreign government has played upon the proclivity of Congressmen for pretty women in lobbying for some greater national good."[19] Stories of South Korean lobbying made headlines in 1976 with the revelation that 90 members of Congress had received donations from that government totaling over $1 million a year. This scandal involved high Korean officials as well as the Reverend Sun Myung Moon.[20] The stakes in such lobbying efforts may involve the survival of a nation, so that their costs are small compared with the potential benefits. South Korea, for instance, depends on U.S. military aid and troops for its security and on U.S. trade for a large portion of its economic growth.

The Public Interest

The public interest is a vague concept, difficult to define and even more difficult to translate into a unified interest group. Two of the best-known public interest groups today are Common Cause, founded by former Secretary of Health, Education and Welfare John Gardner, and the many groups formed by Ralph Nader. They operate in distinctly different ways, but both have the goal of representing the public in opposition to other groups.

Common Cause is devoted to reforming the political process. It does not endorse political candidates but, rather, provides a platform for candidates to express their views to the public. Common Cause also takes legal actions intended to prohibit political practices that it believes to be a violation of the public trust.

Nader's efforts in the public interest originated in the area of consumer affairs and gradually expanded to include political activities such as publishing ratings of congresspeople. "Nader's Raiders" struck a responsive note in many Americans who felt that they were powerless against big business. The large automobile companies were particularly visible targets, and they were an early object of the Nader groups' attention.

There are many other consumer-oriented groups that, taken together, act as a counterforce to the lobbying activities of major interest groups. The main handicap of public interest groups is the fact that their members have many different interests; moreover, individuals do not have a personal stake in governmental policy comparable to that of highly structured

Consumer advocate Ralph Nader testifying before the House-Senate Economic subcommittee. Nader-led groups have influenced government regulations in many areas of consumer concern.

organizations, which necessarily take a longer-range view.

The Washington Lobbyist

There are an estimated 5,000 to 10,000 lobbyists in Washington who are full-time employees of interest groups or work on a retainer basis (many of the latter are partners in large law firms). Former government employees and ex-congresspeople may also be found among the Washington lobbyists. The major part of a lobbyist's job is to give certain individuals or agencies information that might not be available from usual sources or might be overlooked. These contacts with the government may serve a useful purpose in that they represent several alternative positions on a particular issue and reflect the views of the members of the groups they represent. For example, it is necessary for the House Labor Committee be informed of the conflicting views of management and labor if it is considering amendments to the Taft-Hartley Act, which prohibits certain labor practices. Thus, responsive government requires channels of communication between the private sector and the bureaucracy, and the lobbyist's activities serve this function.

The views of a Washington lobbyist explain how important access to the government can be:

I don't think very many people realize how pervasive the 'Feds' are.

The critical area between the Federal Government and the associations and the unions is in the rules and regulations, rather than the legislation itself. Every day, the bureaucracy spews out enough new regulations to fill a good-sized volume called the Federal Register, new rules which have an enormous impact on American business and labor.[21]

Some of the most influential lobbyists represent foreign governments. William F. Rogers, secretary of state in the Nixon administration, currently represents France, and James W. Fulbright, former chairman of the Senate Foreign Relations Committee, represents the United Arab Emirates.[22] Such well-known individuals are able to represent their clients' interests very effectively.

There is a 30-year-old law, the Regulation of Lobbying Act (1946), that requires lobbyists to register and to identify their employers. However, this law is too vague to be effective. Theoretically, lobbyists' activities are limited by this Act, which applies only to the registration of individuals having direct contact with members of Congress. In practice, however, many lobbyists do not bother to register, and their contacts with congressional staff members and the regulatory commissions are not covered by the Act.[23]

In June 1976, the Senate passed a bill clarifying the definition of a lobbyist and requiring lobbies to file public reports of their activities, including whom they meet with and the purpose of the meeting, and how much they spend on their lobbying activities. There was strong opposition to this bill, however, and it failed to clear the House Ethics Committee. The position of public interest groups on this proposed legislation illustrates the difficulty of regulating the activities of lobbyists. Common Cause favored the new controls as a step toward eliminating the abuses that were possible under the old law. However, the ACLU opposed the bill because it would limit the constitutional right of citizens to petition the government.[24]

Many attorneys represent clients before government agencies, but some may be acting as lobbyists and others simply performing professional services. Lobbying is an area of activity in which there are many shades of honesty and dishonesty, and it is hard to separate legitimate contacts with government officials from those that are clearly illegal. There is a fine line between the two, but such a line must be drawn if lobbying is to be controlled.

Summary

The growth of the government has resulted in increased efforts by private interest groups to influence governmental decisions and policies. Interest group activity is a widespread and possibly necessary aspect of the American political system because it provides a more continuous means of communicating with the government than voting. Since a great many decisions are made by the bureaucracy, voting is not enough to communicate the needs of some groups.

Lobbying has two faces, one regarded as beneficial and the other as objectionable. The approved form of lobbying is that which seeks to provide information for lawmakers and regulatory agencies so that they may make better decisions. This also gives the individual a chance to have his or her position in society protected by the interest group with which he or she identifies. Progress in civil rights would have been much slower without active lobbying by interest groups. Similarly, economic interest groups have been able to use lobbies to make sure their interests will be considered.

The objectionable form of lobbying occurs when government officials have a personal stake in their decisions because of past, present, or future ties with particular interests. Also in this category are bribery and the granting of any form of reward for favorable actions by Congress or the bureaucracy.

The competition and conflict within society for favorable action by the government creates a situation in which people with common interests must band together to protect those interests. In this context, interest group activity is an important and beneficial form of political participation.

NOTES

[1] V. O. Key, Jr., *Politics, Parties and Pressure Groups* (New York: Thomas Y. Crowell, 1964), p. 18.

[2] L. Harmon Zeigler and G. Wayne Peak, *Interest Groups in American Society*, 2nd ed. (Englewood Cliffs, N.J.: Prentice-Hall, 1972), p. 73.

[3] Creed Black, "The Labor Bosses Spoke But No One Was Listening," reprinted by permission, *The Philadelphia Inquirer,* May 2, 1976, p. 7-K.

Interest Groups

CHAPTER 7 CROSSWORD PUZZLE

Across

1. ____ among interests may limit the ability of the group to influence policy.
6. Type of skirt; opposite of "mini"
9. Absent without leave (abbr.)
10. Vegetable
12. Opposite of "pleasure"
13. Set of beliefs
15. Interest groups represent individuals or organizations with ____ interests.
17. Arm; branch of a tree
19. Part of the body
20. Soft drinks with caffeine
23. "To ____ or not to be"
24. Wide-mouth earthenware jar
25. Frozen water
26. Coquette
27. 212 in Roman numerals
28. Use a needle and thread
31. Former Japanese prime minister
33. ____ as well as domestic interests are represented in the United States
34. Interest groups are usually represented in their contacts with government by people called ____.

Down

1. Many interest groups are part of political party ____.
2. Interest group activity offers the individual an important form of ____ participation.
3. Greek letter; very small amount
4. Presses clothing
5. Neither/____
7. Totaled
8. One of the major tasks of the lobbyist is to provide ____ to legislators.
11. Land measure
12. Ralph Nader's groups represent the ____ interest.
14. Efforts to ____ the activities of lobbyists have been sporadic and ineffective.
16. Type of beverage
18. Missouri (abbr.)
21. There are many points of ____ through which interest groups can influence government.
22. Gender
23. Very short
29. Spider's ____
30. Enchanted
31. Anger
32. Petroleum

---

[4] Stuart Ditzen, "Gulf Lobbyists Handled $39 Million From 1961 to 1973," in *The Evening Bulletin,* December 12, p. 56A.

[5] Michael C. Jensen, "Corporate Corruption Is Big Business," in *The New York Times,* March 28, 1976, p. 2F.

[6] Ibid., p. 2F.

[7] *Statistical Abstract of the United States, 1975,* p. 93, Table 151.

[8] *U.S. News & World Report,* February 2, 1976, p. 55.

[9] David Burnham, "Unions, Management Ride On S.S. Subsidy," in *The New York Times,* September 14, 1975, p. 3E.

[10] "Tax Panel Kills Investor's Break," in *The Evening Bulletin,* August 6, 1976, p. 52D.

[11] James Tanner, "U.S. Demand for Imported Oil Is Rising Increasing the Reliance on Arab Providers," in *The Wall Street Journal,* November 9, 1976, p. 48.

[12] Eileen Shanahan, "Antitrust Bill Stopped by a Business Lobby," in *The New York Times,* November 16, 1975, p. 1.

[13] Ibid., p. 1.

[14] Thomas R. Dye, *Who's Running America?* (Englewood Cliffs, N.J.: Prentice-Hall, 1976), p. 111.

[15] Quoted by Frances Cerra, "Nader Says Carter Seems Ready to Cater to Corporate Interests," in *The New York Times,* December 8, 1976, p. A22.

[16] Creed Black, "Let's Put the Public Interest Above Special Interests," reprinted by permission, *The Philadelphia Inquirer,* April 25, 1976, p. 7-F.

[17] David Burnham, "Interest Groups Active Before F.C.C. Decision," in *The New York Times,* May 8, 1976, p. 37M.

[18] Quoted by David Binder, "The Israel Lobby in Washington Is Small and Effective," in *The New York Times,* August 8, 1975, p. 2.

[19] John W. Finney, "The S. Koreans Aren't Giving All the Parties," in *The New York Times,* October 31, 1976, p. 3.

[20] Ibid., p. 3.

[21] James F. Bryan, quoted by Richard D. Lyons, "Lobbyists Shifting Quarters to Capital," in *The New York Times,* June 8, 1975, p. 51.

[22] John W. Finney in *The New York Times,* October 31, 1976, p. 3.

[23] Reprinted from "Drive to Tighten Control on Lobbyists," in *U.S. News & World Report,* February 23, 1976, p. 23. Copyright © 1976 U.S. News & World Report, Inc.

[24] David E. Rosenbaum, "Will Lobbying Kill the Proposed Lobbying Bill?" in *The New York Times,* September 12, 1976, p. E3.

CHAPTER 8
POLITICAL PARTIES

CHAPTER OUTLINE

Question to Consider
Introduction
Party Government and Responsible Parties
The Development of American Political Parties
The Role of the Parties
Characteristics of American Political Parties
Party Ideology
    Ideology at the National Level
    Ideology at the State and Local Levels
    Party Government and Political Ideology
The Two-Party System
Third Parties
Party Organizations
    Presidential Parties
    Legislative Parties
    State and Local Parties
Party Leadership
    The Road to the Top
    The Rank and File
Party Performance
    Contesting Elections
    Organizing the Legislature
    The Party and the People
    The Balance of Political Power
The Future of American Political Parties
Summary

QUESTIONS TO CONSIDER

Political parties provide the organizational basis for legislative activity and electoral competition. How well do the Democratic and Republican parties perform these functions? The parties also offer a channel of communication between the government and the people. Is this channel used? If so, with what impact? These questions deal with the basic functions of political parties.

There is no mention of political parties in the Constitution. How and why did they evolve as important political institutions? Is there any particular reason for a two-party system in the United States? Why have third parties been unable to survive? What are the major differences between the Republican and Democratic parties?

In discussing the American party system, we will be aware of many levels of party activity. What is the relationship between party organizations at the local, state, and national levels? What organizational structure are they likely to have? American parties are also marked by varying degrees of activity. What are the characteristics of party leaders and followers? What are the incentives for participating in party activities?

Finally, parties must be judged by how well they perform their basic functions. How effectively do parties choose candidates and contest elections? How effective is their legislative leadership? Party activity is an important element of American politics. An understanding of the role of the parties will help in understanding the relationship between the individual and the government.

Introduction

The Democratic and Republican parties are important political institutions despite their lack of a constitutional foundation. They operate at the local, state, and national levels and provide a basis for political participation by individual citizens as well as a means for the expression of group interests to the government. The major parties try to win elections in order to gain control of the government so that they can achieve their specific goals. This puts them in the mainstream of legislative politics.

At the national level, it has not been unusual during the past twenty-five year for party control to be divided between the Presidency and Congress. Republican Presidents Eisenhower, Nixon, and Ford were faced with Democratic majorities in both the House and the Senate. This sharply limited their ability to win congressional approval for their programs. In contrast, when the President and the legislative majority are members of the same party, the opportunities for new policy directions are greater.

American political parties are divided into a large number of power centers associated with the elective offices for which they compete. This results in a complex party system lacking in organizational unity. The competition for electoral success also encourages attempts to appeal to all sectors of the population, with the result that political philosophy tends to become blurred. While it is accurate to portray the Democrats as more liberal and the Republicans as more conservative, these should be understood as relative terms that have different meanings in different parts of the country and at different times.

Party Government and Responsible Parties

One measure of the effectiveness of political parties is how close they come to the ideal of *responsible parties.* This standard makes the parties responsible for proposing specific programs, maintaining party unity in the legislature in order to carry out these programs, and existing side by side with an opposition party that offers alternative programs and an alternative set of leaders at election time.[1] This type of government, often called *party government,* exists in some European democracies, in which the chief executive is chosen by the majority party in the legislature rather than being elected by the people as in the United States. This makes it impossible for the executive and legislature branches to be controlled by different parties and increases the power of the majority party in carrying out its legislative program.

Responsible parties are usually based on socioeconomic, religious, or linguistic differences that separate the population into clearly defined interest groups. Great Britain's Labor-Conservative party competition is an example of party government. Responsible parties offer the public a clear choice and put their legislative programs into effect if elected.

While those who favor party government lament the inability of American parties to keep their campaign promises, it can be argued that this is a blessing in disguise. Great Britain's current economic problems are largely due to the political actions of past governments. The knowledge that change in party rule will bring with it dramatic changes in economic policies has discouraged the level of investment in industry that is necessary for effective competition in the Western world. In the United States, by contrast, the private sector can count on economic policies that encourage growth over long periods. Such long-term planning is difficult for "responsible" parties because of the tendency for the parties to offer programs that are different enough from each other to attract voter support. With the legislative majority choosing the prime minister, such changes in policy can be put into effect whenever the government changes hands. Since limited resources make it necessary to set priorities, the Labour party has emphasized social welfare programs at the expense of economic investment, while the Conservatives have taken the opposite tack. A more balanced policy would probably have helped Great Britain avoid many of its current problems. Thus, a party government and responsible parties can create a more effective legislative process but run the risk of making such major changes that they upset the balance among political, social, and economic systems.

Party government gives an important role to the opposition party. It is expected to offer the public an alternative to the government in power rather then simply opposition for its own sake. The opposition party forms a "shadow" cabinet whose members monitor the performance of the majority's cabinet departments. If the party wins an election, the members of the "shadow" cabinet are usually appointed to the "real" cabinet posts. The voters thus know in advance who will be prime minister, who will be included in the cabinet, and the legislative program that will be passed if the opposition is successful in gaining control of the government. This contrasts with the American party system in which the Presidential candidates seldom indicate their choice of cabinet officals in advance and run on a party platform that few people take seriously, and in which the political opposition offers an alternative in the form of new faces rather than specific legislative programs. In Great Britain, voters have the choice between voting for the opposition program and voting for that of the incumbent party, while in the United States the choice is usually seen as a positive or negative judgment of the incumbent President.

The Development of American Political Parties

There was no enthusiasm for parties among the nation's early leaders. In his Farewell Address George Washington warned of "the baneful effects of the Spirit of Party." The second President of the United States, John Adams, said that "a division of the republic into great parties . . . is to be dreaded as the greatest political evil under our Constitution." [2] The rise of American parties was a response to political realties rather than the intentions of the founders.

The origins of modern parties can be traced to the 1780s and the debates between those who favored a strong national government to correct the defects of the Articles of Confederation and those who wanted to maintain the dominance of states' rights. The Federalist party, led by Alexander Hamilton, began as a bloc of delgates who were in favor of the new Constitution and grew into an elite party that made no effort to operate at the local level. While the Federalists succeeded in getting the new Constitution passed and ratified, they soon faded from the political scene because of their anti-party attitude. Washington and Adams were Federalists, but when Thomas Jefferson took office in 1801 the Federalists' decline began, and in 1816 the party nominated its last Presidential candidate.

Jefferson opposed the Federalists in the debates over the new Constitution and became the leader of the political opposition during Washington's first terms. Appealing to the anti-Constitution bloc formerly known as the Anti-federalists, Jefferson began to organize this group into a national party and was elected President in 1800 under the Democratic-Republican label. The Democratic-Republicans were the ancestors of today's Democratic party. While the Federalist's influence declined, Jefferson attracted support because of the broad-based appeal of the Democratic-Republicans and his success in winning Federalist support by not making major policy changes. During this period, there was little competition from groups outside the Democratic-Republican coalition, and James Monroe won reelection in 1820 without opposition. [3]

The modern two-party system was born in 1828 with the split within the Democratic-Republicans over the candidacy of Andrew Jackson. John Quincy Adams and Henry Clay, the leaders of the opposition, formed the Whig party—the ancestor of today's Republican party. The Whigs elected William Henry Harrison in 1840, thereby demonstrating the effectiveness of two-party competition.

The years leading to the Civil War were marked by a strengthening of both parties and the extension of party organization to all levels of government. As the government grew, so did the number of job opportunities in government and, hence, the possibility of using jobs as political rewards. In the period leading to the election of Abraham Lincoln, however, the coalitions that had formed the basis of Whig and Democratic strength broke up, largely over the slavery issue. The 1860 election offered a choice among four candidates representing the two major parties plus extremist pro- and anti-slavery views. Lincoln ran as a Republican, and today's Republican party dates from his election.

The development of American political parties has been marked by the success of party appeals to the general public and the failure of elite groups and of third-party or single-issue candidates. As a result, despite the alternation of party power at the national level, most of the policies of previous administrations have remained in effect. Just as Jefferson continued most Federalist policies when he took office, so Eisenhower, Nixon, and Ford continued the more important of their Democratic predecessors' programs. Changes are usually more a matter of style than substance.

The Role of the Parties

The Democratic and Republican parties are really loose coalitions of varied interests that have banded together to pursue certain goals. The party's major area of influence is the electoral process. It is their potential for winning control of legislatures that enables the parties to attract support from various sectors of the public. Their electoral role is what distinguishes them from interest groups such as the AMA or the AFL-CIO, which try to influence governmental policy only in specific areas. Interest groups usually support the party or candidates who favor their views on the issues that concern them most.

Political parties also provide a channel for communication between the individual citizen and the government. Legislators at all levels of government are sensitive and usually responsive to the demands of the public they represent. The electoral role of the parties makes them dependent on the support of individuals as well as groups, and thus gives them indirect access to the government. Ideally, the parties will present alternative policy programs in their attempt to win votes. At the very least, however, they offer the public an alternative between the incumbent officials and the opposition candidates.

Characteristics of American Political Parties

The Democratic and Republican parties are characterized by the large number of party structures that have developed around centers of political power at the federal, state, and local levels. This has resulted in a fragmented party system, with competing factions usually organized under the Democratic or Republican banners but having little in common with other party structures. The rewards for political success are usually found at a particular level of government, and there is little reason to become involved in the interests of party organizations at other levels.[4] County political parties, for example, have a far greater stake in the election of local officials or state legislators than in the election of a President. Yet despite the variety of interests within the parties and the fragmented nature of their organizational structures, the Democratic and Republican parties have long been stable elements of the political system and have provided Americans with a frame of reference for their political perceptions.

Both parties formally state their platforms at their national conventions. These statements of the party's philosophy and programs indicate where the party stands on key issues but do not accurately predict the legislative action that can be expected if it gains control of Congress. While members of Congress are elected as Democrats or Republicans (with few exceptions), they run less on party platforms than on their own ability to serve their state or district, as well as the nation as a whole, if elected.

The many centers of political power in the United States, coupled with the various levels of election competition, encourage the formation of candidate- rather than party-focused political organizations whose chief loyalty is to the individual rather than to party programs, and this tendency weakens the party's control over the congresspeople who are elected under its label. Moreover, owing to the great variety of conflicting interests found in both parties, the majority party in Congress is not a unified bloc. Further, as we have seen, the party with a congressional majority may be faced with a President of the other party and thus subject to the threat of having its programs vetoed. It is this combination of the congressperson's need to control his own campaign structure and the diffuse character of the parties themselves that makes party government in the British sense unlikely in the United States.

A final characteristic of American parties is their tendency to avoid intense political issues. Since the Civil War, American society has been characterized by broad agreement on national goals, with party competition limited to the choice of appropriate ways of achieving those goals. This tends to diffuse political competition somewhat and enable most citizens to comfortably identify with one of the existing parties. Moreover, American parties have traditionally won support from individuals representing various occupational, socioeconomic, ethnic, and religious groups. The parties' attempts to appeal to a wide variety of voters have led them to play down intense political philosophies that would represent only narrow interests and attract only particular individuals.

Party Ideology

An *ideology* is an integrated set of goals, theories, and programs that forms the basis of a political program. The major American parties do not have an ideological basis in this sense, but there are variations in political attitude that have served to differentiate the Democratic and Republican parties. Consider the following characterization of the major parties:

In case you're one of the folks who think there's not a dime's worth of difference between a Democrat and a Republican, here is a guide to some of the differences, published in the Republican Congressional Committee newsletter:

• Democrats buy most of the books that have been banned somewhere. Republicans form censorship committees and read them as a group. • Republicans employ exterminators. Democrats step on the bugs. • Democrats eat the fish they catch. Republicans hang them on the wall. • Republicans date Democratic girls. They plan to marry Republican girls, but they feel they're entitled to a little fun first. • Republicans sleep in twin beds—some in separate rooms. That is why there are more Democrats.

The GOP committee said the author was unknown.[5]

This whimsical passage reflects the popular view of the major American parties, with the Democrats the party of the poorer and more liberal citizens and the Republicans usually richer and more conservative. The traditional roles of the parties has found the Democrats identified with liberal causes and an active government and the Republicans taking positions that favored the status quo and minimal governmental activity in the private sector. To be sure, the differences between the parties have seldom if ever been this clear, and this is one reason for the inability of American parties to serve as "responsible" parties. Still, the liberal—conservative dimension remains the most meaningful way of describing the ideologies of the two major parties.

Ideology at the National Level

The coalitions that have supported the Democratic and Republican parties for the past few decades, and have given the parties their liberal-conservative flavor, were formed in the Roosevelt years. At that time, the Democratic party was seen as the protector of the vast numbers of Americans who were suffering economic hardship or faced racial, religious, or ethnic discrimination. This resulted in a centering of Democratic power in the cities, where the most recent immigrants lived and labor unions were most active. The South was also heavily Democratic, but in this case the reason could be found in the abuses of the Reconstruction which had occurred under Republican administrations. The variety of groups forming the Democratic coalition encouraged a liberal stand, if only because of the need to provide some reward for the loyalty of so many different groups.

While the Democratic party attracted many people at the lower end of the socioeconomic scale, the Republicans won the support of professionals and business people. In addition, rural areas outside of the South remained Republican, and this loyalty was reflected in Republican opposition to many New Deal programs. The description of the two major parties in terms of liberal and conservative ideologics has never been an accurate picture of all who identify with the parties; rather, it is a generalization of the ideologies of the activists in each party.[6] Thus, the Democratic party of the Roosevelt-Truman years counted heavily on the "solid South," which was traditionally conservative, while the Republican party included loyal followers in the East who were more liberal than the rest of the party.

The year 1952 was a turning point in American politics: The coalitions formed during the Roosevelt years began to disintegrate. The Democratic South was dented by Eisenhower's victory, and two-party competition became more active in most states. The big-city Democratic political machines began to decline too, and while they managed to control most local elections, the ability of Democratic leaders to deliver large majorities in Presidential elections diminished rapidly.

The period since 1952 has seen a steady loosening of party ties and a trend toward independent voting in national elections. The influence of the parties in national elections remains strong in the sense that Republican and Democratic candidates dominate the campaign and political administrations are given party labels. However, the stability of the party coalitions has diminished to such an extent that the minority Republicans now have a much better chance of electoral success. These trends have forced the traditionally pragmatic, broad-based American parties to move even closer to the middle of the political road in order to win the support of ever more diverse groups. The concept of group appeal has also changed, with a better-educated public more likely to make independent decisions than to follow the lead of a particular group.

Current party ideology should be viewed on two levels. The party activists retain the liberal-conservative flavor that has been present since the New Deal. Similarly, the members of the party coalitions base their loyalty on the liberal—conservative dimension. Organizations such as the American Bankers Association will usually oppose governmental intervention in the economy, while the United Auto Workers will usually favor such action in periods of high unemployment. However, in appealing to the individual voter there is increased incentive for candidates to take middle-of-the-road positions and take advantage of the voters' willingness to switch parties in Presidential elections. These changes appear to reflect a desire for

'The poor? The sick? The unemployed? What do they have to do with the Republican Party?'

periodic changes in leadership from an active administration to one that is more restrained and then back again. Thus, conservative Presidents, Eisenhower and Ford were followed by the more activist inclined Kennedy and Carter.

Ideology at the State and Local Levels

The local and state levels of party organization are more likely to reflect a consistent liberal or conservative ideology because the public represented is usually more homogeneous, resulting in less pressure for the parties to be all things to all people. The consistent Democratic control of such large cities as Chicago, Philadelphia, and New York during the postwar years illustrates the trouble minority parties face in attempting to unseat an effective majority that represents the coalition of groups who dominate large metropolitan areas—labor, minority groups, religious and ethnic blocs. This also explains the relatively large number of congressional seats that remain under one-party control for long periods.

Stable political identifications may also be seen in rural areas, where Republican organizations have long held control, leaving the Democrats with little power to unseat incumbents. The concept of party loyalty is still valid at the city and town level of American politics. It has become less important at the national level, however, with state political battles somewhere in between.

The fact that the large cities just mentioned have been under Democratic rule for long periods does not mean that their political leaders share the same ideology. But the Democratic leadership in these cities does tend to be more liberal than the Republican opposition in terms of governmental activity. Liberalism and conservatism are relative terms: While local parties tend to reflect a particular ideology, it is not necessarily the same as that of organizations working under the same party label in other areas.

Party Government and Political Ideology

The link between party government and political ideology is strong because the degree of unity necessary for party government can be gained only through an ideology that can attract voter support and serve as a basis for legislative programs. However, American political parties appear to be moving away from ideological appeals and, thus, away from the possibility of party government. This is due in part to voter independence, but it is also due to public doubt that either party can solve the nation's problems. In 1976, both Democratic and Republican candidates stressed the need to slow the growth of the government because this is what they thought the public wanted. In effect, both parties were promising to do less, and this diffused the liberal-conservative distinction in economic matters. Much the same sort of blurring occurred on social issues as the candidates of both parties soft-pedaled busing as a way of achieving quality education while promising to uphold court orders in this area. In short, Carter and Ford stressed their ability to manage the nation rather than promising new, dramatic programs to solve social and economic problems.

The Two-Party System

The stability of the American two-party system and the inability of third parties to survive for long periods or to develop a truly national power base are due to several factors. Major parties can survive the loss of a Presidential election because they have local and state bases of political power around which to regroup. However, the winner-take-all nature of American elections deprives the loser of any reward and thus tends to discourage third parties. Between the two major parties, there is a tradition of reasonable agreement and responsible opposition. However, this respect for the minority does not include third parties. By contrast, nations with proportional representation give legislative power to candidates on the basis of their percentage of the total vote. This arrangement encourages more than two parties because it offers the hope of participation in the government through coalition with a larger party.

The Democratic-Republican rivalry that exists at most levels of American politics is a result of the early formation of two parties. This competition has become a tradition and today represents one of the cornerstones of the American political system. This situation has resulted in a set of informal "rules of the game" that determine the methods that may be used in interparty competition and the roles of the majority and minority parties. (These rules were violated by the Watergate offenders, causing even loyal Republicans to withdraw their support from Nixon when it became clear that he was personally involved in the cover-up.) The political conflict that is most visible during Presidential election campaigns exists in local, state, and national legislatures on a continuing basis. The legislative majority tries to translate its program into law, while the minority often opposes such changes.

There is an important difference between the two-party competition that occurs during elections and the competition involved in legislative organization. The many fractions within the parties make unified legislative efforts difficult, since members of the same party often owe their election to support from varied interest groups. In state legislatures, this problem may be seen in rural-urban competition for the resources controlled by the state and has been complicated by the growth of the suburbs as a political power at the expense of the cities. National politics also mirrors the differences that exist within the parties. However, the difficulty of forming solid party blocs in Congress also reflects the need for congresspeople to organize their own reelection campaigns and maintain their own political organizations—private "armies" loyal to the individual rather than the party. This tends to loosen the ties between individuals who hold public office under the banner of a particular party.

The desire for electoral success is central to party organizations at all levels and is a primary concern in legislative action. Officeholders keep a wary eye on public opinion so that they can avoid finding themselves out of step with the public—a situation that could be politically disastrous. This reinforces the pragmatism that is characteristic of American politics.

Third Parties

There are several reasons for the formation of third parties in the United States, and these differ at the various levels of electoral competition. There are numerous examples of third parties at the state level that have been successful over long periods, but third parties at the national level have generally failed. Such parties are usually spinoffs from the major parties and attract supporters who are either more liberal or more conservative than those of the regular Democratic and Republican organizations. In practice, such parties usually enter candidates in a limited number of contests. This makes it impossible for them to gain control of either national or state legislatures and forces successful third-party candidates to ally themselves with a major party caucus in order to have any effect beyond voting on legislation.

New York State has a strong Liberal party, with its principal strength coming from labor unions in New York City; the state also has a Conservative party that is ideologically to the right of the regular Republican organization. James Buckley was elected to the U.S. Senate from New York on the Conservative ticket in 1970; he then joined the Republican caucus. In 1976, Buckley campaigned for reelection on a Conservative/Republican ticket but was defeated. Candidates in New York try to win the endorsement of these third parties as well as that of the major parties because they have demonstrated their strength in terms of votes.

Other third parties that have achieved success are the Farmer-Labor party in Minnesota and the Progressive party in Wisconsin. Such parties usually owe their success to the leadership of a particular individual or a coalition of groups that share basic interests for a short period.[7] These factors are unlikely to enable third parties to last very long, however, especially since there is no political profit in losing elections and little chance for third parties to elect enough legislators to control the government at any level.

Most third-party efforts at the national level have concentrated on presenting a point of view on a particular issue. These efforts may reflect deep dissatisfaction within one wing of a major party. Or they may represent the views of a small minority who use the media's coverage of national elections as a means of gaining exposure for their proposals.

The Dixiecrats were formed in 1948 as a southern offshoot of the Democratic party that objected to the party's liberal stand on civil rights. They nominated Strom Thurmond of South Carolina for the Presidency and carried on an active campaign, especially in the South. In the same year, former Vice President Henry Wallace was nominated for the Presidency by the Progressive party. This group represented the most liberal sector of the Democratic party and broke away because of what it considered a conservative trend in the party. Both Wallace and Thurmond won over 1 million votes in 1948, and these third-party efforts had a lasting impact on Democratic politics. The Dixiecrat organization faded away after the 1948 election, but not until it had stimulated a movement away from a solidly Democratic South and the beginning of true two-party competition in most southern states. The Progressives also faded away, but they had the effect of discouraging the Democrats from becoming more conservative in response to the Dixiecrats demands.

The most recent third-party effort of any importance was George Wallace's 1968 campaign for the Presidency as the candidate of the American Independent party. Wallace represented another rebellion within the Democratic party over social is-

Wisconsin billboard expressing support for George Wallace in the 1976 Presidential primary. Wallace is one of the few third-party candidates to maintain political influence over a period of years.

sues, the most important being school integration. The Wallace support (almost 10 million votes) affected Democratic politics in that it was impressive evidence that many of the party faithful objected to rapid social change. The McGovern defeat in 1972 carried the same message. Accordingly, in 1976 the key Democratic party candidates took much more moderate positions on issues such as busing in an effort to prevent voters from switching to the Republican party.

Presidential elections have offered third parties a platform for expressing their views to a wider audience than they could reach on their own. As Gus Hall, Communist party candidate for President in 1976, put it, "Ours is not an election party. An election is a continuation of our year-round work to raise issues we're interested in." [8] The 1972 Presidential election included candidates representing the American Independent (Schmitz), Socialist Labor (Fisher), Socialist Worker (Jenness or Reed), Communist (Hall), People's (Spock), Prohibition (Munn), America First (Mihalchik), Libertarian (Hospers), and Universal (Green) parties plus others who entered in only one or a few states. These fringe candidates won a total of about 1.4 million votes, and it can be assumed that some of this support was as much a protest against the policies of the major parties as an endorsement of the candidates' views. Other parties such as the Prohibition party, have contested elections for many years but remain outside of the political mainstream because of their limited appeal. [9]

Party Organizations

There are four levels of American electoral competition: Presidential, congressional, state, and local. Party organizations have developed at each of these levels. The degree of competition at any level may range from intense to nonexistent, and there may be one, two, many, or no parties active in that competition. The common thread running through American politics at all levels is the emphasis on winning elections.

Presidential Parties

Discussions of American parties usually concentrate on Presidential elections and, therefore, on Presidential parties. These parties arise around the candidates who have been nominated for the Presidency. In the Presidential elections held since 1950, it has become increasingly clear that the national committees of the two major parties must take a back seat during the campaign. When the national committee is given a major campaign role, it is staffed by people chosen by the candidate himself.

The growth of Presidential party organizations stems from two factors. First, candidates for nomination must build strong organizations and find financial backers if they are to win the primaries or gain delegate support at state conventions. If this organization is able to win the nomination, it is natural for the candidate to use it in the Presidential race. The national committee does not take an active role in the primary process and plays only a supportive role in the election campaign.

The successful Presidential candidate is usually in a position to control the choice of key national committee members. In effect, the power and status of the Presidency give him as much party control as he wants. In discussing the relationship between the President and the leadership of his party, Robert S. Strauss, Democratic national chairman from 1972 to the inauguration of President Carter, described the chairman's position as follows: "When the party's out of office, you're the head; when a Democrat is President, you're a goddamn clerk." [10]

Legislative Parties

Legislative parties form in Congress as both houses are organized along party lines, with the majority party gaining the chairmanship and majority membership of congressional committees. At this level, the party maintains discipline through persuasion if possible, through gentle pressure if not. In most cases, individuals elected to Congress

Democratic Party Chairman Robert Strauss introducing keynote speaker Barbara Jordan at the 1976 national convention. The election of a Democrtic president in 1976 diminished the potential political power of the party chairman, and Strauss resigned to become U.S. Trade Ambassador.

formed their own campaign and fundraising organizations and received little help from the national committee. This makes them fairly independent. But committee assignments, patronage, and "pork barrel" legislation for their states or districts are closely tied to their party loyalty. They may stray from the party on legislation that could be harmful to the public they represent, but on major issues party loyalty is expected.

The legislative parties formed in the House and the Senate are different in certain ways. Representatives are more numerous and serve for shorter terms, so they do not become as well known as senators. They are therefore more dependent on campaign help from party leaders than senators, who are far more independent of the party organization.

The Federal Election Campaign Act of 1974 contained provisions that might strengthen the position of the Democratic and Republican national committees with respect to the legislative parties. Each committee is allowed to raise $2.5 million for senatorial candidates and $4.8 million for House candidates. In addition, individual contributors can give $20,000 to national party committees.[11] The impact of these fund-raising tools on the relationship between the national committees and the legislative parties cannot be judged until after several elections. At present, however, the relationship between the legislative party and the national committee or the President is largely a matter of the personalities involved. Since it is not uncommon for the President to be a member of the party that does not control Congress, the legislative majority often represents the real power structure of its party.

The nature of the party organization that arises around any member of Congress depends on the amount of electoral competition in that member's district. Most House seats are considered "safe," with the turnover usually amounting to no more than 10 percent of the total. The difficulty of unseating an incumbent representative has kept competition within his or her party low and discouraged efforts by the opposition to conduct extensive campaigns. Effective two-party competition is the exception in most congressional districts, and the incumbent is usually regarded as a leader in the local party organization.

Senators have a different party base. Their six-year term gives them time to solidify their position with the voting public and develop their own political coalitions. Senators have an important voice in state party affairs because they can help the state administration get federal aid. The advantages of incumbency are important in terms of fund-raising as well as organizational effort.

Both representatives and senators have the opportunity to build their own political base and win reelection in that way. The major obstacle to long service is the possibility that major political issues may cause voter dissatisfaction with a particular party. In the 1974 congressional elections, held in the aftermath of Watergate, the Democrats gained 49 House seats. This was the largest congressional swing since the Democrats won 49 additional seats in 1958. Undoubtedly, some of the Republican candidates were victims of voter reaction to the Nixon administration's abuses.

State and Local Parties

The smaller publics represented by state and local parties tend to personalize the political process, since officeholders are able to build loyal political followings. The rewards for political activity are more direct at these levels and this gives the average party worker an incentive to participate.

Local competition is often kept within the party "family." An effective local party depends heavily on patronage in local and state jobs to maintain a loyal group of election workers. Turnouts in local primaries are small, and a small but dedicated group of party workers can have a significant impact on the outcome.

Both state and local parties are under the direction of "committees." These may be controlled by officeholders or by party leaders who seek to maintain their political power without running for elective office. Such committees are organized at local, county, and state levels, and their relationships to other organizations at the same level or to the state committees differ widely. The strength of a committee at any level depends on its electoral success and the personalities of the party leaders.

The degree of party activity and the number of people involved vary according to how soon the primary will take place: The closer the election, the more active the party organization. Each committee raises the bulk of its campaign funds, thereby avoiding obligations to other party groups. Patronage or promises of future support are the prime incentives available to the state party organization in attempts to enlist the support of local committees.

Party Leadership

Party leaders are usually people who have spent much of their adult life in political activity or in aspects of the private sector that are closely allied with the political system. Businesspeople and attorneys, for example, often become interested in political activity.

Party leadership is not always a matter of formal office. It may be simply the recognition of a particular individual as holding a position of power in the organization. This may range from almost complete control over the choice of the party's candidates in primary elections to a certain amount of influence in the legislative process. The following account of a party organization's choice of a congressional candidate illustrates what the term *political clout* means in day-to-day politics:

**CIANFRANI
SUPPORTS MYERS**
State Rep. Michael J. (Ozzie) Myers has received influential Democratic

backing to fill the congressional seat vacated by the death of U.S. Rep. William A. Barrett.

Yesterday, Myers, the 32-year-old leader of the 39th Ward in South Philadelphia, was given the nod by both State Sen. Henry J. Cianfrani and Democratic City Councilman James J. Tayoun. . . .

. . . Cianfrani, who was considered a front runner for the seat, said he definitely would not run. . . .

. . . "I know it's mine for the asking," Cianfrani said, "but I've made my decision and I'm with Ozzie and I'll stay with Ozzie." . . .

. . . "I talked to him briefly yesterday," Cianfrani said. "I was just kidding and I said, 'Ozzie, I'm about to run for Congress. What do you think?'

"I'm with you," he told me, and then I said, "Ozzie, I'm not running but I want you to back who I back." So he said, "O.K., Senator, who do you want?" And I said, "You." [12]

In "safe" congressional districts like the one just described, the ability to choose the candidate amounts to putting him or her into office. In this example, the power was held by a political leader whose only official party position was that of ward leader.

The degree of power available to a political leader depends largely on the strength of the party at that level. The party in power can reward loyal followers, while those who are on the outside have little to offer in exchange for electoral support.

The Road to the Top

Political power is attained in various ways at different levels. Local party organizations have a greater impact on election outcomes than party organizations at any other level, and this puts the successful party in a strong position. Many, if not most, city, township, and county election districts are dominated by one party for long periods. In these organizations, power is usually held by people who have come up through the ranks of precinct workers, committee members, and ward leaders. They may have held elective office, though this is not necessary. Some political activists prefer to maintain a low profile, pursue their private professional or financial interests, and content themselves with the knowledge that they have a major influence on the choice of candidates and on party policy.

Local party organizations are the most stable in the American party system. They are active on a continuing basis, with a core of people involved in party affairs for long periods. The selection of candidates is usually controlled by the party and there are rewards for those who participate. The number of active party workers is small compared to the number of voters registered as party members, but they succeed in keeping the party active and effective.

State politics presents a different picture, with the state organization dominated by political leaders from the more populous areas and by elected officials such as the governor and key legislators. State elections attract more media coverage, and this tends to open up the process of selecting candidates and allow people to run for office without coming up through the party ranks. All a candidate for state office needs is the ability to raise campaign funds without the aid of the party. This enables him or her to enter the primary with a chance of success. Name recognition is extremely important in state contests, and this can be gained through media publicity. This contrasts with the difficulty local candidates face in conducting independent campaigns owing to the high cost of media advertising in local areas.

New York Congresswoman Bella Abzug visiting Cambodia. Such visits are an important way for members of Congress to maintain public visibility.

State political organizations lack the unity of local parties because most of the participants have a firmer base in their local party than they can develop at the state level. This is especially true of states with big-city organizations within the party structure. State parties are most effective in states with largely rural populations. Here, county politics will probably dominate, and political leaders at this level will rise to the top in state organizations.

Some state election laws allow parties to endorse candidates before the primaries. Such laws give more power to the party organizations. In other states, such endorsements are prohibited, and this opens up the nominating process to anyone who can finance a campaign.

The coalition nature of the national parties reduces the influence of the party's national committee and places real power in the hands of individuals who represent important groups within the party. Many of these are chosen by state party organizations to serve on the national committees, but their influence stems from the power of the interest groups they represent. National political power thus differs markedly from local and state political power—the road to the top is less formal and there are more possible routes. National politics is concerned with big stakes—nothing less than control of Congress and the White House so that the goal of the groups that make up the parties may be achieved.

There is much greater fluidity in national politics than in local or state politics. This is due to the meaningful two-party competition that exists in Presidential elections as compared to the tendency toward one-party domination in local and state contests. The realistic opportunity for either party to gain control of the White House leads to a sharing of national power by those who represent major interests within the party and those who have made themselves known as potential Presidential candidates. These individuals have usually proved their political appeal in gubernatorial or congressional races and built upon their positions to establish a political power base. In national politics, therefore, it is not necessary to come up through the party ranks to gain influence. Nothing succeeds like winning, and the person who wins elections at the state or congressional level has a head start toward national office. Senators and representatives provide most of the national political leadership on a continuing basis because of their relatively long terms of office. This gives the party structure some permanence but in no way prevents members of Congress from running for the Presidency.

The Rank and File

It is impossible to define the words Republican and Democrat precisely. The most common uses of these words are based on party identification and voter registration. But these meanings leave out the wide range of political loyalty, activity, and disinterest that exists within both parties. The paid professional staffs of the Republican and Democratic parties are small, and most of the work is done by the relatively small group of party activists who give their time to the organization. These people are attracted to politics for a variety of reasons. Some enjoy the social relationships; some like the feeling of participating in the political system; and others seek personal gain in the form of employment or financial reward. The number of party activists is small in relation to the number of people registered as members of the party.

Elections stimulate the party activists to maximum effort and increase the number of party workers that can be called upon to help. Much of the campaign effort is provided by groups within the party coalition who can recruit their members for party activity. This is the real basis of labor's political power. The extent to which unions can influence the votes of their members is questionable, but their organizational and fund-raising talents have been demonstrated over and over again. These abilities are especially important in primary contests because of the low turnouts for such elections.

The rank-and-file are less ideologically oriented than party leaders and are attracted to a particular party because of shared interests, potential rewards, or the opportunity to associate with people they admire. Since many areas have little or no two-party competition, individuals may have little choice but to work for the dominant party. In contrast, the party leaders are more likely to hold ideological beliefs, and long party service tends to intensify those beliefs.

Party Performance

The effectiveness of parties in the American political system is measured by their success in contesting elections, organizing the legislative branch of the government, and serving as a link between the government and the people. The parties are highly visible political organizations, and much of the recent dissatisfaction with politics is directed at the Republican and Democratic parties. Lack of ideological unity and weaknesses of organizational structure prevent the parties from acting as "responsible" parties. However, more important than whether or not the United States has party government is the contribution the parties make to the political system. Politics is a dynamic force that leads to change and just as the relative power of the Presidency, Congress, and the Supreme Court adjust to new realities, so the party system is continually undergoing change.

Contesting Elections

The major function of the political parties is to contest elections in order to gain control of the government. Obviously, the Democratic and Republican parties carry on intensive campaigns in national elections. The enthusiasm with which local and state

President Harry S Truman holding an early edition of the Chicago Tribune after his upset victory over Thomas E. Dewey in 1948.

elections are contested is related to the chance of success. While a national party organization cannot pick its candidate, it is very unlikely that a Presidential candidate will emerge from obscurity and win the nomination. The success of Jimmy Carter was a rare case in which a candidate with little previous national exposure was able to gain enough recognition through primary victories to win the Democratic party nomination and go on to win the election. However, Carter had an effective political base in the South. Eisenhower was the last President to be elected without an independent political power base, but he was hardly an unknown. Thus, Presidential candidates can come from within party ranks at the state or national level, but the final choice is make as a result of the primary campaign and the nominating convention. This denies the party leadership the power to choose Presidential candidates but opens up participation to larger numbers of people.

The tendency of Presidential candidates to build their own personal campaign organizations rather than using the national committee makes little real difference in the political process. The President is in a position to control the national committee, while the defeated candidate has limited influence unless he regains a political base. Barry Goldwater, George McGovern, and Hubert Humphrey were able to win reelection to the Senate and thus maintain considerable power within the party.

The impression that the parties fail to offer meaningful alternatives in Presidential elections is the most frequent criticism of the party system. This ignores the broad agreement that exists between the major parties on most major questions, with new policies taking the form of small changes rather than sweeping new programs. The Roosevelt years were marked by dramatic change, but such changes have not been called for since the Depression, and the widespread agreement necessary for that degree of change has not occurred. Democratic government cannot move too far ahead of public opinion, regardless of the desires of political leadership.

The Constitutional provision for the election of a President independent of Congress also militates against issue-based elections. Neither the executive branch nor Congress can get its programs passed without the aid of the other, and even in cases of one-party control of both the White House and Congress there is built-in competition between the two branches. While divided government is considered unhealthy by most political scientists, a 1976 Harris survey revealed that by a 40-38 percent margin voters preferred having different parties in control of Congress and the White House.[13] The frequency with which this situation occurs indicates that the public either does not believe it prevents effective government or fears the results of putting too much power in the hands of either party.

Organizing the Legislature

Congressional majorities are often accused of being unable to pass legislation to solve the nation's problems. This inability reflects the diverse interests represented within the parties, the possiblility of veto by the President, limited national resources, and the realization that the government cannot solve all the nation's problems. Any of these factors may be more important than the others at any particular time.

The struggle between President Ford and the Democratic majority in Congress during the economic recession of 1974-1975 caused great national concern and brought forth most of the obstacles to legislative action just mentioned. The recession was accompanied by rising budget deficits, thus putting limits on the spending of even the most liberal congressperson. The President promised to veto any programs calling for large increases in federal spending. This discouraged intensive efforts to pass any legislation that was likely to be vetoed, with little chance that a veto could be overridden.

Perhaps more important than these

political factors was the lack of agreement among economists on how to deal with the problem. Led by Federal Reserve Chairman, Arthur Burns, one group of economists viewed inflation as more serious than unemployment and said, basically, that the nation would have to wait for economic recovery rather than forcing it by means of higher spending. The other economic view was that the nation must provide jobs at any cost, thereby spending its way back to economic health. President Ford followed Burns' advice, and the economic recovery was under way by early 1976.

Party control of Congress can be translated into legislative action only if the congressional majority is unified. The coalitions that make up the American parties represent such varied interests that intraparty differences are unavoidable. The massive soical programs passed in the 1960s are evidence that the legislative majority can act decisively, if not speedily, to make laws that will win popular support. Thus, though the American political system lacks the degree of party government that lends itself to dramatic change, the party leadership in Congress has power and can be effective with popular support, money, and a lack of determined Presidential opposition. It is unlikely that the President would strongly oppose any program that the public clearly favored.

The Party and the People

Local politics is where most of the dialogue between individuals and party leaders occurs. Citizens and politicians at this level are more likely to share common concerns, and the party organization is more likely to be able to act in the local area. In contrast, parties at the national and state levels are concerned primarily with the electoral and legislative processes and are less able to communicate directly with the people. Instead, they depend on the channels of communication provided by the media and interest groups. Likewise, they are seldom in a position to offer as much help to the individual citizen as local party officials.

The dominance of parties in most local districts is evidence that party organizations at this level have succeeded in forging meaningful links with their public. Naturally, as the size of the public increases and party members become more diverse, there is a weakening of the dialogue between people and party.

The Balance of Political Power

The 1976 elections resulted in Democratic victories at all levels of competition. In addition to electing Carter President, the Democratic party emerged with a 3-2 edge in the Senate, more than two-thirds of the House, 38 governorships, control of both houses in 36 state legislatures, and control of most of the nation's major cities. In the words of one political columnist, "Nowhere in the free world does a political party have such an encompassing grip on a country as Democrats presently have in the United States." [14] Given the fact of Democratic political strength, those who predict the end of the Republican party appear to have good reason for concern. However, the diffusion of power among the national, state, and local levels of government makes it impossible for the Democratic party to take full advantage of its overall position.

Even at the national level, there is little reason to believe the Democratic party will be able to use its control of the White House and Congress to keep itself in power for a long time. Political analyst Richard Scammon notes that "with uni-government, monopoly control by one party, people can blame everything, anything—from inflation to the fact that their daughter ran away with the postman—on the Democrats. Then the Republicans will make gains again." [15] Scammon's observation is supported by the fact that in the past four Presidential elections—1964, 1968, 1972, and 1976—Massachusetts and Arizona were the only states in which the electoral votes were won by the candidates of the same party in each election.

The Future of American Political Parties

The impact of the Federal Campaign Spending Act will play an important role in the future of the major parties, especially at the national level. The provision for federal funding of Presidential elections puts power in the hands of the national committees which receive campaign funds in behalf of the candidates as well as funds for the national conventions. These two provisions will probably cause a shift from candidate-controlled organizations to stronger national party organizations. They will also encourage a more effective opposition led by the national committee of the "out" party. [16]

It is likely that many states will pass similar legislation limiting campaign spending in Senate and House contests. If this happens, the same pressures that militate against personality-based Presidential parties will also operate at the congressional level, resulting in more unified, better-disciplined legislative parties whose leaders will have the power to reward those who cooperate and punish those who do not. Such a tightening of the organizational structures of the Presidential and congressional parties would bring the nation closer to party responsibility and party government. The nature of the federal system requires congresspeople to represent their states or districts as well as pursuing the interests of the nation as a whole. This dual role makes the level of party responsibility found in European democracies unlikely but offers the hope of more effective legislative action.

An important barrier to party government in the United States is the existence of interest groups that have access to government at all levels and often bypass the party organizations.

The head of a large organization like the AFL-CIO does not need a party official to arrange for a meeting with the President. This fact reduces the potential rewards of party loyalty, and powerful groups are therefore unwilling to throw their support to either party. If the Democratic or Republican party is sure of the backing of a particular group, this reduces the pressure on the party to support that group's demands. Even groups that are members of the coalitions that make up the major parties often support candidates of the other party in certain election contests. Thus, the political power of interest groups seems to limit the power of political parties.

Summary

American parties appear to be changing from political coalitions dominated by interest groups to broad-based parties depending less on the concept of coalition than on appeals to the individual citizen. Carter's primary victories were marked by his appeal to a cross-section of the public, despite his lack of organized group support and in some cases intense opposition. Many citizens seem to be loosening their emotional ties to the groups with which they formerly identified including the political parties themselves. This does not mean the end of the American party system. Rather it can be viewed as the dawning of a new political day, with Democratic and Republican officals finding it necessary to change their methods in light of the voter's new-found independence from parties and interest groups.

Majority parties in Congress are usually unable to translate their numerical advantage into effective legislative programs. One reason is the variety of the publics represented by congresspeople and the need to build and maintain a personal political base. In addition, the constitutional system of checks and balances leads to competition and conflict between the executive and legislative branches. Thus, even when the congressional majority and the President are members of the same party Congress is unlikely to be able to put a unified legislative program into effect during the President's term of office. Similarly, the President has a national public and this results in restrictions and priorities that are not necessarily the same as those of his fellow party members in Congress.

The structure of the American political system and the many levels of electoral competition appear to prevent the development of a system in which the majority and opposition parties set forth programs that they can be expected to put into effect if they gain control of the White House and Congress. The tendency toward split-ticket voting leads to the strong possibility of a Republican President facing a Democratic Congress, and this type of divided government makes a system of party government and responsible parties impossible. There is no indication that the American people are unhappy with this arrangement, however. The fear of putting too much power in the hands of one group appears to outweigh the untidiness of the system.

NOTES

[1] "Toward a More Responsible Two-Party System," *American Political Science Review,* **XLIV,** Supp. (September 1950), p. 17.

[2] Quoted in Richard Hofstadter, *The Idea of a Party System* (Berkeley: University of California Press, 1969), p. 2.

[3] Hugh A. Bone, *American Politics and the Party System,* 4th ed. (New York: McGraw-Hill, 1971), pp. 28-29.

[4] This thesis is thoroughly explored in James M. Burns, *The Deadlock of Democracy: Four Party Politics in America* (Englewood Cliffs, N.J.: Prentice-Hall, 1963).

[5] Reprinted by permission, *The Philadelphia Inquirer,* October 10, 1974, p. 3-A.

[6] Herbert McClosky, Paul J. Hoffman, and Rosemary O'Hara, "Issue Conflict and Consensus Among Party Leaders and Followers," *American Political Science Review* **54,** No. 2. (June 1960): 425-26.

[7] Judson L. James, *American Political Parties* (New York: Pegasus, 1969), p. 48.

[8] Quoted by Richard Halloran, "Gus Hall, Communist Candidate, Says Goal Is Just to Raise Issues," in *The New York Times,* October 29, 1976, p. A20.

[9] V. O. Key, Jr. *Politics, Parties and Pressure Groups,* 5th ed. (New York: Thomas Y. Crowell, 1964), p. 255.

[10] Quoted by Myra MacPherson, "Party in, Strauss Waltzing Out," in the *New York Post,* November 9, 1976, p. 5.

[11] Warren Weaver, Jr., in *The New York Times,* August 1, 1976, p. E3.

[12] "Cianfrani Supports Myers," *The Evening Bulletin,* April 15, 1976, p. E-3. Reprinted by permission of the Evening and Sunday Bulletin.

[13] *The Harris Survey,* September 27, 1976.

[14] Clayton Fritchey in the *New York Post,* November 9, 1976, p. 33.

[15] Quoted in *Time,* November 15, 1976, p. 37.

[16] Murray S. Stedman, Jr., "Political Parties," in *Modernizing American Government,* Murray S. Stedman, ed. (Englewood Cliffs, N.J.: Prentice-Hall, 1968), pp. 120-121.

CHAPTER 8 CROSSWORD PUZZLE

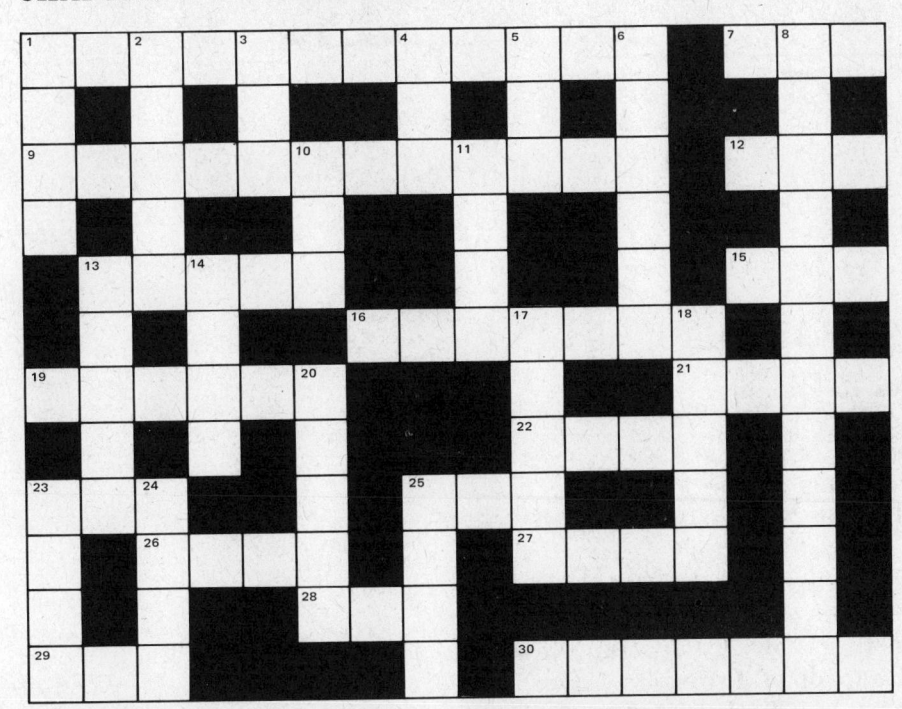

27. Watch or clock face
28. One-member electoral districts have encouraged the development of a ___ party system.
29. Political parties are ___ part of the Constitutional framework.
30. Control of Congress and the Presidency by different parties is called ___ government.

Down
1. Duo
2. The Witch of ___
3. Sprite; elf
4. "Winken, Blinken, and ___"
5. ___ Fleming (creator of James Bond)
6. Levels
8. Party leaders are more likely to reflect liberal-___ ideology than the average party identifier.
10. Terminate
11. Opposite of "odd"
13. Food staple
14. Opposite of "closed"
17. ___ parties have been unable to build followings that have endured in competition with the Democrats and Republicans.
18. Path
20. Mini or maxi ___
23. Idi ___ (Uganda's leader)
24. Thin, pointed weapon
25. Opposite of "rich"

Across
1. Party competition is most notable in ___ elections.
7. ___ cube
9. Most Americans appear to be moving away from party regularity toward a greater degree of voting ___.
12. Writing fluid
13. The Democratic and Republican parties appeal to a ___ base of the electorate.
15. Mediterranean or Aegean
16. Political parties ___ elections in order to control the reins of government.
19. There are many ___ of American party activity.
21. Speak wildly
22. Thought
23. ___, subtract, multiply, and divide
25. ___cent
26. State; verify

CHAPTER 9
THE MEDIA

CHAPTER OUTLINE

Questions to Consider
Introduction
The Modern Media
Characteristics of the Media
To Publish or Not to Publish
    The Bay of Pigs
    Counter-Spy and the CIA
Interpretation of the News
    Reporting Versus Creating News
    The Impact of Intensive Coverage
    Creating a Chain Reaction
Freedom of the Press and the Judicial Process
The Media and the Government
    The Personal Touch
    To the People—with Media Support
    The News Leak
    The Backgrounder
    Trial Balloons
The Media and the Public
Freedom and Fairness
Summary

QUESTIONS TO CONSIDER

The media have become an increasingly important political institution. They are the primary source of political information for most Americans and provide an important link between the people and the political system. But how objective is news reporting? What is the nature of the ownership of the leading television stations and newspapers? Does this have an effect on how news is presented?

There is frequent conflict between the public's right to know and the government's need for secrecy in matters of national security. How can a balance between these two values be achieved? Is freedom of the press an absolute value or should it be limited in order to protect other constitutional rights? Another interesting question is that of whether the media report the news or "create" it. Does intense coverage have the effect of "making" news rather than simply reporting it? Can it have other effects?

The media are the major means by which the government communicates with the people. To what extent should the media cooperate with the government in deciding what to publish? What is a news leak? a backgrounder? a trial balloon?

In addition to their primary role of reporting events, the media have taken an increasingly active investigatory role. Is this an appropriate activity for them? What is its impact on the political environment? Clearly, the media have emerged as an important institution with much potential for political influence.

Introduction

Were it left to me to decide whether we should have a government without newspapers, or newspapers without a government, I should not hesitate a moment to prefer the latter.
—Thomas Jefferson

The strong feelings expressed by Jefferson about the need for a free press are reflected in the First Amendment to the Constitution: "Congress shall make no law...abridging the freedom of speech, or of the press." Few national institutions have been as controversial as the press—or the media—in recent years. While few would argue that the First Amendment guarantees should be abridged, there is increasing debate about the responsibilities implied by such freedom.

Newspapers, periodicals, television, and radio make up what are often called the mass media. The role of the media has not changed very much since the early years of the Republic, but their impact on the nation has changed dramatically. They continue to be the primary source of news for the people and, in turn, offer the administration a chance to find out what impact present or future actions are likely to have on public opinion. While the media support the government in a general sense, they also oppose it. No government official takes kindly to criticism or accusations of wrongdoing, and the media are blamed for any adverse public reaction such as the diminishing popular support for the Vietnam War in the late 1960s or the decline of the Nixon administration after the 1972 election. In a sense, then, the media serve as a watchdog on governmental activity and have the greatest potential for relaying the government's views to the public. However, it is not clear whether the average citizen pays enough attention to news stories or telecasts to be swayed by them.

The watchword of news reporting is to separate objective treatment of events—the presentation of facts in context—from editorializing—subjective value judgments of what the facts mean to the nation. This is perhaps the most difficult part of the media's role. The very choice of which news to headline in newspapers or periodicals, or the choice of the lead story on the nightly television news, involves the news editor's opinion on their importance.

It is also hard to measure the media's influence on public opinion. The question of whether the media are makers or reporters of news, and the extent to which the First Amendment guarantee of press freedom takes precedence over other constitutional guarantees, are matters of controversy.

The Modern Media

The press of Jefferson's time consisted of numerous papers, or pamphlets, distributed locally throughout the colonies. Anyone with access to a printing press could express an opinion, and anyone who was interested could easily be exposed to a variety of political opinions. Today, "the press" (i.e., the media) includes all the major means of communication. A significant difference in the media's news activity today as compared with earlier years is the amount of power and influence in the hands of a few television and radio networks, newspaper chains, and wire services. A 1969 *Wall Street Journal* study estimated that 75 percent of the local, national, and international news available to the American people comes from the Associated Press (AP) and United Press International (UPI).[1] The concentration of ownership of TV stations is even more striking. There were 218 stations in the top 50 markets in the United States in 1971. Only 27 percent of these were singly owned and not associated with any newspaper, while 71.6 percent were part of a group owning more than one station.[2] The high degree of centralization in the mass media should be kept in mind in considering their impact on the American political system.

Characteristics of the Media

Television and radio stations, newspapers, and periodicals are profit-seeking business enterprises. This makes entertainment value a primary concern in determining their policies. The amount of space and time to devote to political news and whether to engage in investigative reporting are primarily economic, not political, decisions. Local news is usually more important to the media audience than national news. Accordingly, the front pages of most newspapers and the TV news are heavily oriented toward local news and information. One has only to watch the daily weather forecast on TV to appreciate this fact.

In their efforts to attract viewers or readers and, thus, advertising revenues, the media try to avoid controversy. "Organized crime" is fair game because most citizens are law-abiding. But taking partisan stands on political issues is a "no win" proposition for most TV stations and newspapers. There is a big difference between news broadcasts that originate with the network and those that come from local stations. The function of network news is to emphasize national issues, but even here controversy is usually avoided, and any management of the news centers on decisions as to what stories to feature rather than interpretation of the news. Similarly, few newspapers reach a national audience. *The New York Times, The Washington Post*, and *The Christian Science Monitor* have a national impact in terms of the type of public they reach—the richer, better educated, and more politically interested and influential citizens, as well as government officials. Both the President and members of Congress need to check the political wind, and these papers are an important source of information.

The Watergate expose, carried on largely by *The Washington Post*, is often mentioned as an example of the importance of a free press in checking out possible abuses of power. However, while the press is important as a safeguard against such abuses, the Watergate revelations are a poor example. It can be assumed that among the several thousand reporters in Washington there were several who had an inkling of the background of the Watergate break-in, but it fell to Robert Woodward and Carl Bernstein, two junior reporters with the *Post* to develop the story. As the plot thickened, the media jumped in *en masse*. By and large, however, the media are establishment-oriented. They are large business enterprises with a stake in political stability. The notion of journalists as wild-eyed radicals seeking to topple the government was popularized by Spiro Agnew and other officials in the Nixon administration and accepted by many Americans, but it is as mistaken as the view that the media are above criticism.

The practical result of the concentration of ownership of the major media is that three TV networks—ABC, NBC, and CBS—and a handful of influential newspapers and wire services are the primary sources of the nation's news. This concentration of power increases the concern over setting legal guidelines for what should be published in the interest of the public's right to know and what should be suppressed in the national interest or in order to protect other constitutional rights. Those who reject any form of governmental regulation of the media as an abridgment of First Amendment freedoms must recognize that no freedom is absolute and that the media have an obligation to consider the national interest and the rights of others.

To Publish or Not to Publish

The major media have reporters throughout the world, and these reporters often become aware of secret military or diplomatic plans. In addition, dissatisfied officials may provide reporters with classified (i.e., secret) information. (It is very difficult to keep anything a secret if the planning involves more than a handful of people with close personal ties to each other.) The press faces a dilemma in deciding whether to publish such information. If it does not publish important news, the press is failing in its responsibility to report the news objectively and keep the public informed. But if it publishes classified information the interests of the nation may be damaged.

While the major news media are most likely to uncover classified information, they are by no means the only ones to face such a dilemma. Two recent examples illustrate the extent of the problem and the difficulty of deciding whether to publish or not to publish.

The Bay of Pigs

The Bay of Pigs affair was intended to give the impression of an invasion by a band of Cuban exiles with no U.S. involvement. Five days before the invasion, on April 12, 1961, President Kennedy told a news conference that "there will not be, under any conditions, any intervention in Cuba by United States armed forces, and this Government will do everything it possibly can... to make sure that there are no Americans involved in actions inside Cuba." [3] In the weeks before the invasion, however, the press had become aware that the United States was recruiting and training Cuban exiles for some type of military operation. [4] *The New York Times* is believed to have received detailed information about the invasion but, after much debate, to have decided against publishing the information in the interest of national security. Later, President Kennedy expressed the wish that the *Times* had exposed the plan and thus caused it to be canceled. [5] News of a secret military nature is usually viewed as not within the public's right to know. In the case of the Bay of Pigs, however, breaking the story might have saved the nation much embarrassment, not to mention the lives of the Cubans who died in the ill-fated invasion.

Counter-Spy and the CIA

Counter-Spy was a small investigative publication that directed most of its efforts toward exposing undercover CIA activities. In the course of its investigations, it uncovered the names of CIA agents stationed at embassies around the world and published them. In early 1976, after the story had appeared, CIA agent Robert Welch was assassinated in Athens. This incident led to heated debate about the responsibilities of the press. David Sanford, managing editor of *The New Republic* responded to the question of whether or not he would have published the agent's name as follows:

Of course I would have published his name. The press is not in the business of serving the interests of the Central Intelligence Agency as the CIA construes them. The threat of death is an occupational hazard suffered by persons who would be covert agents of the CIA abroad.

Part of an agent's job is to withdraw undetected. The press has other duties, one of which is to report fully and accurately the news, without subjecting the story to some arbitrary test of what constituted the "national interest." [6]

John D. Lofton, on the other hand, that "this formulation [is] not only preposterous and outrageous but very, very dangerous to the First Amendment press freedoms enjoyed by those who practice journalism for a living." [7] He went on to say that unless the press exercises self-restraint it faces the danger of having some type of control imposed upon it.

One of the basic problems involved in such issues is the ambiguity of the "national interest." This is a concept that arouses much controversy as people attempt to decide whether the nation's interests will be better served by exposure of all governmental activity or by selective reporting.

Interpretation of the News

The media like to view themselves as objective reporters and observers of political events. When they deal with issues subjectively—that is, present their interpretations of political events—the media usually present contrasting views. For example, a newspaper will print the editor's opinions on the editorial page along with syndicated columnists representing other interpretations of the news. TV and radio stations also label parts of their broadcasts as representing the views of the reporter rather than the opinion of the station's management. In some cases, the announcer may present his or her views as those of the management and invite conflicting opinions.

The problem of objectivity does not arise in connection with these straightforward expressions of opinion. Rather, it comes up in connection with questions of emphasis, such as what should be front-page news or the lead story in a TV newscast. Also, the interpretation of the news by reporters, the impression conveyed by an announcer's tone of voice or facial expressions, or the wording of a headline can have a significant impact on the audience.

Any viewer of the CBS evening news during the course of the Watergate revelations saw Dan Rather speaking, with the White House in the background, Rather's serious manner clearly indicated his view of the efforts of the White House staff to suppress the story. There was no distortion of the facts, but even the most insensitive viewer had no trouble knowing where Rather stood on the issue. This is not a criticism of Mr. Rather but an example of the difficulty the visual media face in separating the objective from the subjective.

Newspapers and periodicals are completely dependent on the written word, plus photos and cartoons. Here again, the issue is not deliberate distortion of the news but the extent to which the impact on the public is a result of the way the news is presented and how often the basic story is headlined.

The way news is presented to the public can often be very subjective. When the media reported the illegal activities of the Nixon administration, they expressed shock and dismay at these abuses of official power. However, when congressional investigations exposed similar activities that had occurred in the Kennedy and Johnson years they reported the findings objectively and showed less indignation. This might have been due to the media's perception that the public had become bored with stories of illegal actions by the executive branch, or it might have resulted from unwillingness to attack former Presidents who had since died.

Everyone has a right to be subjective. However, along with the First Amendment freedom of the press goes the responsibility to strive for a standard of fairness, to present opposing views and examine one's own actions as well as those of others. Revelations of corporate bribes to foreign officials were given maximum publicity in 1975-1976 by the major newspapers and TV networks and condemned in many editorials. But when faced with the accusation that they frequently bribed foreign officials to facilitate the shipment of film for news broadcasts, the TV networks claimed that such bribes were a necessary evil. This sort of double standard makes the media less believable. As John B. Oakes, editor of the *New York Times'* editorial page, wrote,

Newspapermen have a special obligation to retain public confidence through conscious and deliberate efforts to open themselves to the public, to pay particular attention to complaints of unfairness, inaccuracy, bias, vindictiveness—that is, to make ourselves *voluntarily* accountable. Some newspapers have already gone a considerable distance in doing just this—but not many and certainly not enough. [8]

This description of the problems involved in presenting and interpreting the news illustrates the sensitivity of some media leaders to these problems.

The press is in a unique position in American society. Free from governmental control, it could be a meaningful safeguard of a free society. But if it is colored by personal ambition or prejudice, it could bring about a counterreaction that would threaten the freedom it now enjoys. In turn, this would weaken its ability to act as a restraint on the actions of the government.

Reporting Versus Creating News

The media are often accused of "creating" news by emphasizing certain events rather than simply reporting them. They may be accused of being "out to get" a particular political figure, to sabotage court-ordered busing by continuing to report on violence in Louisville and Boston, or to weaken the nation by constantly attacking the FBI and the CIA for engaging in illegal activities. Such stories are not "made up" by journalists any more than Watergate was a media plot to "get" Richard Nixon. The press reports what is happening and may subjectively decide that a particular story should get continued coverage, but there is no indication that the media have the power to make an issue important to the American public or to make Congress take any particular action.

The failure of gun control legislation over the years is a good example of the inability of the media to make news or create intense public opinion. Despite the vivid coverage of the assassinations of John F. Kennedy, Robert Kennedy, and Martin Luther King and a large number of newspaper editorials and TV documentaries calling for gun control, Congress has not passed such legislation. The power of the press to make news is largely in the imagination of those who see the media as the root of the nation's troubles or those within the media who see themselves as "movers and shakers" rather than simply as journalists.

In the final analysis, the media are a channel of communication rather than a tool for shaping public opinions. If a particular event is interesting to the public, there will undoubtedly be greater coverage of that event. But emphasis or even overemphasis does not negate the fact that the media are reporting what is actually happening. One of the safeguards against any attempt to "make" news is the competitive nature of the industry. The 5-year, $5 million contract signed by Barbara Walters in 1976 to co-host the ABC evening news gives some idea of the efforts the media make to attract the viewing audience. With such investments at stake, they will not allow an overzealous journalist "make" news or carry on a crusade against a public figure.

Media leaders are pragmatic about protecting their investments while informing and entertaining the public. This not only keeps them from "creating" news but also makes it unlikely that they will refrain from publishing stories that may be embarrassing to the government on other than national security grounds. This, in turn, leads to the question of the media's ability to emphasize a news story until it becomes important to the public.

The Impact of Intensive Coverage

The resignation of Richard Nixon was followed by a series of congressional investigations into the activities of governmental agencies. At first, revelations of illegal actions by the FBI and the CIA brought cries of indignation from congresspeople, the media, and the public. But after endless revelations and seemingly continuous congressional hearings on the matter, "spy stories" lost their appeal to the public and were moved to the inside pages of the newspapers and the end of the evening news. What accounted for this reduction of emphasis? According to then Senator Walter Mondale, "the public became numb with bad news."[9] Added to this lack of interest were political factors that tended to mute the impact of the news. As Leslie H. Gelb of the *New York Times* put it,

As the details of covert operations, illegal wiretappings and mail openings became old news, public interest waned, and Congressional committees and executive agencies turned inward, settling their disputes along the usual lines of committee turf, bureaucratic tactics and access to information.[10]

The contrast between the intensity of public opinion regarding Watergate and the lack of interest in the CIA and FBI investigations illustrates the role the media can play in arousing public interest in a particular issue and their limited control over the intensity of public opinion. Political events compete for an individual's attention with a great many other, more personal concerns. For such events to arouse intense opinions and more than passing interest, the information in the media must have more than shock value. It must portray the sense that something has happened that could affect the individual in a more personal way than most political events.

Clearly, the steady stream of revelations that followed the Watergate break-in presented a picture of the disintegration of democratic processes that was viewed as a personal threat by most of the American public. But the major factor in the formation of the widely shared opinion that Nixon must resign was the revelation that he and other high administration officials had consistently lied—the so-called cover-up. This was at odds with the basic values of most citizens. In contrast, public interpretation of the "spy stories" appeared to represent disapproval of the methods used by the FBI and the CIA along with general sympathy with their goals. As mentioned in Chapter 2, most Americans agree with the First Amendment freedoms in general but tolerate limitations on those freedoms in a "good cause." Illegal harassment of communists, student radicals, or the Ku Klux Klan does not appear to be viewed as a threat by the average citizen. Thus, the media can present an issue to the public and emphasize its importance by placing it in the limelight, but the competitive nature of the communications business dictates that in the long run such emphasis is determined by public reactions and not by news editors.

Creating a Chain Reaction

One of the troublesome aspects of the impact of a free press is the extent to which sensational reporting may lead to results that are harmful to society. Debate has long raged over the role of TV in encouraging violence, and there appears to be a relationship between intensive coverage of such events as hijackings, bomb scares, and assassinations and a tendency for such events to multiply. For example, on September 22, 1975, Sara Jane Moore tried to shoot President Ford in San

President Ford visiting Sacramento, California, moments before an assassination attempt by Lynn Fromme in 1975. There is controversy over the impact of press sensationalism concerning such events.

Francisco. An earlier assassination attempt by Lynette Alice (Squeaky) Fromme had occurred on September 5 in Sacramento. Many people believed the second attempt had been inspired by the publicity given the first one—both *Time* and *Newsweek* had pictures of Ms. Fromme on the covers of their September 15 issues. Vice President Nelson Rockefeller commented on these events as follows:

Let's stop talking about it. Let's stop putting it on the front pages and on television. Psychiatrists say every time there is any publicity, it is stimulating to the unstable.[11]

Such events raise the question of what degree of self-discipline the media should use in presenting sensational news and, indeed, whether the media have the right to censor news even if such censorship is self-imposed. As Osborne Elliot, editor in chief of *Newsweek* puts it,

Our first responsibility is to report the news to our readers as accurately and as unbiased as possible.

When the President becomes a target twice in 17 days, I don't think it's sensationalizing to report these events. It's far more helpful to report such awful events and to analyze them calmly and with restraint than to bury them and to pretend they didn't happen.[12]

It is a sign of the potential impact of news coverage that such questions became matters of controversy. Even more debatable, however, are cases in which the First Amendment guarantee of freedom of the press conflicts with other constitutional rights.

Freedom of the Press and the Judicial Process

Since the 1960s, there has been an increase in court orders barring the press from pretrial release of facts about a case that might influence potential jurors. The problem involved is the conflict between the rights of the accused and the right of the people to know.

There are no clear guidelines from the courts as to what, if any, restraint may be legally imposed on the press. Participants in the Watergate cover-up trial were ordered by U.S. Judge John J. Sirica not to talk to the press, while Judge Gerhard Gesell, also hearing a Watergate-related trial, told Dwight Chapin, the defendant, that there were no restrictions on his communications with the press.[13] The concern of the court is that guilty people may have their convictions reversed because pretrial publicity made the "fair" trial guaranteed by the Sixth Amendment impossible or, on the other hand, that individuals may be wrongfully convicted because of such publicity. A contrasting opinion was expressed by Harold Medina, a senior judge on the U.S. Court of Appeals for the Seventh Circuit, as follows:

As I never did like censorship of any kind, I have a little unsolicited advice to the news media.

First, I would stand squarely on the First Amendment itself. I used to think guidelines might be helpful. Now I believe them a snare and delusion. And the same is true of legislation....

Second, I would make no compromises and no concessions of any kind.

Third, I say fight like tigers every inch of the way.[14]

The activity of the press in investigating criminal cases often works to the benefit of the accused. Many unjustly indicted or convicted individuals owe their ultimate acquittal to the refusal of the media to believe they are guilty. The presence of reporters at the scene of a crime also acts as an important safeguard of the rights of the accused. However, the press can also have a harmful impact on the interests of both the accused and the public.

The arguments of those who would limit the right of the press to release certain facts during the pretrial period usually refer to cases in which an avalanche of pretrial publicity has occurred. One example is the Charles Manson case, which involved multiple killings by the "Manson family." Others involve convictions being reversed, such as in the case of Sam Sheppard, the Cleveland doctor accused of murdering his wife. In both cases, the impact of pretrial publicity is believed to have made a fair trial by an impartial jury impossible. In 1976, however, the Supreme Court banned judicial orders prohibiting the publication of information about such cases, except in rare circumstances.

Closely allied to the problem of pretrial publicity is that of "leaks" of

Charles Manson being led to the courtroom during his trial for the Tate-LaBianca murders in 1970. Defendants in highly publicized criminal cases, such as Manson, may have their right to a free trial impeded by pretrial publicity.

the public, the fact remains that newscasts attract wide audiences and news magazines have large circulations, while the daily papers use headlines to sell their product. This emphasis on news reporting brings the media into daily contact and often conflict with government at all levels. The relationship between the media and the government is a two-way street in the sense that the media need the government to supply information and the government needs the media as its most important channel of communication with the public; however, the media's emphasis on bad news brings it into conflict with the government's effort to highlight good news.

One of the sources of conflict between the government and the media is the fact that good news is seldom considered newsworthy while bad news tends to dominate newspaper headlines and TV newscasts. High unemployment figures are featured by the press along with the remedies proposed by various political figures. The fact that more people are employed than ever before is mentioned only in passing. Stories of governmental cor-

ruption remain in the headlines as long as editors think the public is interested in the story, but an editor who headlined the honesty of the overwhelming majority of public officials would be considered a fool. The plain fact is that good or usual news is not news to the media, whereas bad or unusual news attracts the attention of the public.

Public officials continually try to get public support for their policies as well as for themselves as individuals. It is hard to separate the two because a person who maintains a high level of public approval is also likely to win widespread support for his or her actions. Nowhere is the effort to win public support more apparent than in the relationship between the media and the White House. The President can dominate the news at will by traveling abroad, making speeches on TV, or appearing in various cities and towns throughout the nation. Such exposure has become an important tool in the effort to maintain public support for the President. It is not news that the President spent seven 16-hour days tending to the nation's busi-

information from grand juries. Grand juries are used to investigate possible crimes, and their activities are supposed to be kept secret. Many states have laws forbidding leaks of information from grand juries, but they are seldom enforced. The danger of publishing such leaks is that those who are being investigated may be innocent and therefore may never be indicted, yet the connection of their names with the grand jury can plant the idea of guilt in the public's mind and damage their reputations.

The Media and the Government

While polls may reveal an alarmingly low level of political knowledge among

President Carter and Walter Cronkite of CBS before the President received telephone calls from citizens during a two-hour radio show from the White House. This was the first such Presidential use of radio to make contact with individual Americans.

ness last week. It was news that Gerald Ford visited Peking in 1975, though the trip was probably less productive than minding the store in the White House might have been.

Public relations efforts to portray officials in a favorable light are often referred to as "media events." The media have some leeway in dealing with such efforts when minor officials are involved. However, in the case of a President or secretary of state it is an unwritten rule that representatives of the media will accompany them on every trip, record every word they speak publicly, photograph the trip, and make every effort to develop behind-the-scenes stories. Because of the high degree of competition among the three major TV networks, none wants to be left behind; the same applies to the news magazines and major newspapers.

The Personal Touch

The media event is an open attempt to create circumstances in which high government officials will appear in a favorable light. More subtle are the behind-the-scenes efforts by the President, the secretary of state, or other public figures to gain sympathetic media treatment of their policies. This reflects the need to maintain a base of support among both the public and the elite groups. The members of the Washington press corps, especially those representing the major media, are at the top of their profession, are proud of their status, and see themselves as companions of those in power rather than mere recorders of political events. It is not hard for an official who is skilled in interpersonal relations to play on their egos in order to gain favorable press coverage. What could be more gratifying to a journalist than late afternoon bourbon with Lyndon Johnson, who might reveal planned policy changes or discuss the problems he faced? Media opposition to Johnson's actions in Vietnam came late in the game, long after the United States was deeply involved in the war. Until the Tet offensive of 1967, Johnson, one of the most persuasive of public figures, was able to keep the major media sympathetic to the U.S. role in Vietnam.

To the People — with Media Support

As we have seen, Ronald Reagan's effort to win the 1976 Republican nomination was an unusually strong challenge to an incumbent President. Reagan needed whatever ammunition he could find. As the most visible official in the Ford administration, Secretary of State Henry Kissinger was also the most vulnerable. He had served in the Nixon-Ford years as national security adviser as well as secretary of state. During that time, the United States' foreign policy dilemmas had not gone away; they had simply changed their appearance. The U.S.-Soviet Union confrontation continued despite the SALT talks, massive U.S. grain sales to the USSR, and a variety of minor agreements. Accordingly, Reagan made Kissinger his number one issue and his main target.

In his own defense, Kissinger made a number of speeches in an effort to retain the support of the public and the continued endorsement of the elite groups. This "barnstorming" approach was intended to attract local media attention and was described in the *New York Times* as follows:

Not since Woodrow Wilson toured the country for the League of Nations has a senior Administration official barnstormed on behalf of a foreign policy issue as Secretary of State Kissinger has done. Mr. Kissinger is doing it for the same political reason as Mr. Wilson. He is running out of support in Washington and has been trying to win arguments in the heartland that he can no longer win in the capital....

Whatever the effects on politics, there is little doubt that the Kissinger campaigns have been well planned and executed. The centerpiece of each visit is a formal address to the local world affairs council or economic club. The address is invariably long and complex, the reaction respectful. Later, Mr. Kissinger meets with the local power elite—a carefully selected group of about 30—for a question-and-answer session....

The local press coverage of his appearances and of the "town meeting" has been spectacular. Virtually guaranteed are major front-page news stories and endless minutes on local television channels. Not infrequently, the television clips show Mr. Kissinger being surrounded in hotel lobbies by approving crowds, as if he were a movie star. [15]

Kissinger's campaign to explain his foreign policy was on a scale usually reserved for Presidential efforts to achieve similar goals. It illustrates the ability of high-ranking officials to gain media coverage under the best possi-

Lyndon Johnson during a briefing with reporters. Johnson made widespread use of such informal contacts to influence media coverage.

ble conditions. There are limits on the positive impact such attempts can have, however. The media can report such events in a favorable light, but they have no control over how the message is received by the public.

The News Leak

The news leak, or unauthorized release of secret or classified information, is the bane of any administration, though questions are often raised regarding the role government officials play in leaking information. Washington has many power centers, each jealously guarding its territory. Like any bureaucracy, it also has many dissatisfied officials who may feel that leaking classified information to the press is the only way they can express their opposition to proposed policies. Responsible journalists will check such information before releasing a story, but even when the story is true the publication of leaked information leads to conflict between the media and the government. It is understandable that officials feel betrayed if classified information is released, and they tend to take out their frustrations on the media. On the other hand, reporters usually see leaks not as matters of national security but as revelations that may be embarrassing to the government. As a result, they feel no guilt about publishing the information if they are sure it is accurate.

Some leaks come from officials seeking favorable coverage by reporters. Revelations of the details of closed congressional hearings are usually of this type. The friendship of reporters is useful to officials who must run for reelection, and supplying news stories is an effective strategy. Other leaks, sometimes called "thrill" leaks, consist of information offered by people who want the feeling of having done something important. Most of the information that appears in political expose columns such as Jack Anderson's "Washington Merry-Go-Round" are supplied in this manner. Les Whitten, Anderson's assistant, has said that his office receives hundreds of such leaks each month. He continues:

It comes from a guy who drops something over the transom, so to speak, and then if we use it, he calls up and says, "that's some story—I'm the one who gave it to you." The guy just gets a kick out of dropping a bombshell. He's not an ideologist with a point of view like so many leakers are. [16]

On the other hand, some news leaks come from individuals with strongly held political ideologies who believe their revelations will have a serious impact on governmental policy. Such leaks are likely to be channeled through major media in order to gain maximum exposure. *The New York Times* is often given such information.

Another type of news leak is provided by officials who want to polish their image by leaking supposedly secret material. Secretary Kissinger engaged in a running battle with congressional committees in 1975, claiming that committee leaks regarding investigations of U.S. foreign policy had done great harm to the United States' ability to hold successful negotiations with other nations. These leaks were front-page news at the time. But shortly after Kissinger had expressed his unhappiness with the press, it was revealed that he himself had leaked transcripts of secret negotiations held during his Mideast "shuttle" diplomacy. These transcripts had led the person who received them to state that Mr. Kissinger's negotiations were "at the apogee of his genius." [17] A leading political columnist pointed out the contradiction involved:

The criterion of classification has become intensely personal. What is embarrassing to Henry Kissinger is "top secret," and the leak must be plugged at all costs; but what makes the Secretary of State appear to be "at the apogee of his genius"—no matter how secret—can be leaked with impunity. [18]

Such cases serve to keep alive the conflict between the media and government over what should be kept secret and what should be published. But even more delicate is the question of the reporter's responsibility to his or her profession and the principle of free speech as opposed to governmental efforts to keep a veil of secrecy around sensitive matters. This issue was raised in dramatic terms when a respected television journalist, Daniel Schorr of CBS, obtained a secret House committee report on its investigation of the CIA. Schorr used some of the information contained in the report in his TV and radio broadcast. He then gave the entire transcript to *The Village Voice,* which printed it on February 16, 1976 under the title, "The Report on the C.I.A. that President Ford Doesn't Want You to Read." [19] The House had voted on January 30 to delete all classified information from the report before it was released. Thus, Schorr had gone against the will of Congress by releasing the still-classified material.

Schorr had offered the report to other newspapers on the condition that nothing be deleted, but they had declined. *The Village Voice,* a New York paper, agreed to Schorr's condition. This case raised fundamental questions about the meaning of freedom of speech, and Schorr was criticized by some journalists as well as by members of Congress. Schorr's response goes to the core of the principle of freedom of speech:

[I am] disappointed in not being able to convey to other journalists the idea that we—all journalists—are engaged in the same battle for press freedom.

If they can hold me in contempt or have me charged with a crime, then they can get any reporter next week. That's the real issue, in all this. [20]

Schorr was subpoenaed by the House Ethics Committee in September 1976 after an investigation failed to find the source of the leak. Schorr refused to reveal his source, and the Ethics Committee voted not to cite him for contempt. Again, the issue was the conflict between the public's right to know, the freedom of the press, and the government's right to keep some information secret. Any of these three values may dominate at any given

Daniel Schorr gets advice from his attorney during his appearance before the House Ethics Committee investigating leaks of classified intelligence reports.

time, but they are clearly hard to define precisely and impossible to separate from one another so that clear standards can be established.

The Backgrounder

One of the favorite methods used by government officials to release information without being quoted is the "backgrounder" or off-the-record briefing. The official is usually in a high position, often the President. The reporters invited to these informal briefings agree not to use the name of the source but, instead, to use such phrases as "sources close to." In this way, the official can express opinions that will appear in the press but will not be attributed to him or her. High officials also use backgrounders to hint at their differences with the President, thus maintaining good relations with the press while not being disloyal to the President.

The backgrounder puts the media at a disadvantage because they have to print a story without naming the source, a story that may even be denied by that source. Thus, they serve the official's purpose while leaving themselves open to accusations of poor or dishonest reporting. Fear of losing out to rival journalists encourages those who are invited to attend backgrounders despite the possibility that they are being "used."

Trial Balloons

Closely related to backgrounders and very often part of them is the practice of sending up trial balloons, or hinting strongly at a possible course of action to see how the public or any group that might be affected will react. These balloons are often launched at backgrounders so that the remarks cannot be directly attributed to a specific official; if the idea fails to catch on, the matter can be dropped without damage to an official's reputation or bargaining position. Trial balloons are also floated by encouraging trusted reporters to report on possible policy changes, again from "a source close to the President." This practice is common in relation to both foreign and domestic affairs. Proposals for a tax increase, a new energy plan, or anything that is likely to arouse strong reactions will be set forth in the form of a trial balloon to determine how widespread and how intense the opposition is likely to be. In matters that may benefit one interest group at the expense of others, the public reaction is a clue to possible congressional reactions.

The use of trial balloons in foreign affairs was evident during the Nixon administration in connection with negotiations with North Vietnam. The latest U.S. position would be set forth by a few journalists based on conversations with an unnamed source. This gave Nixon and Kissinger a chance to judge the possible reaction of the American public as well as that of North Vietnam without actually putting their reputations on the line.

The variety of ways in which the media and the government interact gives some idea of the importance of the relationship to both and helps explain the periodic conflicts between them. The government's use of backgrounders, news leaks, trial balloons, and media events amounts to manipulation of the media. While journalists usually cooperate with such efforts, they often resent being used in these ways and feel free to look behind the scenes for stories that may be embarrassing to the government. The media are the primary means of daily contact between an administration and the public whose support it needs. The interdependence between the media and the government results in a relationship that will never be dull and will often be stormy.

The Media and the Public

The media are the public's window on the political world, since few people have personal contact with officials at any level of government. Election results depend largely on public perceptions that have been influenced by the media. In turn, the kind of news coverage provided by TV and radio networks and print media is intended to attract a wide audience. This means news stories that are not likely to get much attention will be covered briefly, while those that have the potential to attract strong reader and viewer interest will be headlined.

The two principal roles of the media are objective reporting of the news and investigatory reporting, which may be either objective or subjective. However, most members of the media do not take strong positions on political issues simply because their audience is varied and there is no profit to be gained from such a policy.

The desire of the press to interest or amuse the public leads to selective news coverage, which downplays some events and overemphasizes others. An example of overemphasis is the media's coverage of the New Hampshire Presidential primary. There is no political reason to give the small number of delegates at stake in New Hampshire or the fact that it is the first primary such heavy coverage. However, over the years, as the networks and newspapers have competed with each other for news coverage and audience appeal, the New Hampshire primary has taken on great importance to the candidates. The dimensions of the coverage that results may be seen in the following *New York Times* story:

Jimmy Carter, the former Governor of Georgia, told a Democratic forum at a Manchester high school last night that what the voters did here would be "magnified 100 times." As living evidence that this was not a hyperbole, nearly one-third of the audience he was facing was made up of the national press.

The three networks alone have brought about 400 staff members, including 20 camera crews, into the state for the finale of the first and longest campaign of the primary season. By yesterday the Secret Service had issued press credentials to more than 200 reporters and photographers now trailing the candidates around the state. [21]

The closeness of journalists to public figures and events inevitably leads to many stories' being given exaggerated importance. For example, political columns written after Johnson's landslide victory in 1964 described the Republican party as a declining political force. The McGovern defeat in 1972 was accompanied by a similar exaggeration of its long-term impact on the Democratic party. In fact, both parties recovered quite nicely, with the Republicans returning to the White House in 1968 and the Democrats in 1976. There is little question that the role of political parties is changing, but not to the extent that is often implied by the media.

Coverage of Watergate and related stories also exaggerated the impact of these events on the American people. There was great interest and some concern, but it was hardly a traumatic experience for the average citizen, whose way of life was not changed by Nixon's resignation. Rereading articles written at the time would lead one to believe that the nation was going through a major political upheaval. Instead, politics is much as it was before, with the balance of power between Congress and the President changed only on the surface, the public still not very interested in politics as measured by voter turnout, and matters of day-to-day living occupying people's minds more than political issues. Journalists are so close to the political scene that they tend to place more importance on events than they deserve, the way sports writers think of each Super Bowl or World Series as a dramatic event while to the average person such contests often turn out to be rather dull after the buildup they get in the media.

Just as the media can exaggerate the importance of events, they can "bury" stories that they do not consider very interesting. While there is little reason to second-guess the media's view of the public's interests, some events deserve more attention than they get. The starvation in Ethiopia in 1973, the famine in India and Haiti in 1975, and the cholera epidemic in Guinea in 1969 are examples of mass suffering by millions of people and news coverage confined to the inside pages of newspapers and brief reports on television. Perhaps the public is not interested in such tragedies, but the media's downplaying of these events ignores the constructive role

Chicago police arrest a demonstrator during the riots which accompanied the 1968 Democratic National Convention. Television coverage of the convention was interspersed with coverage of turmoil in the streets.

they could play in stimulating people to send help to those who need it.

Freedom and Fairness

Is there a relationship between the constitutional guarantee of freedom of speech and a responsibility for fairness in journalism? This is not a simple question, but it is important because it raises the issue of accountability. Some people argue that freedom of the press means freedom to publish anything and be answerable to no one. Others take the position that freedom of the press also implies a responsible press, responsible in the sense that conflicting views must be offered to the public and caution used in the publication of official secrets.

Print media such as newspapers and periodicals operate without governmental limits on their coverage of the news. In contrast, radio and TV stations are licensed by the Federal Communications Commission (FCC), which has the authority to set standards of proper behavior by these media. Among other things, the FCC has established a "fairness" rule that requires radio and TV stations to present public issues as part of their broadcast schedules and offer a reasonable opportunity for conflicting views on such issues to be expressed. The fairness doctrine is criticized by some people, who feel that it stands in the way of more aggressive programming. Others are unhappy with the rule because it does not require radio and TV stations to give anyone who wants to use this communication medium a chance to do so.

There is a legal double standard in the way the media operate. While the FCC can make radio and TV stations offer certain kinds of programming, there are no restrictions on what newspapers can publish. Nor is there any legal barrier to a newspaper or magazine's presenting one-sided interpretations of the news. The basis for this different treatment lies in the technological limits on the number of radio and TV stations that can operate in any given area. This is one reason for governmental regulation of the industry. However, this control has been expanded to include guidelines for program content, not only in terms of the fairness doctrine but also with regard to the portrayal of violence during "family" viewing hours.

The FCC also has an "equal time" standard that requires stations to give equal broadcast time to opposing candidates. This becomes a major problem when an incumbent President is running for reelection. The basis of this dilemma is simple: Is every Presidential speech or appearance newsworthy by definition? Or can the networks decide which are political in nature and which should be covered because the President is acting in the role of chief executive? In either case, the networks can be accused of not giving the opposing candidate equal time.

Summary

The media have become a target of people who cannot accept the fact that political leaders have human weaknesses that often lead to actions that threaten the political system itself. In reality, the abuses of the democratic process illustrated by Watergate, violations of the law by the CIA and the FBI, and many similar cases are not *caused* by media publicity. The media merely report the findings of others, such as the Senate committee investigating the CIA, though sometimes they may play an investigative role as well. In short, the media reflect rather than shape political events.

Some journalists exaggerate their ability to affect public opinion. But the extent and diversity of the audience they are trying to reach put limits on what is considered acceptable coverage. The nation's mood is reflected on the TV screen and in newspaper headlines and editorials; it is not created by them. The civil rights and campus protests of the 1960s, the antiwar demonstrations toward the end of the Johnson administration, and the economic recession of 1973-1975 were intensively covered by the media, but certainly not caused by them.

On balance, the media do not deserve the criticism they get from dissatisfied Americans who cannot accept the fact that democracy, like life, is not perfect. Nor do they deserve the self-praise media leaders heap on themselves as they defend their constitutional rights at the expense of the rights of other groups. Freedom of the press is no more absolute than the rights of any other group in society. The media are unique in their ability to serve as a watchdog in the name of the people, but along with this ability goes the responsibility to be fair and reasonable in reporting the news of the day.

NOTES

[1] Richard Reeves, "Dateline: White House," in *The New York Times Book Review,* November 30, 1975, p. 20. Copyright © 1975 by The New York Times Company. Reprinted by permission.

[2] *Statistical Abstract of the United States 1975,* No. 862, p. 520.

[3] Irving Janis, *Victims of Groupthink* (Boston: Houghton Mifflin, 1972), p. 21.

[4] Ibid., p. 20.

[5] Sydney J. Harris, "Decency Battles Loyalty," in *The Philadelphia Inquirer,* November 11, 1975, p. 11-A.

[6] Reported by John D. Lofton, Jr., "The Press Should Use Restraint," in *The Philadelphia Inquirer,* February 28, 1976, p. 6-A.

[7] Ibid., p. 6-A.

[8] John B. Oakes, "Confidence in the Press," in *The New York Times,* May 5, 1976, p. 41L. Copyright © 1976 by The New York Times Company. Reprinted by permission.

[9] Quoted by Leslie H. Gelb, "Spy Inquiries Begun Amid Public Outrage End in Indifference," in *The New York Times,* May 12, 1976, p. 20L. Copyright © 1976 by The New York Times Company. Reprinted by permission.

[10] Ibid., p. 20L.

[11] Quoted by Martin Arnold, "Assassination Attempts Spark Controversy over News Media," in *The New York Times,* September 28, 1975, p. 52L. Copyright © 1975 by The New York Times Com-

140 The Media

CHAPTER 9 CROSSWORD PUZZLE

Across
1. The media and the government find themselves in an ___ relationship due to the nature of their responsibilities.
5. Inexpensive
7. Unauthorized release of secret or classified information is called a news ___.
10. Ring; opposite of "square"
12. Station (abbr.)
13. Hawaiian garland of flowers
14. Glimpses
17. Embrace
19. Dispatched
20. Money
21. Foot cover
23. There is an inherent conflict between the public's right to know and the possibility that publication will jeopardize the ___ interest.
26. The media offer an administration the opportunity to explain its program to the ___.
28. The edge of a garment
29. Almond or cashew
30. Opposite of "dry"
31. ___ news is usually more important to the media audience than national affairs.
32. Some observers express fears that media reporting of sensational crimes leads to a ___ reaction.

Down
2. Idiot
3. Long-handled instruments for gathering leaves
4. Large pleasure boat
5. 300 in Roman numerals
6. The media are the prime source of ___ news for most Americans.
8. Part of the head
9. The media often find that their First Amendment freedoms conflict with other Constitutional ___.
11. Symbol of the Republican party
15. Yell
16. "___ and Peace"
18. There is controversy over the extent to which the media ___ news as opposed to reporting events.
19. The mass diversified audience of television networks limits the ability of the media to ___ opinion.
22. "___ nation, under God..."
24. Opposite of "out"
25. Cry of pain
26. Church bench
27. Slippery as an ___

---

pany. Reprinted by permission.

[12] Ibid., p. 52L.

[13] Reprinted from *U.S. News & World Report*, February 23, 1976, pp. 44-45. Copyright © 1976 U.S. News & World Report, Inc.

[14] Quoted in *The New York Times*, November 30, 1975, p. 13E. Copyright © 1975 by The New York Times Company. Reprinted by permission.

[15] Leslie H. Gelb, "On the Road Selling the Kissinger Line," in *The New York Times*, February 29, 1976, p. 4E. Copyright © 1976 by The New York Times Company. Reprinted by permission.

[16] Quoted by Martin Arnold in *The New York Times*, October 8, 1973, p. 29L. Copyright © 1973 by The New York Times Company. Reprinted by permission.

[17] William Safire, "Henry's Leaked Secrets," in *The New York Times*, March 8, 1976, p. 25L. Copyright © 1976 by The New York Times Company. Reprinted by permission.

[18] Ibid., p. 25L.

[19] Quoted by Martin Arnold in *The New York Times*, February 21, 1976, p. 9C. Copyright © 1976 by The New York Times Company. Reprinted by permission.

[20] Ibid., p. 9C.

[21] Joseph Lelyveld, "News Media Magnify Campaign," in *The New York Times*, February 23, 1976, p. 30L. Copyright © 1976 by The New York Times Company. Reprinted by permission.

CHAPTER 10
CONGRESS

CHAPTER OUTLINE

Questions to Consider
Introduction
Congressional Functions
    Representation
    Legislation
    Oversight
The Members of Congress
    Rewards of Congressional Service
    Congressional Ethics
Congressional Constituencies
    The Individual Citizen
    Interest Groups and Elites
    Political Parties
    The Media
The Electoral Process
Congressional Operations
Congressional Politics
    The Leadership
    The House of Representatives
    The Senate
    Party Organization
    Pressures for Party Unity
The Legislative Process
Congressional Committees
    Seniority
    House Committees
    House Subcommittees
    Senate Committees
    Conference Committees
The Budget Committees
The General Accounting Office
Congressional Procedures
    Filibusters and Cloture
    Secrecy
    Classified Information
    The Subpoena Power
    Contempt Citations
Summary

QUESTIONS TO CONSIDER

In many ways, Congress is the hub of the American political system. What are its functions? How does the Senate differ from the House of Representatives? We elect congresspeople to represent us. What kinds of people are most likely to be elected, and do they really carry out our wishes? We know Congress makes laws, but how does it decide which bills to enact into law? What happens from the time a bill is introduced until it is passed or is rejected? We read about congressional committees. What is their role in the legislative process, and how are members of Congress assigned to them? Many traditions and rules of Congress are often included in news reports. What is meant by *seniority? contempt citations? subpoena power? filibustering?* Consider these questions as you read this chapter. The answers will provide some understanding of the legislative branch of the government.

Introduction

Congress is responsible for representing the people to the government. Its principal functions are representation and legislation. From these derive the important tasks of studying the impact of past legislative action and charting the course of future policy. These responsibilities bring Congress and its members into contact with governmental activity at all levels as well as with most groups in the private sector.

The scope of congresspeople's relationships is so broad that they often find themselves subject to conflicting pressures. As we have seen, governmental action leads to a redistribution of resources—economic, social, or political. It is the responsibility of senators and representatives to represent their state or district while keeping the national interest in mind. Thus, almost any congressional action reflects the way legislators have interpreted the demands of various groups and related them to national priorities.

Since Congress is a highly visible institution, it is often criticized for the failure of the government to solve the nation's problems. Many people believe Congress should be able to deal more effectively than it has with a large number of national concerns. But there are some fundamental barriers in the path of congressional action. These will readily be seen as we describe the nature and functions of the legislative branch.

Congressional Functions

Representation

The basic task of Congress is to make laws that will serve the needs of the people. A basic concept of American government is that elected representatives will act in the name of and for the benefit of their constituents (those whom they represent). The electoral process is intended to make sure Congress will be responsive to the people. But there are many conflicts involved in the representative function, since the interests of certain groups do not always parallel those of the nation as a whole. Individuals tend to view events in a short-term context, while the needs of the nation can be effectively met only through long-term planning. The unemployed want jobs *now;* everyone wants suitable housing *now;* and most people see the energy crisis in terms of the price and availability of gasoline *now.* In contrast, the government views the problems of unemployment and housing in terms of the possible inflationary impact of government programs. And the government's concern with the energy crisis centers on the national goal of self-sufficiency rather than the price of gasoline or fuel oil this year. The legislator must somehow balance these contradictory considerations, and this process often leads to compromises that satisfy neither the short-term demands of the people nor the long-term needs of the nation.

Another important part of a congressperson's representative function is providing a channel of communication between the government and the individual. The increasing influence of the national government in the lives of citizens brings more and more people into contact with various government agencies. Representatives and senators have offices in their districts so that their constituents may seek help in dealing with the federal government. Such offices are important in maintaining the image of responsiveness that helps a congressperson win reelection.

Legislation

Congress either rejects or enacts into law legislative proposals that originate in either the executive or the legislative branch. The variety of issues with which Congress must deal and their increasing complexity has led to a legislative system in which each member develops detailed knowledge in a few specific areas as well as a broad understanding of national issues.

There is a degree of conflict between the representative function, which stresses responsiveness to constituents, and the legislative function, which requires that congresspeople view the larger picture and act in the national interest. Citizens in coal-producing states fear the ecological effects of strip mining; those in coastal states are concerned about the impact of offshore oil drilling; people in the Rocky Mountain region view the energy crisis in terms of the impact of development of shale oil deposits on their region. These varied concerns must be balanced against national energy needs, and this puts pressure on members of the House of Representatives, who must stand for election every two years, and on Senators, who seek reelection every six years. (Because of the difference between their terms of office, members of the two houses of Congress have somewhat different perspectives on their representative function. Representatives often do not feel that they can afford to support programs that promise long-term results when they may face voter dissatisfaction in the immediate future.)

The dilemmas posed by the energy crisis illustrate the conflict between the interests of a particular region and the interests of the nation as a whole. Each individual congressperson decides which set of interests deserves higher priority in a particular situation. This clash of interests has a major impact on all governmental planning. It is very difficult for Congress to make long-range plans and get the neccessary support for those plans because of the short-term pressures to meet the needs of constituents. One has only to read the morning paper to see how much criticism is directed at Congress for its failure to deal effectively with the nation's economic and social problems. While such complaints are justified in many cases, it is also true that the political system within which Congress operates discourages the type of effective long-range programs that might produce beneficial results at the expense of short-term gains for a particular group.

Congress works with the President in the legislative process, but political factors often turn this into a battle rather than a cooperative venture. The nation's founders established a framework within which neither the executive nor the legislative branch had constitutional power to dominate the other. This system has worked well, but it has also led to competition. The main reason for the apparently endless conflict between the President and Congress is the fact that they are elected independently and, as a result, Congress is often dominated by a different party than that of the President. In the first televised debate of the 1976 Presidential election campaign, President Ford revealed the frustration he felt in dealing with the Democratic-controlled 94th Congress:

It seems to me instead of anti-Washington feeling being aimed at everybody in Washington, . . . that the focus should be where the problem is, which is the Congress of the United States and particularly the majority in Congress.

They spend too much money on themselves, they have too many employees. There's some question about their morality. [1]

Conflict between Congress and the White House often occurs even when the President and the congressional majority are members of the same party. The members of Congress are always under pressure to serve the needs of their constituents, while the President has the nation as a whole in mind. Legislation to increase taxes is especially distasteful to congresspeople because it is almost always unpopular at home. Lyndon Johnson sought a 6 percent tax surcharge in September 1967 to help pay for the American involvement in Vietnam. Representative Wilbur Mills, chairman of the powerful Ways and Means Committee and a Democrat, blocked the legislation until after March 31, 1968, when Johnson announced that he would not run for reelection. President Johnson's view of this action by a fellow Democrat illustrates the different perspectives of Congress and the President:

I saw Wilbur holding back my bill up there and I knew why he was doing it. Not because he didn't believe in it but because that prissy, prim and proper man was worrying more about saving his face than he was about saving his country. He was afraid to put his reputation behind a risky bill. But when you run around saving your face all day, you end up losing your ass at night. [2]

Congresspeople usually have to run for office with little organizational or financial help besides what they can raise themselves. This reflects the fragmented nature of the American political parties and the tendency of quasi-independent political organizations to arise around each elective office. In turn, this situation weakens party loyalty both in Congress and in the White House, reducing party influence and making it hard to get major legislation passed. Thus, not only do political factors stand in the way of a close working relationship between the President and Congress; they also limit the extent to which a party majority can get legislation through Congress. These cross-currents often result in a legislative impasse.

There is a tendency to think of a high volume of legislation as amounting to progress and a relatively low volume as being due to lack of congressional action. The counterargument is that there are many laws already on the books covering almost any situation and that the efforts of Congress should be directed toward making those laws work more efficiently. There is a good deal of truth in both of these views. There are times when lack of congressional action prevents the nation from achieving widely agreed-upon goals, but this does not mean Congress must be continually engaged in frantic legislative activity.

Oversight

The *oversight*, or investigative, function is an outgrowth of Congress' legislative responsibility. It is the means by which the legislative branch tries to judge the impact of its past actions or the desirability of pending legislation. Congressional committees regularly conduct hearings to gather information on which to base such judgments. These hearings often resemble investigations into possible misdeeds. The post-Watergate atmosphere led to congressional inquiries into such areas of governmental activity as foreign affairs and the nation's intelligence-gathering agencies, which had never been investigated so intensively. Congressional oversight is the chief tool of legislative control over the sprawling federal bureaucracy, most of which has resulted from congressional action. This is how Congress makes sure funds are spent as authorized and policies carried out as intended.

The effectiveness with which the responsibilities of representation, legislation, and oversight are carried out largely determines the political relationship of the legislative branch with other governmental institutions as well as the degree of respect it receives from the people. This brings us back to the role of Congress in a representative democracy. Congress must fulfill its legislative and oversight responsibilities if it is to effectively carry out its primary mission, that of representing the citizen to the government.

The Members of Congress

The only constitutional qualifications for members of Congress are that representatives must be at least 25 years old and have been U.S. citizens for 7 years, while senators must be at least 30 years old and have been citizens for 9 years. Both must be residents of the state in which they are elected. However, the people who serve in Congress are not usually typical of the constituencies they represent. Table 10-1 shows that they are older, better educated, and richer as indicated by their professional backgrounds, and that most are male. Most individuals who

TABLE 10-1

PROFILE OF THE 94th CONGRESS

HOUSE   SENATE

PARTY

House		Senate	
Democrats	290	Democrats	61
Republicans	145	Republicans	38
		Independent	1

SEX

House		Senate	
Men	416	Men	100
Women	19	Women	0

AGE

House		Senate	
Youngest	26	Youngest	33
Oldest	83	Oldest	79
Average	50.8	Average	56

RELIGION

House		Senate	
Protestants	272	Protestants	71
Roman Catholics	108	Roman Catholics	15
Jews	21	Jews	3
Other	34	Other	11

PROFESSION
(Major groups, including some who list themselves in more than one category)

House	Senate
218 lawyers	68 lawyers
108 businessmen and bankers	22 businessmen and bankers
70 educators	8 educators
31 farmers	10 farmers
23 journalists	5 journalists
5 clergymen	

• 19 blacks—18 in the House, 1 in the Senate—are now serving in Congress, as well as 5 Orientals—3 in the House, 2 in the Senate—and 7 who are of Spanish descent—6 in the House, 1 in the Senate.

SOURCE: Reprinted from *U.S. News & World Report,* January 19, 1976. Copyright 1976 by U.S. News & World Report, Inc.

are elected to Congress have shown political ability in local or state government or achieved a certain amount of status in a related field. Without at least some of these characteristics, it would be difficult to gain the support needed to run an effective campaign or win the endorsement of a party organization.

The differences between congresspeople and most of their constituents are likely to be increased by the fact that members of Congress live in Washington during most of the time they are in office. The nation's capital is light years away from Main Street, U.S.A. in political perspective. The longer a representative or senator serves, the more he or she is likely to move away from the perceptions of the people back home. This influence strengthens the impact of the above-average socioeconomic background of congresspeople, and as a result they tend to consider legislation in a broader context than if they were to simply mirror the opinions of the people they represent.

The appearance of responsiveness to the electorate's is probably more important than a congressperson's position on any given issue. As one member of congress has expressed it,

Unless you can keep constantly in contact with your people, serving them and letting them know what you are doing, you are in a bad way. My experience is that people don't care how I vote on foreign aid, federal aid to education, and all those big issues, but they are very much interested in whether I answer their letters and who is going to be the next rural mail carrier or the next postmaster. Those are the things that really count.[3]

Rewards of Congressional Service

The salary of senators and representatives was raised in February 1977 to $57,500. The President pro tem of the Senate and the majority and minority leaders of both houses now receive $65,000. In addition, congresspeople have a very liberal pension plan. Under a 1969 amendment to the federal pension law, an extra 1 percent is added to pension payments every time benefits are adjusted for cost-of-living increases. In fact, a former congressperson has testified before a House subcommittee that the increase in his federal pension is "scandalous":

Former Rep. Hastings Keith (R., Mass.) told a House subcommittee that his pension at retirement was $1,560 a month, but that in 2½ years has increasesd to $2,095, nine percentage points higher than the increase in living costs over the same period. If inflation continues at about 6 percent a year, his pension will nearly triple to $6,000 a month by 1990, Keith testified.[4]

There seems to be a disparity between the income level of congresspeople and the nature of the office they hold. Most have homes in Washington as well as in the district or state they represent. In addition, many had reached higher income levels in private life before seeking election. The importance of the relatively low salary is that practices have developed that enable congresspeople to supplement their official salaries. Some of these raise basic questions of morality and conflict of interest.

Trips by members of Congress—often referred to as *junkets*—are a continuing source of embarrassment to the legislature, but the pleasure received seems to outweigh the public anger aroused by such trips. The total travel budget for both houses of congress was $10.5 million in 1975.[5] This amount is small compared to the total budget, but the problem congressional trips create has more to do with the public's attitude toward such trips than with their cost. Junkets are supposed to be congressional fact-finding or investigative missions, and of course many are legitimate. However, there are no guidelines in this area, and as a result many such trips appear to be unnecessary. The following is a news magazine's description of some questionable 1975 congressional travel:

The federal branch most frequently criticized for nonessential travel is Congress. Much of the travel by lawmakers is justified and necessary, it is generally conceded.... Whether the trips could be justified or not, congressional travelers have had an active year. Some recent tours—Senator William L. Scott (Rep.) of Virginia, made a "fact-finding tour" of 10 Middle Eastern countries and Scandinavia. He met with several foreign leaders. *The Washington Star*, quoting a State Department official, labeled Mr. Scott's journey "a diplo-

A Congressional delegation meeting after their return from a fact-finding trip to Indochina in 1975. Such trips are a continuing source of controversy because of the seeming disparity between costs and benefits derived from the trips.

mat's nightmare." Cost for the Middle East portion: $10,388....

At least two delegations visited Somalia in July at the invitation of the Somali Ambassador. A House group, accompanied by four noncongressional "specialists," three military-escort officers and a photographer, went on an Air Force VC-135 at a cost of $44,717.

The group followed by two days a Somali-bound delegation that included a Senator, 10 Senate and State Department aides, three escort officers and a photographer. Cost: $45,571.[6]

There is often good reason for congresspeople to travel, but the trips just described can hardly be considered essential.

Congressional Ethics

Free travel to faraway places is not the only advantage of being a member of congress. Others include free trips between Washington and home, free photographs of the legislator at work, free long-distance phone calls, inexpensive food in the members' private dining room, and so forth. One senator who disapproves of these advantages is William Proxmire (D., Wis.), who has said that congresspeople "should not be too far removed from the trials and tribulations of the average citizen" and "should not live like kings."[7]

The rewards of congressional service are not limited to financial gain. The status that comes with national office is tremendous. The 435 representatives and 100 senators form the core of the nation's political elite. They have power while in office and easy access to top positions in the private sector if they leave office. They may also have sources of income in the private sector. Many have law practices and other forms of investment that give them additional income, and such income often gives rise to questions of *conflict of interest*.

Efforts to influence congresspeople sometimes take the form of financial support rather than attempts to influence them through public opinion. Legislation affects many sectors of society that may be small in terms of number of voters but have considerable financial influence. Support may also come from sources outside a congressperson's constituency. The need to finance election campaigns makes senators and representatives responsive to such pressures. One of the most objectionable methods used to influence congresspeople is the practice of offering them *honoraria* (i.e., payments) for making speeches at meetings or conventions concerned with matters that fall within their committee responsibilities. The difference between honoraria and campaign contributions is that campaign funds must be spent on campaign activities, while fees for speaking appearances and the like are personal income. The drawbacks of this practice are obvious: There is a thin line between payment for speeches and payment for votes in Congress.

The Senate and House passed legislation in March and April of 1977 that was intended to eliminate abuses of congresspersons' privileges and restrict outside income. The major provisions of the bills limit outside earned income to $8625 (taking effect in January 1979) and provide for financial disclosure of sources and amounts of income as well as financial and real estate holdings (effective May 1978). The responsibility for enforcing the new ethics code falls to the ethics committees in the respective houses of Congress. This change of heart shows the reluctance of Congress to limit its income from honoraria and raises the question of the wisdom of allowing public officials to receive income from private sources that may be affected by their votes on specific legislation. Efforts to influence individual congresspeople in this way again illustrate the dual role of representatives and senators. They are the representatives of the districts or states that send them to Congress, but they are also legislators for the nation as a whole.

Contributions to campaign committees are another, more widespread method of winning congressional support. Contributions by industry leaders to congresspeople serving on committees with pending legislation related to those industries are commonplace. Senator Harrison A. Williams (D., N.J.) reported receiving $131,145 in campaign contributions in June 1975; of this amount, $34,000 was contributed by the securities industry. During the period covered by this report, Williams' Banking, Housing and Urban Affairs Committee was considering a bill to regulate the securities industry.[8] There is no doubt that these campaign donations were legal, but serious questions were raised as to whether such fund raising is proper.

Williams stated at the time that it had nothing to do with the pending of any legislation . . . Anyone who's been in Congress for a little while is involved in many legislative things. The system is that you have to raise money, and questions can be raised.[9]

Williams' statement pinpoints the problem of Congressional ethics. No one accused the senator of wrongdoing. Most agreed that the bill he had introduced was strict. However, the acceptance of contributions or honoraria from interests that a congressperson is dealing with in the course of his or her legislative responsibilities is controversial. Almost any member of Congress is likely to be in this position at one time or another. While the skilled legislator will correctly interpret efforts to influence his or her vote, this does not prevent others from giving in to such pressure. Resisting this kind of temptation is more difficult for senators, who are usually subject to more cross-pressures than representatives. (As we have seen, the latter are more likely to represent a fairly unified district in terms of shared interests, particularly in rural districts.)

On the other hand, the reason interest groups make contributions or offer honoraria to congresspeople is probably to "hedge their bets" rather than to apply pressure. Such payments are intended primarily to give the group access to a member of congress. It is the same type of thinking that leads many groups to contribute to the candidates of both parties. Campaign contributions cannot be held against you, but by not giving you run the risk of having no influence.

Congressional Constituencies

While we usually speak of a congressperson's *constituency* he or she really represents a number of constituencies, each of which is a potential source of support or opposition. These constituencies include the individual citizen, interest groups and elites, the media, and political party organizations. The congressperson must consider all of these constituencies before taking a stand on a controversial question, and all must be given the impression that their elected representative in Washington is responsive to their needs.

The Individual Citizen

Congresspeople serve individual citizens in a variety of ways. Their offices in Washington and in their voting districts try to satisfy personal requests, which may range from assistance in dealing with various government agencies to passes for special White House tours. Representatives and senators may also try to judge the opinions of individual citizens through mail polls or public appearances at which constituents can express their feelings. Congresspeople also make use of their *franking* (free mail for official business) privilege to get across the message that they are interested in their constituents' views and want to help them.

Congresspeople usually spend a lot of time in their states or districts "mending the fences," that is, solidifying political ties and making sure they have not misread the political mood back home. These visits become more frequent as elections approach. This puts an especially heavy burden on representatives because of their two-year term of office. One member of Congress has described service to constituents as follows:

A Congressman has become an expanded messenger boy, an employment agency, getter-outer of the Navy, Army, and Marines, a wardheeler, a wound healer, trouble shooter, law explainer, bill finder, issue translator, resolution interpreter, controversy-oilpourer, glad hand extender, business promoter, veterans affairs adjuster, ex-serviceman's champion, watchdog for the underdog, sympathizer for the upperdog, kisser of babies, . . . and bridge dedicator and ship christener.[10]

Interest Groups and Elites

Congresspeople, as we have seen, are exposed to a variety of pressures from individuals or groups that want to affect their votes on legislation before Congress. These pressures may take the form of electoral support or the threat of withholding such support. Labor unions, interest groups such as the National Rifle Association, or ethnic organizations often try to convince congresspeople that their electoral support is meaningful. Such efforts may be accompanied by letter-writing campaigns concerning specific issues that are important to the group. The NRA is very active in this area and has been effective in blocking gun control legislation in Congress despite public opinion polls showing that gun control has widespread public support.

Pressure on congresspeople may also come from local organizations seeking to influence legislation. The efforts of the AMA to prevent various federal health care or insurance programs from being passed have been accompanied by pressure from county or state medical societies. While congresspeople may have doubts about the ability of any pressure group to influence the votes of its members at election time, they do not like to take chances.

Political Parties

Members of Congress obviously must maintain close ties with state and local parties. The party organizations in the 435 districts that send representatives to the House and the 50 states that elect two senators each vary widely, and so do their relationships with members of Congress. However, the electoral process is a concern shared by all, and the support of an effective party organization is an advantage. Nevertheless, most congresspeople depend largely on their own core of backers for financial and organizational resources. In some cases, this political base enables them to dominate local and state organizations.

The Media

Members of Congress also keep in touch with the media in their constitu-

148   Congress

encies. The media can supply needed information about the degree of concern felt by individuals within the district on a particular issue and also serve as an important bridge to interest groups and elites. Congresspeople usually hold press conferences or briefings when they return home in order to make use of this opportunity to communicate with their constituents. While in Washington, they maintain contact with the media through press releases and by identifying themselves with particular programs. For example, when a military installation is to be located in a state or district, or a large government contract is awarded to a company there, it is customary to allow the member of Congress representing that area to make the announcement. The local media are used for this type of communication.

The Electoral Process

Members of the House of Representatives are elected for two-year terms and the number of representatives has been fixed at 435 since 1912. The U.S. Census is used as a basis for changing the number of representatives per state in line with shifts in population.

Table 10-2 shows the change that resulted from the 1970 census.

The apportionment of representatives among states is accepted practice, but the matter of reapportionment of congressional districts within states has only recently been resolved.

In 1964, the Supreme Court ruled (*Wesberry* v. *Sanders*) that the "one man, one vote" idea was the constitutional basis of apportionment and that congressional districts must meet this test. Until that time, there were wide variations in the size of districts in many states. The practical result was that rural areas were overrepresented in the House of Representatives because district boundaries tended to remain unchanged despite the trend toward an increasingly urban society. Since the *Wesberry* v. *Sanders* decision, the urban and suburban areas have gained representatives so that the House reflects current population patterns more closely than before. There are still some differences in population from one district to another, but the populations of the smallest and largest districts are seldom more than 10 percent above or below the average population per district. The shift in population revealed by the census introduces an element of uncertainty into the careers of representatives because the constituency

TABLE 10-2
Congressional Apportionment

State	1970 Census	1960 Census	State	1970 Census	1960 Census
Alabama	7	8	Montana	2	2
Alaska	1	1	Nebraska	3	3
Arizona	4	3	Nevada	1	1
Arkansas	4	4	New Hampshire	2	2
California	43	38	New Jersey	15	15
Colorado	5	4	New Mexico	2	2
Connecticut	6	6	New York	39	41
Delaware	1	1	North Carolina	11	11
Florida	15	12	North Dakota	1	2
Georgia	10	10	Ohio	23	24
Hawaii	2	2	Oklahoma	6	6
Idaho	2	2	Oregon	4	4
Illinois	24	24	Pennsylvania	25	27
Indiana	11	11	Rhode Island	2	2
Iowa	6	7	South Carolina	6	6
Kansas	5	5	South Dakota	2	2
Kentucky	7	7	Tennessee	8	9
Louisiana	8	8	Texas	24	23
Maine	2	2	Utah	2	2
Maryland	8	8	Vermont	1	1
Massachusetts	12	12	Virginia	10	10
Michigan	19	19	Washington	7	7
Minnesota	8	8	West Virginia	4	5
Mississippi	5	5	Wisconsin	9	10
Missouri	10	10	Wyoming	1	1
			Totals	435	435

that sent them to Congress may be changed by reapportionment.

Because of their six-year term, senators do not have to respond to their constituents on a short-term basis. The terms of senators are staggered so that one-third of the Senate faces election every two years. As a senator's reelection time gets closer, he is likely to spend more time in his home state and be more careful to vote in accordance with the preferences of his constituency.

While the level of electoral competition varies widely among congressional districts and states, the advantage of incumbency is apparent. In the 1970s, about 92 percent of House incumbents and about 86 percent of Senate incumbents have won reelection.[11] In the 1976 congressional elections, only 12 incumbent representatives and 9 incumbent senators failed to win reelection. This is a lower percentage of defeats than in the preceding years, but an unusually large number of congresspeople did not seek reelection. The small number of defeated incumbents is a paradox when one considers the dissatisfaction of many citizens with the political process. Senate Majority Leader Mike Mansfield (D., Mont.) explained it as follows:

People can find fault with the Congress as an institution, but they don't seem to find much fault with their Representatives or Senators. They must like their Congressmen, or they wouldn't keep sending them back. It is the institution of Congress that they're taking it out on, as they do sometimes on the White House and the courts.[12]

The ability of members of Congress to win reelection flows from the opportunity for an incumbent to improve his or her reputation among constituents. Congresspeople are good campaigners who, once successful, usually have little trouble solidifying their relationships with both the individual citizen and the party organization. By providing services to constituents and presenting a favorable media image, the incumbent develops a strong position. It is almost a fact of congressional life that the representative or senator who does his or her homework seldom loses an election.[13] These factors combine to give congresspeople more freedom of action than they are generally believed to have.

Congressional Operations

Despite the relative ease of winning reelection to Congress and the rewards of holding office, congresspeople have been leaving their jobs in record numbers lately. In 1976, 51 members of the House of Representatives chose to retire, while 9 of the 33 senators whose terms were ending also chose not to run again. Their reasons for retirement were varied, and provide some insight into congressional operations and the frustrations faced by individual members. These include inability to achieve goals; the heavy workload, which includes constituent service as well as committee responsibilities; and in many cases, the desire to pursue other careers or simply have more free time.[14]

Senator Robert Byrd of Virginia with staff. The effectiveness of a Congressional staff is a key ingredient in the success of a Senator or Congressperson.

The increased complexity of government has been accompanied by a much larger workload for members of Congress. One sign of this change is the increase in the size of congressional staffs shown in Table 10-3. The increase is due partially to the greater need of congresspeople to help their constituents deal with the ever-growing bureaucracy in Washington (staff budgets depend on the size of the congressperson's constituency). It is also a response to efforts by Congress to get a firmer grip on the complexities of government in order to achieve a status more nearly equal to that of the executive branch.

Another measure of the increase in the congressional workload is the $800 million appropriated in the 1977 budget for the legislative operations, a figure that has increased fourfold in ten years.[15] Thus, whether measured by staff or budget increases, Congress is an expanding institution.

Congressional Politics

Congress is organized along political party lines, with Republican and Democratic majorities and minorities providing the framework for the give and take of legislation. It is customary for the few members elected as third-party or independent candidates to join a major party caucus for organizational purposes.

The legislative party is a key element in the multilevel American party system. It is able to demand a degree of loyalty from party members that may be stronger than their support of the national party organization. Table 10-4 shows how the Democratic party has dominated Congress since 1952, forcing Republican Presidents Eisenhower, Nixon, and Ford to find a way of cooperating with some members of the Democratic party or with its legislative leaders in order to get legislation passed.

The same differences that militate against national party unity also operate in Congress—North against South, conservatives against liberals, labor against industry, and so forth. This adds to the importance of congressional party leaders, who are elected by their fellow party members.

The Leadership

The Democratic and Republican members of the House and Senate meet separately at the beginning of each congressional session to choose their leaders. Such meetings of party members in either house are called *caucuses.* After the party caucuses, each house holds an election, which is really just a formality because the leaders chosen by the majority party are certain to be elected by the full house. There are some significant differences between the House and the Senate in leadership structure; the most meaningful of these stems from the difference in their size.

The most important element in congressional leadership is persuasiveness. It is personal influence rather than formal party position that is the primary tool in maintaining party unity during the legislative process. There are also some individuals who have enough status to play leadership roles without holding formal positions in the party. Hubert Humphrey was a key member of the Senate Democratic leadership in the 94th Congress because of his past service to the party, and Barry Goldwater played a similar role for the Republicans.

The House of Representatives

The Speaker of the House is the House's presiding officer, a position provided for in the Constitution. The Speaker is chosen by the majority party and thus is also the party leader. The Speaker's formal powers were reduced in 1910 after the members of the House rebelled against the heavy-handed leadership of Joseph Cannon (R., Ill.). "Uncle Joe," as he was called, used the Speaker's power to appoint

TABLE 10-3
The Growth of Congressional Staffs

Continuing controversy over the need for additional office space both in the House and Senate illustrates the tremendous growth in congressional staffs since the early 1900s.

Before 1908, when the first House office building — the Cannon building — was constructed, 391 House members and 92 senators and their staffs shared space within the Capitol building itself.

By 1909, both the House and Senate had office buildings in which each member was allotted one room. When the Longworth House Office Building was completed in 1933 each representative was given two rooms.

In 1975, there were three office buildings on the House side and two on the Senate. A third Senate building was authorized in 1972 and money was first appropriated the same year; construction has not yet started. *(1972 Almanac p. 135, 691)*

The following chart shows the growth of Senate and House staffs since 1955:

	House	Increase	Senate	Increase
1955	3,623	—	1,962	—
1960	4,148	+525	2,643	+681
1965	5,672	+1,524	3,219	+576
1970	7,134	+1,462	4,140	+921
1975 (April)	9,951*	+2,817	5,543	+1,403

SOURCE: *Congressional Quarterly,* July 12, 1975, p. 1477.

*The House administration committee March 6 increased the maximum number of staff for each member from 16 to 18, adding a possible 870 staffers to the total House employment.

TABLE 10-4
Party Division in Congress, 1932-1976

	House		Senate	
Year	Democratic	Republican	Democratic	Republican
1932	313	117	59	36
1934	322	103	69	25
1936	333	89	75	17
1938	262	169	69	23
1940	267	162	66	28
1942	222	209	57	38
1944	243	190	57	38
1946	188	246	45	51
1948	263	171	54	42
1950	234	199	48	47
1952	213	221	47	48
1954	232	203	48	47
1956	234	201	49	47
1958	283	154	66	34
1960	263	174	64	36
1962	258	176	68	32
1964	295	140	67	33
1966	248	187	64	36
1968	243	192	58	42
1970	255	180	54	44
1972	255	180	57	43
1974	290	145	62	38
1976	—	—	—	—

President-elect Jimmy Carter and Vice President-elect Walter Mondale meet with Senators Humphrey and Byrd and Representative O'Neill to discuss proposed legislation. A President's potential for success is closely tied to members of his party in Congress.

committee members as a weapon to force representatives to go along with his wishes. Since that time, the power to appoint committee members has been removed from the Speaker, leaving him with the tasks of appointing members of special committees, making parliamentary rulings, and controlling the flow of legislation to appropriate committees. In practice, however, these actions are governed largely by precedent, and the Speaker's political power is due to his status as leader of the majority party rather than his official role.

Both the majority and minority parties also choose *floor leaders,* whose job is to try to unify the party's legislative efforts. This role requires that the majority and minority leaders maintain communication with committee members as well as individual representatives. The floor leaders are assisted by *whips* and *assistant whips,* who line up each party's forces in support of or opposition to pending legislation.

The party leaders share power and influence with major committee chairpeople. As a result, the power structure in the House of Representatives is diffuse with actual influence stemming from an individual's standing with other members than from his or her position in the party structure. As we have seen, members of Congress feel relatively secure when they run for reelection. Therefore, their party loyalty arises largely from the fact that members who cooperate have a better chance of getting support for their own bills.

The Senate

The Constitution provides that the vice president is to be the presiding officer of the Senate. The Senate also elects a *President pro tempore,* who presides when the vice president is absent. These are largely ceremonial positions, though the vice president may vote to break a tie. The real leadership of the Senate is in the hands of majority and minority leaders, who are chosen by their parties. As in the House, the influence of these leaders is more a matter of personal ability and status than formal authority.

Two recent Senate leaders illustrate contrasting leadership styles and different interpretations of the role of majority leader. Lyndon Johnson, who served as minority leader in 1953-1955 and as majority leader in 1955-1960, was one of the most powerful people ever to hold the position of Senate majority leader. He used his limited formal powers to the greatest possible extent. His methods ranged from arranging for foreign travel for senators to more direct methods, usually referred to as "arm twisting." Johnson's biographer, Doris Kearns, described his approach as follows:

The meeting itself might seem like an accidental encounter in a Senate corridor; but Johnson was not a man who roamed through the halls in aimless fashion: when he began to wander, he knew who it was he would find.

After the coincidental encounter and casual greeting, Johnson would remember he had something he would like to talk about. The two men ... would enter an office where they would begin their conversation with small talk over Scotch. As the conversation progressed, Johnson would display an overwhelming combination of praise, scorn, rage and friendship. His voice would rise and fall, moving from the thunder of an orator to the whisper reminiscent of a lover inviting physical touch.... He knew how to make his listeners *see* things he was describing, make them tangible to the senses....

Johnson's argument invoked country and party, loyalty to the leadership, reminders of past services and hints of future satisfactions—but always in a form that disavowed any intention that there was a debt to be paid or trade being offered.[16]

Johnson's successor, Mike Mansfield, led the Democratic majority from 1961 to 1976 and was very reluctant to use his position to influence fellow Democrats. In Mansfield's view, the nature of Senate leadership has changed:

Q. When did you first come to Congress, Senator?
A. It was in 1943.
Q. More than three decades ago. Has the quality of the membership changed in that time?
A. By in large, in spite of the recent publicity, I think the caliber of the members of Congress has improved. Today's members are better educated, younger. Congress is a different institution now than it was when I came.
Q. How do you mean that?

A. For one thing, there's no "inner club" in the Senate any more. That's the way it should be. Nobody is telling anybody else what to do.

Another thing: Younger members are more assertive, as they should be. We don't have wallflowers any more unless a member deliberately sets out to be one.

There is no arm twisting, no threats. I think it's better.[17]

It appears from Mansfield's comments that the Senate, like the rest of American society, has become less willing to accept Johnson's style of leadership. If this is the case and Senators are really more independent than they used to be, the Mansfield leadership style may become more common.

The Senate majority and minority leaders are assisted by whips and assistant whips whose responsibilities are similar to those of their counterparts in the House. In addition, Senate committee chairpeople, like those in the House, are often in a position to reward those who support them.

Party Organization

Electing party leaders and controlling committee assignments are among the responsibilities of the party caucuses (which are called *conferences* in the Senate and by House Republicans). While the influence of these party meetings varies, House Democrats have taken steps to strengthen their caucus so that the Democratic representatives will have a more effective party organization. In large part, these changes were forced by liberal Democrats, who formed the Democratic Study Group in 1959 to challenge the way the Democratic leadership was managing its responsibilities. It was not until 1969, however, that this informal group succeeded in getting the Democratic caucus to meet monthly, a small step but an important one.

In 1975, with a strong legislative majority, Democratic members of the House moved to make major changes in the relative power of the caucus, the Speaker, and committee chairpeople. Responsibility for the Committee on Committees, which has the authority to nominate committee members and chairpeople, was taken away from the Ways and Means Committee and given to the Steering and Policy Committee, which is appointed by the Speaker. This greatly increased the Speaker's power. The changes made at this time also dealt a blow to the *seniority system,* under which length of continuous service on a given committee had determined committee chairmanships. The Democratic caucus removed three incumbents — Hebert of Armed Services, Patman of Banking, and Poage of Agriculture— from committee chairmanships. This action was made possible by a new rule allowing committee nominations from the floor.

All told, these changes in the House Democratic Caucus have strengthened the hand of the party leadership while weakening that of committee chairpeople, who long held power through their seniority regardless of whether they were responsive to the wishes of the majority. Committee nominations now come from the Steering and Policy Committee, which is also active in designing legislative programs and coordinating party action. The reforms instigated by the Democratic Study Group flow in part from the reality of a legislative majority which has the potential for effective action.

The House Republicans have a Committee on Committees, which nominates members and chairpeople, and a House Republican Policy Committee, which handles functions that are theoretically similar to those of the Democratic Steering and Policy Committee. The party organization in the Senate is similar in both parties. The Democratic and Republican Conferences are the party caucuses in the Senate. The relatively small number of senators reduces the importance of these groups and tends to offer more influence to specialized committees. Both parties have policy committees that develop legislative programs and committees that appoint committee members—the Democratic Steering Committee and the Republican Committee on Committees. Senate Republicans have the same minority party status that handicaps House Republicans, but the smaller size of the Senate leads to a higher level of participation by individual members.

TABLE 10-5
Party Unity Scoreboard

The following table shows the proportion of party unity roll calls in 1976, 1975, 1974, 1973, 1972:

	Total Recorded Votes	Party Unity Recorded Votes	Percent of Total
1976			
Both Chambers	1,349	493	37%
Senate	688	256	37
House	661	237	36
1975			
Both Chambers	1,214	584	48
Senate	602	288	48
House	612	296	48
1974			
Both Chambers	1,081	399	37
Senate	544	241	44
House	537	158	29

Definitions

Party Unity Votes. Recorded votes in the Senate and House that split the parties, a majority of voting Democrats opposing a majority of voting Republicans. Votes on which either party divides evenly are excluded.

Party Unity Scores. Percentage of party unity votes on which a member votes "Yea" or "Nay" *in agreement* with a majority of his party. Failure to vote, even if a member announced his stand, lowers his score.

SOURCE: *Congressional Quarterly,* November 13, 1976, p. 3173.

Pressures for Party Unity

Not all issues lead to pressure to go along with the party leadership. The congressperson often has to choose between the likely reaction of his or her constituents and the policy of his or her party. On issues that are not of major importance to the party, there is likely to be little effort by the leadership to influence fellow party members. However, when the issue before the House or Senate is interpreted as a party program, the leadership can be expected to use all possible means to maintain party unity.

One study of the relative impact of party and constituency on congresspeople's voting decisions found that party unity is likely to be strongest on issues such as government management, where there is a clear difference between party programs and constituents are less involved. In contrast, on issues involving civil liberties or social questions the constituency's influence is usually stronger than the drive for party unity.[18]

Table 10-5 illustrates variations in party unity during the 1974-1976 period. Note that party unity dropped in the 1974 and 1976 election years compared to 1975. This shows that congresspeople feel a greater need to vote according to their constituents' preferences during election years and are likely to support their party more strongly in nonelection years. At best, the data in Table 10-5 show that a majority of voting Democrats will oppose a majority of voting Republicans less than half the time in <u>roll call votes</u>, those in which members' votes are recorded.

A major reason for the lack of party unity in Congress is the coalition formed by southern Democrats and Republicans on issues with a liberal-conservative dimension. This conservative coalition usually forms when social issues or military spending are involved. Table 10-6 shows the percentage of votes in the 1961-1976 period in which the coalition appeared, an average of about one-quarter of the recorded votes. It also shows that the southern Democrat-Republican coalition has been successful in over 50 percent of the votes in which it appeared, thus negating the power of the Democratic majority in Congress. Tables 10-5 and 10-6 present evidence that a bipartisan approach is necessary for the passage of most legislation and that party unity is the exception rather than the rule.

The Legislative Process

Legislation can be introduced by any member of either house of Congress. The first step after the introduction of a bill is to refer it to the appropriate committee in the house in which it was introduced. Many bills are unimportant ones reflecting the desires of a particular legislator or constituency. They are introduced so that a congressperson can go on record as having tried to achieve a particular goal that he or she may have promised in an election campaign. Such bills simply fade away in committee for lack of support. Approximately 10,000 bills are introduced each year, and most suffer this fate. Table 10-7 shows the relatively small number that reach the floor of Congress and are voted on.

Proposed legislation that has the support of the leadership or a significant number of members will be acted on by the committee to which it is referred. Hearings are held, with experts both within and outside of the government invited to express their opinions. People who wish to testify before a committee are usually allowed to do so if they are officials of an organization affected by the bill or individuals with recognized status in an appropriate field. The committee then considers possible revisions of the bill—which are usually worked out with its sponsors—and then votes on the bill. If it is passed by the committee, it is sent to the floor of the house in which it originated to be voted on by the full membership.

If the bill is passed by the house in which it was introduced, it is sent to the other house for its vote. If it is passed in this form, it is sent to the President for his signature, and if it is signed it becomes law. Often, however,

TABLE 10-6
The Southern Democrat-Republican Coalition

Coalition Appearances, 1961-1976

Following is the percentage of the recorded votes for both houses of Congress on which the coalition appeared:

1961	28%	1969	27%
1962	14	1970	22
1963	17	1971	30
1964	15	1972	27
1965	24	1973	23
1966	25	1974	24
1967	20	1975	28
1968	24	1976	24

Coalition Victories, 1961-1976

	Total	Senate	House
1961	55%	48%	74%
1962	62	71	44
1963	50	44	67
1964	51	47	67
1965	33	39	25
1966	45	51	32
1967	63	54	73
1968	73	80	63
1969	68	67	71
1970	66	64	70
1971	83	86	79
1972	69	63	79
1973	61	54	67
1974	59	54	67
1975	50	48	52
1976	58	58	59

SOURCE: *Congressional Quarterly,* October 30, 1976, p. 3100.

TABLE 10-7
Number of Bills Reaching the Floor for Vote*

Year	House	Senate	Total
1976	661	688	1,349
1975	612	602	1,214
1974	537	544	1,081
1973	541	594	1,135
1972	329	532	861
1971	320	423	743
1970	266	418	684

SOURCE: *Congressional Quarterly,* October 9, 1976, p. 2877.

*Any of the remaining bills yet to be considered by Ford could be pocket vetoed. The total of 15 vetoes does not include two on bills cleared in the first session but not vetoed until January 1976. These are included in the first session's total.

the second house makes changes in the legislation passed by the other house. If it passes in a different form than that in which it was introduced to the second house, the bill is referred to a conference committee—a committee made up of members of both houses—which reaches a compromise version and sends that version to both houses for another vote.

A Presidential veto is final unless two-thirds of those voting in each house vote to override it, in which case the bill becomes law. Table 10-8 shows the flow of legislation from the introduction of a bill to its enactment into law. The legislative process is a long road with many obstacles to be overcome. As a result, legislation often proceeds at a snail's pace.

The House and the Senate have different constitutional responsibilities that make each dominant in certain legislative areas. For example, appropriation (i.e., money) bills must originate in the House. This means tax legislation is introduced in the House. While both houses must eventually pass all bills, the power to originate legislation is important because it usually establishes the boundaries of debate.

The Senate must ratify treaties with foreign nations and confirm ambassadorial appointments. This theoretically gives it a major role in foreign policy and provides Senate leaders with a chance to participate in the decision-making process. But the use of executive agreements instead of treaties has limited the Senate's role in this area. *Executive agreements* are understandings between the President and other nations—agreements of which Congress often is unaware.

While the Senate's foreign policy role diminished during the Vietnam War, the leadership is now attempting to claim its constitutional rights in this area. An example of the Senate's desire to gain some control over foreign policy was seen in January 1976, when the House voted in favor of a Senate bill that banned U.S. covert action in Angola, the former Portuguese colony that was in the throes of a Soviet-supported rebellion led by Cuban troops. Another congressional act in the foreign policy area in 1974 was the stopping of U.S. arms shipments to Turkey in an effort to limit Turkish military activities in Cyprus. Clearly while the wisdom of congressional involvement in day-to-day diplomatic decisions is debatable, the current trend toward such involvement is strong.

The Senate must also confirm Presidential appointments. This involves it in the selection of high government officials. In general, few Presidential appointments are opposed, but the Senate's confirmation power serves as a check on the President. Several of Nixon's Supreme Court choices were challenged by the Senate, and the President was forced to withdraw the nominations of Clement Haynsworth and Harold Carswell.

Congressional Committees

The meaningful legislative work performed by congresspeople is done in committees and subcommittees. All legislation is referred to committee after it has been introduced. And it is in committee that bills are examined,

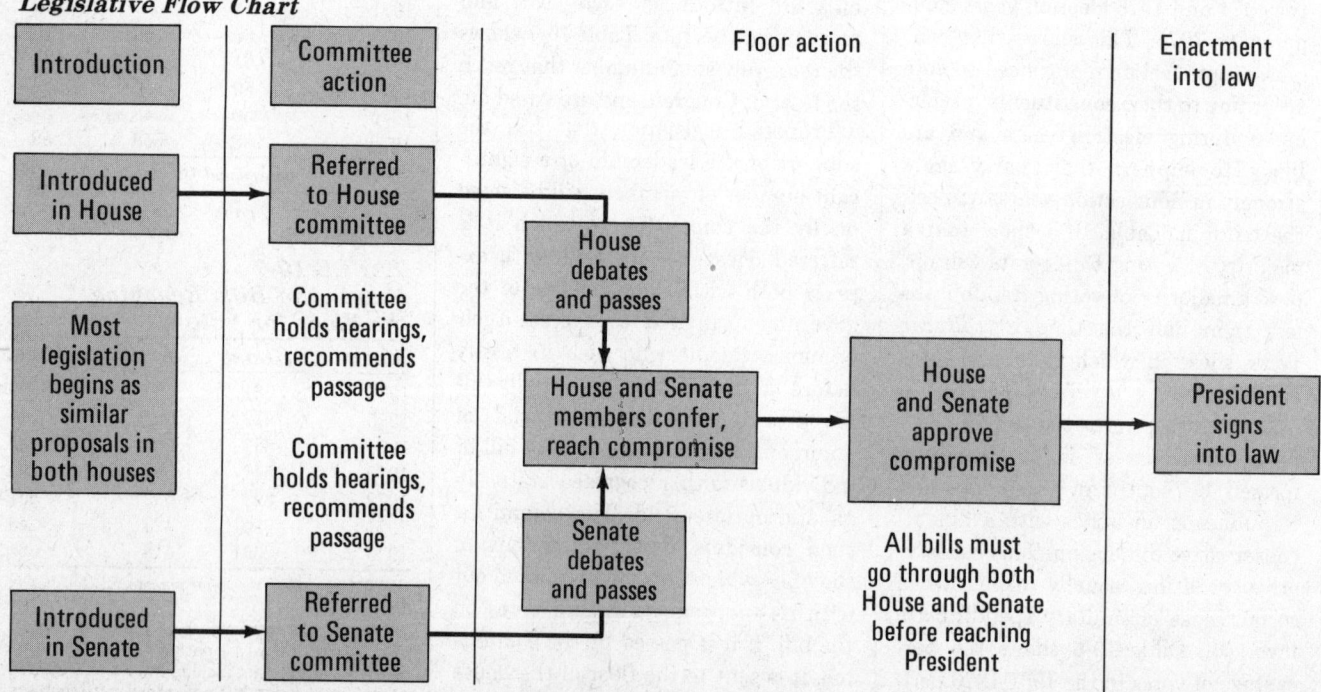

TABLE 10-8
Legislative Flow Chart

Introduction	Committee action	Floor action		Enactment into law
Introduced in House	Referred to House committee	House debates and passes		
Most legislation begins as similar proposals in both houses	Committee holds hearings, recommends passage	House and Senate members confer, reach compromise	House and Senate approve compromise	President signs into law
	Committee holds hearings, recommends passage			
Introduced in Senate	Referred to Senate committee	Senate debates and passes	All bills must go through both House and Senate before reaching President	

SOURCE: Adapted from *Congressional Quarterly Almanac,* 1969, p. 11.

changed, passed, or rejected. The complexity of the government has led members of both houses of Congress to respect the principle of specialization. Members who serve on committees for several terms have a chance to become experts in a particular area. The result of this specialization is that if a bill is voted down in committee it is for all practical purposes a dead issue, while if a bill is sent to the floor of either house of Congress with committee approval, the report of the committee is given great weight by the other legislators, who must ultimately vote on the bill. It is also through committees that congressional oversight of the federal bureaucracy is carried out.

Senators and representatives earn their reputations through their committee assignments and gain the power to influence legislation in their areas of specialization. This arrangement also dictates that any group that wants to influence legislation will do so at the committee and subcommittee level because this is the best time to achieve a meaningful input into the legislative process.

Seniority

The role of seniority in committee assignments is significant in both houses of Congress. Although the seniority rule has been changed in the past few Congresses, it remains an important tradition. Those who favor the seniority system argue that it takes a certain amount of time to become thoroughly familiar with the subject matter of any committee or subcommittee. The seniority system also leads to decentralization of power by offering key positions to members with seniority, giving them some degree of independence from the party leadership. The system also has the advantage of avoiding bitter conflict over each chairmanship, which might be as harmful as the much-criticized abuses of the seniority tradition.

The other side of the seniority argument rests partly on the lack of influence of members who have not served very long. As one representative expressed it after serving one term and retiring,

I could see I wasn't going to get anywhere. Nobody listens to what you have to say until you've been here ten to twelve years. These old men have got everything tied down so you can't do anything. There are only about 40 out of the 435 members who call the shots. They're all committee chairmen and the ranking members, and they're all around 70 or 80. [19]

In addition to the problem of discouraging newly elected members of Congress, the seniority system has produced some chairmen who run their committees like private preserves, ignoring the wishes of fellow committee members and often those of the full House or Senate. However, the reforms discussed earlier have reduced the likelihood of such situations developing in the future.

House Committees

As the 95th Congress opened in 1977, the House of Representatives had 21 standing committees. *Standing committees* are permanent. Each is divided into subcommittees, some of which are *select*, or set up for a specific purpose and abolished once their mission has been accomplished. In the 94th Congress, which opened in January 1975, there were 146 House subcommittees, including select and standing committees. (In the 80th Congress, there were 106.) The increase in the number of subcommittees coupled with the reforms passed in the 1970s have given subcommittees greater influence on the legislative work of the House.

Representatives want to become members of committees that will offer them visibility, improve their standing with their constituents, give them an opportunity to use any expertise gained before coming to Washington, and perhaps most important, increase their power. Power in the government is largely power to influence appropriations or to affect the overall course of legislation.

Accordingly, the most desirable committee assignments in the House are Rules, Appropriations, and Ways and Means. These three committees make the key decisions regarding which bills will be sent to the floor for discussion by the full House (Rules), for what purposes federal money will be spent (Appropriations), and from whom federal revenues will be collected (Ways and Means). Assignment to such committees is a political advantage for a representative because it provides a platform from which he or she can speak out on important issues. Such assignments also have the long-term advantage of allowing members to start out along the road toward seniority that could lead to a chairmanship. And committee chairpeople have long occupied the prime seats of power in the House.

Committee memberships have traditionally been determined by special committees formed by the Democratic and Republican caucuses for this purpose. These "rules of the game" led to a concentration of power in the hands of the party leadership. Committee chairmanships were practically automatic awards of power on a seniority basis. As we have seen, however, in organizing the 94th Congress, the House Democratic Caucus took a significant step away from this procedure. Resenting the autocratic methods used by certain committee chairmen, who often substituted one-man rule for majority rule, they removed these individuals from the chairmanships. This action served notice on committee chairpeople that if a reasonable amount of participation in key decisions by committee members is not made possible, the chairperson's position may well be jeopardized.

House Subcommittees

The power of House subcommittees has been increased in recent years by changes in House rules as well as the reforms just described. The Democratic majority in the House has given that party the freedom to put into effect almost any rules changes it wants. One result is that committee chairpeople are now required to refer bills to subcommittees within two weeks. This makes it impossible for them to block legislation by refusing to act.

One longstanding criticism of House operations had to do with the fact that the seniority system allowed a small group of senior representatives to gain enormous power through their committee and subcommittee chairmanships. The 92nd Congress ruled that no House member can serve as chairperson of more than one subcommittee. With 435 members and 146 subcommittees, this rule has the effect of allowing most members who have served several terms to chair subcommittees. The year it was passed (1971), 16 Democrats who had served since 1958 received their first committee chairmanships. [20]

Committee chairpeople formerly had the authority to choose subcommittee chairpeople. In 1973, however, a caucus was set up within each committee with the authority to choose subcommittee chairpeople and provide them with adequate funding. The decision on whether or not to establish a subcommittee traditionally was made by the committee chairperson. At the opening of the 94th Congress, the Democratic caucus ruled that all committees with more than 20 members must have 4 subcommittees. This automatically results in diffusion of power and weakens the committee chairperson. These changes have been welcomed by those who have long felt that the House was seriously hampered by the practically absolute power in the hands of the chairpeople of a few committees. The new rules also limit committee members to one subcommittee position, which tends to make leadership positions more available to junior representatives.

The question has arisen as to whether these moves aimed at increasing subcommittee influence and limiting the ability of a handful of senior representatives have resulted in an improvement in the legislative process. The problems of the House leadership have been made more complex by the need to deal with the fairly independent chairpeople of 146 subcommittees instead of only 21 committee chairpeople. This increase in the number of power centers within the House has also resulted in a fragmentation of effort and in problems of coordination. There is also considerable overlap among the various committees.

The House reforms have also affected the political process. In the 94th Congress, the Democrats attempted to use their 290 votes to achieve a unified legislative program. The diffusion of power that has resulted from the increased independence of subcommittees and their chairpeople made it more difficult to unify the party.

Senate Committees

Senate committees are organized much like those in the House, with the main differences resulting from the Senate's smaller size.

As the majority party, the Democrats made some changes in the Senate committee system at the beginning of the 95th Congress in 1977. The principal change was to lower the number of committees and subcommittees. The number of committees was set at 25 at the beginning of the session and further reduced to 21 by the time Congress adjourned. The new rules also provide that a senator can sit on only three committees and eight subcommittees. (This will automatically reduce the number of Senate subcommittees.)

Among the most desired committee assignments in the Senate are Foreign Relations, Finance, Appropriations, and Armed Services. Members' preferences are determined, as in the House, by the political exposure and influence a committee assignment can provide. Senate subcommittees are not normally as significant as House subcommittees because there is plenty of room at the committee level to give the 100 senators legislative leeway. A member of the Senate Foreign Affairs Committee describes his subcommittee assignment as follows:

I've been on the European subcommittee for five months and I haven't even heard NATO mentioned, haven't even heard the word. I read my hometown newspaper to find out what's happening to NATO. The subcommittees have displayed absolute irrelevancy in foreign affairs, amazing irrelevancy. [21]

However, select subcommittees formed for a specific purpose such as investigation offer political gains because of the publicity involved. Thus, every member of the Senate is likely to have some influence at one time or another, while new representatives have little real opportunity to affect legislation.

The key to committee and subcommittee operations in both the House and the Senate is the expertise members gain in particular areas and the fact that this knowledge is respected by other members. It is unusual for a bill that is unable to win committee approval to be approved by the full House or Senate if it is sent to the floor for debate. By the same token, the degree of enthusiasm committee members express for certain bills may well influence the votes of other members. The committee system, in short, reflects both the complexity and the scope of the legislative process.

Conference Committees

Legislation approved by committees in either the House or the Senate is sent to the full house for a vote. If a bill passes, it goes to the other house for approval. In matters involving important policy decisions, it is likely that the house to which a bill is sent for final passage will change it considerably. [22] At this point, the bill is sent to a *conference committee,* which consists of members of both houses who meet to iron out differences and produce a bill that will pass in both houses of Congress.

The procedures of conference committees were long kept secret, with senior members of Congress usually appointed to serve on these committees and their meetings customarily closed to the public. It was in conference committees that most real legislative debate occurred, away from cameras or reporters and in an atmosphere of political responsibility. The secretive nature of the conference procedure was changed in 1975 as both houses of Congress voted to open such meetings to the public unless either house voted to keep them closed. (Of course, much legislative activity may still depend on private conversations in which compromises are arrived at informally.)

Theoretically, the conference committees reflect the views of the two houses of Congress as expressed in the original bills. Realistically, the opinions of the members of the conference committee may prevail even though they are markedly different from those of their fellow legislators. The basic task of these important committees is to shape legislation that will be acceptable to both houses of Congress as well as to the President. Without the approval of all three, the bill cannot become law.

The tendency of conference committees to rewrite legislation has been criticized because it is not uncommon for important provisions of the original bills to be completely rewritten or omitted in the final version. This is a problem for which there is no easy cure. The conference committee's job is to reach a compromise, and any attempt to restrict this process would make such compromises harder to achieve. It is not an exaggeration to describe conference committees as the third house of Congress.

The Budget Committees

Congress has been handicapped in dealing with appropriations and Presidential budget requests because of the lack of a unified budget strategy. In the past, Congress has reacted to budget requests on a piecemeal basis. The Congressional Budget and Impoundment Control Act was passed by Congress in 1974 in an effort to deal with this situation. Under this law, Senate and House Budget Committees were set up to prepare overall plans for spending and taxation. The Act also provided for a Congressional Budget Office to provide the Budget Committees with the information necessary for preparing economic forecasts and writing meaningful legislation. It is one thing to demand a reduction in Defense Department spending, but quite another to get detailed information on which to base specific recommendations. In the past, Congress has lacked the necessary information to do much more than oppose Presidential budget requests on a very vague and general basis or pass appropriations bills with little knowledge of their likely impact on the budget as a whole.

The Congressional Budget Act sets deadlines for action on the federal budget. A *concurrent resolution* is to be passed by both houses by April 15. This resolution contains budgetary guidelines for various congressional committees. The second deadline is September 15. At this time, the guidelines are to be replaced by a second concurrent resolution, which sets spending ceilings, determines the deficit (if any), and establishes the revenues needed to put the budget into effect. The law calls for final congressional approval of the budget by November 20 and until this process has been completed.

Table 10-9 presents the budget timetable. The first test of this new system occurred in 1975. The house, where all appropriations bills originate, met its target dates and the spending ceilings foreseen in the first concurrent resolution. The success of the budgetary procedure depends in large part on the attitude of the President because there is always a possibility that he will change spending limits either by using his veto power or by acting aggressively to get bills passed even if they go over the budget ceiling.

There is a difference between passing a law of the kind just described and actually carrying it out. The members of Congress must be willing to work out their differences over spending priorities as well as budgetary limits. As the first chairman of the House Budget Committee, Representative Brock Adams (D., Wash.), said, "If people don't want to be rational and make it work, it can be destroyed."[23] Opposition to congressional budgetary limits was voiced by Senator Russell Long of Louisiana, chairman of the Finance Committee, after part of his

TABLE 10-9
Congressional Budget Timetable

On or before:	Action to be completed:
November 10	President submits current services budget.
15th day after Congress convenes*	President submits his budget.
March 15	Committees submit reports to budget committees.
April 1	Congressional Budget Office submits report to budget committees.
April 15	Budget committees report first concurrent resolution on the budget to their Houses.
May 15	Committees report bills authorizing new budget authority.
May 15	Congress adopts first concurrent resolution on the budget.
7th day after Labor Day	Congress completes action on bills providing budget authority.
September 15	Congress completes actions on second required concurrent resolution on the budget.
September 25	Congress completes action reconciliation process implementing second concurrent resolution.
October 1	Fiscal year begins.

SOURCE: *The United States Budget in Brief, Fiscal Year 1977*, p. 51.
*Public Law 94–186 required the President's 1977 budget to be transmitted to Congress on January 21, 1976, 2 days after Congress convenes.

committee's budget request was changed: "One day we're going to have to fight them to a showdown." [24]

The impact of the new budget operation will be impossible to judge until it has been in effect for a few years; that is, it must become part of the rules of the game. The importance of this effort is indicated by the fact that the chairmanships of the budget committees are already considered prime positions by congresspeople. Money fuels the government, and those who play a key role in determining spending levels and budget priorities are in important positions.

The Congressional Budget Office (CBO) plays a key role in the budgetary process. It is intended to give the Budget Committees the technical expertise and factual information they need in dealing with the executive branch's Office of Management and Budget. The seriousness with which Congress has approached this process is indicated by the CBO's staff of 259 people.[25] Among the information that will be provided by the CBO are five-year estimates of the costs and expected results of all government programs. Obviously, this is an ambitious undertaking, and the CBO will need a highly professional staff and congressional cooperation if it is to be effective.

The General Accounting Office

The General Accounting Office (GAO) was established in 1921 and is under the control of the controller general, who is appointed by the President for a fifteen-year term. Its function is to provide an independent check on governmental expenditures that had been approved by Congress. Accordingly, the GAO has come to be thought of as the congressional watchdog and has steadily enlarged its role from conducting routine audits to investigating a wide range of activities within the federal bureaucracy. The GAO operates with a budget of over $135 million and has a staff of over 3600 people. Still, it is small compared to other government agencies.

The GAO can look into the operations of any government agency except the CIA and the Federal Reserve Board. (The latter plays an extremely sensitive role in handling the nation's money supply and guards its independence as fiercely as the CIA.) While most GAO inquiries are made in response to requests by members of Congress, it undertakes about one-third of its investigations on its own. Its independent status is assured by the controller general's fifteen-year term and strengthened by his or her power to choose assistants without the approval of any other group either within or outside of Congress. Thus insulated from political wars, the GAO is in a unique position to challenge the actions of government officials as well as agencies. For example, during the spring of 1975 the GAO sued President Ford for impounding housing funds, charged 49 officials of the U.S. Geological Survey with owning stock in companies they were supposed to be regulating, and demanded that the FBI give it access to files related to its political intelligence activities. It also withdrew the Secret Service protection that Spiro Agnew had continued to receive long after his resignation from the vice presidency.[26]

The role of the GAO is described by Controller General Elmer B. Staats as follows:

We're the independent auditors for the Congress but we have the right and independent responsibility at our own decision to look into any area. We want to be responsive but at the same time we do have this final responsibility of being the independent auditor for the whole Government.[27]

Congressional Procedures

Filibusters and Cloture

Senate rules allow unlimited debate, and in the past legislation has often been delayed or blocked by filibusters. Filibustering is the practice of gaining and holding the floor of the Senate by talking without stopping. This tactic is most effective when it is used by a bloc of senators, who can keep recognizing each other and thus hold the floor endlessly. In effect, a filibuster can prevent a Senate majority from voting on legislation.

In 1975, in an effort to curb this strategy, the Senate voted to reduce the number of votes needed for *cloture* (a procedure to limit debate) to 60. Formerly, two-thirds of the senators voting had to vote for cloture. The problem of filibusters does not arise in the House because its larger size has caused it to place a five-minute time limit on any member's statement on a particular bill.

Secrecy

Reform bills passed in the 1970s have opened congressional debate to the public to a greater extent than ever before. As noted earlier, most legislative work is done in committee, and it is here that the reforms have occurred. In 1974, the House passed a rule requiring committee sessions to be open to the public and to the press. The Senate adopted a similar rule in 1975. However, committee members can vote in open session to close their meetings under a number of conditions ranging from national security to cases in which information must be kept secret under other governmental regulations. On the whole, this movement to open committee and subcommittee sessions has strengthened the concept of congressional accountability to the public, but again, there is little doubt that congresspeople who want to bargain secretly can do so in private conversations.

Classified Information

The investigations of the government's intelligence organizations conducted by select committees of the House and Senate in 1975 gave rise to new debate over what the executive branch and the agencies under its control should be permitted to keep secret from Congress. The question of what various congressional committees can keep secret from the full membership has also become a matter of concern. Both the House and the Senate have allowed their committees to decide what information should be released to the full membership. This issue is especially important to committees dealing with foreign relations, intelligence oversight, and atomic energy.

Executive privilege was the argument formerly used by government agencies that wanted to withhold certain information from congressional investigators, but this argument fell into disfavor after its excessive use during the Nixon administration. The Ford administration relied more heavily on about 300 regulations covering the release of information.[28]

Governmental secrecy is a controversial matter because while it is necessary to maintain secrecy in some areas, it is just as important to subject all governmental activities to some form of oversight. If this function is left to the executive branch alone, it can by used to cover up misdeeds and to defy the will of Congress. There is evidence that the use of legal action to resolve such questions will be more frequent in the future. The Supreme Court decision in the White House tapes case (1974) implied that executive privilege could be invoked in national security matters but failed to clearly define the process by which material can be classified as top secret.

The Subpoena Power

The right of Congress to subpoena documents and witnesses has become well established in line with the legislative branch's constitutional responsibilities. However, in the murky area of national security or executive privilege the lack of clear guidelines has resulted in conflict between Congress and the President. This issue flared up in November 1975, when the House Select Committee on Inteligence subpoenaed classified information from Secretary of State Kissinger as part of its investigation of the government's intelligence operations. The subpoena involved intelligence reports sent to the White House between 1962 and 1972.[29] Ford and Kissinger claimed that if these reports became public knowledge the nation's foreign relations would be seriously damaged; the House committee, on the other hand, claimed that such information was within the subpoena power of Congress. Neither side chose to take the issue to the courts for a decision, and only limited information was provided.

Contempt Citations

If an individual defies a congressional subpoena, Congress can vote a contempt citation against him or her. A citation must be approved by a majority of the house issuing it. The matter is then referred to the Justice Department for prosecution on criminal charges. Contempt citations for ignoring congressional orders can be voted against administration officials, but this is rarely done because it would lead to a clash between the executive and legislative branches, which are heavily dependent on each other.

Summary

Congress is the people's representative in the government. In addition to its representative function, Congress serves as the nation's legislative body and provides oversight for governmental operations, a function related to legislation. Congresspeople serve several constituencies, ranging from the citizens of their districts and states to interest groups, political parties, and the media. All of these sources of potential support or opposition must be taken into consideration in deciding what position to take on a particular issue.

The politics of Congress changes with changes in leadership. However, the way Congress is organized changes more in form than in substance. The committee system is the basis of legislative activity because of the wide variety of issues that come to the legislature for consideration. Members of Congress specialize in the subjects dealt with by their committees.

A person's judgment of congressional performance is related to what he or she expects Congress to accomplish. Most people would agree that congresspeople try to serve their constituents, whether individuals or interest groups, but their legislative record is more controversial. Congress is damned for doing too much by some people and for doing too little by others. The oversight function provides Congress with its best opportunity to win public approval, since committee investigations are often well publicized and can provide an effective check on governmental abuses. Whatever one's judgment of congressional performance, however, few would call the legislative branch uninteresting.

NOTES

[1] Debate between Jimmy Carter and Gerald R. Ford, Philadelphia, September 24, 1976, as reported in *The New York Times,* September 25, 1976, p. C9. Copyright © 1976 by The New York Times Company. Reprinted by permission.

[2] Quoted by Doris Kearns in *Lyndon Johnson & the American Dream* (New York: Harper & Row, 1976), pp. 301-302.

[3] Quoted in David J. Vogler, *The Politics of Congress* (Boston: Allyn & Bacon, 1974), p. 69.

[4] "His Pension Rises Faster Than Costs," reprinted by permission, *The Philadelphia Inquirer,* November 15, 1975, p. 18-C.

[5] *The New York Times,* January 22, 1975, p. 42.

[6] Reprinted from "Trying to Put a Lid on Government Junketing," in *U.S. News & World Report,* December 22, 1975, p. 59. Copyright © 1975 U.S. News & World Report, Inc.

[7] Quoted by John Pierson in "The Fat Cats of Capitol Hill," *The Wall Street Journal,* July 7, 1975, p. 22.

[8] *U.S. News & World Report,* December 27, 1975, p. 59.

[9] "Securities Industry Gave Senator Williams 28% of Elective Fund," *The New York Times,* June 22, 1975, p. 42. Copyright © 1975 by The New York Times Company. Reprinted by permission.

[10] Former Representative Luther Patrick, quoted in Vogler, p. 9.

CHAPTER 10 CROSSWORD PUZZLE

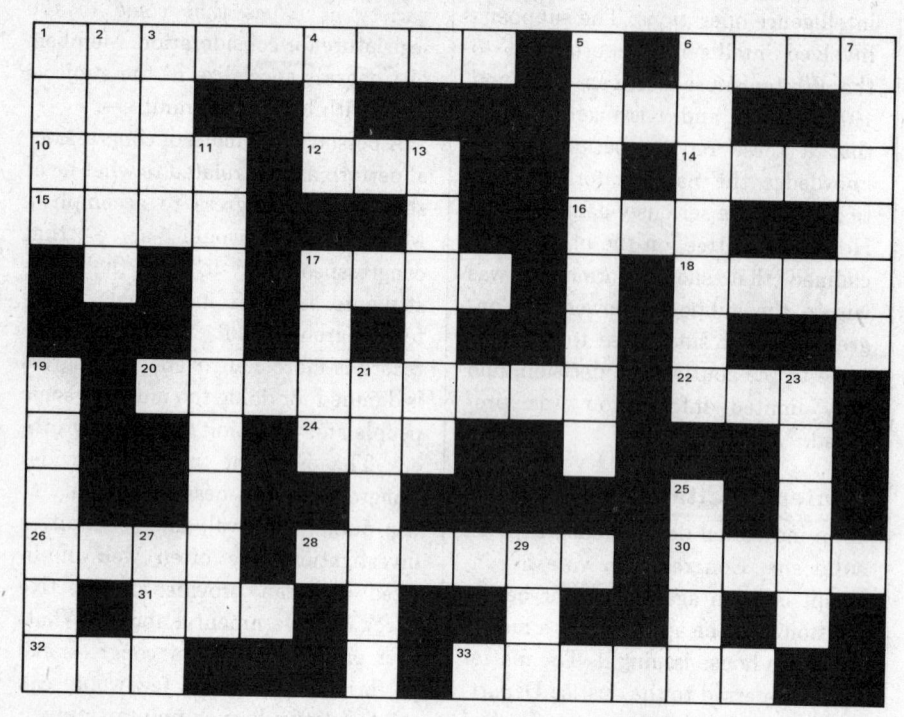

Across
1. Investigations by Congress are an example of its ___ function.
6. Exchange
8. Animal's foot
9. High mountain
10. Grows older
12. Opposite of "no"
14. Repetition of a sound; Greek nymph
15. Entice
16. Central Intelligence Agency (abbr.)
17. Family member
18. Part of a ship; on an even ___
20. Most meaningful legislative work is carried out in ___.
22. Uncooked
24. Three minus two
26. Opposite of "west"
28. The smaller size of the ___ allows individual members more potential influence than afforded members of the House.
30. Entranced
31. Organ of vision
32. Make lace
33. Senators and Representatives represent the ___.

Down
1. Gem stone
2. Indefinite
3. Large, wide-mouthed jar
4. Poison ___
5. Meetings of all party members in one house of the legislature are called ___.
6. The presiding officer of the House is the ___.
7. The average Congressman is better educated and more affluent than the ___ he represents.
11. ___ is the system by which committee assignments are based on length of service in the House or Senate.
13. The ___ must ratify treaties with foreign nations.
17. Ammunition (abbr.)
19. Committees established for a specific purpose with a temporary life are called ___ committees.
21. To have in mind; plan
23. Contact between the leadership of the House and Senate and fellow party members is the responsibility of ___.
25. Type of exam
27. Stage scenery
29. "Blessed be the ___ that binds."

---

[11] Mark J. Green, James M. Fallows, and David R. Zwick, *Who Runs Congress?* (New York: Grossman, 1972), p. 263.

[12] Quoted in *U.S. News & World Report,* August 16, 1976, p. 27. Copyright © 1976 by U.S. News & World Report, Inc.

[13] Quoted in Green, p. 264, Kenneth Harding, head of the House Democratic Campaign Committee.

[14] Richard L. Madden in "Record Total Leaving Congress Voluntarily," *The New York Times,* October 2, 1976, p. 8C.

[15] *The United States Budget in Brief, Fiscal Year 1977,* p. 62, Table 4.

[16] Kearns, p. 123.

[17] Quoted in *U.S. News & World Report,* August 16, 1976, p. 27. Copyright © 1976 by U.S. News & World Report, Inc.

[18] Aage R. Clausen, *How Congressmen Decide* (New York: St. Martin's Press, 1973), pp. 148-149.

[19] Representative Everett Burkhalter, quoted in Green, p. 59.

[20] *Congressional Quarterly,* November 8, 1975, p. 2408.

[21] Quoted in Vogler, p. 132.

[22] Ibid., p. 179.

[23] Quoted in *Congressional Quarterly,* September 6, 1975, p. 1922.

[24] Quoted in Edwin L. Dale, Jr., "Can Congress at Last Control the Money Tree," *The New York Times Magazine,* August 22, 1976, p. 70.

[25] *Congressional Quarterly,* September 6, 1975, p. 1925.

[26] Quoted by Jon Margolis in "The G.A.O. is Congress's Unpopular Watchdog," *The New York Times,* May 18, 1975, p. 7. Copyright © 1975 by The New York Times Company. Reprinted by permission.

[27] Ibid.

[28] *Congressional Quarterly,* October 4, 1975, p. 2099.

[29] "House Unit Seeks Contempt Order Against Kissinger," *The New York Times,* November 15, 1975, p. 8C. Copyright © 1975 by The New York Times Company. Reprinted by permission.

CHAPTER 11
THE PRESIDENCY

CHAPTER OUTLINE

Questions to Consider
Introduction
Presidential Leadership
    Leadership Style
    Presidential Character
The President as Political Leader
The President as Legislator
    The Veto Power
    Impoundment of Funds
    Executive Privilege
The President and the Judiciary
The President and Foreign Policy
    Executive Agreements
    The President as Commander-in-Chief
The President, the Media, and the Public
The President as Administrative Leader
    The White House Staff
    The Executive Office
    The National Security Council
    The Office of Management and Budget
    The Council of Economic Advisers
    The Cabinet
Limitations on Presidential Power
    Commitments and Precedents
    Availability of Resources
    Availability and Quality of Information
    The Political Climate
The Appeal of the Presidency
    The Vice Presidency
    Presidential Succession
Summary

QUESTIONS TO CONSIDER

Few people attract the sort of day-to-day attention that is focused on the President of the United States. The nation's role as a world power coupled with the power of the Presidency itself makes the President's every action newsworthy. American Presidents have differed greatly in terms of character and leadership style. What is *charisma* and how important is it to Presidential performance? What kind of person is most likely to be an effective President? These questions will be discussed in the first section of the chapter.

The President also has a variety of responsibilities. We know that he heads the executive branch, but what agencies and departments are included in the executive branch? How does the President make decisions? What is the relationship between the President and the vice president? These matters will be the subject of the remainder of the chapter. When you complete this chapter, you should have a better understanding of the powers and limitations of the Presidency.

Introduction

The President of the United States is a symbol of American power. But while the President has enormous power and prestige, he is limited by constitutional checks and balances as well as by political realities. He must make a continuous effort to maintain broad-based public support, coerce or persuade an often reluctant Congress into accepting his leadership, and get an often unresponsive bureaucracy to support his programs. The Presidency illustrates the contradiction between appearance of power and the reality of limited authority.

The President's power has increased as the United States' world role has enlarged and the federal government has become an increasingly pervasive force in domestic affairs. The President's role as commander-in-chief of the armed forces has been especially significant in foreign policy matters. There has been an increased tendency to bypass Congress in this area—for example, in the case of the Vietnam War. Presidents since Roosevelt have had increasing leeway in matters of foreign policy, and this has led to greater power for the executive branch.

The growth of Presidential power has made the public increasingly likely to look to the White House for the solution to any problem, foreign or domestic. The public's perception of the Presidency as the zenith of American government has permitted Presidents to surround themselves with the pomp and ceremony of royalty, as evidenced by Kennedy's "Camelot," Johnson's raw display of power, and Nixon's fascination with lavish banquets and extensive foreign travel. Thus, the Presidency has become a far different institution than it was in the Truman-Eisenhower period, to say nothing of the nineteenth century.

Presidential Leadership

The problems facing any modern President are not easy to solve. The successful chief executive controls events as much as possible rather than allowing events to control administration policy. But if he wants to lead rather than be led, the President must set national priorities and develop plans for meeting national goals. The President also serves as a symbol of national pride and purpose.

As Herbert Hoover put it, the presidency is more than an administrative office. It must be the symbol of American ideals. The high and the lowly must be seen with the same eyes, met in the same spirit. It must be the instrument by which the national conscience is livened, and it must under the guidance of the Almighty interpret and follow that conscience. [1]

The crises of government are easier to accept if citizens have confidence in democratic processes that are symbolized by Presidential leadership. Democratic government must be seen as legitimate if it is to function effectively, and the Presidency is the most visible institution of the government. President Nixon's resignation was triggered by his administration's loss of legitimacy in the eyes of the public as well as in the opinion of government leaders. This is a tide no President can withstand.

While events beyond the President's control play an important part in shaping his actions, effective leadership requires strong, imaginative policies. There are few situations in which the chief executive has only one possible course of action. President Truman's announcement of the Marshall Plan is an example of effective leadership. At the end of World War II, many Western democracies faced economic ruin and possible takeover by communist governments. Truman had a variety of choices ranging from total inaction to a strong policy accompanied by a regional economic plan. The Marshall Plan restored the economic base of Western Europe and provided a buffer against further Soviet expansion in Europe.

Leadership Style

Leadership style, or the means by which the chief executive tries to gain support for his programs, has an important effect on his ability to carry out those programs. There is no one style that automatically leads to success. However, the President must gain respect for his ability and trust in his statements.

The last five Presidents had widely differing leadership styles, reflecting both their personalities and their perceptions of the Presidency. Dwight D. Eisenhower took office with a reputation for effective leadership gained during World War II. His style was to avoid the political infighting that had marked the Truman administration. Eisenhower was one of the few Presidents in this century to leave office after two terms with his reputation undamaged. Many criticized him for his nonaggressive style, but the low level of domestic legislation in his administration was accompanied by a low level of military activity abroad. It is possible that the aggressiveness of a Johnson or a Truman in domestic affairs is more likely to be accompanied by activism in foreign affairs. If this is the case, the wars in Korea and Vietnam may have been as much a reflection of Presidential style as an outgrowth of international events.

John F. Kennedy's inaugural address. Kennedy was extremely successful in building support because of his personal magnetism.

Truman and Johnson lacked personal magnetism or charisma but were active in trying to achieve their policy objectives. Neither President was reluctant to clash with his political foes, and both were quick to take their case to the American people. This active style coupled with willingness to fight for desired programs and policies will usually produce results. But, as was demonstrated by the Vietnam War, those results are not always beneficial.

John F. Kennedy was a prime example of a charismatic leader. His personal vitality called forth a positive response from the American people. It was Kennedy's dynamic leadership style that enabled him to maintain a broad base of public support despite a series of foreign policy setbacks that began with the Bay of Pigs invasion in April 1961. This was followed by failure to respond to the building of the Berlin Wall in August of the same year. Despite these setbacks, Kennedy succeeded in maintaining his personal credibility and emerged from the Cuban Missile Crisis in 1962 with an improved reputation for leadership ability. Kennedy's tragic death in 1963 precludes a meaningful evaluation of his success as a leader. However, his leadership style clearly fired the imagination of the American people.

Richard M. Nixon came to the Presidency with considerable experience but without the type of personal magnetism that had worked to Kennedy's advantage. The Watergate affair and Nixon's resignation were basically due to the failure of Nixon and his closest advisers to fully understand the limitations on Presidential power. Nixon's refusal to take responsibility for the Watergate break-in led to a long-drawn-out attempt to cover up the story. This is in strong contrast with Kennedy's action in taking responsibility for the Bay of Pigs failure. It is clear that the people will accept errors of judgment more readily than deception or dishonesty in a leader.

Gerald R. Ford became President as a result of Nixon's resignation. His reputation for frankness and openness was a welcome relief after the secrecy that had characterized the Nixon administration. However, acceptance of the President as a decent human being should not be confused with acceptance of the chief executive as a national leader. Possibly because many people saw him as a "caretaker" President, Ford failed to establish himself as a strong leader despite his appealing personal qualities.

This brief overview of five recent Presidents and their leadership styles leads to the conclusion that no one style will automatically win public approval. Truman, Eisenhower, and Kennedy had contrasting styles, but they all won the trust of the people. Ford had the disadvantage of not having been elected President and was unable to gain a reputation for leadership despite his good personal qualities. Johnson and Nixon were effective leaders until they were faced with adverse circumstances, at which point both resorted to deception, which is something the public will not forgive.

Presidential Character

A President's leadership style is a reflection of his character as an individual. The word *character* refers to an individual's attitudes and personality traits. While any President is aware of the attitudes the American people have come to expect in a chief executive, the character he brings to the White House has an important impact on his performance. The character of the President as a private man affects his view of the political world as well as his reaction to events.

In *The Presidential Character*, James David Barber holds that "the best way to predict a President's character, world view, and style is to see how he constructed them in the first place." [2] Barber describes four patterns of behavior that can be used as a basis for predicting Presidential performance:

1. *Active-Positive*—an individual who enjoys a high rate of activity and believes in a rational approach—"using the brain to move the feet." Such a person is likely to be flexible, with high self-esteem.

2. *Active-Negative*—an individual who works hard, appears ambitious, but believes life is meant to be hard and derives little emotional reward. Such a person is likely to be aggressive as he feels threatened by his environment. This pattern is common among people who are attracted to political life.

3. *Passive-Positive*—an individual who has low self-esteem and whose efforts are directed at receiving the affection of others as a compensation. Such a person remains optimistic, but inner doubts make success unlikely.

4. *Passive-Negative*—an individual who enters politics because of a feeling that it is his duty. Such a person takes a moralistic view, with strong ideas of what is "right." This lack of flexibility is a political detriment. [3]

Barber examines the actions of Presidents Johnson and Kennedy and looks ahead to the potential actions of Richard Nixon. (*The Presidential Character* was written before Nixon's reelection in 1972.) According to Barber, "the struggle in [Johnson's] character was a double battle; of the little lad on teacher's lap wanting to be Davy Crockett, and of the beer hall brawler wanting to rise to high eminence. Those fights went on all his life; in the Presidency they came together in his image of himself as lone defender of the faith, courageously refighting the Alamo in Vietnam." [4] These attitudes are typical of the active-negative personality, whose fear of failure leads to viewing problems as a personal threat. "For him, surrender is suicide, an admission of guilt and weakness. Having invested all his moral capital in the cause, he will—he must—plunge on to the end." [5]

Barber also describes Nixon as an active-negative personality. In the following passage, he sums up Nixon's character and predicts the possible consequences. Barber's words are strikingly prophetic in light of the events that unfolded after *The Presidential Character* was written.

To see in President Nixon the character of Richard Nixon—the character formed and set early in life—one need only read over his speech on the Cambodian invasion, with its themes of power and control, its declaration of independence, its self-concern, its damning of doubters, and its coupling of humiliation with defeat. This character could lead the President on to disaster, following in the path of his heroes Wilson and Hoover and his predecessor Johnson. So far his crises have been bounded dramas, each apparently curtained with the end of the last act. The danger is that crisis will be transformed into tragedy—that Nixon will go from a dramatic experiment to a moral commitment, a commitment to follow his private star, to fly in the face of overwhelming odds. That type of reaction is to be expected when and if Nixon is confronted with a severe threat to his power and sense of virtue.[6]

Barber concludes that active-negative Presidents are potentially dangerous because of the risk of "one man's personal tragedy plunging the nation into massive social tragedy."[7] In contrast, people with active-positive personalities enjoy the power of the Presidency and are comfortable with it. Barber puts Franklin Roosevelt, Harry Truman, and John Kennedy in this category, though they had very different public personalities. As far as the public was concerned, Roosevelt was a father figure, Truman was blunt and honest, and Kennedy was committed to a better life for all Americans. Still, these three Presidents shared an active-positive character, which led each to become highly involved in the Presidency and to face adversity without being handicapped by the fear of failure.

It is impossible to predict with certainty how any individual will fulfill his Presidential responsibilities. President Carter appears to be an active-positive person, but his limited national exposure before the 1976 Presidential campaign makes such a judgment tentative at best.

The President plays many roles, of which some are dictated by the Constitution, and some have evolved with the growth of the nation; together, they give the President more power than the nation's founders could have imagined. The way a President fulfills these roles will vary, depending on his personality. However, there is little opportunity for any chief executive to decrease the range of Presidential activity. The relationships of past Presidents with other nations, with the American public, and with other branches of the government, combined with the President's constitutional duties, have given rise to a prescribed set of Presidential roles.

The President as Political Leader

To any senator, representative, or governor, the Presidency offers the highest challenge and the greatest reward. Anyone who wants to become President must go through a series of campaigns that test his physical stamina, his ability to gain the support of party leaders, his organizational talents, and his fund-raising abilities. The national party organizations usually take a neutral stand during this process, so that the Presidential nominee is very much on his own in the sense that he must build up a personal political organization.

While the President is the formal head of his party, it is more accurate to view him as the leader of a Presidential party that revolves around his office and is responsive to his needs. The inability of the President to control members of his own party in Congress weakens his role as party leader and leads to dependence on the Presidential party, which can be relied on to support his policies. Presidential appointees and some members of Congress may be included in this loose, unofficial group of supporters, but the fact that Congresspeople must seek reelection in their own state or district weakens this base of support. Thus, although the President attains office through the will of the majority, he is often thwarted by members of his own party in Congress. It is necessary for the President to seek bipartisan support for his programs if he is to be successful, and even then he cannot expect too much.

Since 1932, the Democrats have enjoyed a congressional majority in every year except 1946 and 1952. Despite this advantage, lack of party unity has forced Democratic Presidents to attract votes from the Republican minority in order to put their programs into effect. Except during Roosevelt's first two terms, the Democratic edge in itself has not been enough to assure the President of congressional backing. The problem faced by Republican Presidents has been more severe, since they have had to court the political opposition.

A newly elected President is at the peak of his party influence because he has at least four and probably eight years in which to distribute jobs and influence policy in such a way as to reward the faithful and punish the disloyal. Toward the end of his second term, however, a President's influence begins to fade because his ability to affect political events is near an end. There have been few periods during which a President who was blessed with a majority of his own party in Congress could translate this fact into strong congressional support for Presidential programs. The "Great Society" legislation pushed through Congress in 1965-1966 by Lyndon Johnson in the wake of his landslide victory over Barry Goldwater was made possible by such conditions. Johnson's political clout was quickly undermined by the Vietnam War, however, and he left office with little political influence.

Despite the problems any chief executive faces in getting the support of his fellow party members in Congress, the effort goes on. The President can usually be counted on to participate in fund-raising or campaign activities in behalf of party organizations, thereby collecting political I.O.U.'s and increasing his influence. President Ford engaged in a large number of political activities of this sort in the fall of 1975. He expressed his views on this aspect of the Presidency in a press conference as follows: "As President and as a member of the Republican Party and the leader of the Republican Party, I have an obligation to try and strengthen and rebuild the Republican party organization in many, many states. And that's what I've been doing."[8]

Jimmy Carter and his proposed Cabinet meet in Georgia before the inauguration. Carter was the first President to initiate cabinet discussions before an inauguration.

There is an obvious contradiction between the political role of the President in which he is expected to serve his party's interests, and his constitutional role as President of the American people. He cannot react to every issue the way his fellow party members want him to. Thus, he may gain their opposition when he needs their support. The skillful President walks a narrow line between these conflicting responsibilities, convincing his party that he is responsive to their desires while persuading the public that he is acting in the nation's best interests.

The political role of the President is not limited to seeking support from fellow party members or the public as a whole. Effective Presidential leadership also requires support from the more important interest groups in American society. Regardless of his party membership, every President needs the support of the more important farm groups, labor organizations, financial institutions, and business groups. In addition, he must be aware of the elites concerned with particular issues such as foreign policy. The high-level appointments made by President Carter are a good example of how a chief executive works to build a broad base of support. One of Carter's campaign promises was to bring "new faces" to Washington. But when the time came to name the new cabinet many, if not most, of Carter's appointments were members of the "Establishment" who had a record of previous government service or were closely identified with the traditional power structure. Secretary of the Treasury Michael Blumenthal had headed the Bendix Corporation and was influential in American business. Secretary of State Cyrus R. Vance had served in the Johnson administration and was closely identified with the Rockefeller Foundation. UN Ambassador Andrew Young was a well-known civil rights leader. Secretary of Agriculture Robert Berglund had been a well-known farmer and Secretary of the Interior Cecil Andruss an active conservationist. Ideally, cabinet officers represent a cross-section of the important groups in American society and President Carter's cabinet appointments appear to meet that requirement.

The President as Legislator

The President must try to put into effect the policies he has supported in campaign speeches or State of the Union addresses. This is a difficult task because of his lack of political control in Congress. The fact that the President has a national constituency while members of Congress have a state or local base results in markedly different perspectives on most issues. Moreover, because of the lack of party unity within Congress the President must deal with a variety of political blocs on any given issue. In the 1950s and 1960s, for example, a conservative coalition of southern Democrats and Republicans formed around most social legislation to either support or oppose the President's position, depending on whether that position was conservative or liberal.

There are times when the President has a greater chance of success in his legislative role. During periods of war or economic hardship, the President and Congress can more readily agree on legislative goals. The President's impact on legislation can also be affected by his personal relationships with members of key committees, such as the Ways and Means Committee or the Rules Committee in the House, which can either speed or block the President's legislative proposals. President Johnson made use of this type of personal influence and, with large Democratic party majorities in the House and Senate, was able to put into effect a far-reaching legislative program including medicare, massive aid to education, a voting rights bill, large appropriations for research on cancer and heart disease, and rent subsidies for low-income families.

Doris Kearns described the personal touch, Johnson style, in *Lyndon Johnson and the American Dream*. In a phone call thanking the congressperson most responsible for a legislative victory, Johnson said "They tell me you [a liberal Democrat] did a helluva job up there. I'm mighty proud of you and so is *The New York Times*. It was a great day for the House..." And in another conversation: "I want you [a Southern conservative] to know how proud I am of you today, how proud your country is. You did the U.S. a great service. You're a gentleman and

The President as Legislator **167**

Lyndon B. Johnson about to address the nation in 1968; during this speech he announced a halt to the bombing of North Vietnam and his decision not to seek reelection.

a scholar and a producer and I love you." [10]

Johnson's success was unusual, and it is hard to determine the extent to which skill and political influence were the dominant factors and how much was due to the activism of a large Democratic majority pushing through a mass of important legislation that had long been under consideration and whose time had finally come. Usually legislative leaders oppose many of the President's programs; even if they agree with the chief executive, they are often unable to persuade their fellow party members to follow their lead.

Table 11-1 shows the relative success of the President in winning congressional support on roll call votes—in which congresspeople's votes are recorded—between 1953 and 1976. Note that the lowest levels of Presidential success occurred in 1959 (as Eisenhower was completing his two terms), in 1973-1974 (when the Nixon administration was about to collapse), and in the Ford administration. The relatively high level of legislative success enjoyed by Eisenhower until the last year of his term and Nixon's early success demonstrate that minority-party Presidents are not automatically doomed to failure as legislative leaders. However, these data exaggerate the success of the President in dealing with Congress because they do not take into account the fact that many Presidential proposals never reach the floor of Congress. There are also many bills that become law with broad support from both parties. Increases in social security payments and reductions in taxes usually face little opposition; in such cases, a roll call vote is taken so that legislators can get credit from their constituents for voting in favor of the bill.

The President has usually been able to dominate legislation in a few key areas: foreign affairs, military appropriations, and the overall budget. This is because while the President has the opportunity to establish goals in these areas Congress is often unable to provide convincing counterarguments. Thus treaties, defense spending, or foreign aid appropriations may arouse

TABLE 11-1
Presidential Success on Votes, 1953-1974

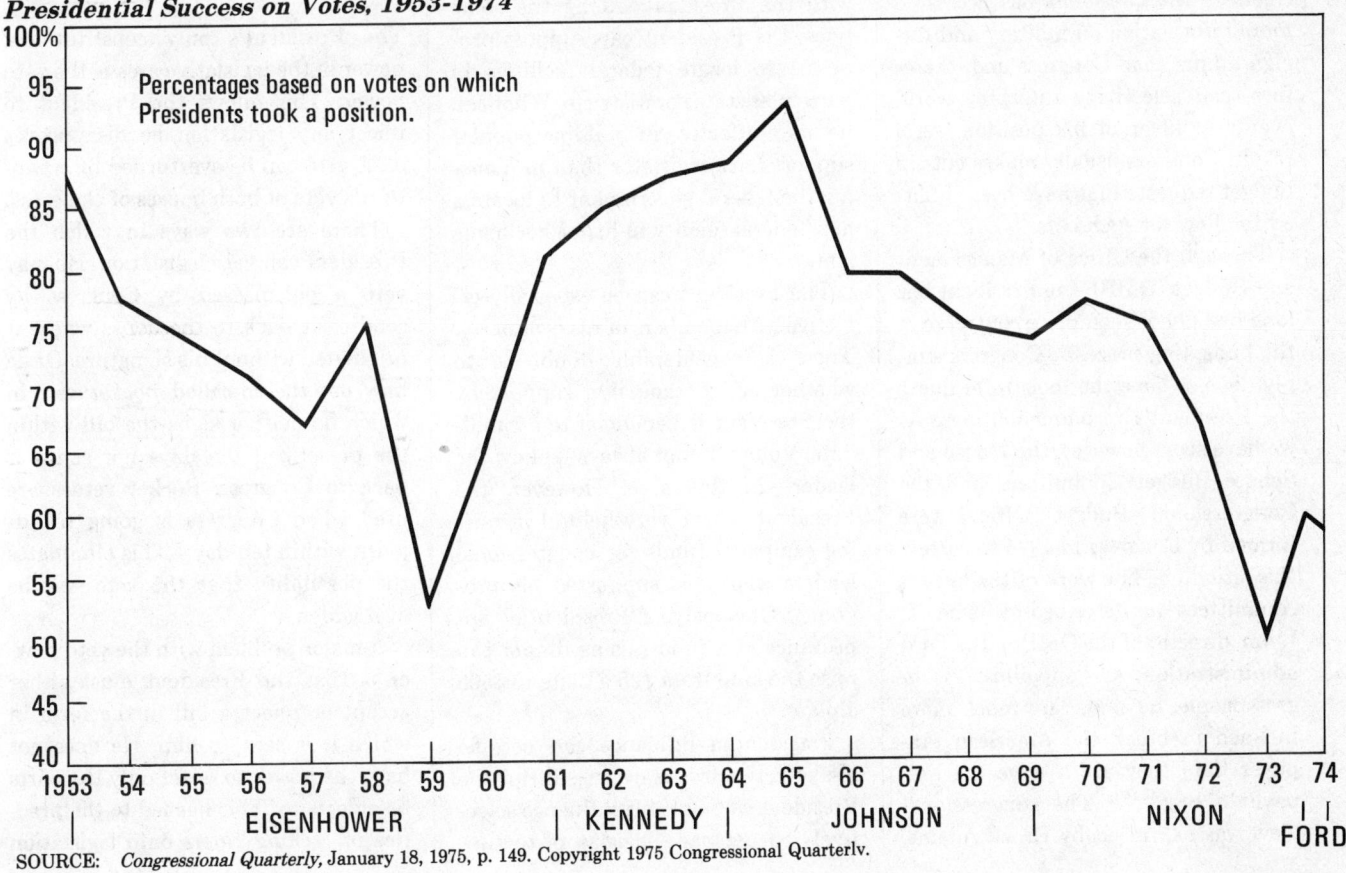

SOURCE: *Congressional Quarterly*, January 18, 1975, p. 149. Copyright 1975 Congressional Quarterly.

some opposition, but the President will usually have his way. As Arthur M. Schlesinger, Jr. has written,

In the 1950s American foreign policy called on the American government to do things that no American government had ever tried to do before. The new American approach to world affairs, nurtured in the sense of omnipresent crisis, set new political objectives, developed new military capabilities, devised new diplomatic techniques, invented new instruments of foreign operations, and instituted a new hierarchy of values. Every one of these innovations encouraged the displacement of power, both practical and constitutional, from an increasingly acquiescent Congress into an increasingly imperial Presidency."

The question of military appropriations is closely tied to the President's foreign policy role because the purpose of the armed forces is to reinforce the nation's foreign policy as well as defend the nation itself. Through the various intelligence agencies in the executive branch—the CIA, the Defense Intelligence Agency, the National Security Council, the National Security Agency—the President has access to more information on military and foreign affairs than Congress and, therefore, can selectively interpret world events in favor of his position. As a result, Congress usually makes cuts in budget requests that have been inflated to allow for such cuts.

Through the Office of Management and Budget (OMB), the President has long had almost complete control over the budgeting process—Congress simply did not have the tools to evaluate the President's recommendations. As we have seen, however, the House and Senate Budget Committees and the Congressional Budget Office were formed by Congress in 1974 to correct this situation. The work of the budget committees was described by James T. Lynn, director of the OMB in the Ford administration, as "appalling." Congresspeople, he said, "are much more inclined to break the American taxpayer than they are to give the taxpayer a break." [12] The congressional view was expressed by Brock Adams, chairman of the House Budget Committee: "For the first time in its history, the Congress has developed and operated a comprehensive national budget for the Federal Government. The successful operation of this new budget process is historic... because it marks the completion of an economic policy that is distinctly that of the Congress—not the President." [13] It is clear from these contrasting opinions that both groups are aware that the new budget process may affect the President's ability to dominate the government's budgetary policies.

There are many important weapons that the President can use in his struggle to persuade Congress to pass his legislative program. The mere fact that the President is involved is significant. The President can be very helpful in building up the reputations of senators or representatives by allowing then to influence his appointments to federal positions of individuals from within their constituencies. This serves to give the legislator greater status and an incentive to cooperate with the President. Along the same lines, the President can support proposals to locate federal facilities in particular states or districts. What can be more effective in building popular support for a legislator than influencing the federal government to locate a new federal facility in his or her home state?

The President can be especially effective with members of his own party. There is considerable doubt as to whether active campaign support by the President is beneficial to a candidate. Voters do not always "follow the leader" in this area. However, the President can be very helpful in raising campaign funds for congressional leaders who have supported his programs. Obviously, a Presidential appearance at a fund-raising dinner can raise the ante from $25 a plate to $500 a plate.

Presidential influence can become less effective if it is overused. But the President who uses his influence selectively to persuade legislators to support his program can be very effective. It is hard to turn down a personal request from the Oval Office. The benefits of cooperating with the President may include invitations to the White House for social occasions. Even a cynic must be impressed when the President and First Lady descend the winding staircase in the White House to the Marine Corps Band's rendition of "Hail to the Chief!" The relationship of the President with members of Congress varies from the close contact he maintains with his party's House and Senate leaders to a nodding acquaintance with low-ranking legislators. The President normally has more influence with members of his own party than with the opposition because he has more to offer in return for their cooperation. But regardless of the personalities or party memberships involved, the office of the Presidency cannot be ignored on Capitol Hill.

The Veto Power

The President's only constitutional power in the legislative area is the veto power. This allows the President to reject any legislation he disapproves of. A veto can be overturned by a two-thirds vote of both houses of Congress.

There are two ways in which the President can veto legislation. He may veto a bill passed by Congress by sending it back to the house where it originated without his signature. Or he may use the so-called *pocket veto* in which he neither signs the bill within the prescribed ten days nor sends it back to Congress. Pocket vetoes are used when Congress is going to adjourn within ten days. This eliminates the possibility that the veto will be overridden.

A major problem with the veto power is that the President must either accept or reject a bill in the form in which it is sent to him. He does not have the power to reject only the parts he objects to. This has led to the practice of tacking *riders* onto legislation that the President wants badly. Many of these riders have nothing to do with the legislation to which they are attached and represent an attempt to avoid a veto. This situation has led to the suggestion that the chief executive be given the power of *item veto*, that is, the power to veto portions of a bill that he objects to while allowing the others to become law. This would strengthen the President's hand and, naturally, is unattractive to those who believe there is already too much power in the Oval Office.

The President's veto power gives him a voice in the writing of legislation as well as its passage. Party leaders in Congress are well aware of the President's position on most proposed legislation, and the threat of a veto will often lead them to make an effort to change a bill so that it will win the President's approval.

The veto power serves as a check on congressional action because of the difficulty of obtaining enough votes to override a veto. However, it can also be used as a political weapon by Congress. Congress can pass legislation that is certain to be vetoed in order to gain public approval at the expense of the President, particularly when the President is a member of the minority party. President Ford vetoed 56 bills in his first two years in office; of these Congress was able to override only 10. The clash of wills and policy differences between Ford and Congress were dramatized by these vetoes and became a subject of debate during the 1976 election campaign.

Impoundment of Funds

Another way the President can thwart the will of Congress is by impounding funds—that is, not spending congressional appropriations as they are intended to be used. *Authorized* is a key word in discussions of impoundment, since most appropriations bills "authorize" rather than "order" spending.

Impoundment was rarely used before the Nixon years. In 1941, Roosevelt refused to spend funds earmarked for public works on the ground that they should be used in the war effort. Similarly, Johnson postponed $5 billion of expenditures in an effort to counteract the inflationary pressures of the Vietnam War. Both actions had the tacit approval of congressional leaders.

Nixon used impoundment to a greater extent than previous Presidents and for a different reason. The examples just given involved decisions to refrain from spending because of economic and other conditions prevailing at the time and after consultation with congressional leaders. In contrast, Nixon used impoundment as a form of item veto.[14] Nixon expressed his right to impound authorized funds as follows: "The constitutional right for the President of the United States to impound funds . . . when the spending of money would mean either increasing prices or increasing taxes . . . is absolutely clear."[15]

Nixon's use of impoundment was challenged before the Supreme Court in 1973 when he refused to spend funds authorized for the Office of Economic Opportunity. The Court ruled against Nixon on the ground that if his position was upheld, "no barrier would remain to the executive ignoring any and all Congressional authorizations, if he deemed them . . . contrary to the needs of the nation."[16] In 1974, Congress passed legislation that limited the President's power to impound funds without the approval of Congress.

Executive Privilege

Executive privilege is the President's right to withhold information from congressional committees, usually on grounds of national security or the national interest. There is no consitutional provision for executive privilege, but it has evolved as part of the concept of separation of powers. The question of what should be regarded as privileged communication within the executive branch and what should be made available to Congress is a controversial one.

This issue made headlines during the Watergate investigations, when executive privilege was used as a means of preventing officials in the executive branch from being forced to testify before the Senate Watergate Committee. The Nixon administration claimed that the President could determine what information could be withheld under executive privilege. However, in *United States* v. *Nixon*, the Supreme Court ruled that the White House tape recordings subpoenaed by the House Judiciary Committee were not in the privileged category and must be released. Since the tapes proved that the President was involved in the Watergate cover-up, the Court's decision played an important role in Nixon's resignation.

A more moderate claim of executive privilege was made by President Ford in relation to discussions and communications involving foreign affairs. In response to a comtempt citation against Secretary of State Kissinger for failing to comply with a House subpoena, Ford said, "This issue involves grave matters affecting our conduct of foreign policy and raises questions which go to the ability of our republic to govern itself effectively."[17]

Obviously, the President and his advisers must have the freedom to discuss governmental policy without being required to make those discussions public. On the other hand, Congress must have information on which to base its legislative decisions. Thus, the issue of executive privilege is likely to remain unresolved, since it is related to the basic conflict between the President and Congress.

The President and the Judiciary

Article II of the Constitution gives the President the power to appoint "Judges of the Supreme Court, and all other Officers of the United States, whose Appointments are not herein otherwise provided for, and which shall be established by Law." The President's power to appoint Supreme

Court justices gives him an opportunity to extend his political philosophy to the judicial branch of the government. Like all federal judges, Supreme Court justices are appointed for life and thus have a voice in Court decisions long after the President leaves office. While the President's appointees must gain approval by a simple majority in the Senate, this does not usually prevent him from appointing people whose political philosophy is similar to his own.

The President usually bases his choices of Supreme Court justices on his perceptions of the nominee's fitness for service on the nation's highest court as well as political philosophy. Once they have joined the Court, however, justices have often become more liberal or conservative than the President expected. For example, Chief Justice Earl Warren, who was appointed by Eisenhower, a conservative, was noted for his liberal influence. In this case, a conservative President appointed a chief justice who had a reputation for middle-of-the-road political views, but proved to be in the vanguard of liberal judicial decision making. Eisenhower has been quoted as calling his appointment of Warren a "damnfool mistake." [18]

Nixon tried to use his power of appointment to place conservative justices on the Court. In Nixon's view, political philosophy was more important than judicial qualifications; as a result, he suffered the embarrassment of having two of his Supreme Court nominees rejected by the Senate. Thus, while the President can affect future Court rulings through his power of appointment, the Senate serves as a check on the appointment of unqualified justices to the Court.

Other judicial appointments are usually made in consultation with influential party leaders and the attorney general. In addition, it is traditional for the President's fellow party members in the Senate to be consulted about appointments to the lower federal courts in their states and for them to have what amounts to veto power over such appointments. This tradition is called *senatorial courtesy*.

The selection of judges for the lower federal courts allows the President to pay political debts or gain new political credits with senators and other prominent politicians. The Supreme Court appointments, in contrast, give the President a chance to have an impact on future interpretations of the Constitution.

The President and Foreign Policy

The international role of the United States makes foreign relations a primary concern of any President. The chief executive is the major force in this area and has the authority to make important decisions such as whether to recognize a new regime or change existing diplomatic relations in any way. The importance of Presidential leadership in this area leads candidates to make every effort to get voters to believe they are competent in foreign affairs. For example, during the debate between President Ford and Jimmy Carter in San Francisco on October 6, 1976, Richard Valeriani, one of the panelists, mentioned Carter's "limited experience in foreign affairs." Carter replied as follows:

I have an adequate background, I believe. I am a graduate of the U.S. Naval Academy, the first military graduate since Eisenhower. I have served as the Governor of Georgia and traveled extensively in foreign countries and South America, Central America, Europe, the Middle East and in Japan. [19]

The fact that one of the three debates between Ford and Carter was concerned solely with foreign affairs illustrated the importance of the President's activities in this area. In the final analysis, the chief executive who must make the basic decisions affecting the relations of the United States with other nations and with international organizations.

Executive Agreements

The President has the constitutional authority (Article II) "by and with the advice and consent of the Senate, to make treaties, provided two-thirds of the Senators present concur." While this provision appears to limit the chief executive's foreign policy role, the use of executive agreements allows the President to chart his own foreign policy course. Executive agreements are understandings reached with other nations and signed by the President on behalf of the nation. Thus, they represent national obligations of which neither Congress nor the public may be aware. Executive agreements are whatever the President says they are. There is no significant difference between such an agreement and a treaty, except that a treaty must be ratified by the Senate.

Congress has tried to regain some control over the President's activities in this area by passing two laws designed to compel the President to inform Congress of understandings reached with other nations. One act requires that all executive agreements related to nuclear arms control be submitted to both houses of Congress for approval. The other, the Case Act of 1972, requires that all executive agreements be submitted to Congress as matters of information; those that are considered secret must be submitted to the Senate Foreign Relations Committee and the House International Relations Committee. However, if the President chooses to call an understanding something else besides an executive agreement, the Case Act is useless. Thus, the proper balance between the powers of the chief executive and the responsibilities of Congress in the area of foreign affairs is still a subject of heated debate.

The President as Commander-in-Chief

The President's diplomatic role is linked to his role as commander-in-chief of the armed forces. Article II,

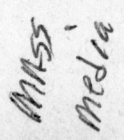

Section 11 of the Constitution provides that "the President shall be Commander-in-Chief of the Army and Navy of the United States, and of the militia of the several States when called into the actual service of the United States."

The authority to command the armed forces coupled with the use of executive agreements has given the President considerable control over foreign affairs. While Congress has the authority to declare war at the request of the President, U.S. armed forces have been involved in numerous major conflicts without congressional approval, notably the Korean and Vietnam Wars. Of course, in a sense Congress must approve of such involvements because it is called upon to fund U.S. military operations.

The questions of whether to seek authorization from Congress before involving U.S. troops in foreign conflicts is a political one. In 1964, President Johnson asked Congress to pass the Gulf of Tonkin Resolution in the wake of reported attacks on two U.S. destroyers in the Gulf of Tonkin. This resolution authorized the President to take "all necessary measures" to repel future attacks and prevent further aggression. The Vietnamese conflict eventually went far beyond the intent of the Resolution and left the President without the support of a substantial majority in Congress. True, Congress did pass the appropriations needed to maintain U.S. forces in Vietnam, but they were presented with significant U.S. involvement and had limited options.

As a result of the Vietnam War, Congress became determined to limit the President's war-making powers. In 1973, it passed the War Powers Act, which provides for a 60-day limitation on the commitment of American troops to combat without congressional approval and an additional 30 days if the President certifies that withdrawal of U.S. forces could take place within that period. After 60 days, Congress has the power to order the President to withdraw American forces. However, public dissatisfaction with the way the Vietnam War was conducted will probably lead future Presidents to seek congressional approval before committing troops except in emergencies.

One reason for the dominance of the President in foreign and military affairs is that he is provided with information by the diplomatic corps and the intelligence agencies—both of which are within the executive branch—and thus is in a position to base his decisions on information that is unlikely to be shared with Congress. It has always been assumed that the commander-in-chief is in a unique position to protect the nation's interests in the areas of national security and foreign affairs and therefore should be given the widest possible latitude in policy-making. Foreign policy debates are given heavy coverage in election years. There is little real disagreement about the direction U.S. policy should take. John F. Kennedy spoke of lowered U.S. prestige abroad and the "missile gap" between the United States and the Soviet Union in his campaign for the Presidency in 1960. Jimmy Carter's criticisms of President Ford's foreign policy revolved around questions of secrecy and morality. Thus, neither candidate's attacks on the incumbent's policies represented a real difference or new approach—both involved style more than substance.

"Politics stops at the water's edge" was an established rule of American foreign policy until the debate over the American involvement in the Vietnam War. However, Gerald Ford became President during a period of widespread distrust of the Presidency. Accordingly, he declared that he would consult fully with Congress before committing U.S. troops abroad. He also pledged to seek Senate approval of U.S. obligations to foreign nations in the form of treaties rather than using executive agreements.

The key to the President's role in foreign and military affairs is his working relationships with high State and Defense Department officials. The President controls the appointment of these officials. He nominates ambassadors, members of the Joint Chiefs of Staff, and the secretaries of state and defense. The Senate has the constitutional right to "advise and consent" to these appointments but seldom challenges a Presidential nomination. In addition to these senior officials, the President chooses the White House staff, which includes assistants who deal with foreign and military affairs. In practice, the President usually avoids controversial appointments in these sensitive areas because such appointments would make it more difficult to deal with Congress on matters of appropriations.

There are differences from one administration to another in the relative importance of the Departments of State and Defense, the CIA, and White House agencies such as the National Security Council. The President often acts as a referee in policy differences between the Departments of State and Defense. Since their responsibilities are different, it is not uncommon for these two departments to hold opposing views on important issues. The negotiations revolving around the Strategic Arms Limitation Talks are an example of the wide gap in perspective between high officials in the Defense and State Departments. Secretary of State Kissinger placed a premium on *detente*—relaxation of tensions—with the Soviet Union, while Secretary of Defense James E. Schlesinger was more concerned with the fact that the United States might be negotiating from a position of relative military weakness. In this case, the President resolved the clash of opinions by firing Schlesinger in November 1975.

The President may also employ special representatives for unofficial diplomatic missions to foreign countries. Their unofficial status may make it easier to conduct negotiations without the publicity that accompanies cabinet secretaries or high-ranking civilian or military officials. Ex-Ambassador Averill Harriman played such a role in negotiations with the Soviet Union during the Kennedy administration.

The President's right to fire military or diplomatic officials is firmly established. Truman's removal of General Douglas MacArthur from the post of U.S. Commander in Korea in 1951 stirred a national controversy, and the fired general received a hero's reception when he addressed a joint session of the houses of Congress. Nevertheless, Truman was regarded as having acted within his rights as President.

In no other area of Presidential activity does the chief executive have freedom of choice he enjoys in foreign affairs and military policy. The major limitation on his actions is the need to seek congressional appropriations to carry out these policies. Such funds have usually been forthcoming, though controversy may arise over the desirability or size of a particular appropriation. However, congressional opposition to appropriations for military aid to Angola in 1975 may signal the end of an era of almost automatic acceptance of Presidential dominance of foreign and military policy.

Diplomacy and military policy have a tendency to become institutionalized. Despite changes in national leadership, policy in these areas remains fairly constant. A President's reputation is greatly affected by his success—or lack of it—in dealing with the international environment. Johnson's impressive legislative record in domestic affairs was overshadowed by the Vietnam War. In contrast, favorable public attitudes toward Nixon's diplomatic moves in relation to the People's Republic of China and the Soviet Union were an important factor in his landslide victory in the 1972 election. In sum, foreign affairs is an area in which the President is able to operate largely independently of the legislative and judicial branches. This offers the potential for firm, constructive action as well as the risk of ill-advised policy.

The President, the Media, and the Public

The President's primary means of communication with the public is through the mass media. This is also the channel through which Americans get most of their political news. Thus, media coverage is an important influence in shaping the public's opinion of the President's performance.

The chief executive and the media often find themselves opposing each other. The media seek news, and bad news or exposure of official wrongdoing is highly newsworthy. The administration makes every effort to interpret events in such a way that the public will view its policies in a favorable light.

Presidential news conferences are a traditional channel of communication with the public, though their importance has decreased in recent years. Ideally, such public appearances by the President give media representatives a chance to ask specific questions about political issues and allow the President to explain his administration's policies. However, in practice

Franklin D. Roosevelt appealing to the nation to elect "Liberal" candidates in the 1938 Congressional elections. Roosevelt was the first President to use electronic media to appeal to citizens.

news conferences have disadvantages from the standpoint of both the media and the President. The President can simply refuse to answer certain questions on national security grounds or, invite questions only from reporters believed to be friendly to his administration and unlikely to raise embarrassing issues. On the other hand, representatives of the media often enjoy the public recognition they receive at news conferences. The large number of media representatives who attend such conferences makes it impossible to explore an issue in any but the most general terms. Despite these limitations, however, the Presidential press conference can serve as a valuable bridge between the President and the public. In the following passage, Arthur M. Schlesinger, Jr. compares the frequency of Roosevelt's press conferences with Nixon's isolation:

For all its abundant vanities and vagaries, the press in the American system served as the champion of the reality principle against the presidential capacity for self-delusion. Reading FDR's press conferences makes it evident how much meeting the press twice a week contributed to the singular vitality and responsiveness of his Presidency. Nixon instead shut himself off from the press, and from the country. If he had, for example, been exposed to constant questioning by the press over the long months after... Watergate, he could hardly have remained in his professed state of invincible ignorance. [20]

Much of the apparent conflict between any administration and the media stems from official efforts to hide embarrassing news from the public. Watergate was not the first government scandal to be covered up. In every administration, there have been events that have served to deepen the distrust between the chief executive and the mass media. For example, when the Soviet Union announced that it had shot down an American U-2 spy plane, the White House claimed that it was a weather observation plane that had gone off course. The capture of pilot Gary Powers forced

Eisenhower to admit that the plane was indeed a spy plane intentionally flying over Soviet territory. Similarly, the administration's account of the Vietnam War was full of misstatements, exaggerated reports of progress and an official attitude that the government had the right to release information selectively to the American people. The official denial of the bombing of Cambodia during the Nixon administration is another example of the tendency to make deceptive statements when the truth might be embarrassing.

The personality of the President has a strong influence on whether his administration is accepted by the media. Sympathetic press coverage is a valuable asset. The press had a fine relationship with President Kennedy and was generous in its treatment of his administration. In contrast, Lyndon Johnson did not trust the media, and the feeling was mutual. In Johnson's words:

Reporters are puppets, they simply respond to the pull of the most powerful strings... There's only one sure way of getting favorable stories from reporters and that is to keep their daily bread—the information, the stories, the plans, and the details they need for their work—in your own hands, so that you can give it out when and to whom you want. Even then nothing's guaranteed, but at least you've got the chance to bargain. [21]

Johnson's poor relations with the media were intensified by the Vietnam War. Johnson felt that it was disloyal to emphasize the lack of progress in Vietnam or to dramatize the horrors of the war. In turn, the administration's efforts to present an optimistic interpretation of those events deepened the media's suspicion of the administration.

Despite the frequent conflicts between the President and the media, every President tries to use the media to his own political advantage. The President is news; every statement he makes, every trip he takes is dutifully reported by a band of correspondents who follow him around the world. This gives the President a unique opportunity to have himself portrayed as a man of action, a leader who cares about the American people, and perhaps most important, a President who is respected by other major powers.

Presidential trips abroad to take part in events such as summit meetings are fully covered by the press and result in at least a shortterm increase in the President's popularity. The televised spectacle of Richard Nixon exchanging toasts with Chinese leaders at a Peking banquet and visiting the Kremlin to discuss arms limitations with Soviet leaders had an enormous impact on the public. While Nixon never had the personal popularity enjoyed by Eisenhower or Kennedy, the press coverage of his foreign travels improved his image as a statesman who could deal effectively with America's problems abroad.

The President's ability to get along with the media is probably as much a result of expectations as it is of circumstances. Eisenhower and Kennedy were quite willing to meet with the press and generally benefited from sympathetic coverage. In contrast, neither Johnson nor Nixon trusted the media to report the news objectively, and the reporters covering the White House returned the compliment.

The President as Administrative Leader

The President heads a vast bureaucracy that employs millions of people and spends hundreds of billions of dollars. The constitutional basis for the large number of Presidential advisers, the Executive Office with its various agencies, and the cabinet departments is found in Article II, which states that "the executive power shall be vested in a President of the United States of America," and that "he may require the opinion, in writing, of the principal officer in each of the executive departments." The huge federal bureaucracy that has developed over the years represents the efforts of a series of presidents to build up the necessary staff to design and carry out governmental policy and programs. Thus the administrative duties of the chief executive are basically concerned with decision making. The executive agencies and the Presidential staff supply the President with the available information as well as the possible choices. The cabinet departments are more directly concerned with administration of the programs that result from the Presidential decision-making process. The responsibility and influence of the various elements of the executive branch differ from one administration to another as each President develops his own system for maintaining control of the federal bureaucracy.

The White House Staff

The growth in the White House staff parallels the increase in Presidential power and the expansion of governmental activity. The top-level staff has grown by leaps and bounds. President Ford requested congressional authorization for an increase in the number of Presidential assistants from 54 to 95,[22] and when President Carter took office, he was determined to reduce the White House staff.

Presidential assistants are given various responsibilities ranging from maintaining day-to-day contact with Congress and government agencies to keeping in touch with large campaign contributors. The staff is chosen by the President and is highly responsive to his needs. The individuals selected by a President range from former governors and members of Congress to people whose only qualification appears to be loyal service during the election campaign.

The formal structure of the White House staff says little about the President's interactions with other individuals and groups. In the words of Kennedy adviser Arthur M. Schlesinger, Jr., "if the White House provided unparalleled facilities to enable a Presi-

President Jimmy Carter confering with aides aboard Air Force One. The influence of Presidential advisors often depends upon their personal relationship to the President.

dent to find out everything that was going on, it also, if a President wanted to be shielded from bad news and vexatious argument, gave him unparalleled facilities to fulfill that ambition too." [23] The degree to which the President is exposed to divergent views depends on his desire for such exposure. The Kennedy years were marked by meetings and contacts with a wide variety of individuals, both within and outside of the government. This led Kennedy to observe that "no one in the country is more assailed by divergent advice and clamorous counsel." [24] In contrast, Nixon worked very much on his own, with his close adviser H.R. Haldeman acting as a filter through which anyone who wanted to see him must pass. The only exception was National Security Adviser Henry Kissinger, who apparently had almost daily access to the President. Nixon preferred to make decisions in the isolation of a small office in the Executive Office Building or the seclusion of Camp David, Maryland. In Nixon's words: "I find that up there on top of a mountain it is easier for me to get on top of things." [25]

It is hard to determine whether advisers influence Presidents or Presidents influence their advisors. The White House staff has an understandable desire to please the President. Only a person who is confident of complete Presidential trust is likely to express views that differ substantially from those expressed by the chief executive. Such advisers see their role as one of presenting the President with all the possible alternatives in a given situation. But perhaps the most important function of most members of the White House staff is to serve as a link between the President and the other branches of the government, as well as within the executive branch. The staff is also responsible for following up Presidential directives to make sure they are carried out. For example, after his landslide victory in 1972, President Nixon assigned White House aides to cabinet departments in an effort to coordinate policy throughout the executive branch.

The Executive Office

The key decisions made by the President usually develop out of background work done in the executive agencies. The people who head these agencies are appointed by the President on the basis of their competence and, perhaps more important, because he has confidence in them. The National Security Council, the Central Intelligence Agency, the Office of Management and Budget, and the Council of Economic Advisers are the most important of these agencies, and their leaders play a major role in shaping the policy alternatives among which the President must choose.

The organization of the Executive Office usually changes with each administration. Some groups may be eliminated while others are added; their relative importance in the policy-making process also changes. However, the National Security Council, Office of Management and Budget, and Council of Economic Advisers appear to be permanent.

The National Security Council

The National Security Council (NSC) was established in 1947 to advise the President on matters of national security and foreign policy. Its role is largely a reflection of the leadership style of the incumbent President. Presidents Kennedy and Johnson consulted many people both within and outside of official positions. The NSC has less influence in such administrations. In contrast, Eisenhower and Nixon approached their responsibilities in a more formal manner and both made significant use of the NSC. Henry Kissinger served as chairman of the NSC in the early years of the Nixon administration and the rapport between Nixon and Kissinger magnified the role of the NSC during that period.

The ability of the NSC to participate in the policy-making process depends on the extent to which other government departments and agencies cooperate with it. The NSC dominated foreign policy during the Nixon administration but became less influential under Ford; Kissinger had transferred his influence to the Department of State. The NSC is an important element in any administration, but only the President's respect for a person like Kissinger can elevate it to a dominant role.

The advantage of having the NSC play a central role in determining foreign policy is that it can synthesize intelligence reports and policy suggestions from various government agencies and present the possible alternatives to the President in an organized manner. The disadvantage is that a President who relies primarily on the NSC becomes isolated from divergent opinions. Even the most objective adviser makes subjective judgments in deciding what information is important and which alternatives deserve the President's attention.

The Office of Management and Budget

The Office of Management and Budget (OMB) was formed in 1970 to replace the Bureau of the Budget. The new agency, headed by a director and a deputy director who are appointed by the President but must be confirmed by the Senate, is responsible for managing the executive branch as well as preparing the federal budget. It examines the budget requests of agencies and departments within the executive branch before they are submitted to Congress and relates these departmental budgets to administration policy. Thus, there is a clash of interests between the cabinet officials, who seek funding for their departments, and the OMB, which is concerned with the overall level of spending within the executive branch.

The OMB's ability to control the budgetary process is limited "because in normal times political influence over domestic programs is too well dispersed in the political system to be gathered back by administrative devices." [26] As with other executive agencies, the role of the OMB depends on the relationship between the director of the OMB and the President. Casper Weinberger, George Schultz, and Roy Ash, who headed the OMB under Nixon and in the early days of the Ford administration, had considerable power because of their access to the President; the OMB's role as an overseer was expanded under these directors.

The Council of Economic Advisers

The Council of Economic Advisers (CEA) was formed in 1946 and consists of three Presidential appointees who must be confirmed by the Senate. The CEA usually plays a key role in economic planning because its members are appointed by the President and its chairperson has ready access to him. However, the contradiction between the President's political role and the need for economic planning complicates the task of the CEA. Every President who seeks reelection has an important stake in the economic health of the nation during election years. Thus, there is a tendency for the government to concentrate on economic expansion at such times. The CEA must weigh economic priorities (e.g., combating inflation) against political pressures and attempt to design an economic program that will serve both goals.

The members of the CEA usually reflect the President's political philosophy. It is unlikely, for instance, that a conservative chief executive would appoint members to the CEA who favored large government deficits. Thus, the members of the CEA serve as advocates of the administration's economic policy in their dealings with Congress and the media. They also appear regularly before private groups to explain and seek support for the administration's policy.

The Cabinet

The *cabinet* consists of the President, the vice president, and the secretaries of the executive departments. There is no specific constitutional basis for the cabinet, and its power as an advisory group has practically disappeared in recent years. The problems of government are complex and require the attention of specialists. Obviously, each cabinet member is somewhat of a specialist in his or her own field but may have little to offer in discussions involving other departmental policies. Presidents today seek advice from close personal advisers rather than depending on the cabinet for guidance.

The selection of cabinet secretaries revolves around political considerations, and this has contributed to the cabinet's loss of influence. In fact, President Nixon fired Interior Secretary Walter Hickel in 1970 after Hickel complained publicly about his

Cabinet meeting with President Carter in the White House. Carter has attempted to reestablish cabinet influence by holding frequent meetings.

lack of access to the President. Some cabinet members may be close to the President, but their influence is due to their personal relationship with the President rather than their membership in the cabinet. Robert McNamara, secretary of defense under Presidents Kennedy and Johnson, was appointed by Kennedy even though they had not met. The appointment was made on the basis of McNamara's professional reputation—he was a highly regarded president of the Ford Motor Company. McNamara became a key adviser to the two Presidents he served, a position he achieved through the personal relationships that developed during that time rather than through his influence as secretary of defense.

Limitations on Presidential Power

A President must use power in a way that is accepted as legitimate both within and outside the government; that is, he must act within his constitutional rights and within established rules of conduct. Excessive use of executive power may diminish public confidence in the President, even though his actions are legal. Nixon's use of the Internal Revenue Service to harass political enemies was on the borderline of lawful activity but clearly violated generally accepted rules of Presidential conduct. Imprudent use of executive agreements or impoundment of funds may also reduce the people's trust in the President, and that trust is his most important asset in dealing with other branches of the government as well as the public. There are two diminsions to the Presidency. One is focused on the office and the other on the individual who holds the office. The President who weakens his credibility also dissipates the respect and prestige routinely accorded the office.

Commitments and Precedents

Just as a President's actions set precedents for the future, so an incumbent is limited by the actions of previous Presidents. This is especially important in foreign affairs because it is understood that changes in the individuals conducting negotiations will not change national policy. To be sure, there is always a period during which a new American President is sized up by other governments. The first foreign policy statement by a new chief executive usually consists of a promise to continue previous policies. The history of U.S. foreign policy since World War II illustrates the importance of such precedents. U.S. support of Israel began during the Truman administration and was maintained by every President since Truman. Likewise, the United States has continued to support Taiwan despite circumstances that have for all practical purposes made this policy obsolete. The current desire for better relations with the People's Republic of China looms larger in American policy than anything the United States could gain from friendship with Taiwan, a friendship that offends the mainland Chinese.

Previous domestic commitments also limit the President's policy choices. Despite the alternation between Democratic and Republican Presidents since 1952, there have been no sudden changes in social policy. There are differences in emphasis between the parties, which are reflected in the priorities of Democratic and Republican Presidents. A Democratic incumbent is likely to expand federal social welfare programs, while a Republican President is more likely to maintain the status quo. However, a Republican President will not attempt to make major reductions in services such as social security. From a political standpoint, it is poor policy to try to deprive either the public or a particular interest group of a benefit to which they have become accustomed.

The President must also recognize the implications of any new commitment he makes. President Ford's opposition to "bail-out" proposals for federal aid to New York City in 1975 was based as much on the implications of such a commitment as the situation itself. Obviously, if such aid was offered to one city it could hardly be withheld from others. Ford settled on a federal loan to New York City and thus set a precedent for future Presidents. This type of limitation on Presidential power exists in almost every area of national life.

Availability of Resources

The President has enormous resources available to be used in carrying out his policies, but these resources are far from unlimited—national needs always exceed available resources. In terms of short-term policy, the question is not the existence of resources but the ability to make use of them fast enough to be effective. For example, North Korea's seizure of the USS Pueblo in 1968 was unopposed because the ship was in a North Korean port before the United States could use military power to recapture the ship. Of course, U.S. forces could have been directed against North Korea, but the risks involved were too high.

Long-term policies are based on the priorities set by the administration. The President customarily gives Congress a "shopping list" of legislative proposals in his State of the Union speech, but behind-the-scenes efforts are directed toward passage of the programs to which the President is prepared to allocate the available resources. The problems the nation faces at any given time exist largely because of lack of resources. The decay of the cities and the energy crisis are examples of problems that must be solved but have received inadequate allocations of resources thus far.

Availability and Quality of Information

The President makes policy decisions with the national interest and his own political philosophy in mind. These decisions are based on the available information, which may be inaccurate or incomplete. Information flows to

Limitations on Presidential Power **177**

Informal meeting between President Carter and Secretary of State Cyrus Vance. Informal confidential meetings such as these often influence important Presidential policy decisions.

The Political Climate

Many of the powers of the Presidency have developed out of congressional grants of authority to deal with specific emergency situations. As a result, the President has far more power than the Constitution intended. These powers go into effect when the President declares a state of national emergency. Such declarations were made by Franklin D. Roosevelt in 1933 during the Depression, by Harry S. Truman in 1950 after the invasion of South Korea, and by Richard Nixon during the postal strike of 1970 and the devaluation of the dollar in 1971. All of these emergencies were still legally in existence as recently as October 1976, along with the President's authority to deal with them. Among the powers the President was given in these emergencies was the right to nationalize private property and commodities, transportation, communications, and means of production. In addition, martial law could be imposed and travel restricted. These emergency Presidential powers were detailed in about 470 laws, with the Chief Executive having wide latitude as to exactly which he wished to invoke. In short, the President had the power to suspend constitutional processes in the name of a declared emergency.

In October 1976, the first step was taken toward a reduction of these Presidential powers with the passage of the National Emergencies Act. This act provided for a review within two years of all existing national emergency legislation and for termination of those that had arisen out of the four emergencies just mentioned. The Act gives the President the authority to declare a state of national emergency, but Congress must be notified in advance and given a statement of exactly which emergency powers the President intends to use. The emergency is automatically terminated within six months, at which time the President can redeclare the emergency if necessary. These procedures are intended to prevent potential abuses of power

the President from every part of the federal bureaucracy and is channelled through his close advisers. At every stage of this process, various officials selectively eliminate information that they do not consider important and emphasize the aspects of the problem that they believe are significant. By the time the President receives the information on which his decisions are based, there may be a gap between the situation to be dealt with and the perceptions of those who are dealing with it.

Urban housing programs undertaken during the past three decades provide an example of government programs based on inadequate information. There is no question about the need to improve living conditions in many cities, but the failure of the programs designed for this purpose suggests that the information on which they were based was inadequate and inaccurate.

The President must base his decisions on evaluations made by others, but he is responsible for the outcome of those decisions. It is fashionable to speak of Presidential decision making as a process of sorting out the available alternatives, but these alternatives are not always what they appear to be; moreover, some possible solutions may be pushed aside by other less appropriate alternatives during the information-gathering process.

In some ways, the limitations on Presidential power are a blessing rather than a handicap. The American people do not want an emperor. They want a President who will combine the seemingly contradictory qualities of bold leadership with responsiveness to the public mood. The changes in administration that result from the electoral process would put a severe strain on the nation if they were accompanied by sweeping policy changes. Thus, the practical limitations on the power of the President are every bit as real as those imposed by the Constitution. These barriers may be a source of frustration to the chief executive, but they act as a check on the abuse of power.

by the President and to provide Congress with new checks on Presidential power.

The Appeal of the Presidency

The Presidency is a position of great power, tremendous responsibility, and many frustrations. It is this combination of power and challenge that makes the nation's highest office the ultimate goal of many public officials. Campaigning in state after state in an effort to win primaries or gain delegate support is very demanding and reduces the number of Presidential candidates to those who not only have a strong desire for the Presidency but also have a political base on which to build. This base may be newly established, as in the case of Dwight D. Eisenhower, or a political following developed during many years in public life, as in the case of Lyndon Johnson. In recent years, the horror of assassination and the disgrace of resignation have elevated two vice presidents to the Presidency, thus highlighting another possible route to the top. There are many pitfalls facing potential candidates, but the opportunity, however remote, of holding the most powerful office in the world remains irresistible to many.

Compensation and Tenure

The President is elected to a four-year term of office and may be reelected to an additional term. The Constitution requires that the President be at least 35 years of age, born in the United States, and a resident of the United States for fourteen years. The President receives a salary of $200,000 a year, plus an expense allowance of $50,000; both are taxable. He also receives a tax-free allowance of $40,000 a year to cover travel expenses and official entertainment. In 1971, Congress provided for a pension of $60,000 a year for ex-Presidents plus $90,000 a year for office staff; former Presidents are also entitled to free office space in a government building and to free postage.

The Vice Presidency

It is hard to imagine a public office with less actual power but more potential than the vice presidency. The potential results from both the political exposure the vice president receives and the possibility that he may succeed to the Presidency upon the death, resignation, or disability of the President. Between 1964 and 1976, the White House was occupied by three former vice presidents: Johnson, Nixon, and Ford.

The Presidential candidate is usually free to choose his running mate, and from the time he is nominated the vice presidential candidate is an appendage of the Presidential candidate. If they win the election, this relationship continues. The vice president's only constitutional responsibility is to preside over the Senate and to vote if there is a tie. This is largely a ceremonial role and has little political importance. The vice president has no other responsibilities unless the President assigns him a role in the administration. As John Nance Garner put it,

Worst damfool mistake I ever made was letting myself be elected Vice-President of the United States. Should have stuck with my old chores as Speaker of the House. I gave up the second most important job in the Government for one that didn't amount to a hill of beans. I spent eight long years as Mr. Roosevelt's spare tire. I might still be Speaker if I didn't let them elect me Vice-President. [27]

The vice presidency became somewhat more important during the Eisenhower administration. Vice President Nixon was given a series of foreign assignments that helped establish him as a political figure in his own right and made him a strong Presidential candidate.

The power of the vice president as a potential Presidential candidate is limited, despite his previous relationship with the chief executive. Nixon

Vice President-elect Walter Mondale holding a Minneapolis Tribune, a single copy printed as a joke after the 1976 Presidential election.

was a junior California senator with little national exposure before he became vice president. Thus, he was indebted to Eisenhower and in no position to establish a positical base of his own. In contrast, Kennedy chose Johnson as his running mate in 1960 to help win southern support at the polls. Johnson had served many years in the Senate and was Senate majority leader when Kennedy made his vice presidential choice. He had an important political base independent of Kennedy and was feared and distrusted by many members of the White House staff. Johnson was given little to do in the Kennedy administration and was literally waiting in the wings for the opportunity to become President. The power of the Presidential candidate to pick his Vice-Presidential candidate is also illustrated by Nixon's choice of Spiro Agnew in 1968. Agnew had served as Governor of Maryland but was a virtual unknown on the national scene. Nixon assigned Agnew "hatchet-man" duties domestically, and Agnew lashed out at the press and groups of individuals, such as the "liberal eastern establishment," that Nixon perceived to be a threat. The role of the Vice-President is completely controlled by the Chief Executive.

The age and citizenship requirements for the vice presidency are similar to those for the Presidency. The vice president receives a salary of $62,500 a year and a $10,000 expense allowance, both taxable. In addition, he receives a staff allowance.

Presidential Succession

The vice president becomes President if the President is removed from office through impeachment, death, or resignation. In addition, the Twenty-fifth Amendment to the Constitution, ratified in 1967, provides that "whenever the President transmits to the President pro tempore of the Senate and the Speaker of the House of Representatives his written declaration that he is unable to discharge the powers and duties of his office, and until he transmits to them a written declaration to the contrary, such powers and duties shall be discharged by the Vice President as Acting President." Thus, if the President becomes temporarily disabled, the vice president takes over until he has recovered.

The Constitution gives the House of Representatives the power of *impeachment*, that is, the right to recommend a trial to determine whether the President shall be removed from office. A majority vote for impeachment in the House sends the matter to the Senate, which conducts the actual hearings. A two-thirds vote of the Senate is needed to remove the President from office.

Impeachment is not designed to force an unpopular President out of office, though it was used in this way in 1868 against Andrew Johnson. The attempt to impeach Johnson arose out of the controversy surrounding the Reconstruction; many members of Congress were angered by Johnson's moderate attitude toward the southern states. Though he was brought before the Senate, Johnson escaped impeachment by one vote.

Article I of the Constitution provides for impeachment and removal of the President from office for "Treason, Bribery or other high Crimes and Misdemeanors." When the House Judiciary Committee examined the conduct of President Nixon, there was much debate over whether Nixon's activities were impeachable offenses or simply examples of poor judgment. Nixon resigned after the Committee had voted to recommend impeachment proceedings before the full House.

The impeachment and removal of a chief executive is an extreme action that is taken reluctantly even by the political opposition. The misuse of the impeachment procedure in the case of President Johnson illustrated the danger that it could be used for political purposes. In the case of President Nixon, it is clear that impeachment can serve as an important safeguard of constitutional government.

Summary

The abuses committed by President Nixon and his closest advisers, which led to the Watergate revelations and Nixon's resignation, appear to have slowed the rate of growth of the Presidency as a center of political power. Congress is insisting on its constitutional rights; the press has maintained an aggressive attitude toward wrongdoing by high government officials; and the public has lost some of its blind faith in the government. Political leaders do, after all, have many of the weaknesses of other human beings.

Despite these changes, however, the Presidency remains the most powerful branch of the government. The nation requires strong leadership, and only the President is in a position to provide it. No legislative body can act with the decisiveness of the President. Accordingly, Congress and the judiciary will probably continue to serve as a check on Presidential power rather than becoming equal partners in the American political system.

While the Presidency is the most visible political office in the nation, it is not synonymous with the executive branch, which includes a large number of agencies, bureaus, and departments. The President's performance depends in part on the amount of cooperation he is able to get from individuals within the federal bureaucracy, many of whom are career officers in the civil service. Any President must channel his policies through these officials, and the way government programs are run has a substantial impact on their success or failure. Thus, while the President faces the constitutional checks and balances of Congress and the judiciary, the federal bureaucracy provides him with either an important ally or a source of continuing frustration.

The President is limited in his ability to make major changes in governmental policy. He is not only bound by the commitments of previous Presidents but must take into account the fact that he is setting precedents for future Presidents. However, limited resources present perhaps the greatest barrier to the full use of Presidential power. There is no shortage of national problems to be solved, but there are real limits on the resources available. In sum, the Presidency presents a picture of awesome power balanced by important political and economic limitations.

NOTES

[1] Quoted in Louis P. Lochner, "Herbert Hoover in His Own Words," *New York Times Magazine,* August 9, 1964, p. 14. Copyright © 1964 by The New York Times Company. Reprinted by permission.

[2] James David Barber, *The Presidential Character* (Englewood Cliffs, N.J.: Prentice-Hall, 1972), p. 9.

[3] Adapted from ibid., pp. 12-13.

[4] Ibid., p. 140.

[5] Ibid., p. 57.

[6] Ibid., p. 441.

[7] Ibid., p. 140.

[8] Quoted in *The New York Times,* October 10, 1975, p. 20L.

[9] *The Gallup Opinion Index,* December 1972, Report No. 90, Princeton, New Jersey.

[10] Doris Kearns, *Lyndon Johnson and the American Dream* (New York: Harper & Row, 1976), p. 237.

[11] Arthur M. Schlesinger, Jr., *The Imperial Presidency* (Boston: Houghton Mifflin, 1972), p. 164.

CHAPTER 11 CROSSWORD PUZZLE

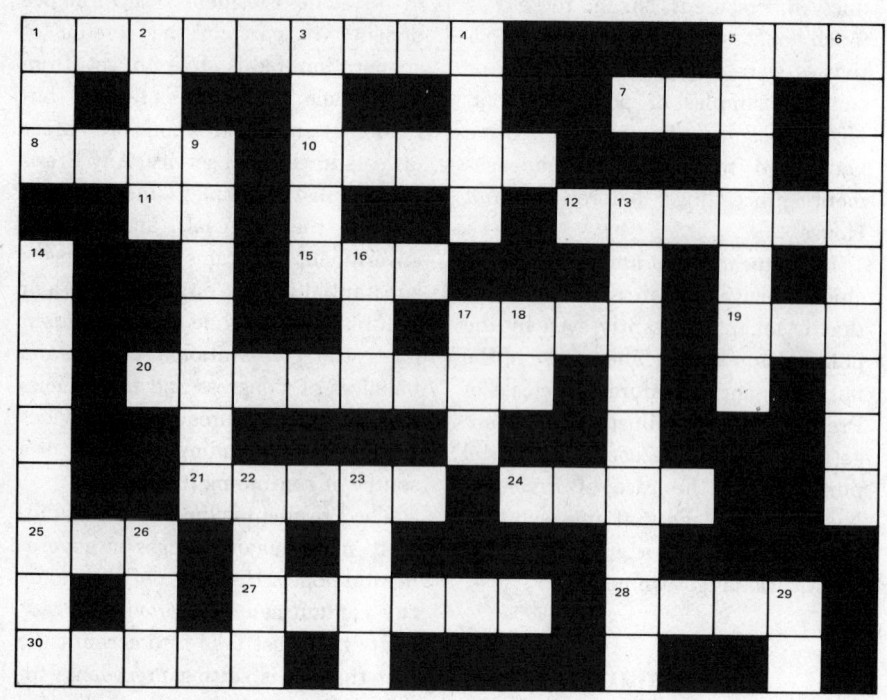

Across

1. The President and the media have an ___ relationship.
5. Federal Communications Commission (abbr.)
7. To and ___
8. Partner
10. The power of the Presidency has ___ dramatically in the 20th century.
11. Opposite of "under"
12. Uncover
15. Family member
17. Very large
19. Obtain
20. The power of the President is limited by ___ commitments.
21. The ___ of leadership adopted by a President reflects personality and perceptions of the Chief Executive's role.
24. Destiny
25. Time period
27. If the President neither signs a bill nor sends it back to Congress within ten days the bill is said to be victim of a ___ veto.
28. Futile; proud
30. Cut hair with a razor

Down

1. Admiral (abbr.)
2. The only Constitutional legislative power the President possesses is the ___.
3. Long narratives
4. Open the mouth wide, from boredom
5. The President usually dominates ___ affairs.
6. In attempting to build support from various segments in society the President attempts to form a ___.
9. Lasts
13. The Presidential prerogative to withhold information from Congress is called ___ privilege.
14. The constitutional framework assures friction between ___ and the President.
16. Wide Japanese sash
17. Humble abode
18. We
22. ___ measure
23. ___ Ness
26. American Medical Association (abbr.)
29. Opposite of "yes"

---

[12] Quoted by Edwin L. Dale, Jr. in "Can Congress at Last Control the Money Tree," *The New York Times Magazine,* August 22, 1976, p. 73.

[13] Ibid., p. 72.

[14] Schlesinger, pp. 236-237.

[15] Quoted in ibid., p. 239.

[16] Decision of District Judge William B. Jones in Local 2677 et al. v. Phillips (1973), quoted in ibid., p. 242.

[17] Quoted in "House Unit Seeks Contempt Order Against Kissinger," *The New York Times,* November 15, 1975, p. 8C. Copyright © 1975 by The New York Times Company. Reprinted by permission.

[18] Joseph W. Bishop, Jr., "The Warren Court Is Not Likely to Be Overruled," *The New York Times Magazine,* September 7, 1969, p. 31.

[19] Quoted in *The New York Times,* October 7, 1976, p. 36L. Copyright © 1976 by The New York Times Company. Reprinted by permission.

[20] Schlesinger, p. 227.

[21] Quoted in Kearns, p. 247.

[22] *Congressional Quarterly,* July 12, 1975, p. 1498.

[23] Schlesinger, p. 215.

[24] Quoted in ibid., p. 214.

[25] Quoted in ibid., p. 218.

[26] Robert J. Sickels, *Presidential Transactions* (Englewood Cliffs, N.J.: Prentice-Hall, 1974), p. 64.

[27] Quoted in Frank X. Tolbert, "What Is Cactus Jack up to Now," *Saturday Evening Post,* November 2, 1963. Copyright © 1963 The Curtis Publishing Company.

CHAPTER 12
THE FEDERAL BUREAUCRACY

CHAPTER OUTLINE

Questions to Consider
Introduction
Characteristics of the Bureaucracy
    Administration and Policy
    Political Orientation
    Influences on the Bureaucracy
Problems of the Bureaucracy
The Super Bureaucrats
Staffing the Bureaucracy
    The Hatch Act
    The Good Old Boy Network
    Unionization and the Right to Strike
The Structure of the Bureaucracy
    The Cabinet Departments
    Subcabinet Departments
    The Executive Agencies
    Semi-Independent Corporations
    The Federal Reserve Board
Governmental Regulation of Business and Industry
    The Independent Agencies and Commissions
    Reform of Governmental Regulation
Bureaucratic Accountability
Summary

QUESTIONS TO CONSIDER

The word *bureaucracy* has become associated with inefficiency and waste. Yet bureaucratic structures are necessary to manage any large organization. The size of the government makes the federal bureaucracy very important, very powerful, and the target of much criticism.

In this chapter, we will describe the federal bureaucracy and its role in the policy-making process. What are the tasks of the federal bureaucracy? Who heads the bureaucracy? How are federal employees hired and under what conditions? What kinds of pressure do they encounter?

We are continually reminded that the government is a major influence in our lives. For example, we read and hear about a wide variety of government regulations. Who makes those regulations? How do the regulators resolve the conflicts that arise when new policies are proposed? What do we mean when we speak of *quasi-legislative* and *quasi-judicial* bureaucratic actions? These questions illustrate the scope of the federal bureaucracy, as well as the way it interacts with Congress, the President, and various interest groups. Indeed, the bureaucracy is sometimes called the fourth branch of the government.

Introduction

The federal bureaucracy carries out the policies and programs proposed by the President and passed by Congress. The growth of the government has been accompanied by an increase in both the size and the power of the bureaucracy so that it has become, in effect, the fourth branch of the government.

The bureaucracy consists of the cabinet departments, regulatory commissions, executive agencies, and government boards and corporations. The heads of these various agencies are usually appointed by the President, often with the approval of the Senate. But the real power is in the hands of the career bureaucrats who have reached the higher ranks of the civil service. These individuals may retain their positions through several Presidential administrations.

The bureaucracy interacts with the President, Congress, the public, and private interest groups. In carrying out its administrative responsibilities, it can make new policies or change existing ones. Executive orders and congressional legislation often take the form of broad guidelines, but the executive agencies make the regulations that determine a program's final characteristics and, often, its effectiveness.

The relationship between the bureaucracy and the individual citizen is different from that between other governmental units and the people. The citizen votes for his or her representatives in Congress and for the President. This makes these officials accountable directly to the people. In contrast, the bureaucracy is not accountable to the public; the only significant way an individual can influence bureaucratic decisions is through an interest group that represents his or her views. The lack of bureaucratic accountability is a problem because bureaucratic decisions affect everyone.

The reason the bureaucracy has been given so much power is that it can function in a nonpartisan manner in carrying out governmental policy. Realistically, however, the various bureaucratic are dealing with conflicts among interest groups and making decisions that will help some people and harm others. Consistent favoring of a particular group or interest is a form of partisanship and defeats the purpose of a nonpartisan bureaucracy.

Table 12-1 shows the rapid growth in the number of civilian employees of the federal government since 1940 and the increase in payroll costs that has accompanied that growth. While these employees are all members of the bureaucracy, we are concerned primarily with those who are in positions of power, who design and interpret governmental policy and are responsible for carrying it out. The word *administration* must be used in its most general sense in describing the federal bureaucracy.

Characteristics of the Bureaucracy

The federal bureaucracy provides the machinery to put government programs into effect. In carrying out this basic responsibility, the upper levels of the bureaucracy must interpret Presidential and congressional guidelines. This brings them into contact with the groups that are directly affected by federal programs. The same process also operates in reverse: Career officials in the various departments and agencies of the executive branch play an important role in the shaping of governmental policy.

Administration and Policy

The federal bureaucracy plays a key role in interpreting executive orders and congressional acts. Some of its functions, such as sending out social security checks, are largely administrative. In this context, bureaucrats are management experts. However, in

TABLE 12-1

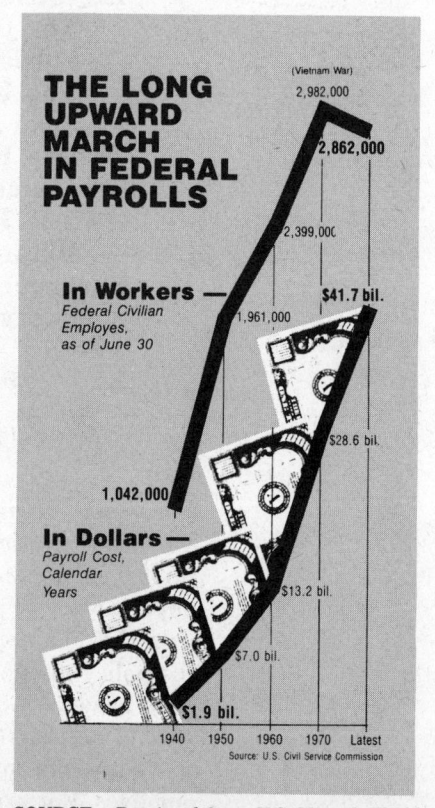

THE LONG UPWARD MARCH IN FEDERAL PAYROLLS

In Workers — Federal Civilian Employees, as of June 30

- 1,042,000
- 1,961,000
- 2,399,000
- 2,862,000
- 2,982,000 (Vietnam War)

In Dollars — Payroll Cost, Calendar Years

- $1.9 bil.
- $7.0 bil.
- $13.2 bil.
- $28.6 bil.
- $41.7 bil.

1940 1950 1960 1970 Latest
Source: U.S. Civil Service Commission

SOURCE: Reprinted from *U.S. News & World Report*, August 16, 1976, p. 22. Copyright 1976 U.S. News & World Report, Inc.

such areas as the collection of income taxes the role of the bureaucracy extends beyond the distribution or collection of federal revenues. The Internal Revenue Service (IRS) issues guidelines for compliance with the income tax legislation passed by Congress and determines how those guidelines will be enforced. This means the IRS is part of the policy-making process: The way taxes are collected determine to a large extent the effects of the tax laws on the individual citizen. It is this type of influence that has enlarged the role of the bureaucracy from a solely administrative one to one that includes significant policy-making functions.

Political Orientation

While the heads of many government agencies are appointed by the President, these officials are largely dependent on information provided by career civil servants. Ideally, the role of these officials in the policy-making process is based on their professional expertise rather than their political views. Theoretically, their advice or interpretations will be politically neutral. However, all decision-making is value laden to some extent, and the federal bureaucracy is no exception. Thus, the concept of the bureaucracy as politically neutral or nonpartisan is unrealistic.

Influences on the Bureaucracy

There are a variety of influences on bureaucratic activity: lobbyists for interest groups and private corporations, the media, public opinion, and most important, the President and Congress. These various groups and individuals, both within the government and in the private sector, seek favorable interpretation of regulations affecting them, strict enforcement or nonenforcement of government regulations, and in general, policies that are favorable to their interests. The need to sort out these often conflicting influences complicates the task of the bureaucracy. Through the bureaucratic structure pass all of the policies, programs and initiatives that represent the aspirations of the administration. A balky bureaucracy can negate the most carefully planned programs while cooperation can insure success.

Problems of the Bureaucracy

The federal bureaucracy has three main problems: (1) the fact that it can defeat the purpose of congressional or Presidential policies; (2) administrative inefficiencies that add to the costs of government and make it less effective; and (3) a tendency to continually expand, adding further to the costs of government and making it less responsive to the people.

The immense size of the federal bureaucracy and the inefficiencies that often result have been criticized both within and outside of the government. Senator Edmund Muskie (D., Maine), a liberal, complains of a government "so big, so complex, so expensive and so unresponsive that it's dragging down every good program we've worked for...." He goes on to ask, "Why can't liberals talk about fiscal responsibility and productivity without feeling uncomfortable?" [1] Such concerns have traditionally been expressed by Republican leaders; the extent of the problem is indicated by the fact that liberal Democrats like Senator Muskie are joining more conservative leaders to protest situations like the following:

The Senate Select Small Business Subcommittee on Government Regulation reported in 1973 that the federal government was using 5,298 different kinds of forms. But that did not include forms used by regulators of the banking industry and the Internal Revenue Service, two of the biggest data collectors in Washington.

Ten billion sheets of paper flow through federal offices every year ... enough to fill 4.5 million cubic feet of space. It is calculated that there are 50 forms to be filled out each year for every man, woman and child in the country. [2]

The concern over the multiplying costs of government illustrated in the passage just quoted led to the creation in 1974 of an independent agency, the Commission on Federal Paperwork, whose fourteen members would be appointed by the President. The Commission was to go into operation on October 3, 1975 with a full-time staff of 80 and a budget of between $4 million and $6 million. [3]

Bureaucrats generally try to increase their area of operations and, thus, their influence. The goal of many governmental units is not only to maintain but to enlarge the programs under their supervision regardless of whether such expansion would be beneficial. In effect, the federal bureaucracy has become one of the most powerful interest groups in the nation, and as a result many bureaucratic actions are self-fulfilling prophecies. Recommendations for new and bigger programs are sent to officials at higher levels, where the need for action is taken for granted, and it is assumed that with enough money progress is inevitable.

The Super Bureaucrats

The key to the power of the federal bureaucracy is the role of the so-called "super bureaucrats," [4] the 10,000 career civil servants who rank below Presidential appointees and above the people who perform the day-to-day administrative tasks. These individuals have the detailed knowledge and experience that enables them to either obstruct federal programs or carry them out effectively. In short, the super bureaucrats are the force that fuels government action, regardless of the party in power. They provide the information that serves as a basis for executive orders and congressional legislation; they interpret governmental policy; and they serve as a channel of communication between the private sector and the government.

The super bureaucrats are usually in the top three ranks of the civil service. Most have been in govern-

President Ford discusses the budget with Budget Director Roy Ash (center) and aide. The Office of Management and Budget is one of the most powerful in the Executive Branch.

their job applications to federal offices that need personnel.

Jobs in the civil service tend to be permanent unless a particular office is closed or reduced in size. An elaborate procedure must be followed before a government employee can be fired. This relative security helps attract well-qualified people but also leads to bureaucratic inefficiency.

Federal employees are assigned a grade or rank on the basis of job specifications and the employee qualifications. Table 12-2 shows the pay scales prevailing in government service in February 1977. There is a wide range of salaries in the bureaucracy, and the top civil service grades offer substantial financial reward.

The civil service has come under attack on the ground that the main problem of government today is inefficiency, not patronage. About 90 percent of the government's civilian employees are covered by the civil service system, with the least productive workers often included in the same grade—and receiving the same salary—as the more capable ones. The National Civil Service League has encouraged the government to replace written tests with broader standards, including experience and merit, for

ment service over fifteen years and earn up to $47,500 a year. Wilbur Cohen, secretary of Health, Education and Welfare under Johnson and a career civil servant, describes the qualifications of these officials as follows: "For a person to get to the top echelons of Government and stay there and handle his job reasonably well, he has to be as good as any top corporate official. He has to handle complex relations with his subordinates, his superiors and with Congress." 5

The tendency of the bureaucracy to expand results from the super bureaucrats' drive for personal benefits and career advancement. This characteristic is not unique to civil servants; it can be found in almost any bureaucratic structure. The problem in the federal bureaucracy arises from its sheer size and from the high costs of unnecessary or wasteful programs.

Staffing the Bureaucracy

There is relatively little political patronage involved in the hiring of federal employees. There are between 2000 and 3000 important jobs filled by Presidential appointment, a small fraction of the total federal payroll. Most government employees qualify for federal employment through the Civil Service Commission. Applicants' names are put on the civil service "register" and the Commission sends

TABLE 12-2
Federal Pay Scale

Grade	Type of Job	Average Pay	Lowest Pay	Top Pay
1	Beginning file clerk	$5,679	$5,559	$7,224
2	Beginning typist	6,479	6,296	8,186
3	Beginning accounting clerk	7,609	7,102	9,235
4	Junior draftsman	8,900	7,976	10,370
5	Beginning engineer	10,131	8,925	11,607
6	Secretary	11,465	9,946	12,934
7	Experienced job analyst	12,399	11,046	14,358
8	Electronics technician	14,123	12,222	15,885
9	Experienced accountant	15,089	13,482	17,523
10	Top engineering technician	17,152	14,824	19,270
11	Buying specialist	18,319	16,255	21,133
12	Experienced auditor	21,793	19,386	25,200
13	Personnel director	25,893	22,906	29,782
14	Chief accountant	30,426	26,861	34,916
15	Chief chemist	35,539	31,309	37,800
16	Administrator	37,720	36,338	37,800
17	Senior administrator	47,500	47,500	47,500
18	Top career official	47,500	47,500	47,500

SOURCE: *U.S. News & World Report*, October 13, 1975, p. 75. Reprinted from *U.S. News & World Report*. Copyright © 1975 by U.S. News & World Report, Inc. (Grades 17 and 18: *Congressional Quarterly*, February 12, 1977.)

the hiring and promotion of government employees. State and local governments have already begun using such standards.⁶

The Hatch Act
The growth of the federal bureaucracy during the New Deal era led to widespread concern over the potential political role of the rapidly expanding number of government employees. In an effort to limit the political activity of civil servants, Congress passed the Hatch Act. This act prohibited federal employees from soliciting campaign funds from fellow workers, becoming candidates in a partisan election, or taking an active part in any partisan election campaign. Federal employees retained the right to express political opinions, make political contributions, and take part in nonpartisan political activity and some local partisan activity in areas with large numbers of federal employees.

The Hatch Act is consistent with the idea that government employees should be free from partisan political pressures. However, the increasing activity of unions of federal employees has sparked demands for liberalization of the Hatch Act on the ground that it deprives federal workers of their constitutional rights. The House Post Office and Civil Service Committee's Subcommittee on Employees' Political Rights and Intergovernmental Relations held hearings in July 1975 on the advisability of amending the Act. The subcommittee's report stated that the Act was "overly broad, vague and repressive in nature"; that the regulations issued by the Civil Service Commission regarding the Act were "contradictory, ambiguous and confusing"; and that in a period of increased emphasis on political participation "almost 3 million federal employees have become politically sterilized."⁷

The argument for maintaining the Act in its original form is based on the fact that it prevents any political party from organizing the bureaucracy along political lines. The Act has resulted in a certain degree of political noninvolvement among government employees, though they often have strong political opinions.

The Good Old Boy Network
The fact that retired federal employees often take jobs with private industries with which they dealt while they were working for the government is a matter of continuing concern. The so-called "good old boy network" can lead to major abuses. Retired employees may contact their old agencies as lobbyists for industry associations or as salespeople for companies doing business with the government, as in the case of retired military officers trying to obtain defense contracts for their companies.

There is a federal law prohibiting former military officers from selling to a military service from which they have retired. In addition, military officers leaving the service to join firms with at least $10 million in defense business must fill out an information form if they held a rank at or above the level of major in the Army or Air Force or lieutenant commander in the Navy. The difficulty of enforcing this law lies in determining exactly what constitutes a sales effort as opposed to a contact intended to promote good will or provide information.

The good old boy network is also found in the flow of officials between the regulatory commissions and the industries they regulate. In appointing the members of regulatory commissions, should the President appoint people who are familiar with the industry to be regulated, or should they have no connection with that industry? If one argues that the members of regulatory agencies should be familiar with the industry they are regulating, it is clear that they must be drawn from companies in that industry. On the other hand, if the commission is not supposed to have any previous link with the industry it will be regulating, there is some question as to whether it will be able to do a good job of regulating that industry. Obviously, there is no simple solution to this dilemma, since either choice has advantages as well as disadvantages.

The dimensions of this problem were outlined by a Common Cause study based on the organization's research as well as investigations by the General Accounting Office and a subcommittee of the House Commerce Committee. Following are some of the facts presented in Common Cause's October 1976 report:

1. 518 officials in 11 Federal agencies had financial holdings in companies they had either regulated or with whom their agencies had contracts.
2. More than half of the 42 commissioners appointed to regulatory agencies in the 1971-75 period formerly were associated with companies regulated by the agency to which they were appointed.
3. From 1969 to 1973, 379 officers and employees of the Defense Department left to join companies with whom they had dealt or who were under their jurisdiction.
4. More than half of the top employees (279 of 429) of the Nuclear Regulatory Commission were formerly associated with companies that held contracts or were regulated by the Commission.⁸

The concept of government officials dealing with private industry at arm's length is attractive but hard to put into effect. The good old boy network affects almost every bureaucratic agency. The limitations on the activities of individuals who leave military service are the most effective means of dealing with this situation developed so far; this appears to be a step in the right direction.

Unionization and the Right to Strike
Increasing numbers of government workers are represented by labor unions in negotiations with the federal government. The largest such union is in the Postal Service, which is almost completely unionized. The relation-

ship between federal employees and the government differs from the relationship between labor and management in private industry in that government employees are forbidden to strike. Despite this rule, strikes have occurred in the Postal Service and among the air traffic controllers at the nation's airports, who are employed by the Federal Aviation Administration.

The future pattern of union-government relations is unclear. Without the ability to strike, the employee's bargaining power is limited. However, civil servants agree to give up the right to strike when they are hired. On the whole, the government has kept the salaries of most of its employees equal to or better than those for comparable positions in private industry, and has been especially generous in relation to fringe benefits such as retirement plans.

The Structure of the Bureaucracy

The Cabinet Departments

There are eleven cabinet or executive departments, each headed by a secretary who is appointed by the President and confirmed by the Senate. These departments are the largest portion of the federal bureaucracy, employing over 1,700,000 people. As shown in Table 12-3, they vary considerably in size. The Department of Defense has over 1 million civilian employees, while the Department of Labor has about 14,000. Each department serves as an umbrella organization for other agencies, boards, or departments. For example, the major components of the Department of Defense (DOD) are the Departments of the Navy, Air Force, and Army, but it also includes smaller organizations such as the Defense Intelligence Agency.

The size of the DOD gives some idea of the management problems faced by the executive departments. While the top level of the DOD consists of Presidential appointees, the super bureaucrats at the next-lower level have immense influence. The secretary of defense depends on these officials to carry out practically all of the DOD's operations and to provide the information on which major decisions are based. In addition to the career bureaucrats and the top-level political appointees—the secretary, under secretaries, assistant secretaries, and deputy under secretaries—the DOD is staffed by military officers who, while under the control of civilian chiefs of staff, head a separate and distinct bureaucracy. The DOD spends over $90 billion a year—over one-fourth of the national budget—and its lines of authority are long, a fact that further complicates the task of the secretary of defense.

The central position of the DOD in American foreign policy is apparent. The civilian officials such as the secretary of defense combine with the joint chiefs of staff to evaluate the nation's ability to carry out foreign policy and to estimate the potential threats posed by foreign powers. This illustrates the department's policy-making role. The DOD's decisions are more vital than those of most executive departments, and its actions are more visible. Whether the Vietnam War or arms control negotiations with the Soviet Union, the DOD has a key role in the formulation and implementation of policy.

In carrying out its responsibilities, the DOD's bureaucracy has developed into a powerful interest group that seeks to influence Congress and the public in favor of maintaining a high level of military preparedness. This sort of thing can be seen throughout the federal bureaucracy. Each department, agency, or commission becomes an advocate of views that emphasize the importance of its area of activity.

The DOD's policy-making role af-

TABLE 12-3
Civilian Employment in Cabinet Departments

Total—1,736,872
State—30,376
Treasury—121,546
Defense—1,041,829
Justice—51,541
Interior—80,198
Agriculture—120,999
Commerce—36,228
Labor—14,834
Health, Education and Welfare—147,125
Housing and Urban Development—17,161
Transportation—75,035

SOURCE: U.S. Civil Service Commission, Manpower Statistics Division, data as of June 30, 1975.

The impressive size of the Pentagon is an indication of the dimensions of the Department of Defense.

fects its relations with other branches of the government, the media, relevant private groups such as defense contractors, and the public. These relations are marked by continuing efforts to gain support for an ever-larger defense budget, new weapons systems, and expanded military facilities. One may view the activities of the super bureaucrats in the DOD as a reflection of their responsibilities. However, they militate against the concept of the career civil servant as an impartial administrator.

The other ten cabinet departments are similar in many ways to the DOD. All are staffed by super bureaucrats with considerable influence on the policy-making process. Just as the DOD is an advocate of military preparedness, so the other departments fight for their share of the federal budget by trying to influence individuals and groups in both the public and private sectors. Each cabinet department is a power center within the bureaucratic structure and wants to maintain or increase its influence and the scope of its activities.

Many of the criticisms of the executive departments arise from the way they carry out government programs. Often the departments develop complicated guidelines for the spending of federal funds, and additional staff must be hired to interpret the guidelines in individual cases. Many programs expand until they have been changed beyond recognition and enormous amounts are spent to pursue goals that the program was never intended to achieve.

The Agriculture Department's food stamp program is a good example of a program that added several layers of bureaucracy in the course of widening its scope of activity. Food stamps were originally intended to supplement the income of about 500,000 people who were living at or below the poverty level. The program began operations in 1965 with a staff of 240. By 1975, the number of employees in the food stamp program had risen to about 2000, in addition to hundreds of local and state government workers, and the number of people receiving food stamps had grown to almost 20 million as a result of changes in the eligibility requirements. While Congress is responsible for the legislation approving such changes, the bureaucracy provided much of the drive for expansion of the program. One result is that the program has been plagued by administrative breakdowns. The Agriculture Department estimated that 26 percent of the people receiving food stamps were getting more stamps than they were entitled to.[9]

It is simplistic to place the responsibility for any expansion of federal programs on the bureaucrats who administer them, but it is obvious that every cabinet department has a stake in increasing its scope of activity, its staff, and its budget. Thus, the executive departments play an important role in the policy-making process. While most government programs have some value in their original form, the tendency of bureaucracy to expand often subverts their original purpose.

Subcabinet Departments

Powerful bureaucracies have developed within the cabinet departments; some of these have so much influence that they have achieved a degree of independence. Within the Department of Transportation, for example, are the Federal Aviation Administration, which supervises the operation of the nation's airports, and the Federal Highway Administration, which funnels federal aid to state and local highway funds. Both organizations are relatively independent from the Transportation Department, despite the fact that they are within its area of activity. In effect, they are "subcabinet" departments.

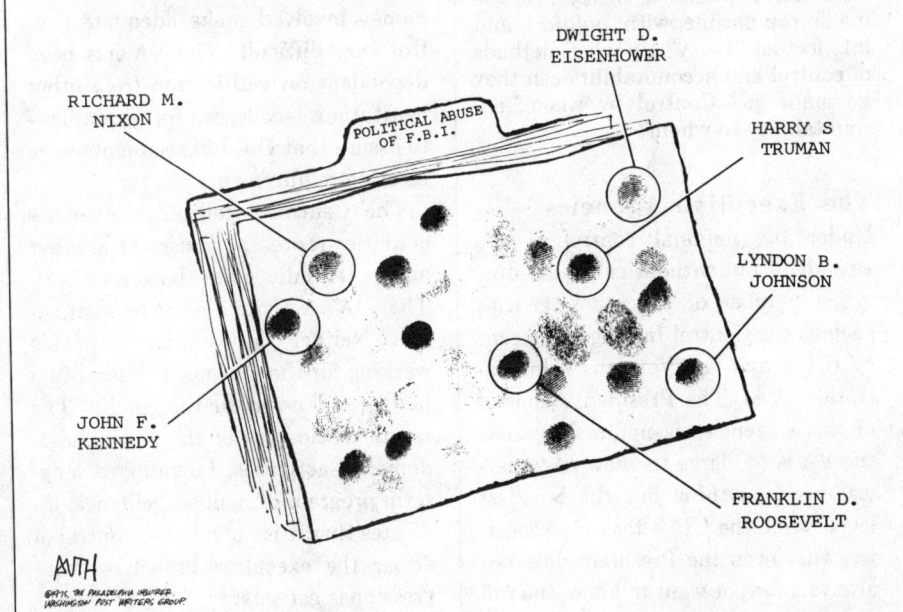

How should subcabinet departments be supervised? This question is especially important in relation to the FBI, which is part of the Department of Justice but largely independent from it. The work of the FBI involves much secrecy but should be free from political control. In 1975, the FBI's activities were the subject of congressional hearings because the constitutional rights of individuals had been violated. The hearings revealed that the FBI was collecting information, often using illegal methods, about citizens who could scarcely be considered a threat to national security, and that this information had been made available to every President since Franklin D. Roosevelt. This has raised a very basic question: How can a government bureau charged with a highly sensitive responsibility be kept under control and out of politics? The political surveillance conducted for American Presidents may not have been done at their request, but there is no indication that any rejected it or curbed this FBI activity.

The difficulty of controlling a large bureaucracy, especially one that engages in secret activities, is illustrated by FBI Director Clarence M. Kelley's admission that he did not know everything that was going on in the FBI. Asked whether he could be certain that his orders to refrain from illegal burglaries were being obeyed, Kelley said, "I wish I could say categorically, unquestionably that this is not going on. I can no longer make categorical, sweeping statements." At another point in the same press conference, Kelley said he had been lied to by subordinates.[10] The task of a Presidential appointee gaining effective control of a large agency is difficult. As the interview with FBI Director Kelley shows, it is difficult to maintain control over department and administration policy. The question of how to control the FBI's activities without seriously limiting its effectiveness goes to the heart of the principle of accountability. As Tom Wicker of the New York Times has pointed out,

No one in Congress or the executive branch has even begun to face—let alone answer—the consequent philosophical and institutional questions. Can secret police agencies ever be made compatible with political and intellectual liberty? By what methods of control and accountability can they be made so? Control by whom, accountability to whom?[11]

The Executive Agencies

Under the nominal control of the President, but without cabinet status, are a number of executive agencies such as the Central Intelligence Agency (CIA) and the Veterans Administration (VA). The President's control of these agencies is nominal because the VA is too large to allow for supervision on anything but the broadest level, while the CIA's task is so sensitive that even the President does not always know, or want to know, the full range of its activities.

The Veterans Administration is the third-largest government agency in terms of number of employees. Its size has become a problem: In October 1975, it was discovered that the VA had overpaid a minimum of $446 million in education benefits under the GI bill. Much of this amount was recovered, but it is unlikely that the actual total of such overpayments will ever be known.[12] Problems of this sort can be expected in most large government programs, but the nature of the VA's programs and the large sums of money involved make adequate control very difficult. The VA has been dependent on verification from other institutions—colleges, for example—to assure that G.I. bill recipients were meeting requirements.

The Central Intelligence Agency's activities represent abuses of another and potentially more dangerous sort. The CIA's activities must be kept secret. Neither the number of people working for the CIA nor the size of its budget is known to the public. The recent disclosures of the CIA's illegal domestic activities, including a long-term program of mail surveillance, indicates that it is outside the control of either the executive branch or congressional safeguards. On the whole, the CIA has developed into what most people believe to be an efficient, professional intelligence organization that has made a significant contribution to the nation's security. However, this does not negate the fact that it has been involved in illegal activities and must be prevented from such involvement in the future.

The problems faced by executive agencies such as the VA and the CIA illustrate the difficulty of making the bureaucracy responsive to the needs of the people. The President's orders cannot guarantee efficiency in the VA or lawful action by the CIA. Officials within the executive bureaucracy need to be persuaded that it is in their own best interest as well as in the national interest to comply with Presidential directives.

Semi-Independent Corporations

A number of government corporations have been set up to undertake tasks that are either too big or too risky for private industry but cannot be accomplished by a bureaucracy. The semi-independent corporation has the advantages of tax exemptions and low-rate loans as well as more freedom of action than would be possible within the federal bureaucracy.

The Tennessee Valley Authority (TVA) was one of the first government corporations. It was formed in 1933 to provide electric power for the Tennessee Valley, a challenge that at the time could not be met by private power companies. The TVA has been remarkably successful, providing relatively cheap electricity to 170 counties in Tennessee, North Carolina, Virginia, Georgia, Alabama, Mississippi, and Kentucky. However, the problems the TVA has encountered in the past ten years illustrate the disadvantages of semi-independent corporations.

Basically, the TVA faces the same problems that private utilities face. Since it must depend on coal because all the suitable dam sites for hydroelectric power have already been used, the TVA has become a polluter of the atmosphere and an advocate of strip mining, which results in serious erosion. Thus, the interests of this government corporation are in conflict with federal attempts to combat the adverse environmental impact of coal burning and the ravages of strip mining. There is also some doubt as to the appropriateness of allowing a tax-exempt government corporation to undersell private power companies that pay taxes.

Like many government agencies, the TVA has shown the bureaucratic tendency to expand. It employs 26,000 people and dominates the industrial development of the 650-mile long Tennessee River Valley. While there was little debate about the need for the TVA when it was founded, there are serious questions about its proper role today.[13]

A different type of semi-independent corporation is illustrated by the U.S. Postal Service, which was formed in 1970 in an effort to provide more efficient mail service. The Postal Service was expected to pay its own way by charging appropriate fees for its services. But instead of becoming self-sufficient it has experienced a series of deficits that reached $850 million in 1975. Tax-exempt status and heavy government subsidies have not solved the problems of the Postal Service which has suffered from the effects of inflation, higher fuel costs, and cost-of-living wage increases for its 600,000 employees.

The change to semi-independent status has succeeded in removing the Postal Service from the patronage system, but is has not yet been given full power over its operations. An independent Postal Rate Commission must pass on postal rates, and this involves the Postal Service in political conflict as the nation's large bulk mailers fight to maintain their rate advantage over first-class mail.

The difficulties experienced by the Postal Service are much like those encountered by private corporations: the pressures of increasing costs and steady union opposition to automation.[14] The early success of the TVA and the current problems of both the TVA and the Postal Service indicate that while there are good reasons for removing some governmental functions from the official bureaucracy, government corporations are not a cure-all for bureaucratic ills.

Despite the difficulties experienced by semi-independent corporations, the concept remains attractive because it attempts to remove such operations from political control. In some cases, the creation of semi-independent corporations is related to the size of the task to be undertaken as well as the advantages of a greater degree of independence. For example, in 1975 President Ford proposed the formation of an Energy Independence Authority to develop U.S. energy resources and end the nation's dependence on Middle Eastern oil. Federal sponsorship of such an effort would permit financial risks that private enterprise would not be willing to take.[15] The magnitude of the proposal—expenditures of $100 billion over the next decade—makes the creation of a semi-independent corporation necessary.

The Federal Reserve Board

The Federal Reserve Board, often called the "Fed," is an indedendent government board with tremendous influence on the nation's economic life. The function of the Federal Reserve Board is to regulate the nation's money supply and, hence, the availability and cost of credit. It has the power to pursue monetary policies that may be at odds with the economic policy of the President or Congress. It is thus in a unique position in the federal bureaucracy.

The seven members of the Fed's Board of Governors are appointed by the President to overlapping 14-year terms and are therefore insulated from partisan politics. The Board of Governors is headed by a chairperson whose four-year term of office does not always coincide with the President's.

The Fed's relative independence has come under increasing criticism from some members of Congress. The economic recession of the mid-1970s was marked by the twin evils of high unemployment and inflation. The Fed claimed that inflation posed the greater threat to the economy, whereas many congresspeople were more concerned with the high level of unemployment. The independence of the Fed allowed its chairman, Arthur Burns, to pursue monetary policies that were designed to slow inflation. This emphasized long-term economic recovery rather than the short-term reduction of the unemployment rate that occupied the attention of Congress.

The lack of accountability of the Federal Reserve System is a question of continuing debate. David P. Eastburn, president of the Federal Reserve Bank of Philadelphia, comments as follows:

I believe it is clear that Congress should retain general oversight but should allow the Fed enough room to make unpopular decisions in the short run that will prove wise in the long run. Also, Congress should not involve itself in the details of monetary policy. For one reason, Congress can be just as susceptible to temporary political pressure as the President. For another, Congress lacks the necessary expertise in monetary policy formation and in its implementation to be calling the day-to-day or even month-to-month monetary signals.[16]

Governmental Regulation of Business and Industry

There are a large number of federal agencies and commissions responsible for enforcing specific laws or achieving specific goals. Most of these agencies have been given the authority to design and enforce government regulations. Thus, they have quasi-legislative and quasi-judicial powers. While many regulatory groups are independent agencies, some cabinet departments also perform regulatory functions. Table 12-4 illustrates the dimensions of the regulatory process.

The Independent Agencies and Commissions

The members of the independent regulatory commissions and agencies are appointed by the President for specific terms of office and must be confirmed by the Senate. The President has limited control over these appointees because of his inability to remove them from office and because their terms of office vary. While the President usually appoints individuals with political philosophies similar to his own, the independent agencies and commissions are legally free from congressional or executive control.

The relationship between the regulatory commissions and the industries they regulate is an important one. The industries are continually trying to influence the rulings and guidelines of the commissions. Obviously, this situ-

TABLE 12-4
Latest Tally of Federal Regulations

A summary of rough estimates by the Office of Management and Budget shows this breakdown of employes in regulatory agencies and workers with regulatory jobs in other agencies—

Agriculture Department (animal and plant-health inspection; Forest Service; stabilization, conservation and marketing services; commodity-credit functions)	25,187
Environmental Protection Agency	11,208
Department of Health, Education and Welfare (food and drug rules, medicare regulation)	9,000
Treasury Department (tax regulation, Comptroller of the Currency, Bureau of Alcohol, Tobacco and Firearms)	7,705
Labor Department (employment standards, occupational safety)	4,790
Commerce Department (Maritime Administration, Patent Office)	4,724
Interior Department (mine safety, land management)	3,713
Federal Energy Administration	3,257
Federal Deposit Insurance Corporation	2,966
National Labor Relations Board	2,404
Department of Transportation (traffic safety, marine safety)	2,285
Equal Employment Opportunity Commission	2,220
Nuclear Regulatory Commission	2,141
Interstate Commerce Commission	2.076
Federal Communications Commission	2,060
Securities and Exchange Commission	1,959
Federal Trade Commission	1,622
Army Corps of Engineers (inland-waterways regulation)	1,500
Federal Reserve Board	1,488
Federal Home Loan Bank Board	1,435
Federal Power Commission	1,316
Consumer Product Safety Commission	1.098
Department of Housing and Urban Development (housing regulations, federal insurance rules)	826
Justice Department (Antitrust Division)	768
Civil Aeronautics Board	718
Other agencies	2,514
Total	100,980

Source: *U.S. News & World Report,* October 6, 1975, p. 31. Reprinted from *U.S. News & World Report.* Copyright© U.S. News & World Report, Inc.

Governmental Regulation of Business and Industry **191**

National Transportation Safety Board official looks at flight recorders taken from Pan Am and KLM airlines that crashed in the Canary Islands in 1977. Government regulation of airlines is an example of the influence of bureaucracy on public concerns.

ation results in intensive lobbying by industry groups as well as pressure in behalf of these groups from members of Congress and other government officials. Like other groups within the bureaucracy, the regulatory agencies tend to grow both in number and in the scope of their activities. Congress has established twelve new agencies in the past ten years, including the Environmental Protection Agency, the Federal Energy Administration, and the Consumer Product Safety Commission. As their names imply, each is intended to oversee or regulate a specific area of activity.

There is increasing concern in both government and private circles that the regulatory agencies are creating unnecessary problems. This concern is based on the fear that in some industries overregulation raises costs and, hence, prices by requiring uneconomical practices, while in other industries competition is discouraged. President Ford expressed his feelings on the matter as follows: "What was begun as a protection for consumers now guarantees that in many cases they will pay higher prices than a free market would call for." [17] An example of the problems created by regulation is the Environmental Protection Agency's requirement that automobile manufacturers install catalytic converters on 1973-model cars in an effort to reduce air pollution. Hundreds of millions of dollars and several years later, this regulation was revoked because it was discovered that the converters emitted harmful sulfuric acid fumes.

Even more serious than the problem of overregulation is the matter of regulations that reduce competition and result in higher prices. This has been the case in the communications, transportation, and energy industries. The Interstate Commerce Commission (ICC) regulates the routes and rates of the nation's truck lines and railroads. It has developed an incredible potpourri of regulations that have restricted competition, raised transportation costs, and encouraged inefficiency. The Civil Aeronautics Board (CAB) regulates the nation's interstate and international airlines in much the same way. If one compares the fares of an airline under CAB regulation with those of intrastate airlines that are free to set their own fares, one finds significant differences. Ticket costs in California's intrastate market — unregulated — range from 4.76 to 7.31 cents per passenger mile. Eastern Air Lines—regulated by the CAB—charges from 8.63 to 11.61 cents per passenger mile. [18] Thus, regulation protects the less efficient airlines at the public's expense. In fact, a former assistant secretary for policy at the Department of Transportation has described the CAB and the ICC as follows:

It is safe to conclude that the CAB is here to stay and that its powers will enlarge, not diminish. I am convinced of this by looking at the survivability of the Interstate Commerce Commission. Even when the majority leader of the Senate proposed the complete elimination of that agency (admittedly in a fit of pique), the ICC went right on cutting out its paper dolls, studying the tariff on yak fat, pondering whether it was all right to abandon the rail line from Overshoe to East Overshoe (even though the trees were so large that no diesel could get through), meanwhile enjoying the spectacle of 60% of the eastern railroads slipping into bankruptcy...the CAB will surely flourish. [19]

The regulatory commissions have come under increasing attack for defending arrangements that are not in the best interests of the public. Along these lines, the reaction of the airline industry to President Ford's call for less regulation and more competition is interesting because it is usually assumed that business and industry do not want governmental regulation. The Air Transport Association protested that "in the guise of regulatory reform, this misconceived plan would in fact . . . disrupt airline service and cause public inconvenience and confusion."[20] In effect, a regulatory commission and the industry it is supposed to regulate were working together for the survival of the companies that make up the industry rather than for the purpose of providing the best possible service at the lowest possible cost.

Reform of Governmental Regulation

Both the House and the Senate have held committee hearings on the state of governmental regulation. These hearings have focused on the following problem areas:[21]

1. *Bureaucratic Delays*— the Food and Drug Administration took eleven years to decide on the percentage of peanuts that should be required in products labeled *peanut butter.* This seems like a frivolous question, but to food processors it is a serious matter. The uncertainties involved in such foot-dragging limit their sales efforts, and an unexpected decision could prove costly.

2. *Overlap and Duplication*—Eleven programs administer the distribution of funds for child care; 14 units within the Department of Health, Education and Welfare deal with programs for education of the handicapped; and over 25 offices in different agencies and departments support water pollution research.[22] In addition to this costly duplication of effort, companies have trouble meeting the requirements of different government agencies, including local and state units. For example, a Philadelphia utility had to get 24 different kinds of approval from 5 federal agencies, 5 state agencies, 2 townships, and a regional commission before it could construct a new facility.[23] This type of overlapping jurisdiction is due in part to the federal system with its layers of government, but the concern of Congress is directed toward the overlap within the federal bureaucracy.

3. *Public Participation*—the role of interest groups and individuals in determining regulatory policy is a matter of concern because the decisions of regulatory agencies inevitably affect the public. A balance must be maintained between the interests of the industries being regulated and the public interest, and this is the reason for the creation of the regulatory agency in the first place.

4. *Agency Independence*— If the regulatory agencies are to act in the public interest, they must be independent of the industries or activities they regulate. When people move freely from the regulatory agencies to the regulated industries and vice versa, there is an obvious conflict of interest. Legislation setting up a "quarantine" period for such individuals is likely to result from the current congressional inquiry.

5. *Priorities*—the question of priorities is important because some agencies have been accused of concentrating on the trees while ignoring the forest. Hasty action can be especially damaging, as we have seen in the case of the auto emission devices described earlier. The National Foundation on the Arts and Humanities received $159 million in fiscal 1975; its $750 award for the seven-word poem "lighght" is an example of the type of action that, though insignificant in terms of money, raises questions of priority.[24]

6. *Congressional Oversight* — The quasi-judicial and quasi-legislative nature of many government regulations have given the regulatory agencies more power than they were intended to have. It has been suggested that some sort of congressional oversight be imposed on the regulatory agencies to prevent them from either circumventing or going beyond the intent of Congress. One proposal would give Congress the power to veto within 60 days of issuance any regulation that carries criminal penalties for its violation. It is argued, on the other hand, that such action would tie the hands of the regulatory agencies and have the effect of turning their rulings into political footballs.

7. *Bureaucratic Inefficiency*—The bureaucrats that run the various regulatory agencies and commissions have gathered enormous power and become less than fully effective. Stories of mismanagement and inefficiency in the regulatory agencies occur frequently in the press, and this intensifies public reaction to the problems of regulation. A case in point is the Supplemental Security Income (SSI) program put into effect by the Social Security Administration on January 1, 1974 to aid 4.2 million blind, aged, or disabled adults. SSI distributed about $8 billion in its first 20 months of operation, and it was disclosed in August 1975 that overpayments of at least $403.8 million were made in the first year and a half.[25] Such disclosures raise serious questions about the ability of even the most efficient agency to administer such programs effectively.

8. *Growth of the Bureaucracy*—The dramatic growth of the bureaucracy in recent years is illustrated by the fact that 236 new federal departments, agencies, and bureaus have been set up in the past 15 years, while only 21 have been eliminated.[26] Even if the task of each new federal agency is distinct from that of existing ones—which is unlikely—it has become commonplace for each agency to strive for self-sufficiency and, therefore, to require a large staff. Consider the government's investigative activities. The General Accounting Office reported on October 13, 1975 that the federal government had spent over $2.6 billion in fiscal 1975 to employ 169,625 people in such activities. These figures do not cover the CIA, the National Security Agency, and certain Defense Department activities,[27] but they do cover a large number of military personnel engaged in security activities, as well as the FBI. The reason for the high totals is that each agency has its own security or intelligence unit.

The problem of bureaucratic growth is magnified by the tendency to build each bureau or department into an independent organization with its own special area of activity, as the following article illustrates:

BUREAUCRAT ADMITS HE JUST LOAFS

Jubal Hale admits he's a bureaucrat with little to do, so he spends his working hours reading and listening to Beethoven records at his office.

Hale says it's not that he doesn't try to earn his $19,693-a-year salary as executive secretary of the Federal Metal and Non-Metallic Safety Board of Review. It's just that the board has never had anything to review in its four years, Hale said in an interview.

"We have been expecting to be abolished for over two years," Hale said. "Bills have been introduced in Congress to abolish us. But nothing happened."

...Apparently, neither Congress nor the Ford Administration has taken the hint. In fact, the administration is asking for $60,000 in annual upkeep for the office in the President's budget for fiscal year 1976.[28]

Bureaucratic Accountability

The question of secrecy in the policy-making process has long troubled observers of the federal bureaucracy. Since the activities of the many bureaus, boards, agencies, and commissions affect various groups of citizens in ways that are not always beneficial, many people believe their meetings should be open. This is a complex issue because in some cases secrecy is necessary. Discussions of criminal investigations, national security, actions that could lead to financial speculation, and matters that involve the privacy of individuals would fall into this category.

In November 1975, the Senate approved legislation that would go far to open bureaucratic activities to public scrutiny. The so-called Sunshine Bill would provide for open meetings of all agencies headed by two or more people appointed by the President and confirmed by the Senate. Closed meetings could be held upon a majority vote of the members, but (with certain exceptions) written accounts of such meetings must be kept and made available to the public. One of the stronger provisions of the bill is a ban on informal contacts between individuals who may be affected by agency rulings and officials of that agency.[29] This would go far to restore the independence of regulatory agencies from the industries or groups they regulate. While the effectiveness of the Sunshine Bill remains to be seen, it reflects Congressional concern over the operations of the bureaucracy and represents an attempt to preserve both the independence and the responsiveness of government agencies.

Closely related to bureaucratic accountability is the question of the extent to which government information should be made available to the public. To deal with this question, the Freedom of Information Act was passed in 1966 and amended in 1974. It provides that government agencies must release information that does not endanger national security; if they believe certain information should be kept secret, they must prove that release of the information would be harmful to national security. The 1974 amendments required government agencies to show individuals the contents of files on their activities. Along the same lines, the Privacy Act of 1975 prohibited the government from releasing information about an individual without his or her consent. This includes the data on military personnel regularly made available to state and local taxing units by the Pentagon.[30]

The impact of these new access-to-information laws is unclear. Reporters seeking information from government agencies still complain of undue delays in the release of information, if not outright lack of cooperation. It is possible to take these matters to court, but the expense and time involved make such action unlikely. People who want to examine the files kept on their

194 The Federal Bureaucracy

activities by agencies such as the FBI and the CIA have also run into bureaucratic roadblocks. The problem of opening the bureaucratic process to public scrutiny is complex, and while the steps taken so far appear to be in the right direction, they are sometimes blocked by the very bureaucratic practices they are designed to overcome.

Summary

It is unlikely that the environment within which the federal bureaucracy operates will change very much in the future. Big government is here to stay, and the only real question is how fast it can be allowed to grow. Thus, the expanded bureaucracy of today is a permanent aspect of American government. Efforts to create a more efficient, more responsive federal bureaucracy will continue, but even these efforts are handicapped by the size of the bureaucracy and the pressures of many conflicting interests. The President, Congress, and a variety of interest groups have a stake in the activities of the bureaucracy.

The administrative and policy-making tasks of the bureaucracy make this fourth branch of the government as powerful as the other three. The President may dominate in the short run, but he is heavily dependent on the willingness of the career civil servants—especially the "super bureaucrats"—to carry out administrative programs in spirit as well as in substance. The ties of mutual interest that bind the federal bureaucracy to Congress are even stronger, since members of Congress usually remain in office longer that the President.

The lack of accountability of the bureaucracy to the people is a major problem. There is clearly a need for oversight of the bureaucracy by the executive and legislative branches. The ability of the super bureaucrats to obstruct policy as well as to participate in its design, in addition to their administrative responsibilities, makes them an important influence on day-to-day operations of American government.

CHAPTER 12 CROSSWORD PUZZLE

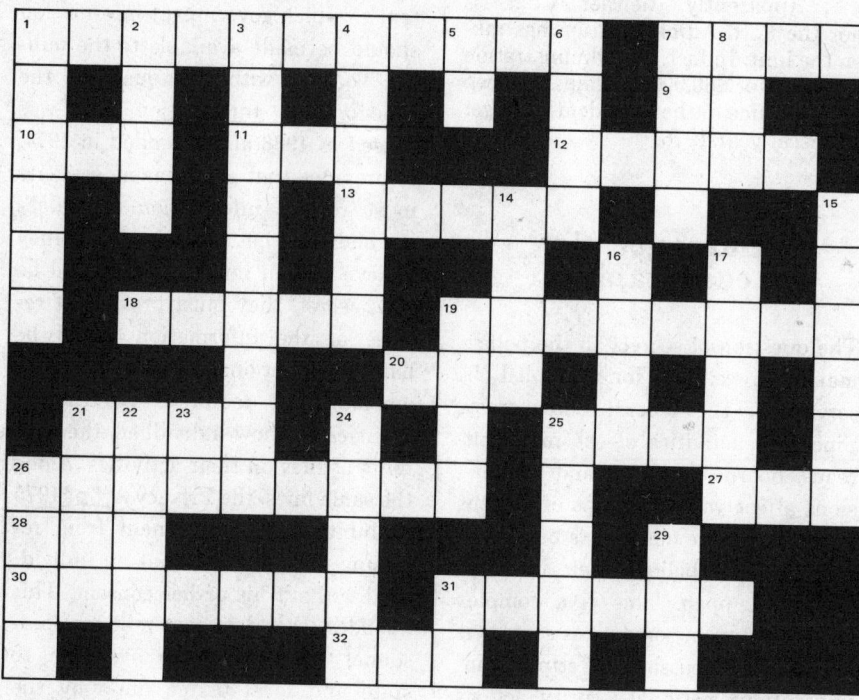

Across
1. The U.S. Postal Service is a semi-independent government ___ .
7. The bureaucracy is marked by a tendency to ___ .
9. Not ___ all
10. American Medical Association (abbr.)
11. Consume
12. Wise men
13. The ___ Act is designed to insulate federal employees from political pressures.
18. Before
19. Government regulatory agencies are endowed with quasi-legislative and quasi- ___ powers.
20. ___ and cheese
21. Money
25. Prefix for colon and circle
26. Ideally the federal bureaucracy is immune to ___ partisanship.
27. ___ it on the line.
28. Muhammed ___ .
30. The Department of Defense is the largest of the ___ Departments.
31. The Veterans Administration is an executive ___ .
32. Terminate

Down
1. Yearns for
2. Posterior
3. Efforts to make the bureaucracy more accountable may take the form of Congressional ___ .
4. Writer
5. ___ , ego, superego
6. Ogden ___ (American humorist)
7. Jokes
8. Route (abbr.)
14. Pal
15. In carving out Congressional mandates, the bureaucracy is often cast in a ___ -making role.
16. An hour is a measure of ___
17. Most federal employees are hired through ___ Service exams.
19. Prison
21. Coca ___
23. Spanish for "yes"
24. Sharp; penetrating
25. The top level bureaucratic employees are sometimes referred to as ___ -bureaucrats.
26. Stride
29. Part of a play
31. Advertisement (abbr.)

NOTES

[1] Robert S. Boyd, "Liberals Read Writing on Wall, Join Big Bureaucracy's Critics," in *The Philadelphia Inquirer,* October 14, 1975, p. 2-A.

[2] *Congressional Quarterly,* October 11, 1975, p. 2167.

[3] Ibid.

[4] From a copyrighted article in *U.S. News & World Report,* November 24, 1975, p. 20.

[5] Ibid., p. 21.

[6] Jonathan R. Laing, "Civil Service Setup, Born as Reform Idea, Now Hit by Reformers," in *The Wall Street Journal,* December 22, 1975, p. 1.

[7] *Congressional Quarterly,* October 25, 1975, p. 2270.

[8] Quoted in "Common Cause Says U.S. Agencies are Hurt by Conduct of Interest," *The New York Times,* October 21, 1976, p. 22C. Copyright © 1976 by The New York Times Company. Reprinted by permission.

[9] *Newsweek,* December 15, 1975, pp. 37-38.

[10] Quoted in *U.S. News & World Report,* August 23, 1976, p. 32.

[11] Tom Wicker, "Power and Corruption," in *The New York Times,* December 5, 1975, p. 39. Copyright © 1975 by The New York Times Company. Reprinted by permission.

[12] "Abuse of G.I. Bill is Disclosed," *The Philadelphia Inquirer,* October 20, 1975, p. 3-A.

[13] "TVA at 42: A Case of Mid-Life Crisis," *The Philadelphia Inquirer,* June 15, 1975, p. 3-L.

[14] James C. Hyatt in "The Postal Service's Bag of Woes," in *The Wall Street Journal,* August 28, 1975, p. 8.

[15] *U.S. News & World Report,* October 6, 1975, p. 53.

[16] David P. Eastburn, "The Fed in a Political World," Federal Reserve Bank of Philadelphia *Business Review,* October 1975, p. 9.

[17] Quoted in *The New York Times,* September 20, 1975, p. 37.

[18] "Winds of Change," *Barron's,* October 13, 1975, p. 7.

[19] Quoted in ibid.

[20] Ibid., p. 7.

[21] *Congressional Quarterly,* November 1, 1975, p. 2325.

[22] *U.S. News & World Report,* November 10, 1975, p. 39.

[23] Ibid., October 6, 1975, p. 28.

[24] Ibid., November 10, 1975, p. 42.

[25] John Fialka in "$403.8 Million is Overpaid in Federal Welfare Foulup," *The Evening Bulletin,* August 16, 1975, p. 20.

[26] *U.S. News & World Report,* November 10, 1975, p. 39.

[27] "Capital Security Tops $2.6 Billion," *The Philadelphia Inquirer,* October 14, 1975, p. 5-A.

[28] "Bureaucrat Admits He Just Loafs," reprinted by permission, *The Philadelphia Inquirer,* May 14, 1975, p. 14-A.

[29] *Congressional Quarterly,* November 15, 1975, p. 2464.

[30] "Two Access-To-Information Laws Cause Chaos," *The Philadelphia Inquirer,* November 9, 1975, p. 10.

CHAPTER 13
THE JUDICIARY

CHAPTER OUTLINE

Questions to Consider
Introduction
Judicial Review—*Marbury* v. *Madison*
Courts and the Political Culture
The Basis of American Law
    Common Law and Civil Law
    Precedents
The American Court System
    State Courts
    Federal Courts
The Judiciary
    Federal Judges
    State Judges
The Role of the Judiciary
    Courts of Original Jurisdiction
    Appellate Courts
The United States Supreme Court
    Activism Versus Restraint
    Accepting Cases for Review
    Court Procedure
    The Impact of Court Opinions
    The Court's Political Philosophy
    Selection of Justices
Administration of Federal Courts
The Historical Role of the Supreme Court
    The Federal-State Relationship
    Government-Business Relations
    Protection of Individual Rights
Landmark Judicial Rulings
    The Fourteenth Amendment
    Racial Discrimination
    Freedom of Expression
The Future of the Judicial Process
Summary

QUESTIONS TO CONSIDER

The Supreme Court makes decisions that appear to change the meaning of the Constitution. Do they really have that effect? What is meant by judicial review? What is the difference between common law and civil law? The answers to these and related questions provide a basis for a discussion of the nation's judicial system. What is the relationship between state and federal courts, and where does the Supreme Court fit into the judicial process? What is meant by judicial activism and judicial restraint? Why do some Court opinions contradict previous rulings? How does the Supreme Court enforce its opinions? Finally, what is the relationship between the judiciary and the other branches of the government? These questions are basic to an understanding of the role of the judiciary in the American political system.

Introduction

The federal judiciary is the third branch of the government, and it has a major influence on national life. The Constitution provided for a Supreme Court, but the role of the Court and the lower judiciary in modern times could not have been foreseen. The Supreme Court began to assert its power in 1803 in *Marbury* v. *Madison*. With its decision in this case, the court established its right of judicial review and thus undertook the responsibility of deciding what the Constitution means. The power of the Court today results from traditions and precedents such as the *Marbury* case rather than the responsibilities assigned to it by the Constitution.

Although the judiciary is an important part of the system of checks and balances, it differs from the executive and legislative branches in several ways. The members of the federal judiciary are nominated by the President and confirmed by the Senate. Their lifetime appointments insulate them from the competitive aspects of the political process and give them more independence than is usually found in other governmental institutions. However, the Supreme Court lacks the power to enforce its actions and is largely dependent on the executive and legislative branches to carry out its directives and comply with its rulings. The power and influence of the Supreme Court flow from its legitimacy in the eyes of the public. Although many of its rulings are controversial, there is little debate about its right to make those rulings.

While the Supreme Court is the most visible judicial institution in the

Chief Justice Warren Burger administers the oath of office to eight cabinet members and four of Carter's top advisors. It is traditional for the Judicial Branch to administer oaths of office.

nation, it is by no means alone. Federal district and appeals courts often serve as testing grounds for changes in interpretation of the Constitution and federal law. State courts also play an important role in reflecting the different attitudes that prevail in various parts of the country.

Judicial Review— Marbury v. Madison

The power of judicial review is simply the authority to declare acts of the legislative or executive branches unconstitutional. Article III of the Constitution did not specifically grant the Court this authority; it fell to Chief Justice John Marshall to establish it in his ruling on *Marbury v. Madison* (1803). The *Marbury* case involved the Judiciary Act of 1789, in which Congress gave the Supreme Court the authority to issue *writs of mandamus* —court orders commanding the performance of a specific act or duty—in cases affecting public officers of the United States and private citizens. William Marbury brought suit to compel an administration official, Secretary of State James Madison, to deliver Marbury's commission as justice of the peace. (Marbury had been appointed by President Adams in the previous administration and his appointment was opposed by the new administration under President Jefferson.) Chief Justice Marshall held that though Marbury was entitled to his commission, the portion of the Judiciary Act of 1789 that gave the Supreme Court the power to issue writs of mandamus was unconstitutional because it expanded the Court's jurisdiction beyond the limits set forth in the Constitution. Marshall's opinion pulled no punches:

It is emphatically the province and duty of the judicial department to say what the law is. Those who apply the rule to particular cases, must of necessity expound and interpret that rule. If two laws conflict with each other, the courts must decide on the operation of each. So if the law be in opposition to the Constitution; if both the law and the Constitution apply to a particular case, so that the court must either decide that case conformably to the law, disregarding the Constitution, or conformably to the Constitution, disregarding the law, the court must determine which of these conflicting rules governs the case. This is the very essence of judicial duty. If, then, the courts are to regard the Constitution, and the Constitution is superior to any ordinary act of the legislature, the Constitution, and not such ordinary act, must govern the case to which they both apply. . . .

The judicial power of the United States is extended to all cases arising under the Constitution.

This decision proved to be extremely important, since it enabled the Supreme Court to maintain its influence and authority despite the immense power of the executive and legislative branches.

Despite Marshall's statement of the principle of judicial review in *Marbury v. Madison* and the intent of the founders as expressed in *The Federalist* (No. 78), the Court did not rule another act of Congress unconstitutional until 1857. The restraint with which the Supreme Court has used its power of judicial review has made this power an accepted constitutional doctrine even though it is not actually stated in the Constitution.

Courts and the Political Culture

The judicial system is very much a part of the political culture, and judicial decisions usually reflect the values of the time. The nation's political mood is like a pendulum. During the 1960s, for example, a liberal trend could be seen in American political life. The Supreme Court's desegregation decisions and the increase in civil rights activity spilled over into other areas such as the rights of the accused in criminal proceedings. In the Nixon-Ford years, there was a clear shift toward more conservative attitudes. Increased resistance to court-ordered busing and demands for tougher sentencing of convicted criminals illustrate this trend.

Courts at all levels usually mirror changes in public perceptions of the proper goals of political and social action. The judiciary does not exist in a vacuum any more than the executive and legislative branches do. Court rulings should be able to win public acceptance if the judicial system is to succeed in carrying out its task. The Supreme Court determines the meaning of the law, but its interpretations must be kept within the limits set by the political culture if they are to survive. While Court rulings often serve as the cutting edge of social change, they must still be consistent with public notions of legitimacy.

The judiciary's activities are not limited to social issues, though these have attracted attention in the past few decades. Judicial decisions have an important impact on the actions of public officials at all levels. Matters such as zoning and licensing procedures in local government often give rise to conflicts that are resolved in court. Similarly, efforts to discourage offensive activities such as massage parlors or pornographic bookstores usually proceed through the court system.

Courts also play an important role in settling economic disputes, and their rulings may have a substantial financial impact. Whether the dispute is between unions and management or between environmentalists and corporations, courts can make decisions that involve millions of dollars. Judicial decisions thus result in redistribution of resources in the same sense as congressional legislation. This puts the supposedly nonpolitical judiciary at the center of many political storms.

A law can have many meanings, depending on how it is interpreted. Most laws, and even the Constitution itself, are written in language that is vague or ambiguous enough to allow for considerable freedom of interpretation. This characteristic of the law brings many cases before the courts and

New York City massage parlor is typical of establishments that are the focus of controversy in many localities over government's right to legislate morality.

make the judiciary an important part of the nation's social, political, and economic system. Thus, the judiciary participates in the political system as well as settling disputes within that system.

The Basis of American Law

Common Law and Civil Law

Interpretation of the law involves more than the Constitution, federal statutes, and administrative regulations. It is influenced strongly by custom, morality, and reason.

Since Anglo-Saxon law provides most of the precedent for American legal concepts and traditions, the judiciary has a legal basis older than the government it serves. There are two basic types of law: *civil law* and *common law*. The major difference between them is that common law is based largely on custom, while civil law has been codified by the government. Civil law is taken largely from the common law in that it arises from notions of acceptable and unacceptable activity based on traditional concepts of morality and reason. As traditional interpretations have become inadequate to changing conditions, governments have found it necessary to resolve such contradictions and to develop formal legal guidelines. Thus, legal change, though slow, is inevitable as a society attempts to interpret common law in a way that is consistent with its changing values and needs. It is the recognition that law is a dynamic value that is at the core of the concept of judicial review by the Supreme Court and reinterpretation of law.

Precedents

Both common and civil law depend heavily on precedent. In this sense, *precedent* (or *stare decisis*) refers to earlier court decisions in similar cases. However, a precedent is not binding in all subsequent cases. The need for change in legal interpretations must be weighed against the force of precedent. Debates that arise over controversial Supreme Court decisions such as the banning of Bible reading in public schools or the legalization of abortion are evidence of the necessity of balancing established traditions against changing values.

The American Court System

The state and federal levels of government are paralleled by the federal and state court systems, which have exclusive jurisdiction in some cases and overlapping jurisdiction in others. This means that there are 51 separate judicial systems in the United States. All legal actions brought under federal laws to which there are no corresponding state laws must be taken to federal courts; maritime law is in this category. However, most criminal suits are brought in state courts because federal law generally applies only to crimes in which state lines are crossed. (This is an example of overlapping jurisdiction, since both state and federal laws are violated.) Civil actions involving citizens of the same state—corporations are treated as citizens under the law—are brought before state courts unless the issue involves questions of constitutional interpretation, in which case the matter may be taken to either a state or a federal court. Civil actions involving amounts over $10,000 and citizens of different states may also be brought before either state or federal courts.

State Courts

There are several levels of courts in every state; while their specific structures differ, their basic framework is the same. The lowest level of courts deals with such matters as traffic violations, actions brought under local ordinances, and minor crimes such as shoplifting. Such courts exist in all but the smallest towns and are headed by a justice of the peace or some similar officer—the title varies. These minor courts usually handle cases in which a decision can be reached without a jury. Jury trials and more important civil and criminal cases are held in trial courts. There are also a variety of lower courts that deal with specialized issues, such as cases involving juveniles, misdemeanors, or small claims (in which the amount is between $100 and $1000).

Most civil suits involving amounts over $1000 or criminal charges other than misdemeanors are brought in state trial courts. It is here that jury trials, if requested, are held and the important cases at the state level are adjudicated. Decisions in such diverse matters as criminal cases and negligence suits vary widely among state courts and even among trial courts within the same state.

Many cases are settled before being brought to trial by means of negotiations between the plaintiff and the defendant, with the judge often playing an important role. It is inexpensive (usually no more than $50) to file suit in state trial courts, and this encourages filing as part of the negotiating process. However, conducting the case itself can be very costly and the outcome is uncertain, so most lawyers try to settle a case after the suit is filed but before the trial begins.

Litigants in state trial courts have the right to appeal to appellate or appeals courts. These courts base their decisions on the trial court's record of the case; their verdicts are reached by a panel of at least three judges. All states have appellate courts, and twenty-two states also have intermediate appellate courts.[1] The top state appellate courts occupy an important place in the nation's judicial system because they are often the first courts to resolve conflicts over important policy questions. Such issues as abortion, pornography, distribution of birth control devices, and the use of property taxes to finance schools were first heard in state courts. While state court decisions involving constitutional questions are not binding on federal courts, their rulings are important indicators of the public's mood in relation to potential governmental actions.

Although the Supreme Court's interpretations of the Constitution take precedence over those of state appellate courts, there has been an increasing tendency for state courts to look to their state constitutions rather than to Supreme Court rulings as the basis of law. This has been especially evident in the area of criminal rights: The Supreme Court has taken the position that convictions can be obtained despite certain violations of an individual's constitutional rights, while many state courts have taken a stand that is more favorable to the defendant. Many such cases revolve around the Supreme Court's *Miranda* decision (*Miranda* v. *Arizona*, 1966), which held that an individual must be informed of his or her right to remain silent because any statements made can be used as evidence. In 1971, the Supreme Court reinterpreted the *Miranda* decision and ruled that statements obtained by illegal means could be introduced if a defendant took the stand in his own defense. However, the state supreme courts of New Jersey, California, and Hawaii have refused to follow the 1971 interpretation and have continued to base their rulings on the 1966 decision. According to the Hawaii supreme court, "the protections which the Supreme Court enumerated in *Miranda* have an independent source in the Hawaii constitution's privilege against self-incrimination."[2]

Other areas in which state courts have taken a more liberal stand than the Supreme Court involve funding of public schools, electronic surveillance, and police searches. These examples show that the state courts occupy an important place in the nation's judicial system in terms of constitutional interpretation as well as day-to-day judicial decisions.

Federal Courts

The federal court system consists of 90 district courts (which are trial courts), 11 appellate courts, and the Supreme Court, which is the nation's highest court. There are also 4 district courts in U.S. territories, as well as special courts such as the Tax Court, the Court of Customs and Patent Appeal, and the Court of Claims.

Federal courts do much more than establish the guilt or innocence of an individual or settle civil disputes. The federal judiciary is an important element in national government, and the fairness of its operations supports the legitimacy of the political system.

The district courts have jurisdiction within specific geographic areas. There is at least one in every state (89 in all) and in the District of Columbia. The number of judges in district courts varies from 1 to 27, with a total of 400 authorized by Congress. In addition, retired district court judges can help in handling the heavy caseload.

In 1975, 160,602 cases were filed in district courts—an average of 402 per judge—and the number of cases is

TABLE 13-1
U.S. District Courts—Trials: 1950 To 1974

For years ending June 30. Through 1960, trials commenced; thereafter, trials completed. Prior to 1965, excludes D.C., Alaska, Hawaii, and outlying areas. A trial is defined as a contested proceeding (other than a hearing on a motion) before either court or jury in which evidence is introduced and final judgment sought.

Type of Trial	1950	1955	1960	1965	1969	1970	1971	1972	1973	1974
Total	7,977	9,258	9,042	11,485	14,397	16,032	17,549	18,780	19,467	18,572
Civil trials	5,663	5,882	6,002	7,613	8,834	9,449	10,093	10,962	10,896	10,972
Nonjury	3,648	3,224	3,161	4,459	5,619	6,078	6,600	7,285	7,289	7,403
Jury	2,015	2,658	3,841	3,154	3,215	3,371	3,493	3,677	3,607	3,569
Criminal trials	2,314	3,376	3,040	3,872	5,563	6,583	7,456	7,818	8,571	7,600
Nonjury	825	1,151	943	1,143	1,883	2,357	2,923	2,968	2,927	2,753
Jury	1,489	2,225	2,097	2,729	3,680	4,226	4,533	4,850	5,644	4,847

SOURCE: *Statistical Abstract of the United States*, 1975, p. 164.

TABLE 13-2
U.S. District Courts—Civil and Criminal Cases: 1950 to 1974

For years ending June 30. Excludes District of Columbia, Canal Zone, Guam, and Virgin Islands, except beginning 1965, civil cases include data for all district courts.

Item	1950	1955	1960	1965	1970	1971	1972	1973	1974
Civil cases: Commenced	44,454	48,308	59,284	67,678	87,321	93,396	96,173	98,560	103,530
Cases terminated*	42,482	47,959	48,847	63,137	79,466	85,638	94,256	97,402	96,701
No court action	(NA)	(NA)	(NA)	29,309	31,056	33,828	37,446	37,024	35,879
Court action, total	(NA)	(NA)	(NA)	33,828	48,410	51,810	56,810	60,378	60,822
Before pretrial	(NA)	(NA)	(NA)	17,089	29,429	32,849	35,590	36,873	38,576
Pretrial	(NA)	(NA)	(NA)	9,442	11,006	11,011	12,739	15,208	13,864
Trials	(NA)	(NA)	(NA)	7,297	7,975	7,950	8,481	8,297	8,382
Percent reaching trial	(NA)	(NA)	NA)	11.6	10.0	9.3	9.0	8.5	8.7
Criminal cases: Commenced**	36,383	35,310	28,137	31,569	38,102	41,290	47,043	38,449	36,105
Dedendants disposed of	37,675	38,990	30,512	33,718	36,356	44,615	49,516	46,724	48,014
Not convicted	4,173	5,135	3,784	4,961	8,178	12,512	12,296	11,741	11,784
Dismissed	3,237	3,792	2,596	3,789	6,608	10,655	10,219	9,757	10,019
Acquitted	936	1,343	1,188	1,172	1,570	1,857	2,077	1,984	1,765
Convicted	33,502	33,855	26,728	28,757	28,178	32,103	37,220	34,983	36,230
By guilty plea or nolo contendere	31,739	31,148	24,245	25,923	24,111	27,544	31,714	29,009	30,660
By court or jury	1,763	2,707	2,483	2,834	4,067	4,559	5,506	5,974	5,570
Imprisonment	14,435	16,889	13,433	13,668	12,415	14,378	16,832	17,540	17,180
Probation	16,046	14,021	10,391	10,779	11,387	13,243	15,395	15,026	16,623
Fine and other	3,021	2,945	2,904	4,310	4,376	4,482	4,993	2,417	2,427

SOURCE: *Statistical Abstract of the United States,* 1975, p. 165.
 (NA) Not available.
 *Excludes land condemnation cases.
 **Excludes transfers.

expected to increase to 180,000 in 1976.[3] Chief Justice Warren E. Burger describes the dimensions of the problem as follows:

The tendency of Americans to try to resolve every sort of problem in the courts continues. Overwhelmed by increased demands for regulatory legislation, for broadened governmental programs of all kinds, Congress enacts legislation, much of which reaches the courts for resolution. There the legislation increasingly presents difficult questions of interpretation because of the uniqueness of the issues.[4]

District court cases are usually heard by one judge; however, either litigant in a case may request a jury trial. Table 13-1 shows the proportions of jury and nonjury trials and civil and criminal actions in district courts. It is interesting to note that about 70 percent of the criminal cases tried in U.S. district courts were heard by juries, but only about 35 percent of the civil cases were settled in that way. This reflects the feeling that civil cases involve points of law that should be interpreted by judges rather than by a jury. In contrast, criminal defendants seek jury trials in the belief that the unanimous verdict required in federal courts is more difficult to obtain and that the chance of conviction is therefore lower.

Table 13-2 shows the small percentage of civil cases that actually come to trial in district courts. As noted earlier, litigants usually try to settle disputes before the trial stage, and most judges encourage out-of-court settlements. The high rate of convictions in criminal cases in federal district courts—about 80 percent—illustrates the professionalism of the U.S. attorney's offices throughout the nation. Cases are not brought to trial by the federal government unless there is enough evidence to make conviction by a jury highly likely.

The decisions of district courts are sometimes made by a panel of three judges, including one circuit court judge. Such panels are formed to hear petitions for injunctions against orders of the Interstate Commerce Commission and various other administrative orders, as well as certain other cases such as those involving civil rights. In 1974, most such cases involved violations of civil rights.[5]

Appeals from district court decisions are usually taken to the appellate court or *circuit* that has jurisdiction over the district court. Circuit courts may base their decisions on either oral or written arguments. There are some situations in which appeals may be taken directly to the Supreme Court. These include appeals from three-judge panels, government appeals in cases where federal statutes have been ruled unconstitutional, and cases of overriding national importance. For example, the refusal of President Nixon to release the White House tapes to the House Judiciary Committee was a matter of such urgency that it was taken directly to the circuit court rather than going through the usual procedure that begins with a district court trial.[6]

There are 11 circuit courts with from 3 to 15 judges each (see Table 13-3); there are 92 circuit court judges, with retired judges filling in when they are needed. Appeals to circuit courts are usually heard by a panel of three judges without a jury. Most such cases are appeals from district court rulings, but circuit courts also consider cases arising from orders of federal regulatory agencies.

The cases heard in circuit courts

usually revolve around issues of law, and decisions made at this level serve as important legal precedents for district and state court cases. Table 13-4 presents information about recent circuit court decisions. Note that about 17 percent of the appeals heard in 1973 resulted in reversals of lower court decisions. The appeals procedure is an important element in the judicial system because rulings at this level involve interpretation of law rather than simply judgment of evidence.

The circuit courts occupy an important place in the judicial system in terms of guaranteeing justice to all litigants as well as serving as a unifying influence on judicial interpretation. All litigants have the right to appeal district court decisions to the circuit courts. The right of appeal stimulates trial judges to be very careful in their interpretation of the law because consistent reversals of their decisions by appeals courts are a poor reflection on their judicial ability.

This factor also encourages trial judges to set aside their personal views in applying the law and to make decisions that are consistent with Supreme Court decisions. This was a significant element in early district court decisions regarding the rights of southern blacks. One study found that while 50 percent of civil rights cases in district courts were decided in favor of the black plaintiff, 75 percent of the decisions in the circuit courts upheld the position of the black plaintiff.[7]

The Judiciary

Federal Judges

Federal judges are appointed by the President for life, subject to Senate confirmation. The reason for appointing judges for life is not only to protect them from political pressure but also to attract highly qualified people to the judiciary. Federal judges can be impeached for misconduct, but this procedure is seldom used. Federal district judges receive $54,500 a year, those in the courts of appeals $57,500, associate justices of the Supreme Court $72,000, and the chief justice $75,000. While these salaries are above those of other government employees, they are modest in relation to the responsibilities involved and the salaries these individuals could earn outside the judiciary. However, federal judgeships are much sought after; there are few positions in public life that command as much respect.

The judges appointed by the President to the lower federal judiciary are usually recommended by the senators from their state who are members of the President's party (referred to as Senatorial courtesy) and approved by an American Bar Association committee. Federal judges may have been active politically or have strong political ties to public officials. These associations play an important role in shaping their perceptions of the issues that reach the courts.

TABLE 13-3
District and Appeals Court Boundaries

SOURCE: Sheldon Goldman and Thomas P. Jahnige, *The Federal Courts as a Political System* (New York: Harper & Row, 1976), p. 27.

TABLE 13-4
U.S. Courts of Appeals: 1950 To 1974 (For years ending June 30.)

Item	1950	1955	1960	1965	1968	1969	1970	1971	1972	1973	1974
Cases commenced	2,830	3,695	3,899	6,766	9,116	10,248	11,662	12,788	14,535	15,629	16,436
Criminal	308	677	623	1,223	2,098	2,508	2,660	3,197	3,980	4,453	4,067
U.S. civil	708	811	788	1,387	1,500	1,823	2,167	2,367	2,604	2,704	3,267
Private civil	1,114	1,363	1,534	2,677	3,569	4,197	4,834	5,234	5,795	6,172	6,157
Administrative appeals	485	576	737	1,106	1,545	1,345	1,522	1,383	1,509	1,616	2,205
Other	215	268	217	373	404	375	479	607	647	684	740
Cases disposed of*	2,355	2,809	2,681	3,546	4,668	5,121	6,139	7,606	8,537	9,618	8,451
Affirmed or granted	1,700	1,907	1,924	2,635	3,499	3,838	4,626	5,765	6,207	7,163	6,429
Reversed or denied	528	777	656	773	1,009	1,072	1,280	1,377	1,664	1,693	1,579
Percent of total	22.4	26.9	24.5	22.0	21.6	20.9	20.9	18.1	19.4	17.5	18.6
Other	127	125	101	138	160	211	233	464	666	762	443
Cases terminated	3,064	3,654	3,713	5,771	8,264	9,014	10,699	12,368	13,828	15,112	15,422
Criminal	342	670	580	1,014	1,754	2,022	2,581	3,047	3,799	4,210	4,299
U.S. civil	783	893	750	1,229	1,356	1,559	1,912	2,258	2,512	2,722	2,791
Private civil	1,184	1,289	1,517	2,183	3,268	3,679	4,367	5,065	5,399	6,030	5,847
Administrative appeals	541	523	660	1,004	1,512	1,394	1,407	1,503	1,448	1,493	1,734
Other	214	279	206	341	374	360	432	495	670	657	751
Median months **	7.1	7.3	6.8	8.0	7.8	8.3	8.2	7.6	6.6	6.4	6.8

SOURCE: Statistical *Abstract of the United States*, 1975, p. 164.
*Beginning 1974, data not comparable with earlier years due to changes in criteria after hearing or submission.
** Median time interval from filing of complete record to final disposition.

Federal judges do not always agree in their legal philosophy. They are individuals with liberal or conservative leanings and tendencies toward activism or restraint. They also have different perceptions of the law as a result of their varied personal experiences. These differences are reflected in the decisions reached by federal courts. While Supreme Court decisions provide broad guidelines for lower court action, there is enough diversity among the matters that reach the lower courts to allow for different interpretations.

State Judges

Political considerations play an important role in the selection of state court judges. Some are appointed and some elected (usually for a long term); most have been active in politics. Indeed, the position of state court judge is often granted as a reward for faithful party service. There is a wide range in the salaries of state judges, and the range in their judicial ability is equally wide. The local judiciary is similar to the state judiciary except that political factors weigh even more heavily and there is a corresponding drop in professionalism.

Various plans to upgrade the judiciary have been proposed; their goal is to limit the list of nominees for judgeships to those approved by local and state bar associations. These groups investigate the background and record of potential judges and weed out those who lack the necessary experience, legal knowledge, or judicial temperament. In states or localities that elect judges, the bar associations often make public their approval or disapproval of a judge's performance. Then they seek the backing of the state party organizations in electing those they approve of and witholding support from those they consider unfit for further service. Thus, whereas long-term or lifetime appointments insulate judges from political pressure, the need to seek reelection serves as a check on abuses of judicial authority.

The Role of the Judiciary

Courts of Original Jurisdiction

The functions of federal and state judges vary, but there are some that are common to most judicial jurisdictions. The Supreme Court cannot be included in a general description of the judiciary because of its unique position in American government. It will be discussed later in the chapter.

In addition to deciding on the merits of the cases that are brought before them, judges usually perform administrative functions such as scheduling and disposing of cases. Cases are listed for trial after the appropriate papers—usually a complaint and an answer—have been filed. Certain types of cases may be given precedence over others because a quick decision is needed. Labor disputes involving hospitals, which pose a threat to public welfare, get this kind of treatment. Many judges have considerable leeway in deciding the order in which cases will be heard, but such decisions are usually made by administrators in the court system. Reducing the backlog of cases is a high-priority matter in almost every court.

Much of the judge's work is done in his or her chambers rather than in open court. As we have seen, many judges encourage litigants to settle cases out of court rather than bringing them to trial. This not only reduces the court's backlog but also avoids the expense of a trial.

In most cases, including criminal

trials, the evidence is not so clear-cut as to preclude an effective defense and, hence, a lengthy trial. In criminal cases, long, expensive trials can be avoided through the use of *plea bargaining*, in which the defendant pleads guilty to a lesser crime than the one he or she is charged with in return for the promise of a lighter sentence. The use of plea bargaining is controversial because the agreement reached is seldom completely satisfactory to either the defendant or the prosecution. A defendant may be confronted with what appears to be strong evidence of his or her guilt and encouraged to bargain for a lighter sentence than might have resulted from a trial. However, the accused is denied the opportunity to establish his or her innocence and may be settling for a conviction when a trial might have resulted in acquittal. The prosecution may also be settling for a less than desirable outcome. Often defendants are allowed to plead guilty to lesser offenses when they are guilty of worse crimes and thus get lighter sentences than they deserve. However, while plea bargaining is a poor substitute for a trial, the huge backlog of court cases encourages the use of this procedure.

Once a trial begins, the judge acts as a referee and rules on what evidence may be introduced, keeps the questioning of witnesses within legal limits, and ultimately makes a decision on the case. If it is a jury trial, the judge instructs the jurors on the legal matters involved in the case. In criminal cases, the judge usually retains the power of sentencing, while in civil cases the jury often fixes the amount of compensation, if any, in addition to reaching a decision. The judge may reduce this amount if he or she considers it unfair.

Appellate Courts

Appellate courts are appeals courts. Cases are brought to these courts in an attempt to reverse or modify the decisions of lower courts. These courts differ from lower courts in that there is no jury and the cases are decided on the basis of the trial record. Cases that come before appellate courts are heard by at least three judges, and the decision of the majority holds. Because there are often contradictions in the evidence presented in court cases and many ambiguities in the law, the appeals procedure provides ample opportunity to overturn lower court decisions. This procedure emphasizes interpretation of the law, so that judges at this level are in effect judicial policy makers.

The nation's ultimate appeals court, and the court that has the final word in interpreting the Constitution, is the United States Supreme Court. The responsibilities of the Supreme Court are as unique as its method of operation. At this level, judicial decisions often become quasi-legislative acts because of their potential impact on the nation. They also have an important effect on the relationship between the government and the people.

The United States Supreme Court

The Supreme Court is unique in that it is both a legal and a political institution. It makes its own rules, chooses the cases it will hear, rejects cases it does not want to rule on, and reaches decisions that have the force of law even though the Court is not a legislative body. The power of judicial review has placed the Court at the center of a variety of issues, and its impact has gone far beyond mere interpretation of the Constitution. The Court is both a leader of public opinion, as in the *school desegregation cases*, and a follower of the public mood in that it seldom takes positions that conflict with its perception of the views of the majority.

The Court will often find itself involved in controversy if it does not confine itself to narrow constitutional questions. Judging from the actions of the Court during the past few decades, it does not hesitate to become entangled in controversial political and social issues, from the rights of the accused to the question of executive privilege. The extent to which the Supreme Court deals with such issues is a reflection of the philosophy of the nine Court justices. The justices have the power to either rule on such issues or avoid them, and this is the basis for much criticism of the Court. On the one hand, the justices are accused of overstepping their bounds; on the other, they are accused of judicial timidity.

Activism Versus Restraint

Perhaps the most important aspect of a justice's perception of the role of the Supreme Court is the question of whether it is appropriate for the Court to deal with political or social issues that Congress has not resolved. The argument for judicial restraint was expressed by Associate Justice John Marshall Harlan as follows:

The activist view, in a nutshell, is that every major social ill in this country can find its cure in some constitutional "principle," and that this Court should "take the lead" in promoting reform when other branches of government fail to act. The Constitution is not a panacea for every blot upon the public welfare, nor should this Court, ordained as a judicial body, be thought of as a general haven for reform movements. [8]

The activist philosophy, by contrast, is based on the idea that in the absence of congressional action the Court has a duty to guarantee all citizens their constitutional rights. Thus, the issue of whether or not the Supreme Court should hear cases that revolve around political questions is a controversial one.

It can be argued that equality under the law is guaranteed by the Constitution, and there was good reason for Court action in the school desegregation cases. However, the Court's action in *Baker* v. *Carr* (1962), was more debatable. This was the case in which the Court issued its "one man, one vote" ruling, which had the effect of forcing the states to provide for proportional representation in both houses of their legislatures. The justices objected to the widespread practice of *gerrymandering*, or drawing election district boundaries in ways that favored the candidates of the party in power.

The argument against the Court's involvement in such matters is best expressed in the minority opinion written by Justice Frankfurter for *Baker* v. *Carr* (Frankfurter often expressed the opinion that the Court should stay out of the "political thicket" [9]):

There is not under our Constitution a judicial remedy for every political mischief. In a democratic society like ours, relief must come through aroused popular conscience that sears the conscience of the people's representatives. [10]

The opposing view is presented by a well-known legal expert as follows: "But the majority had seen one attempt to 'sear the conscience' after another frustrated for generations. Indeed, in many of the transgressing states the very imbalance of representative districts rendered 'an aroused public conscience' impossible." [11]

Accepting Cases for Review

For a case to be accepted for review by the Supreme Court, a major constitutional question must be involved and the litigants must have *standing,* that is, they must be directly affected by the case. This requirement is intended to eliminate cases that are brought for the sole purpose of testing Constitutional interpretation.

Cases brought to the Court for review come from state appellate courts, U.S. courts of appeals, three-judge district courts, and special courts (such as Customs and Patent Appeals) in which the United States is a litigant. The Court also accepts district court cases involving federal communication, antitrust, and commerce laws.

The Supreme Court hears a case only if four justices agree to bring it before the full Court. A *writ of certiorari* must be issued to bring the case to the attention of the full Court. In deciding whether to grant or deny certiorari, the justices influence the extent to which Court decisions shape governmental policy. The late Justice Louis D. Brandeis is quoted as saying, "The most important thing we do is not doing." [12] Brandeis believed the Supreme Court should resist the temptation to adjudicate every controversy that comes to its attention which would result in the establishment of many new constitutional principles.

It is also important for the Court to confine its rulings to questions that have applications beyond the case being decided. Hence, it accepts only cases that raise "substantial" federal issues, avoiding cases that hinge on constitutional interpretation but raise issues that are unique to a particular situation. The philosophy that determines the Court's granting of writs of certiorari is often criticized as either too activist in that in involves the Court in too many issues or too passive in that it avoids dealing with important matters.

There is another important consideration in the Court's decision on whether or not to grant a hearing. The Court will usually refuse to hear cases that have not yet received much public attention, even though they may involve important issues. This policy is sometimes referred to as the principle of "ripeness." In following this policy, the Court is not trying to make sure all its actions are popular. It simply wants to know its decisions will be accepted as fair and just. The death penalty, pornography, and abortion are areas in which early Court rulings avoided the basic issue so that it would be raised again when the public was ready to accept a change in the Court's interpretation of the Constitution. *Brown* v. *Board of Education* (1954) was a watershed in the drive for equality of black Americans and until the reapportionment cases were adjudicated in 1962 *(Baker* v. *Carr),* the Court had usually refused to even consider cases involving political questions.

Like any powerful institution, the Court runs the risk of losing legitimacy if it makes frequent rulings affecting the social or political life of the nation. Therefore, cases that place the Court in a quasi-legislative position must be chosen carefully and, if possible avoided until there is widespread support for judicial action in a particular area or at least until there is little chance of strong public disapproval of the Court's ruling. As Table 13-5 shows, only 169 cases were decided during the Court's 1973 term out of 5340 that were on the docket. This is

TABLE 13-5
U.S. Supreme Court—Cases Filed and Disposition During October Terms: 1969 to 1974

Action	1969	1970	1971	1972	1973	1974*
Total cases on docket	4,202	4,212	4,533	4,640	5,340	3,028**
Appellate cases on docket	1,758	1,903	2,070	2,183	2,480	1,457
From prior term	271	325	362	442	412	612
Docketed during present term	1,487	1,578	1,708	1,741	2,068	845
Cases acted upon	1,529	1,613	1,752	1,834	1,948	964
Granted review	222	214	238	217	229	143
Denied, dismissed, or withdrawn	1,219	1,285	1,409	1,397	1,572	770
Summarily decided	88	114	105	220	147	51
Cases not acted upon	229	324	318	349	532	493
Pauper cases on docket	2,429	2,289	2,445	2,436	2,585	1,407
Cases acted upon	1,971	1,802	2,023	1,982	2,013	919
Granted review	30	41	61	35	30	19
Denied, dismissed, or withdrawn	1,916	1,683	1,781	1,902	1,942	889
Summarily decided	25	78	181	45	41	11
Cases not acted upon	458	487	422	454	572	488
Original cases on docket	15	20	18	21	14	10
Cases disposed of during term	5	7	8	8	4	1
Total cases available for argument	241	267	280	256	261	164
Cases disposed of	147	160	181	180	172	82
Cases argued	144	151	176	177	170	81
Cases dismissed or remanded without argument	3	9	5	3	2	1
Cases remaining	94	107	99	76	89	82
Cases decided by signed opinion	105	126	143	159	161	22
Cases decided by per curiam opinion	21	22	24	18	8	1
Number of signed opinions	88	109	129	140	140	13

SOURCE: *Statistical Abstract of the United States*, 1975, p. 164.
*Preliminary
**Through Jan. 10, 1975.

an indication of the selectivity with which the Court decides which cases it will consider.

Court Procedure

The Court normally is in session from October through June. Because it is an appellate court, most of its decisions are based on the written records of cases tried in lower courts. However, about 5 percent of the cases granted writs of certiorari are heard in open court with oral arguments presented by lawyers. These hearings are brief, and the justices may ask questions during the presentation of the arguments.

The Court may also issue decisions without using written opinions or oral arguments. These are called <u>summary opinions</u> and have the same force as decisions that are accompanied by opinions. Such decisions have been criticized by several justices. For example, Justices William J. Brennan, Jr. and Thurgood Marshall have said that "if significant constitutional issues are to be decided summarily without any briefing or oral argument and with only momentary and offhanded conference discussion, and if these summary opinions nevertheless bind the courts of the 50 states and all lower Federal courts, respect for our constitutional decision making must inevitably be impaired."[13] Summary opinions are usually confined to appeals from circuit court decisions, but the potential impact of such decisions is a matter of conern.

Discussions regarding which cases to accept and how to rule on those cases are held in private with no one but the justices taking part. The chief justice chairs these conferences, and an active chief justice can have a significant impact on the Court. In addition to assigning the writing of opinions, the chief justice can influence the choice of cases to be accepted. Chief Justice Earl Warren was an effective leader in the sense that he was able to convince the other justices to accept his activist philosophy, thereby propelling the Court into controversial areas.

Associate justices can also influence their fellow justices, but no meaningful generalization can be made about the interaction of the justices during their weekly conferences. While the chief justice has more authority in procedural matters, the extent to which this authority carries over to substantive discussions depends on the personalities and philosophies of the members of the Court.[14]

In a 1976 speech to an American Bar Association meeting, Justice Lewis F. Powell, Jr. described the way the members of the Court conduct their business. He said, "Perhaps as much as 90 percent of our time we function very much as nine separate, small, independent law firms." Powell went on to say that informal discussions among the justices about business before the Court was "minimal," with most communication "being by correspondence or memoranda."[15]

Supreme Court decisions require a majority vote of the justices participating. The setting of important legal precedents by 5-4 or 6-3 majorities is often criticized on the ground that it is inconsistent to require unanimous jury verdicts in most cases but to allow important changes in American law to be passed by slim margins. It was with this criticism in mind that Chief Justice Warren persuaded the Court to reach a unanimous decision in *Brown v. Board of Education*, the key school desegregation case. The Court also issued a unanimous decision in the White House tapes case. The recognition that unanimity is desirable on major issues helps soften the criticism of split votes on other cases.

The Impact of Court Opinions

The impact of Supreme Court opinions depends on the nature of the case and the support the majority opinion reflects. Unanimous decisions are usually accompanied by a strong opinion that will serve as an important legal precedent in other jurisdictions and in future cases. When a decision is based on a divided vote, a minority opinion is often issued along with the majority opinion and may be widely cited in future tests of the issue in question. The prestige of the Supreme Court is such that even legal viewpoints that failed to win majority support must be taken seriously. Minority opinions are often more definite than the majority opinion because there is less need to reach a middle ground that other justices can accept. In some cases, there may be more than one concurring or dissenting opinion if the justices on either side are unable to agree on an opinion.

In addition to setting legal precedents, Supreme Court opinions send a message to the executive and legislative branches as well as the interest groups affected by a particular issue. The Court may choose to rule on rather narrow constitutional grounds or may make a sweeping statement of legal doctrine. If the grounds for a ruling are limited, there is plenty of opportunity for Congress or state legislatures to change the portions of their statutes that have been declared unconstitutional without changing the intent of the law. An example is provided by Supreme Court rulings in capital punishment cases. The Court ruled in 1972 *(Furman* v. *Georgia)* that capital punishment was unconstitutional in the form in which it was being applied because it represented cruel and unusual punishment. However, the majority in the 5-4 decision expressed three different opinions, and only two justices were unalterably opposed to the death penalty. The other three justices voting with the majority merely stated that the law in question was unconstitutional because it was applied unfairly. This type of opinion says, in effect, that new laws that are applied more evenly may meet the Court's approval. Accordingly, in February 1977 Idaho carried out its death penalty with the execution of Gary Gilmore.

The Court's Political Philosophy

The Court is an ever-changing political institution that fluctuates between liberalism and conservatism as well as between activism and restraint. It is customary to refer to periods of Court history by the name of the chief justice. Thus, we refer to the Warren Court or the Burger Court in discussing the trends of the past 25 years. The Warren Court was considered both liberal and activist, issuing many opinions that had a profound effect on American social life and individual rights. The decisions in the school desegregation cases (1954) are the ones most closely associated with the Warren Court, but they are by no means the only ones made by that Court that protected the individual against unjust governmental action. Table 13-6 shows the more important Warren Court rulings (as well as those of the Burger Court) in the areas of individual freedom, procedural rights, and equal protection under the law.

The Burger Court is usually viewed as more conservative than the Warren Court, as well as more restrained. The major change in the Court's rulings under Chief Justice Burger has been in the field of defendants' rights—some of the Warren Court rulings that protected the accused have been abridged. Restrictions on police searches without a warrant have been eased; the grounds on which a defendant can plead entrapment have been narrowed; and federal courts have been barred from reviewing criminal convictions based on illegal seizure of evidence. On the other hand, the Burger Court has consistently upheld the First Amendment freedoms of speech and the press. It has banned judicial "gag" orders designed to restrict news stories about criminal cases and removed restrictions on campaign spending by candidates in their own behalf.

The relative restraint of the Burger Court may be seen in its tendency to delegate responsibility to state courts rather than attempting to adjudicate certain cases on a national level. For example, it has made local officials responsible for defining what constitutes pornography and upheld the right of local police forces to establish their own procedures for handling citizen grievances and to set their own dress codes for officers.[16] In addition, the Burger Court reversed a Warren Court precedent that allowed Congress to set minimum wage and hour standards for state and local employees. In explaining the reasoning behind the latter decision, Burger said, "We took steps to arrest the denigration of states to a role comparable to the departments of France, governed entirely out of the national capital."[17] This ruling was based on a 5-4 vote, with the dissenting Justices calling the ruling a "catastrophic body blow" to Congress' power to regulate commerce.

In the past 40 years, the Supreme Court has been more inclined to void congressional actions than previously. In the 1969-1976 period, for example, the Burger Court declared provisions in 27 federal laws unconstitutional, bringing to 59 the number voided since 1937.[18] This is an indication of the willingness of recent Courts to exercise the power of judicial review despite their different political philosophies.

Identifying the Court's decisions during a specific period with the name of the chief justice is an oversimplification because the justices' votes have equal weight and because the composition of the Court changes from time to time while the chief justice remains the same. The political attitudes of the associate justices are an important element in the Court's rulings. These elements interact with prevailing national values to influence the direction of Court decisions as well as their content.

Selection of Justices

Supreme Court justices are nominated by the President and confirmed by the Senate. While this process is similar to the way all federal judges are appointed, the selection of Supreme Court justices is more significant because of the long-range impact their political philosophies are likely to have on the nation. While the judges of district and circuit courts generally must have the approval of the senators from their states (if they are members of the President's party) as well as that of the Standing Committee on Federal Judiciary of the American Bar Association (ABA), the selection of Supreme Court justices is made on a different basis. The endorsement of the ABA is usually necessary, but there are numerous exceptions. The President will always try to nominate a justice whose political philosophy is similar to his own, and may ignore the ABA committee in the process.

Traditionally, the ABA has been a conservative influence on the selection of justices. In 1916, however, President Wilson nominated the liberal Louis Brandeis over the ABA's opposition. Today, though it is still relatively conservative, the ABA reflects many shades of political philosophy, and the President has less trouble finding nominees who will be considered qualified regardless of their political outlook. The influence of the ABA can be seen in President Johnson's experience when he nominated Francis X. Morrissey to the Supreme Court. Morrissey had the support of Senator Edward Kennedy (D., Mass.) and the Massachusetts Bar Association, but was considered unqualified by the ABA Committee. The storm of criticism of the Morrissey nomination made it obvious that it would not be confirmed, and it was accordingly withdrawn.[19]

President Nixon had a similar experience, though he had agreed not to nominate justices who had been rated "not qualified" by the ABA Committee. After several of his nominees had been rejected, by the ABA, Nixon nominated Justices William Rehnquist and Lewis Powell without ABA endorsement. In contrast, President Ford sought ABA approval when he nominated John Paul Stevens to the Court. Stevens was approved by the

TABLE 13-6
Fundamental Freedom Cases

Title	Constitutional Right Protected	Court
Aptheker v. Rusk, 378 U.S. 500 (1964)	Right to travel protected by the Fifth Amendment	Warren
Lamont v. Day, 381 U.S. 301 (1965)	Right to receive mail from Communist countries protected by First Amendment	Warren
U.S. v. Robel, 389 U.S. 258 (1967)	Freedom of association protected by First Amendment	Warren
SACB v. Boorda, 397 U.S. 1042 (1970) denying cert. to 421 F. 2d 1142 (1969)	Freedom of association protected by First Amendment	Burger
Schacht v. U.S. 398 U.S. 58 (1970)	Freedom of expression protected by First Amendment	Burger
Blount v. Rizzi, 400 U.S. 410 (1971)	Freedom of expression protected by First Amendment (TWO PROVISIONS VOIDED)	Burger
Tilton v. Richardson, 403 U.S. 672 (1971)	Separation of church and state required by First Amendment	Burger
Chief of Capitol Police v. Jeannette Rankin Brigade, 409 U.S. 972 (1972) affirming judgment of 342 F. Supp 575 (1972)	Freedom of assembly protected by First Amendment	Burger
Buckley v. Valeo, 96 S. Ct. 612 (1976)	Freedom of expression and association protected by First Amendment (THREE PROVISIONS VOIDED)	Burger

Lower Court Decisions Which Were Not Appealed by the United States

Reed v. Gardner, 261 f. Supp 87 (1966)	Freedom of association protected by First Amendment	
Stewart v. Washington, 301 F. Supp 610 (1969)	Freedom of association protected by First Amendment (TWO PROVISIONS VOIDED)	
U.S. v. Brown, 381 U.S. 437 (1965)	Bill of attainder prohibited by Constitution, Art. 1, sec. 9	Warren
Albertson v. SACB, 382 U.S. 70 (1965)	Fifth Amendment prohibits compulsory self-incrimination	Warren
U.S. v. Roman, 382 U.S. 136 (1965)	Fifth Amendment prohibits presumption of guilt	Warren
U.S. v. Jackson, 390 U.S. 570 (1968)	Sixth Amendment prohibits forced waiver of right to trial by jury	Warren
Marchetti v. U.S., 390 U.S. 39 (1968) (and) Grosso v. U.S., 390 U.S. 62 (1968)	Fifth Amendment prohibits compulsory self-incrimination (TWO PROVISIONS VOIDED)	
Haynes v. U.S., 390 U.S. 85 (1968)	Fifth Amendment prohibits compulsory self-incrimination (TWO PROVISIONS VOIDED)	Warren
Leary v. U.S., 395 U.S. 6 (1969)	Fifth Amendment prohibits compulsory self-incrimination and presumption of guilt (TWO PROVISIONS VOIDED)	
U.S. v. U.S. Coin and Currency, 401 U.S. 715 (1971)	Forfeiture of money by person failing to register as gambler void under Fifth Amendment	Burger

Title	*Equal Protection Cases* Constitutional Principle	Court
Bolling v. Sharpe, 347 U.S. 497 (1954)	Fifth Amendment prohibits segregated schools in District of Columbia	Warren
Washington v. Legrant, 394 U.S. 618 (1969)	Fifth Amendment prohibits residence requirement for welfare recipients	Warren

Richardson v. Davis, 409 U.S. 1069 (1972) affirming judgment of 342 F. Supp 588 (1972) and of Richardson v. Griffin, 346 F. Supp 1226 (1972)	Fifth Amendment prohibits discrimination in sharing of benefits by legitimate and illegitimate children	Burger
Frontiero v. Richardson, 411 U.S. 677 (1973)	Fifth Amendment prohibits discrimination against women members of armed forces (TWO PROVISIONS VOIDED)	Burger
Department of Agriculture v. Moreno, 413 U.S. 508 (1973)	Fifth Amendment prohibits unreasonable statutory classifications	Burger
Jiminez v. Weinberger, 417 U.S. 628 (1974)	Fifth Amendment prohibits unreasonable statutory classifications	Burger
Weinberger v. Wiesenfeld, 420 U.S., 636 (1975)	Fifth Amendment prohibits unreasonable statutory classification	Burger

SOURCE: Adapted from P. Allan Dionisopoulos, "The Supreme Court: Four Decades of Activism," *DEA News American Political Science Association,* Fall 1976, pp. 19–20, Tables I, II, V.

ABA Committee and eventually appointed to the Court.

To gain Senate confirmation, a nominee must have demonstrated considerable legal talent in prior positions, though not necessarily in the judiciary. It is also important that the candidate's record not contain actions or associations that might affect his ability to judge impartially. The failure of Harold G. Carswell and Clement Haynsworth to win Senate confirmation was due to prior involvement by both nominees in activities that raised doubts about their suitability for the Court. Thus, though the President can nominate justices whose political philosophy he approves of, the nominee must be able to win acceptance in the Senate as well as the approval of the ABA, and other experts in the legal field.

Ford's nomination of Justice Stevens was greeted with widespread approval because of Stevens' record as an appeals court judge for the Seventh Circuit in Chicago. Stevens' philosophy appeared to be in keeping with the President's own political and social views. However, one cannot predict how a justice will act after being appointed. Just as Chief Justice Warren proved to be more liberal than Eisenhower expected, Justice White turned out to be more conservative than Kennedy expected. Neither Warren nor White had served as a judge before being appointed to the Court.

The media always give considerable attention to the potential impact of Supreme Court appointments on future Court decisions. While the philosophy of the justices has an important effect on their rulings, it should be remembered that the Court is an integral part of the American political system rather than an adjunct to it. Thus, it is influenced by the shifting tides of public opinion and the political views of elected officials. Justices who argue for judicial restraint do so as much out of the feeling that the Court should not risk its prestige unduly as because of their conservative philosophy.

Administration Of Federal Courts

The administrative body of the federal judiciary is the Judicial Conference of the United States. Led by the chief justice, the Conference includes the chief judges of the circuit courts and one district judge from each circuit. This group decides on policy for the federal court system, but its decisions are not binding on the eleven circuits. The latter may either accept or reject the Conference's proposals.

Chief Justice Burger has been an outspoken Conference leader and has made an effort to get Congress to increase the number of federal judges in order to cope with the steadily growing backlog of cases in federal courts. Thus, the Conference gives the judiciary a way of expressing its views and a means of dealing with Congress.

The Conference also deals with procedural matters. For example, one of Chief Justice Burger's concerns is the lack of professionalism among trial lawyers practicing in federal courts. In an effort to improve this situation, the Judicial Conference proposed rules that would require attorneys practicing in federal courts to take five additional law courses. However, the Second Circuit Court of Appeals voted against this proposal despite its acceptance throughout much of the federal judiciary.[20]

Despite its lack of absolute authority, the Judicial Conference has become an important adjunct to federal court activity; as its leader, the chief justice is able to make his views known on a wide range of issues. This administrative role adds to the influence of the Supreme Court.

The Historical Role Of the Supreme Court

The Federal-State Relationship

The growth of the nation is mirrored in the cases brought to the Supreme Court as well as in the Court's rulings.

Chief Justice Warren Burger. Burger's court is considered more conservative than that of his predecessor, Chief Justice Earl Warren.

John Marshall served as chief justice from 1800 to 1835, and it was during this period that some of the most crucial constitutional issues were decided.

From 1789 to the Civil War, the leading political issue dealt with by the Supreme Court was the relationship between the states and the federal government. The Court consistently ruled in favor of federal law and thus played an important role in the development of national power at the expense of the states. The first case in which a state law was declared unconstitutional was *Fletcher* v. *Peck* (1810). Georgia legislators had been bribed to approve the sale of large tracts of land that were later resold for large profits. A new state legislature tried to rescind the titles to the land. The case eventually came before the Supreme Court, which ruled the rescinding act unconstitutional. This decision established the supremacy of the Constitution over state laws and expanded the principle of judicial review to state actions.

In 1816, the Virginia Court of Appeals ruled *(Martin* v. *Hunter's Leesee)* that the state had the right to interpret the Constitution. Of course, this was one of the key issues facing the Constitutional Convention, which ultimately decided in favor of the supremacy of national law. The Court supported this principle, stating that the people had given the federal government the power to void state law. Similar Court decisions protected the property rights of individuals against state action.

Chief Justice Roger B. Taney served during the pre-Civil War period (1836-1864). As mentioned earlier, Court action is similar to legislative and executive activity in that it resembles a pendulum that swings to one side until public reaction stimulates a swing in the opposite direction. The Taney Court tried to correct what many people had come to believe was an imbalance of power in favor of the federal government. At the same time, the Court upheld the ownership of slaves in the name of protecting property rights. In 1857, the Court ruled *(Dred Scott* v. *Sanford)* that slaves could not bring suit in federal courts because Negroes were not citizens under the Constitution. The Taney Court also ruled that Congress could not control slavery in U.S. territories.

Government-Business Relations

The Civil War settled the issues of slavery and federal supremacy. The postwar period was marked by the expansion of capitalism, and the relationship between government and business was at the core of most legal issues for the rest of the nineteenth century and the early years of the twentieth. During this period, the Court extended the doctrine of federal supremacy to include control of interstate commerce and affirmed the constitutional authority of the states over the actions of their citizens. The due process clauses of the Fifth and Fourteenth Amendments were interpreted as requiring that the states use their power "reasonably," an ambiguous term that has been refined in a series of Court decisions since that time and is still the basis of many appeals.

The rule that the government must act reasonably in restricting the actions of citizens—including corporations—is referred to as *procedural* due process. The idea of *substantive* due process—also emerged during this period which refers to the object of regulation—The actions of the Court in ruling on such issues as the reasonableness of freight rates (procedural due process) and the objects of taxation (substantive due process) involved it in almost every aspect of the nation's economy. Between 1899 and 1937, numerous state laws were ruled unconstitutional because they violated either the due process guarantees or constitutional guarantees of equal protection under the law.

In 1934, the nation was experiencing a severe economic depression and unprecedented legislation was being passed by Congress to cope with the situation. In 1935, however, the Court ruled unconstitutional the National Industrial Recovery Act, the Bituminous Coal Act, and the Agricultural Adjustment Act; in 1936, it ruled against a New York State law setting minimum wages for women. This marked a watershed in the protection of property rights at the expense of

This U.S. Steel plant in Pittsburgh was among those seized by the Truman administration in 1952 to avert a strike. The Supreme Court ruled the seizure unconstitutional.

A 1930 picture of the Supreme Court led by Chief Justice Charles Evans Hughes. It was this court that resisted many of Roosevelt's New Deal programs until 1937, when it began to recognize most government action in the economic area as constitutional.

either governmental policy or individual rights. Roosevelt won a landslide victory in the 1936 election, and in 1937 he proposed legislation that would enable him to appoint a new justice to the Court for each justice over the age of 70 (the total would be limited to 15). This would have had the effect of adding six justices to the Court. Popularly known as the "court-packing" scheme, this ill-advised proposal was never pushed through Congress. However, Roosevelt's victory combined with public dismay at the Court's actions to change the direction of Court rulings. The minimum wage law that had been rejected nine months earlier was brought before the Supreme Court again and was upheld, and in 1938 the Court ruled that regulatory legislation is constitutional unless it cannot be assumed that it is within the knowledge and experience of the legislators (*United States* v. *Carolene Products*).

Protection of Individual Rights

The Supreme Court's actions since 1937 have centered on the protection of individual freedom. The basic problem that must be resolved in most such cases is that of providing the maximum freedom possible while guaranteeing the safety and welfare of the community. During the past forty years, the Court has interpreted the constitutional rights of the individual in such a way as to limit the authority of the government in a number of areas.

Landmark Judicial Rulings

The Fourteenth Amendment

The Fourteenth Amendment was adopted in 1868 in order to grant full citizenship to the newly freed slaves and to guarantee their basic political rights. The Amendment declares that "no State shall make or enforce any law which shall abridge the privileges or immunities of citizens of the United States; nor shall any State deprive any person of life, liberty or property without due process of law; nor deny to any person within its jurisdiction the equal protection of the laws." As with other parts of the Constitution, the Supreme Court's interpretation of the Fourteenth Amendment has changed over the years. This amendment has provided the legal basis for many of the Court's decisions in the area of individual freedom.

At first, there was considerable debate over the intent of the Fourteenth Amendment, with some justices applying it only in the narrow sense of protecting the political rights of blacks. However, the interpretation that has become generally accepted is that the Amendment "incorporates" the Bill of Rights as binding on the states. The doctrine of incorporation was set forth in the opinion of Justice Sanford in *Gitlow* v. *New York* (1925) and since then has often been cited in extending the protection of the Bill of Rights to citizens in their relations with states. Since 1937, it has enabled the Supreme Court to play an active role in protecting individual rights against the actions of the government.

Racial Discrimination

The first modern case dealing with discrimination was *Missouri* v. *Canada* (1938), which overturned the doctrine, established in *Plessy* v. *Ferguson* (1896), that separate but equal treatment under the law was constitutional. The Court ruled that "equal" must be truly equal rather than the best that could be offered under the circumstances. This trend in Court rulings reached its climax in *Brown* v. *Board of Education* (1954), in which the Court stated the doctrine that separate was automatically unequal:

> We come then to the question presented: Does segregation of children in public schools solely on the basis of race, even though the physical facilities and other "tangible" factors may be equal, deprive the children of the minority group of equal educational opportunity? We believe that it does.[21]

Much of the nation's educational system was segregated at the time of this ruling. Accordingly, the Court ordered federal district courts to oversee desegregation "with all deliberate speed."

The first challenge was to *de jure*—legal—school segregation in the South. Despite some widely publicized resistance, such as the refusal of Alabama Governor George Wallace to allow integration and President Eisenhower's use of the National Guard to overcome the resistance of Arkansas Governor Orval Faubus, most southern states complied with court orders. Opposition was largely limited to filing countless appeals from district court orders. While the process has been slower than many would have liked, the federal judiciary has largely succeeded in achieving integration in the South.

The struggle for desegregation in northern states and the larger southern cities has been more difficult: Segregation that results from residential patterns—*de facto* segregation—is harder to overcome than *de jure* segregation. Cities such as Philadelpia, New York, and Boston still have what amount to segregated schools, especially at the elementary level. In many cases, busing students from one district to another appeared to be the only answer. But resistance to busing orders has been the rule rather than the exception, and as a result integration of northern schools has progressed slowly. This situation illustrates the dependence of the Court on legislative and executive action to carry out its orders. The judiciary can deal effectively with legal challenges but is ill-equipped to deal with widespread public resistance.

Freedom of Expression

The best-known legal standard by which freedom of expression is judged is the "clear and present danger" test. Stated in 1919 by Justice Holmes:

The character of every act depends upon the circumstances in which it is done...The most stringent protection of free speech would not protect a man in falsely shouting "fire" in a theatre and causing a panic... The question in every case is whether the words used are used in such circumstances and are of such a nature as to create a clear and present danger that they will bring about the substantive evils that Congress has a right to prevent. [22]

It is hard to apply the "clear and present danger" test because each case brought before the Court is different. However, such rulings provide reasonable guidelines in that they protect both the individual and the public.

Judicial interpretations of freedom of expression put the burden of proof on the government. For the most part, courts at all levels of the federal judiciary have chosen to protect the rights of the individual and the press unless there was strong evidence that the action in question posed a major threat to the public safety.

The Future of the Judicial Process

The increase in the number of cases reaching federal courts in recent years is shown in Tables 6-1 and 6-2. The tendency to seek legal solutions to variety of problems has also affected state courts. The process of government by bureaucracy produces a multitude of regulations and directives issued by state and federal departments and agencies; as a result, the courts must deal with an ever-larger number of cases. The obvious solution is to increase the number of judicial jurisdictions and the number of judges assigned to courts at all levels. Such proposals are currently before Congress and many state legislatures.

The restructuring of the judicial process includes changes in the jury system. The tradition of unanimous verdicts by juries of twelve men and women is viewed as unnecessarily costly and time-consuming. Various states have shifted to eight-, seven-, or even six-person juries. The concept of unanimity has also changed, so that a verdict may be reached by a 6-2 or 5-1 vote. The Judicial Conference has announced its support for a bill that will set the number of jurors at six in civil cases brought in federal courts. However, there is widespread disagreement about the shift to smaller juries and nonunanimous verdicts in criminal trials. Some states have established a variety of jury sizes depending on the charge involved. Virginia provides for juries of twelve for felony cases and five for misdemeanors. Felony convictions may be accompanied by prison sentences while misdemeanors are punished by fines or penalties short of jail. The extent to which these changes in the American jury system will reduce the cost of a trial in terms of time and money remains to be seen.

Summary

Changes in the structure and procedures of the judicial process do not represent fundamental shifts in legal values or the role of the judiciary. They simply reflect the fact that the judiciary is a political institution and, like other branches of the government, must change its practices with changing conditions. The increased caseload and the tendency to turn to the courts for solutions to many problems has increased the impact of the judiciary and made its rulings very important in all sectors of society.

The judiciary provides a balance to the actions of the executive and legislative branches. The Supreme Court in particular provides protection against governmental restriction of individual freedom. The Supreme Court is also the final authority in the interpretation of the rights of the individual versus those of society. Reinterpretations of the Constitution reflect the need to keep pace with new circumstances, shifting values, and the tendency of individuals to look to the Court for solutions to problems that could also be solved by legislative action.

The importance of the judiciary in the nation's political system is illustrated by the interest and, often, controversy surrounding judicial appointments—especially appointments of Supreme Court justices. The lifetime appointments of federal judges give the judicial branch a degree of independence that is not possible in the elected executive or legislative branches and insulates them from political pressure or temporary public sentiment. At the same time, however, the judiciary is very much a part of the political system, and its rulings usually take into account what the public expects and will accept.

CHAPTER 13 CROSSWORD PUZZLE

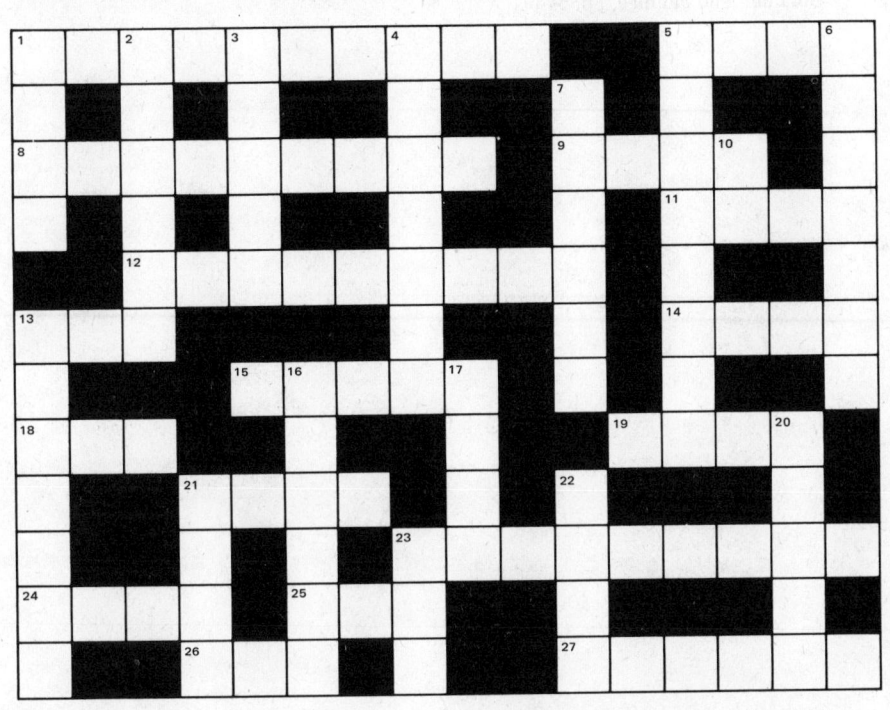

Across

1. The Constitutional principle of "incorporation" is stated explicitly in the ____ Amendment.
5. Ado
8. Courts that hear appeals from lower court decisions are called ____ courts.
9. Young horse
11. Machines for weaving
12. Judicial activities must be balanced against judicial ____.
13. Hint; long tapered rod used in billiards
14. ____ and tear
15. Mechanical device used for fastening pieces of wood or metal together
18. Purpose
19. "A Farewell to ____" (Hemingway novel)
21. Equal
23. The nation's judicial system is an integral part of the ____ process.
24. Wicked
25. Instrument used for rowing a boat
26. Appendage on a fish
27. Marbury vs. Madison established the principle of judicial ____.

Down

1. Cloth emblem of a country
2. Person who rules on plays in baseball
3. Stories
4. Chemical; type of fertilizer
5. The Supreme Court is both a leader and ____ of opinion.
6. Supreme Court decisions that are issued without written opinions or oral arguments are called ____ opinions.
7. Whiskey or tape
10. ____ and fro
13. The political philosophy of the Supreme Court ____ over time.
16. American law is based upon ____ law and civil law.
17. Drunken derelict
20. The matters that the Supreme Court dealt with after the ratification of the Constitution primarily concerned federal-____ relationships.
21. The Miranda decision dealt with ____-incrimination.
22. Place where ships dock
23. Snoop

NOTES

[1] Herbert Jacob, *Justice in America*, 2d ed. (Boston: Little, Brown, 1972), p. 150.

[2] Quoted by Durham Monsma in "State Courts Lead in Liberalism Now," *The Philadelphia Inquirer*, May 3, 1976, p. 14-A.

[3] Warren F. Burger, quoted in "More Judges Are Needed Now," reprinted by permission, *The Philadelphia Inquirer*, January 4, 1976, p. 1-E.

[4] Ibid.

[5] Sheldon Goldman and Thomas Jahnige, *The Federal Courts as a Political System*, 2d ed. (New York: Harper & Row, 1976), p. 26.

[6] Ibid., p. 28.

[7] Kenneth N. Vines, quoted in Jacob, p. 192.

[8] Quoted in *The Apollo Book of American Quotations*, selected and arranged by Bruce Bohle (New York: Dodd, Mead, 1967), p. 95.

[9] Henry J. Abraham, *Freedom and the Court* (London: Oxford University Press, 1967), p. 17.

[10] 269 U.S., dissenting opinion, at 270.

[11] Ibid., Abraham, p. 17.

[12] Linda Matthews in "Why the Supreme Court Is Doing by Not Doing," *The Philadelphia Inquirer*, July 20, 1975, p. 2-F.

[13] "Two Justices Say Court Endangers Its Repute by Summary Decisions," *The New York Times*, November 9, 1976, p. 24L. Copyright © 1976 by The New York Times Company. Reprinted by permission.

[14] David J. Danielski, "The Influence of the Chief Justice in the Decisional Process of the Supreme Court," in Thomas P. Jahnige and Sheldon Goldman, eds., *The Federal Judicial System* (New York: Holt, Rinehart, Winston, 1968), pp. 151-160.

[15] Quoted by Lesley Oslander in "Powell Finds High Court Showing 'Sounder Balance,'" *The New York Times,* August 12, 1976, p. 18L.

[16] John P. Mackenzie in "Recent Decisions Show a Burger Court is Emerging," *The Philadelphia Inquirer,* July 18, 1976, p. 5-E.

[17] Ibid.

[18] P. Allan Dionisopoulis, "The Supreme Court: Four Decades of Activism," *DEA NEWS, American Political Science Association,* Fall 1976, p. 20.

[19] Goldman and Jahnige, pp. 54-55.

[20] Tom Goldstein in "Judges Here Reject Rules for U.S. Court Lawyers," *The New York Times,* December 21, 1975, p. 33. Copyright © 1975 by The New York Times Company. Reprinted by permission.

[21] *Brown* v. *Board of Education of Topeka, et al.,* U.S. 483, at 492. 1954.

[22] *Schenck* v. *United States,* 249 U.S. 47 (1919).

CHAPTER 14
THE POLITICAL ECONOMY

CHAPTER OUTLINE

Questions to Consider
Introduction
Setting Priorities
Inflation
Unemployment
Designing Economic Policy
    Arguments for Long-Range Planning
    Arguments Against Long-Range Planning
The Economic Role of Congress
The President's Economic Role
The Budgetary Process
    The President Initiates
    Congress Acts
    Review and Audit
    Budget Execution and Control
The Budget
Sources of Revenue
    The National Debt
    Taxation
    Tax Reform
The U.S. Economy
Fiscal and Monetary Policy
    Fiscal Policy
    Monetary Policy
The Economic Power Structure
    Financial Institutions
    Employee Pension Funds
    Labor Unions
    Large Corporations
The Role of the Government
    Direct Impact on the Economy
    The Role of Foreign Trade
Summary

QUESTIONS TO CONSIDER

Political institutions determine how national resources are allocated. Economic factors therefore loom large in the political world. For the individual, it is likely that the state of the economy is the most important political issue most of the time. In this chapter, we will discuss several questions that are at the heart of most economic issues: What is the relationship between unemployment and inflation? What is involved in the debate over long-range economic planning? How is the federal budget prepared? Why are taxes so high? What is the difference between fiscal and monetary policy? Who owns the lion's share of American wealth? What is the government's role in the economy? The answers to these questions will provide an overview of the American political economy and make the media's coverage of economic affairs easier to understand.

Introduction

No aspect of governmental activity has a more direct impact on the lifestyle of the individual than economic policy. The public has shown that while it may tolerate corruption or mismanagement in its leaders, it will not accept a lower standard of living. Accordingly, the government must chart its economic course with one eye on the next election and the other on economic conditions.

Economic policy may be viewed in the context of two broad issues. First, in doing its job the government becomes a major economic force: A large portion of the nation's economic resources are devoted to paying the costs of the political system itself, such as maintaining the bureaucracy or paying for national defense. Second, economic resources are an important tool in the achievement of social goals—they fund programs ranging from unemployment insurance to subsidies for higher education. Thus, while the American political economy is based on the right of the individual to own property, to seek any job he or she wants, and to invest his or her savings in any of a variety of ways, the economic well-being of the individual is highly dependent on the actions of the government.

As the government has grown, it has magnified the economic impact of federal spending while increasing its control over many industries through numerous regulatory agencies. The traditional capitalist economic theory, expressed in the writings of Adam Smith (e.g., *The Wealth of Nations*), was based on the idea that the supply and demand for goods and services were self-adjusting. When supply increased faster than demand, the prices of goods and the wages paid to workers would drop. When demand rose faster than supply, the prices of goods and services would rise. This is a very basic economic notion, but it works less well as actions of the government or the private sector create artificially higher prices or wages, stimulate demand faster than supply (which produces inflation), or increase supply faster than demand (which results in unemployment). Modern society has built-in safeguards that prevent labor from receiving lower wages and offer unemployment compensation to cushion the shock of layoffs. As a result, while industry reacts to economic difficulties by trying to lower employment levels, inflation persists even during recessions. In short, market forces no longer operate as Smith believed they would. The economy does not adjust quickly enough to changing conditions, so that governmental action becomes necessary to solve economic problems.

Setting Priorities

One of the government's primary tasks is to allocate resources according to national priorities. Many interest groups compete for larger portions of the federal budget, and government officials make the final decisions on how these resources will be distributed. President Ford's 1976 budget message to Congress dealt with the question of priorities in the 1977 budget and in the years to come. As the President put it, the budget sought to "achieve fairness and balance"

—between the taxpayer and those who will benefit by Federal spending;
—between national security and other pressing needs;
—between our generation and the world we want to leave to our children;
—between those in some need and those in most need;
—between the programs we already have and those we would like to have;
—between aid to individuals and aid to State and local governments;
—between immediate implementation of a good idea and the need to allow time for transition;
—between the desire to solve our problems quickly and the realization that for some problems, good solutions will take more time; and
—between Federal control and direction to assure achievement of common goals and the recognition that State and local governments and individuals may do as well or better without restraints.[1]

This statement of the dilemmas involved in setting priorities was made during a period of rapid growth in government spending, with the preceding period of high inflation fresh in everyone's mind and continued high levels of unemployment a national concern. There is never enough federal revenue to satisfy all the needs of society, but the present economic situation makes the problem of setting priorities even more troublesome. The built-in increase in the cost of existing government programs leaves little flexibility to deal with new demands.

Table 14-1 shows the dramatic growth that has taken place in govern-

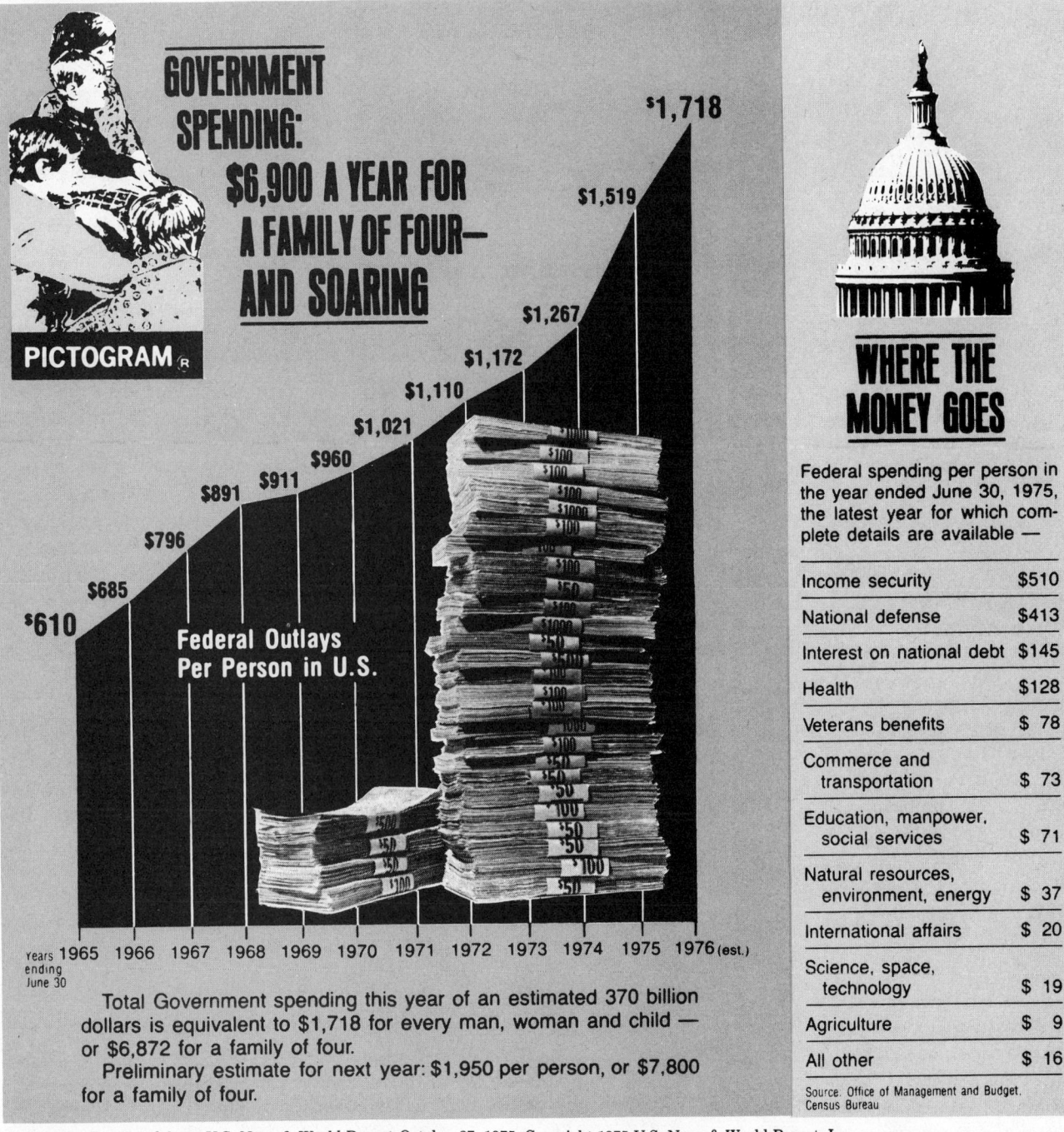

Setting Priorities **217**

TABLE 14-1

GOVERNMENT SPENDING: $6,900 A YEAR FOR A FAMILY OF FOUR—AND SOARING

Federal Outlays Per Person in U.S.

Year (ending June 30)	Amount
1965	$610
1966	$685
1967	$796
1968	$891
1969	$911
1970	$960
1971	$1,021
1972	$1,110
1973	$1,172
1974	$1,267
1975	$1,519
1976 (est.)	$1,718

Total Government spending this year of an estimated 370 billion dollars is equivalent to $1,718 for every man, woman and child — or $6,872 for a family of four.

Preliminary estimate for next year: $1,950 per person, or $7,800 for a family of four.

WHERE THE MONEY GOES

Federal spending per person in the year ended June 30, 1975, the latest year for which complete details are available —

Income security	$510
National defense	$413
Interest on national debt	$145
Health	$128
Veterans benefits	$ 78
Commerce and transportation	$ 73
Education, manpower, social services	$ 71
Natural resources, environment, energy	$ 37
International affairs	$ 20
Science, space, technology	$ 19
Agriculture	$ 9
All other	$ 16

Source: Office of Management and Budget, Census Bureau

SOURCE: Reprinted from *U.S. News & World Report,* October 27, 1975. Copyright 1975 U.S. News & World Report, Inc.

ment spending per family since 1965 and the purposes for which government funds were spent in 1976. Note the large percentages allocated to income security (which includes social security), national defense, and interest on the national debt—these items are hard to trim and will rise during periods of inflation. Tables 14-2 and 14-3 bring the economic problems of the individual citizen into focus. The high cost of a college education is no surprise, but the rate of increase in the past ten years means that a markedly larger portion of the family budget must be allocated to a college education. Few family incomes have kept pace with this increase. The difficulty most families face in buying a house is illustrated in Table 14-3. Only 20 percent of American families could afford to purchase an old house in 1974, and housing costs have continued to rise since then.

The problems faced in financing a college education or buying a house are but two examples of needs that must be dealt with by the government if the national standard of living is to be maintained or improved. The limit-

TABLE 14-2

THE SOARING COST OF COLLEGE

Average Outlays Per Academic Year

	1966-67	1971-72	1976-77	In 10 years
Private four-year colleges	$3,539	$3,626	$4,568	Up 29%
Public four-year colleges	$1,587	$1,934	$2,790	Up 76%
Private two-year colleges	$2,229	$2,736	$3,907	Up 75%
Public two-year colleges	$1,260	$1,623	$2,454	Up 95%

Expenses at many colleges and universities will be well above these averages, in some cases exceeding $7,000 a year — meaning a four-year cost of close to $30,000 for some students.

Note: Included are tuition and fees, room and board, books and supplies, and personal expenses and transportation.

Basic data: College Scholarship Service, National Center for Education Statistics

SOURCE: Reprinted from *U.S. News & World Report*, May 24, 1976, p. 73. Copyright, 1976 U.S. News & World Report, Inc.

ed resources available to the government make it more difficult to solve such problems. And overshadowing these economic problems are the need to provide enough jobs for a growing population and maintain the individual's purchasing power by keeping inflation at a reasonable level.

Inflation

Few conditions are more unsettling to the nation's economy than inflation. Caused by a demand for goods and services that exceeds supply, inflation reduces the purchasing power of the dollar. Table 14-4 illustrates how persistent inflation has been in the 1970s, and shows the potential result of inflation in terms of family expenses. Inflation hits hardest at people living on fixed incomes, usually retired people who cannot supplement their pensions, which do not change. While the government has raised social security benefits in an effort to deal with this problem, these increases have not been enough to offset the effects of inflation.

The aspect of inflation that is hardest to deal with is its tendency to spiral as labor seeks ever-larger wage increases to offset higher prices—prices that have been raised in order to pay for higher labor costs. As prices rise, consumer demand usually drops, though the fear of inflation may stimulate some purchasing as a "hedge." Reduced demand discourages new investment in inflationary times, and as a result the facilities needed to meet future demand are not likely to be built.

The government has trouble solving the problem of inflation because the usual solution is painful in social and political terms. By reducing federal spending or slowing the rate of increase in such spending, the government can lower spending throughout the economy. However, any action that limits spending leads to increased unemployment, lower consumer spending, and, hence, the threat of recession. An alternate approach is to end monopolistic practices in labor and industry and reduce governmental regulation, which tend to frustrate market forces that, if left alone, might produce an equilibrium between supply and demand.

Inflation and unemployment seem to be related in that the inflationary spiral can be slowed if the nation is willing to pay the price of economic recession—lower production rates and higher unemployment. Sometimes the political question that faces the administration is one of balancing the rate of unemployment against the rate of inflation. At best, this balancing act does not lend itself to accurate predictions, and the human costs of unem-

TABLE 14-3
The Cost of Owning a Home

	Median Price	Monthly Expense	Minimum Income	Percentage of Families With Minimum Income
		New Houses		
1970	$35,500	$373	$17,900	14.9%
1971	36,300	364	17,470	18.0
1972	37,300	375	18,000	20.8
1973	37,100	397	19,060	21.5
1974	41,300	486	23,330	15.0
		Old Houses		
1970	30,000	319	15,310	21.5
1971	31,700	330	15,840	22.5
1972	33,400	349	16,750	24.8
1973	31,200	348	16,700	29.6
1974	35,600	441	21,170	20.0

SOURCE: *The New York Times*, May 11, 1975, p. 9E. Copyright © 1975 by The New York Times Company. Reprinted by permission.

Sign outside a grocery store protesting coffee prices. Informal consumer boycotts have been organized to combat inflationary pressures.

ployment also are an important element that must be taken into consideration.

Unemployment

Unemployment is a persistent problem that is noticed less during periods of full production but flares up during recessions. The government's policy toward unemployment reflects both economic and social values. In economic terms, it is argued that the government should be the employer of last resort, that by gaining the productivity of the unemployed, government programs will cost little or nothing and contribute to economic health. The counterargument is that any such action by the government must be financed by higher taxes or by increased budget deficits (which lead to inflation). Unemployment is expensive to society both in terms of lost tax revenue and in terms of the reduced purchasing power of consumers.

From the standpoint of social values, it is hard to balance the responsibility of the individual in a free enterprise system for his or her own economic well-being against the government's responsibility for the welfare of every citizen. As Table 14-5 shows, unemployment does not have an equal impact on all groups in society. The less educated and least trained are the first to be let go when business falls off and the last to be rehired when the economy perks up. One of the basic problems involved is the type of employment a technological society can provide for the untrained workers. This involves social as well as economic factors. For example, if students drop out of high school and reject job training opportunities, they will suffer chronic unemployment throughout their lives.

Another side of the unemployment question is the matter of the wages paid in government-sponsored programs. If the government pays the minimum wage, people will be tempted to leave other jobs and switch to these programs—about 4 million people are currently earning the legal minimum wage and another 3 million whose jobs are not covered by minimum wage laws are earning less. It is often suggested that untrained individuals, especially teenagers, be offered jobs at less than the minimum wage until they are ready to compete in the labor market. Obviously, such proposals are opposed by labor unions, which view them as a step backward. Partly owing to this attitude, the government spent $19.4 billion in unemployment compensation benefits in 1976 in addition to public assistance payments to the long-term unemployed.[3] The problem thus demands solution, and periods of high unemployment make this a high-priority political issue.

One of the problems involved in deciding how to deal with unemployment is the difficulty of predicting the potential impact of governmental action. Like any statistic, the figures for unemployment can be judged in different ways. For example, it was reported in March 1976 that the unemployment rate was 7.5 percent. Some considered this figure exaggerated because it included teenaged children living at home, working wives whose husbands were employed, people who were out of work for a few weeks, and people who were unskilled, untrained, or unwilling to work. On the other hand, some argue that the official unemployment figure represents only half of the true total because it does not include people who are too discouraged to look for work or who are underemployed—working at jobs that do not make full use of their skills. It should be noted that even though the unemployment level remained above 7

Harlem youth are among those that will be disadvantaged in the job market.

percent in 1976 as the nation recovered from recession, the number of Americans who were employed reached new highs each month.

The creation of new jobs is at the heart of the question of how to deal with inflation and recession and is the best guarantee of economic prosperity. The labor force is growing rapidly; as one official has noted, "We've got to keep running just to stand still." [4] A 5 percent unemployment rate is often cited as the maximum that is tolerable in terms of the well-being of the nation's economy and of the individual. But reduction of unemployment to 5 percent by 1980 would require 2 million new jobs a year, twice as many as have ever been created in peacetime. [5] This illustrates the complexity of the unemployment dilemma: The ability of the government to deal with the problems of recession and unemployment determines its ability to allocate federal revenues to new programs or to expanding existing ones.

Designing Economic Policy

There has never been an economic policy in the United States that was a result of long-range planning, the setting of long-range goals, and consistent application of long-range policies. Rather, the political system has dealt with the economy on a catch-as-catch-can basis. The days of popular sentiment and economic orthodoxy rejecting continued budget deficits is long past. Today's economic decisions are as much a product of political expediency as anything else.

Modern economic philosophy is a result of the depression of the 1930s and the efforts of democratic governments throughout the world to deal with its devastating impact. The New Deal programs of the Roosevelt administration reflected the economic theories of John Maynard Keynes, a British economist who stressed the need for governmental spending and tax policies to stimulate a lagging

TABLE 14-4
PICTOGRAM®

THE SHRINKING DOLLAR..

1970
100 cents

NOW
72 cents

1980
51 cents

Measured by how much the consumer's dollar will buy

If prices rise by an average of 6.9 per cent a year in the next five years — as they have in the past five — 21 cents more will be chipped away from the buying power of the 1970 dollar. The dollar will then have lost almost half its value since 1970.

SOURCE: Reprinted from *U.S. News & World Report*, October 6, 1975. Copyright 1975, U.S. News & World Report, Inc.

Designing Economic Policy **221**

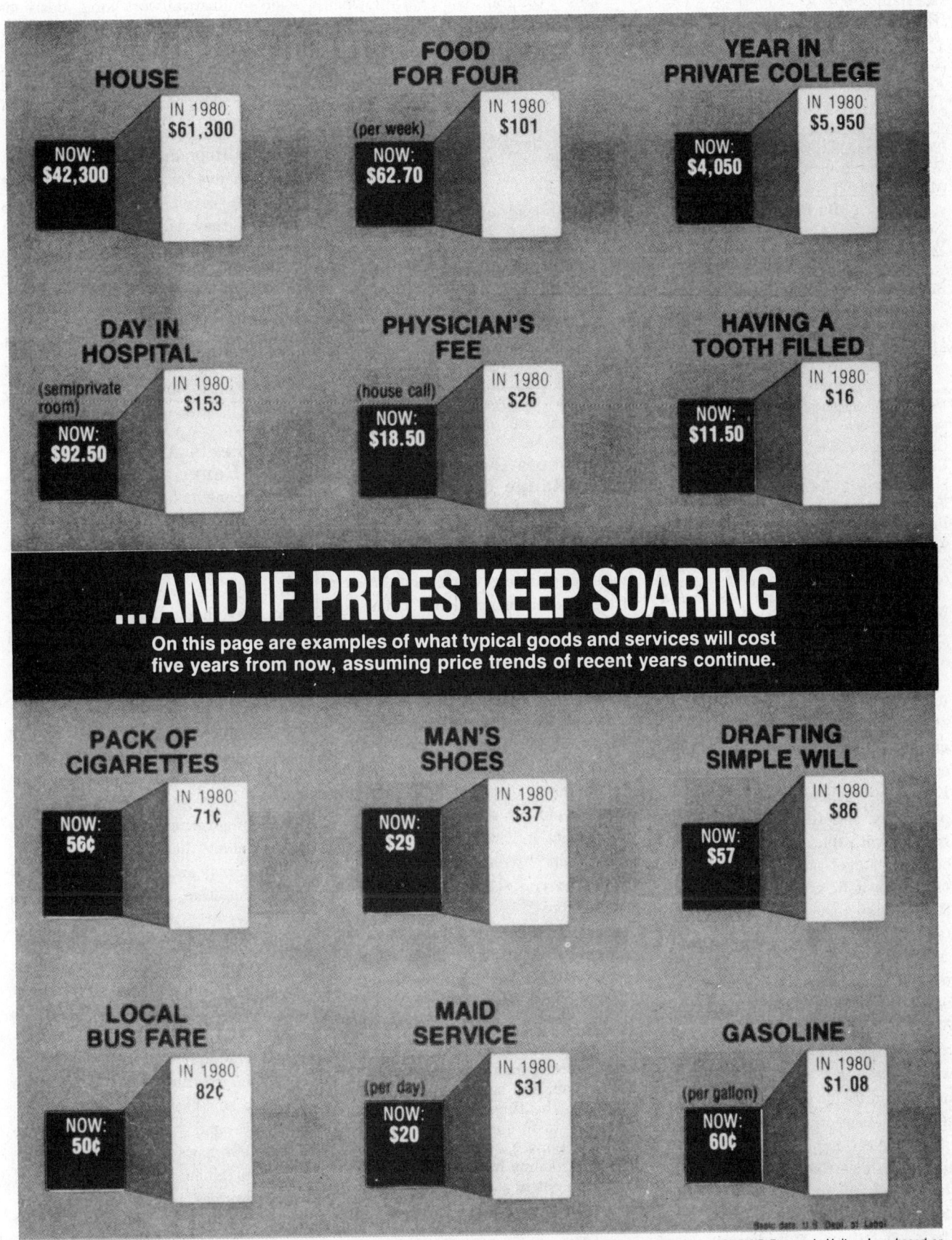

HOUSE
NOW: $42,300
IN 1980: $61,300

FOOD FOR FOUR
(per week)
NOW: $62.70
IN 1980: $101

YEAR IN PRIVATE COLLEGE
NOW: $4,050
IN 1980: $5,950

DAY IN HOSPITAL
(semiprivate room)
NOW: $92.50
IN 1980: $153

PHYSICIAN'S FEE
(house call)
NOW: $18.50
IN 1980: $26

HAVING A TOOTH FILLED
NOW: $11.50
IN 1980: $16

...AND IF PRICES KEEP SOARING

On this page are examples of what typical goods and services will cost five years from now, assuming price trends of recent years continue.

PACK OF CIGARETTES
NOW: 56¢
IN 1980: 71¢

MAN'S SHOES
NOW: $29
IN 1980: $37

DRAFTING SIMPLE WILL
NOW: $57
IN 1980: $86

LOCAL BUS FARE
NOW: 50¢
IN 1980: 82¢

MAID SERVICE
(per day)
NOW: $20
IN 1980: $31

GASOLINE
(per gallon)
NOW: 60¢
IN 1980: $1.08

Basic data: U.S. Dept. of Labor

Note: Today's costs are typical current prices, as compiled in Government surveys. Projections for 1980 are by USN&WR Economic Unit and are based on price changes since 1970, a period in which over-all living costs rose an average of 6.9 per cent a year — considerably less than the rate in past year

TABLE 14-5
Where Jobless Rate Runs Highest

Based on unemployment figures as of February, 1976—

By Age and Sex	
Teen-age males	19.3%
Teen-age females	19.1
Women, age 20 and over	7.5
Men, age 20 and over	5.7

By Race	
Nonwhites	13.7
Whites	6.8

By Marital Status	
Single men	16.8
Single women	11.9
Married women	7.2
Married men	4.1

By Occupation	
Laborers	14.1
Production workers	9.8
Service workers	8.9
Craftsmen, foremen	6.7
Clerical help	6.1
Sales workers	5.2
Farm workers	3.9
Professional, technical	3.6
Managers, administrators	2.9

SOURCE: U.S. News & World Report, March 22, 1976, p. 62. Reprinted from *U.S. News & World Report.* Copyright © 1976 U.S. News & World Report, Inc.

Note: Figures are seasonally adjusted except for single men, women.

economy. Keynesian theory has been used to justify budget deficits and the creation of a multitude of programs and tax incentives designed to provide economic stimulation. However, Keynes also believed that in periods of prosperity and full employment the government's role should be diminished and budget surpluses created to offset the deficits of recession years. But bureaucracies are unwilling to take away benefits that have been granted to particular groups even though those benefits are no longer needed. Thus, for example, the oil depletion allowance, which was designed to encourage oil exploration at a time when this was a very risky activity, has been difficult to eliminate despite the sophistication of current methods of geological exploration. Similarly, farm subsidies that originated in the dust bowls of the 1930s have been trimmed only in recent years, though the need for such subsidies has long since passed.

This is the framework within which the discussion of national economic planning takes place. Those who support such planning believe long-range plans can include review processes that will eliminate outdated programs and implement new ones. Opponents are afraid that governmental regulation in the form of long-range planning will lead to excessive political influence on the economy and encourage inefficiency. There are very real questions as to the ability of any government to harness economic forces for the good of the nation. The arguments for and against national planning focus on the basic political questions of the government's functions, limitations, and abilities.

Arguments for Long-Range Planning

The Balanced Growth and Planning Act, introduced in Congress in 1975, is the cornerstone of the arguments for national planning. Under this Act the federal government would set goals for personal income, inflation, and unemployment levels for short- and long-term periods. Congress would be presented with the planners' priorities and would pass legislation with these goals in mind. Tax incentives, regulations, and spending programs would be the major tools used. The government would not set production levels for private industry, but through its use of incentives and penalties it would have a significant impact on production.

Senator Hubert Humphrey, a strong supporter of national planning, has expressed his views on the issue as follows:

America has lost much, and wasted more, because we did not have coherent planning long ago. We have suffered again and again because we did not take the time—or have the machinery—to foresee the consequences of our actions....

This economy is already "planned"; although not in a rational or coherent way. In the private sector, where the 200 largest industrial corporations control two-thirds of industry's assets and employ fully one-half of the nation's industrial work force, decisions are made every day that profoundly affect the lives of all Americans. And they are made on the basis of planning that is expensive and confidential, and which may or may not be in the best interests of the American people. [6]

Senator Humphrey's argument is that it is possible for government planners to make better economic judgments because they will be centralized. His view also assumes that economic plans will not be subject to political infighting, which could multiply existing federal programs without increasing their effectiveness in line with increased costs. The key to any kind of planning is flexibility, and this is hard to achieve in bureaucratic environments.

Arguments Against Long-Range Planning

The opponents of long-range economic planning base their arguments on two major points. First, they hold that while existing markets do not work precisely the way economic theory says they should, the fact is they do work. Resources tend to be allocated according to the demands of consumers as expressed in the marketplace. Also, many people are skeptical about the potential effectiveness of planning that is based on goals rather than on market forces. The failure of price controls is often pointed to as an example of governmental interference in the economy that did not achieve its goal and may actually have contributed to inflation by creating pent-up price pressure.

The second objection is more relevant in a political sense because it raises the fundamental question of who should decide what is best for society, the individual or the government. The large-car, small-car debate that emerged during the energy crisis involved this basic question. Gasoline shortages and higher prices led to greater emphasis on small-car production. But when the shortages ended and fuel prices stabilized, the consumer began asking for larger cars. Large cars use more gasoline, and gasoline is expected to become increasingly more expensive. Should the government decide that no large cars can be made in the interest of energy conservation, or should the marketplace make the decision as it mirrors consumer demand? To put it another way, should Washington decide that it is wasteful to burn larger quantities of gasoline in larger cars, which forces prices up, or should this choice be made by the individual, who may be willing to pay the price for the luxury of driving a larger car?

The problems faced by the government in dealing with such matters are discussed by C. Jackson Grayson, chairperson of the Price Commission during the Nixon administration, in his book, *Confessions of a Price Controller*. Grayson states that the difficulties of using federal controls "have convinced me that it is impossible to improve on the system in which billions of daily market decisions by the public determine our resource allocations."[7] Thus, the dispute between those who argue for a planned economy and those who would trust to market forces is related to the question of how to achieve a balance between individual freedom and responsibility on the one hand and the government's duty to promote the general welfare on the other.

The Economic Role Of Congress

Congress' formal role in the economic planning process consists of performing its budgetary duties, passing tax legislation, and granting standby powers to the President so that he can move quickly if necessary. All of these functions interact with Congress' responsibilities to specific constituencies as well as to the nation as a whole. Any legislation involving large sums of money will bring pressure from individuals and groups who may be affected by the final decision, and the nature of politics is such that it is easier to say yes than to say no. This tendency, coupled with limited resources, helps explain the difficulty of balancing the budget or creating federal programs that serve their intended purpose and then are ended. Once Congress moves to aid a particular group or industry, the program expands rather than contracting. This is as true of tax relief for a particular industry as it is of welfare programs.

Since money fuels government programs, the budget occupies a central position in congressional legislation. Budgetary considerations influence tax legislation, proposed government programs, and almost any federal effort to deal with economic matters. They reflect the need to match demands from many sectors of American society—demands that often contradict one another—with the limited resources available.

The President's Economic Role

The President sets the tone of economic policy as in most areas of governmental activity. Through his choice of economic advisers and his own economic philosophy, the President has considerable influence on the economy. The Ford administration provides an example of both these points. Ford was an economic conservative; he believed market forces would be more effective than massive federal spending in bringing the nation out of the recession of 1973-1975. In keeping with his economic philosophy, Ford chose Alan Greenspan, who was generally known as a capable but conservative economist, as chairperson of the Council of Economic Advisers.

Ford was under pressure from the Democratic-controlled Congress to increase federal spending, which would enlarge the already massive federal deficit. However, he resisted most such attempts and maintained his position through a series of vetoes. This illustrates the potential power of the Presidency in economic matters. Nor is the President's economic power confined to such matters as the budget or tax legislation. As the chief designer of U.S. foreign policy, the President can negotiate trade agreements with other nations. Similarly, decisions dealing with foreign and military affairs are intertwined with domestic economic policy. For example, large grain sales to the Soviet Union, which are largely under Presidential control, have important economic effects in the United States.

The President's economic powers, sweeping as they may appear, should not be overestimated. While the President can initiate or block programs and policies that have an economic impact, he must be aware of the need to maintain broad-based public support as well as the backing of key interest groups. Any action that lacks this type of backing is likely to be blocked by Congress or by the agencies that are supposed to administer the program. Ford's refusal to fund certain programs during the 1974-1976 period was backed by key business groups and many respected economists. There was also a lack of public support for new programs; those who were employed viewed programs intended to increase employment as welfare by another name.

The Budgetary Process

The budgetary process consists of four distinct phases. First, the executive branch prepares the budget and send it to Congress. Second, Congress amends, approves, or otherwise changes the budget and returns it to the President for his signature; at this point, it becomes law. The third step is the execution and control of budgetary expeditures. Finally, the review and audit stage serves as a check on wasteful or ineffective spending and provides guidelines for the following year's budget. All four steps are interrelated, and effective action at all points is necessary.

The President Initiates

The budgetary process begins when the President submits estimates of the expenditures necessary to carry on existing programs and services in the next fiscal year. These estimates have been made by the Office of Management and Budget. At this point, Congress begins its task of reviewing the budget (this is done by the Congressional Budget Office); the President submits his final budget fifteen days after Congress begins its new session. The early estimate gives Congress more time to work on the budget than was formerly the case, when Congress' first real exposure to the specific contents of the budget occurred when it was submitted in its final form.

Congess Acts

If Congress wants to initiate a new program, it first passes legislation authorizing—or enabling—a government agency to carry out the program. Some programs require annual authorization—defense expenditures and foreign aid are examples— while others are automatically extended—social security and welfare programs are of this type. Obviously, programs whose appropriations must be approved annually are subject to greater political pressure than those that are automatically extended.

Revenue and appropriation bills are introduced in the House, with the Ways and Means Committee handling revenue bills and the Appropriations Committee appropriations bills. After the full House has voted its approval, the bills are sent to the Senate, where a similar process is followed. Differences between the House and Senate versions of a bill are settled by a conference committee, and a final bill is sent to both houses for approval. During this process, committee members are approached by lobbyists representing interest groups that may be affected by the legislation in question.

Review and Audit

Since most government spending is done by the executive branch, it falls to the Executive Office to oversee programs and check on their effectiveness and efficiency. The Office of Management and Budget (OMB) performs this task on behalf of the President, but Presidential aides are often assigned to follow up on high-priority programs. Congressional oversight is largely left to the General Accounting Office (GAO), though congressional committees often investigate charges of waste or noncompliance. Both the OMB and the GAO have been strengthened in recent years and provided with the staff and facilities necessary to perform their oversight functions more effectively. They have also gained a certain amount of independence from other agencies in the executive and legislative branches, which is essential for any group with the responsibility for auditing other groups.

Budget Execution and Control

The OMB allocates funds to various departments in line with the appropriations bills passed by Congress. The Executive office may change the rate of spending or postpone certain projects, but these are temporary measures that cannot last beyond the fiscal year and must be approved by Congress within 45 days. These provisions are contained in the Impoundment Control Act of 1974, which was passed in response to the Nixon administration's practice of withholding funds that had been appropriated by Congress but were opposed by the White House.

The Budget

Few, if any, economic subjects get as much publicity as the seemingly endless debates over the federal budget. Political candidates promise to spend more for this and less for that. Defense spending is an attractive target for most candidates because it is an annual appropriation and spending money for weapons that we hope will never be used is easy to criticize. Behind the headlines, however, is the seldom-recognized fact that about three-fourths of the budget is allocated to programs that it is almost impossible to decrease or eliminate. Table 14-6 presents the fiscal year 1975 budget. Clearly, only defense spending and civilian programs can be reduced, and even these areas cannot be reduced by much. The 1977 budget calls for over $66 billion in defense appropriations. (This figure excludes money for personnel, retirement pay, and veterans' benefits.) The increase in defense spending, despite protests from many sectors of society, results from the realities of the international situation and the unwillingness of the government to take chances with national security. Note that in 1976 both parties supported a strong national defense.

Civilian programs offer a somewhat greater possibility of reductions in government spending. Table 14-7 lists the groups that benefit from a variety of federal programs. There has been much debate over school lunch and food stamp programs, which appear to have been taken advantage of by many people who do not need such aid. Also note the tens of millions of Americans who are receiving some form of regular income from the government. This is an important stabilizing factor in the economy and helps cushion the shock of recession, but it makes a balanced budget hard to achieve. One of the obstacles to a balanced budget is the fact that so many individuals are receiving so many benefits from government programs that it is difficult to agree on what should be cut. Since most programs increase their payout to keep up with inflation or must pay for increased costs for the same reason, the government is constantly trying to find adequate sources of revenue.

Sources of Revenue

The federal government has two sources of revenue. The primary source is taxes, and the alternative is to borrow money. As the government borrows without repaying the princi-

TABLE 14-6

MAJOR PROBLEM: MOST SPENDING IS "RELATIVELY UNCONTROLLABLE"

Of the 324.6 billion dollars spent by the U.S. Government in the year that ended June 30, 1975—

72% was relatively "uncontrollable"—expenditures fixed by law and thus hard to cut

	(billions)
Social Security, medicare, rail retirement	$83.3
Expenditures required by prior-year contracts	$49.1
Medicaid, public assistance, housing payments	$24.4
Interest	$23.3
Unemployment assistance	$14.0
Retirement pay, military and civilian	$13.3
Veterans' benefits	$12.5
Revenue sharing	$ 6.1
Miscellaneous	$ 8.7
TOTAL	$234.7

Thus: Barely more than $1 in $4 of spending was "relatively controllable"

For national-defense programs	$58.2
For Government pay, other civilian programs	$31.7
TOTAL	$89.9

Source: Office of Management and Budget

SOURCE: Reprinted from *U.S. News & World Report,* October 27, 1975, p. 72. Copyright 1975 U.S. News & World Report, Inc.

pal, the national debt increases and the interest on the debt also rises.

The National Debt

The inflationary spiral of the past ten years has heightened the problem of budget deficits as well as increasing the interest rate to holders of government debt instruments. Most of this debt is owed to the public and to financial institutions in the form of interest-bearing bonds, notes, and treasury bills that are offered in a wide variety of denominations and pay interest at the going market rate. The government cannot simply print money to pay for its programs. It must raise the cash either by selling new debt instruments or through taxation.

As of 1977, the estimated government debt is $709.7 billion, with $45 billion (about 11 percent of the national budget) needed to pay interest charges. Or, to bring the matter closer to home, the 1977 debt amounts to about $3266 per person.[8] The Keynesian approach of incurring budget deficits to stimulate a lagging economy and repaying the debt in times of prosperity has gone by the board. The first part of the proposition is honored annually, but there is little hope of repaying the debt.

Taxation

The individual citizen bears much of the financial burden of government. In fiscal year 1977, individual income taxes will account for 39 percent of governmental revenue, compared to 13 percent from corporate income tax-es. There is a continuing struggle over the way taxes are allocated, and "tax breaks" or preferences created over the years have resulted in many inequalities in the tax structure. In theory, tax breaks achieve a specific purpose that is judged to be in the public interest. Thus, industry is given tax incentives for new investment and individuals are entitled to exemptions according to the number of their dependents. The result is the pattern illustrated in Tables 14-8 and 14-9. Note the differences among corporate as well as personal income tax categories. If one looks at the four groups that pay the lowest taxes (see Table 14-9), a clear picture emerges of where the economic power lies.

Tax legislation results from congressional action, which, in turn, is heavily influenced by lobbyists for particular interest groups. To appreciate the extent of the tax preferences achieved through such lobbying, the percentage of income tax should be compared to the flat 48 percent that applies to all corporate earnings over $50,000. Ninety percent of all corporate income is derived from firms earning more than this amount; thus, the total received by the government from corporations would be only slightly less than 48 percent if there were no tax preferences. However, various tax saving laws reduced corporate taxes to 28.7 percent in 1972.[9]

The usual reason given for tax breaks for industry is that they result in industrial expansion, which, in turn, creates new jobs. But consider the following (based on a 1975 Congressional Budget Office study):

A $1-billion increase in government purchasing would create from 20,000 to 50,000 jobs and reduce unemployment by as much as .05 percent, while a $1-billion accelerated public works program would create from 16,000 to 46,000 jobs and reduce unemployment by as much as .08 percent over two years, the CBO said.

CBO ranked tax cuts as the most expensive way of creating jobs. According to the report, a $1-billion tax reduction would create from 8,000 to 15,000 jobs and reduce unemployment

TABLE 14-7

5 WAYS TO PUT THE BUDGET

IT TAKES FEWER AND FEWER YEARS TO ADD $100 BILLION TO THE BUDGET

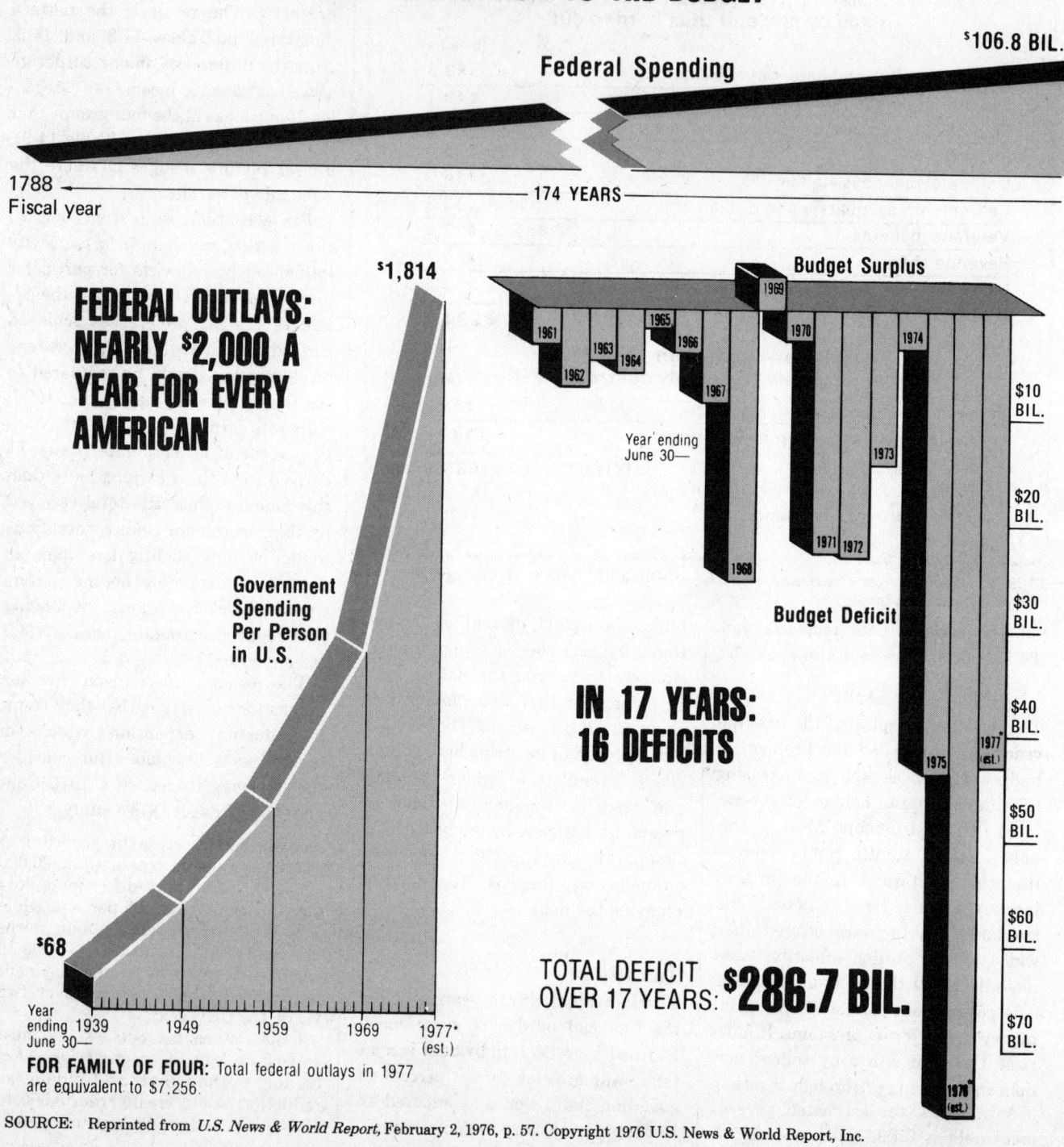

Federal Spending — $106.8 BIL.

1788 Fiscal year — 174 YEARS

FEDERAL OUTLAYS: NEARLY $2,000 A YEAR FOR EVERY AMERICAN

Government Spending Per Person in U.S.

$1,814

$68

Year ending June 30— 1939, 1949, 1959, 1969, 1977* (est.)

FOR FAMILY OF FOUR: Total federal outlays in 1977 are equivalent to $7,256.

Budget Surplus: 1961, 1962, 1963, 1964, 1965, 1966, 1967, 1969, 1970

Year ending June 30—

Budget Deficit: 1968, 1971, 1972, 1973, 1974, 1975, 1977 (est.), 1976 (est.)

$10 BIL. / $20 BIL. / $30 BIL. / $40 BIL. / $50 BIL. / $60 BIL. / $70 BIL.

IN 17 YEARS: 16 DEFICITS

TOTAL DEFICIT OVER 17 YEARS: $286.7 BIL.

SOURCE: Reprinted from *U.S. News & World Report*, February 2, 1976, p. 57. Copyright 1976 U.S. News & World Report, Inc.

Sources of Revenue **227**

IN PERSPECTIVE

$394.2 BIL.

$324.6 BIL.

Spending in 1977, by the time Congress acts on President Ford's proposed budget, is all-but certain to surpass the 400-billion mark.

$211.4 BIL.

← 9 YEARS → ← 4 YEARS → ← 2 YEARS →

$400 BIL.
$300 BIL.
$200 BIL.
$100 BIL.
0

→ 1962　　　　　　　1971　　　1975　1977* (est.)

RISING TIDE OF FEDERAL DEBT...

$709.7 BIL.

Total Public Debt

$40.4 BIL.

At midyear— 1939 1944 1949 1954 1959 1964 1969 1974 1977*(est.)

...AND A SOARING INTEREST BURDEN

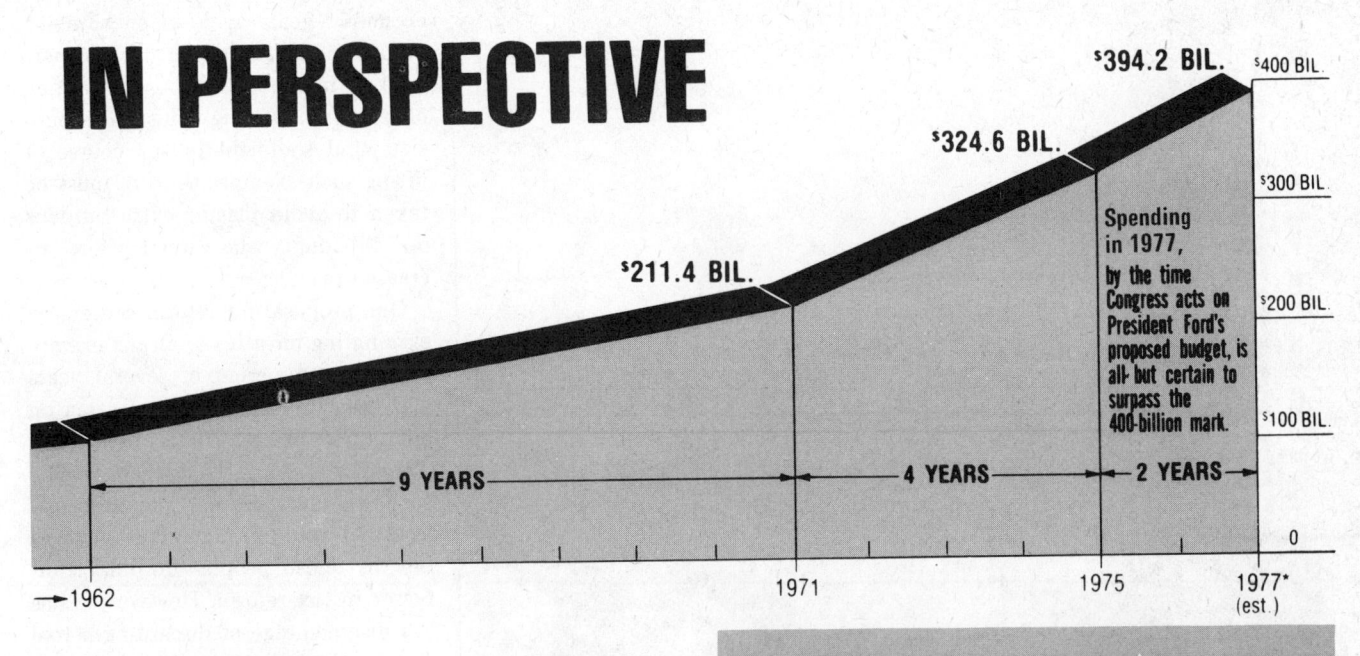

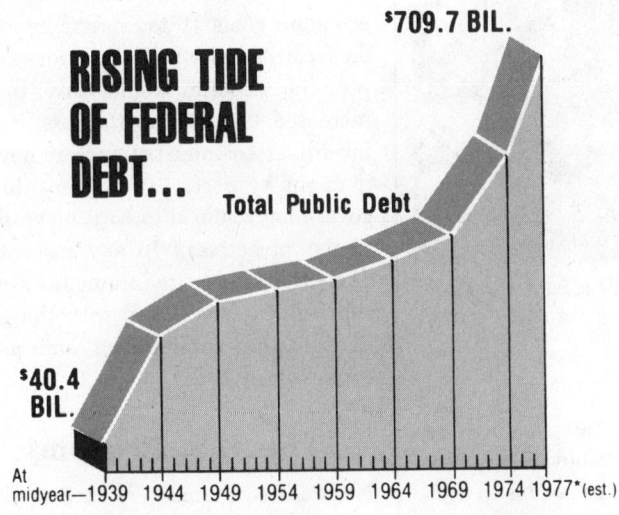

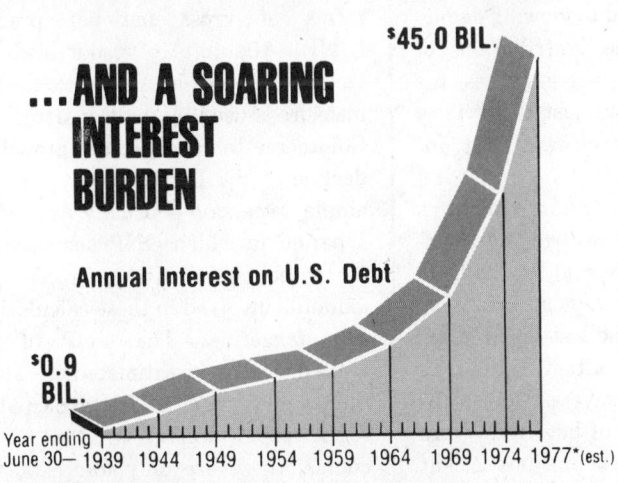

$45.0 BIL.

Annual Interest on U.S. Debt

$0.9 BIL.

Year ending June 30— 1939 1944 1949 1954 1959 1964 1969 1974 1977*(est.)

BY 1977: U.S. debt will amount to $3,266 per person. Paying interest for that debt will account for more than 11 per cent of all federal spending.

*Starting in 1977, fiscal years will end on September 30.

NEARLY EVERY AMERICAN HAS A PIECE OF U.S. BUDGET

Some of the millions who share in federal spending programs under this year's budget –

People collecting Social Security: **32,100,000**
Medicaid beneficiaries: **23,200,000**
People receiving food stamps: **18,400,000**
People helped under medicare: **13,200,000**
Children in school-lunch programs: **26,600,000**
Railroad-retirement beneficiaries: **1,000,000**
Members of families receiving aid for dependent children: **11,500,000**
Workers on unemployment compensation: **11,500,000**
Disabled coal miners: **500,000**
Civil Service retirees: **1,500,000**
Military personnel: **2,100,000**
Military retirees: **1,100,000**
Aged, blind, disabled receiving aid: **4,600,000**
Government workers: **2,800,000**
Veterans or survivors collecting pensions or compensation: **4,900,000**

AND THAT'S NOT ALL. Millions of Americans are helped by other programs — federally subsidized housing, small-business loans, farm price supports, college-student loans, GI benefits, for example. Result: Practically everybody is directly involved in some federal spending program or other.

Note: Figures cannot add to a total because many people receive Government help under more than one program.

Source Office of Management and Budget, U S Depts. of Treasury and Commerce

World War II, four-story, red, white and blue cash register set up in Times Square to record purchases of War Bonds. Selling government securities is one way the government borrows money.

by .03 percent at most within two years.[10]

There are other kinds of tax exemptions granted to corporations for specific purposes. Many people doubt the wisdom of such exemptions because they remain in effect long after they are needed. The nature of the political process has led to the creation of something for everyone in the way of tax breaks. This situation favors the richer citizens and major business interests because they have more influence on the bargaining process.

Tax Reform

While newspapers often feature stories about the seven people with incomes of over $1 million who pay no income tax (see Table 14-8), the problem of tax exemptions is much more complex. Table 14-10 shows the increase in tax subsidies in the past decade and the distribution of these benefits among various groups in society. We are not used to viewing deductions for charitable contributions or interest on home mortgages as tax breaks, but they are just that: They favor one group of citizens over another.

Tax reform is growing in popular as well as political appeal because Internal Revenue Service regulations have become overly numerous and cumbersome and the income lost through tax exemptions is increasingly unfair to the majority of taxpayers. More difficult is the problem of how and where to start cutting out exemptions so that a fair tax structure can be achieved without too much damage to some individuals. The existing tax incentives were intended to achieve specific economic goals such as encouraging homeownership, relieving pensioners and the unemployed from the burden of taxes, stimulating industrial expansion, and so forth. In the course of lifting such exemptions, care must be taken to avoid placing extra burdens on individuals who cannot afford increased taxes.

One proposal for reform centers on eliminating most if not all tax exemptions over a period of several years and then imposing a flat rate tax on all individual and corporate income. This proposal has the appeal of being easy to understand and simple to collect, and would probably be viewed as fair by most people—an important factor in tax reform. However, it has the disadvantage of discarding a tool that can be used to achieve specific economic goals. (If taxes were imposed on social security recipients, for example, the benefits would have to be increased to make up the loss; if tax incentives to industry were removed, it might be necessary to grant direct government subsidies to achieve particular objectives.) In any case, it is likely that the entire income tax structure will be overhauled with the goal of designing a simplified and more equal system.

The U.S. Economy

National economies are measured in terms of gross national product (GNP)—the total of goods and services produced in the nation. This measure is used by the Department of Commerce to calculate the growth or decline of the U.S. economy. For example, *recession* is usually defined as a period in which GNP has declined for three consecutive quarters. The amounts involved in these calculations are staggering:—The GNP of the United States is estimated at $1890 billion as of 1977 and is expected to reach $2877 billion in 1981.[11] (Of course, these are only forecasts, but economists have been rather accurate in predicting GNP.) The expected growth in the 1977-1981 period can be achieved only through new industries,

TABLE 14-8

PERSONAL INCOME TAXES

Based on federal returns for 1973 income —

Who Pays Tax

Income Group	Taxable Returns	Returns With No Tax Due
Under $5,000	11,545,788	15,491,830
$5,000-$10,000	19,784,124	797,608
$10,000-$15,000	15,726,664	77,445
$15,000-$25,000	12,991,983	43,011
$25,000-$50,000	3,489,385	12,443
$50,000-$100,000	594,197	2,466
$100,000-$200,000	109,718	458
$200,000-$500,000	21,787	142
$500,000-$1,000,000	2,620	15
$1,000,000 and over	896	7

How Heavy a Load

Based on taxable returns —

Income Group	Average Income	Average Tax	Average Tax Rate
Under $5,000	$ 3,571	$ 188	5.3%
$5,000-$10,000	$ 7,469	$ 674	9.0%
$10,000-$15,000	$ 12,470	$ 1,350	10.8%
$15,000-$25,000	$ 18,879	$ 2,473	13.1%
$25,000-$50,000	$ 33,018	$ 5,676	17.2%
$50,000-$100,000	$ 69,945	$ 17,448	24.9%
$100,000-$200,000	$ 146,002	$ 44,864	30.7%
$200,000-$500,000	$ 344,012	$113,822	33.1%
$500,000-$1,000,000	$ 920,229	$305,568	33.2%
$1,000,000 and over	$2,909,598	$934,863	32.1%
All taxable returns	$ 12,692	$ 1,682	13.3%

Note: Income groups are based on "adjusted gross income." Average income figures shown include 100 per cent of net long-term capital gains as estimated by USN&WR Economic Unit on the basis of official data.

Basic data: Internal Revenue Service

SOURCE: Reprinted from *U.S. News & World Report,* November 24, 1975, p. 90. Copyright 1975 U.S. News & World Report, Inc.

---

more jobs, and more disposable consumer income, that is, income available for spending.

Consumer spending accounts for almost two-thirds of GNP and is a key element in the U.S. economy. Several surveys are taken on a continuing basis to measure consumer attitudes toward matters such as purchasing a new car or buying a house, as well as general attitudes toward the economy. These indexes are watched closely by government planners as well as private industry for clues as to the future of the economy.

The U.S. economy consists of a multitude of businesses and industries competing with one another for the consumer dollar (which leads to corporate profits). The government does not sit idly by during this process. It actively attempts to create and maintain an economic climate in which prosperity is possible. In pursuing this goal, it uses economic tools such as control of the money supply, tax policy, and government spending.

Fiscal and Monetary Policy

Efforts to control the economy through governmental action usually center on fiscal policy (taxation and government spending) and monetary policy (the supply of money and its cost). Economists are often described as advocates of either fiscal or monetary policy. In practice, however, economic policy includes both approaches.

Fiscal Policy

Fiscal policy is mirrored in the budget as the administration tries to stimulate the economy by incurring deficits—spending more than it takes in through taxation—or lowering taxes in order to create more consumer and corporate income. In an inflationary period, the government can reduce its spending, raise taxes, and create budget surpluses. This sounds much simpler that it is in reality. As Table 14-6 illustrates, most government spending cannot be reduced, regardless of conditions, and the remainder is not easily cut either. Similarly, the rate of inflation shown in Table 14-4 militates against any major increase in spending in periods of recession be-

TABLE 14-9
The Taxes

Corporations Pay—U.S. Taxes as a Percentage of Net Income

Motor vehicles	39.9
Printing, publishing	38.8
Apparel	38.2
Textiles	38.1
Food processing	36.0
Metal products	36.0
Transport equipment (except motor vehicles)	35.5
Rubber	35.5
Chemicals	34.8
Electrical equipment	34.2
Utilities, transportation companies	33.6
Paper	33.2
Nonelectric machinery	31.9
Lumber	31.7
Insurance	30.4
Retail, wholesale trade	30.1
Primary metals	27.3
Construction	26.8
Real estate	25.7
Miscellaneous services	24.9
Banking	16.7
Petroleum refining	9.9
Investment and holding companies	4.9
Oil and gas production	3.8

SOURCE: U.S. News & World Report, November 24, 1975, p. 91. Reprinted from *U.S. News & World Report.* Copyright © 1975 U.S. News & World Report, Inc.

Note: Tax rates—based on 1972 data, latest available—are figured after deducting credits for investment and foreign taxes.

cause budget deficits erode the value of the dollar. Nor can taxes be increased without the risk of lowered consumer spending—which would lead to recession—nor can they be decreased very much without making the budget deficit worse.

Fiscal policy is based on Keynesian theory but, as noted earlier, the nation has been unable or unwilling to take advantage of prosperous periods to reduce the national debt so that it could again be increased to fight recession. Today the government has much less flexibility in its use of fiscal policy because of past misuses of such policy.

Monetary Policy

Monetary policy is carried out by the Federal Reserve Board, an independent agency that regulates the supply of money, thus having a direct impact on the amount of credit available to industry and the interest rate it has to pay. The Fed faces the dilemma of how to create enough monetary growth for industry to expand in line with demand without providing too much growth and encouraging inflation or unnecessary expansion (which leads to recession). This is a difficult balance to achieve. As Arthur Burns, chairperson of the Federal Reserve Board, has said, "Our objective in life is not to hit the target, but the best possible performance of the economy. We will not be slaves of a number. I should give up my job if we were."[12]

The Fed uses a variety of methods to control money supply and interest. Money supply is usually defined as currency in circulation plus checking accounts at commercial banks. The Fed functions as a lending institution to banks that are members of the Federal Reserve System. It sets the interest rates for such loans; this is called the *rediscount rate.* More important is the Fed's authority to set interest rates for *Federal funds* — overnight loans among banks. It also controls the reserves banks must keep on deposit against loans. If it raises the reserve requirement, less money can be lent by banks to businesses and individuals, and interest rates may rise as a result. By lowering the requirement, the Fed encourages banks to offer money at lower interest rates.

The Fed also carries on *open market operations,* in which it buys and sells government securities. If it buys securities from banks, the banks have more money on deposit against which to lend to customers; by selling securities, the Fed reduces the supply of money. This is probably the Fed's most important control over the nation's money supply.

The Fed is responsible for providing balance to the economic system. In times of economic expansion, the Fed takes a conservative approach, gradually decreasing the supply of money and raising interest rates and the reserve requirement in order to counteract inflationary tendencies. The trick is to prevent inflation without denying the economy the money supply necessary for economic health. The Fed will take an opposite tack during periods of recession, forcing interest rates down and the money supply up in an effort to encourage economic growth.

The activities of the Fed have become increasingly controversial because of their potential impact and because the Fed is a relatively independent agency. This independence was built into the system so that sensitive economic tools such as money supply and interest rates could not be used as political footballs. However, many people are disturbed by the Fed's power to pursue economic strategies that are not in harmony with those of Congress and the President.

The impact of Fed actions on the economy is hard to evaluate. While lower interest rates probably stimulate such industries as auto manufacture and homebuilding (in which purchases are financed by banks), interest rates are at their lowest in recessionary periods, when business in these industries is at a low ebb. As the economy perks up, the interest rates rise—yet so do sales of cars and homes. Thus, there is a lag in the economy's response to interest rate changes, and this carries over to consumer response. The simple economic truth is that the U.S. economy is heavily dependent on the consumer, and the level of consumer confidence is the most important part of any economic equation.

The Economic Power Structure

In recent years, control of American industrial and financial interests has become increasingly concentrated. This is partially due to the fact that "the big get bigger," but other changes are more significant. Almost 30 million people own stock in American corporations listed on the New York Stock Exchange. While this figure indicates widespread public ownership of listed corporations, it is misleading. Control of American industry is increasingly passing into the hands of a relatively few financial institutions and pension funds representing corporate employees.

TABLE 14-10

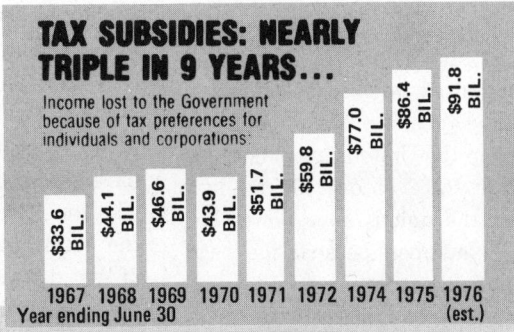

TAX SUBSIDIES: NEARLY TRIPLE IN 9 YEARS...

Income lost to the Government because of tax preferences for individuals and corporations:

Year ending June 30	Amount
1967	$33.6 BIL.
1968	$44.1 BIL.
1969	$46.6 BIL.
1970	$43.9 BIL.
1971	$51.7 BIL.
1972	$59.8 BIL.
1974	$77.0 BIL.
1975	$86.4 BIL.
1976 (est.)	$91.8 BIL.

...WHO GETS THE BILLIONS

INDIVIDUALS .... $66 BILLION

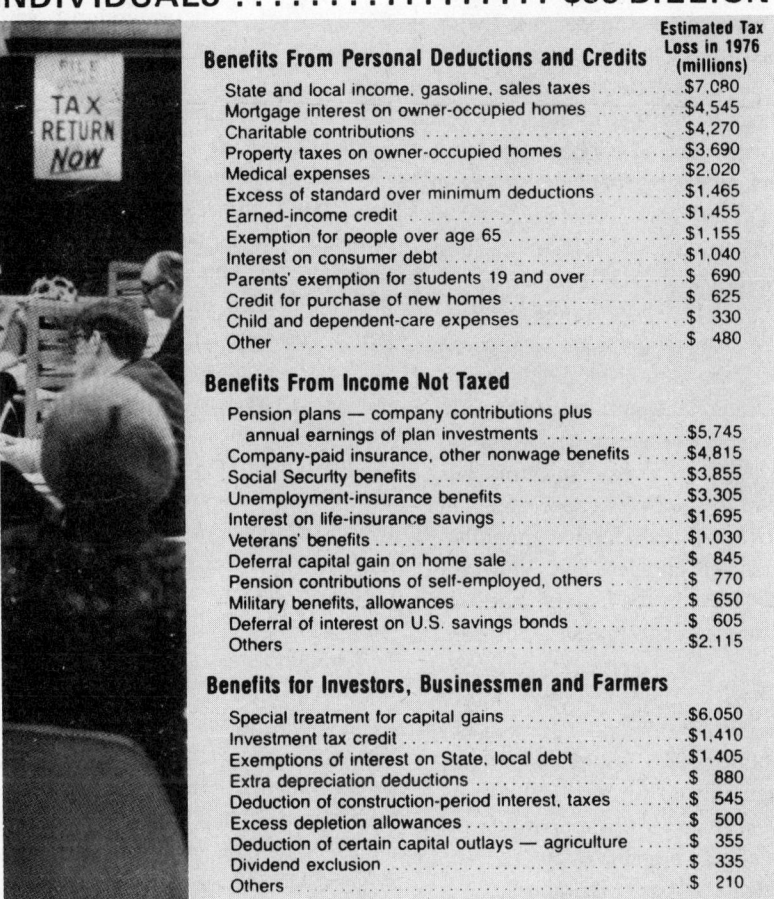

Benefits From Personal Deductions and Credits — Estimated Tax Loss in 1976 (millions)

State and local income, gasoline, sales taxes	$7,080
Mortgage interest on owner-occupied homes	$4,545
Charitable contributions	$4,270
Property taxes on owner-occupied homes	$3,690
Medical expenses	$2,020
Excess of standard over minimum deductions	$1,465
Earned-income credit	$1,455
Exemption for people over age 65	$1,155
Interest on consumer debt	$1,040
Parents' exemption for students 19 and over	$ 690
Credit for purchase of new homes	$ 625
Child and dependent-care expenses	$ 330
Other	$ 480

Benefits From Income Not Taxed

Pension plans — company contributions plus annual earnings of plan investments	$5,745
Company-paid insurance, other nonwage benefits	$4,815
Social Security benefits	$3,855
Unemployment-insurance benefits	$3,305
Interest on life-insurance savings	$1,695
Veterans' benefits	$1,030
Deferral capital gain on home sale	$ 845
Pension contributions of self-employed, others	$ 770
Military benefits, allowances	$ 650
Deferral of interest on U.S. savings bonds	$ 605
Others	$2,115

Benefits for Investors, Businessmen and Farmers

Special treatment for capital gains	$6,050
Investment tax credit	$1,410
Exemptions of interest on State, local debt	$1,405
Extra depreciation deductions	$ 880
Deduction of construction-period interest, taxes	$ 545
Excess depletion allowances	$ 500
Deduction of certain capital outlays — agriculture	$ 355
Dividend exclusion	$ 335
Others	$ 210

CORPORATIONS .... $25.8 BILLION

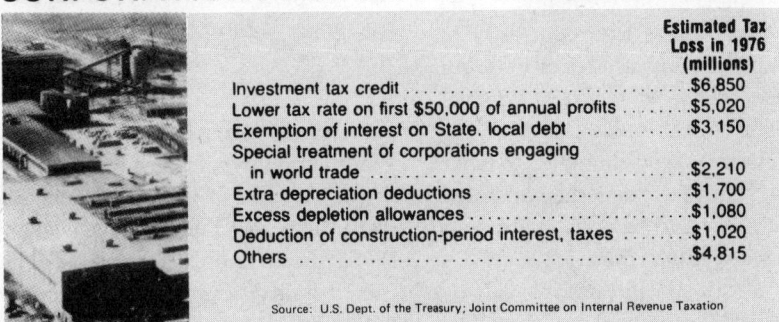

Estimated Tax Loss in 1976 (millions)

Investment tax credit	$6,850
Lower tax rate on first $50,000 of annual profits	$5,020
Exemption of interest on State, local debt	$3,150
Special treatment of corporations engaging in world trade	$2,210
Extra depreciation deductions	$1,700
Excess depletion allowances	$1,080
Deduction of construction-period interest, taxes	$1,020
Others	$4,815

Source: U.S. Dept. of the Treasury; Joint Committee on Internal Revenue Taxation

SOURCE: Reprinted from *U.S. News & World Report*, May 10, 1976, p. 76. Copyright 1976 U.S. News & World Report, Inc.

The changes in ownership of industry are also changing the shape of economic policy. Employees and the unions representing them now have a common interest in profits— the fuel of the free enterprise system. It is profits that allow industrial expansion, expansion that creates new jobs for an expanding work force, and increased wealth in the hands of labor that maintains economic prosperity. Alone, the government cannot achieve these goals, but they must be achieved or a democratic political system is in trouble. Political and economic stability are inseperably linked.

Financial Institutions

Financial institutions include large banks, insurance companies, mutual funds, and pension plans. These institutions invest large amounts of money on behalf of their clients, stockholders, or beneficiaries. In so doing, they provide the funds that enable industry to grow.

Financial institutions have become the dominant force on Wall Street and in the international financial markets. Together they account for 70 percent of the dollar volume on the New York Stock Exchange, about double their 1963 share and three times their 1954 share. It is estimated that Americans own $840 billion in stocks of various kinds, and that institutions own 40 percent of those stocks.[13]

The concentration of wealth in the hands of financial institutions is a significant economic fact. Political influence follows wealth, and through such economic interest groups as the Council of Economic Development, those who control the nation's wealth have much to say about how the government will participate—or not participate—in the economic system.

Financial institutions tend to look at the overall economic picture. They put pressure on the government to avoid overly restrictive control of the money supply, and they seek tax advantages for the nation's money managers. As Table 14-9 shows, banks pay corporate taxes at low average rates. One example of the preferential treatment of banks is the regulation that allows banks to borrow money, deduct the interest as an expense, and put the proceeds into tax-exempt municipal bonds. It is illegal for anyone else to deduct interest on loans used for this purpose.

The power of banks goes far beyond the influence that flows from their own wealth. They are trust managers; that is, they invest money that belongs to others. The largest bank conducting trust operations, Morgan Guaranty Trust Company, controls 2 percent of the total national investment in securities—over $15 billion.[14] The trust manager's right to vote the shares of a corporation gives the trust an influential voice in the management of that corporation.

Employee Pension Funds

Most trust funds come from employee pension plans, which have grown to enormous proportions and signal a new era in management-employee relations. In 1976, it was estimated that employee pension funds owned more than one-third of the equity capital— or common stock—in the nation's publicly held companies (those that offer their stock to the public). It is calculated that by 1985 this ownership will exceed 50 percent. This means that control of the nation's corporations will have passed to pension fund trustees (like Morgan Guaranty), which administer the funds for the benefit of employees.[15]

While the employees collectively own most of the larger corporations, it is the trustees who have the power through their control of the voting rights of the stocks in the trusts they administer. This enables them to play a key role in election of the Board of Directors, the individuals who make the major policy decisions. The rapid growth and size of the employee pension funds bring about a mutuality of interest between employees and corporate management. They both have a vested stake in the vitality of the nation's economy as well as in healthy corporate profits.

Labor Unions

Labor unions represent a major source of economic power, which, in turn, has given organized labor political influence. There are about 20 million union members in the United States out of a total work force of over 85 million. However, the unions have power beyond their numbers because the wage settlements they obtain set the pattern for nonunion labor as well.

The American labor movement has become increasingly conservative in its approach to the government's role in the economy. No longer faced with the need to establish its place in the economic power structure, union leadership has found that its interests coincide with those of big business. Like business, labor objects to any proposal for wage and price controls. Only a growing economy can offer more jobs and higher wages and benefits.

Table 14-11 reflects the relative costs of American labor compared with Western European and Japanese labor. Americans are no longer the highest-paid workers in the world (in terms of productivity) and this has benefited the nation's exports as well as motivating such foreign manufacturers as Volkswagen and Volvo to build facilities in the United States to serve the American market. The productivity of the American worker has also exceeded that of workers in other nations. Productivity—measured in terms of the unit cost of labor—has increased only 33 percent in the United States since 1970. Comparable increases abroad amount to 105 percent in Sweden and Great Britain, 90 percent in Japan, 70 percent in France, and 50 percent in Germany.[16] The trend toward greater productivity in the United States, as shown by lower increases in the unit cost of production, is a favorable one. Much of the credit for this trend should go to labor unions, which have generally accepted *cost-of-living increases* in major contract negotiations during the 1970's rather than insist on excessive gains.

The positive part labor has played in building a strong economy has earned the respect of business leaders. While there is a basic conflict between management's desire to keep labor cost down and the unions' desire to improve their members' standard of living, a reasonable balance appears to have been achieved in the past decade. The long period of economic growth the nation has enjoyed since the end of World War II, marred only by a few recessions, has brought the unions into the economic mainstream. The fringe benefits they have won for their members, such as pension plans, have also created a shared interest with management in improved productivity.

It would be simplistic to view all labor unions as positive economic forces. One of the factors that encourage labor to be reasonable in its demands is the challenge posed by nonunion labor. The experience of the building trades unions is a case in point. There are about 1 million workers in the building trades, and the largest contracting firms are unionized. Work rules that far exceeded productivity drastically raised the cost of building with union labor. Union featherbedding—the practice of requiring employers to hire more labor than is necessary—allowed nonunion contractors to win 78 projects worth $7.2 billion, in the 1971-1973 period, according to the National Contractors Association. Competitive pressures of this sort have forced the building trades unions to take a more cooperative attitude. They have signed agreements that ban strikes during a project, offered to work Saturday at regular wages to make up for weekday rain delays, and agreed to allow contractors to determine the size of work crews.[17]

Large Corporations

While large corporations share many of the concerns of the major financial institutions, their interests are likely to be more limited in nature. The responsibility of corporate officers is to produce increased earnings per share; anything else is secondary. This

TABLE 14-11

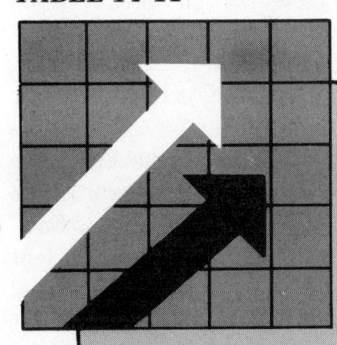

PAY SCALES: THE 5-YEAR RECORD

Recent changes in currency rates, along with steadily rising wage costs in foreign countries, mean that the U.S. no longer heads the list of "high labor cost" nations. The record —

(total labor costs per hour, including "fringes")

	1970	1975	Change
Sweden	$3.01	$7.12	Up 137%
Norway	$2.49	$6.56	Up 163%
Denmark	$2.37	$6.32	Up 167%
Canada	$3.49	$6.19	Up 77%
UNITED STATES	$4.25	$6.06	Up 43%
Belgium	$2.08	$6.05	Up 191%
West Germany	$2.43	$5.64	Up 132%
Netherlands	$2.12	$5.54	Up 161%
Switzerland	$1.99	$5.03	Up 153%
Italy	$1.87	$4.36	Up 133%
Austria	$1.54	$4.07	Up 164%
France	$1.74	$4.01	Up 130%
Britain	$1.68	$3.70	Up 120%
Japan	$1.10	$3.45	Up 214%

Source: Swedish Employers' Confederation

SOURCE: Reprinted from *U.S. News & World Report,* February 9, 1976, p. 65. Copyright 1976 U.S. News & World Report, Inc.

motive encourages corporate executives to use all possible influence on government officials at all levels (including the regulatory agencies, and the political party system) whose decisions may have an impact on the corporation's earnings. At times, attempts to maintain or increase corporate influence lead to illegal activities.

The Watergate Special Prosecutor's Office won convictions against 18 corporations and 22 individuals for illegal political contributions. The companies involved were among the nation's largest, including Phillips Petroleum, Minnesota Mining and Manufacturing, Goodyear, and American Airlines. The use of political "slush" funds was not confined to the United States— Gulf Oil admitted making contributions of $12 million to parties, candidates, and public officials both here and abroad.[18] These contributions were intended to give the company an influence on any legislative action that might affect it.

Corporate efforts to influence governmental action are just as legitimate as those of any interest group. The illegalities just mentioned are the exception, not the rule, but they demonstrate the dangers that exist when the stakes in federal decisions are high. The outcry over illegal contributions together with the recognition that business does have a legitimate interest in who is elected to public office led to a provision in the 1974 Campaign Finance Act that allows corporations to set up political committees, though the earlier limits on the use of corporate funds are still in effect.

The economic health of the nation's large corporations cannot be separated from the well-being of the average citizen. While the systems of taxation and regulation may give business an unfair advantage, this does not change the fact that high levels of employment at adequate wages depend on an efficient, profitable corporate structure. The policies of any administration, Democratic or Republican, are intended to maintain an economic climate in which corporate interests can prosper. As the nation's population increases, so does the need for more jobs. The government is unable to do much more than provide temporary public works jobs in times of economic crisis. The long-range solutions to the problems of providing jobs and a rising standard of living fall to the private sector. If corporate profits are not high enough, the funds for new jobs will not be available. A major task of the federal government, then, is to strike a balance between providing incentive for economic expansion while protecting the citizen from corporate greed.

The Role of the Government

Governmental activity in the economic sector paralleled the rise of giant financial institutions after the Civil War. While many government agencies and departments have a voice in economic decisions, the activities of the Federal Trade Commission provide an index of the relationship between the government and the private sector (see Table 14-12). Note the variety of the FTC's activities—the FTC has been involved in matters ranging from violations of antitrust law to truth in advertising. This is an indication of the degree of freedom it enjoys in dealing with the economy.

As the government has expanded its economic activities, a large number of regulations have been made by the bureaucracy. The effectiveness of these regulations is hard to judge in economic terms. Some industries, such as airlines and trucking, have become so dependent on regulation of their routes and fares or rates that they oppose deregulations. Other industries, such as the auto manufacturers, have found the regulations imposed by the government very costly, and many have passed these costs on to the consumer in the form of higher prices. For example, an estimated $3 billion was spent on 1974 model cars to install devices that prevented cars from being started until the seat belts were fastened. The National Safety Council estimated that two out of every five motorists had this device disconnected. The government finally withdrew the regulation,[19] but not before it had led to tremendous financial waste.

There were about 75,000 people employed in governmental regulatory functions in 1976 at a cost of over $3 billion.[20] Add to this the cost to the consumer of almost any regulation, which usually increases manufacturers' costs and leads to higher prices. The drive for pollution control is affecting almost every industry, since there are few that do not emit waste products into the environment. Environmental concerns are important because the present and potential dangers are real. But what kind of pollution control should be imposed over what period of time? Regulatory questions of this sort give rise to much debate. As with any other government expenditure, the only certainty is that the individual citizen will bear the financial burden, either as a taxpayer (if subsidies are used to pay the cost) or as a consumer (if industry foots the bill and passes the costs on to the consumer).

Direct Impact on the Economy

The government's major economic impact comes from its role as the nation's largest employer and as the largest customer for business products. These expenditures are an important prop to the economy because even during periods of recession government employment and spending are stable. Payments to individuals under various assistance programs totalled about 55.4 percent of total federal outlays in 1977.[21]

The growth of the government has made it the dominant economic force in the nation. This is an asset in the sense that it offers stability; however, it is a mixed blessing in that whenever the government performs a function that might have been performed by the private sector, a degree of economic freedom is lost because of the regulations that accompany any government program. There is also the danger that the future funding of existing programs will require higher taxes.

In addition to direct payments to individuals and programs in which the federal government shares the costs with the states (such as unemploy-

TABLE 14-12
Federal Trade Commission Actions

1914 Federal Trade Commission Act declares unfair methods of competition in commerce illegal. Clayton Act forbids mergers or takeovers that might substantially lessen competition or tend to create a monopoly.

1915 First FTC commissioners sworn into office.

1920-24 Congress sours on agency. Allegations that it is a hotbed of socialism. Agency loses string of test cases in supreme court.

1925 Pro-business Coolidge administration chooses as FTC chairman Mr. William Humphrey, a republican congressman, who grumbles that agency has become "an instrument of oppression and disturbance instead of a help to business." FTC shunted into writing "studies."

1929-32 Great depression revives populist sentiment against big business.

1936 Robinson-Patman Act seeks to make sure all merchants can buy goods at same price from the same supplier.

1938 Wheeler-Lea Act amends FTC Act to outlaw "unfair or deceptive acts or practices in commerce" in addition to unfair methods of competition.

1948 FTC versus Cement Institute. Supreme court sustains finding against so-called basing point pricing system, in which companies charge customers a freight fee calculated on delivery from the same city, even when the product is delivered from another city. Steel industry, which had a similar "phantom freight" system, fell into line with this ruling.

1950 FTC versus Morton Salt. Supreme court confirms agency's authority to require corporations to file special reports in answer to specific questions.

1964-65 FTC successfully prods Congress to pass law to require health warnings on cigarette packets.

1967 Supreme court upholds first formal challenge by FTC to conglomerate merger when it requires Procter and Gamble to divest itself of Clorox, America's leading manufacturer of household liquid bleach.

1969 Truth in Lending Act requires full disclosure of credit terms to customer before credit transaction is completed.

1972 FTC versus Sperry and Hutchinson, America's largest and oldest stamp trading company. Supreme court decides FTC has power "to define and proscribe an unfair competitive practice, even though the practice does not infringe either the letter or the spirit of the antitrust laws," 1972 Pfizer and Firestone. FTC establishes illegality of advertisements that make claims that cannot be substantiated by advertiser.

1975 Magnusson-Moss Warranty-Federal Trade Commission Improvement Act expands FTC's authority to promulgate substantive trade regulation rules in consumer protection, to obtain civil penalties and consumer redress for violations of FTC Act and to pursue unlawful acts "affecting commerce," not just those "in commerce."

1976 FTC regulations restrict centuries-old holder in due course doctrine. Banks and others that finance instalment credit transactions no longer aloof from disputes between shops and shoppers. All consumer credit contracts must include provision that preserves customer's right to dispute the obligation to pay instalments, even to the financial middlemen, if goods are defective.

SOURCE: *The Economist (London),* May 29, 1976, p. 73.

Ohio Highway Patrol attempts to keep traffic moving as truckers block the highway to protest government-imposed speed limit and increased fuel prices.

ment compensation), the government makes direct subsidies to industries such as airlines and shipbuilding, subsidizes some farm products in the form of price supports, and makes a variety of other payments (as well as allowing tax exemptions). All of these devices are intended to serve as a cushion against adverse economic conditions. As with most governmental actions, many payments and subsidies are continued long after they have served their original purpose.

The Role of Foreign Trade

The United States has an important stake in foreign trade, and the government plays a major role in maintaining positive foreign relations that encourage U.S. investment. It is not only desirable but necessary to cooperate with other nations to prevent inflationary spirals like that of 1971-1973, in which increases in international oil and food prices had an adverse impact on the United States and throughout the Western World. Widespread recessions are accompanied by severe currency fluctuations as market forces lead to revaluation of world currencies. The United States, as the world's leading industrial power, is directly affected by such events.

The basic thrust of U.S. foreign trade policy is to encourage free trade—that is, to remove barriers to trade among nations—though efforts are made to protect specific industries for limited periods. The Trade Act of 1974 gave the President the right to negotiate the lowering of trade barriers with other nations. It also allowed the government to take actions such as restricting imports if they threaten domestic industries. Since World War II, the United States has lost markets in labor-intensive industries because U.S. labor was more expensive than foreign labor, particularly in places like Pakistan or Taiwan. The gap has narrowed between the United States and other industrialized nations, but the manufacture of items such as sneakers and inexpensive blouses has been practically wiped out in the United States by foreign competition. The government cannot protect such industries without raising consumer prices in the United States and causing foreign governments to take similar action against imports of American products.

Summary

The political system plays a major role in maintaining an acceptable level of economic growth. Providing enough

Soviet cargo ship loads American wheat at the port of Longview, Washington. Foreign grain sales have become increasingly important to American agriculture.

jobs for the expanding work force without causing inflation will be the most important challenge to the government in the years ahead. Though raw material shortages may be offset by technological advances (past crises such as the lack of rubber and tin during World War II have been overcome through the use of synthetic materials), the employment-inflation problem is as much political as economic because it involves the government's basic task of setting national goals and adjusting its policies to achieve those goals. Thus, the government makes decisions that determine the extent to which various groups in society benefit from and pay the costs of economic progress.

The goal of continued prosperity and a steadily rising standard of living also depends on powerful interest groups—such as big business and big labor—acting with the nation's long-range economic well-being in mind rather than seeking the maximum short-term gain for themselves. The competition between various interest groups is part and parcel of the American economic system, just as it is basic to the political system. But unless the more powerful groups in the economy recognize the legitimate interests of other groups, moderation will be replaced by unwillingness to compromise. In short, while the economic role of the government is crucial, the private sector shares the task of maintaining a healthy economy.

CHAPTER 14 CROSSWORD PUZZLE

Across
1. The ___ is the nation's largest employer and largest customer for business products.
6. Series of images occurring while asleep
9. Footwear
10. Beverage
12. Congress participates in economic planning through its ___ responsibilities.
16. Angry
18. Opposite of "odd"
19. In establishing economic policy the nation's priorities must be balanced against available ___.
20. ___ and fauna
21. Shade of a color; hue
23. Information
24. The basic foreign trade policy of the U.S. is to encourage ___ trade.
27. ___ and feather
29. High rock
30. The functions of review and ___ of government spending are carried out by the Office of Management and Budget (OMB).
31. Place to cook in
32. The creation of ___ jobs is probably the best guarantee of economic prosperity.
34. Teen, middle, or old ___

Down
1. Seize; type of bag
2. Competed with
3. Anger
4. Word used with green or lasting
5. Cooking abbreviation
6. "I ___" (wedding vow)
7. Posterior
8. Actions designed to regulate the money supply are referred to as ___ policy
11. Entice
13. Phantom; spirit
14. List of duties imposed by a government on goods
15. Opposite of "no"
16. When demand for goods and services exceeds supply, ___ is the likely result.
17. Opposite of "below"
21. The government raises money by either selling debt securities or levying ___.
22. Almond or cashew
23. National spending which exceeds revenues increases the national ___.
25. Ill-mannered
26. There has been increased emphasis on the need for ___-term economic planning
28. Uncooked
29. Orange or pekoe ___

NOTES

[1] *The United States Budget in Brief, Fiscal Year 1977,* p. 4.

[2] *U.S. News & World Report,* March 22, 1976, p. 64.

[3] *The United States Budget in Brief, Fiscal Year 1977,* p. 62.

[4] Julius Shishkin, Director of the Bureau of Labor Statistics, quoted in *The Economist,* London, April 17, 1976, p. 38.

[5] Ibid.

[6] Quoted in *The New York Times,* December 21, 1975, p. 12F. Copyright © 1975 by The New York Times Company. Reprinted by permission.

[7] Quoted by Thomas A. Murphy in "National Economic Planning—Pro and Con," *The New York Times,* December 21, 1975, p. 12F. Copyright © 1975 by The New York Times Company. Reprinted by permission.

[8] *U.S. News & World Report,* February 2, 1976, p. 57.

[9] *U.S. News & World Report,* November 24, 1975, p. 91. Copyright © 1975 U.S. News & World Report, Inc.

[10] *Congressional Quarterly,* September 6, 1975, p. 1926.

[11] *The United States Budget in Brief, Fiscal Year 1977,* pp. 15-16.

[12] "Monetary Policy: A Shifting Target," *The New York Times,* January 4, 1976, p. 20.

[13] Dan Rottenberg in "The Moneyweight Champion," *The New York Times Magazine,* February 22, 1976, p. 16.

[14] Ibid., p. 16.

[15] Peter F. Drucker in "American Business's New Owners," *The Wall Street Journal,* May 27, 1976, p. 22.

[16] *U.S. News & World Report,* February 8, 1976, p. 66.

[17] James C. Hyatt in *The New York Times,* December 18, 1976, p. 23.

[18] Robert M. Smith in "Big Business and the Plans," *The New York Times,* February 1, 1976, p. 3E.

[19] *U.S. News & World Report,* June 14, 1976, p. 31.

[20] Ibid.

[21] *The United States Budget in Brief, Fiscal Year 1977,* p. 19.

CHAPTER 15
MILITARY AND FOREIGN POLICY

CHAPTER OUTLINE

Questions to Consider
Introduction
The Interdependence of Nations
The National Interest
The Role of Diplomacy
The Foreign Policy Establishment
    Presidential Advisers
    The Foreign Policy Elite
    The Foreign Policy Bureaucracy
    The Professional Diplomats
    The Intelligence Agencies
    The Military
Congress and Foreign Policy
The Defense Industry
    The Military-Industrial Complex
    Arms Exports
Public Opinion and Foreign Policy
The Conduct of Foreign Policy
Making Foreign Policy Decisions
A Foreign Policy Overview
    Europe
    The Middle East
    Asia
    Latin America
    Africa
Summary

QUESTIONS TO CONSIDER

What is the relationship between domestic politics and U.S. foreign and military policy? Why should the United States care about what happens in nations thousands of miles away? These questions are important because international events have a direct impact on domestic conditions.

In this chapter, we will concentrate on questions like the following: How is U.S. foreign policy made? Does the President make all the key decisions? What is the role of the various intelligence agencies? What is the "military-industrial complex"? How does it affect foreign policy? What are our foreign policy interests in various parts of the globe? It will soon become clear that foreign policy and domestic politics are highly interdependent.

Introduction

The United States devotes over 25 percent of its national budget to military and diplomatic activities. About 40 percent of the government's civilian employees are in the Department of Defense and the State Department, in addition to over 2 million military personnel. The size of the defense and diplomatic establishments makes them a matter of concern to any administration and has a profound impact on all citizens. The resources allocated to America's relations with the rest of the world account for a large percentage of the taxes the average citizen pays, and the benefits of these expenditures are also shared by all.

Domestic security and prosperity are possible only in an international atmosphere that is favorable to U.S. interests. These interests are political (the security of the nation from attack) and economic (the freedom of U.S. businesses to export their products and to import manufactured goods and raw materials). Our dependence on imported oil is the most obvious example of such an interest, but there are many other raw materials that must be bought overseas. Similarly, the creation of jobs for an expanding population requires the maintenance of export markets. Thus, foreign interference with either export or import activities is viewed as a threat to national security.

A strong military establishment is needed to back up American diplomacy. The basic goal of U.S. foreign policy is to maximize American opportunities abroad and minimize the risks. The military offers a security umbrella to allies and acts as a deterrent to adversaries.

It is impossible to consider foreign policy without including the military. The size of the military and foreign policy establishment has both a political and an economic impact. The economic effect of military spending goes far beyond the $100 billion defense budget. The communities in which this money is spent depend on continued high levels of military spending for employment. In 1975, $37.3 billion was spent on prime military contracts. The twenty states that benefited from these expenditures control two-thirds of the seats in the House of Representatives.[1] This relationship illustrates the political-economic-military linkage that is at the core of all congressional appropriations.

The President, as commander-in-chief of the armed forces, has direct control over the military. He is also the chief diplomat, since the State Department operates within the executive branch. Congress also plays a role in foreign and military affairs through activities ranging from passing appropriations to approving Presidential appointments of senior diplomats and military officers and ratifying treaties with other nations. But decision making in relation to foreign affairs involves not only people in official positions but also interest groups with a direct stake in U.S. policy abroad and, of course, the public, whose continuing support is needed if any policy is to succeed.

The Interdependence of Nations

If the United States were free to devote all its energies to domestic concerns, there would be no reason for its enormous expenditures on foreign affairs. However, since the late nineteenth century there has been a steady expansion of the nation's interests in other parts of the globe. Fueled by two world wars and the Korean and Vietnamese wars, foreign affairs have become a major concern of every President and a source of much debate both within and outside the government. While few people will argue that the United States can withdraw from its worldwide economic and political activities, the point at which American interests are threatened by the actions of other nations is often hard to determine.

The dependence of the nation on raw materials from abroad leads to U.S. involvement in the economies of other nations. Such involvement is also required in order to maintain export markets for American raw materials and manufactured goods. The health of the domestic economy is closely tied to that of its trading partners. It would be naive to imagine that

President Carter and Japanese Prime Minister Takeo Fukudo at welcoming ceremonies on the White House lawn in 1977. Visits between world leaders have become commonplace with modern air transport.

the United States can remain prosperous while the rest of the world does not. The U.S. recession and inflation of 1973-1975 was accompanied by similar conditions in other Western nations and Japan. Likewise, the emergence from the recession and the increase in employment in 1976 were shared by most of the industrialized nations.

The interdependence of nations has been heightened as U.S. raw material supplies have been depleted. The impact of the 1973 Arab oil embargo is an example of the nation's dependence on foreign markets, and the opportunities these markets provide for domestic interests are illustrated by U.S. grain sales to the Soviet Union. Economic relations with other nations are a two-way street. If the United States wants to export its products, it must be willing to import products from abroad. Thus, economic prosperity at home is closely tied to foreign relations, and this gives all citizens an important stake in foreign affairs.

The National Interest

A nation's goals both at home and abroad are usually referred to as the *national interest*. While the specific goals of U.S. foreign policy change over time, there are two basic goals that are always top priority: (1) maintenance of foreign markets for American products and protection of American investments abroad, and (2) national security.

There are many interpretations of exactly where and in what form U.S. interests are threatened. The Japanese attack on Pearl Harbor in 1941 was an obvious threat—it was a direct attack on U.S. territory. However, few questions of national security can be answered as clearly. In 1950, President Truman responded to North Korean aggression by launching a massive military effort under UN sponsorship in order to maintain the independence of South Korea. In this case, an action that occurred far from U.S. borders was seen as a threat to American interests. The basis of Truman's action and the efforts to "contain" communism that have marked foreign policy since the end of World War II is the belief that the Soviet Union will expand its domination of other nations and eventually isolate the United States unless it is prevented from doing so.

It was this perception of the national interest that led to the U.S. involvement in the Vietnam War. The Vietnamese conflict was interpreted as part of the larger threat of world communism rather than as a local political struggle. The unhappy U.S. experience in Vietnam illustrates the difficulties involved in foreign affairs: There is always a danger that foreign actions will be misinterpreted.

The mistakes made in Vietnam led to a hands-off policy in 1970's. In 1975-1976, when Cuban forces were involved in the conflict in Angola, the administration wanted to aid the anti-communist forces but Congress was unwilling to commit U.S. resources to a situation that did not affect the nation directly. As a result, the Soviet-backed forces were successful in setting up a socialist government in Angola. Most international political situations, like the Angolan conflict are ambiguous and require careful interpretation. In the words of Hans J. Morgenthau, "In every political situation contradictory tendencies are at play. One of these tendencies is more likely to prevail under certain circumstances." [2]

Foreign policy involves both diplomatic and military activities; neither is adequate in itself. The following passage reflects the uncertainties involved in judging how to blend these two elements:

DIPLOMACY AND WAR

In foreign policy, the most difficult issues are those whose necessity you cannot prove when the decisions are made. You act on the basis of an assessment that in the nature of things is a guess, so that public opinion knows, usually only when it is too late to act, when some catastrophe has become overwhelming.

The necessity of the measures one takes to avoid the catastrophe can almost never be proved. For that reason you require a great deal, or at least a certain amount of confidence in leadership and that becomes difficult in all societies. [3]

Arabian American Oil Company oil rigs form a backdrop for camels in Saudi Arabia. Energy shortages have propelled such underdeveloped nations into important positions in international affairs.

The Role of Diplomacy

Diplomacy is the art of conducting foreign relations. It requires skill under the best of conditions and is complicated by the often conflicting interest of both allies and adversaries. U.S.-French relations since the end of World War II provide an example of how a traditional friendship between nations can be damaged by a clash of interests. After the war the United States made every effort to halt the spread of nuclear weapons and offered to serve as a shield for NATO forces. France, however, insisted on developing its own nuclear weapons, though these obviously would be inadequate to protect France in the event of a major war between eastern and western nations. Similarly, the NATO nations may have economic interests that are different from those of the United States. Skilled diplomacy is needed to adjust these differences in such a way that traditional friendships may be maintained.

Foreign affairs are conducted in a very realistic atmosphere. Adversaries admit their divergent interests just as readily as allies point to their interdependence. The areas in which cooperation is possible are fewer in relations with adversaries, and a strong military is more important in such cases. It would be unthinkable for the United States to even imply that it might use force against its Western European allies, but it would be just as unthinkable for it to negotiate with an adversary like the Soviet Union without the military strength to back up its policies.

War is always a possibility when national interests clash. The U.S. involvement in the Korean and Vietnamese conflicts, the Soviet suppression of independent political action in Poland, Hungary, and Czechoslovakia, and the almost continuous strife between Israel and the Arab states are examples of the pervasiveness of armed conflict. Successful diplomacy is intended to prevent the use of force, but all nations must be prepared to use military means to protect their interests if diplomacy fails. This is the reason for the huge U.S. defense establishment and the large share of the nation's resources devoted to foreign affairs. The continuing problem in matters of national defense is to determine what military action—or lack of it—is consistent with the nation's diplomatic needs. Power without purpose is wasteful, but inadequate power could be self-destructive.

The Foreign Policy Establishment

Foreign policy decisions involve individuals whose official positions give them access to the President, those whose positions in the private sector give them a certain amount of influence, and those whom the President trusts. The decisionmakers are aware, however, that foreign policy must ultimately be acceptable to the public. Policy decisions are based on evaluations of the probable actions of other nations, their probable reaction to American actions, and the ability of the United States to successfully carry out a particular policy. Foreign policy, therefore, is based on probabilities and "ifs." One of the problems involved in judging these probabilities is the fact that incorrect information may prevent an accurate evaluation of all useful alternatives. [4]

Since the President has the ultimate responsibility for the decision-making process, much depends on his relationship with the heads of the executive departments, members of Congress, and influential private citizens. The support of all is needed, but no individual or group is dominant. Presidents Kennedy, Johnson, and Nixon kept a tight rein on foreign affairs and, in effect, made their own policy with the help of a small core of advisers. In contrast, Presidents Eisenhower and Ford assigned more responsibility to their secretaries of state, John Foster Dulles and Henry Kissinger. Regardless of Presidential style, however, a specific group of institutions, public and private, play an important role in the process of determining foreign policy.

Presidential Advisers

The National Security Council (NSC) was established in 1947 to advise the President on foreign affairs. While the composition of this group varies according to the desires of the President, it usually includes ranking officials from Departments of State and Defense, and the CIA as well as the President's National Security adviser. The power of the NSC was at its peak during the Nixon administration, when Henry Kissinger served as National Security adviser.

The major function of the NSC is to provide the President with information about foreign policy alternatives based on the intelligence received from various government departments and agencies and the NSC's evaluation of that information. One of the strengths of the NSC is its ability to call upon all parts of the bureaucracy for information. However, the NSC is not the President's only source of advice on foreign policy. Here again, as in any area of Presidential activity, the style of the chief executive determines which individuals or groups will have the greatest influence. There are a number of experts in foreign affairs who may be called upon for their advice. Averill Harriman, for example, has held official diplomatic posts in many administrations and has also been active in the informal policymaking process.

Many of the President's informal advisers represent interest groups such as military contractors or the international banks and law firms. These individuals form a foreign policy elite and are likely to be consulted if the subject matter of decision is within their area of activity. Many have served the government in the past, and this experience makes their advice more valuable.

The Foreign Policy Elite

It is unlikely that the President would consider any policy unless he thought it would win the support of the foreign policy elite. President Nixon's diplomatic relations with the People's Republic of China were described as a bold move because of the hostility that had been created during the Korean War and Mao Tse-Tung's support of North Vietnam. However, Nixon could not have taken this new policy direction without the approval of the foreign policy elite.

The foreign policy elite offers the President more than advice. It is an important source of support in gaining the approval of Congress, the bureaucracy, and the media and, through them, public approval. As is true in any area of Presidential action, the authority to command does not always lead to successful implementation. The wholehearted cooperation of many individuals is necessary, and the elite usually has influence throughout government circles and the private sector. It supplies many of the upper-level officials to cabinet departments, and these individuals usually serve several years and then return to professional or business careers.

The Council on Foreign Relations (CFR) is the most influential foreign policy interest group in the nation. Founded in 1921, the CFR is supported by grants from the Rockefeller, Ford, and Carnegie Foundations, as well as contributions from leading corporations. From it have come a large percentage of the nation's secretaries of state and other officials in the Departments of Defense and State. In addition, Presidential advisers are usually members of the CFR. [5]

The CFR's influence is not affected by changes in administration. Secretaries of State Dean Acheson, John Foster Dulles, Dean Rusk, Henry Kissinger, and Cyrus Vance were members of the CFR, and all had served as advisors to the government before being appointed to the cabinet. Political scientist Lester Milbraith has noted that "the Council on Foreign Relations, while not financed by government, works so closely with it that it is difficult to distinguish Council actions stimulated by government from autonomous actions." [6]

The CFR represents a cross-section of the nation's financial, industrial, and academic elites. This distinguishes it from other interest groups or elites, which often are more narrowly based. The implication is that the views of the CFR represent the opinions of several elites, and this has enabled it to maintain its influence in the foreign policy area. The common denominator that links the various groups within the foreign policy elite is their emphasis on the importance of the U.S. role in international affairs. It is this outlook that keeps the nation from withdrawing from its foreign commitments. The post-Vietnam rhetoric about reducing America's world role was inconsistent with the interests of the elites that influence foreign policy.

The Foreign Policy Bureaucracy

The foreign policy bureaucracy consists of the individuals within the executive branch who are active in the policy-making process. Most are middle-level career bureaucrats who keep their jobs through several changes of administration. Like any bureaucracy, the foreign policy bureaucracy tends to continually enlarge its area of activity. This helps explain the difficulty of changing the direction of military or foreign policy. Once a policy has been established, the professional reputations of those who support that policy are on the line. Rather than admitting the possibility of error, they will try to salvage something from the policy regardless of what this may cost. The U.S. experience in Vietnam was largely a result of this bureaucratic tendency. Military officers are asked for their evaluation of the relative strength of the United States and its adversaries under a variety of conditions. Once this estimate has been provided, any errors in judgment are submerged. For example, the U.S. bombing of North Vietnam was intended to weaken the will of the people as well as to destroy supply lines to the south. It failed to do either effectively, but the solution agreed upon was not to halt the bombing but to expand the war into Cambodia.

There are many levels of bureaucracy in the Departments of Defense and State. As policy proposals rise to the upper levels, alternatives that do not have influential backers are weeded out. There is a tendency to strike a policy balance that everyone involved at the upper levels can support. As Henry Kissinger has written, "If one wishes to influence American foreign policy, the time to do it is in the formative period, and in the middle level of the bureaucracy—that of the assistant secretary and his immediate advisors. That is the highest level in which people can still think." [7] Kissinger also expressed the idea that the principal job of foreign policy advisers is to present the President with alternatives. In practice, however, objectivity is difficult to achieve because the alternatives proposed will reflect the biases of those who are involved in the planning.

The Professional Diplomats

Table 15-1 presents the organizational structure of the Department of State. Most of the high-level positions are filled by career diplomats who have the experience to make policy recommendations, though the secretary of state and some ambassadors are presidential appointees.

The influence of the State Department has declined since the end of World War II, though individual secretaries have been influential. John Foster Dulles (in the Eisenhower administration) and Henry Kissinger (in the Ford administration) dominated American foreign policy, but the State Department itself played a less important role. Increasingly, the intelligence

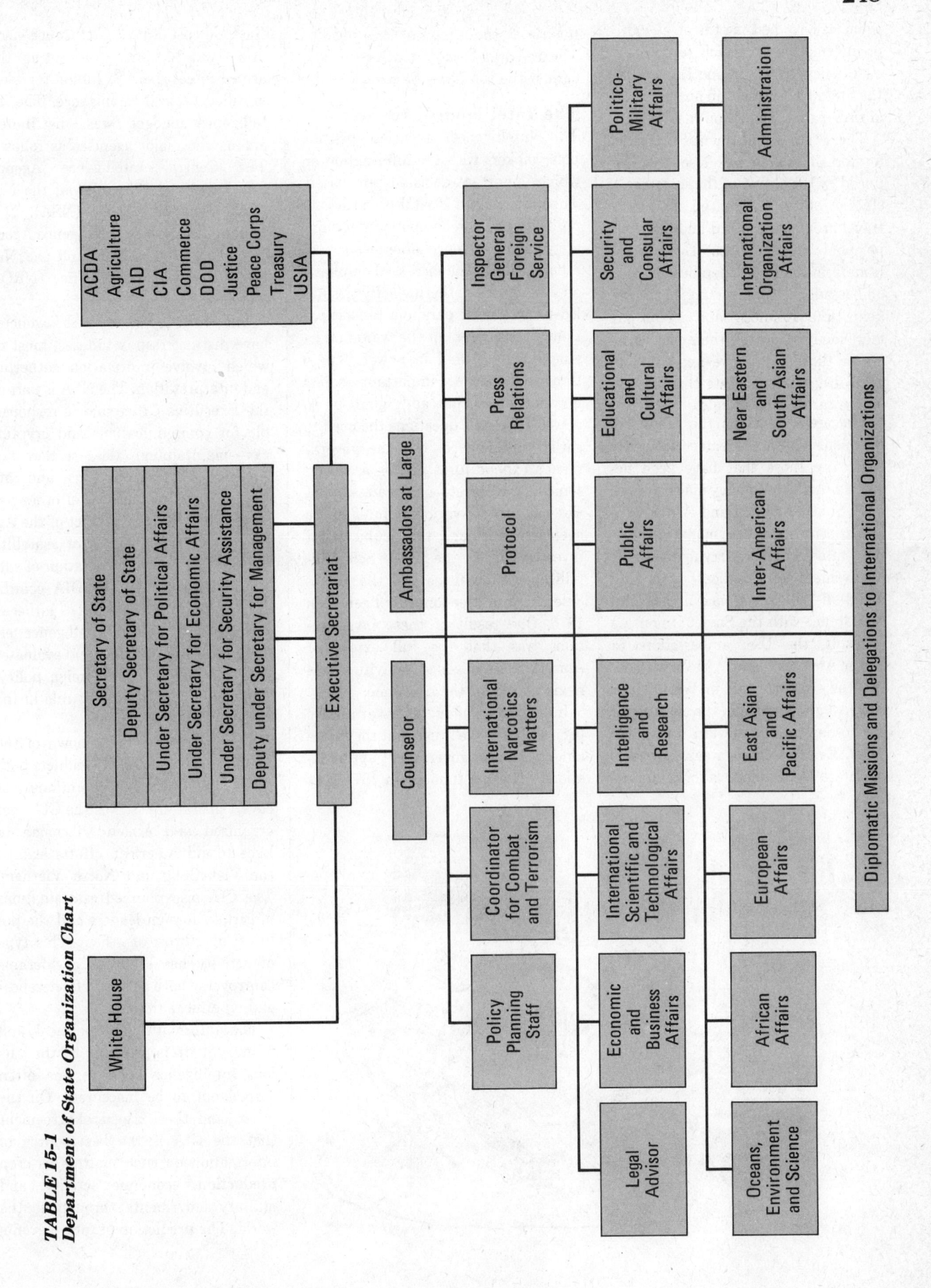

TABLE 15-1
Department of State Organization Chart

agencies have become the chief source of information on which to base foreign policy decisions, and this has left the State Department in an operational rather than a decision-making role.

The State Department's influence on foreign policy has also been reduced by the ability of the secretary of state or other Presidential advisers to travel around the world and maintain personal contact with key foreign leaders instead of depending on U.S. ambassadors. Moreover, activist Presidents like Kennedy and Nixon are more likely to consult their own advisers or those they have appointed to State Department posts than to rely on the career bureaucrats.

The areas in which the State Department has the greatest influence today are those that have been neglected by the top policy makers in the past. South America and Africa were low-priority areas for many years as the United States was trying to end its involvement in Southeast Asia and maintain the appearance of peaceful coexistence with the Soviet Union. As a result, the U.S. ambassadors to South American and African nations and the support staff in Washington played a greater role in the charting of day-to-day policy toward these regions. Even in these areas, however, the State Department is losing its influence as the affairs of the so-called Third World become matters of concern at the top levels of government.

The Intelligence Agencies

The intelligence agencies provide policymakers with the information on which important decisions are based. This information is vital because U.S. military and foreign policy decisions are geared to the probable response of other nations. The increased emphasis on intelligence-gathering activities has led to an almost paranoid preoccupation with secrecy. In the words of Irving Kristol, "Men in power like to think that there are important 'secrets of state' since that adds glamour to power." [9] No one questions the need to gather intelligence, but the government's expenditures in this area and some of the secret—or *covert*—activities of the various intelligence agencies became the subject of investigations by the Senate Select Intelligence Committee and the House Select Committee on Intelligence in 1975. One result of these investigations was that the full extent of American intelligence activities was made public for the first time.

Intelligence budgets have always been secret in the sense that they were hidden in other government appropriations. It was estimated in 1975 that the total cost of U.S. intelligence operations was $4 billion. In addition, the armed forces spent $2 billion for what is called tactical intelligence. The intelligence budget was distributed among the major agencies as follows: The Central Intelligence Agency (CIA) received $750 million; the National Security Agency (NSA), $1.2 billion; the Defense Intelligence Agency (DIA), $100 million; and the National Reconnaissance Office (NRO), $2 billion.[8]

The various intelligence agencies have distinct responsibilities, most of which involve information gathering and interpretation. The NSA is part of the Executive Office and is responsible for communications and cryptology—maintaining the secrecy of American communications and attempting to decode those of other nations. The NRO, an adjunct of the Air Force, is responsible for satellite surveillance and interpretation of satellite photography. The DIA coordinates the information gathered through the tactical intelligence efforts of the armed forces and evaluates it in the light of U.S. foreign policy, thus playing an important role in the policy-making process.

The CIA is the best known of the intelligence agencies. It conducts both intelligence-gathering operations and covert operations. It was the CIA that organized and armed tribesmen in Laos to aid American efforts against the Viet Cong and North Vietnam. The CIA also planned assassinations of certain foreign leaders and the political overthrow of others. This type of activity has aroused considerable controversy both as to its effectiveness and on ethical grounds.

The information on political and military matters provided by the various intelligence agencies has often turned out to be inaccurate. On the other hand, there is general agreement that the CIA is the best source of information on such matters as crop production, economic activity, and military movements throughout the world. The prediction of future events that involve human decisions is more uncertain but more important. Policy makers do not like surprises, but this is what they often have to deal with on the international scene.

U.S. intelligence failed to forecast the 1967 Tet offensive in Vietnam, the 1973 Yom Kippur War in the Middle East, the Turkish invasion of Cyprus in 1974, and the 1974 coup in Portugal. These failures have raised questions as to the value of U.S. intelligence efforts and the expenditures made for this purpose. In the words of a former CIA official, the intelligence official is a "speculative evaluator." However, such guesswork, "subject to error as it has to be, is far preferable to the alternative—the crystal ball." [10]

The information provided by the intelligence agencies has not always been defective. Sometimes it has been ignored. For example, an intelligence estimate made available to Lyndon B. Johnson before the commitment of U.S. troops to Vietnam in 1965 warned, "We will find ourselves mired down in combat that we cannot win and from which we will have extreme difficulty extracting ourselves." [11]

The failures just described illustrate the problems of accuracy and timeliness, as well as responsiveness of policy makers, faced by the intelligence agencies. These problems are significant because the line between intelligence estimates and policy recommendations is a thin one. Intelligence estimates often offer only limited alternatives, and this has sometimes resulted in covert operations that might have been avoided if other alternatives had been considered.

As defined in the Senate Select Committee's *Report on the Foreign and Domestic Intelligence Activities of the United States,* "covert action is the attempt to influence the internal affairs of other nations in support of United States foreign policy in a manner that conceals the participation of the United States Government. Covert action includes political and economic action, propaganda and paramilitary activities." The Senate Committee reported that the CIA had conducted 900 major projects and several thousand smaller projects since 1961. The activities listed ranged from the attempted assassinations of Fidel Castro of Cuba and Patrice Lumumba of the Congo (both failed), to support of the coup against Ngo Dinh Diem, president of South Vietnam. There were also efforts to prevent Chile's President Salvador Allende from taking office, as well as paramilitary operations in Southeast Asia. These activities were under the control of the 40 Committee, established in 1969. The composition of this committee varied, but it always included a total of five members from the Departments of State and Defense and the CIA.

One of the major problems involved in covert activities is that their secrecy precludes high-level supervision. Once the 40 Committee had approved such projects, the operational responsibility passed to the CIA and they were beyond effective oversight. However, the end of the American military commitment in Indochina coupled with congressional investigations has led to a decline in covert operations by the CIA. It has been estimated that the percentage of the CIA's budget allocated to covert activities has declined to 2 percent from a peak of 60 percent. [12]

The extent to which the national interest is helped by covert activities must be measured against the ill will and distrust that are created when such activities become public knowledge. Perhaps a larger question is that of the desirability of covert activities in a nation that prides itself on democratic processes and on moral leadership in international affairs. In response to such questions, the Senate voted in 1976 to establish a 15-person Oversight Committee that would have exclusive authority over the CIA, including budgetary authority, and share oversight responsibilities over the NSA, the DIA, and other military intelligence agencies with the armed services. This should prevent activities such as attempts to assassinate foreign leaders, since it is unlikely that 15 senators would go along with such plans. It is likely that future intelligence activities will concentrate on gathering information to serve U.S. diplomatic efforts rather than on covert activities.

The Military

The military is a major influence on U.S. foreign policy. The almost continual conflict between the United States and the communist world has prevented the military from shrinking to its pre-World War II status. Table 15-2 gives a clear picture of the military presence around the globe.

The tendency to expand and to demand an ever-larger share of the nation's resources may be seen in the Pentagon as in all bureaucracies. Table 15-3 compares the salaries of military and civilian personnel; note the impact of the benefits received by career military officers.

The military is responsible for maintaining the strength to back up American diplomacy. The nature of this task makes it better to overestimate the strength of adversaries and underestimate U.S. power than vice versa: Since the Pentagon wants U.S. strength to be second to none, its evaluations are made on the premise that too much is better than too little. This is particularly true when the defense budget is under attack:

Just like the flowers that bloom in the spring, ominous intelligence estimates about Soviet military developments seem to crop up every time the United States defense budget is in trouble on Capitol Hill.... The intelligence estimates are available only for selective use by a few officials who can emphasize threatening new Soviet developments while ignoring or concealing areas in which the Soviets may be weak. The result is self-serving abuse of intelligence information by officials whose overriding desire is to sell a defense program to Congress. [13]

Congresspeople use military spending as a target when they want to impress the voters with their concern over the federal budget. However,

TABLE 15-2

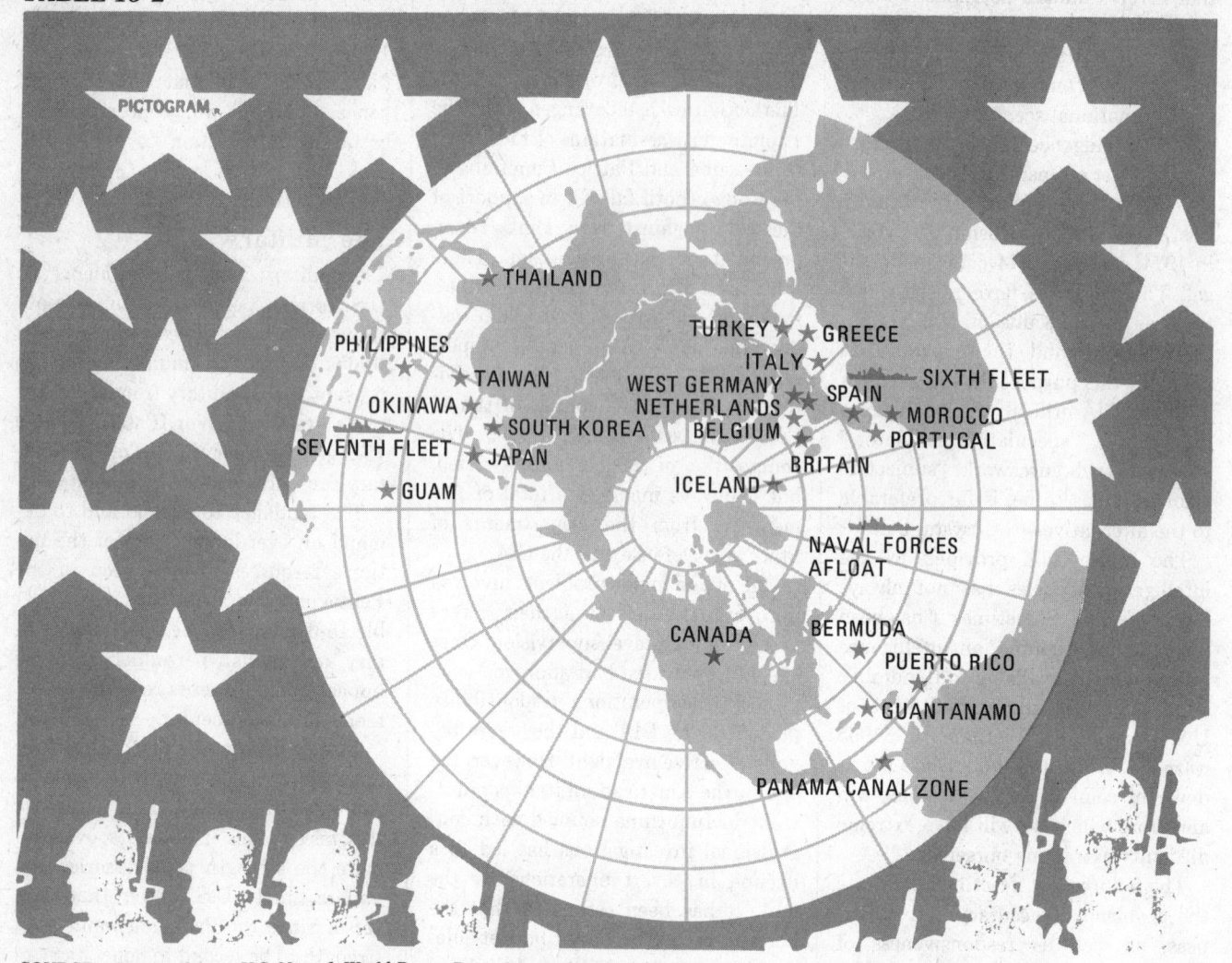

SOURCE: Reprinted from *U.S. News & World Report,* December 29, 1975, p. 21. Copyright 1975 U.S. News & World Report, Inc.

their descriptions of wasteful military expenditures become muted when it comes to bases located in their districts or defense contracts that will benefit their constituents. Usually the liberals in Congress attack the high level of defense spending while the conservatives support the Pentagon's budget requests, but this pattern breaks down when political gains are involved. The issue of military spending was raised in an interesting way in 1975, when Representative William J. Green (Dem., Pa.) proposed an amendment to the defense appropriations bill that would forbid the Defense Department to spend any money on closing the Frankford Arsenal, a munitions works in Green's district, as well as 77 other facilities in 42 states that the Pentagon wanted to close for the sake of economy. The amendment was defeated, but the list of those who voted for the restriction and, in effect, for the continuation of wasteful military spending included several congresspeople who were known for their oppositions to high levels of military spending. As reported at the time,

Where were Congresspersons Bella "Down with the Military" Abzug and Elizabeth "Peace Now" Holtzman? Why, they were right with the "Save Our Bases" bunch. Pacifism may be in fashion but Fort Drum, Fort Hamilton, Fort Wadsworth, the Brooklyn Naval Air station, and the historic Watervliet Arsenal are in New York.

And where was Massachusetts' Father Drinan? Why, voting to hang onto the Weymouth Naval Air Station. And Illinois' Abner Mikva, the great liberal who once said that waste in defense spending exceeded our annual deficit? He was saving the Savanna (Ill.) Army Depot for Savanna.[14]

The preceding passage is from an article written by a conservative newsman who was obviously dissatisfied with what he called the hypocrisy of

TOTAL OF SERVICEMEN NOW OVERSEAS: 497,000

CHANGE IN 1975: DOWN 21,000

IN PACIFIC AND FAR EAST

NOW:	155,000
CHANGE IN 1975:	DOWN 26,000

	Now	Change in 1975
JAPAN, OKINAWA	48,000	DOWN 10,000
SOUTH KOREA	42,000	UP 2,000
THAILAND	10,000	DOWN 16,000
PHILIPPINES	14,000	DOWN 4,000
GUAM	10,000	NONE
TAIWAN	3,000	DOWN 2,000
SEVENTH FLEET	28,000	UP 4,000

IN LATIN AMERICA

NOW:	15,000
CHANGE IN 1975:	DOWN 3,000

	Now	Change in 1975
PANAMA CANAL ZONE	9,000	DOWN 1,000
PUERTO RICO	4,000	DOWN 1,000
GUANTANAMO	2,000	DOWN 1,000

IN EUROPE

NOW:	309,000
CHANGE IN 1975:	UP 11,000

	Now	Change in 1975
WEST GERMANY	220,000	UP 13,000
BRITAIN	21,000	NONE
ITALY	11,000	DOWN 1,000
SPAIN	9,000	NONE
TURKEY	7,000	NONE
GREECE	2,000	DOWN 2,000
ICELAND	3,000	NONE
BELGIUM	2,000	NONE
NETHERLANDS	2,000	NONE
PORTUGAL	1,000	NONE
OTHER COUNTRIES	1,000	NONE
SIXTH FLEET	30,000	UP 1,000

IN OTHER AREAS

NOW:	18,000
CHANGE IN 1975:	DOWN 3,000

	Now	Change in 1975
CANADA	1,000	DOWN 1,000
BERMUDA	1,000	NONE
MOROCCO	1,000	NONE
OTHER COUNTRIES	5,000	DOWN 2,000
NAVAL FORCES AFLOAT	10,000	NONE

Source: U.S. Dept. of Defense

---

blasting military spending on one hand and then voting to keep certain programs for constituents. However, it is more than an attack on the congresspeople named; it is an illustration of the political and economic realities of defense. Defense-related spending is so great that it has gained a momentum of its own and a purpose that goes beyond purely military considerations and spills over into the nation's economic life. It would be politically difficult for any congressperson to vote to slash funds for his or her state or district, despite a desire to cut down on military spending in general. It is likely that many of those who voted for the Green amendment were encouraged to do so by the realization that it could not pass. They gained political points with their constituents while suffering only a degree of embarrassment when the contradictions in their position were exposed. The military thus is in the advantageous position of having the support of congresspeople who will vote for any new weapons system or any increase in force as well as the votes of those who feel that they must back specific portions of defense appropriations bills.

It has been customary for the Pentagon to ask for more money than it actually needs in light of the fact that this figure will almost certainly be reduced by Congress. Since the complexity of military appropriations requests makes specific criticism difficult, the requested budget is usually cut by 4 or 5 percent. However, the 1977 budget was reduced by less than 1 percent and represented a $15.5 billion increase over the budget for the previous year.[15] Clearly, the antimilitary feeling that has arisen in Congress and among the public since the Vietnam War is fading. Any optimism about the possibility of a prolonged peace that would lead to lower defense spending was diminished by the Soviet action in Angola and the fact that the USSR clearly intends to continue its course of intervention in "people's struggles."

The military has always been an inviting target for critics of large government budgets. Its 25 percent share of the budget is highly visible, and the idea of spending enormous amounts to develop weapons systems runs against the grain of a nation that is interested in peace. Yet there is little doubt that the American military establishment will maintain or increase its role because of the continued instability of international relations.

Congress and Foreign Policy

The Vietnam War had a profound impact on the way Congress views its responsibilities in relation to military affairs and foreign policy. There had always been debate over these matters, but most members of Congress had tended to rely on the judgment of the senior members of the armed service and foreign affairs committees. In turn, these senior members rarely opposed the administration's policies. In the early 1970s, however, many congresspeople had the feeling that they had been deceived by President Johnson with regard to Vietnam and that the support they had expressed in the Gulf of Tonkin Resolution had been carried beyond its original intent.

The resignation of President Nixon spurred Congress to establish a more equal relationship with the executive branch. There was a new tendency to challenge U.S. policy and to block it if the majority of congresspeople were opposed. Revelations of the CIA's covert activities in several foreign countries further aroused Congress.

In 1976, Secretary of State Kissinger proposed U.S. financial and military aid to friendly forces in Angola. This was a classic case of a small nation experiencing internal conflict serving as the focus of a confrontation

TABLE 15-3
Military Pay Scales
SOME COMPARISONS
Based on a report by the Senate Appropriations Committee—

	Total Annual Compensation Including Benefits*	
Military Rank	**Military**	**Comparable Civilian Grades**
Major General	$54,815	$41,350
Brigadier General	48,886	41,350
Colonel	43,305	38,849
Lieutenant Colonel	35,101	31,131
Major	29,188	24,485
Captain	24,004	19,749
Top-level Sergeants	20,964	12,813
Lower-level Sergeants	14,711	11,551
Corporal	9,915	10,375
Privates, recruits	7,821	8,326

*Includes estimated cash value of retirement, medical-care, other benefits to service personnel, federal workers.

WHEN YOU ADD UP MILITARY PAY AND BENEFITS—

Rank	Basic Pay	Value of Retirement Benefits	Quarters Allowance	Federal Tax Advantage*	Health Care	Subsistence, Commissary, Benefits	Total Compensation
General	$37,800	$7,709	$3,830	$3,627	$869	$776	$54,611
Lieutenant General or Major General	37,800	7,696	3,830	3,541	1,172	776	54,815
Brigadier General	33,142	6,923	3,830	3,043	1,172	776	48,886
Colonel	29,113	6,155	3,434	2,350	1,477	776	43,305
Lieutenant Colonel	22,950	5,085	3,175	1,638	1,477	776	35,101
Major	18,522	4,314	2,866	1,234	1,477	776	29,188
Captain	14,630	3,638	2,599	884	1,477	776	24,004
First Lieutenant	10,058	588	2,336	675	1,172	776	15,606
Chief Warrant Officer	18,371	4,269	2,765	1,188	1,477	776	28,845
Sergeant Major	14,350	3,619	2,448	905	1,477	1,062	23,861
Master Sergeant	11,948	3,077	2,290	693	1,477	1,062	20,547
Sergeant First Class	10,404	2,730	2,146	667	1,477	1,062	18,486
Staff Sergeant	8,849	2,382	1,994	662	1,477	1,062	16,427
Sergeant	6,466	1,853	1,843	559	1,172	1,062	12,995
Corporal	5,512	322	1,613	537	869	1,062	9,915
Private First Class	5,018	294	961	467	564	946	8,251
Recruit	4,334	254	799	406	564	946	7,305

Note: A number of assumptions were made in the Senate Appropriations Committee's computation of pay and benefits listed. Among these: Basic pay is for average length of service in each grade. Military retirement benefits are not counted for the grades that most people leave before retirement. Numbers of dependents may differ from rank to rank, a factor in health-care benefits and other extras.
*Represents tax savings resulting from tax exempt status of certain allowances.
SOURCE: *U.S. News & World Report,* December 8, 1975, p. 79. Reprinted from *U.S. News & World Report.* Copyright © 1975 U.S. News & World Report, Inc.

TABLE 15-4
The Biggest Defense Contractors (1975 contracts)

Lockheed	$2,080,303,000
Boeing	1,560,827,000
United Technologies	1,407,447,000
McDonnell Douglas	1,397,939,000
Grumman	1,343,335,000
General Dynamics	1,288,756,000
General Electric	1,264,180,000
Litton	1,038,050,000
Hughes Aircraft	1,026,021,000
Rockwell Int'l	732,306,000
Raytheon	680,566,000
Northrop	620,324,000
Textron	545,904,000
A.T.&T.	510,076,000
Sperry Rand	437,103,000
Total top 15	$15,933,137,000
Total contracts	$39,500,615,000

SOURCE: *The New York Times,* May 23, 1976, p. 4F. Copyright © 1976 by The New York Times Company. Reprinted by permission.

between the United States and the Soviet Union. In Angola, the symbolic confrontation was more important than the actual conflict. Kissinger feared that unless the United States showed its willingness to oppose Soviet moves in Africa, there would be other confrontations that could pose greater threats. To the members of Congress who opposed this view, this logic sounded too much like the reasoning behind U.S. involvement in Vietnam. Accordingly, Congress rejected Kissinger's proposal.

The extent to which Congress will involve itself in future foreign policy decisions is unclear. It is possible that Congress will be less interested in participating in the policy-making process as the Carter administration takes hold in 1977. However, one change in congressional attitude is probably permanent: The State Department and the military establishment have more trouble than ever selling the idea that their expertise is beyond question.

The Defense Industry

The Military-Industrial Complex

Defense is big business, and many major corporations depend on government contracts for most of their sales volume. At stake in military contracts is more than the profits of large corporations, however. The economic health of particular areas and jobs for the people who live in those areas also depend on an uninterrupted flow of defense spending. Thus, the interests of the defense contractors and the Pentagon coincide. The former have an economic interest while the latter want all the modern military hardware they can get. The resulting alliance between the military and the defense contractors is one of the most powerful interests in American society.

One of the major reasons for the continued high level of defense spending is the fact that technological advances will always make today's weapons systems obsolete within a decade—the 1977 defense budget includes $11 billion for military research and testing.[16] An additional problem is that no one really knows how much hardware is enough. As noted earlier in the chapter, the military would rather have too much than too little, and this view is reinforced by the interests of the defense contractors. The shared interests of the military and the defense contractors are also strengthened by the good old boy system, which provides the government with highly qualified officials but contributes to a unified view of the nation's defense requirements.

Few will argue about the need to maintain a strong defense. However, some potentially harmful effects can result from the military-industrial influence if it is given free rein. In his farewell address, President Eisenhower described this as follows:

This conjunction of an immense military establishment and a large arms industry is new in the American experience. In the councils of Government, we must guard against the acquisition of unwarranted influence, whether sought or unsought, by the military-industrial complex. The potential for the disastrous rise of misplaced power exists and will persist.[17]

Eisenhower's warning was prophetic. Even advocates of a strong defense will admit that there are numerous cases of waste in the development of weapons systems. The question is how to eliminate such waste without adversely affecting national security.

Arms Exports

Closely allied with the influence of the military-industrial complex in foreign affairs is the matter of arms exports. Such exports have become big business for defense contractors and, as such, offer obvious economic benefits in terms of jobs and profits. Table 15-4 shows the stake the arms industry has in the continuation of such exports. The military supports arms sales because they involve it in the training of foreign armed forces. This expands the military's influence.

There are two strong arguments in favor of the arms trade. The first is economic: It is good for business in the United States. Second, it increases U.S. influence abroad through the need for spare parts for U.S.-made weapons. Also, if we do not sell arms other nations will; this will not only hurt American manufacturers but also deny the United States whatever influence such sales may yield. The Turkish-Greek conflict over Cyprus in 1975 shows how little that influence may be. Both nations were equipped with American weapons, which are sold on the condition that they be used only for defense purposes. Such conditions are impossible to enforce however, and illustrate the limited control of any nation over the actions of another.

Congressional pressure to limit arms sales surfaces periodically. In May 1976, for example, legislation requiring quarterly accounting to Congress was added to a foreign aid bill but vetoed by President Ford. The massive lobbying by the arms industry to defeat the bill is evidence of the importance of arms exports to many of the nation's large corporations. The "white paper" circulated in opposition to the bill stressed the number of jobs that depend on arms exports. "It estimated that 450,000 jobs were 'directly' involved, another 450,000 with subcontractors and suppliers, and another 900,000 'diffused throughout the economy.' " [18] Pressure of this sort is hard to ignore. While the lobbyists' figures are probably inflated, there is little question about the economic significance of arms exports.

The influence of the military and the arms suppliers on foreign policy leans toward maximum American involvement throughout the world. Only in this way can the military achieve what it sees as its mission—the protection of the nation's security—and the defense contractors achieve their goal—steadily increasing sales and profits. The military-industrial complex represents the nation's capability to support policy with strength, but undue influence could lead to a pattern of supporting strength with policy.

Public Opinion and Foreign Policy

The policy alternatives that are discussed at the decision-making level are seldom discussed in the media. It is assumed that the ordinary citizen has little knowledge of and a low level of interest in foreign affairs. There is little question that this has been true in the past. The "politics stops at the water's edge" maxim led to agreement on U.S. policy during the period from 1941 to the Vietnam War years. During the war, however there was a marked shift in public opinion from support to dissatisfaction (after the Tet offensive in 1967) to disillusionment (as the "withdrawal with honor" took place). [19] However, in this case the shift in public opinion was accompanied by a similar change of heart among influential elites and within the government itself. It is hard to tell whether the public grew tired of the war because of increased opposition from respected elites or whether the elites followed the public. In any case, there is little question that we have entered a new era in public attitudes toward foreign policy. In response to the public's demand to be better informed on matters of foreign policy, Jimmy Carter said in a televised debate with President Ford, "Every time we've made a serious mistake in foreign affairs it's been because the American people have been excluded from the process." [20]

Before the Vietnam War anyone who spoke too loudly against defense spending or foreign policy was accused of being "soft on communism." To be sure, there were those who protested against the "brinkmanship" of John Foster Dulles, but these were debates over style rather than substance. Now, for the first time since the end of World War II, the substance of policy has become a subject of controversy. As a result, it is no longer considered unpatriotic to question American involvement in foreign conflicts.

During the early 1970's, public dissatisfaction with U.S. foreign and military policy led to the development of an all-volunteer army to replace the military draft. There was also an attempt to cut military expenditures as if to punish the armed forces for their part in the Vietnam War. The pendulum of public opinion has begun to swing back toward a middle-of-the-road position, however, and during the 1976 Presidential campaign all the candidates called for more effective military spending.

The Conduct of Foreign Policy

The primary goal of U.S. foreign policy is to protect the nation's interests; these include both economic and security considerations. The question of national security is dominated by the rivalry with the Soviet Union that has existed since the end of World War II. The high level of military preparedness, the huge defense budget, and the billions appropriated for the development of still another generation of weapons are evidence of the belief that the Soviet Union continues to pose a major threat to U.S. security. The fact that both the USSR and the United States possess enough nuclear force to destroy the other makes direct threats unthinkable. Accordingly, the conflict has taken the form of confrontations in areas where Soviet and U.S. interests do not clash. The USSR's actions against Hungary, Czechoslovakia and Poland, its support of socialist forces in Angola, and its policy of supplying arms to Arab nations are examples of aggressive actions that did not run the risk of war with the United States. Soviet Premier Khrushchev's placing of missiles in Cuba in 1962 was the most direct such confrontation, and when faced with determined opposition the USSR backed away from the risk of war. Similarly, the United States has fought major wars in Korea

President Carter and aides meeting with NATO Secretary General Josef Luns (left). NATO is the cornerstone of America's military commitment to Western Europe.

and Vietnam but in neither case risked conflict with the USSR.

In protecting their interests, the superpowers are rational enough to confine their military activities to areas in which there is a *power vacuum,* that is, areas in which there are few established major power interests. Power vacuums exist primarily in countries that have little political stability, an inadequate economic base, and no strong ties to either superpower. The existence of a power vacuum encouraged the Soviet Union to intervene in the Angolan conflict through the supply of arms and the use of Cuban troops.

The rivalry between the two superpowers is based on more than the normal economic competition to be expected between two populous industrial nations. The apparent incompatibility of the capitalist and communist systems colors the perceptions of each nation toward the other. Soviet leaders have made it clear that their interpretation of detente in no way precludes efforts to expand communist influence. Nor is the United States likely to refrain from trying to influence other nations in favor of capitalism. The CIA's efforts to unseat the Marxist Allende regime in Chile and to prevent a communist government in Italy in the 1976 election show that when U.S. diplomats speak of the virtue of free elections they do not include elections in which communist candidates are running. The opposition of each superpower to the other's political system results in continued hostility.

In sum, America's world role is dominated by two major considerations. One is the need for an international political presence to buttress American economic interests. The other is the East-West competition that has existed since World War II and poses a threat so serious that it dominates foreign policy. At the same time, the domestic political situation has changed markedly. Although the President is still the primary force in foreign policy, he must take into account the views of several interest groups with a stake in U.S. policy abroad. Moreover, there is greater need to consult with Congress and to win public approval of American activities in foreign countries.

Making Foreign Policy Decisions

While the President has the final authority to negotiate with other nations and to chart America's foreign policy

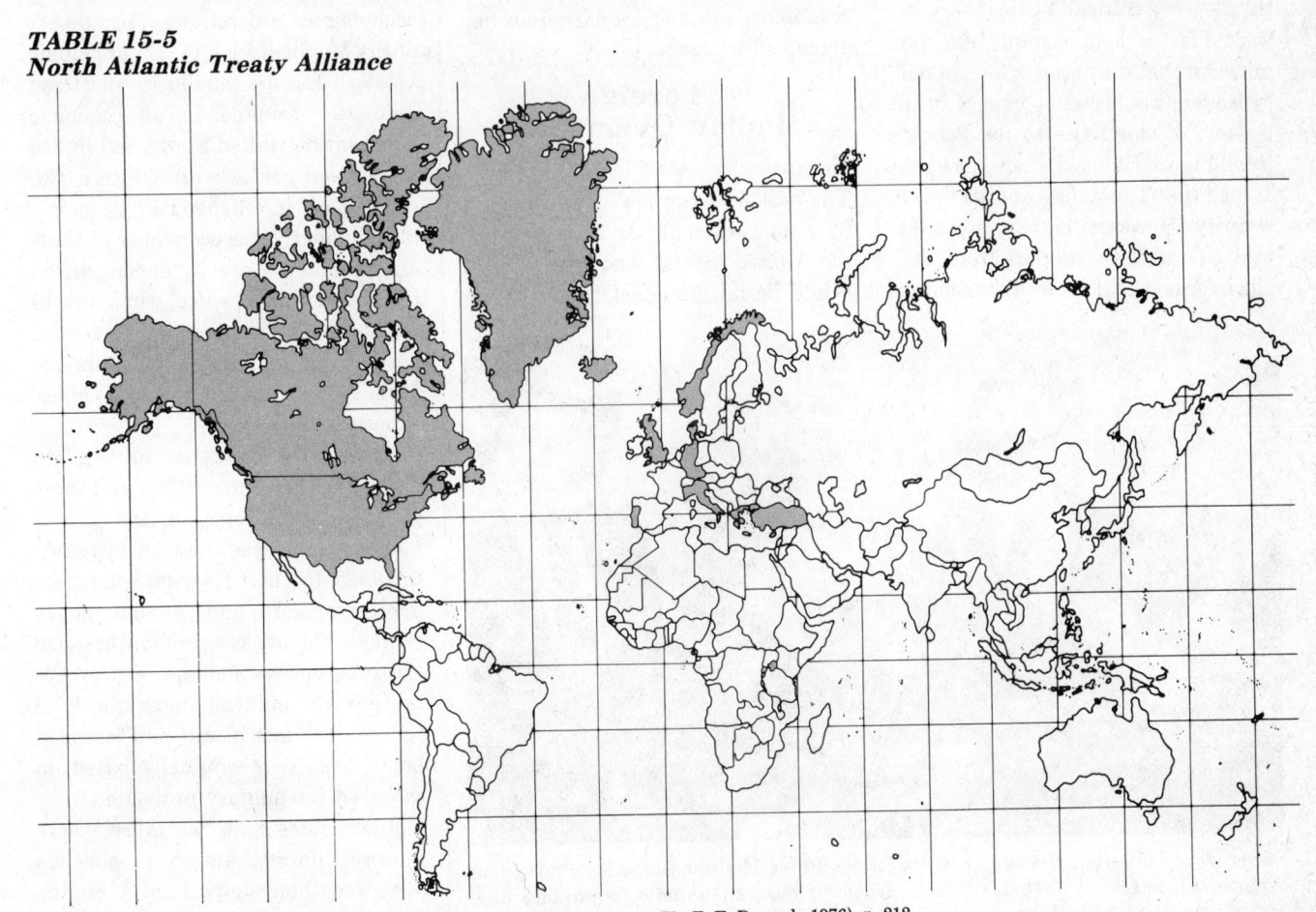

TABLE 15-5
North Atlantic Treaty Alliance

SOURCE: Robert D. Cantor, *Introduction to International Politics* (Itasca, Ill.: F. E. Peacock, 1976), p. 212.

course, his choices are limited by the long-term goals of U.S. policy. Containment of communism has been the cornerstone of U.S. policy since the end of World War II, and American involvement abroad has been directed toward this goal. It was the main reason for U.S. involvement in Korea and Vietnam; it is the reason for continued U.S. support of NATO; and it plays a role in current diplomatic activities. In its broadest sense, this policy has the support of the elite, the bureaucracy, Congress, and the public. Debate is confined to the question of whether or not particular events abroad pose a threat to U.S. security.

The President's choices are also limited by the commitments made by previous administrations. Thus, President Carter is mindful of the commitment of all Presidents since Truman to the survival of Israel and the defense of Japan and Europe. While it is possible to change these obligations, this is very difficult. U.S. policy toward Taiwan is an example of a commitment that the nation's foreign policy leaders would like to change in the interest of closer ties to the People's Republic of China. It can hardly be argued that Taiwan is essential to U.S. security. However, nations are reluctant to withdraw support from their allies for fear that their other commitments will be questioned. Thus, continued presence of U.S. troops in Western Europe is as much to assure our NATO allies of our intent to help them resist any Soviet aggression as it is a result of military considerations.

The nation's policy makers are faced with the facts of increased economic interdependence among nations and the continued rivalry between the capitalist and communist blocs. This mutual distrust makes negotiations between the United States and the Soviet Union more complex than normal international bargaining, which is, in itself, a major task. Political scientist Stanley Hoffman has observed that "there is a risk in international negotiations that whatever are presented as maximum concessions and minimum demands become treated as minimum concessions and maximum demands." [21] In this atmosphere, it is no wonder that the making of foreign policy decisions is an uncertain process among allies and a dangerous one among adversaries.

A Foreign Policy Overview

Europe

The past 30 years have been marked by a series of confrontations between the United States and the USSR. While Berlin, occupied by the Allies (the United States, the USSR, Great Britian, and France), during World War II was the first point of friction between the superpowers, it has proved to be only the tip of the iceberg. After the war, both nations made every effort to solidify their European alliances. These efforts led to the NATO alliance (see Table 15-5), joining the United States, Canada, and the Western European democracies along with Greece and Turkey, and the Soviet-led Warsaw Pact.

During the postwar years, the Soviet Union crushed all resistance to its influence in Eastern Europe, while the West expressed its determination to see these nations regain their independence. However the United States can do little to change the political situation in Eastern Europe, and the Soviet Union is faced with the necessity of coexisting with the Western capitalist countries. The division of Europe into two areas of influence is reinforced by economic considerations. The success of the Marshall Plan (1947) in helping Western Europe rebuild its shattered industries resulted in an economic boom in the United States and linked the United States with Western Europe in an interdependent economic bloc. Similarly, the economies of Eastern Europe are heavily dependent on the Soviet Union, which, while unwilling to give substantial aid, possesses needed raw materials and offers the promise of a large market for its allies' exports.

Despite the close ties of Western Europe to the United States and those of Eastern Europe to the Soviet Union, these areas show an increased tendency to chart their own independent economic and foreign policy courses. The nuclear standoff between the superpowers and the tacit acceptance of the political status quo have reduced the fear of war and loosened bonds that were originally based on the need for military protection. The United States now has allies whose interests do not always parallel its own, and their support for U.S. foreign policy is no longer automatic.

Secretary of State Henry Kissinger meets Israel's Prime Minister Golda Meir during his "shuttle diplomacy" in 1974. Kissinger conducted foreign affairs on a face-to-face basis rather than through usual channels of diplomacy.

Secretary Kissinger meeting King Faisal of Saudi Arabia at the Ri'Assa Palace in Riyadh in 1975.

The Middle East

American policy in the Middle East has been tied to support for Israel, but the economic crisis brought about by the increase in the price of imported oil has changed the situation in that area. A larger portion of the nation's wealth must now be devoted to purchasing oil from the Middle East. This raises the prices of other products and services and leaves less for the consumer to spend.

The tremendous wealth that has accrued to the oil-producing nations has stimulated a new arms race: Iran and Saudi Arabia are purchasing arms far beyond their foreseeable needs. The wisdom of the U.S. arms trade in this region is certain to become a source of debate as the Carter Administration designs its own foreign policy. In the past, the United States has sold enough arms to Israel to enable it to offset its manpower disadvantage in conflicts with surrounding Arab states. However, the newfound wealth of the Arab nations together with increasing U.S. dependence on oil as an energy source have brought about a shift from all-out support for Israel to a supportive but more balanced approach.

The Middle East offers U.S. industry tremendous economic potential, and future U.S. policy in that area will be affected by economic considerations to a greater extent than in the past. Previous U.S. policy toward Israel was based on the need to support a democratic nation against Soviet influence. Today, by contrast, the economic ties that link the United States with the Middle East appear to have become more significant than the East-West conflict. However, the future of U.S. relations with Middle Eastern nations will be largely determined by the ability of the United States to bring about a diplomatic solution to the festering Arab-Israeli dispute.

Asia

The United States' interests in Asia are closely allied with those of Japan, which serves both as an important trading partner and as a buffer to potential expansion by the People's Republic of China. Since the end of World War II, Japan has relied on a defense pact with the United States for its security. The U.S. garrison of 40,000 troops in South Korea is considered part of the defense of Japan.

China and Japan dominate Asia, and the future direction of U.S. policy in Asia depends more on the actions of the new Chinese leadership than on policy decisions made in Washington.

President Idi Amin celebrates his seven years as leader of Uganda. Allegations of Amin's repressive methods have raised fundamental questions concerning our role in the internal affairs of other nations.

If the Soviet Union and the People's Republic develop closer relations, this will be perceived as a potential threat to Japan and therefore, to U.S. interests in Asia. However, if the conflict between the two most populous communist nations continues, there will be little reason for direct U.S. involvement in future Asian conflicts.

Latin America

Latin America is the only major region of the world that has been relatively untouched by the U.S.-Soviet rivalry (except during the Cuban missile crisis). As a result of Castro's failure to successfully "export" his revolution to other Latin American nations, the communist regime in Cuba is no longer regarded as a threat to U.S. security. To be sure, there are communist movements in most Latin American countries, but none appear to be closely allied to the USSR.

Because Latin America has been relatively free from international conflict, it has received little attention from the United States despite its important economic investment in this area. Presidents Roosevelt, Kennedy, and Johnson included better relations with Latin America among their foreign policy goals, but other events diverted their attention. Moreover, the Latin American nations maintained their diplomatic distance; while the region is considered to be within the American sphere of influence, it has for the most part followed its own course. The failure of American policy makers to pay more attention to Latin America despite its nearness and its economic potential illustrates the pecking order of diplomatic priorities: Areas that are in a state of turmoil get top priority while others get much less attention.

Africa

The developing nations of Africa had been neglected by the United States until Soviet and Cuban aid to Angola in 1975-1976 led to the establishment of a socialist regime in that nation. The reasons for the shift from disinterest to attention provide some insight into the motivations behind foreign policy. Lack of political stability in many of the newly formed African nations has discouraged economic investment despite the mineral riches of the continent. Economic activity and political influence go hand in hand; thus, there was little reason for the United States to involve itself politically in Africa until the USSR attempted to expand its influence there. However, wherever one superpower goes the other is sure to follow.

The major internal threats to stability in Africa are posed by the white minority rule in Rhodesia and South Africa. These regimes are under increasing pressure to change their policies and allow black majority rule. The probability of war in Africa is hard to judge, but it is unlikely that either the United States or the USSR would be uninvolved in such a conflict.

Summary

The United States is heavily involved in economic and political activities throughout the world. Since the world situation is always in a state of flux, the United States must maintain the intelligence agencies that provide policy makers with accurate information and the military strength that backs up its diplomatic efforts. The nation cannot withdraw from its international role without suffering heavy economic losses and risking Soviet expansion, which might ultimately threaten its very survival.

Foreign policy is intertwined with domestic politics because national resources are limited; the government's spending in one area of national life often limits its spending in other areas. There was optimistic talk in the late 1960s about the "peace dividend" that would result from withdrawal from the Vietnam War; it was anticipated that large sums of money would become available to domestic programs. Instead, military expenditures have remained high and the American commitment abroad has changed little. Thus, owing "to" the facts of international life there is no easy way for the United States to maintain its position of relative power without a heavy investment in foreign and military policy.

NOTES

[1] *U.S. News & World Report,* April 26, 1976, p. 16.

[2] Hans J. Morgenthau, *Politics Among Nations,* 5th ed. (New York: Knopf, 1973), p. 21.

[3] Henry Kissinger, quoted by James Reston in *The New York Times,* October 13, 1974, p. 34L. Copyright © 1974 by The New York Times Company. Reprinted by permision.

[4] Raymond F. Hopkins and Richard W. Mansbach, *Structure and Process in International Politics* (New York: Harper & Row, 1973), p. 156.

[5] Thomas R. Dye, *Who's Running America?* (Englewood Cliffs, N.J.: Prentice-Hall, 1976), p. 112.

[6] Lester Milbrath, "Interest Groups in Foreign Policy," in James N. Rosenau, ed., *Domestic Sources of Foreign Policy* (New York: Free Press, 1967), p. 247.

[7] Henry Kissinger, "Bureaucracy and Policymaking: The Effects of Insiders and Outsiders on the Policy Process," in Morton H. Halperin and Arnold Kanter, eds., *Readings in American Foreign Policy: A Bureaucratic Perspective* (Boston: Little, Brown, 1973), p. 85.

[8] Leslie H. Gelb in "Spy Inquiries, Begun Among Public Outrage, End in Indifference," *The Philadelphia Inquirer,* May 12, 1976, p. 4-A.

[9] Irving Kristol in "Secrets of State," *The Wall Street Journal,* November 14, 1974, p. 18.

[10] Sherman Kent, quoted by Arthur Cox in "U.S. Intelligence: Why It Failed and What to Do," *The Philadelphia Inquirer,* November 2, 1975, p. 1-L.

[11] Ibid, p. 2-L.

[12] *The Wall Street Journal,* September 24, 1976, p. 1.

[13] John W. Finney in "Soviet Might Grows and Grows at U.S. Budget Time," *The New York Times,* November 2, 1975, p. 4E. Copyright © 1975 by The New York Times Company. Reprinted by permission.

[14] Michael Killian in "Military Spending Has Strange Allies," *The Philadelphia Inquirer,* November 5, 1975, p. 15-A.

[15] John W. Finney in "Cut in Arms Bill in House Is Smallest in Decade," *The New York Times,* May 14, 1976, p. 1.

[16] Paul Lewis in "All Systems Are Go for the Arms Makers," *The New York Times,* May 23, 1976, p. 4F.

CHAPTER 15 CROSSWORD PUZZLE

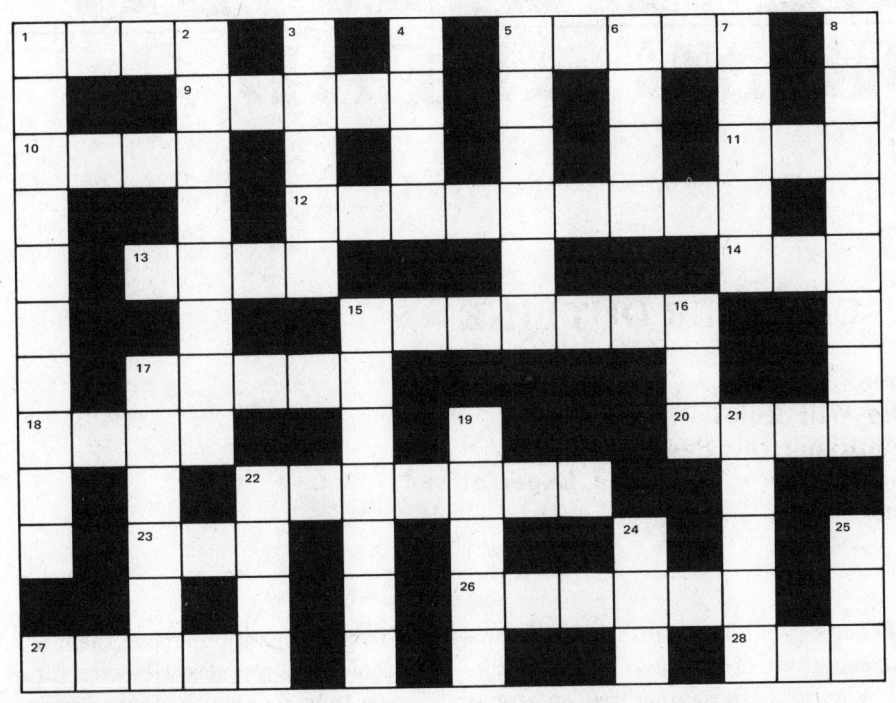

Across
1. "The Man in the ___ Mask"
5. The energy crisis serves to emphasize the ___-dependence of nations.
9. Helped
10. Type of mop or storm
11. Nothing; zero
12. The ___ has the greatest impact on foreign policy.
13. ___ of living
14. Drunkard
15. Domestic prosperity is closely related to the nation's ___ interests
17. Group of people on a jury
18. Matinee ___
20. Withhold; refuse to acknowledge
22. Post World War II foreign policy has been marked by ___ with the Soviet Union
23. Frozen water
26. ___ operations attempt to influence the actions of other nations while concealing the involvement of the United States
27. Rendezvous
28. Hearing organ

Down
1. The military-___ complex forms one of the most influential interest groups in the nation.
2. The ordering of priorities in the international sphere is often called the ___ interest.
3. Highly skilled
4. Out of work
5. Ask (to a party)
6. Opposite of "false"
7. Landlords' incomes
8. The nation's diplomatic efforts are often dependent on the potential strength of the ___.
15. Strawberry, chocolate, vanilla, etc.
16. ___ out (fall asleep)
17. There is a fine line between presenting options and suggesting ___ initiatives.
19. Cut into broad, thin pieces
21. Those individuals who maintain influence in foreign policy deliberations are referred to as the foreign policy ___.
22. Relax
24. Wager
25. Diplomacy and ___ are closely related.

---

[17] Quoted by John J. Finney in "The Military-Industrial Complex Grows More So," *The New York Times,* April 11, 1976, p. 2E. Copyright © 1976 by The New York Times Company. Reprinted by permission.

[18] James McCartney in "How Arms Makers Won the Day," *The Philadelphia Inquirer,* May 12, 1976, p. 4-A.

[19] Louis Harris, *The Anguish of Change* (New York: W. F. Norton, 1973), pp. 58-67.

[20] Quoted in *The New York Times,* p. 36L.

[21] Stanley Hoffman in "Time for a Sweeping Israeli Initiative," *The New York Times,* March 27, 1975, p. 31.

CHAPTER 16
LOOKING AHEAD

CHAPTER OUTLINE

Introduction
Who Will Rule?
Mobilizing the People
The Politics of Lowered Expectations
Conclusion

Introduction

American politics could well be described as the politics of change. The only prediction that can safely be made about the nation's political future is that the relationship between the government and the people will be different than it is now, and the growth of the government in the twentieth century offers little reason to believe this relationship will become less complicated. Among other things, the nation's diplomatic and economic role has led to interdependence among nations as well as among individuals. Domestically, this puts the government in the position of mediating conflicts among competing groups.

The nation's political traditions stress the freedom of the individual to pursue his or her destiny with a minimum of governmental interference. However, the trend toward big government has replaced the word *minimum* with *maximum*. It is the balance between individual freedom, individual responsibility, and the role of the government that is at the core of many of today's political dilemmas. However, the individual is not alone in the expectation, if not the demand, that the government be more helpful. Representatives of the nation's largest corporations praise the free enterprise system while demanding a variety of government programs to insulate them from the uncertainties of the economic world.

Clearly, neither individuals nor corporations can have it both ways. If they see the government as the answer to all their problems, they can hardly complain about the increase in governmental power. Only a government with enough power to control the activities of individuals and groups in society will have access to the resources needed to meet such demands. There is a price that must be paid for every benefit of government action in terms of restriction and regulation; those who are unhappy about "big" government must be willing to settle for "little" government aid. And those who seek ever-increasing aid must recognize that it will be accompanied by increased regulation.

Who Will Rule?

More groups have become active in the political process than formerly, and the competition among them has become more complex. However, it remains to be seen which of these groups will emerge as dominant political forces. One of the paradoxes of American politics is that the individuals with the most to gain from political participation are the most reluctant to do so. For that matter, those in the lower socioeconomic groups are least likely to vote. If this situation continues, the nation will be led by people who reflect the views of the more politically active groups. In short, the nation will be led in the future, as in the past, by representatives of a numerically small but economically powerful elite. However, if minority groups can mobilize their members into an effective political force the ground rules will change and more weight will be given to the demands of groups that formerly were excluded from the political process. While there is little evidence that such a change is taking place, rising educational levels may result in a rearrangement of the power structure in the near future.

The ability of the government to provide an economic climate that offers most citizens a rising standard of living is probably the most important factor in encouraging political participation. Political activism is effective only when a cause is considered worth working for. "Preservation of democracy" or "good government" crusades lack the emotional appeal that might accompany citizen protest during an economic depression.

Mobilizing the People

Traditionally, political parties have served as a means of mobilizing the public for political participation. However, the parties appear to have lost the ability to perform this function. The inability of legislative majorities to maintain a high degree of party unity illustrates the decline in the importance of party labels. The rise of interest groups with the resources to appeal to the government in their own behalf has also made parties less active in national politics. While interest groups formerly formed coalitions in support of major parties, there is an increasing tendency for groups to avoid "partisan" conflicts, saving their energies for the narrower range of issues that directly affect them. It is possible that the Federal Election Campaign Act will place more power in the hands of the party organizations, but similar action will be required at the state level before one can talk of renewed party influence. Until then, however, it is likely that powerful interest groups will continue to dominate American politics.

The Politics of Lowered Expectations

Public acceptance of the way the government allocates resources is based on the recognition that there is not enough to go around. Not everyone will be content with his or her share, but few will be dissatisfied enough to threaten the nation's political stability.

Recently, it has become fashionable to speak of the need to lower the expectations of the American people. Basically, this notion springs from the realization that resources are limited and that some will be used up within our lifetimes. In addition, whatever resources remain will undoubtedly cost more. This fact has serious political implications. It is impossible to separate the vitality of a political system from its ability to provide its citizens with a standard of living that comes close to their expectations. To put it simply, will the American people lower their expectations because of the need to devote more income to necessities? Or will the inability of many people to afford luxuries that they have become accustomed to result in increasing demands on the government to reallocate resources? These are not abstract questions, though they represent the kind of problems Americans have not had to deal with in the past.

Perhaps the most significant fact presented in this book is that the economy must provide over 2 million new jobs a year to prevent unemployment from climbing, a far higher number of jobs than have been created each year in the past. Where will these jobs come from? And what will be the political result of failure to create these jobs?

It is generally believed that it is the function of the government to do what people can not do for themselves, and that our political institutions will succeed in creating the necessary jobs. Maybe so, but this is the sort of test that the government has not met successfully in the past. However, the political institutions provided in the Constitution have proved very flexible in adjusting to new conditions. The threat of scarce resources may well pose a new and different kind of challenge.

Conclusion

It is easier to point to the problems facing American society than to suggest solutions. The nation's political system has always been in a state of flux, and perhaps major obstacles will be overcome in the future as they have in the past. Certainly it should be possible for a nation to adjust to changing conditions, whether through changes in the political power structure or by reexamining the way resources are allocated. However, such changes require a return to cooperation rather than conflict among groups. Moreover, adjusting to change will require that the more powerful groups recognize the claims of groups that have been politically inactive in the past. This is the essence of democratic self-rule. If competing groups in society are unable to cooperate in solving their problems, their disputes will be decided by the government. With every governmental action, a little bit of individual freedom is lost. And it is the preservation of individual freedom that should be the nation's highest priority.

APPENDIX

CONSTITUTION OF THE UNITED STATES

WE THE PEOPLE of the United States, in Order to form a more perfect Union, establish Justice, insure domestic Tranquility, provide for the common defence, promote the general Welfare, and secure the Blessings of Liberty to ourselves and our Posterity, do ordain and establish this CONSTITUTION for the United States of America.

ARTICLE 1

SECTION 1. All legislative Powers herein granted shall be vested in a Congress of the United States, which shall consist of a Senate and House of Representatives.

SECTION 2. [1] The House of Representatives shall be composed of Members chosen every second Year by the People of the several States, and the Electors in each State shall have the Qualifications requisite for Electors of the most numerous Branch of the State Legislature.

[2] No Person shall be a Representative who shall not have attained to the Age of twenty-five Years, and been seven Years a Citizen of the United States, and who shall not, when elected, be an Inhabitant of that State in which he shall be chosen.

[3] *[Representatives and direct Taxes shall be apportioned among the several States which may be included within this Union, according to their respective Numbers, which shall be determined by adding to the whole Number of free Persons, including those bound to Service for a Term of Years, and excluding Indians not taxed, three fifths of all other Persons.] The actual Enumeration shall be made within three Years after the first Meeting of the Congress of the United States, and within every subsequent Term of ten Years, in such Manner as they shall by Law direct. The Number of Representatives shall not exceed one for every thirty Thousand, but each State shall have at Least one Representative; and until such enumeration shall be made, the State of New Hampshire shall be entitled to chuse three, Massachusetts eight, Rhode-Island and Providence Plantations one, Connecticut five, New-York six, New Jersey four, Pennsylvania eight, Delaware one, Maryland six, Virginia ten, North Carolina five, South Carolina five, and Georgia three.

[4] When vacancies happen in the Representation from any State, the Executive Authority thereof shall issue Writs of Election to fill such vacancies.

[5] The House of Representatives shall chuse their Speaker and other Officers; and shall have the sole Power of Impeachment.

[1] SECTION 3. **The Senate of the United States shall be composed of two Senators from each State, [chosen by the Legislature] thereof, for six Years; and each Senator shall have one Vote.

[2] Immediately after they shall be assembled in Consequence of the first Election, they shall be divided as equally as may be into three Classes. The Seats of the Senators of the first Class shall be vacated at the Expiration of the Second Year, of the second Class at the Expiration of the fourth Year, and of the third Class at the Expiration of the sixth Year, so that one third may be chosen every second Year; [and if Vacancies happen by Resignation, or otherwise, during the Recess of the Legislature of any State, the Executive thereof may make temporary Appointments until the next Meeting of the Legislature, which shall then fill such Vacancies]. ***

[3] No Person shall be a Senator who shall not have attained to the Age of thirty Years, and been nine Years a Citizen of the United States, and who shall not, when elected, be an inhabitant of that State for which he shall be chosen.

*The part included in heavy brackets was repealed by section 2 of Amendment XIV.
**The part included in heavy brackets was repealed by section 1 of Amendment XVII.
***The part included in heavy brackets was changed by clause 2 of Amendment XVII.
NOTE.—The superior number preceding the paragraphs designates the number of the clause.

[4] The Vice President of the United States shall be President of the Senate, but shall have no Vote, unless they be equally divided.

[5] The Senate shall chuse their other Officers, and also a President pro tempore, in the absence of the Vice President, or when he shall exercise the Office of President of the United States.

[6] The Senate shall have the sole Power to try all Impeachments. When sitting for that Purpose, they shall be on Oath or Affirmation. When the President of the United States is tried, the Chief Justice shall preside: And no Person shall be convicted without the Concurrence of two thirds of the Members present.

[7] Judgment in Cases of Impeachment shall not extend further than to removal from Office, and disqualification to hold and enjoy any Office of honor, Trust, or Profit under the United States: but the Party convicted shall nevertheless be liable and subject to Indictment, Trial, Judgment, and Punishment, according to Law.

SECTION 4. [1] The Times, Places and Manner of holding Elections for Senators and Representatives, shall be prescribed in each State by the Legislature thereof; but the Congress may at any time by Law make or alter such Regulations, except as to the Places of chusing Senators.

[2] The Congress shall assembly at least once in every Year, and such Meeting shall [be on the first Monday in December,] unless they shall by Law appoint a different Day.*

SECTION 5. [1] Each House shall be the Judge of the Elections, Returns, and Qualifications of its own Members, and a Majority of each shall constitute a Quorum to do Business; but a smaller Number may adjourn from day to day, and may be authorized to compel the Attendance of absent Members, in such Manner, and under such Penalties as each House may provide.

[2] Each House may determine the Rules of its Proceedings, punish its Members for disorderly Behavior, and, with the Concurrence of two thirds, expel a Member.

[3] Each House shall keep a Journal of its Proceedings, and from time to time publish the same, excepting such Parts as may in their Judgment require Secrecy; and the Yeas and Nays of the Members of either House on any question shall, at the Desire of one fifth of those Present, be entered on the Journal.

[4] Neither House, during the Session of Congress, shall, without the Consent of the other, adjourn for more than three days, nor to any other Place than that in which the two Houses shall be sitting.

SECTION 6. [1] The Senators and Representatives shall receive a Compensation for their Services, to be ascertained by Law, and paid out of the Treasury of the United States. They shall in all Cases, except Treason, Felony and Breach of the Peace, be privileged from Arrest during their Attendance at the Session of their respective Houses, and in going to and returning from the same; and for any Speech or Debate in either House, they shall not be questioned in any other Place.

[2] No Senator or Representative shall, during the Time for which he was elected, be appointed to any civil Office under the Authority of the United States, which shall have been created, or the Emoluments whereof shall have been encreased during such time; and no Person holding any Office under the United States, shall be a Member of either House during his Continuance in Office.

SECTION 7. [1] All Bills for raising Revenue shall originate in the House of Representatives; but the Senate may propose or concur with Amendments as on other Bills.

[2] Every Bill which shall have passed the House of Representatives and the Senate, shall, before it become a Law, be presented to the President of the United States; if he approve he shall sign it, but if not he shall return it, with his Objections to that House in which it shall have originated, who shall enter the Objections at large on their Journal, and proceed to reconsider it. If after such Reconsideration two thirds of that House shall agree to pass the Bill, it shall be sent, together with the Objections, to the other House, by which it shall likewise be reconsidered, and if approved by two thirds of that House, it shall become a Law. But in all such Cases the Votes of both Houses shall be determined by Yeas and Nays, and the Names of the Persons voting for and against the Bill shall be entered on the Journal of each House respectively. If any Bill shall not be returned by the President within ten Days (Sundays excepted) after it shall have been presented to him, the Same shall be a Law, in like Manner as if he had signed it, unless the Congress by their Adjournment prevent its Return, in which Case it shall not be a Law.

*The part included in heavy brackets was changed by section 2 of Amendment XX.

[3] Every Order, Resolution, or Vote to which the Concurrence of the Senate and House of Representatives may be necessary (except on a question of Adjournment) shall be presented to the President of the United States; and before the Same shall take Effect, shall be approved by him, or being disapproved by him, shall be repassed by two thirds of the Senate and House of Representatives, according to the Rules and Limitations prescribed in the Case of a Bill.

SECTION 8. The Congress shall have Power To lay and collect Taxes, Duties, Imposts and Excises, to pay the Debts and provide for the common Defence and general Welfare of the United States; but all Duties, Imposts and Excises shall be uniform throughout the United States;

[2] To borrow money on the credit of the United States;

[3] To regulate Commerce with foreign Nations, and among the several States, and with the Indian Tribes;

[4] To establish an uniform Rule of Naturalization, and uniform Laws on the subject of Bankruptcies throughout the United States;

[5] To coin Money, regulate the Value thereof, and of foreign Coin, and fix the Standard of Weights and Measures;

[6] To provide for the Punishment of counterfeiting the Securities and current Coin of the United States;

[7] To Establish Post Offices and post Roads;

[8] To promote the Progress of Science and useful Arts, by securing for limited Times to Authors and Inventors the exclusive Right to their respective Writings and Discoveries;

[9] To constitute Tribunals inferior to the supreme Court;

[10] To define and punish Piracies and Felonies committed on the high Seas, and Offenses against the Law of Nations;

[11] To declare War, grant Letters of Marque and Reprisal, and make Rules concerning Captures on Land and Water;

[12] To raise and support Armies, but no Appropriation of Money to that Use shall be for a longer Term than two Years;

[13] To provide and maintain a Navy;

[14] To make Rules for the Government and Regulation of the land and naval Forces;

[15] To provide for calling forth the Militia to execute the Laws of the Union, suppress insurrections and repel Invasions;

[16] To provide for organizing, arming, and disciplining the Militia, and for governing such Part of them as may be employed in the Service of the United States, reserving to the States respectively, the Appointment of the Officers, and the Authority of training the Militia according to the discipline prescribed by Congress;

[17] To exercise exclusive Legislation in all Cases whatsoever, over such District (not exceeding ten Miles square) as may, by Cession of particular States, and the acceptance of Congress, become the Seat of the Government of the United States, and to exercise like Authority over all Places purchased by the Consent of the Legislature of the State in which the Same shall be, for the Erection of Forts, Magazines, Arsenals, dock-Yards, and other needful Buildings;—And

[18] To make all Laws which shall be necessary and proper for carrying into Execution the foregoing Powers, and all other Powers vested by this Constitution in the Government of the United States, or in any Department or Officer thereof.

SECTION 9. [1] The Migration or Importation of Such Persons as any of the States now existing shall think proper to admit, shall not be prohibited by the Congress prior to the Year one thousand eight hundred and eight, but a tax or duty may be imposed on such Importation, not exceeding ten dollars for each Person.

[2] The privilege of the Writ of Habeas Corpus shall not be suspended, unless when in Cases of Rebellion or Invasion the public Safety may require it.

[3] No Bill of Attainder or ex post facto Law shall be passed.

[4] *No capitation, or other direct, Tax shall be laid, unless in Proportion to the Census or Enumeration herein before directed to be taken.

[5] No Tax or Duty shall be laid on Articles exported from any State.

[6] No preference shall be given by any Regulation of Commerce or Revenue to the Ports of one State over those of another: nor shall Vessels bound to, or from, one State be obliged to enter, clear, or pay Duties in another.

[7] No money shall be drawn from the Treasury, but in Consequence of Appropriations made by Law; and a regular Statement and Account of the Receipts and Expenditures of all public Money shall be published from time to time.

*See also Amendment XVI.

[8] No title of Nobility shall be granted by the United States: And no Person holding any Office of Profit or Trust under them, shall, without the Consent of the Congress, accept of any present, Emolument, Office, or Title, of any kind whatever, from any King, Prince, or foreign State.

SECTION 10. [1] No State shall enter into any Treaty, Alliance, or Confederation; grant Letters of Marque and Reprisal; coin Money; emit Bills of Credit; make any Thing but gold and silver Coin a Tender in Payment of Debts; pass any Bill of Attainder, ex post facto Law, or Law impairing the Obligation of Contracts, or grant any Title of Nobility.

[2] No State shall, without the Consent of the Congress, lay any Imposts or Duties on Imports or Exports, except what may be absolutely necessary for executing its inspection Laws; and the net Produce of all Duties and Imposts, laid by any State on Imports or Exports, shall be

for the Use of the Treasury of the United States; and all such Laws shall be subject to the Revision and Control of the Congress.

³ No State shall, without the Consent of Congress, lay any duty of Tonnage, keep Troops, or Ships of War in time of Peace, enter into any Agreement or Compact with another State, or with a foreign Power, or engage in War, unless actually invaded, or in such imminent Danger as will not admit of delay.

ARTICLE II

SECTION 1. ¹ The executive Power shall be vested in a President of the United States of America. He shall hold his Office during the Term of four Years, and together with the Vice-President, chosen for the same Term, be elected, as follows:

² Each State shall appoint, in such Manner as the Legislature thereof may direct, a Number of Electors, equal to the whole Number of Senators and Representatives to which the State may be entitled in the Congress: but no Senator or Representative, or Person holding an Office of Trust or Profit under the United States, shall be appointed an Elector.

*[The Electors shall meet in their respective States, and vote by Ballot for two persons of whom one at least shall not be an Inhabitant of the same State with themselves. And they shall make a list of all the Persons voted for, and of the Number of Votes for each; which List they shall sign and certify, and transmit sealed to the Seat of the Government of the United States, directed to the President of the Senate. The President of the Senate shall, in the Presence of the Senate and House of Representatives, open all the Certificates, and the Votes shall then be counted. The Person having the greatest Number of votes shall be the President, if such Number by a Majority of the whole Number of Electors appointed; and if there be more than one who have such Majority, and have an equal Number of Votes, then the House of Representatives shall immediately chuse by Ballot one of them for President; and if no Person have a Majority, then from the five highest on the List the said House shall in like Manner chuse the President. But in chusing the President, the Votes shall be taken by States, the Representation from each State having one Vote; A quorum for this Purpose shall consist of a Member or Members from two thirds of the States, and a Majority of all the States shall be necessary to a Choice. In every Case, after the Choice of the President the Person having the greatest Number of Votes of the Electors shall be the Vice President. But if there should remain two or more who have equal Votes, the Senate shall chuse from them by Ballot the Vice-President.]

³ The Congress may determine the Time of chusing the Electors and the Day on which they shall give their Votes; which Day shall be the same throughout the United States.

⁴ No person except a natural born Citizen, or a Citizen of the United States, at the time of the Adoption of this Constitution, shall be eligible to the Office of President; neither shall any Person be eligible to that Office who shall not have attained to the Age of thirty-five Years, and been fourteen Years a Resident within the United States.

⁵ In case of the removal of the President from Office, or of his Death, Resignation or Inability to discharge the Powers and Duties of the said Office, the same shall devolve on the Vice President, and the Congress may by Law provide for the Case of Removal, Death, Resignation or Inability, both of the President, and Vice President, declaring what Officer shall then act as President, and such Officer shall act accordingly, until the Disability be removed, or a President shall be elected.

*This paragraph has been superseded by Amendment XII.

⁶ The President shall, at stated Times, receive for his Services, a Compensation, which shall neither be encreased nor diminished during the Period for which he shall have been elected, and he shall not receive within that Period any other Emolument from the United States, or any of them.

⁷ Before he enter on the Execution of his Office, he shall take the following Oath or Affirmation:—"I do solemnly swear (or affirm) that I will faithfully execute the Office of President of the United States, and will to the best of my Ability, preserve, protect and defend the Constitution of the United States."

SECTION 2. ¹ The President shall be Commander in Chief of the Army and Navy of the United States, and of the Militia of the several States, when called into the actual Service of the United States; he may require the Opinion, in writing, of the principal Officer in each of the executive Departments, upon any subject relating to the Duties of their respective Offices, and he shall have Power to grant Reprieves and Pardons for Offences against the United States, except in Cases of Impeachment.

² He shall have Power, by and with the Advice and Consent of the Senate, to make Treaties, provided two thirds of the Senators present concur; and he shall nominate, and by and with the Advice and Consent of the Senate, shall appoint Ambassadors, other public Ministers and

Consuls, Judges of the supreme Court, and all other Officers of the United States, whose Appointments are not herein otherwise provided for, and which shall be established by Law; but the Congress may by Law vest the Appointment of such inferior Officers, as they think proper, in the President alone, in the Courts of Law, or in the Heads of Departments.

[3] The President shall have Power to fill up all Vacancies that may happen during the Recess of the Senate, by granting Commissions which shall expire at the End of their next Session.

SECTION 3. He shall from time to time give to the Congress Information of the State of the Union, and recommend to their Consideration such Measures as he shall judge necessary and expedient; he may, on extraordinary Occasions, convene both Houses, or either of them, and in Case of Disagreement between them, with Respect to the Time of Adjournment, he may adjourn them to such Time as he shall think proper; he shall receive Ambassadors and other public Ministers; he shall take Care that the Laws be faithfully executed, and shall Commission all the Officers of the United States.

SECTION 4. The President, Vice President and all civil Officers of the United States, shall be removed from Office on Impeachment for, and Conviction of, Treason, Bribery, or other high Crimes and Misdemeanors.

ARTICLE III

SECTION 1. The judicial Power of the United States, shall be vested in one supreme Court, and in such inferior Courts as the Congress may from time to time ordain and establish. The Judges, both of the supreme and inferior Courts, shall hold their Offices during good Behavior, and shall, at stated Times, receive for their Services a Compensation which shall not be diminished during their Continuance in Office.

SECTION 2. [1] The judicial Power shall extend to all Cases, in Law and Equity, arising under this Constitution, the Laws of the United States, and Treaties made, or which shall be made, under their Authority;—to all Cases affecting Ambassadors, other public Ministers and Consuls;—to all Cases of admiralty and maritime Jurisdiction;—to Controversies to which the United States shall be a Party;—to Controversies between two or more States;—between a State and Citizens of another State;*—between Citizens of different States;— between Citizens of the same State claiming Lands under Grants of different States, and between a State, or the Citizens thereof, and foreign States, Citizens or Subjects.

[2] In all Cases affecting Ambassadors, other public Ministers and Consuls, and those in which a State shall be Party, the supreme Court shall have original Jurisdiction. In all the other Cases before mentioned, the supreme Court shall have appellate Jurisdiction, both as to Law and Fact, with such Exceptions, and under such Regulations as the Congress shall make.

[3] The trial of all Crimes except in Cases of Impeachment shall be by Jury; and such Trial shall be held in the State where the said Crimes shall have been committed; but when not committed within any State, the Trial shall be at such Place or Places as the Congress may by Law have directed.

SECTION 3. [1] Treason against the United States shall consist only in levying War against them, or, in adhering to their Enemies, giving them Aid and Comfort.

*This clause has been affected by Amendment XI.

No Person shall be convicted of Treason unless on the Testimony of two Witnesses to the same overt Act, or on Confession in open Court.

[2] The Congress shall have power to declare the Punishment of Treason, but no Attainder of Treason shall work Corruption of Blood, or Forfeiture except during the Life of the Person attainted.

ARTICLE IV

SECTION 1. Full Faith and Credit shall be given in each State to the public Acts, Records, and judicial Proceedings of every other State. And the Congress may by general Laws prescribe the Manner in which such Acts, Records and Proceedings shall be proved, and the Effect thereof.

SECTION 2. [1] The Citizens of each State shall be entitled to all Privileges and Immunities of Citizens in the several States.

[2] A Person charged in any State with Treason, Felony, or other Crime, who shall flee from Justice, and be found in another State, shall on demand of the executive Authority of the State from which he fled, be delivered up, to be removed to the State having Jurisdiction of the Crime.

[3] *[No person held to Service or Labour in one State, under the Laws thereof, escaping into another, shall, in Consequence of any Law or Regulation therein, be discharged from such

Service or Labour, but shall be delivered up on Claim of the Party to whom such Service or Labour may be due.]

SECTION 3. ¹ New States may be admitted by the Congress into this Union; but no new State shall be formed or erected within the Jurisdiction of any other State; not any State be formed by the Junction of two or more States, or parts of States, without the Consent of the Legislatures of the States concerned as well as of the Congress.

² The Congress shall have Power to dispose of and make all needful Rules and Regulations respecting the Territory or other Property belonging to the United States; and nothing in this Constitution shall be so construed as to Prejudice any Claims of the United States, or of any particular State.

SECTION 4. The United States shall guarantee to every State in this Union a Republican Form of Government, and shall protect each of them against Invasion; and on Application of the Legislature, or of the Executive (when the Legislature cannot be convened) against domestic Violence.

ARTICLE V

The Congress, whenever two thirds of both Houses shall deem it necessary, shall propose Amendments to this Constitution, or, on the Application of the Legislatures of two thirds of the several States, shall call a Convention for proposing Amendments, which, in either Case, shall be valid to all Intents and Purposes, as part of this Constitution when ratified by the Legislatures of three fourths of the several States, or by Conventions in three fourths thereof, as the one or the other Mode of Ratification may be proposed by the Congress; Provided that no Amendment which may be made prior to the Year One thousand eight hundred and eight shall in any Manner affect the first and fourth Clauses in the Ninth Section of the first Article; and that no State, without its Consent, shall be deprived of its equal Suffrage in the Senate.

ARTICLE VI

¹ All Debts contracted and Engagements entered into, before the Adoption of this Constitution shall be as valid against the United States under this Constitution, as under the Confederation.

² This Constitution, and the Laws of the United States which shall be made in Pursuance thereof; and all Treaties made, or which shall be made, under the Authority of the United States, shall be the supreme Law of the Land; and the Judges in every State shall be bound thereby, any Thing in the Constitution or Laws of any State to the Contrary notwithstanding.

³ The Senators and Representatives before mentioned, and the Members of the several State Legislatures, and all executive and judicial Officers, both of the United States and of the several States, shall be bound by Oath or Affirmation, to support this Constitution; but no religious Test shall ever be required as a Qualification to any Office or public Trust under the United States.

ARTICLE VII

The Ratification of the Conventions of nine States, shall be sufficient for the Establishment of this Constitution between the States so ratifying the Same.

DONE in Convention by the Unanimous Consent of the States present the Seventeenth Day of September in the Year of our Lord one thousand seven hundred and Eighty seven and of the Independence of the United States of America the Twelfth. IN WITNESS whereof We have hereto subscribed our Names,

GO WASHINGTON—
Presidt. and deputy from Virginia.

[Signed also by the deputies of twelve States.]

New Hampshire.
JOHN LANGDON,   NICHOLAS GILMAN.
Massachusetts.
NATHANIEL GORHAM, RUFUS KING.
Connecticut.
WM. SAML. JOHNSON, ROGER SHERMAN.
New York.
ALEXANDER HAMILTON.
New Jersey.
WIL: LIVINGSTON,   WM. PATERSON,
DAVID BREARLEY,   JONA: DAYTON.

B FRANKLIN,
ROBT MORRIS,
THOS. FITZSIMONS,
JAMES WILSON,

GEO: READ,
JOHN DICKINSON,
JACO: BROOM,

JAMES McHENRY,
DANL CARROLL.

JOHN BLAIR—

WM. BLOUNT,
HU WILLIAMSON.

J. RUTLEDGE,
CHARLES PINCKNEY,

WILLIAM FEW,
Attest:

Pennsylvania.
THOMAS MIFFLIN,
GEO. CLYMER,
JARED INGERSOLL,
GOUV MORRIS.

Delaware.
GUNNING BEDFORD, jun,
RICHARD BASSETT.

Maryland.
DAN OF ST THOS. JENIFER,

Virginia.
JAMES MADISON Jr.

North Carolina.
RICH'D DOBBS SPAIGHT,

South Carolina.
CHARLES COTESWORTH PINCKNEY,
PIERCE BUTLER.

Georgia.
ABR BALDWIN.
WILLIAM JACKSON, *Secretary.*

RATIFICATION OF THE CONSTITUTION

The Constitution was adopted by a convention of the States on September 17, 1787, and was subsequently ratified by the several States, on the following dates: Delaware, December 7, 1787; Pennsylvania, December 12, 1787; New Jersey, December 18, 1787; Georgia, January 2, 1788; Connecticut, January 9, 1788; Massachusetts, February 6, 1788; Maryland, April 28, 1788; South Carolina, May 23, 1788; New Hampshire, June 21, 1788; Virginia, June 25, 1788; New York, July 26, 1788; North Carolina, November 21, 1789; Rhode Island, May 29, 1790. It was declared in operation September 13, 1788; by a resolution of the Continental Congress.

ARTICLES IN ADDITION TO, AND AMENDMENT OF, THE CONSTITUTION OF THE UNITED STATES OF AMERICA, PROPOSED BY CONGRESS, AND RATIFIED BY THE LEGISLATURES OF THE SEVERAL STATES, PURSUANT TO THE FIFTH ARTICLE OF THE ORIGINAL CONSTITUTION

AMENDMENT I

Congress shall make no law respecting an establishment of religion, or prohibiting the free exercise thereof; or abridging the freedom of speech, or of the press; or the right of the people peaceably to assemble and to petition the Government for a redress of grievances.

AMENDMENT II

A well regulated Militia, being necessary to the security of a free State, the right of the people to keep and bear Arms, shall not be infringed.

AMENDMENT III

No Soldier shall, in time of peace be quartered in any house, without the consent of the Owner, not in time of war, but in a manner to be prescribed by law.

AMENDMENT IV

The right of the people to be secure in their persons, houses, papers, and effects, against unreasonable searches and seizures, shall not be violated, and no Warrants shall issue, but upon probable cause, supported by Oath or affirmation and particularly describing the place to be searched, and the persons or things to be seized.

AMENDMENT V

No person shall be held to answer for a capital, or otherwise infamous crime, unless on a presentment or indictment of a Grand Jury, except in cases arising in the land or naval forces, or in the Militia, when in actual service in time of War or public danger; nor shall any person be subject for the same offence to be twice put in jeopardy of life or limb; nor shall be compelled in any criminal case to be a witness against himself, nor be deprived of life, liberty, or property, without due process of law; nor shall private property be taken for public use, without just compensation.

AMENDMENT VI

In all criminal prosecutions, the accused shall enjoy the right to a speedy and public trial, by an impartial jury of the State and district wherein the crime shall have been committed, which district shall have been previously ascertained by law, and to be informed of the nature and cause of the accusation: to be confronted with the witnesses against him; to have compulsory process for obtaining witnesses in his favor, and to have the Assistance of Counsel for his defence.

AMENDMENT VII

In suits at common law, where the value in controversy shall exceed twenty dollars, the right of trial by jury shall be preserved, and no fact tried by jury, shall be otherwise reexamined in any Court of the United States, than according to the rules of the common law.

AMENDMENT VIII

Excessive bail shall not be required, nor excessive fines imposed, nor cruel and unusual punishments inflicted.

AMENDMENT IX

The enumeration in the Constitution, of certain rights, shall not be construed to deny or disparage others retained by the people.

AMENDMENT X

The powers not delegated to the United States by the Constitution, nor prohibited by it to the States, are reserved to the States respectively, or to the people.
(Ratification of first ten amendments completed December 15, 1791.)

AMENDMENT XI

The Judicial power of the United States shall not be construed to extend to any suit in law or equity, commenced or prosecuted against one of the United States by Citizens of another State, or by Citizens or Subjects of any Foreign State.
(Declared ratified January 8, 1798.)

AMENDMENT XII

The electors shall meet in their respective states and vote by ballot for President and Vice-President, one of whom, at least, shall not be an inhabitant of the same state with themselves; they shall name in their ballots the person voted for as President, and in distinct ballots the person voted for as Vice-President, and they shall make distinct lists of all persons voted for as President, and of all persons voted for as Vice-President, and of the number of votes for each, which lists they shall sign and certify, and transmit sealed to the seat of the government of the United States, directed to the President of the Senate;—The President of the Senate shall, in presence of the Senate and House of Representatives, open all the certificates and the votes shall then be counted;—The person having the greatest number of votes for President, shall be the President, if such number be a majority of the whole number of Electors appointed; and if no person have such majority, then from the persons having the highest numbers not exceeding three on the list of those voted for as President, the House of Representatives shall choose immediately, by ballot, the President. But in choosing the President, the votes shall be taken by states, the representation from each state having one vote; a quorum for this purpose shall consist of a member or members from two thirds of the states, and a majority of all the states shall be necessary to a choice. *[And if the House of Representatives shall not choose a President whenever the right of choice shall devolve upon them, before the fourth day of March next following, then the Vice-President shall act as President, as in the case of the death or other constitutional disability of the President.]— The person having the greatest number of votes as Vice-President, shall be the Vice-

President, if such number be a majority of the whole number of Electors appointed, and if no person have a majority, then from the two highest numbers on the list, the Senate shall choose the Vice-President; a quorum for the purpose shall consist of two thirds of the whole number of Senators, and a majority of the whole number shall be necessary to a choice. But no person constitutionally ineligible to the office of President shall be eligible to that of Vice-President of the United States.

(Declared ratified September 25, 1804.)

AMENDMENT XIII

SECTION 1. Neither slavery nor involuntary servitude, except as a punishment for crime whereof the party shall have been duly convicted, shall exist within the United States, or any place subject to their jurisdiction.

SECTION 2. Congress shall have power to enforce this article by appropriate legislation.

(Declared ratified December 18, 1865.)

AMENDMENT XIV

SECTION 1. All persons born or naturalized in the United States, and subject to the jurisdiction thereof, are citizens of the United States and of the State wherein they reside. No State shall make or enforce any law which shall abridge the privileges or immunities of citizens of the United States; nor shall any State deprive any person of life, liberty, or property, without due process of law; nor deny to any person within its jurisdiction the equal protection of the laws.

*The part included in heavy brackets has been superseded by section 3 of Amendment XX.

SECTION 2. Representatives shall be apportioned among the several States according to their respective numbers, counting the whole number of persons in each State, excluding Indians not taxed. But when the right to vote at any election for the choice of electors for President and Vice-President of the United States, Representatives in Congress, the Executive and Judicial officers of a State, or the members of the Legislature thereof, is denied to any of the male inhabitants of such State, being twenty-one years of age, and citizens of the United States, or in any way abridged, except for participation in rebellion, or other crime, the basis of representation therein shall be reduced in the proportion which the number of such male citizens shall bear to the whole number of male citizens twenty-one years of age in such State.

SECTION 3. No person shall be a Senator or Representative in Congress, or elector of President and Vice-President, or hold any office, civil or military, under the United States, or under any State, who, having previously taken an oath, as a member of Congress, or as an officer of the United States, or as a member of any State legislature, or as an executive or judicial officer of any State, to support the Constitution of the United States, shall have engaged in insurrection or rebellion against the same, or given aid or comfort to the enemies thereof. But Congress may by a vote of two thirds of each House, remove such disability.

SECTION 4. The validity of the public debt of the United States, authorized by law, including debts incurred for payment of pensions and bounties for services in suppressing insurrection or rebellion, shall not be questioned. But neither the United States nor any State shall assume or pay any debt or obligation incurred in aid of insurrection or rebellion against the United States, or any claim for the loss or emancipation of any slave; but all such debts, obligations and claims shall be held illegal and void.

SECTION 5. The Congress shall have power to enforce, by appropriate legislation, the provisions of this article.

(Declared ratified July 28, 1868.)

AMENDMENT XV

SECTION 1. The right of citizens of the United States to vote shall not be denied or abridged by the United States or by any State on account of race, color, or previous condition of servitude.

SECTION 2. The Congress shall have power to enforce this article by appropriate legislation.

(Declared ratified March 30, 1870.)

AMENDMENT XVI

The Congress shall have power to lay and collect taxes on incomes, from whatever source derived, without apportionment among the several States, and without regard to any census or enumeration.

(Declared ratified February 25, 1913.)

AMENDMENT XVII

The Senate of the United States shall be composed of two Senators from each State, elected by the people thereof, for six years; and each Senator shall have one vote. The electors in each State shall have the qualifications requisite for electors of the most numerous branch of the State legislatures.

When vacancies happen in the representation of any State in the Senate, the executive authority of such State shall issue writs of election to fill such vacancies: *Provided,* That the legislature of any State may empower the executive thereof to make temporary appointments until the people fill the vacancies by election as the legislature may direct.

This amendment shall not be so construed as to affect the election or term of any Senator chosen before it becomes valid as part of the Constitution.

(Declared ratified May 31, 1913.)

[AMENDMENT XVIII

[SECTION 1. After one year from the ratification of this article the manufacture, sale, or transportation of intoxicating liquors within, the importation thereof into, or the exportation thereof from the United States and all territory subject to the jurisdiction thereof for beverage purposes is hereby prohibited.

[SECTION 2. The Congress and the several States shall have concurrent power to enforce this article by appropriate legislation.

[SECTION 3. This article shall be inoperative unless it shall have been ratified as an amendment to the Constitution by the legislatures of the several States, as provided in the Constitution, within seven years from the date of the submission hereof to the States by the Congress.]*

(Declared ratified January 29, 1919.)

AMENDMENT XIX

The right of citizens of the United States to vote shall not be denied or abridged by the United States or by any State on account of sex.

Congress shall have power to enforce this article by appropriate legislation.

(Declared ratified August 26, 1920.)

AMENDMENT XX

SECTION 1. The terms of the President and Vice-President shall end at noon on the 20th day of January, and the terms of Senators and Representatives at noon on the 3d day of January, of the years in which such terms would have ended if this article had not been ratified; and the terms of their successors shall then begin.

SECTION 2. The Congress shall assemble at least once in every year, and such meeting shall begin at noon on the 3d day of January, unless they shall by law appoint a different day.

SECTION 3. If, at the time for the beginning of the term of the President, the President elect shall have died, the Vice-President elect shall become President. If a President shall not have been chosen before the time fixed for the beginning of his term, or if the President elect shall have failed to qualify, then the Vice-President elect shall act as President until a President shall have qualified; and the Congress may by law provide for the case wherein neither a President elect nor a Vice-President elect shall have qualified, declaring who shall then act as President, or the manner in which one who is to act shall be selected, and such person shall act accordingly until a President or Vice-President shall have qualified.

SECTION 4. The Congress may by law provide for the case of the death of any of the persons from whom the House of Representatives may choose a President whenever the right of choice shall have devolved upon them and for the case of the death of any of the persons from whom the Senate may choose a Vice-President whenever the right of choice shall have devolved upon them.

SECTION 5. Sections 1 and 2 shall take effect on the 15th day of October following the ratification of this article.

SECTION 6. This article shall be inoperative unless it shall have been ratified as an amendment to the Constitution by the legislatures of three-fourths of the several States within seven years from the date of its submission.

(Declared ratified February 6, 1933.)

AMENDMENT XXI

SECTION 1. The eighteenth article of amendment to the Constitution of the United States is hereby repealed.

SECTION 2. The transportation or importation into any State, Territory, or possession of the United States for delivery or use therein of intoxicating liquors, in violation of the laws thereof, is hereby prohibited.

SECTION 3. This article shall be inoperative unless it shall have been ratified as an amendment to the Constitution by conventions in the several States, as provided in the Constitution, within seven years from the date of the submission hereof to the States by the Congress.

(Declared ratified December 5, 1933.)

AMENDMENT XXII

SECTION 1. No person shall be elected to the office of the President more than twice, and no person who has held the office of President, or acted as President, for more than two years of a term to which some other person was elected President shall be elected to the office of the President more than once. But this article shall not apply to any person holding the office of President when this Article was proposed by the Congress, and shall not prevent any person who may be holding the office of President, or acting as President, during the term within which this Article becomes operative from holding the office of President or acting as President during the remainder of such term.

SECTION 2. This article shall be inoperative unless it shall have been ratified as an amendment to the Constitution by the legislatures of three-fourths of the several States within seven years from the date of its submission to the States by the Congress.

(Declared ratified March 1, 1951.)

*Amendment XVIII was repealed by section 1 of Amendment XXI.

AMENDMENT XXIII

SECTION 1. The District constituting the seat of Government of the United States shall appoint in such manner as the Congress may direct:

A number of electors of President and Vice President equal to the whole number of Senators and Representatives in Congress to which the District would be entitled if it were a State, but in no event more than the least populous State; they shall be in addition to those appointed by the States, but they shall be considered, for the purposes of the election of President and Vice President, to be electors appointed by a State; and they shall meet in the District and perform such duties as provided by the twelfth article of amendment.

SECTION 2. The Congress shall have power to enforce this article by appropriate legislation.

(Declared ratified April 3, 1961.)

AMENDMENT XXIV

SECTION 1. The right of citizens of the United States to vote in any primary or other election for President or Vice President, for electors for President or Vice President, or for Senator or Representative in Congress, shall not be denied or abridged by the United States or any State by reason of failure to pay any poll tax or other tax.

SECTION 2. The Congress shall have power to enforce this article by appropriate legislation.

(Declared ratified February 4, 1962.)

AMENDMENT XXV

SECTION 1. In case of the removal of the President from office or of his death or resignation, the Vice President shall become President.

SECTION 2. Whenever there is a vacancy in the office of the Vice President, the President shall nominate a Vice President who shall take office upon confirmation by a majority vote of both Houses of Congress.

SECTION 3. Whenever the President transmits to the President pro tempore of the Senate and the Speaker of the House of Representatives his written declaration that he is unable to discharge the powers and duties of his office, and until he transmits to them a written declaration to the contrary, such powers and duties shall be discharged by the Vice President as Acting President.

SECTION 4. Whenever the Vice President and a majority of either the principal officers of the executive departments or of such other body as Congress may by law provide, transmit to the President pro tempore of the Senate and the Speaker of the House of Representatives their written declaration that the President is unable to discharge the powers and duties of his office, the Vice President shall immediately assume the powers and the duties of the office as Acting President.

Thereafter, when the President transmits to the President pro tempore of the Senate and Speaker of the House of Representatives his written declaration that no inability exists, he shall resume the powers and duties of his office unless the Vice President and a majority of either the principal officers of the executive department or of such other body as Congress may by law provide, transmit within four days to the President pro tempore of the Senate and the Speaker of the House of Representatives their written declaration that the President is unable to discharge the powers and duties of his office. Thereupon Congress shall decide the issue, assembling within forty-eight hours for that purpose if not in session. If the Congress, within twenty-one days after receipt of the latter written declaration, or, if Congress is not in session, within twenty-one days after Congress is required to assemble, determines by two-thirds vote of both Houses that the President is unable to discharge the powers and duties of his office, the Vice President shall continue to discharge the same as Acting President; otherwise, the President shall resume the powers and duties of his office.

(Declared ratified February 10, 1967)

AMENDMENT XXVI

SECTION 1. The right of citizens of the United States, who are eighteen years of age or older, to vote shall not be denied or abridged by the United States or by any State on account of age.

SECTION 2. The Congress shall have power to enforce this article by appropriate legislation.

(Declared ratified July 1, 1971)

PROPOSED AMENDMENT

SECTION 1. Equality of rights under the law shall not be denied or abridged by the United States or by any State on account of sex.

SECTION 2. The Congress shall have the power to enforce, by appropriate legislation, the provisions of this Article.

(Passed Congress March 24, 1972)

BIBLIOGRAPHY

Chapter 1—The American Political System

Bachrach, P., *The Theory of Democratic Elitism* (Boston: Little, Brown, 1967).

Becker, Carl, *Freedom and Responsibility in the American Way of Life* (New York: Vintage Books, 1960).

Boorstin, D., *The Genius of American Politics* (Chicago: University of Chicago Press, 1953).

Charlesworth, J. C., ed., *Contemporary Political Analysis* (New York: Free Press, 1967).

Dahl, Robert A., *Pluralist Democracy in the United States: Conflict and Consent* (Chicago: Rand McNally, 1967).

Davies, James C., *Human Nature in Politics* (New York: Wiley, 1963).

Downs, A., *An Economic Theory of Democracy* (New York: Harper & Row, 1957).

Easton, D., *A Framework for Political Analysis* (Englewood Cliffs, N.J.: Prentice-Hall, 1965).

Hartz, Louis M., *The Liberal Tradition in America* (New York: Harcourt Brace Jovanovich, 1955).

Held, V., *The Public Interest and Individual Interests* (New York: Basic Books, 1970).

Kariel, H. S., *The Decline of American Pluralism* (Stanford, Cal.: Stanford University Press, 1961).

Lasswell, Harold, *Politics: Who Gets What, When, How* (Cleveland: Meridian Books, 1936).

Lindblom, C. E., *The Intelligence of Democracy* (New York: Free Press, 1965).

Lowi, T. J., *The End of Liberalism* (New York: W. W. Norton, 1969).

McCoy, Charles A., and Playford, John, *Apolitical Politics: A Critique of Behavioralism* (New York: Thomas Y. Crowell, 1967).

McNeil, Elton B., *The Nature of Human Conflict* (Englewood Cliffs, N.J.: Prentice-Hall, 1965).

Newfield, J., and J. Greenfield, *A Populist Manifesto* (New York: Warner Books, 1972).

Toqueville, A. de, *Democracy in America* (Garden City, N.Y.: Doubleday, 1969).

Chapter 2—The Constitution

Beard, C. A., *An Economic Interpretation of the Constitution of the United States* (New York: Macmillan, 1954). Originally published in 1913.

Becker, C. L., *The Declaration of Independence* (New York: Knopf, 1942).

Boorstin, D. J., *The Americans: The Colonial Experience* (New York: Random House, 1958).

Commager, H. S., *Majority Rule and Minority Rights* (New York: Oxford University Press, 1943).

Craven, W. F., *The Legend of the Founding Fathers* (New York: New York University Press, 1956).

Dahl, R. A., *A Preface to Democratic Theory* (Chicago: University of Chicago Press, 1956).

Hofstadter, R., *The American Political Tradition and the Men Who Made It* (New York: Knopf, 1973).

Jay, J., J. Madison, and A. Hamilton, *The Federalist Papers* (New York: New American Library, 1961). Originally published in 1788.

Mason, A. T., *The States Rights Debate: Antifederalism and the Constitution* 2d ed. (New York: Oxford University Press, 1972).

Miller, J. C., *Origins of the American Revolution* (Stanford, Cal.: Stanford University Press, 1959).

Pritchett, C. H., *The American Constitution* (New York: McGraw-Hill, 1968).

Rossiter, C., *1787: The Grand Convention* (New York: Macmillan, 1966).

Smith, D. G., *The Convention and the Constitution: The Political Ideas of the Founding Fathers* (New York: St. Martin's Press, 1965).

Smith, J. A., *The Spirit of American Government* (Cambridge, Mass.: Harvard University Press, 1965).

Sutherland, A. E., *Constitutionalism in America: Origin and Evolution of its Fundamental Ideas* (New York: Blaisdell, 1965).

Tugwell, R. G., *The Emerging Constitution* (New York: Harper's Magazine Press, 1974).

Warren, C., *The Making of the Constitution* (Boston: Little, Brown, 1937).

Wood, G. S., *The Creation of the American Republic: 1776-1787* (Chapel Hill: University of North Carolina Press, 1969).

Chapter 3—American Federalism

Bennett, W. H., *American Theories of Federalism* (University, Ala.: University of Alabama Press, 1964).

Elazar, D. J., *American Federalism: A View from the States*, 2d ed. (New York: Thomas Y. Crowell, 1972).

——— et al., eds., *Cooperation and Conflict: Readings in American Federalism* (Itasca, Ill.: F. E. Peacock, 1969).

Goldwin, R. A., ed., *A Nation of States: Essays on the American Federal System*, 2d ed. (Chicago: Rand McNally, 1974).

Grodzins, M., *The American System*, ed. D. J. Elazar (Chicago: Rand McNally, 1966).

Leach, R. H., *American Federalism* (New York: W. W. Norton, 1970).

Patterson, J. T., *The New Deal and the States: Federalism in Transition* (Princeton: Princeton University Press, 1969).

Reagan, M. D., *The New Federalism* (New York: Oxford University Press, 1972).

Reuss, H. S., *Revenue-Sharing: Crutch or Catalyst for State and Local Government?* (New York: Praeger, 1970).

Riker, W. H., *Federalism: Origin, Operation, Significance* (Boston: Little, Brown, 1964).

Schmidhauser, J. R., *The Supreme Court as Final Arbiter in Federal-State Relations, 1789-1957* (Chapel Hill: University of North Carolina Press, 1958).

Sharkansky, I., *The Maligned States: Policy Accomplishments, Problems, and Opportunities* (New York: McGraw-Hill, 1972).

Sundquist, J. L., with D. W. Davis, *Making Federalism Work: A Study of Program Coordination at the Community Level* (Washington, D.C.: Brookings Institution, 1969).

Wright, D. S., *Federal Grants-in-Aid: Perspectives and Alternatives* (Washington, D.C.: American Enterprise Institute for Public Policy Research, 1968).

Chapter 4—The American Dream

Abraham, H. J., *Freedom and the Court: Civil Rights and Liberties in the United*

States, 2d ed. (New York: Oxford University Press, 1972).

Arendt, H., *Crisis of the Republic: Lying in Politics; Civil Disobedience: On Violence; Thoughts on Politics and Revolution* (New York: Harcourt Brace Jovanovich, 1972).

Berman, W. C., *The Politics of Civil Rights in the Truman Administration* (Columbus: Ohio State University Press, 1970).

Carmichael, S., and C. V. Hamilton, *Black Power: The Politics of Liberation in America* (New York: Vintage, 1967).

Claude, R., *The Supreme Court and the Electoral Process* (Baltimore: Johns Hopkins Press, 1970).

Epstein, J., *The Great Conspiracy Trial: An Essay on Law, Liberty, and the Constitution* (New York: Random House, 1970).

Ernst, M. L., and A. V. Schwartz, *Censorship: The Search for the Obscene* (New York: Macmillan, 1964).

Gillette, W., *The Right to Vote: Politics and the Passage of the Fifteenth Amendment* (Baltimore: Johns Hopkins Press, 1965).

Gillmor, D. M., *Free Press and Fair Trial* (Washington, D.C.: Public Affairs Press, 1966).

Krislov, S., *The Supreme Court and Political Freedom* (New York: Free Press, 1968).

Longaker, R. P., *The President and Individual Liberties* (Ithaca, N.Y.: Cornell University Press, 1961).

Lundberg, Ferdinand, *The Rich and the Super Rich* (New York: Bantam Books, 1968).

Matthews, Donald R., *Social Background of Political Decision-Makers* (Garden City, N.Y.: Doubleday, 1954).

Morgan, R. E., *The Supreme Court and Religion* (New York: Free Press, 1972).

Murphy, P. L., *The Meaning of Freedom of Speech: First Amendment Freedoms from Wilson to FDR* (Westport, Conn.: Greenwood, 1972).

Shapiro, M., *Freedom of Speech: The Supreme Court and Judicial Review* (Englewood Cliffs, N.J.: Prentice-Hall, 1966).

Chapter 5—Public Opinion and Political Participation

Bogart, L., *Silent Politics: Polls and Awareness of Public Opinion* (New York: Wiley, 1972).

Clausen, John A., ed. *Socialization and Society* (Boston: Little, Brown, 1968).

Converse, Philip, "The Nature of Belief Systems in Mass Publics," in David Apter, ed., *Ideology and Discontent* (New York: Free Press, 1964).

Dawson, Richard, and Kenneth Prewitt, *Political Socialization* (Boston: Little, Brown, 1969).

Easton, David, and Jack Dennis, *Children in the Political System* (New York: McGraw-Hill, 1969).

Free, L. A., and H. Cantril, *Political Beliefs of Americans: A Study of Public Opinion* (New Brunswick, N.J.: Rutgers University Press, 1967).

Greenstein, Fred I., *Children and Politics*, rev. ed. (New Haven, Conn.: Yale University Press, 1968).

Katz, E., and P. F. Lazarsfeld, *Personal Influence: The Part Played by People in the Flow of Mass Communications* (New York: Free Press, 1955).

Key, V. O., Jr., *Public Opinion and American Democracy* (New York: Knopf, 1961).

Lane, R. E., and D. O. Sears, *Public Opinion* (Englewood Cliffs, N.J.: Prentice-Hall, 1964).

Langton, Kenneth, *Political Socialization* (New York: Oxford University Press, 1969).

Luttbeg, N. R., ed., *Public Opinion and Public Policy: Models of Political Linkage* (Homewood, Ill.: Dorsey Press, 1968).

Mendelsohn, H., and I. Crespi, *Polls, Television and the New Politics* (Scranton, Pa.: Chandler, 1970).

Milbrath, L. W., *Political Participation: How and Why Do People Get Involved in Politics?* (Chicago: Rand McNally, 1965).

Novak, M., *The Rise of the Unmeltable Ethnics: The New Political Force of the Seventies* (New York: Macmillan, 1972).

Smith, M. Brewster, Jerome S. Bruner, and Robert W. White, *Opinions and Personality* (New York: Wiley, 1956).

Verba, S., and N. H. Nie, *Participation in America* (New York: Harper & Row, 1972).

Wilcox, A. R., *Public Opinion and Political Attitudes* (New York: Wiley, 1974).

Chapter 6—Voting Behavior and the Electoral Process

Berelson, B. R., P. E. Lazarsfeld, and W. N. McPhee, *Voting* (Chicago: University of Chicago Press, 1954).

Burnham, W. D., *Critical Elections and the Mainsprings of American Politics* (New York: W. W. Norton, 1970).

Campbell, A., P. E. Converse, W. E. Miller, and D. E. Stokes, *Elections and the Political Order* (New York: Wiley, 1966).

———et al., *The American Voter* (New York: Wiley, 1960).

Campbell, A., G. Gurin, and W. E. Miller, *The Voter Decides* (New York: Harper & Row, 1954).

Cantor, R. D., *Voting Behavior and Presidential Elections* (Itasca, Ill.: F. E. Peacock, 1975).

DeVries, W., and V. L. Tarrance, *The Ticket-Splitter: A New Force in American Politics* (Grand Rapids, Mich.: Eerdmans, 1971).

Key, V. O., Jr., *The Responsible Electorate* (Cambridge, Mass.: Harvard University Press, 1966).

Kraus, S., ed., *The Great Debates* (Bloomington: Indiana University Press, 1962).

Lamb, K., and P. Smith, *Campaign Decision-Making* (Belmont, Cal.: Wadsworth, 1968).

Longley, L. D., and A. G. Braun, *The Politics of Electoral College Reform* (New Haven, Conn.: Yale University Press, 1972).

Napolitan, J., *The Election Game and How to Win It* (Garden City, N.Y.: Doubleday, 1972).

Peirce, N. R., *The People's President* (New York: Simon & Schuster, 1968).

Polsby, N. W., and A. B. Wildavsky, *Presidential Elections*, 4th ed. (New York: Charles Scribner's Sons, 1976).

Pomper, G. M., *Elections in America: Control and Influence in Democratic Politics* (New York: Dodd, Mead, 1968).

Pool, I. de S., R. P. Abelson, and S. Popkin, *Candidates, Issues, and Strategies* (Cambridge, Mass.: M.I.T. Press, 1965).

Sayre, W. S., and J. H. Parris, *Voting for President: The Electoral College and the American Party System* (Washington, D.C.: Brookings Institution, 1970).

Chapter 7—Interest Groups

Bauer, R. A., I. de Sola Pool, and L. A. Dexter, *American Business and Public Policy*, 2d ed. (Chicago: Aldine-Atherton, 1972).

Cater, D., *Power in Washington* (New York: Random House, 1964).

Cobb, R. W., and C. D. Elder, *Participation in American Politics: The Dynamics of Agenda-Building* (Boston: Allyn & Bacon, 1972).

Dexter, L., *How Organizations are Represented in Washington* (Indianapolis: Bobbs-Merrill, 1969).

Domhoff, G. W., *The Higher Circles: The Governing Class in America* (New York: Random House, 1970).

Hall, D., *Cooperative Lobbying—The Power of Pressure* (Tucson: University of Arizona Press, 1969).

Halberstam, D., *The Best and The Brightest* (New York: Random House, 1972).

James, M., *The People's Lawyers* (New York: Holt, Rinehart & Winston, 1973).

Mahood, H. R., ed., *Pressure Groups in*

American Politics (New York: Charles Scribner's Sons, 1967).
McConnell, G., *Private Power and American Democracy* (New York: Knopf, 1966).
Milbrath, L. W., *The Washington Lobbyists* (Chicago: Rand McNally, 1963).
Mitchell, W. C., *Public Choice in America* (Chicago: Markham, 1971).
Pechman, J. A., and B. A. Okun, *Who Bears the Tax Burden?* (Washington, D.C.: Brookings Institution, 1974).
Prewitt, K., and A. Stone, *The Ruling Elites* (New York: Harper & Row, 1973).
Salisbury, R. H., ed., *Interest Group Politics in America* (New York: Harper & Row, 1970).
Wilson, J. Q., *Political Organizations* (New York: Basic Books, 1973).
Ziegler, H., and G. W. Peak, *Interest Groups in American Society*, 2d ed. (Englewood Cliffs, N.J.: Prentice-Hall, 1972).

Chapter 8—Political Parties

Broder, D. S., *The Party's Over* (New York: Harper & Row, 1972).
Burns, J. M., *The Deadlock of Democracy: Four-Party Politics in America* (Englewood Cliffs, N.J.: Prentice-Hall, 1963).
Crotty, W. J., *Approaches to the Study of Party Organization* (Boston: Allyn & Bacon, 1968).
David, P. T., R. M. Goldman, and R. C. Bain, *The Politics of National Party Conventions* (Washington, D.C.: Brookings Institution, 1960).
Davis, J. W., *Presidential Primaries: Road to the White House* (New York: Thomas Y. Crowell, 1967).
Greeley, A. M., *Building Coalitions* (New York: New Viewpoints, 1974)
Greenstein, F., *The American Party System and the American People*, 2d ed. (Englewood Cliffs, N.J.: Prentice-Hall, 1970).
Hofstadter, R., *The Idea of a Party System* (Berkeley: University of California Press, 1969).
Jones, C. O., *The Republican Party in American Politics* (New York: Macmillan, 1965).
Ladd, E. C., Jr., *American Political Parties: Social Change and Political Response* (New York: W. W. Norton, 1970).
Mazmanian, D. A., *Third Parties in Presidential Elections* (Washington, D.C.: Brookings Institution, 1974).
Michels, R., *Political Parties* (New York: Dover, 1915; reprinted 1949).
Nash, H. P., Jr., *Third Parties in American Politics* (Washington, D.C.: Public Affairs Press, 1959).

Ranney, A., *Curing the Mischiefs of Faction: Party Reform in America* (Berkeley: University of California Press, 1975).
Saloma, J. S., III, and F. H. Sontag, *Parties* (New York: Knopf, 1972).
Schattschneider, E. E., *Party Government* (New York: Farrar & Rinehart, 1942).
———, *The Struggle for Party Government* (College Park: University of Maryland Press, 1948).
Sorauf, F. J., *Party Politics in America* (Boston: Little, Brown, 1968).

Chapter 9—The Media

Bagdikian, B. H., *The Effete Conspiracy and Other Crimes by the Press* (New York: Harper & Row, 1972).
Blumler, Jay G., and Elihu Katz, eds., *The Uses of Mass Communications* (Beverly Hills: Sage, 1974).
Carlson, Robert O., *Communications and Public Opinion* (New York: Praeger, 1975).
Cohen, B. C., *The Press and Foreign Policy* (Princeton, N.J.: Princeton University Press, 1963).
Dunn, D. D., *Public Officials and the Press* (Reading, Mass.: Addison-Wesley, 1969).
Efron, Edith, *The News Twisters* (Los Angeles: Nash, 1971).
Emerson, Thomas I., *The System of Freedom of Expression* (New York: Random House, 1970).
Emery, Edwin, *The Press and America*, 3d ed. (Englewood Cliffs, N.J.: Prentice-Hall 1972).
Fagen, R. R., *Politics and Communication* (Boston: Little, Brown, 1966).
Lacy, Dan, *Freedom and Communications*, 2d ed. (Urbana: University of Illinois Press, 1965).
McLuhan, Marshall, *Understanding Media* (New York: McGraw-Hill, 1964).
Minow, N., J. B. Martin, and L. M. Mitchell, *Presidential Television* (New York: Basic Books, 1973).
Mott, F. L., *American Journalism* (New York: Macmillan, 1941).
Nimmo, D. D., *Newsgathering in Washington: A Study in Political Communication* (New York: Atherton, 1964).
Schiller, Herbert I., *Mass Communications and American Empire* (New York: A. M. Kelley, 1969).
——— *The Mind Managers* (Boston: Beacon Press, 1973).

Chapter 10—Congress

Bailey, S.K., *Congress Makes a Law* (New York: Columbia University Press, 1950).
Bolling, R., *House Out of Order* (New York: E. P. Dutton, 1965).

Clausen, A., *How Congressmen Decide: A Policy Focus* (New York: St. Martin's Press, 1973).
Eagleton, T. F., *War and Presidential Power: A Chronicle of Congressional Surrender* (New York: Liveright, 1974).
Fenno, R. F., Jr., *Congressmen in Committees* (Boston: Little, Brown, 1973).
Fishel, J., *Party and Opposition: Congressional Challengers in American Politics* (New York: McKay, 1973).
Fisher, L., *President and Congress: Power and Policy* (New York: Free Press, 1972).
Green, M., et al., *Who Runs Congress?* (New York: Bantam Books, 1972).
Horn, S., *The Cabinet and Congress* (New York: Columbia University Press, 1960).
Kingdon, J., *Congressmen's Voting Decisions* (New York: Harper & Row, 1973).
Matthews, D. R., *U.S. Senators and Their World* (Chapel Hill: University of North Carolina Press, 1960).
Mayhew D. R., *Congress: The Electoral Connection* (New Haven, Conn.: Yale University Press, 1974).
Morrow, W. L., *Congressional Committees* (New York: Charles Scribner's Sons, 1969).
Polsby, N.W., *Congress and the Presidency*, 2d ed. (Englewood Cliffs, N.J.: Prentice-Hall, 1971).
Turner, J., and E. V. Schneier, Jr., *Party and Constituency*, rev. ed. (Baltimore: Johns Hopkins Press, 1970).

Chapter 11—The Presidency

Anderson, P., *The Presidents' Men* (Garden City, N.Y.: Doubleday, 1968).
Barber, J. D., *The Presidential Character* (Englewood Cliffs, N.J.: Prentice-Hall, 1972).
Berger, R., *Impeachment: The Constitutional Problems* (Cambridge, Mass.: Harvard University Press, 1973).
Burns, J. M., *Presidential Government: The Crucible of Leadership* (Boston: Houghton Mifflin, 1966).
Cronin, T. E., *The State of the Presidency* (Boston: Little, Brown, 1975).
Destler, I. M., *Presidents, Bureaucrats, and Foreign Policy* (Princeton, N.J.: Princeton University Press, 1972).
Eisenhower, M. S., *The President is Calling* (Garden City, N.Y.: Doubleday, 1974).
Fenno, R. F., *The President's Cabinet* (Cambridge, Mass.: Harvard University Press, 1959).
Mueller, J. E., *War, Presidents and Public Opinion* (New York: Wiley, 1973).
Neustadt, R., *Presidential Power* (New York: Wiley, 1960).
O'Brien, L. J., *No Final Victories* (Garden City, N.Y.: Doubleday, 1974).

Phillips, C., *The Truman Presidency: The History of a Triumphant Succession* (New York: Macmillan, 1966).

Polsby, N., ed., *The Modern Presidency* (New York: Random House, 1973).

Reedy, G. E., *The Twilight of the Presidency* (New York: World, 1970).

Schubert, G. A., Jr., *The Presidency in the Courts* (Minneapolis: University of Minnesota Press, 1957).

Sorensen, T. C., *Decision-Making in the White House: The Olive Branch or the Arrows* (New York: Columbia University Press, 1963).

Chapter 12—The Federal Bureaucracy

Altshuler, A. A., ed., *The Politics of the Federal Bureaucracy* (New York: Harper & Row, 1968).

Bennis, W. G., ed., *American Bureaucracy* (New Brunswick, N.J.: Transaction Press, 1970).

Berkman, R. L., and W. K. Viscusi, *Damming the West* (New York: Ralph Nader Study Reports, Grossman, 1973).

Downs, A., *Inside Bureaucracy* (Boston: Little, Brown, 1967).

Jacoby, H., *The Bureaucratization of the World* (Berkeley: University of California Press, 1973).

Kilpatrick, F. P., M. C. Cummings, Jr., and M. K. Jennings, *The Image of the Federal Service* (Washington, D.C.: Brookings Institute, 1964).

Ostrom, V., *The Intellectual Crisis in American Public Administration*, rev. ed. (University, Ala.: University of Alabama Press, 1974).

Parkinson, C. N., *Parkinson's Law* (New York: Ballantine, 1957).

Pressman, J. L., and A. Wildavsky, *Implementation: How Great Expectations in Washington Are Dashed in Oakland* (Berkeley: University of California Press, 1973).

Redford, E. S., *Democracy in the Administrative State* (New York: Oxford University Press, 1969).

Schon, D. A., *Beyond the Stable State* (New York: Norton, 1971).

Schulz, C. L., *The Politics and Economics of Public Spending* (Washington, D.C.: Brookings Institute, 1969).

Tullock, G., *The Politics of Bureaucracy* (Washington, D.C.: Public Affairs Press, 1965).

Vaughn, R. G., *The Spoiled System: A Call for Civil Service Reform* (New York: David McKay, 1975).

Wildavsky, A., *The Politics of the Budgetary Process*, rev. ed. (Boston: Little, Brown, 1974).

Wilensky, H. L., *Organizational Intelligence* (New York: Basic Books, 1967).

Chapter 13—The Judiciary

Abraham, H. J., *Justices & Presidents: A Political History of Appointments to the Supreme Court* (New York: Oxford University Press, 1974).

Bickel, A. M., *The Least Dangerous Branch: The Supreme Court at the Bar of Politics* (New York: Bobbs-Merrill, 1962).

Black, C. L., Jr., *Structure and Relationship in Constitutional Law* (Baton Rouge: Louisiana State University Press, 1969).

Chase, H. W., *Federal Judges: The Appointing Process* (Minneapolis: University of Minnesota Press, 1972).

Cox, Archibald, *The Warren Court: Constitutional Decision as an Instrument of Reform* (Cambridge, Mass.: Harvard University Press, 1968).

Eisenstein, J., *Politics and the Legal Process* (New York: Harper & Row, 1973).

Jahnige, T., and S. Goldman, eds., *The Federal Judicial System* (Hinsdale, Ill.: Dryden Press, 1968).

Murphy, W. F., *Congress and the Court* (Hinsdale, Ill.: Dryden Press, 1965).

———, and C. H. Pritchett, eds., *Courts, Judges, and Politics*, 2d ed. (Chicago: University of Chicago Press, 1974).

Rosen, P. L., *The Supreme Court and Social Science* (Chicago: University of Chicago Press, 1972).

Schubert, G. R., *The Judicial Mind: Attitudes and Ideologies of Supreme Court Justices, 1946-1963* (Evanston, Ill.: Northwestern University Press, 1965).

Scigliano, R., *The Supreme Court and the Presidency* (New York: Free Press, 1971).

Strum, P., *The Supreme Court and "Political Questions": A Study in Judicial Evasion* (University, Ala.: University of Alabama Press, 1974).

Chapter 14—The Political Economy

Baran, Paul A., and Paul M. Sweezey, *Monopoly Capital* (New York: Monthly Review Press, 1966).

Clark, Kenneth B., and Jeannette Hopkins, *A Relevant War on Poverty* (New York: Harper & Row, 1969).

Donovan, John C., *The Politics of Poverty* (Indianapolis, Ind.: Pegasus, 1973).

Friedman, Milton, *Capitalism and Freedom* (Chicago: University of Chicago Press, 1963).

Galbraith, John K., *American Capitalism—The Concept of Countervailing Power* (New York: Houghton Mifflin, 1956).

———, *The Affluent Society* (New York: Houghton Mifflin, 1958).

———, *The New Industrial State* (New York: Houghton Mifflin, 1968).

Kolko, Gabriel, *Wealth and Power in America* (New York: Praeger, 1962).

Moynihan, Daniel, *Maximum Feasible Misunderstanding* (New York: Free Press, 1969).

Musolf, Lloyd D., *Government and Economy* (Glenview, Ill.: Scott, Foresman, 1965)

Reagan, Michael, *The Managed Economy* (New York: Oxford University Press, 1967).

Rostow, Walter W., *The Stages of Economic Growth* (New York: Cambridge University Press, 1960).

Samuelson, Paul A., *Economics*, 10th ed. (New York: McGraw-Hill, 1976).

Sexton, Patricia C., *Education and Income* (New York: Viking Press, 1964).

Wildavsky, Aaron, *The Politics of the Budgetary Process* (Boston: Little, Brown, 1974)

Chapter 15—Military and Foreign Affairs

Bailey, Thomas A., *The Art of Diplomacy: The American Experience* (Englewood Cliffs, N.J.: Prentice-Hall, 1968).

Benson, Leonard G., *National Purpose: Ideology and Ambivalence in America* (Washington, D.C.: Public Affairs Press, 1963).

Bohlen, Charles E., *The Transformation of American Foreign Policy* (New York: W. W. Norton, 1969).

Brzezinski, Zbigniew, *Between Two Ages: America's Role in the Technetronic Revolution* (New York: Viking Press, 1970).

Chomsky, Noam, *American Power and the New Mandarins* (New York: Vintage Books, 1969).

Cobb, Roger W., and Charles Elder, *International Community: A Regional and Global Study* (New York: Holt, Rinehart & Winston, 1970).

Dietze, Gottfried, *America's Political Dilemma: From Limited to Unlimited Democracy* (Baltimore: Johns Hopkins Press, 1968).

Hoffman, Stanley, *Gulliver's Troubles, or the Setting of American Foreign Policy* (New York: McGraw-Hill, 1968).

Kolko, Gabriel, *The Roots of American Foreign Policy: An Analysis of Power and Purpose* (Boston: Beacon Press, 1969).

Landecker, Manfred, *The President and Public Opinion: Leadership in Foreign Affairs* (Washington, D.C.: Public Affairs Press, 1968).

McCarthy, Eugene J., *The Limits of Power: America's Role in the World* (New York: Holt, Rinehart & Winston, 1967).

Morgenthau, Hans J., *A New Foreign Policy for the United States* (New York: Praeger, 1969).

Paolucci, Henry, *War, Peace, and the Presidency* (New York: McGraw-Hill, 1968).

Waltz, Kenneth N., *Foreign Policy and Democratic Politics: The American and British Experience* (Boston: Little, Brown, 1967).

ANSWERS TO CROSSWORD PUZZLES

CHAPTER 1

	1 L	2 O	N	G		3 P	4 E	R	S	U	A	D	E		5	6 D
	E				7 R	8 A	9 T		E		R					E
	10 G	L	O	O	M	Y			V		N		11 C	12 A	R	P
	I		U		13 P	O	W	E	R		M	14 O	M			E
	15 T	R	I	P		E			R		16 P	I	E		17 I	N
	I		18 S	19 I		20 D	21 I	E		22 E	N	D		23 A	D
	24 M	25 A	T		26 N	E	A	T		27 Z	O	O		28 A	G	E
	A	29	E	C			30 E		31 P	R		32 C	O	N
	C	I			33 C	O	34 N	F	L	I	C	T		O		T
	35	36 Y	E	L	L	37 O	W		38 S	U	E		T		39	40
		A		N		39 O	40 U	S		41 Y	A	R	D	42
		43 R	E	S	O	U	R	C	E	S			44 S	O	N

CHAPTER 2

	1 F	2 E	D	E	R	A	L	I	S	T		4 P	5 A	6 R	7 T	Y
	I		A		I							8 I	D	E	A
	R		9 S	T	O	10 V	E		11 C	O	T	S		12 M	Y
	13 S	14 O		I		15 I	N	C	H					E
	16 T	R	Y		17 F	18 E	N	D		19 E		20 O	V	21 E	R
		E		22 S	I	N	G	S		23 C	H	A	I	R		24 P
			25 S	E	C				K		26 T	R	A	I	L
		27 A	T	T	A	R		28 B				G		O
		29 M	A	S	T		30 J	U	D	I	C	I	31 A	32 L
	33 W	I	T		34 I	N	35 K		R			36 N	N	E
	E		37 E	38 G	O		I	S		39 T	I		40 M	P
	41 B	I	S	O	N		42 N	A	T	I	O	N	A	L

275

Answers to Crossword Puzzles

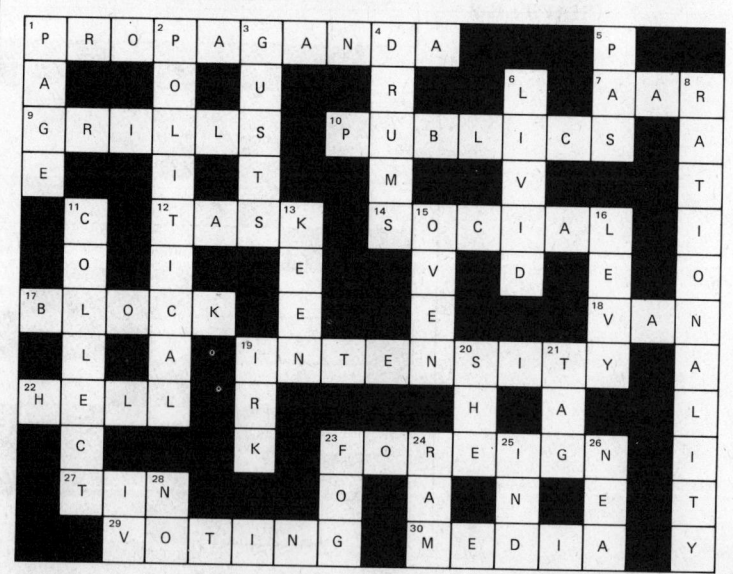

CHAPTER 3, **CHAPTER 4**, and **CHAPTER 5** crossword puzzle answer grids.

Answers to Crossword Puzzles **277**

CHAPTER 6

Crossword answer grid for Chapter 6 with the following entries:
- 1 Across: DELEGATES
- 7: E
- 8 Down: L
- 1 Down: DO
- 9: VAN
- 10: QUILT
- 11: SPY
- 12: CATER
- 13 Down: AI CK
- 14: RUE
- 15 Down: RA
- 16 Down: TH
- 17: ELECTIONS
- 19: P
- 20: PRESIDENT
- 21: TINT
- 22: TET
- 23: REAL
- 25: ID
- 26: AWE
- 28: LAUGH
- 29 Down: HAN
- 30: FIRST
- 33: TIP
- 35: ISSUES
- 36: IMAGE

CHAPTER 7

Crossword answer grid for Chapter 7:
- 1 Across: COMPETITION
- 6: MAXI
- 9: AWOL
- 10: OKRA
- 12: PAIN
- 13: CREDO
- 15: SHARED
- 17: LIMB
- 19: LEG
- 20: COLAS
- 23: BE
- 24: OLLA
- 25: ICE
- 26: FLIRT
- 27: CCXII
- 28: SEW
- 31: ITO
- 33: FOREIGN
- 34: LOBBYISTS

CHAPTER 8

Crossword answer grid for Chapter 8:
- 1 Across: PRESIDENTIAL
- 7: ICE
- 9: INDEPENDENCY
- 12: INK
- 13: BROAD
- 15: SEA
- 16: CONTEST
- 19: LEVELS
- 21: RAVE
- 22: IDEA
- 23: ADD
- 25: PER
- 26: AVER
- 27: DIAL
- 28: TWO
- 29: NOT
- 30: DIVIDED

278 Answers to Crossword Puzzles

CHAPTER 9

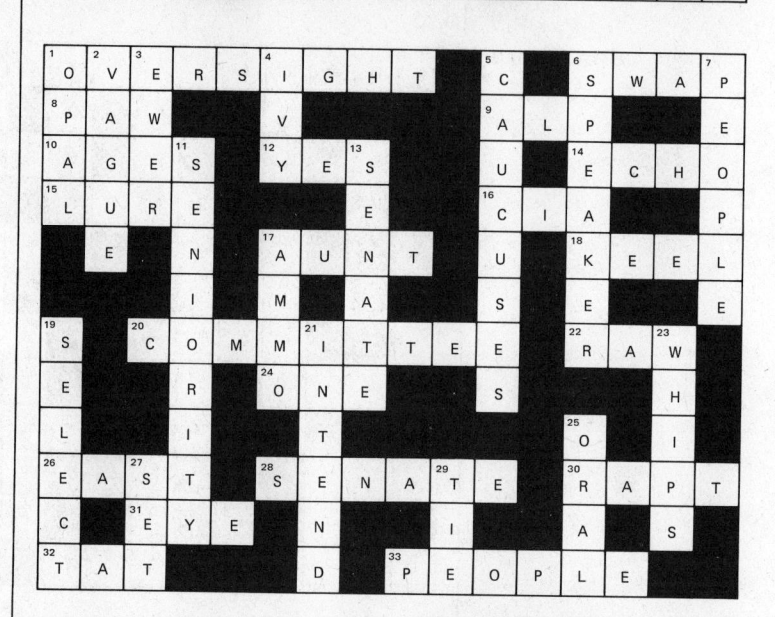

	1	2 A	D	3 V	E	R	S	A	R	4 Y		5 C	H	E	A	6 P
		O		A				A				C				O
		7 L	8 E	A	K		9 R		10 C	I	R	C	11 L	E		L
	12 S	T	A		E		I		H				13 L	E	I
			R		14 S	I	G	H	T	S		15 S		16 W	E	T
					H				17 C	L	A	S	P			I
		18 M		19 S	E	N	T		R		R		H			C
	20 C	A	S	H			21 S	22 H	O	E			A			A
		K		A				23 N	A	24 T	25 I	O	N	A	L
	26 P	E	O	P	L	27 E		28 H	E	M		29 N	U	T	
	E			E		E						C			
	30 W	E	T			31 L	O	C	A	L		32 C	H	A	I	N

CHAPTER 10

1 O	2 V	3 E	R	4 S	I	G	H	T		5 C		6 S	W	A	7 P
8 P	A	W		V						9 A	L	P			E
10 A	G	E	11 S		12 Y	E	13 S			U		14 E	C	H	O
15 L	U	R	E				E		16 C	I	A				P
			N		17 A	U	N	T		U		18 K	E	E	L
			I		M		A			S		E			E
19 S		20 C	O	M	M	I	T	21 T	E	E		22 R	A	23 W	
E		R					24 O	N	E					H	
L		I					T					25 O		I	
26 E	A	27 S	T		28 S	E	N	A	29 T	E		30 R	A	P	T
C		31 E	Y	E					I			A			S
32 T	A	T					D		33 P	E	O	P	L	E	

CHAPTER 11

1 A	2 D	V	3 E	R	S	A	R	4 Y			5 F	C	6 C
	D		E		A			A			7 F	R	O		O
8 M	A	T	9 E		10 G	R	O	W	N		R		12 R	E	V	E	A	L
		11 O	N		A			N					I
14 C			D		15 S	16 O	N			X			I
O			U			B		17 H	18 U	G	E		19 G	E	T
N		20 P	R	E	V	I	O	U	S		C		N		I
G			E					T			U				O
R			21 S	22 T	Y	23 L	E		24 F	A	T	E			N
25 E	R	26 A			A		O			I			
S		M		27 P	O	C	K	E	T		28 V	A	I	29 N
30 S	H	A	V	E			H				E			O

Answers to Crossword Puzzles 279

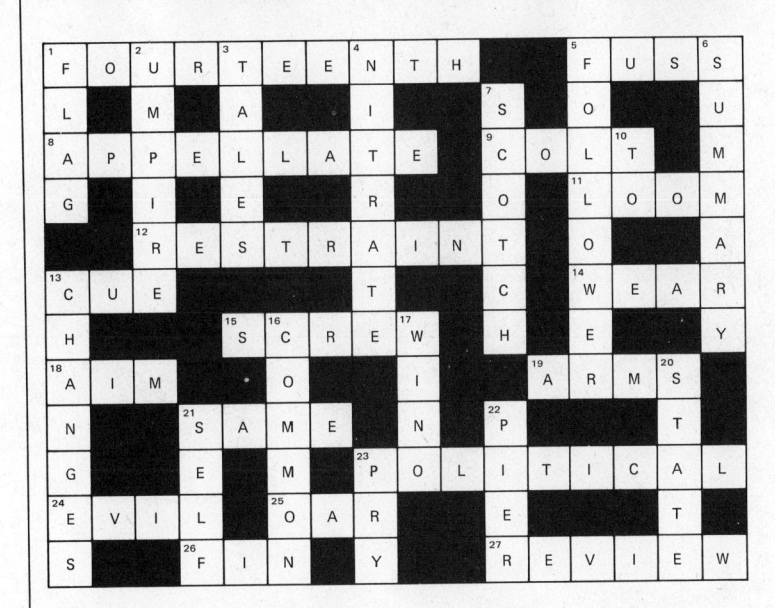

CHAPTER 12

Across: 1 CORPORATION, 7 GROW, 9 AT, 10 AMA, 11 EAT, 12 SAGES, 13 HATCH, 17 C, 18 PRIOR, 19 JUDICIAL, 20 HAM, 21 CASH, 25 SEMI, 26 POLITICAL, 27 LAY, 28 ALI, 29 A, 30 CABINET, 31 AGENCY, 32 END

CHAPTER 13

Across: 1 FOURTEENTH, 5 FUSS, 8 APPELLATE, 9 COLT, 11 LOOM, 12 RESTRAINT, 13 CUE, 14 WEAR, 15 SCREW, 18 AIM, 19 ARMS, 21 SAME, 23 POLITICAL, 24 EVIL, 25 OAR, 26 FIN, 27 REVIEW

CHAPTER 14

Across: 1 GOVERNMENT, 6 DREAM, 9 SHOE, 10 A, 12 BUDGETARY, 16 IRATE, 18 EVEN, 19 RESOURCES, 20 FLORA, 21 TINT, 23 DATA, 24 FREE, 27 TAR, 28 TUB, 29 TOR, 30 AUDIT, 31 OVEN, 32 NEW, 33 GUN, 34 AGE

CHAPTER 15

INDEX

Abortion, 2, 26, 69
Abzug, Bella, 246
Acheson, Dean, 107, 242
Adams, Brock, 157, 168
Adams, John, 115
Adams, John Quincy, 95, 115
Adams, Samuel, 16
Advisory Commission on Intergovernmental Relations (ACIR), 32, 33
AFL-CIO Committee on Political Education (COPE), 105
Africa, U.S. policy in, 254
Agnew, Spiro, 27, 130, 158, 178
Agriculture, Department of, 11, 75, 105, 187
Alexander, Herbert, 89
Allende, Salvador, 245, 251
Ambassadorships, sale of, 88
America First party, 120
American Airlines, 233
American Bankers Association, 101, 117
American Bar Association (ABA), 5-6, 101, 108, 202, 208
American Civil Liberties Union (ACLU), 48, 108, 111
American Independent party, 119, 120
American Israel Public Affairs Committee, 110
American Medical Association (AMA), 100, 101, 105, 147
American Petroleum Institute (API), 106
American Revolution, 15, 16
Americans for Democratic Action (ADA), 83, 108
American Telephone & Telegraph (AT&T), 103, 106
Amitay, Morris, 110
Anderson, Jack, 136
Andruss, Cecil, 166
Angola, 70, 154, 172, 248, 249, 250, 254
Antifederalists, 20, 23, 24, 115
Antiwar movement, 47, 65, 73
Appellate courts, 200-204
Arab nations, 241, 250, 253
Arab oil embargo, 10, 240
Armed forces. *See* Military
Arms, right to bear, 24
Arms exports, 249, 253
Articles of Confederation, 17-19, 115
Ash, Roy, 175
Asia, U.S. policy in, 253
Assembly, freedom of, 24, 45, 47, 65
Assistant whips, 151
Associated Milk Producers, 105
Associated Press (AP), 129

Backgrounders, 137
Bailey, F. Lee, 51
Baker v. Carr (1962), 205
Balanced Growth and Planning Act of 1975, 222
Banfield, Edwin C., 38
Barber, James David, 164-165
Bayh, Birch, 85
Bay of Pigs invasion, 130, 163
Beard, Charles A., 21
Berglund, Robert, 166
Bernstein, Carl, 130
Biden, Joseph, Jr., 57
Bill of attainder, 23
Bill of Rights, 21, 23-25, 211
Blacks
    education, 49
    elected officials, 50
    employment, 52-53, 222
    equality and, 48-50
    income, 52-53
    interest groups, 104-105
    migration to cities, 49
    political awareness, 6
    public opinion, 67
    voting, 49, 50
Blumenthal, Michael, 166
B'nai B'rith, 100
Bogart, Leo, 62
Brandeis, Louis D., 205, 208
Brazil, 7
Brennan, William J., Jr., 46, 206
Brooke, Edward W., 57
Brown, Robert E., 21
Brown v. Board of Education (1954), 49, 56, 205, 206, 211
Buckley, James, 119
Budget, 10, 157, 168, 224-227, 239
Bureaucracy. *See* Federal bureaucracy
Burger, Warren E., 46, 201, 207, 209
Burns, Arthur, 125, 230
Burr, Aaron, 26
Business Roundtable, 106
Busing, 56-57, 69, 198, 212

Cabinet, 28, 107, 166, 175-176
Cabinet departments, 186-187
Caddell, Patrick H., 80, 81
Campaign Finance Act of 1974, 233
Campaign financing, 87-89, 105-106
Campaigns. *See* Congressional election campaigns; Presidential election campaigns
Canada, 252
Cannon, Joseph, 150

Capital punishment, 25, 207
Carnegie Foundation, 242
Carswell, Harold G., 154, 209
Carter, Jimmy, 118
    cabinet, 107, 166
    character, 165
    domestic programs, 10
    foreign policy, 70, 170-171, 250
    presidential campaign (1976), 32, 69, 80-82, 84-85, 90-96, 104, 124, 126
    White House staff, 173
Case Act of 1972, 170
Castro, Fidel, 245, 254
Caucuses, 150
Censorship, 133
Census Bureau, 94
Center for Community Changes, 41
Center for National Policy Review, 41
Central Intelligence Agency (CIA), 5, 130-131, 132, 136, 168, 174, 188, 193, 241, 244-245, 248, 251
Certiorari, writ of, 205
Chapin, Dwight, 133
Charles A. Beard and the Constitution (Brown), 21
Chase Manhattan Bank, 107
Checks and balances, 21, 22
Chile, 251
Christian Science Monitor, The, 130,
Christian Scientists, 48
Church and state, separation of, 48
Circuit courts, 201-202
Cities, 11, 177
    changing composition of, 37-38
    decay of, 38
    job market, 39
    migration to, 35
Civil Aeronautics Board (CAB), 191
Civil disobedience, 8, 50
Civilian programs, 224, 225
Civil law, 199
Civil Rights Act of 1957, 50
Civil Rights Act of 1960, 50
Civil Rights Act of 1964, 50
Civil rights movement, 2, 8, 44, 47, 49-50, 73, 75
Civil rights organizations, 6, 103, 108
Civil Service Commission, 184, 185
Civil service system, 184
Clay, Henry, 115
Clear and present danger, 212
Cloture, 158
Clusters, 70-71
Cohen, Wilbur, 184
Colonies, 3, 15-17

Commission on Federal Paperwork, 183
Committee to Re-Elect the President, 88
Common Cause, 105, 110, 111, 185
Common Law, 199
Communication, 33
Communism, 45, 70
Communist party, 120
Concord, battle of, 16
Confessions of a Price Controller (Grayson), 223
Conflict, 2, 74
Conflict of interest, 146-147
Congressional Budget and Impoundment Control Act of 1974, 157, 224
Congressional Budget Office (CBO), 158, 168, 224, 225, 228
Congressional elections campaigns, 81
  financing, 88, 89
  voter participation, 94
  1974, 121
  1976, 149
Congress of Racial Equality (CORE), 100
Congress of the United States, 141-159
  amendment process, 25-26
  under Articles of Confederation, 17
  budgetary process, 157-158, 223, 224
  checks and balances, 21, 22
  civil rights legislation, 49-50
  committees, 154-158
  constituencies, 147-148
  on death penalty, 25
  economic role of, 223, 224
  electoral process, 148-149
  ethics, 146-147
  foreign policy, 154, 170-172, 239, 248-249
  functions of, 142-144
  General Accounting Office and, 158
  interest groups and, 106, 147
  judicial review and, 23
  junkets, 145-146
  leadership, 150-152
  legislative parties, 82, 120-121, 152, 153
  legislative process, 142-143, 153-154
  media and, 147-148
  members of, 144-147
  military spending and, 246
  operations, 149
  oversight, 143-144
  Presidency and, 15, 20, 124-125, 143, 159, 162, 165-169
  procedures, 158-159
  salaries in, 145
  secrecy, 158-159
  seniority system, 152, 155, 156
  separation of powers, 22
  staffs, 149, 150
  subpoena power, 159
  taxation and, 23, 27
  welfare and, 35
Connecticut Compromise, 19
Conscientious objectors, 47
Conservatism, 64, 67-70, 118
Conservative party, 119
Constitutional Convention, 15, 18-20
Constitution of the United States, 14-15
  amendment process, 25-27. *See also specific amendments*

Bill of Rights, 21, 23-25, 211
  checks and balances, 21, 22
  Constitutional Convention, 15, 18-20
  due process, 25, 26
  enumerated powers, 23
  flexibility of, 15, 29
  individual rights, 15, 21, 23-25, 45
  judicial review, 22-23
  limited government, 21-22
  majority rule, 7
  meaning of, 21-23
  Presidency and, 20, 177, 178
  ratification, 20-21
  separation of powers, 22
  slavery and, 19, 49
  text of, 258-269
Consumer Product Safety Commission (CPSC), 191
Continental Congress, 16
Coolidge, Calvin, 9
Corporations, 6
  campaign financing, 105
  in economic power structure, 232-233
  international, 109
  taxation of, 230, 231-232
Cost of living, 69, 232
Council of Economic Advisers (CEA), 174, 175, 223
Council of Economic Development (CED), 231
Council on Foreign Relations (CFR), 107, 242
Counsel, right to, 25, 51
Counter-Spy, 130
Crime, 11, 68
Criminal law, 51
Cruel and unusual punishment, 25
Cuba, 70, 130, 163, 254
Cyprus, 154, 245, 249
Czechoslovakia, 241, 250

Dade County, Florida, 39
Deardourff, John, 91-92
Death penalty, 25, 207
Debates, presidential, 92, 170
Declaration of Independence, 16-17, 44
De facto segregation, 56, 212
Defense, Department of, 109, 171, 186-187, 193, 238, 241, 243, 245
Defense industry, 109, 249
Defense Intelligence Agency (DIA), 168, 244
Defense spending, 224, 225, 249
De jure segregation, 56, 212
Delegate selection, 84
Democracy, 3-8, 70
  defined, 3
  group basis of American politics, 2, 6-7
  legitimacy, 4-5
  majority rule vs. minority rights, 7
  political institutions, 5-6
  pragmatism, 7-8
  representative government, 3-4
Democratic party. *See* Electoral process; Political parties; Presidential election campaigns
Democratic-Republicans, 115

Democratic Study Group, 152
Dennis, Eugene, 45
Dennis v. United States (1951), 45-46
Desegregation, 49, 56, 204-207, 211
Dewey, Thomas E., 49, 96
Diem, Ngo Dinh, 245
Diplomacy, 241
Diplomats, professional, 242-244
Direction of opinion, 62
Discrimination, 44, 48-50, 53
  reverse, 44, 53, 56
District courts, 198, 200-201
Dixiecrats, 119
Domestic issues, public opinion and, 68-70
Double jeopardy, 25
Douglas, William O., 45
Dred Scott v. Sanford (1857), 217
Due process, 25, 26, 210
Dulles, John Foster, 107, 242, 250

Eagleton, Thomas, 87
Eastburn, David P., 190
Economic Interpretation of the Constitution, An (Beard), 21
Economic policy. *See* Political economy
Education
  busing, 56-57, 69, 198, 212
  desegregation cases, 49, 56, 204-207, 211
  equal opportunity in, 56-57
  interest groups, 102
  property taxes and, 35, 37, 56
  public opinion and, 65-66
  relationship between income and, 65
  voting behavior and, 94
Eighteenth Amendment, 4, 26, 27
Eighth Amendment, 25
Eisenhower, Dwight D., 49, 96, 115, 117, 118, 124, 170
  leadership style, 163
  as legislator, 167
  media and, 173
  on military-industrial complex, 249
  U-2 incident, 173
Electoral college, 20, 95-96
Electoral process, 78-96. *See also* Presidential election campaigns
  campaign financing, 87-89, 105-106
  national conventions, 86-87
  nominating process, 83-86
  primaries, 81, 83-86, 89, 90, 104
Eleventh Amendment, 26
Elite groups, 65, 75
Elliot, Osborne, 133
Ellsberg, Daniel, 8, 46
Ellsworth, Oliver, 19
Employment, 9, 10, 52-56
Energy, 2, 8, 10, 11, 44
Environmental groups, 2, 100, 108
Environmental Protection Agency, 191
Equality, 44-45, 48-51
  economic, 51-53, 56
  education and, 56-57
  employment and, 52-56
  justice and, 48, 50-51
  racial, 49-50
Equal Rights Amendment, 26, 27
Europe, U.S. policy in, 252

Executive agencies, 188
Executive agreements, 154, 170
Executive branch. *See* Presidency
Executive Office, 174-176, 224, 244
Executive privilege, 159, 169
Ex post facto laws, 23

Fairness doctrine, 139
Faisal, King, 253
Farmer-Labor party, 119
Faubus, Orval, 212
Favorite sons, 85
Featherbedding, 232
Federal Aviation Administration (FAA), 186, 187
Federal bureaucracy, 173-176, 181-194
    accountability, 193-194
    cabinet departments, 186-187
    characteristics of, 182-183
    executive agencies, 188
    foreign policy and, 242-243
    good old boy network, 185
    influences on, 183
    problems of, 183
    regulation. *See* Government regulation
    role in political economy, 233-235
    semi-independent corporations, 188-189
    size of, 182, 183
    staffing, 184-186
    structure of, 186-190
    subcabinet departments, 187-188
    super bureaucrats, 183-184
    unionization, 185-186
Federal Bureau of Investigation (FBI), 5, 75, 132, 187-188, 193
Federal Communications Commission (FCC), 108, 139
Federal courts, 198, 200-202, 209
Federal Election Campaign Act of 1971, 88
Federal Election Campaign Act of 1974, 88-89, 105, 121, 257
Federal Election Commission, 89
Federal Energy Administration, 191
Federal government. *See* Congress of the United States; Federal bureaucracy; Federalism; Government regulation
Federal Highway Administration, 187
Federalism, 29, 31-41
    cities and suburbs, 37-39
    defined, 32
    federal-state-local revenue balance, 34
    grants-in-aid, 40
    spending, imbalance of, 33-34
    growth of, 32-33
    McCulloch v. Maryland, 32-33
    property taxes as education revenue, 35, 37, 56
    revenue sharing, 34, 40-41
    values and resources, 34-36
Federalist Papers, The (Madison, Hamilton, and Jay), 21, 22, 27-28, 198
Federalists, 20-21, 24, 115
Federal Maritime Commission, 109
Federal Reserve Board, 189-190, 230
Federal Reserve System, 230
Federal Trade Commission (FTC), 234
Federal Voting Rights Act of 1970, 94

Fifteenth Amendment, 49
Fifth Amendment, 24-25
Filibusters, 158
Financial institutions, 231-232
First Amendment, 24, 45-48, 129
First Continental Congress, 16
Fiscal Assistance Act, 40-41
Fiscal policy, 229-230
Fletcher v. Peck (1810), 210
Floor leaders, 151
Florida primary, 85
Food and Drug Administration (FDA), 192
Ford, Gerald, 27, 32, 115, 118, 176, 249
    appointments, 208, 209
    assassination attempts, 132-133
    Congress and, 124-125, 143
    economic policy, 124-125, 216, 223
    executive privilege, 169
    foreign policy, 70, 170, 171
    impoundment of funds, 158
    leadership style, 163-164
    as political leader, 165
    presidential campaign (1976), 80-82, 84-85, 90-96
    White House staff, 173
Ford Foundation, 242
Foreign policy, 9, 10, 176, 186, 238-254
    Carter and, 70, 170-171, 250
    conduct of, 250
    Congress and, 154, 170-172, 239, 248-249
    decision-making, 240-247, 251-252
    defense industry and, 109, 249-250
    diplomacy, role of, 241
    federal bureaucracy and, 242
    Ford and, 70, 170, 171
    interdependence of nations, 239-240
    Johnson, Lyndon and, 241, 254
    Kennedy, John and, 130, 163, 171, 241, 244, 254
    Nixon and, 62, 172, 173, 241, 244
    overview, 252-254
    Presidency and, 162, 168, 170-172, 176, 223, 239, 240-241, 251-252
    propaganda and, 75
    public opinion and, 68-70, 250
    Roosevelt, Franklin and, 254
Foreign trade, 235, 239-240
Fourteenth Amendment, 25, 26, 49, 211
Fourth Amendment, 24
France, 232, 241, 252
Franklin, Benjamin, 20
Frankfurter, Felix, 205
Free-enterprise system, 9
Fromme, Lynette Alice (Squeaky), 133
Fulbright, James W., 111
Funds, impoundment of, 158, 169
Furman v. Georgia (1972), 207

Gag orders, 46, 207
Gardner, John, 110
Garner, John Nance, 178
Gelb, Leslie H., 132
General Accounting Office (GAO), 158, 193, 224
General Electric Company, 107
General Motors Corporation, 107
Germany, 232

Gerrymandering, 205
Gesell, Gerhard, 133
Gitlow v. New York (1925), 211
Goldwater, Barry, 7, 82, 90, 92, 96, 124, 150, 165
Good old boy network, 185
Goodyear Tire and Rubber Company, 233
Governmental secrecy, 158-159
Government regulation, 190-193
    Federal Trade Commission, 234
    inflation and, 218
    planned-economy concept and, 223
    reform of, 192-193
Grand juries, 134
Grants-in-aid, 40
Grayson, C. Jackson, 223
Great Britain, 15-17, 232, 252
    political parties in, 114-115
Great Depression, 33
Greece, 252
Green, William J., 246
Greenspan, Alan, 223
Gross National Product (GNP), 9, 228-229
Group basis of American politics, 2, 6-7
Gulf of Tonkin Resolution, 171, 248
Gulf Oil Corporation, 107, 233
Gun control, 24, 132, 147

Habeas corpus, 23
Haldeman, H. R., 174
Hall, Gus, 120
Hamilton, Alexander, 20-22, 27-28, 115, 124
Hancock, John, 16
Harlan, John Marshall, 205
Harriman, Averill, 172, 241
Harris, Fred, 85
Harrison, Benjamin, 95
Harrison, William Henry, 115
Hatch Act, 185
Hayes, Rutherford B., 95
Haynsworth, Clement, 154, 209
Head Start, 37
Health, Education, and Welfare (HEW), Department of, 11, 192
Health care, 105
Health Research Group, 11
Hearst, Patricia, 51
Hebert, F. Edward, 152
Heinz, H. J., 89
Hickel, Walter, 176
Holmes, Oliver Wendell, 45, 212
Holtzman, Elizabeth, 246
Hoover, Herbert C., 96, 162
House of Representatives. *See* Congress of the United States
Humphrey, Hubert H., 80, 85, 91, 93, 96, 104, 124, 150, 222
Hungary, 241, 250

Ideology of political parties, 116-118
Immigration, 33, 44
Impeachment, 179
Implied powers, 28, 32-33
Impoundment of funds, 158, 169

Income
  differences in, 52
  public opinion and, 65-66
  relationship between education, 65
Income taxes, 34
Individual rights, 15, 21, 23-25, 45
Industry organizations, 74
Inflation, 10, 12, 53, 67, 69, 125, 216, 218-219, 229-230, 240
Intensity of opinion, 62
Interest groups, 5, 6, 28, 72, 91, 99-111, 116, 223, 224, 257
  Congress and, 106, 147
  education, 102
  electoral role of, 104-105
  financial role of, 105-106
  foreign interests and, 109-110, 251
  goals of, 101-102
  judiciary and, 108
  lobbyists, 106, 109-111
  media and, 108
  nature of, 100-101
  political parties and, 103-106
  political system and, 102-103
  Presidency and, 106-107
  public interest, 110
  regulatory commissions and, 107-108
  structure of, 101
  within government, 108-109
Internal Revenue Service (IRS), 176, 183, 228
Interstate Commerce Commission (ICC), 191
Iran, 253
Irish-Americans, 67
Israel, 109, 110, 176, 241, 253
Italy, 251
Item veto, 169

Jackson, Andrew, 115
Jackson, Henry M., 81, 85, 104
Japan, 240, 253
Jay, John, 21
Jefferson, Thomas, 24, 26, 115, 129
Johnson, Andrew, 179
Johnson, Lyndon B., 80, 87, 93, 96, 245
  appointments, 208
  character, 164
  domestic programs, 165-167, 172
  foreign policy, 241, 254
  leadership style, 163
  media and, 135, 172
  National Security Council and, 174
  as Senate majority leader, 151
  as Vice President, 178
  Vietnam War, 5, 12, 22, 69, 75, 135, 171, 172, 248
Johnson, Michael, 104
Johnson, William S., 20
Joint Chiefs of Staff, 171
Judges. *See* Judiciary
Judicial Conference of the United States, 209, 212
Judicial review, 22-23, 28, 197, 198
Judiciary, 196-213. *See also* Supreme Court of the United States
  appellate courts, 200-203
  checks and balances, 21, 22
  common and civil law, 199
  federal courts, 198, 200-202, 209
  future of, 212
  interest groups and, 108
  judges, 202-203
  political culture and, 198-199
  precedents, 199
  Presidency and, 169-170
  separation of powers, 22
  state courts, 198, 199-200
Judiciary Act of 1789, 198
Junkets, congressional, 145
Jury trial, right to, 25
Justice, Department of, 50, 187
Justice, equality and, 48, 50-51

Kearns, Doris, 151, 166
Keith, Hastings, 145
Kelley, Clarence M., 188
Kennedy, Edward M., 208
Kennedy, John F., 80, 87, 92, 96, 118, 132
  character, 164
  foreign policy, 130, 163, 171, 242, 244, 254
  media and, 172
  National Security Council and, 174
  Vietnam War, 22
  White House staff, 174
Kennedy, Robert F., 132
Key, V. O., Jr., 61
Keynes, John Maynard, 220, 222
Khrushchev, Nikita, 250
King, Martin Luther, Jr., 50, 75, 132
King, Rufus, 20
Kissinger, Henry A., 70, 107, 135-137, 169, 171, 174-175, 241, 243, 244, 248, 253
Korean War, 239, 240, 241, 250
Kristol, Erving, 244

Labor, Department of, 75, 186
Labor unions, 72-74, 100, 101, 103-105, 108, 123
  in economic power structure, 232
  federal employees and, 185-186
  minimum wages and, 219
Landon, Alfred M., 96
Laos, 244
Latin America, U.S. policy in, 254
Law, 8, 199. *See also* Judiciary
Law Enforcement Assistance Administration, 51
League of Women Voters Education Fund, 41
Legislative branch. *See* Congress of the United States
Legislative parties, 120-121, 150
Legitimacy, 4-5
Lexington, battle of, 16
Libel, 47
Liberalism, 64, 67-68, 118
Liberal party, 119
Libertarian party, 120
Limited government, 21-22
Lincoln, Abraham, 115
Lippmann, Walter, 65
Literacy tests, 49, 50
Lobbyists, 106, 109-111
Local party organizations, 121, 122
Lofton, John D., 131
Long, Russell, 157
Lowered expectations, politics of, 257
Lubell, Samuel, 12
Lumumba, Patrice, 245
Lyndon Johnson and the American Dream (Kearns), 166
Lynn, James T., 168

MacArthur, Douglas, 172
McCarthy, Eugene, 79, 95
McCarthyism, 45
McCulloch v. Maryland (1819), 32-33
McGovern, George, 7, 82, 87, 90, 96, 120, 124
McNamara, Robert, 176
Madison, James, 18, 20, 21, 22, 24, 198
Mahoney, James, 104
Majority rule, 7
Mandamus, writ of, 198
Mansfield, Mike, 149, 151-152
Manson, Charles, 133
Mao Tse-Tung, 242
Marbury, William, 198
Marbury v. Madison (1803), 197, 198
Maritime industry, 105
Marshall, John, 32-33, 198, 210
Marshall, Thurgood, 206
Marshall Plan, 163, 252
Martin v. Hunter's Leesee (1816), 210
Meany, George, 104
Measurement of public opinion, 70-71
Media, 3-4, 5, 22, 128-139
  backgrounders, 137
  characteristics of, 129-130
  Congress and, 147-148
  fairness doctrine, 139
  government and, 134-137
  interest groups and, 108
  interpretation of news, 131-133
  judicial process and, 133-134
  news leaks, 130-131, 136
  political information and, 71-72
  Presidency and, 134-135, 172-173
  presidential campaigns and, 91-92
  press, freedom of, 24, 46, 129, 133-134, 139, 207
  public and, 137-139
  trial balloons, 137
Medina, Harold, 133
Mexican-Americans, 48
Middle East, U.S. policy in, 253
Mikva, Abner, 246
Milbraith, Lester, 242
Military, 109, 110, 239, 244
  arms exports and, 249
  desegregation of, 49
  influence on foreign policy, 247-248, 249
Military-industrial complex, 109, 249
Miller, Warren, 92
Miller v. California (1973), 47
Minimum wage, 74, 219

Minnesota Mining and Manufacturing Company, 233
Minority rights, 7
Miranda v. Arizona (1966), 200
Missouri v. Canada (1938), 211
Mondale, Walter, 132
Monetary policy, 230
Monroe, James, 115
Moore, Sara Jane, 132
Morgan Guaranty Trust Company, 232
Morris, Gouverneur, 20
Morrissey, Francis X., 208
Muskie, Edmund, 85, 183

Nader, Ralph, 107, 110
National Association for the Advancement of Colored People (NAACP), 6, 100, 101, 108
National Chamber of Commerce, 83
National Civil Service League, 184
National Contractors Association, 232
National conventions, 86-87
National debt, 224-225
National Emergencies Act, 177
National emergency, 177
National Farmers Union, 100
National Foundation on the Arts and Humanities, 192
National government. *See* Congress of the United States; Federal bureaucracy; Federalism; Government regulation
National health insurance, 105
National interest, 130-131
National Reconnaisance Office (NRO), 244-245
National Rifle Association (NRA), 101, 147
National Safety Council, 234
National Security Agency (NSA), 168, 193, 244, 245
National Security Council (NSC), 168, 174-175, 241
National Urban Coalition, 41
National Urban League, 53
Natural gas, 2
New Hampshire primary, 84, 138
New Jersey Plan, 19
News leaks, 130-131, 136
Newspapers. *See* Media
New York City, financial crisis (1975), 12, 34, 176
New York Times, The, 46, 130, 136
Nie, Norman, 74
Nineteenth Amendment, 27
Ninth Amendment, 25
Nixon, Richard M., 80, 115, 248
  appointments, 154, 170, 208
  character, 164-165
  foreign policy, 62, 172, 173, 241, 244
  impoundment of funds, 169
  leadership style, 163
  as legislator, 167
  media and, 172, 173
  national emergency and, 177
  National Security Council and, 174
  opinion polls and, 74
  presidential campaign (1968), 91, 96

presidential campaign (1972), 93, 96
  resignation, 4, 5, 27, 162-163, 169, 179
  revenue-sharing, 34
  as Vice President, 178
  Vietnam War, 22, 137
  wage and price controls, 74
  Watergate, 118, 132, 163, 169, 172
  White House staff, 174
North Atlantic Treaty Alliance, 252
North Atlantic Treaty Organization (NATO), 241, 252
North Vietnam, 243, 244

Oakes, John B., 131
Obscenity, 46-47
Office of Management and Budget (OMB), 158, 168, 174, 175, 224
Open market operations, 230
Opinion leaders, 72
Opinion polls, 61-63, 70-72, 74, 90, 91, 93
Opinion trends, 61-62

Pakistan, 235
Participation in America (Verba and Nie), 74
Party government, 114, 125
Party loyalty, 118
Party platform, 86
Party responsibility, 125
Patman, Wright, 152
Peer groups, political information and, 71, 72
Pennsylvania primary, 85
Pension funds, 232
Pentagon, 245, 249
Pentagon papers, 8, 46, 65
People's party, 120
People's Republic of China, 172, 176, 241, 253
Periodicals. *See* Media
Petition, freedom of, 45, 47
Philippines, 7
Phillips Petroleum Company, 233
Picket, right to, 74
Plea bargaining, 204
Plessy v. Ferguson (1896), 49, 211
Poage, W. R., 152
Pocket veto, 168
Poland, 241, 250
Political culture, 64-65
Political economy, 215-236
  budget, 224-227, 239
  budgetary priorities, 216-218
  budgetary process, 223-224
  Congress, role of, 223, 224
  fiscal policy, 229-230
  foreign trade, role of, 235, 239-240
  government, role of, 233-235
  inflation, 216, 218-219, 229-230, 240
  long-range planning, issue of, 220, 222-223
  monetary policy, 229, 230
  power structure of, 230-233
  Presidency and, 223-224
  revenue sources, 224-225, 228-231
  unemployment, 216, 218-222

U.S. economy, elements of, 228-229
Political environment, 2-3
Political information, 71-72
Political institutions, 5-6
Political participation. *See* Voting behavior
Political parties, 5, 28, 65, 69, 113-126, 257
  characteristics of, 116
  development of, 115
  future of, 125-126
  in Great Britain, 114-115
  identification, 81-82
  ideology, 116-118
  interest groups and, 103-106
  leadership, 121-123
  legislative organization, 120-121
  organization in Congress, 152-153
  performance, 123-125
  Presidential party organization, 120
  responsible, 114-115
  role of, 115-116
  state and local organization, 121
  third parties, 89, 95, 118-120
  two-party system, 115, 118-119
Political theory of opinion formation, 64
Polls, 61-63, 70-72, 74, 90, 91, 93
Poll taxes, 49
Population growth, 33
Population shifts, 66-67, 148
Portugal, 245
Postal Service, 185, 189
Powell, Lewis F., Jr., 206, 208
Power, 2, 3
Powers, Gary, 172
Power vacuums, 251
Pragmatism, 7-8, 67
Precedent (stare decisis), 199
Presidency, 161-179. *See also* Presidential election campaigns
  as administrative leader, 173-176
  appointments, 154, 169-171, 207-209, 239
  budget, 157, 168
  cabinet, 28, 107, 166, 175-176
  character, 164-165
  as Commander-in-Chief, 170-171
  Congress and, 15, 20, 124-125, 143, 159, 162, 165-169
  Constitution on, 20, 177, 178
  economic role of, 223-224
  executive agreements, 154, 170
  executive privilege, 159, 169
  foreign policy, 162, 168, 170-172, 176, 223, 239, 241-242, 251-252
  impeachment, 179
  implied powers, 28, 32-33
  impoundment of funds, 158, 169
  interest groups and, 106-107
  judiciary and, 169-170
  leadership style, 163-164
  as legislator, 166-168, 176
  media and, 134-135, 172-173
  as political leader, 165-166
  power, limitations on, 176-178
  succession to, 27, 179
  term of office, 27, 178
  veto power, 164, 168-169

Presidential Character, The (Barber), 164-165
Presidential debates, 92, 170
Presidential election campaigns, 89-93
 electoral college, 20, 95-96
 financing, 87-89, 105-106
 impact of, 92-93
 as media event, 91-92
 organization, 90-91
 popular vote (1932-1976), 96
 primaries, 81, 83-86, 89, 90, 104
 strategy, 90
 voter participation, 93-95
 1800, 26
 1820, 115
 1824, 95
 1840, 115
 1860, 115
 1876, 95
 1888, 95
 1936, 96, 211
 1948, 49, 119
 1952, 117
 1960, 80, 93, 96
 1964, 7, 50, 80, 82, 83, 90, 92, 93, 96, 125, 138, 165
 1968, 79, 80, 83, 85, 91, 92, 93, 96, 119-120, 125
 1972, 7, 82, 83, 90, 92, 93, 120, 125, 138
 1976, 32, 65, 69, 80-82, 84-85, 89-96, 104, 118, 125, 126
President pro tempore of the Senate, 151
Press, freedom of, 24, 46, 129, 133-134, 139, 207
Pressure groups. *See* Interest groups
Pretrial publicity, 133
Price Commission, 223
Price fixing, 106
Primary campaigns, 81, 83-86, 89, 90, 104
Priorities, setting, 10-11, 216-218
Prior restraint, 46
Procedural due process, 210
Progressive party, 119
Prohibition, 4, 27
Prohibition party, 120
Propaganda, 75
Property taxes, 35, 37, 56
Proxmire, William, 146
Psychological predispositions of voters, 82
Psychological theory of opinion formation, 63
Public interest, 110
Public knowledge of political questions, 69
Public opinion, 3, 4, 22, 60-76
 attitudes, 62
 characteristics of, 62-63
 direction of, 62
 domestic issues and, 68-70
 education and, 65-66
 ethnic influence on, 67
 foreign policy and, 68-70, 250
 governmental efforts to influence, 75
 group membership and, 64
 income and, 65-66
 information flow, 71-72
 intensity of, 62, 69, 71, 72
 issue types and, 68-70
 liberal-conservative dimension, 67-68
 measurement of, 70-71
 opinion trends, 61-62
 political culture and, 64-65
 political theory of formation of, 64
 polls, 61-63, 70-72, 74, 90, 91, 93
 population shifts and, 66-67
 propaganda and, 75
 psychological theory of formation of, 63
 public, defined, 61
 rationality of, 62
 sociological theory of formation of, 63-64
 stability of, 62, 69, 71
 value systems, 62, 63, 65
 voting and, 82-83
Public trust, 5
Pueblo incident, 176

Quartering Act, 15
Quota system, 56

Radio. *See* Media
Rafshoon, Gerald, 92
Railroads, 33
Randolph, Edmund, 18
Rather, Dan, 131
Rationality of opinions, 62
Reagan, Ronald, 34, 84, 85, 135
Recessions, 12, 53, 124-125, 228, 230, 235, 240
Rediscount rate, 230
Regionalism, 39
Regulation of Lobbying Act of 1946, 111
Regulatory commissions, 107-108
Rehnquist, William, 208
Religion, freedom of, 24, 45, 47-48, 65
Religious groups, 103
Reporting requirements (campaign financing), 88-89
Representation, 142
Representative government, 3-4
Republican party. *See* Electoral process; Political parties; Presidential election campaigns
Residency requirements, 94
Revenue, sources of, 224-225, 228-236
Revenue bills, 224
Revenue sharing, 34, 40-41
Reverse discrimination, 44, 53, 56
Rhodesia, 254
Roberts, Owen J., 47
Rockefeller, Nelson, 133
Rockefeller Foundation, 242
Rodriguez v. San Antonio School District (1973), 37
Rogers, William F., 111
Roosevelt, Eleanor, 49
Roosevelt, Franklin D., 96, 220
 character, 165
 foreign policy, 254
 media and, 172
 national emergency, 177
 Supreme Court and, 211
Roth case (1957), 46-47
Rusk, Dean, 107, 242

Salk, Jonas, 72
Sampling, 70-71
Sanford, David, 130
Sanford, Edward T., 211
Saudi Arabia, 253
Scammon, Richard, 125
Schlesinger, Arthur M., Jr., 168, 172, 173
Schlesinger, James E., 171
School desegregation cases (1954), 49, 56, 204-207, 211
School prayers, 26
Schorr, Daniel, 136
Schultz, George, 175
Scott, William L., 145
Search and seizure, 24
Second Amendment, 24
Second Continental Congress, 16
Segregation, 49, 50, 56
Self-interest, 63
Semi-independent government corporations, 188-189
Senate. *See* Congress of the United States
Senatorial courtesy, 170, 202
Seniority system, 152, 155, 156
Separate but equal doctrine, 49
Separation of powers, 22
Seventeenth Amendment, 27
Shapp, Milton, 85
Shays' Rebellion, 18
Sherman, Roger, 19
Shriver, Sargent, 85
Sierra Club, 108
Simants, Erwin, 46
Simon, William, 53
Sirica, John J., 133
Sixteenth Amendment, 26
Sixth Amendment, 25, 51, 133
Slavery, 19, 26, 49, 115
Slush funds, 233
Smith, Adam, 216
Smith Act of 1940, 45
Social issues, 69
Socialist Labor party, 120
Socialist Worker party, 120
Social opportunity, 51-52
Social security, 33, 65
Social values, 8
Sociological theory of opinion formation, 63-64
South Africa, 254
Southern Rim, 64, 66-67
South Korea, 110, 253
Spanish-American War, 33
Speaker of the House, 150-151
Speech, freedom of, 24, 45-47, 65, 136, 207
Split-ticket voting, 66, 93
Staats, Elmer B., 158
Stability of opinions, 62
Stamp Act, 16

Standard of living, 44, 52
Stare decisis, 199
State, Department of, 171, 239, 242-244, 249
State conventions, 104
State courts, 198, 199-200
State party organization, 121, 123
State primary conventions, 86
States' rights, 25
Stevenson, Adlai E., 87, 96
Strategic Arms Limitation Talks (SALT), 171
Strauss, Robert S., 120
Strikes, 232
Subcabinet departments, 187-188
Subsidies, 235
Substantive due process, 210
Suburbs, 37-39
Subversive activity, 45-46
Sun Myung Moon, 110
Sunshine Bill of 1975, 193
Super bureaucrats, 183-184
Supplemental Security Income (SSI) program, 193
Supreme Court of the United States
   activism vs. restraint, 205
   appointment of justices, 23, 169-170, 207-209
   campaign financing, 88, 89
   capital punishment, 25, 207
   civil rights, 49-50, 198
   clear and present danger, 212
   Constitution on, 197
   counsel, right to, 25, 51
   criminal rights, 200
   due process, 26, 210, 211
   executive privilege, 159, 169
   federal-state relationship, 32, 209-210
   government-business relations, 210-211
   gun control, 24
   impact of opinions, 206-207
   impoundment of funds, 169
   individual rights, 24, 45-48, 211-212
   judicial review, 22-23, 28, 197, 198, 204
   libel, 47
   "one man, one vote" ruling, 205
   political philosophy, 207
   privacy, right to, 25
   procedures, 206
   property taxes for school funding, 37
   school desegregation, 48, 204-207, 211-212
   search and seizure, 24
   separate but equal doctrine, 49
   slavery, 210, 211
   writs of certiorari, 205
Sweden, 232

Taft-Hartley Act, 111
Taiwan, 176, 235
Taney, Roger B., 210
Tanzler, Hans, 39
Taxation, 2, 4, 23, 65
   budgetary considerations and, 223
   colonial, 16
   of corporations, 230, 231-232
   education and, 35, 37
   federal-state-local revenue balance, 34
   fiscal policy and, 229
   government unemployment programs and, 219
   imbalance of federal spending, 33
   reform, 228, 231
   as source of revenue, 225, 228-231
   state and local, 40
Tea Act of 1773, 16
Teenagers, employment of, 52, 53, 56
Telegraph, 33
Television. *See* Media
Texas primary, 84
Tennessee Valley Authority (TVA), 189
Tenth Amendment, 25
Third Amendment, 24
Third parties, 89, 95, 118-120
Thirteenth Amendment, 26, 49
Thurmond, Strom, 49, 119
Ticket splitting, 66, 93
Trade and professional associations, 72
Transportation, 33
Treason, 23-24
Treaties, 154, 170
Trial balloons, 137
Trilateral Commission, 107
Truman, Harry S., 49, 96
   character, 165
   leadership style, 163
   national emergency, 177
Turkey, 154, 245, 249, 252
Twentieth Amendment, 27
Twenty-fifth Amendment, 27, 179
Twenty-first Amendment, 4, 26, 27
Twenty-second Amendment, 27
Twenty-seventh Amendment, 26, 27

U-2 incident, 172-173
Udall, Morris, 85
Unemployment, 10, 52-53, 69, 216, 218-222
Unemployment compensation, 2, 33, 65
Union of Soviet Socialist Republics, 70, 171-172, 240, 245-247, 252-254
Unions. *See* Labor unions
United Auto Workers, 117
United Press International (UPI), 129
United States v. Carolene Products (1938), 211
United States v. Nixon, 169
Universal party, 120

Valeriani, Richard, 170
Value systems, 62, 63, 65
Vance, Cyrus R., 107, 166, 241
Verba, Sidney, 74
Veterans Administration, 188
Veto power, 164, 168-169
Vice Presidency, 27, 87, 151, 178-179
Vietnam War, 3-5, 12, 22, 62, 69, 75, 135, 137, 171-173, 239, 240, 243, 244, 246, 249-250
Village Voice, The, 136
Vinson, Frederick M., 45
Virginia Plan, 18-19
Vote, right to, 26, 27, 49, 50
Voting behavior, 78-96. *See also* Presidential election campaigns
   candidates, 80-81
   education and, 94
   issues, 80
   participation, 65, 72-74, 93-95
   parties, 81-82
   patterns, 93-95
   primaries, 81, 85-86, 89, 90, 104
   psychological predispositions, 82
   public opinion and, 82-83
   socioeconomic factors, 82-83
   ticket splitting, 66, 93
Voting Rights Act of 1965, 50

Wage and price controls, 61, 67, 74, 222
Wallace, George, 85, 91, 93, 119-120, 212
War Powers Act of 1973, 22-23, 171
Warren, Earl, 170, 206, 209
Warsaw Pact, 252
Washington, George, 16, 18, 115
Washington Post, The, 130
Watergate, 4, 5, 7, 8, 22, 118, 121, 130-132, 138, 163, 169, 172
Watergate Special Prosecutor's Office, 233
Wealth, 52, 230-232
Wealth of Nations, The (Smith), 216
Weinberger, Casper, 175
Welfare, 34, 35, 45
Wesberry v. Sanders (1964), 148
Whig party, 115
Whips, 151
White, Byron R., 209
White House staff, 171, 173-174
Whitten, Les, 136
Wicker, Tom, 188
Williams, Harrison A., 146-147
Willkie, Wendell L., 96
Wilson, Woodrow, 6, 208
Women
   discrimination against, 48
   employment, 52-56
   vote, right to, 27
Women's rights movement, 6, 102, 103, 108
Woodward, Robert, 130
Work ethic, 65
World War II, 241
Writ of certiorari, 205
Writs of mandamus, 198

Yates v. United States (1957), 46
Yom Kippur War, 245
Young, Andrew, 166

Zoning codes, 45

78 79 80 9 8 7 6 5 4 3 2 1